Major Problems in
Texas History

MAJOR PROBLEMS IN AMERICAN HISTORY SERIES

GENERAL EDITOR
THOMAS G. PATERSON

Major Problems in Texas History

DOCUMENTS AND ESSAYS

EDITED BY

SAM W. HAYNES

UNIVERSITY OF TEXAS AT ARLINGTON

CARY D. WINTZ

TEXAS SOUTHERN UNIVERSITY

HOUGHTON MIFFLIN COMPANY
Boston   New York

Editor in chief: Jean Woy
Senior associate editor: Fran Gay
Senior project editor: Rosemary Winfield
Production/design coordinator: Christine Gervais
Senior manufacturing coordinator: Priscilla Bailey
Marketing manager: Sandra McGuire

Cover: *Oil in the Sandhills,* 1944, by Alexander Hogue. Collections Musée National d'Art
Moderne/Cci, Centre Georges Pompidou

Printed in the U.S.A.

Library of Congress Control Number: 98-72039

ISBN: 0-395-85833-X

56789-CRS-09 08

To Adrian Haynes, Jason Wintz, and Alexander Wintz,
a new generation of Texans

Contents

C H A P T E R   4
Populating Texas During the Late Spanish and Mexican Periods, 1810–1835
Page 79

C H A P T E R   5
Revolutionary Texas, 1835–1836
Page 111

C H A P T E R   6
The Fragile Republic: Building New Communities, 1836–1845
Page 146

C H A P T E R   7
Texas Joins the Union: Changing Roles for Tejanos and Women in the New State, 1845–1860
Page 175

C H A P T E R   8
Secession and Civil War, 1861–1865
Page 208

D O C U M E N T S

C H A P T E R   9
Race, Politics, and Reconstruction, 1865–1875
Page 238

D O C U M E N T S

C H A P T E R   1 0
*Conquering and Populating the Frontiers,
1860–1890*
Page 271

D O C U M E N T S

CHAPTER 11
Suffrage and Beyond: Texas Women and Reform, 1885–1925
Page 307

CHAPTER 12
Oil, Industrialization, and Urbanization, 1900–1940
Page 337

C H A P T E R   1 5
*The Rise of the Republican Party and the Transformation
of Texas Politics, 1960–2000*
Page 437

Preface

More scholarly and popular history has been written about Texas than perhaps any other state. Indeed, so much attention has been devoted to some of the more colorful aspects of Texas history—the Revolution, the cattle drives, and the oil boom spring instantly to mind—that they have become etched indelibly on the American popular consciousness. In recent years, however, scholars have begun to challenge some of the most basic and time-honored assumptions about the state's past. To a large degree, they have been inclined to reject the Anglocentric perspective that has shaped much of the scholarship on the American West—a view steeped in lore and insulated by myth. In its place, they have constructed a new narrative, one that is informed by a greater appreciation of the state's multiethnic character.

Today, historians are much more inclined than their predecessors to view the state's past through the broadest possible lens. In addition to adopting a more inclusive approach with regard to issues of ethnicity and race, they have employed the categories of gender, technology, urbanization, class formation, and community development to expand our knowledge of the state's past and, in so doing, link it to the history of the nation. At the same time, Texas historians have come to appreciate the power of myth in shaping historical memory, recognizing that the way we create myths about the past can often tell us as much about ourselves today as the past itself.

At the start of the twenty-first century, scholars at colleges and universities in Texas and throughout the country are actively engaged in the process of creating a new synthesis for Texas history. But historians alone do not deserve all the credit for these major contributions to the field. Their work has been sponsored and assisted by professional organizations and publishers who have helped redefine Texas history and dramatically raised the standards of scholarship. For example, the Texas State Historical Association and its journal, *Southwestern Historical Quarterly* (both of which recently celebrated their one-hundredth anniversaries) have embraced the new perspectives on Texas history, and they have provided important forums for the new scholarship. For information about the association and journal, see their website at www.tsha.utexas.edu. In addition, Texas A&M University Press (which recently celebrated its twenty-fifth birthday) has published a disproportionate number of the new books on Texas history in recent years, contributing greatly to our knowledge of the state's past.

To fully understand Texas, one must first come to terms with the myths that have played such a central role in defining it. In Chapter 1, Mark E. Nackman argues that Anglo-Texans developed a unique identity during the early decades of the nineteenth century. Walter Buenger and Robert A. Calvert view the process of identity formation as one grounded more in misconception than reality and suggest that Texas historians deserve a fair share of the responsibility for promoting and perpetuating the myth of Texas exceptionalism. Yet these stereotypes about the state continue to thrive today, Benjamin Soskis reminds us, because they serve the agendas and interests of those who employ them. The process by which Texans have developed and promoted certain myths about the state is also the focus of several essays in subsequent chapters. In Chapter 5, David J. Weber explains how Texans have romanticized their struggle for independence with Mexico. In a similar vein, Chapter 12 challenges the stereotype of the freewheeling Texas entrepreneur, noting that urban growth in early twentieth-century Texas took advantage of national and international economic and political developments and was accompanied by a rather "un-Texas" concern with urban planning. Chapter 15 chronicles and attempts to explain the unraveling of another Texas myth—the Texas Democratic Party's absolute control over Texas politics.

In view of the ethnic diversity that has long been one of the region's constant features, it should come as no surprise that racial conflict and accommodation are dominant themes in several of the chapters that follow. Chapter 2, for example, examines the dislocating effects that the arrival of Europeans in Texas had on Native Americans and studies the ways in which indigenous peoples sought to adapt to those upheavals. Chapter 4 deals with the tensions that arose soon after large numbers of Anglo-Americans moved into Mexican Texas. In Chapter 5, which focuses on the Texas Revolutionary period, Eugene Barker portrays the conflict as a clash of disparate political cultures. At the same time, however, the interaction of ethnic groups must not always be viewed strictly in terms of a collision between immutable, monolithic forces. As Gregg Cantrell (in Chapter 4), David J. Weber (in Chapter 5), and David Montejano and Jane Dysart (in Chapter 7) remind us, Anglo-Mexican relations were nothing if not complex and frequently characterized by cooperation and collaboration. The challenges faced by African Americans in Texas in the nineteenth and twentieth centuries are also given attention in several chapters. In Chapter 8, slavery historian Randolph B. Campbell examines the "peculiar institution" as it existed in Texas. In Chapter 9, Barry Crouch, who has written extensively on the state's Freedman's Bureau, details the violence that freedmen confronted during this period, while Carl Moneyhon demonstrates how some blacks assumed positions of political power, albeit briefly.

While the issue of ethnic conflict is woven throughout the fabric of the book, another theme that figures prominently in several chapters is the process of community building and formation. Chapter 3, for example, focuses on the obstacles Spain encountered in its attempts to establish a permanent presence north of the Rio Grande, while Chapter 6 examines the challenges Anglo-Texans faced as they set about the task of nation-building after the Revolution. In Chapter 8, Walter L. Buenger seeks to place antebellum Texas firmly in a southern regional context and thereby helps to explain the path Texans chose in their decision to join the Confederacy in 1861. Similarly, Chapter 10 examines the settlement of the frontier in post-Civil War Texas, emphasizing the diversity of the cultural forces and human participants in this process.

Several chapters also reflect historians' interest in gender issues. Chapter 7 focuses in part on the special challenges that Mexican American and Anglo American women faced in the new state. Chapter 11 focuses on the role of women in the political and social movements of the late nineteenth and early twentieth centuries. Subsequent chapters also focus particular attention on the role that women have played in the struggle for racial and civil rights. In Chapter 13, Irene Ledesma examines Mexican American women who challenged the norms of their own community as well as the Anglo male-dominated labor movement as they struggled for their rights in the workplace, while Merline Pitre and Yvonne Davis Freer describe, in Chapter 14, the leadership role of African American women in the state's early civil rights movement.

This volume adheres to the format of other volumes in the Major Problems series, introducing students to some of the most important issues in the field of Texas history through a mix of primary sources and scholarly interpretations. Chapter introductions and headnotes for the documents and essays seek to provide historical context, as well as to help students view the material in a conceptual manner by posing questions for further consideration. Organized chronologically, the documents and essays in each chapter highlight a particular problem or theme in Texas history and are designed to encourage students' critical thinking skills and stimulate classroom discussion. The documents are drawn from a wide variety of sources, including letters, diaries, oral histories, poems, songs, broadsides, government reports, political and institutional papers, court rulings, legislative acts, and newspaper editorials and columns. The interpretive essays represent classic writers of the state's history and the most innovative scholars working in the field of Texas history today. Some essays were selected because they draw wholly divergent conclusions from the same materials; others were chosen for the way in which they complement one another, by approaching a particular topic from different perspectives. In both cases, the selections are intended to demonstrate that the past should be viewed not as a single narrative but from multiple viewpoints, each valid in its own way. At the end of each chapter is a Further Reading section that alerts students to some of the most significant new scholarship as well as classic studies.

The authors would like to thank Thomas G. Paterson, general editor of the Major Problems in American History series, and Jean Woy, sponsoring editor at Houghton Mifflin, for asking us to prepare a volume of documents and essays on Texas history. Our editor at Houghton Mifflin, Frances Gay, patiently shepherded this manuscript through every stage of the publication process, while Rosemary Winfield kept us on task during the production phase of the project.

The authors are indebted to many historians who gave freely of their time and expertise for this project. Walter Buenger of Texas A&M University helped us rethink the direction and focus of significant portions of this book. Juliana Barr of Rutgers University, and David E. Narrett of the University of Texas at Arlington offered numerous helpful suggestions regarding the documents and essays that appear in some of the early chapters. Jimmy L. Bryan, a graduate student at Southern Methodist University, helped track down some particularly elusive documents that appear in Chapter 6. Tom Kreneck, of Texas A&M, Corpus Christi, and Barry Crouch of Gallaudet University provided suggestions, advice, and guidance in identifying and locating documents for the later chapters. Equally helpful was the staff of the Special Collections of the University of Texas at Arlington and at the Barker Center for American History at the University of Texas at Austin. Francine Cronshaw translated Spanish-language documents into English, and Adrian Anderson contributed suggestions and inspiration. Although most of the selected essays are reprinted from previously published sources, four historians—Gregg Cantrell of the University of North Texas, Robert Fairbanks of the University of Texas at Arlington, Merline Pitre of Texas Southern University, and Yvonne Davis Freer of Texas A&M University—kindly agreed to write essays specifically for this volume. We also thank the following reviewers of this volume: Walter Buenger, Texas A&M University; Caroline Castillo Crimm, Sam Houston State University; Arnoldo De Leon, Angelo State University; Charles H. Martin, University of Texas at El Paso; and James A. Wilson, Southwest Texas State University, who offered numerous helpful comments and specific citations for documents and essays when this project was in its earliest stages of development.

Most of all, we want to acknowledge the role that our friend and colleague Robert A. Calvert played in the inception and development of this project. Initially he planned to be a coeditor but was obliged to withdraw as his health failed. We know he would recognize his influence on the organization of the book, and we hope that he would be pleased with the way it turned out. We regret that he will not be with us to celebrate the publication, but we will toast his memory.

Finally, this book is dedicated to Adrian Haynes, Jason Wintz, and Alexander Wintz, a new generation of Texans.

S. W. H.
C. D. W.

Major Problems in
Texas History

Enduring Myths and

the Land

Texas has always been defined as much by its myths as by its past. Perhaps more than any other state, Texas can claim a vibrant popular history, one that is familiar not only to natives of the state, but to many people far beyond its borders. At the core of this popular history are such events as the revolution against Mexico, Indian wars, the cattle drives and the open range, the oil boom—episodes that are often cited as evidence of the state's unique frontier heritage and the spirit of individualism that it purportedly engendered. Yet these images are so deeply ingrained in the popular consciousness that they often tend to obscure other facets of the historical record. To regard Texas history as the narrative of Anglo males engaged in a process of triumphant conquest over alien enemies and a hostile environment is to provide an unbalanced and distorted view of the state's past.

This popular version of the state's history has proven remarkably resilient to revisionist challenge. Certainly Hollywood and television—the twin engines of American cultural myth production—have done their part to promote Texas stereotypes, inoculating Texans from the disquieting realities of change and modernization. For much of the twentieth century, Texas historians were also willing recruits on behalf of this traditional interpretation. To a large degree, scholars took their cue from the American historian Frederick Jackson Turner, who attached special importance to the Anglo-American westward push across the continent in his famous address, "The Significance of the Frontier in American History," in 1893. According to Turner, the process of "taming the wilderness" endowed earlier generations with a frontiering spirit that became embedded in the American character. Texas, with its history of violent conflict with Mexico and various Indian tribes, appeared to be a template for Turner's frontier thesis. Some scholars even set about to prove what the general public had long suspected—that the state's frontier heritage had stamped Texans with a unique identity, an exaggerated form of "Americanness."

In recent years, Texas historians have tended to reject this interpretation, and the chauvinism that has so often accompanied it. Reflecting the concerns of historians in other fields, they have pursued new areas of interest that include gender relations, ethnicity, class formation, and urban and technological change. In short, they are no longer fixated on the martial heroics of Anglo alpha males. The state's

1

demographic and economic landscape has also led historians to move in new his-
toriographical directions. It is estimated that Hispanic Americans will become
the state's largest ethnic group by 2025. Oil and gas, the mainstays of the Texas
economy in the twentieth century, are being eclipsed by a burgeoning information
technologies industry. Texas, still often characterized in popular literature as a
rugged wilderness, has become an urban state: 85 percent of its population lives
in cities. As Texas enters a new century, it offers few vestiges of its frontier heritage,
prompting present-day historians to question whether that period of the state's past
has been given undue emphasis.

These debates serve to highlight the fundamental but frequently overlooked
fact that history and historical memory are rarely if ever the same. The traditional
interpretation of Texas history may continue to appeal to many Anglo-Texas males,
but it cannot have the same resonance for women, nor for non-white ethnic groups,
such as Mexican Americans and African Americans. The past can be seen from
multiple perspectives, each valid in its own way, but necessarily incomplete. Only
by adopting a more inclusionary approach can historians hope to present a reason-
ably complete version of the past.

✹ E S S A Y S

The study of history is rarely static; more often it is subject to constant revision,
shaped and reshaped according to the shifting perspectives of those who write it. The
three essays offered in this chapter are indicative of the manifold changes that have
occurred in the study of Texas during the last twenty-five years.

In the first essay, Mark E. Nackman, author of a 1975 study on Texas nationalism,
offers a vigorous defense of the orthodox view that Anglo-Texans possessed a unique
identity, one that set them apart from other Americans. According to Nackman, notions
of Texas exceptionalism have their roots in the 1830s and 1840s, when Anglo settlers
won their independence from Mexico and set about to establish a sovereign nation. This
brief, turbulent chapter in its history, Nackman argues, enabled Texas to claim a mythic
past that was the foundation of the state's identity for the next century and a half.

While Nackman concedes that Texas nationality had no meaning for ethnic minorities, his exclusively Anglo focus puts him at odds with newly developing trends
in Texas scholarship. In the second essay, written in 1991, Walter L. Buenger, an historian at Texas A&M University, and the late Robert A. Calvert offer a critique of the
traditional interpretation, which has enjoyed an unduly long "shelf life," and more
generally fault Texas historians for their slowness in incorporating new historio-
graphical developments into their scholarship.

In the third and most recent essay, written on the eve of the 2000 presidential
election, journalist Benjamin Soskis examines some of the modern day myths—
favorable and unfavorable—that continue to be an integral part of popular perceptions
of the state's identity. According to Soskis, the modern state of Texas bears little relation to the heroic stereotypes of legend, but resembles other parts of the country in its
attitude toward responsible urban growth, environmental controls, and ethnic accommodation. Yet despite the state's high-tech economy, diverse population, and a political culture that is progressive in a number of respects, Texas is still often defined by its
frontier myths. The "New Texas" Soskis describes is a curious amalgam of nineteenth
century stereotypes and caricatures, grafted anachronistically onto a modern, complex society. Perhaps, one might argue, in its readiness to cling to the past even as it
embraces the future, Texas is exceptional, after all.

The Roots of Texas Exceptionalism

MARK E. NACKMAN

Texan nationalism, like American nationalism, did not give birth to the nation-state. Both nationalisms surfaced with the creation of the state itself. The Texas nation was from the start a homogeneous one and national unity through social integration was achieved almost immediately. The "nation" spoken of in this study is the "Anglo" nation, embracing white Americans and Europeans. Other racial and ethnic groups on the land—Mexicans, blacks, and Indians—were not assimilated and remained powerless. With rare exceptions, they did not contribute to the political state. Language, religion, and custom isolated the Mexican, race and slavery excluded the black, and a wide cultural chasm separated the Indian. Thus, Texan nationality had little or no meaning for these groups. The Anglo-Americans dominated and enjoyed certain advantages in the quest for nationhood: a common language, religion, ethnicity, and political heritage. Even class differences were slight among the generations up to the Civil War. They made a coherent group and a credible petitioner for nationality. Like all nationalists, they wanted to convince others (particularly other governments) that they were entitled to a nation-state. No one could deny their territorial conquests, least of all the Mexicans. From a cultural standpoint, however, did they truly constitute a nation? To be recognized as a separate and distinct people, they should have certain distinguishing characteristics. Wherein did the Texans differ from the American friends and relatives they had left behind in the States?

I must say at the outset that a separate culture is not a *sine qua non* of nationality. Nor must there be, where there is a separate nationalism, a culture of equivalent separateness. Whether the Zionists of the twentieth century who settled in Palestine and founded the state of Israel became culturally distinguishable from the Jews remaining in their native countries is a moot question. Whatever the verdict, it is undeniable that they considered themselves deserving of their own nation and nationalism was a natural outgrowth of that determination. One might also observe that Americans of the revolutionary era were highly Anglicized. It may then seem paradoxical that they revolted from England at the very time they most resembled their English rulers. Where cultural antagonisms exist (as between the Anglo-Americans in Texas and their Mexican masters), the potential for revolt is greater, but the drive for self-determination does not depend on cultural differentiae. Whether the Texans differed significantly from their American brethren or from other frontiersmen is not germane to the rise of nationalism. But it should be borne in mind that personal circumstances cast them into a similar mold and that their subsequent historical experience departed from the American norm.

Up to 1846, they had this in common: they were all expatriates. The very fact that they had abandoned home and country to settle in an unknown and untamed wilderness marked them as a breed apart. We may ask why any sober individual would choose Texas, a country infested with "wild" Indians and banditti, and threatened continually after 1836 by a hostile Mexico. Why should they volunteer for such a land in preference to their own American frontier, which at least enjoyed the protection of federal laws and a national army? A good many, it seems, were debtors or criminals seeking refuge from economic hardship or the hot breath of the law. Some fancied themselves empire-builders who never blinked at national boundaries, many more wished only for anonymity and a place in the vast landscape to hide from a hounding wife, or creditor, or sheriff. Others, doubtless, were ordinary farmers and businessmen no more ambitious or desperate than their counterparts in Iowa or Arkansas. Or were they? The vexing question remains: why should they take their chances in Texas?

An army wife stationed in Texas in the 1850s encountered an individual whom she considered the epitome of the Texan. This was one Henry Clay Davis of Rio Grande City, who had in a few years established himself as a prosperous ranchero while earning a reputation for fighting prowess as the leader of a local ranger company. "Clay Davis was a true specimen of the Texan, tall and athletic," she wrote. Indeed, Davis's past seemed to fit perfectly into the mold of the typical Texan. Seeking adventure, he had left his Kentucky home at the age of fifteen and while still a youth got into a bloody fight on a Mississippi steamboat, apparently killing a man. He took off for Arkansas, a fugitive from justice, without friends or money. As he grew to manhood, he learned the necessity of self-reliance. His many escapes from danger imparted to him a recklessness which he would put to good use in the Texas Revolution. When he reached Texas, the woman concluded, "He found himself among men of tastes and dispositions similar to his own. . . . Fighting simply for the love of it, he cared less for the result than for the pleasurable excitement it produced."

Many American visitors came away convinced that Davis was the stuff of which the average Texan was made. Whether from the security of the United States or in the nerve-fraying atmosphere of Texas itself, persons acquainted with Texans before the Civil War concluded that a daredevil spirit and volatile temperament were part of their being. Those who got to know them at first hand sometimes felt themselves rubbing elbows in situations too cozy for comfort. "I saw at the breakfast table one morning," related one, "four murderers who had sought safety in this country; and a gentleman assured me, that on one occasion, he had set down with eleven." Another reported that he had once spent the night at an inn where he found himself in the company of fourteen men, "all of whom freely acknowledged that they had absconded from their native country, and were drawn into Texas as a last resort." Samuel E. Chamberlain, whose knowledge of Texans came from what he saw of them in the Mexican War, did not hesitate to generalize: "Take them all together with their uncouth costume, bearded faces, lean and brawny forms, fierce wild eyes and swaggering manners, they were fit representatives of the outlaws who made up the population of the Lone Star State."

Contemporaries also testified to certain ennobling qualities. "What a race!" marveled the French minister to the Republic in 1839. "What can the Mexicans do against men of this kidney!" An English settler found the country "full of enterprising and persevering people" ("the timid and the lazy generly [sic] return to the States"), and the British chargé in Austin doubted there was anywhere in the world a race of men "more enterprising and energetic." To a traveler from Germany, the Texans fully deserved "all the praises which impartial observers have heaped upon them in the past. Even the really bad Texan is no common, low, vulgar, debased criminal, but in his character and conduct there is still discernible a certain degree of greatness." The Scotch militarist, General Arthur Wavell, had known the men of Texas since the days of the early filibusters. In 1844, he offered this assessment to the British Foreign Office:

> To as much if not more natural Talent, and energy to call it into play, and knowledge of all which is practically useful under every Emergency of the most Civilized Nations, they add a reckless hardihood, a restless spirit of adventure, resources and confidence in themselves, keen perception, coolness, contempt of other men, usages, and Laws, and of Death, equal to the Wild Indian.

The many travelers who visited Texas during the antebellum years tried to fathom what they felt certain was a distinct Texan character. In doing so, they made the Texans acutely conscious of their specialness. The Texan found himself to be a curiosity, almost a legendary figure in his own lifetime. Half-alligator, half-horse; villain, desperado, Indian fighter, wild man—he personified the exoticism of the far western frontier. Some, like William "Bigfoot" Wallace, enjoyed telling tall tales and yarns to the folks back home in Virginny, and the very dimensions of his physique persuaded his eager listeners that the mythical Texan was real. Texans could not depart the boundaries of their country without being surrounded by curiosity seekers. "What has contributed very much to my daily annoyance is the circumstance of my being a Texian," wrote Sam Maverick to his wife from Charleston in 1846. "I leave it to you to imagine for I cannot describe the fatigue I constantly suffer by continual calls from my very friendly but exceedingly uninformed acquaintance & kindred." From London, the self-effacing Texan ambassador to the Court of St. James related a diplomat's experience:

> I dined a few evenings since, by special invitation, with Sir John Herschell the great astronomer, and Mr. Tytler the eminent Scotch historian. Several other literary gentlemen of distinction were present. . . . I of course was modest and reserved in such company—and yet they would bring me out on the subject of Texas and the U states— we discussed the affairs of the two nations—their prominent men—institutions etc. They listened with much deference to all I said about those countries—but evidently with delight to the accounts of our Indian fights—prarie [sic] life—buffalo hunting etc.

As every historian of Texas will insist, the majority, perhaps the vast majority of settlers were decent, law-abiding folk. Visitors to the country gratefully commented upon their friendliness and hospitality, while admitting to their intelligence, their fortitude, and even their morality. It may have been a goodly flock; nevertheless one is struck by the evident profusion of black sheep in it. Their ubiquity was remarked upon by nearly every traveler who journeyed to the country in the formative years.

> Texas generally may with safety be regarded as a place of refuge for rascality and criminality of all kinds—the sanctuary to which pirates, murderers, thieves, and swindlers fly for protection from the laws they have violated in other countries, and under other governments. . . . Many innocent and deluded people are certainly mixed up with this vile population, and some mercantile men of respectability, education, and probity; but, in the main, scoundrelism, under one shape or another, constitutes the larger portion of the present population of Texas.

As early as 1822, the *Niles' Register* called Texas "a rendezvous for criminals," and soon the initials "G.T.T." ("Gone to Texas") would become infamous. As an American explained to an Englishman, "When we want to say shortly that it's all up with a fellow, we just say 'G.T.T.', just as you'd say gone to the devil, or the dogs." The place was known as the "Elysium of rogues," and its people as "renegades and ruffians." Anson Jones, who later became a president of the Texas Republic, was living in New Orleans and failing in business in 1833 when he was urged to try his luck in Texas. "My impressions of Texas were extremely unfavorable," he recalled. "I had known it only as a harbor for pirates and banditti." When the fires of the Texas Revolution were about to blaze in 1835, the Opelousas, Louisiana *Gazette* opined that if Texas and Mexico went to war, "The world would lose many bad citizens and the devil would gain some faithful servants—that everybody knew that the immigrants to Texas were vagabonds and refugees from justice." The heroics of the Revolution made Texans world renowned for their fighting prowess but did nothing to diminish their notoriety for plunder and thievery. The widely circulated exposés of Benjamin Lundy, William Ellery Channing, and others stigmatized the revolutionary effort as a land-stealing escapade and a conspiracy to advance the domain of slavery. Purportedly executed by a cadre of audacious adventurers, the Revolution made the names Sam Houston, Jim Bowie, William Travis, and Davy Crockett household words in America and kept Texas in the public mind for years to come.

As a fledgling nation, Texas fared little better with the American press that it had as a Mexican province, particularly as the question of annexation rose and fell. The New York *Sun* remarked in 1839 that few Texans had "the conscience to abstain from plundering whatever they can lay their hands on," and gave the country faint praise by declaring its president, Mirabeau B. Lamar, "the only man in Texas, whether of high or low degree, who possessed a character unstained by villainy of some sort or other." As annexation came to be more and more an issue in the midforties, an avalanche of epithets descended upon the Texans. Horace Greeley in the *Clay Tribune* cast Texas as a "den of thieves" and a "rendezvous for rascals of all the continent." At an anti-annexation meeting in New York, Philip Hone was shocked by the behavior of a gang of "prizefighters and pardoned felons" who riotously broke up the gathering by hissing, groaning, and shouting, "Hurrah for Texas!" The Hartford *Courant* labeled Texas " the land of Bowie knives and Toothpicks." In a scathing editorial against annexation, the paper urged the nation's legislators not to sully America's good name by adding a population "composed mainly of a wild and desperate set of men." The debate over Texas in the 1844 presidential campaign featured a widely disseminated cartoon showing candidates Polk and Dallas wooing "Lady Texas," while a sanctimonious Henry Clay stood to the side with folded arms, saying: "Stand back, Madam Texas! for we are more holy than thou! Do you think we will have anything to do with gamblers, horse-racers, and licentious profligates?"

The leading spokesmen for Texas had for some time deplored the sayings of the "foreign press." "We have been most dreadfully slandered in the U.S. papers," complained Stephen F. Austin to a Philadelphian. "Such publications have injured us dreadfully . . . it is really a cruel & unjust thing to have the best interests of a whole community, and a new & rising one, injured and men jeopardised by a set of silly scribblers." Texans suspected that a conspiracy of sorts existed to discourage desirable citizens and families from emigrating. The Houston *Telegraph and Texas Register* in 1841 accused American publicists of "unwarranted and reckless jibes and taunts," which had darkly colored the image of the Republic. "It is to be regretted, that so many blackguards and grossly ignorant men are still conducting public journals in the United States; while this state of things continues, we must expect to experience the effect of calumny and detraction."

Texans were, of course, aware of the political considerations operating against them. Their stuttering bid for annexation to the United States marshaled an array of forces, particularly in New England, opposed to the extension of slavery. In answer to William Ellery Channing's open letter to Henry Clay in 1837, a modest Texan, George L. Hammeken, allowed that if the Bostonian's denunciation of the Revolution contained merely his objections to slavery and to annexation, he would have left it to "abler pens" to respond. "But no man of honor and feeling, however incompetent to cope in fine language," he asserted, "should remain quiet when the character and motives of his friends and countrymen are so unjustly vilified." Hammeken conceded that Texas was filled with men who had been "unfortunate in commerce, or been ruined by their kindness to swindlers," but he insisted that there were no more than three or four hundred fugitives from justice, and they had no influence on the inhabitants in general.

Still, the Texan reputation was not confined to Northern opinion subserving the purposes of political anti-slavery. Southerners, too, entertained the notion that Texans were, according to William H. Wharton, "a set of adventurers, of young men of desperate fortunes" bent on conquest and glory. "To the contrary," argued Wharton, the first Texas minister to the United States, "the people of Texas [are] generally unpretending farmers and planters from the middle walks of life, [and] all they desired on earth was the privilege of cultivating in peace those fertile lands which they had so dearly earned by the perils and privations consequent upon the colonizing of a wilderness." Other Texans stoutly maintained that theirs was a decorous society, that young men did not come to town loaded down with pistols and knives, and that Texas had no call for an "anti-Duelling and Peace-Making Society" such as had been organized in Mississippi in 1844. Moreover, as Guy M. Bryan grandly announced to his Kenyon College mate, Rutherford B. Hayes, Texas could boast its "circles of beauty & accomplishment & intellect that will vie or bear comparison with the proudest & best of your land." Upon Texas's debut as a state in 1846, local editors implored the voters to exercise discretion in their selection of U.S. congressmen. We should impart to the world, the LaGrange *Intelligencer* admonished, "a just and proper impression of our moral and intellectual character."

> It is a matter of infinite moment on our first entrance into the fold of the confederacy, that a gross delusion under which a great many honest and intellectual minds have long labored, in regard to our moral, social, and intellectual condition should be at once and forever removed. We should take a peculiar degree of pride and satisfaction in convincing our sister states, that we . . . possess a large fund of moral and intellectual wealth . . . by sending to the councils of the nation gentlemen who will compare to advantage with any of their fellow members. . . . We should delight to show such puny snarlers [revilers of Texas], not only that something good can come out of Texas, but some of the most precious and elevating goods which this world may boast.

A Matagorda newspaper in 1844 observed that since the Revolution eight years earlier, "It has been the fate of Texas to attract the attention of the world to a greater extent than was ever done by the same number of the human family in any age." It was a fair estimation. If nothing else, the unwelcomed publicity advertised Texas to an audience far and wide. Foreigners were perhaps more amused than disheartened by the halo of evil surrounding the Lone Star. "When every other land rejects us," the Englishman William Bollaert punned, "here is the land which freely takes us (Texas)." . . .

For all these refugees, Texas became a homeland. Its broad boundaries gave them room to roam and enveloped them in a protective shell. They, in turn, embraced Texas. As a society of pariahs, the Texans could achieve self-respect and self-realization through identification with a virile state. The citizen's supreme loyalty went eagerly to his fellow nationals, and the vehicle of their joint aspirations was the state. The achievement of nationhood, reinforced by such palpable effects as a constitution, a flag, an army, a navy, fired their nationalism. Nationhood gave them security; nationality told them who they were. With the Republic of Texas they became "Texians" and nothing else. No longer need they be men without a country.

The Shelf Life of Truth in Texas

WALTER L. BUENGER AND ROBERT A. CALVERT

Professional historians often see their mission as stripping away myth and exposing unvarnished truth. Yet cultural biases bind historians just as they do society at large. As purveyors of written culture historians may arrive at only the near-truth, a truth relevant to current problems. This should cause no dismay, for understanding what historical truth has been releases society from the blinders of tradition. Realizing the limited shelf life of history allows for the pursuit of a new understanding of our past and present culture.

Escaping the enfolding snares of past writings on a society requires understanding their origin. Scholars must investigate not only the past, but how past generations looked at the past. Practitioners of history call this process historiography: the history of historical writings and changing intellectual points of view. For Texas the key historiographic question is: Why have historians not subjected the myths of the state to rigorous cyclical examination? Certainly, different cultures interpret their myths of origin differently. A "diversity of Texas myths" exists based on which ethnic group describes its origins. Nevertheless, the dominant culture has created and added to the myth in such a way that few openly challenge its premises. Thus the macho myth of Anglo Texas still reigns.

The Texas myth has been both a part of and separate from the older frontier myth of the Anglo United States, which was born in the Puritan heritage of the City

Walter L. Buenger and Robert A. Calvert, *Texas Through Time: Evolving Interpretations* (College Station: Texas A&M University Press, 1991), xi–xv, xviii–xxi, xxxi–xxxv. Reprinted by permission of the Texas A&M University Press.

on the Hill and honed by the Manifest Destiny advocates of the mid-nineteenth century. The North American myth celebrated the past. It assumed, at least until the Vietnam War, that the United States was invincible in wartime, magnanimous in peacetime, and destined to bring peace, prosperity, Christianity, and democracy to first the continent and then to the globe.

The Texas myth accepted the North American version, adopted it, and typically exaggerated it. The outlines of the Texas myth are well known. For all practical purposes it begins with the Alamo and ends with San Jacinto. Mythic Anglo Texan male heroes—Crockett, Bowie, and Travis—die for the nation. Women are either subservient and supportive—Susanna Dickinson carries the message of heroism to Sam Houston—or sultry and seductive—Emily Morgan gives her all to detain the dictator. A foreigner, Moses Rose, refuses to cross Travis's line and flees the battle. A loyal black slave, Joe, a noncombatant, accompanies Susanna and describes the fall of the Alamo. A Tejano, Juan Seguín, leaves the Alamo as a messenger and then serves as a scout. Later disillusioned, Seguín goes to Mexico, but still represents the "good" Mexican as compared to the barbarous Santa Anna, who is saved from the cruel death he dealt to Texas heroes by Houston, the generous Anglo victor at San Jacinto, who went on to help found a republic based on freedom. The creation of the nation—the Texas Republic—separates the Texas myth from the Anglo North American myth and gives to the culture a Texas nationalism and romantic vision that transcends geography and creates, as Willie Nelson sings, a Texas state of mind.

Only recently has cyclical revisionism appeared in Texas history and the myth come under considerable criticism. Like other myths it is only partially true. The actual character of the historic individuals no doubt has little correlation to their mythic presence, but debunking them makes scant difference in the perception of the myth. Selective historical memory persists and Texas elites in particular still profess at least a limited subscription to that romantic concept of Texas. The myth then creates a sense of what a Texan is that precludes many of the state's citizens from identifying themselves as Texans. Moreover, the myth also defines the presumed role of all of Texas' multicultural citizens and describes the alleged characteristics of non-Anglo males. The result is that in much the way that oral myths sustained a cultural identity and gave a society shared values and common goals, written myths and folklore have shaped the goals and perceptions of those who have governed and controlled Texas for most of the twentieth century. . . .

Demands for an inclusionary history, for intellectual toughness and honesty, however, have usually run aground on the rock of Texas provincialism. One root of this provincialism grows from the mixed perception that Texans have of their own identity. Partial responsibility for this unfocused identity rests with historians who have failed to nurture cyclical revisionism. Affected by a frontier heritage that is depicted as larger than life in both fiction and folklore, university professors translated into the official history of Texas what many citizens viewed as the unique experience of Anglo-Saxon males wresting the wilderness from savage Indians and venal Mexicans. The universities were largely Anglo male preserves and research and teaching represented that bias. Further, as late as the 1950s, historians still worked within the intellectual constructs of Frederick Jackson Turner's frontier thesis. They saw the frontier as the agent that shaped and made the United States unique. In this Texas historians simply followed the lead of their teachers.

At the University of Texas, which dominated the training of professional historians interested in Texas as a field of study, the first generation of historians who came on the scene in the early twentieth century took Turner's concept and applied it to the history of the state. Although judicious, some still saw a war of civilized Anglos versus barbaric cultures. George P. Garrison, for whom the building that houses the University of Texas history department is named, entitled one of his books *Texas: A Contest of Civilizations* and argued that competition on the frontier produced the superior Texas character that civilized the state and vanquished aboriginal and Spanish cultures. Garrison believed strongly in scientific history. He also believed that history demonstrated progress, and that social Darwinism caused progress. The Texas frontier represented for Garrison the movement across the North American West of the Teutonic values that gave western European culture world domination. Where Garrison left off Eugene C. Barker picked up. Although his work was highly professional and more dispassionate than most, as the subtitle of his most famous work reveals, Barker also saw a "manifest destiny" in the expansion of Anglo Texas. For him the Texas Revolution was a clash of Anglo and Hispanic cultures that was almost inevitable once Spain and Mexico invited energetic and freedom-loving Anglos into Texas.

The tendency to romanticize the frontier continued into the second generation of historians working in the 1930s. Both Walter Prescott Webb, who was influenced by Garrison, and J. Frank Dobie, who was not an historian but certainly shaped intellectual life in Texas through the 1950s, saw the frontier as a source of positive values relevant to modern life. They feared that the loss of the frontier heritage of Texas would weaken the state and make it like all others. This need to glorify the past led novelist Larry McMurtry to ask if there existed an unsentimental Texas historian. . . .

The tendency to look toward historic Texas frontiers and Anglo culture as explanations for the causes for most events also skewed the direction of historical studies. It gave Texas history a strong nineteenth-century bias that is still in effect. . . . Until recently most historians simply did not write on twentieth-century topics. By ignoring them they were not forced to ask critical questions about cultural and economic injustices. The historians were not forced to look at the limited shelf life of history.

This avoidance of culturally relevant topics and the concentration on writings in the heroic mode was also at least partially subconsciously defensive, and this defensiveness sprang from anticolonialism, another root of Texas provincialism. In a state whose economy was clearly a colonial one and whose cultural developments were limited by its rural heritage and its commitment to a yeomanlike concept of agrarian goodness, memories of the frontier past saved the society from looking deeply into the bleakness and poverty of much of the historical period through the 1930s. . . .

This resentment did not recede when the prosperity of World War II turned into the recently ended sustained economic growth. Expansion forced Texans to consider the issues of urban growth, outside population migrations, and a transition into an industrial economy. Texans both welcomed the changes and feared them as intellectual and cultural colonialism. Some believed that the frontier produced an expansive imagination and a concept of risk taking that would be lost if the frontier heritage were lost; others insisted that modernization would make Texas like all other states and that its folk culture and heritage should be preserved to protect Texans' sense of place.

Clearly both groups wanted a usable myth for the twentieth century. The Texas macho myth hung on—less pronounced but more damaging. Once it had given many Texans purpose and identity. Now for many it had become a "Hollywood" caricature that encouraged greed and a lack of individual responsibility for society as a whole. Others saw attacks on the Anglo Texas tradition as an elitist endeavor that would destroy the past and therefore the state's *Zeitgeist*. Historical writings became a battleground between proponents representing both parts of the state's identity crisis: modernists who welcomed change and wanted to verify it historically, and traditionalists who wanted writings that preserved the perceived cultural heritage. The more numerous traditionalists glorified the historic past to deter the onslaught of technocratic and cultural vandals and proclaimed that frontier individualism explained the present economic accomplishments and social stability of the state. . . .

Perhaps this identity crisis also springs from the inability of Texans to place themselves within the broader region of West or South. Not knowing if Texas belongs with the slaveholding South or the cattle-ranching West has allowed Texans to ignore the more innovative scholarship in those areas and to argue that Texas has always been unique. The insistence on uniqueness, added to the persistent impact of past scholars, precluded until recently a full-scale study of Texas slavery. Just as Texans cannot place themselves in the Sunbelt, then, they cannot place their history or their identity in the analytical framework of either the South or the West. The insistence by some Texas historians on the state's uniqueness and an inability to accept an analytical framework had encouraged the provincialism of outsiders who observe the doings of Texas historians. Often deservedly, historians from outside the state minimize the work done on Texas, because it fails both to draw comparisons between Texas and other similar places and to set Texas in a larger national focus.

Nowhere has this identity crisis come into sharper focus than in the economic history of the state. Historians . . . have exhibited a curious "flight from modernity." On the one hand they celebrate growth and profits. On the other they flee the implications of a modern life created by growth and profits. The ranch remains the most studied and probably least significant major aspect of the Texas economy. Besides being a traditional topic acceptable to the old masters, ranches are romantic, close to a preindustrial past, and uniquely Texan—at least in the popular view. Texas historians choose ranch histories as ideal topics, for they fit within the framework of past giants, and they fire another round at the modernists. Popular culture also supports such ventures, for, tellingly, ranch histories usually outsell all other Texas books.

Moreover, most economic and business histories record a fascination with a golden age, a bygone age, where things were better and the heroes and villains were clearly discernible. In this golden era the old myth of the Anglo-Saxon male triumphing over all odds without the aid of government runs rampant. Issues of class, community, gender, and ethnicity are ignored because they conflict with the pristine past. Current legends are perfect examples of the avoidance of modern realities by editing out all complexities and subtleties. Unlike history, in legends events are resolved without contradictions. The writers often ignore the evolution of twentieth-century Texas, because its development challenges earlier legends. Ironically, then, descriptions of the business would have inherited and adapted the Anglo Texan myth, encapsulated in the Alamo. Even possibly more ironic, the part of the historical discipline most closely linked to the "dismal science" of economics and to factual data seems currently to also be the one that is most enamored with myth and chained by an identity crisis. . . .

A new history would be particularly useful if it adjusted our myths and values to our current situation, if it helped to resolve the identity crisis associated with being Texan, if it demonstrated the importance of opening up new ways of looking at ourselves. . . . The image of Texas as a homogeneous state has only recently come under attack and the critique of that image has not been widespread. The strength of earlier writings on Texas history was that they perpetuated a pride in the state, a myth of what it meant to be a Texan that could lead us to value the past and refuse to accept a second-rate status. Yet until all of the population feel a part of the myth, excluded groups will be alienated from the state's history and potentially from the state itself.

The New Texas

BENJAMIN SOSKIS

Election 2000 may come down to Texas—not its electoral votes, which are safely in the pocket of George W. Bush, but its political identity. Both presidential campaigns realize that Texas is to this race what Massachusetts was to 1988: if you can define the state, you can define its governor. For Bush, that means aligning himself with his state's reputation for boundless opportunity, vast self-confidence, and relaxed good humor. In their answer to the Clinton campaign's legendary *The Man From Hope,* the biographical film that introduced the Arkansas governor to the country in 1992, the Bush campaign at the Philadelphia GOP convention showed W. on a prairie in Crawford, Texas, site of his yet-to-be completed ranch. He spoke about his hometown. "There used to be a slogan in Midland that said 'The sky is the limit,' which really is such an optimistic slogan," Bush mused. "It's how I feel about America, really." Clad in blue jeans and a cowboy hat, he extolled the virtues of the Texas frontier. He waxed lyrical about "dreamers—the doers who take risks and sometimes failed, but then rose above failure to achieve greater good things." Then he climbed into his blue pickup truck and, passing a well-placed calf, drove off toward the horizon.

Al Gore, of course, is trying to evoke a different image: Texas as economic and cultural backwater. If Bush has the "Proud of Texas Committee," which touts the

Benjamin Soskis, "Lone Star Joining: Why Texas Is Like America," *The New Republic,* September 18, 2000. Copyright © 2000. Reprinted with permission.

state's old-fashioned virtues, Gore has the "Texas Truth Squad," which notes end-lessly that Texas ranks near the bottom of the nation in categories that connote enlightenment (child health care, clean air) and near the top in those that connote primitivism (incarceration, gun violence, cow-manure production). By Election Day, one Democratic strategist boasts, Gore will have turned Texas "into a Third World country."

Gore and Bush aren't trying to create stereotypes of Texas. They're doing something far easier—tapping into stereotypes that already exist. They're playing on the flip side of Texas's reputation as exceptional, a state whose cultural distinc-tiveness has uniquely withstood homogenizing national influences. Even before this campaign, many liberals viewed Texas as a world apart, a state where, in the words of lefty *New York Times* columnist Bob Herbert, "compassion is virtually illegal." Just as conservatives didn't need much convincing to believe that Massa-chusetts was a place of oppressive taxation and rampant political correctness, lib-erals already believed that Texas abused its poor—Al Gore just filled in the details. Likewise, conservatives didn't need much convincing to believe that Bush supports self-reliance and personal freedom, because, after all, his state is one of the few places where they still reign.

There is, of course, some truth to both images. It probably is easier to start a business in Texas than in New York. And swaths of the Lone Star State really do suffer from deep social underdevelopment and government neglect—neglect Gore and the press would be derelict to ignore. But the odd thing about the Bush-Gore fight over the meaning of Texas is that its very premise, Texas exceptionalism, is increasingly anachronistic. By buying into one side or another of the Texas frontier myth—by accepting that the state is somehow set apart, either by its rugged in-dividualism or by its prideful backwardness—the candidates and the press have ignored the striking new reality on the ground: Texas is becoming more like the rest of the nation than anyone, Texan or non-Texan, wants to admit.

It started with the oil bust. For much of the postwar era, Texas's reputation as distinct from the rest of the country stood on firm economic ground: its economy was countercyclical. When the price of oil was high, as in the Carter years, the na-tion foundered but Texas boomed. When the price of oil dropped and the country rebounded under Ronald Reagan, Texas crashed. "When I first came here," says Rice University sociologist Stephen Klineberg, "the rule of thumb was, if things are good in Boston, they're going to be bad for us in Houston, and vice versa."

But the 1980s oil bust, which hit harder and lasted longer than almost anyone had predicted, changed that. Third-lowest in the country in 1980, the state's un-employment rate was ninth-highest by 1990. Over the same period, the number of Texans living in poverty grew 47 percent. Slowly and painfully, the economy began to diversify, as companies that once fixed oil rigs retooled to service computers and televisions. In 1982, around 30 percent of state revenue came from severance taxes on oil and gas; by 1988, that figure had dropped to 8 percent.

Since then, the state has nursed itself back to economic health by embracing the same industry that has remade the economy nationally: technology. Two decades ago, high tech accounted for just over 5 percent of the state's economic output; today, it accounts for nearly 9 percent. Indeed, more Texans now work in high tech as work in oil, gas drilling, refining, and agriculture combined. According to a recent study by the American Electronics Association, Texas ranks second in semiconductor and office-computer manufacturing and is the nation's second-largest electronics exporter. In fact, according to a study by Bernard Weinstein of the University of North Texas, the state's economy has so dramatically aligned itself with the rest of the country's that, for the first time in modern history, rising gas prices do Texas more harm than good: every $1 increase in the price of natural gas cuts economic activity by some $3.4 billion a year and adds another 35,000 people to the ranks of the unemployed. "For a long time Texas was different," Weinstein explains. "Well, it ain't another country anymore."

That could be the unofficial motto of Tyler, Texas. A few months ago, I visited this friendly town of 84,000 in the green, eastern part of the state. Tyler is best known for its fall Rose Festival—an archaic, lavish blend of debutante ball and Mardi Gras. Recently, though, the town has gained another distinction: it is one of the state's hottest technology hubs, ranked the fourteenth-fastest-growing tech town in the nation by the California-based Milken Institute.

For most of the twentieth century, Tyler's economic fortunes depended on oil. In 1930, a 70-year-old wildcatter struck black gold at the Daisy Bradford Farm, 20 miles away. The discovery ushered in the East Texas oil boom, and Tyler, whose paved streets distinguished it from many nearby towns, became the regional service center for the fledgling industry. Tyler shrugged off the Depression and thrived for the next few decades, attracting a number of major manufacturing firms. Then the bust hit. Between 1981 and 1989, the number of residents employed in the oil and gas industries dropped by more than half. "It knocked everyone out of the saddle," says Kevin Eltife, the town's 41-year-old mayor. "We had to create a whole new city."

Now Tyler is a boomtown again. But it's a different sort of boom. The town boasts two nationally ranked not-for-profit hospitals, and medicine has become one of its largest employers. Three years ago, the University of Texas granted its Tyler satellite full four-year status, and soon afterward, a College of Engineering opened, followed by a $20 million cultural center. The College of Engineering, which will churn out 30 graduates a year, helps provide Tyler with the kind of tech-savvy labor pool that attracts employers. Indeed, the number of tech employees in town has doubled in the last decade to nearly 3,000, twice as many people as are employed in the town's famed oil and gas sector.

To be sure, Tyler retains touches of East Texas folksiness: just as Eltife, the son of Lebanese immigrants, brandishes a convincing drawl, so the downtown eateries have names like "The Feed Lott" written in lasso-like fonts. But mostly Tyler is co-opting old images to serve a new reality, appropriating styles and symbols of the nineteenth century to adorn the twenty-first. At the Jordan Plaza technology park, for example, the architectural style is distinctively ranchlike: twelve wide, low-roofed buildings face a 20-acre wooded park, which will be allowed to remain "wild." But it is as thoroughly "new economy" as anything you'd find in Boston or San Jose: the 60-acre complex is full of firms like SPEA International, a company based in Turin, Italy, that builds microchip testers and plans to recruit 50 engineers to the town in the next five years; GeoInfo Ltd., whose 50 employees specialize in geographic information systems and mapping technology; and Fair Point Communication, a 25-person telecommunications firm.

Tyler still has a ways to go before it becomes another Silicon Valley. Its nightlife, according to some of the town's younger residents, could use some work. David Buhrkuhl, a semiretired businessman who serves as head of SPEA's American division, actually worries that until the nightlife improves, SPEA might have a hard time attracting twentysomething engineers. " You can't compare Tyler to South Hampton," admits Eltife. But when I ask the Birkenstock-clad mayor whether Tyler might look more like Austin after a decade of development, he pauses for a moment—perhaps contemplating images of Austin's frolicking hippies and militant environmentalists—smiles, and replies, "Sure."

And the transformation I saw in Tyler is playing out on a much grander scale in Texas's large metropolitan centers. In 1940, the state was 80 percent rural; now it is 85 percent urban. Of the 570,000 domestic migrants to Texas in the '90s, more than 80 percent settled in the high-tech suburbs outside Houston, Dallas, Fort Worth, and Austin. Last year, for instance, Yahoo! set up shop in an abandoned warehouse in Dallas's Deep Ellum district, once one of the nation's most infamous skid rows, prompting at least a dozen Internet-related firms to follow; Dell Computer has called Austin home for years. Dallas now ranks fourth nationally in number of high-tech workers; Houston ranks fourteenth; Austin, fifteenth. Even Waco, a city that doesn't exactly enjoy a reputation for forward thinking, has witnessed a 60 percent growth in high-tech output over the last five years.

Texas's economic changes are sparking social ones. The state has experienced surges of professional migration before. The greatest expansion of Anglos in the state, for instance, occurred during its 1970s oil boom, when nearly one million people settled in Houston alone. But to attract today's high-tech migrants, the state is not simply relying on its traditional enticements—low cost of living, low taxes, minimal regulation, and an oil-rich substratum. The new migrants, according to conventional wisdom, demand a healthy environment and functioning social services. And this has led a growing number of Texans to challenge a prominent tenet of their state's secular religion: the unfaltering belief that development is always good, you can always use another highway, and there is always more land. Last year, in a highly publicized statewide poll, more than half the respondents named urban sprawl as a major concern. "This reflects a real change in Texas attitudes," state historian T. R. Fehrenbach told a local newspaper at the time. Previously," it was practically considered Communistic to oppose growth."

Ground zero for this insurgency is Austin, where environmentalists routinely play kingmaker in city elections—this year, every candidate elected to the city council ran on an environmentally friendly platform. And today, after years of feuding, business groups (spurred by local high-tech leaders) have joined Greens to promote "smart growth" and improve the city's quality of life. According to Robin Rather, a former chairwoman of Save Our Springs (Austin's largest environmental organization) and currently head of a reform-minded alliance of high-tech CEOs, a local consensus is emerging that the imperatives of the market require some attention to environmental standards. "I think what we've proven is that if you cut through the rhetoric and look at what's in everybody's best interest, it's quality of life." she says. In fact, Save Our Springs has joined forces with the city's Chamber of Commerce and the Real Estate Council to buy 50,000 acres of open space in the nearby Hill Country, to protect the city's aquifer. "It's sort of an anti-sprawl measure," Rather suggests, a bit taken aback by the phrase.

Texans, of course, have long viewed Austin as an exotic isle of liberalism, toler-ated as if it were the older sister who cut her hair short and went off to Berkeley. But notions of smart growth are also catching on in Houston, a city whose name is prac-tically synonymous with sprawl. Last April, Houston's environmentalists won a stunning victory over development titans when the city council voted down a pro-posal to build an airport on the Katy Prairie, a wildlife-rich wetland 30 miles outside the city. In the wake of the victory, environmentalists established a political action committee, Houston Conservation Voters, to push for clean air and open-space poli-cies. The refineries and developers "are still in control," says Jim Blackburn, the PAC's director. "But there is certainly more willingness to discuss issues, and to be open to ideas, than I have previously seen in this part of the world."

The stats bear out Blackburn's wary optimism. According to Rice University's Klineberg, who has been polling Houstonians for nearly two decades, as many voters support spending city funds on inner-city mass transit as support funding highways to the suburbs, and they prefer investments in education and public serv-ices to tax cuts—both stark changes from the past. In 1999, 70 percent of those Klineberg polled supported emissions testing for all vehicles in Houston, up from 38 percent just four years earlier. And Houston's business community is finally catching on. This June, the city's largest business organization, the Greater Houston Partnership, officially came out in support of "sensible growth." Even Tom DeLay has taken notice. After the House majority whip, who represents the southwest Houston suburbs, shot down federal funding for an inner-city rail system, he re-ceived a significant number of complaints from his conservative constituents. "I think he was surprised by how much sentiment there was out there in the suburbs to quit just pouring concrete and think about new solutions," says Richard Murray, a political scientist at the University of Houston. This July, in a rare slap in the face to the third-highest-ranking congressional Republican, city officials chose to ignore DeLay's opposition and, if necessary, give up on federal funding and finance the rail project locally.

If Texas's high-tech migration is upsetting a long-held consensus on develop-ment and the environment, a broader migration is challenging long-standing stereotypes about the state's racial identity. For decades an unofficial demarca-tion, running from San Antonio to Corpus Christi, separated Texas's Hispanic south from its more Anglicized north, which was itself starkly divided between white and black. But in recent years a tide of Mexicanization has breached that divide, reshaping the political and cultural identities of the state's largest cities. Houston, for example is now one of the most racially diverse cities in America— 34 percent Hispanic, 31 percent white, 29 percent black, 6 percent Asian. Austin, too, is now more than one-quarter Hispanic, with a rapidly growing Asian com-munity that includes a large population of Indian techies who left Silicon Valley, lured by Austin's cheaper rents and multicultural vibrancy. In fact, at current growth rates, in 20 years Asians will surpass blacks as Austin's second-largest minority. Even Dallas, epicenter of good-old-boyism, is now nearly one-quarter

Hispanic. And, according to census projections, that number will reach 40 percent in 30 years.

More impressive than the ethnic diversification itself is that Texas has experienced it without much of the violence and antagonism that has plagued its supposedly more liberal counterpart, California. The Lone Star State has produced no successful Proposition 187-style campaigns to restrict the rights and benefits of immigrants, and politicians hostile to the largely Hispanic immigrant community frequently suffer at the polls. For instance, after Jim Mattox, a former state attorney general and front-runner for the Democratic senatorial spot in 1994, suggested using the military to patrol the border, his campaign plummeted. When Bush ran for governor, by contrast, he made a point of signaling to voters that he supported immigration and considered Texas's relationship with Mexico one of the state's most valuable assets. Bush won in 1994 "because he wasn't Pete Wilson," says Andrew Hernandez, author of the *Almanac of Latino Politics,* referring to the California governor who championed Prop 187. "He got credit for saying, 'We are not that kind of state.'"

This isn't to say Texas is always racially enlightened. The state's shamefully decrepit criminal justice system leaves many poor black and Hispanic defendants without competent counsel. Texas still witnesses spasms of racial violence—the brutal dragging death of Jasper resident James Byrd two years ago being among the most terrifying. In parts of East Texas, the tolerance enjoyed by Texas Latinos is often denied to African Americans; and in the border regions the poverty and dropout rates among Tejanos remain much higher than the statewide averages. For the most part, however, race relations in Texas confound the traditional liberal paradigm of a white majority oppressing a brown or black underclass. The state's supposedly reactionary business elite, for instance, has largely accepted multiculturalism as a way of life. Houston and Dallas, neither of which has a black majority, both recently elected black mayors, and they did so without much of the racial hostility that accompanied similar breakthroughs in Los Angeles, Chicago, and New York. "There is an understanding that the future is increasingly a non-Anglo future," notes Klineberg, "an understanding that if you're going to make money in the twenty-first century, you're going to have to make coalitions."

One reason for the absence of ethnic vendettas is that in Texas, Hispanic and Anglo culture are more deeply intertwined than in California or even New York. "Texas Latinos are more likely to be multigenerational Americans and have greater distance from the immigrant experience than do their counterparts in California," writes Gregory Rodriguez, a fellow at the New America Foundation, a Washington, D.C., think tank. Three years ago, when a town across the border from El Paso hoisted a gigantic Mexican flag and the local paper polled residents about whether it should plant an American flag in response, a greater percentage of Hispanics than non-Hispanics said yes.

And if Hispanic Texans don't see a contradiction between being culturally Mexican and fully American, neither, it seems, do the state's Anglos. Unlike in California, Texas's white politicians have never crusaded against bilingual education; George W. explicitly supports it. In fact, in more than 30 districts—from El Paso to Dallas to Houston—schools encourage "two-way" bilingualism so that Anglo students can also gain proficiency in Spanish. According to Josefina V. Tinajero, president of the National Association for Bilingual Education, attitudes toward bilingual education in California are hampered by a sort of liberal paternalism, which she describes as a "let's help these poor little kids who don't speak English" attitude. In Texas, on the other hand, where more than 70 percent of all English-as-a-second-language elementary school students are educated in both Spanish and English, compared to just 30 percent in California, bilingualism is considered "an asset . . . an intellectual accomplishment," and a wise business investment. She points to a partnership between the San Antonio Chamber of Commerce and the city's school districts to ensure that all high school graduates are fluent in both languages. "From an economic point of view," Tinajero says, "the leadership in Texas has seen that bilingual education is good for our kids."

But prognosticators who expect that Texas's "sleeping giant" Hispanic population will usher in an era of Lone Star liberalism when Hispanics become a plurality of the state's population (expected by 2025) are probably deluding themselves. Texas, unlike California, boasts a Hispanic Republican congressman and a Hispanic Republican state official. And even many Hispanic Democrats, like El Paso's law-and-order, pro-life Representative Silvestre Reyes, hold political views far to the right of national Latino advocacy groups like the National Council of La Raza.

But if one explanation for Texas's lack of a white backlash is the political moderation of its Hispanic population, another is the underappreciated moderation of its white population as well. In fact, despite the high-profile antics of the state's Republican Party, whose recent platform demanded the abolition of the IRS and the Federal Reserve, there is substantial evidence that, on a host of social issues, Texans are not much more conservative than the nation as a whole. According to a March Scripps Howard Texas Poll, 44 percent of Texans consider themselves pro-choice, while 46 percent lean pro-life (the national figures, according to a March Gallup Poll, are 48 percent pro-choice, 43 percent pro-life). And, according to statewide polling by Rice's Klineberg, nearly half of all Texans believe that "government should do more to solve our country's problems" and that homosexuals should be granted equal civil rights. For years, writes Rice sociologist Chandler Davidson, Texas has suffered from a "myth of overwhelming conservatism," encouraged by hard-right politicians who "self-servingly portray themselves as spokesman for a homogenous conservative population." But now, despite the Gore camp's best intentions, that myth, like the 25,000 abandoned oil wells that litter the state, might finally run dry.

Or maybe not. Because it's not just the presidential candidates who seem determined to wrap Texas in outdated caricatures; so do many Texans themselves. Dallas residents might complain about the unfair portrayal of their city as a gaudy boomtown and tout their cosmopolitan art scene. But in the next breath they'll proudly advertise their city's second-largest tourist attraction: Southfork, the ranch from the TV show "Dallas," which celebrates exactly the image they claim to loathe. And linguists have recently discovered that the much-maligned Lone Star drawl correlates not so much with geographic location or time spent in the state as with positive feelings about Texas. A 1993 statewide poll found that more than 60 percent of Texans believed themselves to be "particularly unique" compared with other Americans.

Ironically, Texans have historically promoted their state's cultural uniqueness so strenuously precisely because of its lack of true unity and cohesion. In the nineteenth century, the legends of the cowboy (appropriated from eighteenth-century northern Mexican folk culture) and the Alamo held together a fragile coalition of five ministates, each with its peculiar culture, topography and climate. (The annexation treaty of 1845, which incorporated Texas into the Union, included a provision allowing the state to splinter into those five regions if it chose to do so.) Politicians, in particular, have burnished the old myths to stoke Texas chauvinism and unite the populace. Lyndon Johnson, for instance, used the image of the spirited rancher to transcend his Germanic, peach-farming, central Texas origins and broaden his appeal to the entire state. And, once Johnson became president, the national press eagerly bought into the stereotype he and his Texas constituents had worked so hard to create. If, along with self-sufficiency, entrepreneurial savvy, and bravado, that stereotype included buffoonery, anti-intellectualism, and violence, LBJ and the rest of the state seemed happy with the bargain. They would take the bad rap if they could keep the swagger.

And today's Texans, no matter how much they change their state's reality, seem just as happy with the deal. Back in May, Bush admitted to *U.S. News & World Report* that, compared to "bigger-than-life characters" like LBJ and John Connally, he represented "the newer Texas," someone who didn't "fill the screen quite as big." But then there he was, in that convention film, leading a camera crew in his pickup truck around the site of his future ranch, singing Midland's praises. How ironic, since few Texas cities have done a worse job of adapting to the state's new realities. Midland, which once boasted one of the highest per capita rates of millionaires in the nation, has proved unable to tap into Texas's high-tech boom and is now an economic disaster; last year the city's unemployment rate reached 9 percent. In April, town elders invited Tyler Mayor Eltife to come explain how he turned his East Texas town around.

It is Tyler, not Midland, that represents the real story of "entrepreneurial pioneers" and Texas optimism—a story about how the state revived itself by becoming more like the rest of America. Yet each presidential candidate, for his own, very different reason, seems determined to bury it. And the people of Texas appear happy to play along.

 F U R T H E R   R E A D I N G

Daniel D. Arreola, "The Texas-Mexican Homeland," *Journal of Cultural Geography* 13 (Spring/Summer 1993)

Walter L. Buenger, "Texas and the South," *Southwestern Historical Quarterly* 103 (January 2000)

Walter L. Buenger and Robert A. Calvert, *Texas Through Time: Evolving Interpretations* (1991)

Robert A. Calvert and Arnoldo de León, *The History of Texas* (1990)

Richard Francaviglia, *The Shape of Texas, Maps as Metaphors* (1995)

Don Graham, *Giant Country: Essays on Texas* (1998)

John H. Jenkins, *Basic Texas Books* (1988)

Terry G. Jordan, "The Anglo-Texan Homeland," *Journal of Cultural Geography* 13 (Spring/Summer 1993)

D. W. Meinig, *Imperial Texas: An Interpretive Essay in Cultural Geography* (1969)

Robert F. O'Connor, ed., *Texas Myths*, (1986)

Rupert N. Richardson, Earnest Wallace, Adrian N. Anderson and Cary Wintz, *Texas the Lone Star State* (rev. ed. 2000)

Texas State Historical Association, *Handbook of Texas* (rev. ed., 1996)

Emilio Zamora, Cynthia Orozco, and Rodolfo Rocha, *Mexican Americans in Texas History: Selected Essays* (2000)

CHAPTER
2

Contested Empires:
The Native Americans of Texas
and European Contact

The first Europeans to arrive in Texas encountered a complex set of distinct tribal cultures of nomadic hunters and sedentary agriculturalists, perhaps numbering as many as 50,000 people in the late seventeenth century.

Although conflict and accommodation were not new to Texas—or to North America—prior to European contact, the arrival of the Spanish and French profoundly upset the geopolitical and cultural equilibrium of the Texas tribes. As the documents and essays in this chapter indicate, a vast cultural divide separated Native Americans and Europeans. Throughout the western hemisphere, devastating pandemics wreaked havoc on Native Americans when they first encountered Europeans, and Texas was no exception.

Yet the Indians of Texas were not simply passive victims of European disease. Despite the debilitating effects of depopulation, many Texas tribal groups emerged as active agents in the contest for empire between France and Spain. Indeed, European forays into Texas during the first two centuries of Indian-European contact proved so sporadic and tentative that Native Americans were usually in a position to dictate the terms of their encounters with European visitors. Not until the eighteenth century, with the arrival of the Spanish in sufficient numbers, coupled with the rapid decline of the indigenous population, was Spain able to establish a limited degree of political and cultural sovereignty over east and south central Texas. How did Europeans and Native Americans attempt to bridge the cultural chasm that separated them during the early years of contact? What forces and conditions often stood in the way of mutual understanding?

DOCUMENTS

Document 1 is an excerpt from the memoir of Alvar Nunez Cabeza de Vaca. The treasurer of the ill-fated Narvaez expedition, Cabeza de Vaca was one of 600 soldiers and colonists who sailed from Cuba in June 1527, in search of riches in Florida. After several setbacks, Narvaez' men attempted the following year to sail to Mexico in make-shift boats. De Vaca was one of about one hundred and sixty members of the expedition who were washed up along the Texas coast. After a lengthy captivity by coastal Indian tribes, De Vaca and three survivors trekked across Texas, Mexico, and the American Southwest, reaching the Spanish settlements of Sinaloa, in western Mexico, in 1536.

Cabeza de Vaca's peregrinations encouraged Spanish authorities to undertake further expeditions into the borderlands, two of which converged on Texas in the early 1540s. Francisco Vásquez de Coronado followed rumors of golden cities into the southwest, crossing the Texas panhandle and traveling as far east as Kansas be-fore returning to Mexico. Hernando De Soto led an expedition from Florida across the Gulf Coast region. When De Soto died near the Mississippi River, Luis de Moscoso assumed command and led his men into East Texas. Document 2 is an ac-count of Moscoso's trek to the Trinity River. Discouraged by the failure to uncover new sources of mineral wealth, Spanish authorities declined to authorize any new expeditions into the borderlands until the end of the century.

Almost one hundred and fifty years would pass before European adventurers would return to Texas. In 1682, René La Robert Cavalier, Sieur de la Salle, sailed down the Mississippi River and claimed the region for the French. Two years later he embarked on a second expedition from France, accompanied by 280 colonists, but was unable to find the mouth of the river and landed on the Texas coast. LaSalle was murdered by disgruntled members of the expedition in 1687. Henri Joutel, one of La Salle's loyal subordinates, lived among the Caddoes before leading a group of survivors to Canada. In Document 3, Joutel describes a Caddo war party.

Alarmed by reports of the French presence in Texas, the Spanish government promptly renewed its efforts to control the area, authorizing several expeditions under Alonso de León. In Document 4, Father Damian Massanet describes the rem-nants of Fort St. Louis, built by La Salle and his men on Matagorda Bay in 1685. Father Francisco Casanas de Jesús Maria spent a year and a half among the Caddo Indians; his report to the viceroy of Mexico on the favorable conditions for under-taking missionary work in East Texas is excerpted in Document 5. As Jesus Maria had anticipated, however, the absence of Spanish women posed a serious obstacle to amicable Hispanic-Indian relations. Sexual depredations committed by the male soldiery, coupled with the dramatic increase in Indian mortality rates as a result of exposure to European disease, soon antagonized the Caddoes, and Spain was obliged to close its mission in 1694.

1. Cabeza de Vaca Encounters the Indians of Texas, 1535

Castillo and Estevanico went inland to the Yguazes. This people are universally good archers and of a fine symmetry, although not so large as those we left. They have a nipple and a lip bored. Their support is principally roots, of two or three kinds, and they look for them over the face of all the country. The food is poor and gripes the persons who eat it. The roots require roasting two days: many are very bitter, and withal difficult to be dug. They are sought the distance of two or three

Frederick W. Hodge and Theodore H. Lewis, eds., *Spanish Explorers in the Southern United States 1528–1543* (Austin: Texas State Historical Association, 1990): 64–66; 95–97. Copyright Texas State Historical Association. Reprinted with permission.

leagues, and so great is the want these people experience, that they cannot get through the year without them. Occasionally they kill deer, and at times take fish; but the quantity is so small and the famine so great, that they eat spiders and the eggs of ants, worms, lizards, salamanders, snakes, and vipers that kill whom they strike; and they eat earth and wood, and all that there is, the dung of deer, and other things that I omit to mention; and I honestly believe that were there stones in that land they would eat them. They save the bones of the fishes they consume, of snakes and other animals, that they may afterwards beat them together and eat the powder. The men bear no burthens, nor carry anything of weight; such are borne by women and old men who are of the least esteem. They have not so great love for their children as those we have before spoken of. Some among them are accustomed to sin against nature. The women work very hard, and do a great deal; of the twenty-four hours they have only six of repose; the rest of the night they pass in heating the ovens to bake those roots they eat. At daybreak they begin to dig them, to bring wood and water to their houses and get in readiness other things that may be necessary. The majority of the people are great thieves; for though they are free to divide with each other, on turning the head, even a son or a father will take what he can. They are great liars, and also great drunkards, which they became from the use of a certain liquor.

These Indians are so accustomed to running, that without rest or fatigue they follow a deer from morning to night. In this way they kill many. They pursue them until tired down, and sometimes overtake them in the race. Their houses are of matting, placed upon four hoops. They carry them on the back, and remove every two or three days in search of food. Nothing is planted for support. They are a merry people, considering the hunger they suffer; for they never cease, notwithstanding, to observe their festivities and *areytos*. To them the happiest part of the year is the season of eating prickly pears; they have hunger then no longer, pass all the time in dancing, and eat day and night. While these last, they squeeze out the juice, open and set them to dry, and when dry they are put in hampers like figs. These they keep to eat on their way back. The peel is beaten to powder.

It occurred to us many times while we were among this people, and there was no food, to be three or four days without eating, when they, to revive our spirits, would tell us not to be sad, that soon there would be prickly pears when we should eat a plenty and drink of the juice, when our bellies would be very big and we should be content and joyful, having no hunger. From the time they first told us this, to that at which the earliest were ripe enough to be eaten, was an interval of five or six months; so having tarried until the lapse of this period, and the season had come, we went to eat the fruit.

We found mosquitos of three sorts, and all of them abundant in every part of the country. They poison and inflame, and during the greater part of the summer gave us great annoyance. As a protection we made fires, encircling the people with them, burning rotten and wet wood to produce smoke without flame. The remedy brought another trouble, and the night long we did little else than shed tears from the smoke that came into our eyes, besides feeling intense heat from the many fires, and if at any time we went out for repose to the seaside and fell asleep, we were reminded with blows to make up the fires. The Indians of the interior have a different method, as intolerable, and worse even than the one I have spoken of, which is to go with brands in the hand firing the plains and forests within their reach, that the mosquitos may fly away, and at the same time to drive out lizards and other like things from the earth for them to eat.

They are accustomed also to kill deer by encircling them with fires. The pasturage is taken from the cattle by burning, that necessity may drive them to seek it in places where it is desired they should go. They encamp only where there are wood and water; and sometimes all carry loads of these when they go to hunt deer, which are usually found where neither is to be got. On the day of their arrival, they kill the deer and other animals which they can, and consume all the water and all the wood in cooking and on the fires they make to relieve them of mosquitos. They remain the next day to get something to sustain them on their return; and when they go, such is their state from those insects that they appear to have the affliction of holy Lazarus. In this way do they appease their hunger, two or three times in the year, at the cost I have mentioned. From my own experience, I can state there is no torment known in this world that can equal it. . . .

. . . Among the articles given us, Andrés Dorantes received a hawk-bell of copper, thick and large, figured with a face, which the natives had shown, greatly prizing it. They told him that they had received it from others, their neighbors; we asked them whence the others had obtained it, and they said it had been brought from the northern direction, where there was much copper, which was highly esteemed. We concluded that whencesoever it came there was a foundry, and that work was done in hollow form.

We departed the next day, and traversed a ridge seven leagues in extent. The stones on it are scoria of iron. At night we arrived at many houses seated on the banks of a very beautiful river. The owners of them came half way out on the road to meet us, bringing their children on their backs. They gave us many little bags of margarite and pulverized galena, with which they rub the face. They presented us many beads, and blankets of cowhide, loading all who accompanied us with some of every thing they had. They eat prickly pears and the seed of pine. In that country are small pine trees, the cones like little eggs; but the seed is better than that of Castile, as its husk is very thin, and while green is beaten and made into balls, to be thus eaten. If the seed be dry, it is pounded in the husk, and consumed in the form of flour.

Those who there received us, after they had touched us went running to their houses and directly returned, and did not stop running, going and coming, to bring us in this manner many things for support on the way. They fetched a man to me and stated that a long time since he had been wounded by an arrow in the right shoulder, and that the point of the shaft was lodged above his heart, which, he said, gave him much pain, and in consequence, he was always sick. Probing the wound I felt the arrow-head, and found it had passed through the cartilage. With a knife I carried, I opened the breast to the place, and saw the point was aslant and troublesome to take out. I continued to cut, and, putting in the point of the knife, at last with great difficulty I drew the head forth. It was very large. With the bone of a deer, and by virtue of my calling, I made two stitches that threw the blood over me, and with hair from a skin I stanched the flow. They asked me for the arrowhead after I had taken it out, which I gave, when the whole town came to look at it. They sent it into the back country that the people there might view it. In consequence of this operation they had many of their customary dances and festivities. The next day I cut the two stitches and the Indian was well. The wound I made appeared only like a seam in the palm of the hand. He said he felt no pain or sensitiveness in it whatsoever. This cure gave us control throughout the country in all that the inhabitants had power, or deemed of any value, or cherished. We showed them the hawk-bell we brought, and they told us that in the place whence that had come, were buried many plates of the same material; it was a thing they greatly esteemed, and where it came from were fixed habitations. The country we considered to be on the South Sea, which we had ever understood to be richer than the one of the North.

2. Luis de Moscoso Explores East Texas, 1542

The Governor set out from Nondacao for Soacatino, and on the fifth day came to a province called Aays. The inhabitants had never heard of the Christians. So soon as they observed them entering the territory the people were called out, who, as fast as they could get together, came by fifties and hundreds on the road, to give battle. While some encountered us, others fell upon our rear; and when we followed up those, these pursued us. The attack continued during the greater part of the day, until we arrived at their town. Some men were injured, and some horses, but nothing so as to hinder travel, there being not one dangerous wound among all. The Indians suffered great slaughter.

The day on which the Governor departed, the guide told him he had heard it said in Nondacao, that the Indians of Soacatino had seen other Christians; at which we were all delighted, thinking it might be true, and that they could have come by the way of New Spain; for if it were so, finding nothing in Florida of value, we should be able to go out of it, there being fear we might perish in some wilderness. The Governor, having been led for two days out of the way, ordered that the Indian be put to the torture, when he confessed that his master, the cacique of Nondacao, had ordered him to take them in that manner, we being his enemies, and he, as his vassal, was bound to obey him. He was commanded to be cast to the dogs, and another Indian guided us to Soacatino, where we came the following day.

The country was very poor, and the want of maize was greatly felt. The natives being asked if they had any knowledge of other Christians, said they had heard that near there, towards the south, such men were moving about. For twenty days the march was through a very thinly peopled country, where great privation and toil were endured; the little maize there was, the Indians having buried in the scrub, where the Christians, at the close of the day's march, when they were well weary, went trailing, to seek for what they needed of it to eat.

Arrived at a province called Guasco, they found maize, with which they loaded the horses and the Indians; thence they went to another settlement, called Naquiscoça, the inhabitants of which said that they had no knowledge of any other

Frederick W. Hodge and Theodore H. Lewis, eds., *Spanish Explorers in the Southern United States 1528–1543* (Austin: Texas State Historical Association, 1990): 243–246. Copyright Texas State Historical Association. Reprinted with permission.

Christians. The Governor ordered them put to torture, when they stated that farther on, in the territories of another chief, called Naçacahoz, the Christians had arrived, and gone back toward the west, whence they came. He reached there in two days, and took some women, among whom was one who said that she had seen Christians, and, having been in their hands, had made her escape from them. The Governor sent a captain with fifteen cavalry to where she said they were seen, to discover if there were any marks of horses, or signs of any Christians having been there; and after travelling three or four leagues, she who was the guide declared that all she had said was false; and so it was deemed of everything else the Indians had told of having seen Christians in Florida.

As the region thereabout was scarce of maize, and no information could be got of any inhabited country to the west, the Governor went back to Guasco. The residents stated, that ten days' journey from there, toward the sunset, was a river called Daycao, whither they sometimes went to drive and kill deer, and whence they had seen persons on the other bank, but without knowing what people they were. The Christians took as much maize as they could find, to carry with them; and journeying ten days through a wilderness, they arrived at the river of which the Indians had spoken. Ten horsemen sent in advance by the Governor had crossed; and, following a road leading up from the bank, they came upon an encampment of Indians living in very small huts, who, directly as they saw the Christians, took to flight, leaving what they had, indications only of poverty and misery. So wretched was the country, that what was found everywhere, put together, was not half an alqueire of maize. Taking two natives, they went back to the river, where the Governor waited; and on coming to question the captives, to ascertain what towns there might be to the west, no Indian was found in the camp who knew their language.

The Governor commanded the captains and principal personages to be called together that he might determine now by their opinions what was best to do. The majority declared it their judgment to return to the River Grande of Guachoya, because in Anilco and thereabout was much maize; that during the winter they would build brigantines, and the following spring go down the river in them in quest of the sea, where having arrived, they would follow the coast thence along to New Spain,—an enterprise which, although it appeared to be one difficult to accomplish, yet from their experience it offered the only course to be pursued. They could not travel by land, for want of an interpreter; and they considered the country farther on, beyond the River Daycao, on which they were, to be that which Cabeça de Vaca had said in his narrative should have to be traversed, where the Indians wandered like Arabs, having no settled place of residence, living on prickly pears, the roots of plants, and game; and that if this should be so, and they, entering upon that tract, found no provision for sustenance during winter, they must inevitably perish, it being already the beginning of October; and if they remained any longer where they were, what with rains and snow, they should neither be able to fall back, nor, in a land so poor as that, to subsist.

The Governor, who longed to be again where he could get his full measure of sleep, rather than govern and go conquering a country so beset for him with hardships, directly returned, getting back from whence he came.

3. A Caddo War Party Returns Home, 1687

One morning at daybreak a troop of women enter our hut who were painted and smeared. When they had all entered, they began to sing various songs in their language at the top of their voices; after which, they began a kind of circle dance holding each other's hands. For what purpose were they performing this ceremony that lasted a good two or three hours? We learned that it was because their people had come back victorious over their enemies. As soon as the village had heard it, they all gathered in the way that I have told. Their dance ended with a few presents of tobacco that those in the hut made to the women who had come. I noticed during their dance that, from time to time, some of them took one of the scalps that was in the hut and made a show of it, presenting it first from one side, then the other, as if to jeer at the tribe from which the scalp had come. At noon, one of the warriors also arrived at our hut, apparently the one who had brought the news of the enemies' defeat.

This Indian told us that the people of his village had indeed killed 40 of the enemy and that the others had taken flight; at this news, everyone displayed great joy. But what disturbed me then was to see that, as joyful as these women were, they broke out crying. I was fearful, as always, of some malicious plan against us according to what I had heard in the past. After all these ceremonies, the women went to work; pounding corn, some parching it and others making bread. They were preparing to bring the food to the warriors. . . .

We learned then of the way they had proceeded: they had met, surprised and struck terror into their enemies with a few gunshots fired by our men who, having killed a few of them, drove the others to flee. Indeed, before any of them had been killed, the enemy was waiting staunchly, not demonstrating any fear. But hearing the shots from the guns, of which they had no understanding, they ran as fast as possible. In this way, our Indians killed or captured 48 individuals, men as well as women and children. They killed several women who had climbed trees to hide as they could not escape by running, not having enough time to follow along with the others.

Few men found themselves thus defeated, but the women were left for victims because it was not the Indians' custom to give any mercy except to children. They cut off the scalp of a woman still alive, after which they asked our people for a charge of powder and a bullet which they gave the woman and sent her back to her tribe telling her to give that to her people as a warning that they should expect the same treatment in the future.

I believe I have spoken elsewhere of this practice of taking scalps. In involves cutting the skin all around the head down to the ears and the forehead. They then lift the entire skin which they take care to clean and taw to preserve and display in their huts. They thus leave the sufferer with an exposed skull, as they did with this woman whom they sent back with word to her tribe.

William Foster, ed., *The LaSalle Expedition to Texas: The Journal of Henri Joutel, 1684–1687*, (Austin: Texas State Historical Association, 1998): 204–207. Copyright William C. Foster. Reprinted with permission.

The warriors brought another woman to the women and girls who came to meet them with food. Then they gave to the women and girls this unfortunate captured woman to be sacrificed to their rage and passion according to the account of our men who were witnesses. When these women arrived and learned that there was a captive, they armed themselves, some with short heavy sticks, others with wooden skewers they had sharpened, and each one struck her as caprice seized her, vying with each other. The unfortunate woman could do nothing but await the finishing stroke, suffering as it were the martyr's role, for one tore away a handful of hair, another cut off a finger, another dug out an eye. Each one made a point of torturing her in some way; and in the end there was one who struck a hard blow to her head and another who drove a skewer into her body. After that she died. They then cut her up into several pieces which the victors carried with them, and they forced several other slaves taken earlier to eat the pieces. Thus the Indians returned triumphant from their war. Of the 48 persons whom they took, they gave mercy only to the young children. All their scalps were brought back, and several women who had gone to war with the others even carried some heads they brought back. . . .

On the next day, the 20th, the Indians assembled and went to the chief's hut where all the scalps were carried as trophies along with the heads. Then they began to rejoice which continued all day in that hut, and the ceremony continued for three more days. After that, they proceeded to the huts belonging to the most eminent among them whom they called *cadis* which means chiefs or captains. They invited the six Frenchmen who had accompanied them to participate in their festivities just as they had participated in their victory. As we were staying in one of the most important chief's huts, they came there after concluding their celebration at the hut of the head chief.

I was astonished at the way they conducted themselves. After all had arrived, the elders and the *cadis* took their places on the mats upon which they sat down. Then one of these elders, who had not been with them but who seemed to be an orator, began to speak as master of ceremonies. He delivered a kind of eulogy or oration of which I understood nothing. A short time later, each warrior who had killed in battle and had scalps marched forward preceded by a woman carrying a tall cane and a deer skin. Then came the wife of the warrior carrying the scalp; the warrior followed with his bow and two arrows. When they arrived before the orator or master of ceremonies, the warrior took the scalp and placed it in the hands of the orator who, on receiving it, presented it to the four quarters of the compass, saying many things that I did not understand. After this he placed the scalp on the ground on a mat spread for this purpose. Another warrior approached in the same manner until each one had brought his scalp as a trophy. When all this was done, the orator gave a kind of address, and they were served food. The women of the hut had cooked *sagamité* in several large pots knowing the assembly would come. After they had eaten and smoked, they began to dance in an unclosed circle formation. They set a sort of rhythm that they stamped with their feet and waved with fans made from turkey feathers; in this way they adapted all this to their songs which seemed too long to me because I could not understand anything.

Their ceremony ended with a few presents of tobacco which those from the hut gave to the elders and the warriors. I must mention too that the master of ceremonies brought food and tobacco to the scalps as if they were in condition to eat or smoke. They also had two young boys whom they had captured and given mercy. One was wounded and could not walk; therefore they had put him on a horse. They brought pieces of flesh of the woman they had tortured, and they made these two young boys eat some of it. They made a few other slaves, whom they had captured another time, eat pieces of her flesh as well. As for them, I did not notice whether they ate any themselves. After they had finished, they went off to a few other huts, and this ceremony lasted there for three days.

4. Spain Reacts to the French Presence in Texas, 1689

We left Coahuila on the twenty-sixth of March in the year 1689, and went as far as the Rio del Norte, which, in the said province of Coahuila, is called the Rio Grande, our guide still being the Indian Juanillo, and when we reached the said river, I sent for the Indian who knew the country and had been among the Frenchmen, whom I call Quems, because he belonged to the Indian nation of that name. We travelled on towards the northeast and at times east-northeast, until we reached the river of Our Lady of Guadalupe. And here I asked this Indian whether the dwellings of the French were still a long way off, thinking that when we should be distant from them a day and night's journey, some of us might push forward in order, unnoticed, to take a survey of the village. The Indian replied that the village was about fifteen leagues distant from that river.

On the morning of the next day Captain Alonso de León asked me what we should do in order to ascertain the number of Frenchmen and the condition of things in their village. With regard to this there were various opinions, mine being that, since we had with us the Quems Indian, who was well acquainted with the country, we should all have a mass sung in honor of the Blessed Virgin of Guadalupe that very morning, at the very place in which we were; also that when we should succeed in the reaching the dwellings of the Frenchmen we should have another mass celebrated, in honor of Saint Anthony of Padua. All consented very readily to this, and, soon, at about nine o'clock in the morning, the mass to the Virgin was sung.

After that it was arranged that, the two Indians, Juanillo the Papul and the Quems Indian, serving as guides, twenty-five men should travel on with us until we should come upon the French village in the early morning, while the remaining soldiers with the beasts of burden should come behind us and camp when they reached a suitable spot. This spot they should then not leave until we returned, unless by the express command of Captain Alonso de Leon. When we started out, the rear-guard received orders to proceed slowly, watching cautiously lest any Indian should appear; in case any did, they were to seize him without doing him the least harm, and notify us of the capture.

After travelling some four leagues, the rear-guard saw an Indian come out of a dense wood, and called to him, and he went towards them without any show of resistance. They sent us word, and we halted. On the arrival of the Indian the two we

---

"Letter of Father Massanet to Don Carlos de Siguenza, 1690," Herbert E. Bolton, *Spain's Exploration in the Southwest, 1542–1706* (New York: Scribner's, 1916): 355–364.

had along asked him whether there were thereabouts any of the white people who dwelt further on. He said that, as to those living further, they used to inhabit houses which now no longer existed, for, two moons previous, the Indians of the coast had killed all but a few boys, whom they had carried off; that he himself lived in the ranchería of the Emet and Lavas Indians, which was about two leagues out of the route which we were following towards the bay of Espiritu Santo. We went with this Indian to the ranchería of which he spoke, and reached it at about three in the afternoon. As soon as the Indians became aware of our presence, they made for the wood, leaving to us the ranchería, together with the laden dogs, which they had not been able to drive fast enough when they fled. The Indian who served as our guide himself entered the wood, and called to the others, declaring that we were friends, and that they should have no fear. Some of them—and among these was their captain—came out and embraced us, saying: *"Thechas! techas!"* which means "Friends! friends!" One of those who came out first was a big young fellow about twenty years old, who wore a Recollect friar's cloak, and when we saw that it was the cloak of a friar, we gave him a blanket, and I took the robe from him.

The said Indians told how, two days previous, two Frenchmen had passed by with the Tejas Indians. That very afternoon we started in pursuit of the said Frenchmen, and at sunset, we reached the ranchería of the Toxo and Toaa Indians, who told us that the said Frenchmen had passed by with the said Tejas, and had been unwilling to remain there with them. That night we slept near the ranchería, and at eight in the evening some Indians came to the place where we were, one of them dressed after the fashion of the French. And they brought some French books and a Holy Bible. The next morning we set out in quest of the said Frenchmen, passing through some very dense woods; and at about two o'clock in the afternoon we came to some ranchitos of Emet Indians. On our inquiring concerning the Frenchmen, these Indians pointed out to us an Indian who had just arrived and who had conducted them (the Frenchmen) as far as the San Marcos River, and when we wished to cross they told us that we would not be able to cross the said river. We told the Indian who had led the Frenchmen that if he would take them a paper and bring an answer we would give him a horse, and that he should take the answer to the houses where the Frenchmen lived. Captain Francisco Martinez wrote the letter in the French language because he was master of it.

We returned where the camp was, five leagues beyond the Guadalupe River, and we learned that three days previous the horses had stampeded, and a number having been recovered, fifty were still missing, and in pursuit a soldier had lost his way. This man remained missing four days, and in the meantime he met with some Indians who were skinning a buffalo, who took him home with them at nightfall to their ranchería, giving him to eat of the buffalo meat, and whatever else they themselves had. On the day after this, an Indian belonging to the same ranchería came there with a small bundle of tobacco. This Indian was the one who had been with us, and he made a long harangue to all the Indians who were in the ranchería. As to the soldier who was lost, when he met with the Indians who had the buffalo, they spoke to him by signs, and he understood them to tell him to make a fire. This he must have inferred from seeing the meat they had, or he was frightened at seeing himself lost among barbarian Indians; he spilled on his cloak the powder he was carrying in a flask, and on his striking the light a spark fell on the powder, and it burned his whole side from head to foot. When the Indians learned that we were in their territory they must have come to the conclusion that, since that man was lost, his comrades would be sure to look for him. The next day they brought him his horse, and, since he was so badly burned that he could not help himself, the Indians themselves saddled it for him, and assisted him to mount, telling him by signs to go with them. They brought him very near to the place where we were, just a couple of shots away. The Indians who brought him, not wishing to approach us, signified to him that he should go on, using signs to indicate to him where we were, at the foot of a hill which he saw there. At the foot of that hill, on the other side, they left him, and he reached us at nine in the morning, which was for all a source of great satisfaction. We felt very sorry when we saw how badly burnt he was.

On the following day we left for the settlement of the Frenchmen, and when we were about three leagues from it there came out some twenty-five Indians. Now the old Frenchman who accompanied us took occasion to say that the settlement of the Frenchmen was not in the place to which the two Indian guides were taking us. On the way this Frenchman tried several times, by means of an Indian of the Cavas nation whom he had with him, to make our two Indians desert us, or say that it was very far, and that we should not be able to cross the rivers which were on the way. I resented so much that the Frenchman should be given occasion to speak that I grew angry, and Captain Alonso de Leon said to me: "Father, we are going wherever you wish." We continued following the two guides quite three leagues; we arrived at a stream of very good drinking water, and the two Indians said to me: "Lower down on the bank of this stream are the houses of the French, which must be about three leagues off." Then the old Frenchman saw that there was no help, and that we were certain to come upon the village. He then said: "Sir, now I know very well, yea, very well, that the houses are on this little river."

We started the next morning, and three leagues off we found the village of the Frenchmen on the bank of the stream, as I had been told by the two Indians, the Quems and Juanillo the Papul. We arrived at about eleven in the forenoon, and found six houses, not very large, built with poles plastered with mud, and roofed over with buffalo hides, another larger house where pigs were fattened, and a wooden fort made from the hulk of a wrecked vessel. The fort had one lower room which was used as a chapel for saying mass, and three other rooms below; above the three rooms was an upper story serving for a store-house, wherein we found some six loads of iron, not counting scattered pieces, and some steel, also eight small guns and three swivels made of iron, the largest pieces being for a charge of about six pounds of shot. The pieces and one swivel were buried, and Captain Alonso de Leon carried off two of the swivels. There was a great lot of shattered weapons, broken by the Indians—firelocks, carbines, cutlasses—but they had not left the cannon, only one being found. We found two unburied bodies, which I interred, setting up a cross over the grave. There were many torn-up books, and many dead pigs.

These Frenchmen had a piece of land fenced in with stakes, where they sowed just a little corn, and had an asparagus bed; we found also very good endive. This place affords no advantages as to situation, for good drinking-water is very far off, and timber still further. The water of the stream is very brackish, so much so that in five days during which the camp was pitched there all the horses sickened from the brackish water.

The next day we went down to explore the bay of Espíritu Santo, and coasted it until we succeeded in finding the mouth; in the middle of this there is a flat rock, and all along the shore of the bay there are many lagoons which it is very difficult to cross. Blackberries are abundant, large and fine, and there are a number of stocks which seem to be those of grape vines, but no trees, and no fresh water. The Indians dig wells for drinking water.

After exploring the bay we returned to the main body of our party, whom we had left in the village; we arrived there at noon, and remained there that afternoon, and the next day they bent the large iron bars, making them up into bundles, in order to carry them with ease. We found the Indian with the reply to the letter which we had written to the Frenchmen; they said that we should wait for them, that they would soon come, that another Frenchman was further on, and that they were waiting for him in order that they might come all together. The Indian received the horse, as we had ordered. As to the fort, Captain Alonso de Leon would not have it burnt down, and it remained as it was.

The next day we set out on our return trip to the Guadalupe River, and when we got halfway, since we saw that the Frenchmen did not come, Captain Alonso de Leon, with twenty-five men, went to the ranchería where they were, and the main party went on as far as the Guadalupe River, where it remained waiting three days. The Frenchmen were in the ranchería of the Toaa Indians, with the Tejas; they came to the Guadalupe with Captain Alonso de Leon and arrived there on the 2d of May, '89. Two Frenchmen came, naked except for an antelope's skin, and with their faces, breasts, and arms painted like the Indians, and with them came the governor of the Tejas and eight of his Indians. Through that day and night I tried my utmost to show all possible consideration to the said governor, giving him two horses, and the blanket in which I slept, for I had nothing else which I could give him. Speaking Spanish, and using as an interpreter one of the Frenchmen whom we had with us, I said to the governor that his people should become Christians, and bring into their lands priest who should baptize them, since otherwise they could not save their souls, adding that if he wished, I would go to his lands. Soon the afore-mentioned governor said he would very willingly take me there, and I promised him to go, and to take with me other priests like myself, repeating to him that I would be there in the following year, at the time of sowing corn. The governor seemed well pleased, and I was still more so, seeing the harvest to be reaped among the many souls in those lands who know not God.

The next day was the day of the Holy Cross—the 3d of May; after mass the governor of the Tejas left for his home and we for this place. We arrived at Coahuila, and Captain Alonso de Leon sent two Frenchmen—the one named Juan Archebepe, of Bayonne, the other Santiago Grollette—from Coahuila to Mexico, with Captain Francisco Martinez, and His Excellency the Conde de Galbe had the Frenchmen provided with suitable clothes and dispatched to Spain on shipboard in the same year, '89.

All this news did not fail to create excitement and to give satisfaction not only to His Excellency but also to other men of note in Mexico, and there were several meetings held in order to consider measures not only for keeping the French from gaining control of those regions and settling in them, but also for the introduction of religious ministers.

5. A Franciscan Reports on Prospects for Converting the Caddo Indians, 1691

I trust that by the grace of the Most High, through the protection of our Most Holy Mother and the good wishes of our Catholic Majesty and of your Excellency, all these tribes will be subdued. This will be true if those who come from Spain to this country to live will furnish a good example. This done, and the spirit of the evangelical ministers being joined therewith, it is inevitable that much glory and fruit for the two Majesties can be expected. . . .

The dissatisfaction of all the Indians is great when the Spaniards live among them without their wives. I say also from what I have experienced that, if it be possible, it would be to our interest if no man came without his wife. . . . Before I left the mission of Santiago, a letter was written me giving me information of the people that were on their way to Texas, and of the flocks they were bringing. I read this letter to the captains and nobles who were altogether in a council. The first thing they noticed in the letter was that the men were coming without their wives, and they knew that there would [necessarily] be additional men to guard the stock. If objections be made to these few, how much greater objection will be raised, your Excellency, if a great number come into this country to stay. Every day these Indians ask me whether the Spaniards are going to bring their wives with them when they come back. I tell them yes. But in spite of everything they do not give me any credence. They tell me that I must write to Your Excellency, their great captain, and tell you in this missive that they want to be friends, but if the Spaniards want to live among them it must be under such conditions that no harm will be done the Indians by the Spaniards if they do come without their wives; but, if the Spaniards bring their wives, the Indians will be satisfied.

I must say that the demand of these Indians is just and reasonable. And it has already been agreed to. I know from experience gained upon two occasions when duty to the church called me to the work of conversion that this will be wise; and it will be well to leave for my protection three or four unmarried men. I have been much distressed and feared to lose all the fruit that might be produced; and, therefore, prostrate at your feet, I beg of Your Excellency to look with favor upon this work which is so pleasing to the Lord, that it should not be lost. And do not send criminals taken from the prisons, or bachelors, or vagabonds, who, when they are here, away from home where there are no Christians, would commit great atrocities, and, by their depraved lives and bad example, counteract the efforts of the minister, depriving them of the fruit of these souls of the Indians. It would be better for that class of men to be sent somewhere else where they can be kept down with lash in hand. In this way, and in no other, may their souls be saved. For, God knows, souls cannot be saved by one who does not regard his own soul; by one who does not believe in human justice nor acknowledge the justice of God. What a pity. But the evangelical ministers can be confident, since they know that they have the

"Descriptions of the Tejas or Asinai Indians, 1691–1722," trans. Mattie Austin Hatcher, *Southwestern Historical Quarterly,* vol. 29 (July, 1925–April, 1926): 287–290; 300–303. Copyright Texas State Historical Association. Reprinted with permission.

protection of Your Excellency whom we all know watches over the work with more ardent love and desire than we do ourselves. . . .

I trust by the Grace of God that, as soon as the ministers are able to speak the language perfectly and when we have the protection and watchful care of the Spaniards, we will uproot all the discord which the mortal enemy of our souls has sown in this country and that the faith will be planted with greater perfection than in other sections; especially as we enjoy the protection of our Catholic king and of Your Excellency who tries to encourage this work with so much zeal and order by sending ministers and by doing everything else which you may think necessary, since it is for the service of God, our Lord, without which all that has already been done will be lost, if God does not intervene. I say all this because the devil will lay many snares and hindrances in our way in order that the cause of the Most High may not triumph.

Most Excellent Sir, from the information I possess my pen might run on concerning the things I have so far recorded, particularly in regard to their ceremonies, rites, and superstitions, which are so great that those I have myself seen and carefully examined would fill a quire of paper. However, time offers me only the alternative of closing this work. However, what I have related so far contains the most essential features. If Your Excellency will permit me to amplify these notes in greater detail, I shall be very prompt in executing the order. The Lord knows that in this whole matter I am inspired only by the desire I have that not a single soul shall be lost and that these poor miserable people may die only after receiving the holy baptism. It would certainly be a great misfortune if they should perish for want of encouragement because it has not yet been ascertained, nor is it not known, whether there are other unconverted tribes who are more civilized and settled than these Indians and their more immediate neighbors; for all of them cultivate their fields. They do not lack for food. They never abandon their houses nor their country, although they do go to war with their enemies.

They are an industrious people and apply themselves to all kind of work. Indeed, if during the year and three months I have been among them if I had had some bells, some small clasp knives, some glass beads, and some blue cloth—which they greatly prize,—some blankets, and other little things to exchange with these Indians, I could have started a convent with the articles it would have been possible to make from the best materials that are abundant here. I, therefore, declare that it will be well for the ministers to have some of these things—not that one person only should have them—because the Indians are of such a nature that they have no love save for the person who gives them something. So strong is this characteristic that only the person who gives them something is good while all others are bad. They do not even want to receive the holy sacrament of baptism except from some person who has given them a great many things. Even the ministers are not able to persuade them, nor will it ever be possible to develop the mission without these presents. During my stay of one year and three months in this country and during the ten months since I started this, Your Excellency's mission, under the name of Santíssima Nombre de María, I have not had a scrap or anything else. I have torn even my tattered garments up to give to some Indian for helping me. The governor of this mission of yours can vouch for this. . . .

All the ministers may take courage and comfort themselves, first because the language of all these tribes is easy to learn; and then because all the infidels of this section of the country are very tractable. The ministers should not be discouraged even when some of the Indians are very obstinate and are not willing to receive the holy baptism. In two cases I realized that it was impossible to succeed in inducing them to receive it and so they died without it. But cases have come up that demand great prudence so that the fruit may not be lost through some unimportant thing. I do not prophesy what may happen, but it will be well for the ministers who come to this country to know that, in time and upon a closer acquaintance, they will discover cruelties which the Indians practice. Mothers have killed their newborn children because the fathers did not want them. On one occasion they set fire to a house and left two little children to burn, declaring that they were good for nothing.

Most Excellent Sir, according to the information I have received about three thousand persons among all the friendly tribes of the *Tejias* must have died during the epidemic which the Lord sent during the month of March, 1691. The disease was worse in some provinces than in others. As to our own province, I have already stated that the deaths probably reached the number of three hundred—in other provinces the number was sometimes greater, sometimes less.

I have information that the *Cadaudacho* have hopes that the French will return, because they promised when leaving the country that they would return when the cold season again set in, and that a great many of them would have to come in order to occupy the country completely. This is nothing but Indian gossip, though for several reasons it is to be feared that they speak as they are instructed to speak. The French may also be compelled to return on account of their companions whom they left here. I know nothing more of this matter than that in the month of February there were nine or ten Frenchmen at a feast which the Indians had in a neighboring province, about thirty leagues from us called the province of *Nacaos.*

Most Excellent Sir, I know well that much of what I have related does not concern me, but I have had no motive in so doing save the desire I have of bringing souls to the Lord. Although there are many of the tribes who have died, there is no lack of material for conversion for all the ministers who may come. In the name of our Saviour and that of the blessed Mary, prostrate at their feet, I pray for aid and protection and that His Divine Majesty may grant you good health in order that Your Excellency may be the patron of a work which is so pleasing to God.

❧ E S S A Y S

The area today known as Texas experienced rapid depopulation as a result of European diseases. The first essay, by the late Smithsonian anthropologist John C. Ewers, presents a grim picture of the devastating toll which these epidemics took on the indigenous peoples of Texas, a process that was well underway even before Europeans arrived in large numbers. Nonetheless, as the second essay by Daniel A. Hickerson reminds us, the disastrous impact of disease was only one component, albeit the most important one, of the sociocultural changes which the Indians of East Texas experienced as a result of European contact. When the Spanish, spurred by reports of French encroachment, arrived in the pine forests of East Texas in the late seventeenth century to establish their claim to the region, they encountered an agricultural people, the Caddo Indians, living under a highly developed political system as members of the Hasinai Confederation. But the lives of the Caddoes had already been profoundly altered by the Spanish presence in North America. Hickerson offers several reasons for the creation of the confederacy, all of which suggest the extent to which the prior arrival of the Spanish in distant regions of the borderlands had transformed native cultures in Texas even before direct contact occurred there.

The Impact of European Diseases on Texas Indians

JOHN C. EWERS

That Europeans introduced epidemic diseases into the Americas which drastically reduced the numbers of Indians during the historic period is a fact well know to both historians and anthropologists. But the long range effects of successive epidemics on the populations of particular tribes have not been sufficiently studied, and the effects of these epidemics on the beliefs and customs of the Indians who survived them have been little considered by scholars.

Texas provides a fertile field for studying the influences of epidemics on neighboring tribes of different cultures over an extended period. Nowhere else in the American West did tribes of so many cultures live in such close proximity in the historic period. In Texas alone, buffalo-hunting nomads of the plains met not only horticultural tribes of the plains and woodlands, but also hunter-gatherers of the southwestern deserts and fishermen of the Gulf Coast. . . .

In view of the difficulties in evaluating early estimates of Indian populations, it is not surprising that most anthropologists have relied upon the figures cited in James Mooney's posthumously published study, *The Aboriginal Population of America North of Mexico*. Because Mooney's industry was enormous, his knowledge of Indians and of the literature was great, and his integrity was beyond question, this study of Indian population became the classic work in its field. Nevertheless, A. L. Kroeber, who carefully reviewed Mooney's estimates for the entire North American continent, concluded that "the best of Mooney's estimates can hardly pretend to be nearer than 10 per cent of the probable truth, and some may be 50 per cent or more from it" [see Table 1]. . . .

On the whole, Mooney's estimates for the Indian tribes of Texas appear to be conservative. He may have erred more grievously in underestimating some of the more populous tribes than in overestimating some of the smaller ones. A total population for the tribes considered of at least 50,000 might not be excessive.

By 1890 census figures for these same tribes indicate that their total populations had declined to 12,243, or less than 25% of Mooney's "aboriginal" total for these tribes (Table 1, columns 5–6). Before 1890 the Karankawan, Atakapan, and Coahuiltecan tribes had become extinct. The Caddoan and Tonkawan tribes, as well as the Lipan Apache and Comanche, appear to have suffered reductions of more than 75%. Only the Kiowa, Kiowa-Apache, Mescalero Apache, Arapaho, and Cheyenne appear to have been reduced by less than 50%. It is noteworthy that, with the exception of the Mescalero Apache, all of the last group of tribes

John C. Ewers, "The Influence of Epidemics on the Indian Populations and Cultures of Texas," *Plains Anthropologist: Journal of the Plains Conference,* vol. 19, no. 60 (May 1973): 104–113. Reprinted by permission from Plains Anthropologist. Copyright © 1973 by Plains Anthropological Society.

Table 1. The Depopulation of the Indian Tribes of Texas

Tribe or Group of Related Tribes	Linguistic Stock	Mooney Est. for 1690	Mooney Est. for 1780	Census for 1890	Per Cent Reduction
Karankawan tribes	Karankawan	2,800		Extinct	100%
Akokisa	Atakapan	500		Extinct	100%
Bidai	Atakapan	500		Extinct	100%
Coahuiltecan tribes	Coahuiltecan	7,500*		Extinct	100%
Tonkawan tribes	Tonkawan	1,600		56	97%
Caddoan tribes of East Texas	Caddoan	8,500		536	94%
Wichita group of tribes	Caddoan	3,200		358	89%
Kichai	Caddoan	500		66	87%
Lipan Apache	Athapascan	500		60**	88%
Mescalero Apache	Athapascan	700		473	32%
Kiowa-Apache	Athapascan		300+	326	+9%
Comanche	Shoshonean	7,000		1,598	77%
Kiowa	Kiowa-Tanoan		2,000	1,140	43%
‡Arapaho	Algonquian		3,000⎫	5,630	13%
‡Cheyenne	Algonquian		3,500⎭		

* Coahuiltecan tribes in Texas estimated at one-half Mooney's total for these tribes in Mexico and Texas.
** Includes 20 Lipan among Tonkawa and 40 among Mescalero Apache in 1890.
\+ Yet Mooney (1898:253) states: "They have probably never numbered much over three hundred and fifty."
‡ All figures for Cheyenne and Arapaho include both Northern and Southern divisions, although only the Southern ones lived on the frontiers of Texas.

had limited contacts with whites prior to 1790, and none of them were missionized during the Spanish Period.

Epidemics certainly were not the sole cause of this radical reduction of more than 75% in the population of these tribes during the period prior to 1890. Intertribal warfare and wars with Spaniards, Mexicans, Texans, and citizens of the United States also took their toll. Overindulgence in liquor on the part of Indians living near white settlements also contributed to this decrease, as did venereal disease, malnutrition, and starvation. Nevertheless, Mooney's contention that epidemics were *the major cause* of marked population decrease among the tribes of North America prior to 1900 appears to have been true of the Indians of Texas.

Mooney listed but five "great epidemics" in Plains Indian history which decimated some or all of the tribes of Texas: an unidentified disease reported to have killed 3000 Caddoans in East Texas in 1691; widespread smallpox epidemics in 1778, 1801, and during the late 1830's; and a widespread cholera epidemic in 1849. Yet I found references to no less than *thirty* epidemics which appeared among one or more of the tribes of Texas (as I define them) between 1528 and 1890. There was still another one in 1892. Even this may not be a complete record. The absence of references to any epidemic among these Indians during the 146-year-period 1528–1674 may reflect our paucity of information more accurately than it does their state of health, or freedom from epidemics.

Contemporary writers did not identify the diseases involved in a number of the epidemics of the pre-1800 period. However, Dr. Pat Nixon, a San Antonio physician who reviewed the literature on these early epidemics, suggested the diseases on the basis of the symptoms described. Throughout the entire period, smallpox was the most common cause of epidemics.

There were smallpox epidemics in 1674–5, 1688–9, 1739, about 1746, 1750, 1759, 1763, 1766, 1778, 1801–02, 1816, 1839–40, 1861–2, and 1864. Although the Indians of present Oklahoma were vaccinated against smallpox in 1865, an epidemic of this disease occurred among the Mescalero Apache in New Mexico in 1877. Yet another smallpox epidemic was averted among the Mescalero during the winter of 1882–1883, when timely vaccination enabled these Indians to escape "without a single case of smallpox."

Next to smallpox, measles and cholera appear to have been the most deadly, although epidemics of malaria, whooping cough, and influenza also took their tolls of Indian lives.

The frequency of epidemics within a tribe must be regarded as a very important factor in the progressive decline of Indian population, for it inhibited the recovery and growth of tribal populations. The French biologist, Jean Louis Berlandier, who explored Texas in 1828 and subsequent years, reported that smallpox occurred among the Indian tribes "every sixteen years, making great ravages for a year at a time." He was not precisely accurate in defining the interval between epidemics, but the record is clear that there was a smallpox epidemic among one or more of the tribes of Texas at least once each generation from 1739 to 1877. Losses in these epidemics must have been high among children and teenagers who never lived to reproduce. Older people (including women beyond child-bearing age), who gained immunity by exposure to previous epidemics, presumably survived. . . .

Indian beliefs regarding the causes of epidemics varied. Interestingly enough, the fragmentary records of two of the earliest epidemics indicate that the afflicted Indians initially, and probably correctly, blamed the whites for these plagues. Cabeza de Vaca wrote that the Karankawa at *first* blamed his Spanish party for communicating the epidemic of 1528 to them, "believing we had killed them and holding it to be certain, they agreed among themselves to kill those of us who survived." But one Indian saved the Spaniards' lives by pointing out that if the white men had "so much power" they would not have suffered so many of their own men to perish.

Caddoan survivors of the disastrous epidemic of 1691 among the Indians of the East Texas missions at first blamed the high mortality upon the priests' practice of baptizing the stricken Indians during their death throes. But Father Casañas believed that he convinced even the most hostile Indian medicine men that the priests attentions had not caused the Indian deaths. . . .

The common practice among the nomadic tribes of scattering once an epidemic struck one of their camps, as well as their avoidance of the locality of the initial outbreak for a considerable time thereafter, must have helped to minimize losses among them. The desertion of the missions by some of the missionized Indians during the epidemic of the 18th century must have had a similar effect. The loyal neophytes who remained with their priests perished, while many of the dispersed apostates survived.

Significantly, the greatest population losses during the 18th century and the early years of the 19th century were suffered by the least mobile tribes. These were the mission Indians and the Caddoan farming tribes. The latter, as well as the Wichita and the tribes of East Texas, lived in compact, semi-permanent villages of multi-family lodges, where conditions were as favorable for the rapid communication of diseases as they were in the mission compounds. . . .

Early accounts of the Karankawan and Caddoan tribes of East Texas refer to the common practice of infanticide. It was also the custom of the Caddo to bury a live, nursing infant with its dead mother, and of the Comanche to kill a warrior's wife at his grave. These customs do not appear to have survived among these tribes beyond the middle of the 19th century. Why? Did not the continued decline in tribal population encourage the abandonment of customs so wasteful of human life?

The population decline also may have brought about significant changes in Indian war practices during the 19th century. Eighteenth century accounts indicate that the eating of prisoners, the hideous torture of captives, and the trade of captives as slaves were common among the Indian tribes of Texas. As the 19th century progressed only the Tonkawa continued to practice cannibalism to any extent, and both the torture and sale of captives became less common. Captives became more valuable as adopted members of a family—to replace children, wives, and husbands who had been lost in epidemics—than as human sacrifices or human trade goods. . . .

Epidemics strongly affected Indian tribal organization—or more properly disorganization and reorganization. Certainly the Karankawan, Atakapan and Coahuiltecan tribes, all of whom were repeated victims of epidemics, suffered the ultimate in social disorganization—extinction. The Lipan Apache lost their political and social autonomy and survived only as minority groups of a few individuals living among friendly Apache tribes in Oklahoma and New Mexico. Remnants of the Tonkawa were preserved from extinction under the protection of the United States Army at Fort Griffin during the waning years of the intertribal wars. The horticultural Caddoans, who numbered nearly thirty tribes before the epidemic of 1691, were reduced to three small tribes, identified as Caddo, Kichai, and Wichita, by the end of the frontier period.

There is need for a thorough study of the process by which the Caddoans managed to survive, through repeated combinations and reorganizations into fewer and fewer units as their numbers declined. In this process the names of many of the earlier tribes became almost forgotten. But they survived (to a degree) biologically long after they lost their political identity. There are indicators of tribal combinations following the deaths of important chiefs and many of their followers during the 18th century epidemics. Why the names of some of these tribes, such as Anadarko, survived, while those of other once equally numerous and prominent tribes disappeared, needs explanation. . . .

The cumulative effect of 30 or more epidemics among the Indians of Texas played a major role in the marked decline in population among these tribes during the historic period prior to 1890. Even though our best available set of early population estimates for these tribes, those of James Mooney, cannot be considered exact, comparison of them with 1890 census figures for the surviving tribes clearly indicates both a general population decline and a differential rate of decline among the different tribes. The sedentary, missionized and horticultural tribes suffered the most severe losses. Some of them became extinct; others sacrificed their tribal independence as their numbers decreased but insured their biological survival by combining with other linguistically and culturally related tribes. This practice was most common among the Caddoan tribes of East Texas. The nomadic tribes of the northern periphery appear to have suffered least, due to a combination of factors such as their relative remoteness from Whites until the early years of the 19th century, their common practice of scattering once they learned of the presence of disease among their people, and their very positive efforts to recruit additional tribal members through raiding for captives—both Indian and non-Indian.

The Caddo Confederacy

DANIEL A. HICKERSON

The Hasinai Confederacy was a loosely centralized group of Caddoan agricultural communities located along the Neches and Angelina Rivers in eastern Texas during the seventeenth and eighteenth centuries. Recent research has focused on introduced disease, and resulting population coalescences, during the protohistoric period (ca. A.D. 1520–1680) as an important factor in the formation of this confederacy and other similar groupings. Though the importance of disease cannot be denied, other factors contributed to the political and social situation of the Hasinai in the early historic era. Among these factors were trade in European goods, Apache aggression, and the natural defensive advantages of the Hasinai region. . . .

. . . Once the disease factor has been recognized, there exists a strong temptation to overstate its impact on bringing about those cultural changes, protohistoric or historic population movements, and shifts in settlement or subsistence patterns, and political and economic life for which evidence is found. This temptation can be dangerous for at least two reasons. First, despite recent attempts to use demographic research to interpret the archaeological record, the true extent of demographic decline in the Caddoan region has yet to be adequately established. And second, the protohistoric period in this region (ca. 1520–1680) was characterized by a number of large-scale historical changes, each of which culturally affected local populations over a wide area, and only one of which was the introduction of Old World epidemic diseases to the New World.

In other words, we should view disease within a larger context, as one of several large-scale processes of change that resulted directly or indirectly from European activity in North America and Mesoamerica. Each of these historical processes contributed to sociocultural changes among the Caddo and other Native American peoples. Even where disease plays a significant and documented role in a sociocultural change, it cannot entirely determine how the change is played out. For example, the spread of disease may have brought about the abandonment of some areas in North America, but other social, political, and environmental factors may have played a role in determining or influencing where the survivors moved.

Daniel A. Hickerson, "Historical Processes, Epidemic Disease, and the Formation of the Hasinai Confederacy," *Ethnohistory,* 44:1 (Winter 1997): 31–48. Copyright © 1997, American Society for Ethnohistory. All rights reserved. Reprinted by permission of Duke University Press.

I begin with the premise that the Hasinai area of eastern Texas was the site of a protohistoric population coalescence, that the core of the historic Hasinai Confederacy was a combination of groups or communities long resident in the area, and that they were joined by other Caddoan communities during the late protohistoric period, possibly during the mid- to late seventeenth century. Several such amalgamations took place in the protohistoric southeast. The Creeks and the Choctaws were both societies that developed as a result of protohistoric population coalescences. The spread of epidemic disease may have been one event that brought about pressure for such coalescences. The abandonment of some areas, and subsequent amalgamations of survivors in a diminished number of continuing or new settlements, has been identified as a response to depopulation from epidemic disease.

But population movements took place for other reasons in addition to depopulation. During the protohistoric and early historic periods there were many political and economic changes, some originating many miles away, with far-reaching impacts; and there were social and environmental factors other than disease that influenced the movements of groups of people—that influenced whether or not they moved their settlements, and to what destinations. In this article I briefly discuss the role of disease in protohistoric population movements. I then focus attention on three additional factors—warfare, the physical environment, and trade—and discuss how changes in these factors combined to influence the creation of the historic alliance known as the Hasinai Confederacy.

The Hasinai Confederacy in the Seventeenth Century

The Hasinai Caddo occupied the Neches and Angelina river valleys and neighboring areas in eastern Texas. In the late seventeenth and early eighteenth centuries, the Hasinai lived in nine to twelve communities. Collectively, these communities were grouped politically into what anthropologists have called a "confederacy," and which we might think of as a loosely centralized chiefdom. The Hasinai Confederacy was one of three such groupings in the late seventeenth and early eighteenth centuries in the Caddoan area of present-day northeastern Texas, northwestern Louisiana, southwestern Arkansas, and southeastern Oklahoma. The other two, the Kadohadacho and Natchitoches confederacies, were located on the Red River, to the north and east of the Hasinai.

In 1691, the Spanish missionary Fray Francisco Casanas de Jesus Maria listed the following communities as comprising the Hasinai: Nabadachos, Nechas, Nechavis, Naconos, Nacachaus, Nazadachotzis, Cachaes, Nabitis, and Nasayayas. Later lists, made after 1715, differed slightly, with additions and omissions of certain names. To what extent these inconsistencies reflect changes in the composition of the Hasinai, and to what extent they resulted from errors in observation or in the recording of names, is unclear. There is little doubt, however, that changes in the makeup of the Hasinai Confederacy occurred, both before and after European entry into the region.

Each Hasinai community consisted of several widely separated hamlets, which were probably the residences of local lineage groups. Each hamlet consisted of seven to fifteen houses, which were usually located in or near river or creek bottoms and were surrounded by fields of corn, beans, squash, melons, tobacco, and other crops. Father Anastius Douay noted of a Hasinai community in 1686, "This village is one of the largest and most populous that I have seen in America. It is at least twenty leagues long, not that it is constantly inhabited, but in hamlets of ten or twelve cabins."

Hasinai society was hierarchical, with several status positions, the two highest of which were hereditary and probably reserved for members of a central lineage. The xinesi was the recognized leader of the Hasinai Confederacy. He performed no labor, and his household was supported with tribute collected from the members of the communities. The duties of the xinesi were primarily ceremonial, including the performance of numerous rituals, many connected to the agricultural cycle, regular sacrifices of food to supernatural beings, and the maintenance of the sacred, perpetual fire in a ceremonial structure near his house.

Each community was governed by a caddi (pl. caddices), or chief. Like the xinesi, the caddices performed ritual functions, but they also had a number of politcal duties. The caddi of each community coordinated communal work efforts, acted as judge in disputes between individuals or kin groups, and had some authority in the conduct of war. On most matters of importance, the caddi consulted a council of elders, who were probably heads of the lineages that made up each community. Each caddi also acted as an intermediary between his own and other communities. This last function included receiving visiting representatives of other communities and groups, both Caddoan and non-Caddoan, who regularly came to trade with the Hasinai.

The first Europeans to enter the territory of the Hasinai were the surviving members of the de Soto expedition, who briefly entered eastern Texas in 1542 before they were forced to turn back to the Mississippi River. The next European contact was not made until 1686, when the ill-fated French party led by LaSalle, stranded on Matagorda Bay on the Texas Gulf Coast, twice passed through the Hasinai territory while in search of a route to the Mississippi. Shortly thereafter, in 1690, Spanish officials, alarmed by reports of the French settlement, sent missionaries to the Hasinai, with the primary purpose of reinforcing Spanish claims to the territory. French fur traders began to make regular visits to the Hasinai by the first decade of the eighteenth century, visits that became more frequent after the establishment of a French post at Natchitoches, on the Red River in western Louisiana, in 1716. For nearly a century thereafter, the Hasinai would occupy the frontier between Spanish and French colonial territory.

Hasinai Population and Epidemic Disease

... When drawing comparisons with the demographic trends elsewhere in the protohistoric Southeast, it must be kept in mind that settlements in the Caddoan area were, in general, more dispersed and less densely populated than the Mississippian period settlement systems of the Southeast, and thus were likely to be less susceptible to the spread of epidemics. Within the Caddoan culture area, the populations of eastern Texas, particularly those of the relatively lightly settled Hasinai area, appear to have been less severely affected by introduced diseases than the populations of the more densely populated Arkansas and Ouachita river valleys, both of which

were abandoned before direct contact with Europeans could take place.'
party, which passed through the Caddoan area early in the protohist
found it to be less densely populated, with smaller and more scattered
than those areas of the Southeast through which they had passed earlie
was first noted during their passage through Naguatex, located on the R
their point of entrance into eastern Texas.

Epidemics of introduced diseases might be sufficient to explain the abandonment of, or significant demographic reduction in, some areas, and the concentration of settlements in others, in the Arkansas, Ouachita, and Red river regions
during the protohistoric period. However, given available information, comparisons of settlement patterns and epidemic disease trends are not adequate to explain
the abandonment of the less densely populated upper Cypress Creek basin toward
the end of the protohistoric or the very early historic period. Nor do these factors
adequately explain the coalescence of population around this time along the
Neches and Angelina Rivers, the site of the historic Hasinai Confederacy. . . .

Warfare

One political factor that clearly influenced population movements during the protohistoric period is warfare—specifically, the increased aggression by the Apaches in
the southern Plains. The inroads of Apache Indians were a major concern for the
Hasinai and their neighbors, and violent encounters that frequently took place with
the Apaches were noted by nearly all of the European observers who lived for an extended time among the Hasinai. It is important to understand that, although the
Spanish priests may have believed the wars between the Hasinai and the Apaches to
be the result of the "ancient hostility between them," the rise of the Apaches as a
major threat to the settled tribes at the margins of the Plains was actually, as of the
late seventeenth century, of quite recent origin. Before the seventeenth century, the
Apaches wandered the western Plains on foot, hunting bison and other game, and
trading with the Pueblo peoples who lived along the Rio Grande to the west of the
Plains. Indeed, it appears that the Apaches only became a significant threat to their
eastern neighbors around the middle of the seventeenth century. The development
that created this threat took place several hundred miles to the west, with the introduction of the horse into New Mexico by the Spanish colonists who occupied the
Rio Grande valley.

The first horses, and the knowledge required to ride and maintain them, were
probably acquired by the Apaches through trade with Puebloan Indians. The possession and mastery of those first horses gave the Apaches the means to build up their
supplies through raiding, and by 1660 they were taking horses in frequent attacks on
the Spanish and Puebloan Indian settlements in New Mexico. It was around this
time that the Apaches acquired their reputation among the Spanish as the fearsome
and hostile warriors who dominated the southern Plains, a reputation that stayed
with them well into the eighteenth century.

Horses, along with Spanish weapons acquired in New Mexico, made the
Apaches a serious threat to the settled agricultural villages occupied by Caddoan Indians on the eastern fringe of the Plains. They became, in the words of one Spanish
observer, "enemies of one and all" on and near the Plains. In 1690 Alonso de Leon,

who led the initial Spanish expeditions to the territory of the Hasinai, noted that "the war that the Tejas (Hasinai) fight continuously is with the Apache Indians, who are from the land to the west of their settlements." Father Massanet, a Franciscan missionary who worked among the Hasinai, reported in 1691 that the Apaches "are at war with all the other nations. . . . they dominate all the other Indians." Father Isidro Felix de Espinosa, a Franciscan missionary priest who chronicled the Franciscan effort in this area, noted that when the Hasinai went to the Plains to hunt bison, they "go well-armed, because at this time, if they encounter the Apaches, they cruelly murder each other."

Other tribes that had lived on the southern Plains, and had served as a buffer between the Apaches and the Caddoan groups, had been driven south and west by the 1680s, as the Apaches expanded across the entire width of the Plains. In 1686 Alonso de Posada described the Apache nation, "which possesses and is owner of all the plains of Cibola [the southern Great Plains]. . . . The Indians of this nation are so arrogant, haughty and such boastful warriors that they are the common enemy of all nations who live below the northern region. . . . They have destroyed, ruined, or driven most of them from their lands." Posada noted that the Apaches were at war with the Hasinai, and listed several nations, including the Jumanos, that they had driven from the region of the Nueces River southward to the Rio Grande.

The Hasinai themselves began to acquire horses and Spanish weapons of their own through trade some time before the 1680s. In 1686 the French party under René Robert Cavelier Sieur de LaSalle found among the Hasinai many horses, which they freely traded to the French explorers. Father Espinosa stated that the Hasinai had possessed many horses "since the first entry of the Spaniards," which had taken place in 1690. The acquisition of horses allowed the Hasinai and their allies to meet the Apache on more equal terms, and occasionally to take the offensive in battle.

However, at the same time, they were also actively seeking allies to stand with them in these battles. These allies included a large number of native groups, both Caddoan and non-Caddoan, which the Hasinai hosted regularly at feasts and trading fairs. Father Espinosa described the loyalty of these allies, who, he says, "are so faithful in observing their treaties that they do not delay even one day from the appointed time, to gather all together for the march in search of their enemies, the most adamant of which are the Apaches." In the eyes of Hasinai leaders, their potential allies also included European newcomers. In 1687, according to Father Douay of the LaSalle party, a party of Hasinais persuaded some of the French colonists to join them in battle with the Canoatinno, which may have been an Apache group living on or near the Colorado River. Indeed, military alliance may have been expected, even assumed, of the friends and neighbors of the Hasinai. A few years later, in a letter of 1693, Father Massanet noted that among the reasons for the dissatisfaction that the Hasinai had with the Spanish, "they have said many times that if we do not go with them to their wars and to kill their enemies, that we should return to our land."

The rise of hostility between the Hasinai and the Apache on the southern Plains, and the resulting increased danger from raiding and warfare, clearly exerted pressure on the Hasinai and their neighbors, both Caddoan and non-Caddoan, to seek close alliances and in some instances to concentrate their settlements for the benefit of mutual protection. This factor alone, however, does not explain the selection of the specific region of the Neches and Angelina Rivers, the homeland of the Hasinai, as the site of a population coalescence.

Environment

The location of the Hasinai in the woodlands along the Neches and Angelina Rivers in itself provided a measure of protection from mounted raiders of the Plains. Many Titus phase settlements, particularly those on the upper reaches of the Big Cypress Creek and on the nearby Lake Fork Creek, were located in oak-hickory forest that was less dense, and closer to the Plains, than the oak-pine forest occupied by the historic Hasinai. The threat from the Apaches, and other real or potential enemies, may have been a significant factor that determined or influenced the movement of populations into this area during the seventeenth century.

The dense forest that covered most of this area was a hindrance to travel by any means, but especially to horseback warriors wishing to strike suddenly and then retreat quickly. The advantages of this natural protective barrier were noted by European observers. In 1690 Father Massanet described the two roads from the south by which the Hasinai could be reached. The first road "goes straight north to the Texas. But the Apaches are in the habit of coming to it, and these Apaches are enemies both of the Texas [i.e., the Hasinai] and of the Spanish." The second road ran to the northeast, and was "more secure, because there are no enemies, nor do the Apaches come to it because of the dense forest and the distance." . . .

Historical accounts also indicate that during part of the year river flooding presented as significant a barrier to travel as did the dense forest. The most difficult period of travel was in the fall, which coincides with one of the two peak rainfall periods for eastern Texas, late September or October; the other peak period occurs in May. In 1689 a Jumano Indian being questioned by Spanish authorities investigating French activity on the Gulf coast was asked about the approach to the country of the Hasinai. He replied, "When the rains begin it is not easy to enter or come out of that land because of the flooded rivers and marshes which do not permit passage. . . . After it begins to rain in those parts it is not possible to come out until winter sets in." Father Massanet wrote, in 1693, to the Viceroy Conde de Galve, explaining why a promised report from the province of the Hasinai, which he had sent in the care of two soldiers in October, was several months late. "It pleased the majesty of God," he explained, "that the Colorado River would not allow them to pass, nor lessen its flow until the past month of April." . . .

The combination of the dense forest and the sometimes impassable rivers made travel in the country of the Hasinai always difficult, and sometimes impossible, for anyone unfamiliar with the territory, whether they be horseback raiders from the Plains or Franciscan priests from New Spain. As the Apaches, supplied with horses taken from the Spanish settlements of New Mexico, expanded their hunting territory on the Plains, threatening all challengers, such a country must have provided a particularly attractive homeland for displaced or remnant Caddoan groups from the country farther north and northwest. Caddoan peoples had occupied the Neches and Angelina basin long before horses were introduced to the Plains peoples. However, in the early to mid-seventeenth century, when those Plains peoples began their rapid expansion, this quality of the country around the

Neches and Angelina could hardly have been overlooked by Caddoans who had previously occupied the less densely forested, more exposed territory to the north and northwest, closer to the edge of the Plains.

Trade

Another aspect of the geographic position of the Hasinai may have exerted an equally strong attraction for the Caddoan peoples who occupied eastern Texas during the protohistoric period. Although archaeological data are not conclusive on this point, there is strong historical evidence that during the mid- to late seventeenth century, the Hasinai communities were a gateway for trade in European goods and horses brought from Spanish settlements in northern Mexico and New Mexico.

Evidence exists for trade contacts between the East Texas Caddo and the regions to the west, particularly the Puebloan area of New Mexico, in both the archaeological and the historical records. Father Douay, with the LaSalle party, noted in 1686 that the Hasinai "have intercourse with the Spaniards through the Choumans [Jumano], their allies." These allies brought to the Hasinai "many things which undoubtedly came from the Spaniards, such as dollars and other pieces of money, silver spoons, lace . . . clothes and horses." Douay also noted the presence of several Jumano "ambassadors" among the Hasinai. A few months later, on their second passage through the territory of the Hasinai, the LaSalle party was greeted by a Hasinai man dressed in Spanish clothing, and saw several others who carried Spanish sword blades. . . .

The Jumanos are most frequently mentioned as middlemen who brought Spanish goods to the Hasinai. However, there is no reason to suppose that other groups, including the Coahuiltecans, were not involved in this trade network as well. Jumanos, displaced from the southern Plains, are known to have been present in northern Coahuila around the time of the report cited above, and Coahuiltecan groups resident in that area may have accompanied the Jumanos on their trading visits to eastern Texas. Indeed, the "Coahuiles" mentioned by the Bishop of Guadalajara may have even included Jumanos. European observers, including the members of the Teran de los Rios expedition of 1691–92, noted the presence of members of a number of other tribes, probably "Coahuiltecan," who accompanied the Jumanos on their journeys to the Hasinai around 1690.

If the reports concerning the Hasinai made to the Bishop of Guadalajara by the Indians were accurate, which we have no reason to doubt, then it would appear that the xinesi (the "Great Lord" mentioned in the quote above) maintained strict control of the border regions of the Hasinai territory. The local chiefs, the caddices, of the outlying provinces or communities of the Hasinai Confederacy, appear to have been instrumental in maintaining this border control. These caddices, or "casique(s) . . . named by the Great Lord," were probably members of the same lineage as the xinesi, if the Hasinai conformed to the pattern of southeastern chiefdoms, in which status positions were held by members of a central lineage within a system of ranked clans and lineages.

There is no direct evidence from the historical descriptions of the Hasinai, other than this one indirect account, that the xinesi appointed the caddices. It is more likely that the xinesi rose from the ranks of the caddices, either through seniority or through personal influence—he may have been, as Kathleen Gilmore termed it, the "biggest big man" among big men. An observation by Father Casanas suggests that this may have been the case, when he requests that the viceroy of New Spain direct that a gift be sent for him to present to the xinesi, the "principle chief of all this province." He then reveals that this chief, whom Casanas had already presented with a baton symbolizing his command, "is no more than a Caddi, subject with those of the other eight of these nine nations to the Grand Xinesi," but that because of the gifts and recognition by the Spanish, "it will be impossible that he should not be recognized as the Xinesi."

However, it is also quite likely that the xinesi could direct the placement of caddices, who were probably younger relatives, among the Hasinai villages. The purpose of their control of the frontier and the points of entry into the Hasinai territory would have been, at least in part, to control the inflow and distribution of incoming trade goods, both among their supporters among the Hasinai and to representatives of other groups allied with them.

Identification of the historical processes taking place in the material and social environment are important to any understanding of the influences on sociocultural changes, such as those that created the late-seventeenth-century Hasinai Confederacy. It is also important to remember that such historical processes can have their origins in far-flung locations, hundreds or even thousands of miles distant from the point of observation.

This article has addressed four separate historical factors that, at the end of the protohistoric period and the beginning of the historic period, were present and which exerted significant pressure on the Caddoan peoples that comprised the Hasinai Confederacy. These factors were epidemic disease, the rise of Apache aggression and hostility on the southern Plains, the development of a regular trade in European goods and horses from Spanish colonial settlements in northern Mexico and New Mexico, and the location of defensible territory. This combination of factors led to the migration of Caddoan populations south to the protohistoric and early historic Hasinai territory. This migration provided the foundation for the subsequent development, during the late protohistoric period, of a formal political alliance and nascent chiefdom . . . first called the Hasinai Confederacy. . . .

. . . Ewers emphasizes that the movement of groups and their combination with other communities was a frequent response to demographic decline among the historic period Caddo, and notes that the population of a Caddo community rarely dropped below 150 before it would leave its territory and join another group. Of course, the population of a village would not have to drop to this critical level if other factors dictated a decision to shift to a new location. And other pressures besides disease could have made it advantageous for communities to move nearer to more well-positioned allies and trading partners, and thus might have been responsible for population movements.

The Spanish occupation of northern New Spain, accompanied by the introduction of Spanish goods and horses, encouraged the creation of a native trade economy centered on the movement of European goods and horses across the southern Plains, from New Mexico and far western Texas to the Caddoan region of eastern Texas. The groups involved in this trade network probably included many of the same peoples who were involved in earlier exchange in native objects, which had brought goods from the Puebloan region to the Caddoan villages along the Red River.

However, during the late seventeenth century, middleman groups, notably the Jumano, began to follow a more southerly route across the Plains than did the earlier traders, a development that was almost certainly a response to Apache expansion and aggression. As a result of this southerly shift in the native trade route across the Plains, the Hasinai communities of northeastern Texas became the eastern terminus of this route, and thus became the regional gateway for the entrance of Spanish trade goods and horses into the Caddoan region.

Apache hostility also made it advantageous for other Caddoan peoples to concentrate their settlements near the Hasinai, for its relatively protected positions, for the safety to be found in numbers, and for the Spanish horses and weapons to be found there, which allowed them to meet the Apaches on relatively equal ground. The Hasinai leaders were able to use their position as a gateway for the distribution of trade goods to help them gain a close circle of Caddoan allies, forming the Hasinai Confederacy, as it is now known to historians and anthropologists. They were also able to attract a looser, less formal, alliance network of groups, both Caddoan and non-Caddoan, that they could count on as allies and as trade partners. Finally, the desire of the Hasinai and Jumano Indians, and their allies, to maintain open trade routes across the southern Plains in the face of increasing Apache raiding may, by the late 1600s, have led the Hasinai to encourage the establishment of Spanish missions in their territory.

 F U R T H E R   R E A D I N G

Herbert E. Bolton, *The Hasinais: Southern Caddoans as Seen by the Earliest Europeans,* Russell M. Magnaghi, ed. (1987)
———, *Coronado on the Tourquoise Trail: Knight of Pueblo and Plains* (1940)
Donald E. Chipman, *Spanish Texas, 1519–1821* (1992)
Donald E. Chipman and Harriet Denise Joseph, *Notable Men and Women of Spanish Texas* (1999)
William C. Foster, *Spanish Expeditions into Texas, 1689–1768* (1995)
Jack Jackson, *Flags Along the Coast: Charting the Gulf of Mexico, 1519–1759* (1995)
———, *Shooting the Sun: Cartographic Results of Military Activities in Texas, 1689–1829* (1999)
Elizabeth John, *Storms Brewed in Other Men's Worlds: The Confrontation of Indians, Spanish, and French in the Southwest, 1540–1795* (1975)
David La Vere, *Caddo Economics and Politics, 700–1835* (1998)
William W. Newcomb, Jr., *The Indians of Texas: From Prehistoric to Modern Times* (1961)
Martin Salinas, *Indians of the Rio Grande Delta: Their Role in the History of Southern Texas and Northern Mexico* (1990)
F. Todd Smith, *The Caddo Indians: Tribes at the Convergence of Empires, 1542–1854* (1995)
David J. Weber, *The Spanish Frontier in North America* (1992)
Robert S. Weddle, *Spanish Sea: The Gulf of Mexico in North American Discovery, 1500–1685* (1985)

CHAPTER
3

The Challenges of
Spanish Colonization:
Struggles and Accommodation
in the Eighteenth Century

Spain's program to Hispanicize the borderlands met with decidedly mixed results. Vast distances, poor communications, and warring Indian tribes were only a few of the obstacles Spain faced. By the mid-eighteenth century, the religious communities and civil settlements established by Spain remained little more than isolated islands in a vast region very much dominated by its indigenous peoples. As the century drew to a close, Spain, like other European colonial powers, sought to implement a more streamlined, efficient administrative system designed to reduce government expenditures. Known as the Bourbon reforms, they included a complete review of Spain's borderlands empire. Accompanied by the diminishing political influence of the Catholic Church, these reforms also led Spain to cut costs by secularizing many of the missions it had built in Texas and the American Southwest.

Students of early Texas and the American Southwest owe a great debt to Herbert E. Bolton, an historian writing in the early twentieth century whose work inspired a generation of borderlands scholarship. Rejecting an Anglocentric view of early American history that focused primarily on the English colonies of the eastern seaboard, Bolton called attention to Spain's colonization efforts and urged historians to integrate the Hispanic Southwest into the narrative of European settlement in North America. Bolton and the many historians he influenced viewed the borderlands as part of a larger process of Spanish imperial expansion in the western hemisphere. This perspective gave particular attention to the institutional structures of Spain's empire, a grand design imposed on the borderlands by Spanish officialdom in which colonists, clerics, and Indians were all dutiful participants.

More recently, however, historians (including the two whose works are excerpted in this chapter) have devoted less attention to royal policies and edicts

49

*and more attention to the inhabitants themselves. By emphasizing community
formation and development, a new generation of historians has gained a better
understanding of the obstacles and challenges which the peoples of the borderlands faced in their efforts to settle Texas in the seventeenth and eighteenth
centuries. Challenging, at least implicitly, traditional assumptions of European
"conquest," some historians have stressed the ways in which Native Americans
resisted and ultimately shaped Spanish rule. Similarly, Spanish settlers are
viewed less as obedient subjects of the crown than as active participants in the
creation of a unique borderlands community, who managed to adapt to the harsh
realities of their wilderness environment. An understanding of the problems
which these communities faced will enable students to see why Mexico turned to
external sources to populate Texas in the early nineteenth century (see Chapter 4).
What problems did Hispanics encounter in their struggles to establish permanent
settlements in the Texas borderlands? To what extent were Native Americans
successfully assimilated into these communities?*

❧ D O C U M E N T S

The first two documents in this chapter reflect the squabbling and discord that initially characterized relations between the Franciscan missionaries and civil settlers of
Spain's borderlands communities. In 1731, fifteen families from the Canary Islands
arrived in Villa San Fernando de Bexar (later known as San Antonio), and promptly
found themselves in competition with the local missionaries and presidial soldiers
for the area's limited resources. In Document 1, the Canary Islanders complain to the
viceroy in Mexico City of the hardships and difficulties which they have encountered
in San Antonio. In Document 2, the Franciscans present their version of the reasons
for the friction between the isleños and the area missions in an appeal written by
Father Benito Fernández. On the basis of Father Fernández' statements, the viceroy
rejected the isleños' petition.

The five missions of the San Antonio area became the centerpiece of the
Spanish mission system in Texas in the eighteenth century. In Document 3, Father
Gaspar José de Solís gives an enthusiastic report on productivity at the San José
mission. Franciscan efforts to establish a Catholic presence in northern Texas, on the
other hand, encountered far stiffer resistance from indigenous tribes. In Document 4,
Father Miguel de Molina gives an account of the attack on the San Sabá mission by
Comanches and Wichitas in 1758.

During the second half of the eighteenth century, Spanish authorities gradually
reached the conclusion that their northernmost American holdings were more of a
burden to the empire than an asset. Document 5 is an excerpt from the Rubi Dictamen,
issued by Marqués de Rubí following his extensive inspection of presidios and civil
settlements in the Southwest. Rubi recommended the consolidation of Spain's frontier
population in Texas, urging the abandonment of all missions and settlements with
the exception of San Antonio and La Bahía. By the end of the century, ecclesiastical
authorities, bowing to royal pressures to administer the mission system with a greater
degree of economic efficiency, were also ready to give up their efforts in Texas. In
Document 6, Father José Francisco López, president of the Texas Missions, advocates
the secularization of the five missions in San Antonio, in order to release missionaries
for evangelical work elsewhere.

1. The Canary Islanders State Their Grievances to the Viceroy, 1741

The first hardship which these miserable people suffer is the lack of a church in which Mass can be said and divine services held. They must, therefore, attend services in a room of the presidio, and during the rainy season this cannot be done because of the heavy rains. Mass is then said in the room of the guard, which is an open porch. Both places are unbecoming for the celebration of the august Mystery. Some citizens, who want a decent church, have agreed to contribute towards building a church, in so far as their meagre means allow. This is clear from the testimony given by the governor of this province, which I duly present. But they have been unable to contribute what they promised because of their great needs. Would Your Excellency be so kind as to give orders to proceed with the building of a church and assign from the royal treasury the amount Your Excellency would be pleased to grant, and appoint a person to look after the accounts. The citizens are ready to help with their personal labor.

Likewise, may I mention to Your Excellency that these miserable settlers have no way whatsoever to maintain themselves, because this province has no trade or anything which can give them work, unless it be farming their land, which they cultivate with their own hands. Even by this one occupation that they have, they cannot obtain a life's sustenance, because there is no place to sell the corn they harvest. If they want to go outside the province, besides the danger from savages, their expenses soar so high, that they have nothing left. On the other hand, if they want to sell in the presidios, the captains do not want to buy, even though the Marqués de Casafuerte has given regulations for the captains to buy at the price of three pesos to supply the presidios. The reason why the captains do not buy from the Islanders is the fact that the missionaries sell corn at two pesos, since they have no expense in harvesting it. The Indians of the missions are obliged to work for the missionaries and cultivate the fields, but the settlers are unable to get the Indians for work in their fields even though they pay them. In view of this, would Your Excellency order those captains, especially Captain Don Gabriel Costales to buy the corn they need from these citizens who are ready to sell at two pesos, which is a very moderate price.

Also, my parties feel the disadvantage of not being able to obtain from the missionaries permission for the Indians to work in their fields, though they would be paid in cash for their work. The missionaries have put a stop to all communication between the Spaniards and the Indians; they also prevent the Indians from cultivating the fields of the Spaniards. . . .

Since my parties also suffer continuous damage in their fields from the cattle of the missions, though the fields are fenced in, would Your Excellency give orders so that these cattle do not enter the fields of the Islanders; also, because their animals and horses are harmed, would Your Excellency command Captain Don Joseph de Urrutia to see to it with all care that the citizens suffer no harm in themselves, in

"Memorial of Father Benito Fernández, 1741," *Southwestern Historical Quarterly,* vol. 79 (January, 1979): 274–276. Copyright Texas State Historical Association. Reprinted with permission.

their fields, nor among their cattle and animals? For all that has been here requested, may a penalty be imposed to insure observance, and the needed dispatch be issued and sent to Captain Urrutia with a penalty attached to enforce it; and may the writings I have presented be returned to me, as they are needed by my parties? Therefore, I ask Your Excellency that after the presentation of these writings or provisions, would you give orders as I have requested, and give your decision to the general auditor?

2. Father Benito Fernández Refutes the Canary Islanders' Complaints, 1741

The hardships and labor, which the families have endured since the first days of their arrival, are ordinary ones which human nature must put up with in all parts of the world; compensation is had by obtaining help from others who are in the same difficulties in this Kingdom of New Spain. The lands given by the King our Lord were opened and cleared, and they vie in richness with lands in the rest of the world. The land was fertilized already and a great supply of running water was ready to be drawn. This work had been done previously by the soldiers and settlers. During the time the Islanders were building their homes, they lived with the citizens and soldiers. With help from the royal treasury they were decently clothed and were supplied with implements, seed, and other needed items. To no one did they pay tax, nor do they now pay tribute to the King our Lord; a few extortions took place, but they were common in the entire province. There is war with the Apache Indians; and problems that cause war in Europe are met with. These problems loom large but are far less than the problems caused by hostile Indians in these regions. And so the notable discomforts and hardships which (as the Islanders say) they suffer, are, or seem to be, those of delicate women rather than those of manly men, who are called the first founders and settlers of a villa in the vast province of Texas. . . .

If the citizens of the Villa San Fernando would work together to build a new church (whose walls are already almost finished, for they had more than two years to do this and the wood was cut [for them]), without doubt the building now would be complete and they would not have to ask the royal treasury to pay all the expenses. It is not true to say that they were ready to work together and give personal labor to build their church, for, as I have said, there is not much more to do to finish it, and the soldiers and citizens are not refusing cooperation in doing what they can in that construction, if only the families would divide the work and would not engage in quibbling and walkouts that end up in untruths.

The attorneys say that the only work the families have to maintain their livelihood is farming. If this is true, then the Islanders are lazy, for their fields are full of undergrowth. When the King our Lord gave them the land, it was clean and cleared. Since it is not just to accuse them of the crime of laziness, for then the purpose of His Majesty in bringing them to this province from the Islands would be frustrated

"Memorial of Father Benito Fernández, 1741," *Southwestern Historical Quarterly,* vol. 79 (January, 1979): 277–278. Copyright Texas State Historical Association. Reprinted with permission.

with rising cost for the royal treasury, it must be stated that the families do not have only one kind of work, that of farming, for many of them roam about. In truth, the families of the Canary Islands could not exceed sixteen, and those who are only farmers are least in number. It is a fact that one of the attorneys is not a farmer; he is the high constable; neither are Señor Francisco Arrocha, Señor Antonio Rodríguez, Dionis [Manuel de Niz?], and others [farmers]. Señor [Antonio] Santos works more at bricklaying than at farming. The three Leales are more merchants than farmers. One of the Islanders is a carpenter and four are soldiers. The breeding of cattle, raising vegetables and fruit, and making cheese do not bring exceptional profit in these regions. And so the attorneys do not speak well in saying that the only work of the families is farming their lands.

They also say that in this province one cannot engage in trade and so it is necessary to be employed only in the work of farming. They ought to cite the family of the deceased Don Miguel Núñez and of Joseph Antonio Rodríguez, citizens, as also the high constable, an Islander, who maintain themselves quite comfortably by trading; there are others who maintain a livelihood by trade alone. And so it is not true to say that in the province there is no trade nor that one cannot be sustained by this work but that all are forced to the hard work of farming. . . .

The missionaries do not allow the Indians to work for outsiders not because of personal interest but to safeguard the spiritual and temporal welfare of the Indians and to reach the goal set by His Majesty and the Most Excellent Lord the Viceroy. And that goal is to have the Indians, after their conversion to the holy faith, form a new settlement for the Crown, where the new children and subjects live as comfortably as they can (this is what our royal monarch desires). . . .

. . . These Indians of the missions (as said before) are born in the forest and do not do the work which civilized life brings with it; now they work in their own pueblos with great moderation and even this means great hardship for them and some Indians leave the mission for that reason. If these Indians would be obliged to do a day's work to keep alive and clothe themselves, it seems certain that they would draw back and revert to the full freedom of the forest and live only to hunt and in complete liberty. . . .

Every day the missionaries see to it that the Indians of all ages and conditions of life recite the Christian Doctrine and by this gentle influence gain good knowledge; at the same time the missionaries go on explaining the sacred mysteries. This could not be done if the Indians were day laborers; they could not then be maintained as they are now cared for at the mission; nor could they attend catechism instruction regularly. The missionary thinks it best for the Indians to form their pueblo leisurely and attend daily catechism and not be forced to work every day. Besides—the planting done in the missions and all the work is performed by the community. Only the Indian who is a Christian and is strong enough to take care of the old, the infirm, and the non-Christian unfamiliar with work, is capable of becoming a day laborer. When these Indians become day laborers, they and their wives and children maintain themselves with difficulty. If those who can work daily are working for the Islanders, then the others in the mission would necessarily die, for no planting would be done in the mission. Not only would the Indians suffer hardship, as was said, but the rest of the province would be forced to go to the granaries of the Islanders and buy food at rising prices, which is the purpose of the petition presented to the higher tribunal of His Excellency by the attorneys for the families. That this would be so is very evident. In each mission there is only one corn field and only one granary for all the Indians and beyond this there is no planting done, neither by the missionaries nor by anyone else. This would be ascribed then to them, to the missionaries, and to their own interests; in the end no mission would plant and products could be sold at the price desired by the Islanders. I spoke to Señor Juan Leal, one of the lawyers, and made the same remark to him. He replied that it was not his intention to hinder the planting done by the Indians but only that they should not sell corn that is left over at the regular price. But this is what they intend in their dubious claim, which I hold to be unjust in both Spains, for it is completely opposed to natural reason. These Indians are settlers and natives; the Islanders are settlers and foreigners. . . . The King our Lord wants and commands that the natives live a civilized life and go clothed and walk in our holy Faith. Means are not wanting for the Islanders to clothe themselves. It seems to be something beyond reason to expect these pueblos of Indians to give out goods they need themselves for clothing, and other items needed to live a civilized life and establish their pueblos. It is something beyond an irremediable crime to begin to think that the King our Lord brought from the Canary Islands men who thought to justify such injustice to the natives. And so the claim of the lawyers made that they found things unreasonable is contrary to what our royal monarch wants and commands.

3. Father Gaspar José de Solís Praises the Productivity of Indians at the San José Mission, 1768

The condition of this mission of Señor San Joseph de San Miguel de Aguayo, as I saw it in the inspection which I made personally in this year of 1768, is as follows: it is so pretty and well arranged both in a material and in a spiritual way that I have no voice, words or figures with which to describe its beauty. The structure consists of a perfect square of stone and lime, each side is two hundred and twenty varas long and has a door; there are towers in opposite corners, each one guarding its two sides. The dwellings of the Indians are built against the wall from five to six varas in length and four in width. Within each there is a little kitchen of four varas in length, a chimney and loopholes which fall on the outside for defence against the enemy; there is an arched granary of stone and lime, [and] three cannon; there is a work-shop where woolen blankets and very good cotton and woolen cloth is woven. They make a great deal of the latter. They have a carpenter shop, an iron shop, a tailor shop, a furnace in which to burn lime and brick, and an irrigating ditch so large and carrying so much water that it seems like a small river, and it has a great number of fish in it. This canal waters many fertile fields, all of which are fenced in for more than a league. In these fields they have sown corn, brown beans, lentils, melons, water-melons, peaches, sweet potatoes, Irish potatoes, sugar-cane. From all of these things they take large and abundant harvests, so that this mission

"Diary of Fray Gaspar José de Solís, 1767–68," *Southwestern Historical Quarterly,* vol. 35 (July, 1931): 50–52. Copyright Texas State Historical Association. Reprinted with permission.

gives food to others, and to the presidio of San Antonio, Bahía del Espíritu Santo, San Saba, the Orcoquisac and Los Adais. It has a garden in which they grow all kinds of vegetables and many fruit trees, especially peaches, one now and then of a pound in weight, little more or less.

Although this mission does not actually have a church it is building a very adequate one of stone and lime in the shape of an arch which serves as a church. Some of the closed arches of the *portales* of the dwellings of the ministers are of fair size. They are sufficient for all of the offices that are necessary. The jewels of silver, the sacred vessels, the large cup of the *custodia,* the ornaments and all things pertaining to the Divine Worship, are good and neatly arranged. Its baptismal font, its shell, and small vials for the Holy Oil are made of silver, also small vessels for the Holy Water and hyssop are of silver. This mission has from ten to twelve leagues of ranch that is called El Atascosa, where there are about ten droves of mares, four droves of burros, about thirty pair, and about fifteen hundred yoke of oxen for plowing. It has all of the tools, such as rakes, plows, hoes, sticks, axes, varas and all that are necessary; and about five thousand head of sheep and goats.

The Indians take care of all of this without the necessity of having white people to look after it and administer it. The same Indians serve in the work-shop, in the carpenter shop, the iron shop, the tailor shop and the quarry; in short for all that is to be done in the mission. They are industrious workers and very skilful in every thing; they serve as mule drivers, stone-masons, cow-herders, shepherds and in short do everything, since they do not employ any one for anything who does not belong to the mission.

The nations among whom this mission of Señor San Joseph and San Miguel de Aguayo was founded, in the year 1716 or '17, by the Minister Reverend Father Friar Antonio Margil de Jesús, are the Pampoas, Mesquites, Pastias, Camamas, Cacames (Tacames), Canos, Aguastallas and Xaunaes. Between young and old of both sexes, there are about three hundred and fifty men advanced in years, learning and experience; and of these skilled in managing arms there are about one hundred and ten, forty-five of whom are armed with guns, sixty-five with bows and arrows, lances and other arms. All the Indian men and women are very well trained in civilized customs and christianity. All of them know how to pray the christian doctrine and the mysteries of our Holy Faith; all speak the Spanish language, except those who came from the forest when grown and who have remained untamed and wild, but all know how to pray and have been baptized. Most of them are skilled in playing on the guitar, some on the violin and others on the harp. All have sonorous voices, and on Saturdays, each 19th day and the feast days of the Christ and the Most Holy Mary they take out their rosary, singing with four voices, soprano, alto, tenor and bass, being accompanied with the corresponding instruments, and it is glorious to hear them. . . .

All of the Indians, both men and women, know how to sing and dance after the manner of the white people from the land outside, and perhaps with more skill and beauty; they are all decently dressed, each having two suits, one for work days and another better one for feast days. The Indians are not ugly, and the Indian women are comely and very graceful, except one now and then who is surly and lazy. The Indian men occupy themselves with the work that is to be done. The old men make arrows for the soldiers; the young Indian women spin and untangle the wool and sew; the old women spend their time fishing in order that the Fathers may eat; the boys and girls go to school and pray in their turn.

Although the mission is so cultured, following the inclination that the Indians have for their *mitotes* at times when the Fathers are careless, the men and the women go off to the woods and dance the *mitotes* with the pagan Indians. This is carefully watched for, and those who are caught are punished severely. They all have their beds in high places with their large warm blankets of cotton and wool, woven in the work-shop of the mission, their sheets and blankets, and their buffalo hides which serve them as a mattress. In short the Indians of this mission are so well trained in civilized life and so cultured that the Indians from the outside, who are among white people, and for a long time have been reduced and settled, will need time to become like them.

4. Father Miguel de Molina Describes the Attack on the San Sabá Mission, 1758

I certify fully and swear upon my word as a priest that shortly after sunrise . . . a furious outburst of yells and war cries was heard outside the gate of the enclosure. It seemed to come from the distance of a musket shot in the direction of the fords of the river, which at that point flows northward. Soon afterward, some of the men and women of the Mission cried out that the Indians were upon us. I immediately went to the church to warn the Father who was starting to say his Mass, of what was going on, and to advise him, in view of the state of affairs, not to continue. He followed my advice, removing his sacred vestments, but remained in the church.

I returned very quickly to the quarters of the Father President, where several persons had taken refuge, while others had sought safety in various buildings and offices, for a great horde of Indians, firing their muskets, had surrounded the stockade and houses. The barbarians took note of our precautions and our preparations for defense, and they found out too that the gates were not open and that it would not be easy to carry out their evil designs without effort or risk, as they had supposed. Therefore they resorted to offers of peace and friendship, which they made from outside the enclosure, some in the Castilian language, and some by means of signs and gestures.

They succeeded in convincing Corporal Ascencio and another soldier, the son of Juan Antonio Gutiérrez and the two soldiers entered the quarters of the Reverend Father President to inform us of the good will and peaceful intentions of the Indians. The Corporal assured us that the promises of the Indians were genuine, and that he recognized them as members of the Texas, Tancague, Vidae, and other nations from farther inland, with whom he had had experience on many previous occasions.

Thereupon the Father President went out into the courtyard. I accompanied him, filled with amazement and fear when I saw nothing but Indians on every hand, armed with guns and arrayed in the most horrible attire. Besides the paint on their

Paul D. Nathan, trans., Lesley Byrd Simpson, ed., *The San Saba Papers: A Documentary Account of the Founding and Destruction of the San Saba Mission* (San Francisco: John Howell-Books, 1959), 84–91. Copyright Southern Methodist University Press. Reprinted with permission.

faces, red and black, they were adorned with the pelts and tails of wild beasts, wrapped around them or hanging down from their heads, as well as deer horns. Some were disguised as various kinds of animals, and some wore feather head-dresses. All were armed with muskets, swords, and lances (or pikes, as they are generally called), and I noticed also that they had brought with them some youths armed with bows and arrows, doubtless to train and encourage them in their cruel and bloody way of life.

As soon as the wily enemy became aware of the confidence we placed in them, many dismounted and, without waiting for us to unlock the gates, opened them by wrenching off the crossbars with their hands. This done, they crowded into the inner stockade, as many of them as it would hold, about 300, a few more or less. They resorted to the stratagem of extending their arms toward our people and making gestures of civility and friendliness. When I noticed that many chieftains had approached with similar gestures, I advised and persuaded the Father President to order that they be given bundles of tobacco and other things they prize highly. This he did most generously. I myself presented four bundles to an Indian who never did dismount and whom the others acknowledged as their Great Chief. He was a Comanche, according to the barbarians themselves, and worthy of respect. His war dress and his red jacket were well-decorated, after the manner of French uniforms, and he was fully armed. His face was hideous and extremely grave.

When I gave him the four bundles of tobacco, he accepted them cautiously, but with a contemptuous laugh, and gave no other sign of acknowledgment. I was dis-concerted at this, all the more so because I had already seen that the Indians, heed-less of their promises of peace, were stealing the kettles and utensils from the kitchen, and the capes of the soldiers. They also took the horses from the corral, and then demanded more. When they were told there were no more, they asked whether there were many horses at the Presidio. The Fathers and soldiers told them that there were indeed many horses at the Presidio, as well as equipment and supplies of all kinds—a reply we thought expedient to make them fully aware that nothing was lacking for the defense of the Presidio. When we asked the cunning enemy whether they intended to visit the Commandant at the Presidio, they replied that they did, and asked us to give them a note to him. We did not consider this request inoppor-tune, but rather thought it might be an effective way of clearing the Mission of the enemy, for they still had it completely surrounded and were causing great damage by their thievery, as they boldly ransacked all the buildings and offices.

The Father President decided to give them the paper, which was taken by a chieftain of the Texas Nation, who went to the corral and took one of the remaining horses, the personal mount of the Father President, saying he needed it to take the note to the Presidio. When the Father President objected, he took up his musket and aimed it at the horse, whereupon the Father let him keep the horse and resumed his conversation with several Indians, who were telling him about the state of affairs in the Texas country, concerning which the Father, having visited there, had some knowledge. All this while the barbarians persisted in their hostile actions, surround-ing, searching, and looting the various buildings.

Meanwhile, other Indians were talking with me and my companions, trying to convince us that they had no intention other than to fight the Apaches, who had killed some of their people. They asked whether there were any at the Mission; but, since the enemy had already declared their desire to kill Apaches, we had managed to shelter and conceal [the latter] in the quarters of the Father President, the entrance to which was protected by a constant guard of soldiers.

I further certify that, a short time after the departure of the Texas Indian from the Mission post, he returned with a large number of his followers, saying that he had not been allowed to enter the Presidio and that three of his companions had been killed and another wounded with knife cuts. To which the Father President and I answered that he must have approached the Presidio with too large a party and they must have behaved badly; that, if he wished to go again, the Father President would go with him. He replied that he would do so. With this decision the Father ordered the horse saddled that had been left for him, and another for a soldier.

The Father President and the soldier Joseph García mounted in order to accompany the Indian. I observed the Father President looking for the Indian chief who was to go with him, but without finding him; nor was he to be seen among the rabble that thronged the courtyard. Therefore the Father President started toward the gate to look for him outside the enclosure; but, as he approached the gate, a shot was heard and the said Father President cried out. At once other shots were fired at the mounted soldier, and then began a cruel attack against all, and thus I became fully convinced of the treachery and falsehood of the enemy and my suspicion of evil intentions on their part was confirmed. I was now certain that the story of the crafty Texas chieftain about the killing of his Indians was a lie and a snare. I managed to escape to the quarters of the Father President; others did likewise, and still others sought refuge elsewhere. I also assert that, at the very moment the Father President and the soldier Joseph García were shot, [the Indians] set raging fires on all sides of the stockade, where they had provided themselves with ample supplies of firewood. All this I and the other refugees saw through the loopholes in our room. Therefore I believe—indeed, I am sure—that they had been planning and preparing their violence from the start, and that they began it as soon as they had the wood ready, the buildings reconnoitered, and the roads occupied. It is my opinion that their number exceeded 2,000—an estimate I made by observing for more than half an hour the space they occupied while carrying on their trickery and mischief.

From our closed room we fired through loopholes prepared in advance and thus defended ourselves until after midday. The Indians busied themselves meanwhile with pillage and plunder of the provisions stored for the Apaches who were to be settled at the Mission. They were confident that the fires they had set in and around the Mission post would consume us all without any further effort on their part. Therefore they became careless and afforded us the opportunity to make our way to a house next the church, because our former quarters were already burning. But our move was discovered by the enemy, who again attacked us with shots and fed the fires they had previously set, so that we had to flee once more. We went into the church itself, which was less badly ruined, although it too was on fire. There we remained until past midnight, when all of us escaped except Juan Antonio Gutiérrez, who could not on account of a serious wound in the thigh. . . .

The number and resourcefulness of these enemies of religion, divine and human, is very great, and the inhabitants of this region cannot be converted, even by the strongest efforts and the best planning, unless the territory between this river and our own settlements is occupied by our troops. For it is likely, if in this case the attackers numbered about 2,000 equipped with at least 1,000 firearms, that in another attack their numbers will be still greater because of the many nations now involved in the war. Intent as they are on robbery and plunder, they will not desist from such activities, nor cease to carry out their diabolic schemes. Therefore I consider it impossible to reduce and settle these Apache Indians along the San Sabá, or for many leagues roundabout, even with the aid of the King's forces; nor will they be pacified by the utmost favor and aid. For having become aware, as they have done, of the evident threat and danger from their enemies, they are certain to try to escape from them, as they are now doing. It is well-known that the home of the Apaches is far away, closer to our settlements along the rivers. I am of the opinion that it would be an inhuman action to try to reduce them to this region, for experience shows that it is not proper or right to subject them to the dread of ill treatment and cruelty by their more numerous and warlike barbarian enemies. Nor is it possible, as is being attempted, to reduce all the Apaches [into Christian settlements].

Although it is only a little more than two months since I arrived at this post, obeying the orders of my College, I have become well-versed in the affairs, events, and actions affecting the Apache Indians and their objections to being reduced and settled in this region. I believe that the strongest reason for their reluctance is dread and fear of their enemies. They have not openly said so, even when given the opportunity, so as not to admit their terror or show their anxiety and fear, for they are well-known to be very proud, haughty, and petulant. I am well-aware that some of them have often admitted their uneasiness to our soldiers. These fears, together with the ice, snow, cold weather, and the continual high winds of winter in this region, make it difficult for them to take care of their horses and other animals, and since we have experienced the cruel and hateful conduct of the enemies of the Apaches, we must give the latter some credence and continue trying to find refuge for them in other parts, where they will be able to support themselves and be less reluctant to accept conversion. This is my unalterable opinion.

5. Retrenchment in the Borderlands: The Rubí Dictamen of April 10, 1768

Let the presidio and town of San Antonio de Béxar remain, . . . because they have been so much expense to the royal treasury, in the conveying of families from the Canary Islands; in the building of a church, which could be sumptuous; in the inducements distributed to the settlers for the provision of tools for their tilled fields, which they neglect, and arms for the service, which they do not perform except at the cost of new inducements from the accounts of the King. Also let the five missions—not composed of Indians native to that spot, but of those brought or extracted from the coast of the Colony of Nuevo Santander and from other, more interior locations to which the missionaries go to do their spiritual recruiting—remain in their pleasant valleys. However, since this settlement is more than a degree

Pedro de Rivera, in Jack Jackson and William C. Foster, eds., *Imaginary Kingdom: Texas as Seen by the Rivera and Rubí Military Expeditions, 1727 and 1767* (Austin: Texas State Historical Association, 1995), 183–185, 196, 197. Copyright Jack Jackson. Reprinted with permission.

farther north than the other presidios placed on a line along the banks of the Rio Grande, it is necessary to take precautions, in the best way possible, against the risks which are presented by its location and distance of more than fifty leagues from the Presidio of San Juan Bautista del Río Grande.

With San Sabá evacuated as has been advised, and with the presidio and the little settlement of Los Adaes (presently being finished off by its own misfortune) extinguished or incorporated into the Department of New Orleans—the extremely unsuitable Presidio of Orcoquizá being withdrawn at the same time to this town [San Antonio] or another location in its vicinity—the town of San Antonio will remain finally the most advanced of our frontier in the province of Texas. . . .

For a greater increase of forces, trade, circulation, and consumption of merchandise and money, it will be convenient that the governor, relieved of the cumbersome care of Los Adaes, should reside in this settlement [San Antonio] adding to it the command of the Presidio of San Juan Bautista del Río Grande, which would then be taken away from that of the governor of Coahuila. Perhaps the governor of Texas will propose to bring the other presidios located on the banks of the Rio Grande, beginning with the presidio at the confluence of this river with the Conchos, in Vizcaya, closer to this settlement of San Antonio, according to the respective distance at which they may then be located. If so, it may be at the cost of moving this Presidio of San Juan Bautista somewhat forward from its present location on the banks of the river in order to shorten and even up the distance from the latter to the aforementioned settlement of San Antonio. . . .

From the Presidio of Los Adaes, distant only seven leagues from the Fort of Natchitoches [of the colony] of New Orleans, it is 240 [leagues] to the town of San Antonio de Béxar, which I have set as the most advanced limit of our frontier; and 200 leagues, approximately, to the Presidio of La Bahía, the last one of our line. For these two lines of communication, which are the only ones frequently used for entering Los Adaes, we have two narrow paths. These we share with the various subdivisions of the coastal Indians, the reduction of whom leaves this transit somewhat open, but not completely free of their petty larcenies. In this whole extension there is not one single settlement of ours to be found, nor should we promise ourselves one for many years, as far as the Mission of Nacodoches, distant forty-six leagues from Los Adaes, where, without there being a single converted or catechized Indian, there has been a friar established since the last entry made by the Marqués de San Miguel de Aguayo in the year 1721.

Next after this mission, on the same route, at a distance of less than twenty leagues, is the Mission of Los Aes, with the appellation of Los Dolores, where two other friars reside in the same inaction, having only one Indian for whom to carry out their ministry. From this mission one comes to Los Adaes, in which—besides the company, the stationing of which costs 27,765 pesos per year—the King maintains another mission with two friars. Frustrated in their principal purpose of converting the heathen, they administer spiritual nourishment to the troops of the presidio and to the small neighboring population of its surrounding farms. These are becoming depopulated by misfortunes and by the scarcity of water, and did not number even thirty families at the time of my review. To the south-southwest of this presidio, at a distance of 120 leagues, is located, among a thousand inconveniences and infelicities, the Presidio of Orcoquizá with its company of thirty-one enlistees.

Here is also an imaginary mission—without Indians, with two missionary ministers, and no citizenry—for it was found to be impracticable, despite the offer to construct it, which the founder and creator of this presidio pledged himself to do.

This region's two presidios, and the stipends for the religious at the four cited missions, are a cost to the King of 44,151 pesos per year. Multiplied by the number of years since their creation, beginning with the twenty-first year of this century [1721], it is a very considerable sum, without our being compensated for this exorbitant expense in any manner at all, either spiritual or political. As to the conversion of the heathen, we will not lose a single Christian, nor even a single neophyte, if the aforementioned four missions are suppressed. And as to the defense of our true dominions, more than two hundred leagues from this imaginary frontier, we shall substitute for this weak barrier one that is being established in a more respectable fashion along the Colorado [Red] and Missouri Rivers by the present governor of that colony [Louisiana], Don Antonio de Ulloa, and thus the communication and transit therefrom to the dominions of this kingdom will be made much more difficult, as the King intends.

So it may be legitimate for me to ask now if, in the abandonment of the presidios of Los Adaes and Orcoquizá, and their imaginary missions, the King will lose the vaunted extension of his dominions, or if he will obtain the saving of more than 44,000 pesos that their [annual] maintenance costs him? Therewith I satisfy this objection, which has seemed to me an essential one.

6. Father José Francisco Lopez Advocates Secularizing the Missions in San Antonio, 1792

The first point I make is obvious from the fact that in the sixty and more leagues surrounding these missions of Béjar there is no nation of pagan Indians which can be converted. Those who are at a greater distance to the east, north, and south, cannot be taken out of their land without violence to their nature, without offending the laws of humanity, the pontifical regulations, and repeated decrees of his Majesty, nor has it been possible for the missionaries to win them over by favors and kindness, so that they freely leave their lands and congregate in one of the missions. At different times from 1703 till the present year of 1792 various and costly experiments have been made in vain toward this end.

Secondly, it is evidently true, shown not only by the long time of eighty-nine years since the mission of San Antonio was founded, bur felt also in the trade and communication with those Indians, that although they have not given up entirely the traits that are proper to and inseparable from their natural low way of living and their fickleness, they nevertheless are seen to be more civilized and cultured than many other Indians and pueblos in lands beyond.

Finally, the experience of so many years has taught us that the best fruit we can promise ourselves for the future of these Indians will be only to preserve in them the

"Report on the San Antonio Missions in 1792," trans., Benedict Leutenegger, *Southwestern Historical Quarterly,* vol. 77, no. 4 (April, 1974): 490–497. Copyright Texas State Historical Association. Reprinted with permission.

faith and Christianity they have received, just as it is preserved in the other christian pueblos by the help and preaching of their pastors. But no apostolic increase in spreading the faith can be made among them, and yet this is the proper and special office of the missionaries, to which alone our efforts ought to be directed. . . .

. . . I consider it highly important that without making any changes in the Missions of Espíritu Santo and Nuestra Señora del Rosario de la Bahía, the other four missions on the River of San Antonio be reduced to two by joining Mission Espada to Mission San José, and Mission San Juan Capistrano to Mission Purísima Concepción, both because of the advantage of having the first two on one side of the river and the last two on the other side, and also because the lands and goods are joined in their respective boundaries, and those of Mission Concepción are also adjacent to those of San Juan Capistrano. Thus only two missionaries will be in charge, and they should reside in Mission San José and Concepción, since their churches and the houses for the missionary are larger and better. The other two missions will be pueblos or settlements of visitation [mission-stations]. In this way and by giving over the Mission of San Antonio and the administration of Nacogdoches to the bishop, the holy College can make greater progress in converting the infidels, which is the main objective of its apostolic zeal and the only purpose I have in writing this report. In this way the King Our Lord will be spared new expenses, and our College, without increasing the number of missionaries, will be able to use these five superfluous missionaries for new conversions which, it seems, can be made on the coast of San Bernardo, in Refugio, Brazos de Dios, and Orcoquiza. Thus the faith will be spread in that direction and the aforesaid missions will not be abandoned. At the beginning of their foundations it was judged necessary to have more missionaries, but at the present time they can be adequately maintained by only two missionaries, if the union which I have suggested is accepted.

But one must remember that this is possible only by leaving the administration of temporal affairs to the Indians, by keeping them in their respective pueblos without merging their lands and goods, and by freeing the missionaries from the administration and care of temporalities, so that they will look after only the spiritual welfare of the Indians, who will work for themselves and seek their own well-being. . . .

It is certain that as soon as the Indians receive the goods, they will misuse them, sell them and give them to the Spaniards, and by using up their small patrimony in games, drunkenness, and other vices, they will want more when they return to the house of their Father missionary, asking for help to alleviate their hunger and to clothe them; and when the poor missionary will have to dismiss them from his door in sorrow, not being able to help them sufficiently, even by sharing with them the bread of his own sustenance, he will have to practice patience, charity, and compassion, and will see many of his poor Indians go hungry, naked, and dejected, and exposed to serve the Spaniards to get food. But since these are consequences that will follow from transferring the goods to their awkward management and misconduct, they are also unavoidable conditions which keep the Indians in the natural sphere with all the rest of them. This is neither surprising to the Indians, nor is it proper for the apostolic institute to strive to suspend the course of divine Providence, which in its hidden design maintains all the natives of this America in the condition of the most lowly, humble, poor and abject men.

The most zealous, prudent, and holy missionaries, who have been in these Indies from the beginning of the conquest up to this day, as we know from history and as can be seen in the abundant fruit obtained by their evangelical preaching in all the converted pueblos, thought undoubtedly that they fulfilled their task of preaching and exercised their apostolic zeal by instructing the Indians in the catholic religion, by teaching them to live as Christians, as obedient sons of the holy Church and true subjects of our Sovereign. The true charity, which impelled them to win so many souls, did not influence them to draw the Indians from their natural place of abode, to help them in their bodily miseries, to lift them up from their humble dejection, and to throw on their shoulders the duty of protecting and defending these helpless men, except in so far as these duties were conducive to the teaching and instruction by which they tried to educate them. And when, through the goodness of God our Lord we can say that in these four missions of which we speak our missionaries have now done all the duties imposed by the apostolic institute, having all the Indians in their care (except a few who have come recently) well instructed and nourished in Christianity, and in all that is required by necessity and precept to reach salvation if they want to be saved. We sympathize surely on seeing the miserable state in which they would be left by the surrender of their goods, and we shall be content in having, after all, imitated our venerable predecessors. We shall make known to all who till now have been deceived, and who have entrusted to us the management of temporalities, that we have used them only in so far as they have been conducive to keeping the Indians together and as a help in instructing and teaching them. This, for the most part, has been achieved. . . .

Finally, some could object to this report, claiming that the Indians, should they lack the shelter and protection from the missionary, would abandon themselves and become lazy by not cultivating their land, by leaving the missions, and some perhaps would join pagan nations to make war against us, tired of the heavy yoke of Christianity and apostatizing in great numbers from the faith and thus lose their souls. But just as the pastor, the preacher, the confessor are not responsible for these and greater willful evils committed by bad Christians because of temporal discomfort and not because of lack of instruction and teaching, neither can the apostolic missionary be held responsible for the fatal results that come to the bad Indians of his mission because of the lack of material things. In truth, if the Indians have not apostatized up to this day and have remained in the mission, submitting to the yoke of Jesus Christ after so many years of instruction, if this has been due to the temporal comfort which they have had under the protection of the missionary, little or nothing has our apostolic institute achieved. This is not easy to believe when we see that the more unskilled Indians of these missions, with the exception of one or the other, have received more instructions than many other pueblos in lands beyond. Thus if perchance they are lost, we can tell them what God told Israel: *perditio tua ex te*. These Indians will perish . . . because of the evil inclination which prompts all evil Christians to permit themselves to be carried to perdition. Although the missionaries must deplore their perdition, it is not their task to try to remedy the situation by means of material help. Otherwise, charity would compel them to care for the widows, orphans, helpless men and women, who perhaps would not be given to so many vices, if the help of clothing and food would be given to them as it is given to the Indians.

Y S

ing two essays examine the problems and challenges of community build-
n's northern frontier, each from a different perspective. In the first essay,
Hinojosa, an historian at the University of Texas at San Antonio, focuses
on the mission system in Texas, which was modeled after the Franciscans' long tradition of Indian conversion in Mexico and South America. Contrary to the widely held
view that the Franciscans were primarily dedicated to the goal of assimilating native
groups into Hispanic society, Hinojosa argues that the monastic orders of Texas sought
instead to build separate utopian communities, and for the most part abandoned integration as a long-range goal. For almost a century, the Franciscans endeavored to build
permanent, self-sustaining communities; ultimately, however, economic and demographic pressures led to the absorption of the missions into the larger community of
San Antonio.

In the villa of San Antonio, the same need for self-sufficiency resulted in a very
different set of solutions. As Jesús F. de la Teja, an historian at Southwest Texas State
University, argues in the second essay, the region's limited resources tended to erode
social divisions based on race and caste. Rejecting the long-held view that the Isleños
represented a traditional ruling elite over the San Antonio community, de la Teja argues
convincingly that the town's small size and remote position on the edge of Spain's northern frontier required a significant level of cooperation among San Antonio residents.

Self-Sufficiency and the San Antonio Missions

GILBERTO M. HINOJOSA

Forces of Exclusivity in Mission Life

Although certain facets of mission life seemed to encourage the eventual integration
of the Indians into Hispanic colonial society, overall the padres strove to build and
maintain communities that were completely separate from the neighboring settlement of San Fernando. In the missions natives were to become acquainted with
farming and grazing and certain crafts, gain some fluency in the Spanish language,
and adopt selected cultural traditions. The overriding goal of the friars was, after all,
to settle the Indians and inculcate in them the Christian faith and the moral virtues it
required, all very important elements of Spanish society and culture. However, acculturation of the natives was not absolutely essential to the functioning of mission
pueblos and the fulfillment of the friars' goals. As for assimilation of the Indians
into the Hispanic society of San Fernando, it does not appear to have been seriously
considered. Quite the contrary, the work and life in the missions and the building
programs directed by the padres were designed to create permanent communities
completely separate from the other institutions on the frontier. The survival and development of the missions for almost a century attests to the strength of those ideals
of segregation and independence.

Gilberto M. Hinojosa, "The Religious-Indian Communities," in Gerald E. Poyo and Gilberto M. Hinojosa,
eds., *Tejano Origins in Eighteenth Century San Antonio* (Austin: University of Texas Press, 1991), 68–82.
Copyright © 1991. By permission of the University of Texas Press.

A dispute in 1736 between the missionaries and the governor in San Antonio concerning a bridge over the river that separated Mission San Antonio de Valero and the town-presidio settlement exemplifies this commitment of the friars to build and maintain separate communities. The bridge had been built by the Indians under the direction of the padres to facilitate mission business with the presidio, but no sooner had the crude span been set up than settlers and soldiers began using it to visit the Indian pueblo for personal reasons. This unrestricted access to the mission interfered with the scheduled work, the teaching of crafts, and catechism and prayer. Some of the intruders allegedly cheated the neophytes out of food and household goods or stole these outright. Supposedly the soldiers also slaughtered mission cattle, indulged in public drunkenness, and molested native women. To prevent these disruptions and abuses the missionaries removed the beams that served as a bridge. Thereupon the settlers and soldiers affected by this action took their objections to the top provincial authority, Carlos Franquis de Lugo, who eagerly jumped into the fray on their side. Without hesitation the governor brazenly ordered the missionaries to send some Indians to help reconstruct the bridge. The friars refused, but the soldiers forced a handful of natives to carry out the governor's wishes nonetheless. The padres retaliated by posting a guard in front of the mission, an action that enraged Franquis de Lugo. Set on resolving the conflict personally, he dashed across the river, forced his way into the mission, and confronted the religious superior in his cell, threatening him with his cane. The missionary stood his ground, however, and, although the bridge remained, the friars discontinued the tradition of allowing settlers and soldiers to worship in the mission chapel.

The bridge story is illustrative of the friars' attempts to control all interaction between the natives and all others and to protect mission property. Fray Benito Fernández de Santa Ana observed that, while presidiales and townspeople could trade with the mission residents, these outsiders should not be allowed to enter the Indian pueblo or even talk to the natives unless supervised by a missionary. By the same token, intruders and squatters on mission lands were to be assessed the stiff penalty of 200 pesos and evicted. The maintenance of two distinct societies was critical to the functioning of the friars' institutions. Indeed, as padre Mariano Francisco de los Dolores y Viana reminded the governor, strict separation of Indians and Spaniards was decreed by the laws of the realm.

As prescribed by the friars, life and work within the mission walls was directed to the exclusivity and permanence of those institutions. The friars set out to teach the Indians to farm and graze livestock and to build suitable dwellings, but they did so at the most elementary levels. The evidence suggests that the missionaries utilized the neophytes mostly in work gangs that provided unskilled manual labor. Bolstered by supply trains which brought a variety of finished or nearly finished goods to the missions, the padres could direct the energies of the residents to clearing the fields, constructing the irrigation canals, and erecting the buildings needed in the pueblo. Occasionally some Indians took up butchering, tanning, tailoring and sewing, smithing, carving, and sculpturing. Most frequently, however, Spaniards or mestizos from the villa or from central Mexico were in charge of these skilled tasks, while the natives were engaged in the labor-intensive functions that ensured the subsistence, profit, and long-range endurance of the missions.

These overriding objectives interfered with goals directed to the acculturation of the natives, such as teaching the Spanish language. The padres did prefer their own mother tongue over Indian dialects which lacked the terms for the new tools and crops and, most importantly for the abstract concepts of Christianity. But teaching Spanish to the natives proved to be more difficult than learning the Indian languages. The use of a Coahuiltecan dictionary-catechism in the missions bears this out and in fact suggests that the padres even attempted to establish a Coahuiltecan lingua franca among the natives. To have carried out an efficient acculturation program as their ideals called for, the friars would have needed to have started each mission with only a few Indians, as one friar advised, and increased their numbers only gradually. But that process would have impeded the construction projects, which involved many workers, and learning Spanish did not appear to be as important for missionization and Christianization as did the work habits and moral behavior fostered by a settled village life.

The friars had, in fact, directed substantial efforts in the early years to Hispanicizing the Indians, but these endeavors were thwarted by their own manpower limitations. Ideally one of the two friars stationed at a mission was to devote himself entirely to teaching the new language, Spanish customs, and Christian doctrine and morals, but, given the relatively large number of Indians, this was hardly sufficient for effective cultural change. Consequently the friars demanded that some mission families send their young boys to reside in the monastery wing in order to imbue them with the European world view, values, and traditions. By midcentury, when widespread commitments drained available personnel and only one priest was assigned to each mission, the friars deemphasized cultural endeavors and at times even spiritual ideals and placed more attention on the "temporalities" in order to guarantee the primary goal of institutional survival.

The building program reflected the self-sustaining impulse pervasive in the missions. Generally the first structures erected after a mission's founding were makeshift, temporary jacales (mud and stick, thatched-roof huts) because the padres wanted to ascertain the location's suitability and because priority was given to clearing the fields and digging the acequias, undertakings that required a couple of decades to complete. However, small stone churches were built shortly after a permanent site was selected. Typically these structures were converted into other uses once the major projects were well on the way in the 1740s and construction began on bigger churches and on conventos (monasteries for the friars). In the following decade storage buildings and workshops were erected. Later, stone houses were built for the residents, and the pueblos were enclosed. Within these fortresslike villages the friars then expanded the churches and conventos, impressing residents and visitors alike with the success of the mission enterprises. From their pulpits and offices the padres directed mission life and operations, fully confident that their institutions would always form important, separate communities in the area.

Even serious demographic changes did not alter for a long time the direction of these institutions towards exclusivity. When a decline in the mission population became evident in the 1780s, the friars shifted construction priorities from the addition of decorative features in the churches to the expansion of utilitarian structures such as mills, granaries, and workshops. Most of the buildings had, in fact, been erected previously, in the early period which coincided with population peaks (from the 1740s to the 1770s).

During those years, and indeed since their foundation in the 1720s, the San Antonio missions had averaged more than 150 residents, having at times as many as 260 (in one exceptional year Mission San Jose reported 350 Indians). But in the mid-1770s the population of each institution declined by 50 to 100 natives. Then, in the late 1780s, it dropped precipitously, reaching the lowest marks after 1792, approximately when partial secularization began. In those twilight years the still physically imposing structures housed very few Indians (from twenty-seven to forty-five residents each). However, given the more than sixty years of sustained relatively high populations and strong support from the interior of the colony, the mission communities stood apart and independent from the other institutions in San Fernando.

This trend towards creating insular communities, so evident in the drive for mission self-sufficiency and in the physical barriers, minimized the need for interaction between Indians and the soldier-settlers and town dwellers. Consequently the movement of acculturated natives to San Fernando—if, in fact, it was ever intended—appears minimal until the end of the century. The number of mission Indians marrying outside their racial group was inconsequential. The mission system was simply not designed towards making integration a reality. Indeed, contrary to prevailing historical interpretation, the padres did not, until the very end, contemplate the demise of their institutions and full assimilation of the natives into the Hispanic society. Throughout most of the century the letters and reports of the missionaries never expressed a desire for a fully integrated society. Quite the opposite, the padres' words and actions attest to the hope of permanent, separate towns. Up until the 1790s the friars launched new building programs, continued to consolidate their institutions, and even made efforts to expand their landholdings. These mission complexes, with prominent churches and conventos, reflected a large-scale, somewhat utopian, plan to create distinct Indian communities directed by the friars—a re-creation of the centuries-old República de Indios common to central Mexico.

The independence of the missions could not be sustained indefinitely, however. Along with the pull towards exclusion, the system contained internal pressures directing it towards integration. Furthermore, external forces, such as governmental policies and economic and social developments beyond the control of the padres, interfered with mission objectives. The friars themselves also had a change of heart, or at least of interest, in their work in Texas, and this also weakened the intrinsic institutional drive for autonomy. Consequently by the end of the century the missions were shorn of their corporate status and secularized. Lands were deeded to residents and opened to settlers, while the religious duties of missionaries were turned over to the diocesan clergy. The dissolution of these once-separate religious entities broke down the barriers to their becoming a part of the larger Béxar community.

To a certain extent, the seeds of the dissolution of the missions were evident in the very foundation of the province. The padres had never been able to implement their goals in East Texas, where large groups, such as the Hasinai, who lived on isolated farms, proved "insolent" and "obstinate," resisting the padres pressures to congregate them. For a time the missionaries were heartened by the number of deathbed baptisms (it appears that the Indians who were seriously ill hedged their bets on the hereafter by availing themselves of both Indian and Spanish rituals). Eventually, however, since the padres were unable to procure the military support to create the necessary social structure for conversion, they became disillusioned with their work among these Indians and retreated to the San Antonio River valley.

The Béxar "way stations" quickly became the core religious settlements from which missions for the large northern Indian groups were planned and launched. However, these ambitious new efforts failed. The Comanches, the Wichitas, and other northern tribes were prospering in their commerce with the French and remained beyond direct Spanish control throughout the colonial period. When Spain did try to bring the Norteños (Nations of the North) into its sphere in the mid-1700s, the Crown adopted a policy of trading with these natives rather than attempting to settle them. For geopolitical reasons, the government also refused to assist the missionaries in reducing and Christianizing the Apaches. Still, in the face of these failures and constraints, the padres never questioned their strategy for evangelization; rather, they continued to be committed to their vision of creating permanent Indian villages.

Unable to evangelize the larger native groups, the missionaries contented themselves with recruiting from small Central-Texas and coastal bands, a limitation which was an asset in many respects but which ultimately proved to be the undoing of the missions as separate communities. Small bands of Coahuiltecans and Karankawas, which were easily recruited and controlled, were the most likely candidates for missionization. Having a dozen or so of these groups in a mission provided an element of stability to the work force because, if one band left with all its members (as happened on one occasion at San José), the entire pueblo's population would not suffer significantly, and the construction projects could continue without interruption. This strategy of depending on small bands worked well until the last quarter of the eighteenth century. At that time, these groups no longer subjected themselves to the padres' demands for social and cultural conformity to Spanish ways and turned instead to the Norteños to improve their lot. The lack of neophytes to replenish mission populations would in time spell the end of those institutions.

Recruitment was critical for the survival of the missions since the Indian towns were unable to increase, or even maintain themselves, numerically. At Valero, for example, during the sixty years for which data is available (which includes mostly years with high populations), births outnumbered deaths only in five years. On the average, for every seven babies born annually, ten persons died. The disproportionate death rate was directly linked to a high infant and childhood mortality. Over two-thirds of 319 Indians baptized and buried at Valero died during the first three years of life. Only fifty reached what may have been considered adulthood, twelve years of age. Of these, only fourteen lived into their twenties, and a mere eight into maturity (thirty to forty-five years).

Various factors contributed to the overall low rate of natural increase among mission Indians. For example, there were considerably fewer women than men, a phenomenon that resulted from the numerous deaths of mothers while giving birth and possibly from female infanticide. This latter practice appears to have been a common form of population control among Indians facing limited resources, and the natives may have continued this custom even after missionization. Fatal accidents, murders, and deaths at the hands of attacking Indians contributed minimally. Plagues also took their toll on the mission residents because of the Indians' lack of immunity to European diseases, but the data suggests that deaths occurring during epidemic years were not considerably higher than usual. It appears, however, that the most important contributor to the high death rate was the generally poor health of the mission Indians.

According to the missionaries, the Indians themselves were to blame for this condition. Fray Mariano observed that common illnesses were fatal to the natives because they ate unwholesome foods gathered in el monte (the wilderness) nearby. Supposedly these had debilitating effects on all, especially on nursing infants. Moreover, the padre noted, the Indians were usually dirty and did not use purges, sweating, or other accepted remedies, relying instead on wild herbs for their cures. They also engaged in " sexual excesses" which resulted in the spread of venereal diseases. Fray Mariano also complained that the natives did not adequately protect themselves from the elements. They appeared more concerned with eating and roaming than with building comfortable houses and weaving in order to clothe themselves. While Fray Mariano's observations may reflect a strong European prejudice, they may also suggest that the missions were not attracting physically strong bands and that life in the mission did not substantially alter the lifestyles of those Indians or make up for the poor health in which they arrived.

Indeed, mission life itself may have had limited effects on the Indians and may have, in fact, exacerbated the Indians' health problems. Undoubtedly the nutrition of mission residents improved—sufficient corn and beef appears to have been distributed year-round, and vegetables and fruits were available seasonally—but the very change of diet may have affected the Indians' health. Whereas, during the roaming days the natives had eaten a large variety of roots, fruits, nuts, wild game, and fish, their mission fare was largely starches (corn) and red meats (beef). Then, too, while their caloric intake may have been suitable for moderate activity, Indians were made to work in different and more demanding work patterns than their previous tasks required. The highly supervised life of labor, prayer, and learning was probably very stressful for these once-free natives, and constant psychological pressures, we now know, are as injurious to health as any virus or malnutrition.

Besides being more constrained and crowded in the Indian pueblos than they had been in el monte, the natives actually did not enjoy adequate housing in the missions. The construction program had concentrated on clearing the fields, digging the acequias, and building the churches and storage rooms. Indeed, as late as 1776, Fray Benito Fernández de Santa Ana admitted that some "Indian houses . . . [were still] impermanent and rickety, their household goods . . . [were] few, not much more than a metate [corn-grinding stone], a skillet, and a thin mat on which to sleep." Despite benefits natives received by accepting the padres' invitation, life in their new surroundings apparently did not improve their health significantly and may have worsened it. Whatever the cause, the troubling reality was that mission populations had serious difficulties maintaining themselves.

Indian resistance to demands of mission life also contributed to the demise of those institutions. The task of changing the natives' cultural outlook and lifestyles was a major challenge for the missionaries, who continually had to exhort and pressure backsliding neophytes to comply with their new religious responsibilities. The padres' charges did not easily give up their sexual mores or their mitotes (nature-dance rituals). Under the observant eye of friars and soldiers, the mission Indians were marched to church like schoolchildren to attend mass, sing the alabanzas (hymns), and fulfill the Easter duty of receiving the Sacrament of Penance. In the confessional the neophytes rarely volunteered any information of their offenses, acknowledging them only when prodded and excusing their reticence by claiming "You did not ask me" or "I thought it would upset you." When pressed to admit sexual sins, they usually denied these were willful acts. But the missionaries were not discouraged by their limited success in changing the natives. They merely doubled their efforts of persuasion and force, including greater supervision and the use of whips and stocks to discipline those remiss in their obligations.

Chafing under the monastic work-and-prayer routine, the Indians resorted to passive protests such as carelessness and work slowdowns or desertion. "It takes four of them to accomplish what I can do alone," grumbled one missionary, adding that the simple task of cleaning the sanctuary lamp would not get done unless the priest supervised the assignment. The neophytes often claimed ignorance or lack of dexterity as reasons for not performing their duties, or they feigned illnesses, a strong sign, according to one friar, that they were preparing to desert. Indeed, when pressed too severely to comply with the work rules or to change their ways, many residents simply ran away. "These Indians are not difficult to convert," observed one padre, meaning that they could be easily persuaded to enter the mission, "but they are bothersome [to keep]," thus explaining the large population turnover in the missions.

Desertions aggravated the demographic crisis. Unbeknownst to the natives, in joining the missions they had entered into a binding legal commitment, equivalent to receiving baptism, matrimony, or Holy Orders, or to taking religious vows. Thus, when the Indians abandoned their new homes to go back to their old habitats, they became "apostates," individuals rejecting the faith or abandoning the monastery. Usually soldiers accompanied the padres to ensure the return of escapees, but the padres did not receive this assistance after midcentury. By then the government had adopted a policy of befriending and trading with the larger Indian nations and refused to alienate them by demanding they surrender mission runaways who had joined them. This inability to retrieve escapees, coupled with a decline in new recruits, dealt a heavy blow to the missions.

The demographic crisis led to the greater contact between the religious institutions and the town. Despite restrictions, mission residents had, in fact, always traded with the soldier-settlers and interacted with them in various other settings. On occasion Indians accompanied the presidial companies on military campaigns against warring Indians, and some soldiers were almost always stationed in the missions because their assistance, as Fray Mariano observed, was indispensable "in order to direct and instruct them [the natives] in their work, and to subdue, teach, control, and punish" them. Without the soldiers' help, another missionary advised, the Indians would revert to their inherent laziness, neglect to plant and harvest the corn crop, and commit all kinds of excesses and crimes right under the very roof of the mission. Furthermore, unless closely watched, the natives might just run away. Two or three soldiers sufficed to maintain order and work because their presence reminded the Indians that the entire presidial company was nearby. Towards the end of the century the influence of these few presidiales increased as fewer natives remained in the missions.

The same happened with other outsiders. The padres had always hired some five to ten vecinos (townspeople) in each mission for skilled crafts. As the Indian population declined, additional outsiders worked at the missions in order to keep them economically viable. The vecinos residing in the Indian pueblos increased not only in absolute numbers but also in proportion to the declining native population. For every one Spaniard, mestizo, or mulatto living in the missions, there was an average of twenty-eight Indian residents in 1772, thirteen in 1792, and only six in 1806. As the proportion of vecinos from San Fernando working and living in the missions grew, their cultural impact on the remaining natives increased, a situation that hastened secularization. Thus, while the friars had at first insisted on segregation, in time they increasingly brought into the missions more soldiers and townspeople who unavoidably acted as agents of acculturation for the mission residents, and by the end of the century, the once-Indian pueblos came to resemble Hispanic villas in practically everything save legal status.

A downturn in the economic fortunes of the missions further weakened those once self-sufficient institutions and threatened their very survival as separate communities. In the 1750s San José had been a thriving enterprise with approximately 2,000 sheep and 3,000 head of cattle, bustling carpentry and smithing workshops, active looms where the Indians made most of their clothing, a full granary, and a sugarcane storage building. But "now [three decades later] everything, everything is turned around," lamented one of the friars. "There are few Indians and many hired hands. There are few cattle, and even so, no one to sell them to because there are too many grazers. Even if the missions had an abundance of corn, there are too many farmers, so many that some have abandoned agriculture. The resources that [once] sustained the missions have [now] been reduced." As this observer suggested, part of the padres' problem stemmed from developments outside the mission walls. By the second half of the century some of the town dwellers from San Fernando had not only secured their agricultural resources but also had expanded their cattle-grazing enterprises. These ranchers had found a market for their herds in Louisiana and prospered from this trade, openly disregarding the royal decrees prohibiting it. The padres, who relied on subsidies from the Crown, could not act so boldly. Furthermore, as the roundup of wandering, unbranded cattle spread throughout the river valley down to the coast, the rancheros competed vigorously with the missions, with the result that the institutional herds dwindled considerably and the padres found themselves in a serious economic impasse. . . .

Yet these economically depressed and demographically small communities continued to control immense properties, resources that the town dwellers and the soldiers quite naturally wished to exploit. To achieve that goal, the latter urged the government to end the corporate privileges of the missions and allow them (the settlers) to exploit the lands and herds used by so few residents, who were only technically "Indian."

The Crown agreed in part with the petitioners and applied to the mission herds the same tax it collected on all mesteños (unclaimed livestock on the range). The vecinos avoided the assessment on their herds by various appeals and by ignoring the decree altogether, but the padres apparently lacked the stamina for the long, drawn-out legal battle and, more importantly, did not have the manpower to compete with the settlers in the race to round up the remaining livestock. By the end of the century the herds were largely depleted, and the issue of the tax became moot, even though the padres repeatedly blamed the decline of the missions on the levy on mesteños. Faced with all these difficulties, the friars found the governing of the missions an all-consuming task. Overseeing the farming and grazing operations took so much time, one padre complained, that he had little time for the doctrina (religious education for the natives) and even for his own prayer and meditation. Maintaining the missions was draining the resources available locally and straining the order's assets and its ability to raise funds for the San Antonio institutions. Furthermore, the expulsion of the Jesuits from the Spanish Empire in 1767 had left an enormous vacuum in the northwestern frontier, a vacuum the Franciscans were called upon to fill. Facing this new challenge and disappointed by their ventures in Texas, the friars willingly agreed to partial secularization in the 1790s and all but abandoned the province in the early 1800s.

When the missions were secularized, title to many of their lands was turned over to individual residents. Some Franciscans remained to minister spiritually to their former charges, but the mission era was over. The institutions that had dominated the San Antonio valley from the early 1700s to the 1780s experienced a rapid decline in the last decade of the century. Originally established with the idealistic goal of "civilizing" and Christianizing the natives, the missions developed into separate Indian pueblos but ended as Hispanic communities barley distinguishable from the neighboring town of San Fernando. At the close of the century that villa, its military establishment, and the missions merged into the settlement later known as San Antonio.

In a sense, the closing of the missions and the distribution of lands was in keeping with the friars' long-range goal of integrating the Indians into the Hispanic society, and to that extent the missions accomplished the purpose for which they were founded originally. In reality, however, the friars had not operated their institutions with this end in mind. They had set out to establish segregated Indian towns with certain corporate legal rights and a very distinct character. Many aspects of mission life were geared towards self-sufficiency, permanence, and the exclusion of external influences. Nevertheless, critical demographic patterns beyond the control of the padres worked against the survival of those autonomous Indian pueblos. In this regard, the problem of desertions was aggravated by minimal or nonexistent population growth, leaving the missions dependent on continued immigration, which ceased once the economically dependent bands found a better alternative in joining the Norteños. When the prospects of recruiting neophytes at the earlier levels faded, it then became impossible to justify the cost and personnel involved in maintaining those large enterprises for so few residents. Challenges by the townspeople and the government resulted in the termination of the autonomous corporate status the missions had enjoyed. By the time this happened, those institutions were already changing. Vecinos and soldiers had moved into the missions, and Indians had been drifting into the civilian town. Thus the once-separate Franciscan-Indian pueblos merged with the larger community of the villa of San Fernando de Béxar.

The Making of a Tejano Community

JESÚS F. DE LA TEJA

To understand community development in San Antonio during its first eighty years of existence, it is first necessary to agree on the meaning of the term "community." At its simplest, community is synonymous with place, and historians often use the two terms interchangeably. Community, however, can be defined as the product of shared attitudes, experiences, and cultural traits without reference to place. . . . In a broader perspective, community may also embody shared space and shared experience. . . .

To analyze the development of the San Antonio community, one must examine its origins. In 1718 Governor Martín de Alarcón led an expedition that resulted in the founding of San Antonio. Crown officials perceived the new settlement as a multifaceted project, not a purely military one, even though San Antonio's primary function remained strategically defensive in nature. The presidio was to serve as a way station between the Río Grande missions and the Louisiana-border outpost of Los Adaes and to protect area missions as they began the work of bringing the natives into the Spanish fold. The original settlement also was to be the nucleus for a Spanish town. With these purposes in mind, Alarcón was instructed to recruit civilians with families, not just soldiers. Accordingly, many of Béxar's first residents came to settle as much as to protect imperial interests. They were not professional soldiers but frontiersmen recruited in Coahuila and Nuevo León to tame the wild new province.

Isolation and shared purpose made the forging of community ties natural. The presidio formed the settlement's core, and all inhabitants, military and civilian, looked to its commander for political and judicial as well as military leadership. Families, many of whom were interrelated, lived in a compact settlement, civilians and military residing side-by-side. The soldiers shared many responsibilities with the handful of civilians—farmers, muleteers, construction workers, and assistants to the missionaries. As their enlistments expired, soldiers became civilian settlers, but their roles remained much the same. In essence, the settlement consisted of families facing the dangers, duties, and adventures of the frontier.

Mission records at San Antonio de Valero bear witness to the emergence of this early community. Beginning in 1720, marriages between soldiers and the daughters of soldiers occurred frequently, and those unions produced the first generation of native Bexareños. From its founding in 1718 to 1731, forty-seven couples married and 107 children were baptized at Mission Valero. Some weddings were performed for people from other Texas outposts, but most of these marriages helped forge communal bonds within the new settlement.

The small, isolated population's need for unity required a loosening of caste boundaries. Although evidence indicates that San Antonio's original population was ethnically mixed, it was not a matter to which the settlers paid undue attention.

Jesús F. de la Teja, "Indians, Soldiers and Canary Islanders: The Making of a Texas Frontier Community," *Locus: An Historical Journal of Regional Perspectives on National Topics,* vol. 2, no. 1 (Fall 1990), 84–96. Reprinted by permission of the author.

In registering the civilian population, the missionaries at Valero did not indicate an individual's ethnic status unless he or she was considered Spanish. For instance, there is evidence of only one interracial marriage at San Antonio, that between a Spanish settler and an Indian servant of the commander. Even when a groom was identified as the son of a Spaniard and an Indian, he was listed as Spanish, not mestizo, in the marriage register. Such obfuscation permitted descendants of racially mixed individuals to "pass" as Spaniards, the preferred social category in the larger colonial society. Clearly, the society that developed at San Antonio between 1718 and 1731 reflected the unifying influence of a number of factors. The necessities of survival in a frontier outpost, including protection from hostile Indians and production of food, drew the settlers together both physically and in terms of shared experiences.

In order to understand fully the impact of the Isleños upon this nascent community, and vice versa, it is important to realize that prior to 1731 the settlement at San Antonio bore little resemblance to an organized town. In the absence of a civil government, the presidial commander was the sole source of political authority. The arrival of the Canary Islanders in 1731 and the creation of a formal municipality altered this situation and completely disrupted the existing community.

Concerns for defending northern New Spain's mining districts led the crown and the Council of the Indies to consider various plans for fostering the growth of Texas, including the settlement of Old World families. Although a proposal to recruit Canary Islanders was first presented in 1719, not until February 14, 1729, did a group of ten Isleño families arrive at Veracruz en route to the San Antonio area. Preceding the new settlers were directives from the viceroy of New Spain to Juan Antonio Pérez de Almazán, captain of the presidio, which explained the economic, social, and political position that the Islanders were to occupy. Among other things, the instructions required that the immigrants be settled apart from the existing presidial community in order to avoid conflict. It was this part of the instructions that Captain Almazán felt compelled by circumstances—Apache hostilities, availability of irrigation water—to set aside.

Following procedures established by the Laws of the Indies, which codified Spanish colonial law, each of the Isleño founders of the new town, called San Fernando de Béxar, received a promotion to the rank of nobility, carrying with it the title of hidalgo. Only the hidalgos had the right to hold places on the town council and to serve in other town offices, including sheriff (*alguacil*) and official secretary (*escribano de cabildo*). In addition, only these town officers could elect local alcaldes to administer justice.

Along with the foreordained political power, the Isleños received daily allowances during their first year in Texas, and they were provided with the seeds necessary for raising their first crop. Each family also received a quantity of sheep, goats, cattle, and horses. In addition to the already cleared agricultural land given to them, Captain Almazán distributed among the Isleños other arable land as well as town lots on or near the main plaza of the new town. All of this was done to the exclusion of San Antonio's creole settlers.

The privileged position of the Canary Islanders produced considerable rancor as well as numerous petitions and appeals to Spanish officials by the original settlers and, in response, by the Isleños. It worked, however, to define more clearly the status of the various groups within the new, complex social structure that evolved in the town's first years. At the bottom of the emerging hierarchy stood the soldiers and a growing number of *agregados,* who took advantage of the availability of town land to build homes and start gardens and orchards. Most of them lived in *jacales* that stood in marked contrast to the stone homes of the wealthy few. In spite of vice-regal efforts to regulate prices for goods going to the presidos, venality in the system kept most soldiers on the edge of poverty. The same was true of the agregados. With nowhere else to go, some became servants or day laborer, others lived off the products of their gardens and small herds. By 1745 the agregados numbered forty-nine families, all of whom chafed under the predominance of the Canary Islanders.

Above the mass of agregados were a smaller group of civilian settlers, some of whom had been present at San Antonio's founding in 1718 and had amassed enough property to be of some consequence. Along with the handful of craftsmen, black-smiths, carpenters, and tailors, at least a few farmers and ranchers made a living supplying the presidios of Texas with horses, cattle, and maize. Besides those who received grants from Governor Manuel de Sandoval, or had not been affected by Captain Almazán's redistribution of lands to the Islanders, a group existed with enough wealth to buy out completely some Isleños. It is from this group of men that the first non-Islander officeholders came.

The Canary Islanders stood at the top of the hierarchy but were not a monolithic block. Their bid to exclude anyone else from power was not a unified effort. As the settlers observed, there were deep divisions within the Islander group. Having been brought together in the Mexico City suburbs from at least two different parties, the immigrants were ill prepared to work together. The many civil and criminal proceedings between Islanders, the lawsuits between them and the missionaries, presidio commanders, and governors, all attest to the absence of community in the years following the Canary Islanders' arrival. One frustrated official commented in 1745: "The fourteen families from the Canary Islands complain against the reverend fathers of the five missions, against the Indians that reside therein, against the captain of the presidio, and against the other forty-nine families settled there, so that it seems they desire to be left alone in undisputed possession. Perhaps even then they may not find enough room in the vast area of the entire province." He might well have added that the Isleños complained about each other, too. By the mid-1740s one Islander had renounced membership in the cabildo and departed the province, four had sold their farmland to non-Islanders, and four others had enlisted at the three Texas presidios.

Despite the divisions, social, economic, and political realities broke down the barriers that separated the group and fostered the process of community building. In the year the immigrants arrived, ritual kinship bonds began to be forged. For example, María Rosa Padrón, the first Canary Islander offspring born in San Antonio, had Gertrudes Flores de Valdez, a creole settler, as godmother. More important, the Isleño group's small size determined the inevitability of intermarriage with other settlers. For example, Joseph Leal and Ana de los Santos arranged marriages for their nine children, all of whom were born in San Antonio, to non-Islanders. Among the few Isleño offspring who married each other, their children in turn married into creole families. Within four generations in San Antonio, there remained no pure-blooded Canary Islander descendants.

The Isleño population's biological integration was part of a greater process of racial amalgamation common to the Spanish colonial world in general. In San Antonio, as elsewhere in the Mexican north, being "Spanish" was more a function of socio-economic success than ethnic purity. The continual influx of soldiers and their dependents, the incorporation of Hispanicized Indians, and limited opportunity for marriage within one's declared ethnic group contributed to creating a racially mixed community. Fray Juan Agustín Morfi, during his visit to San Antonio in 1777, described the town's leading men, its cabildo members, as "a ragged band of men of all colors."

Economic integration of the two groups quickly took place as the new arrivals needed the expertise of frontier survival possessed by the presidial population. Apart from learning to tend livestock and to fire guns, skills that Captain Almazán said were lacking in the Isleños, the creole settlers almost certainly introduced the newcomers to the variety of native American crops that made up the frontier diet. Not all were suited to agriculture, however, as evidenced by four young Islanders who left their property for military service in the province's presidios. Other Islanders established business ties with the more powerful members of the greater community, the captain, the governor, or the wealthier creole settlers. . . .

Circumstances, particularly geographic isolation and Indian depredations, also prevented the Islanders from remaining aloof and distinct from the rest of the population. San Antonio was over 250 miles distant from the most important avenue of contact with central New Spain, the presidio-mission complex of San Juan Bautista, over 100 miles from the nearest Spanish settlement, La Bahía, and more than 400 miles from the East Texas area of settlement. Remoteness and isolation were even more tangible during periods when the town was cut off from the outside world. Flooding of streams separating Béxar from San Juan Bautista on the Río Grande, as much as hostile Indians, could delay the mail for months. Distance often precluded the arrival of timely assistance in periods of Indian assault. In the summer of 1768, for example, Captain Luis Antonio Menchaca fended off a twenty-two day siege of the settlement without any help from the outside.

Indian hostilities also had much impact on Béxar's development. A principal reason for establishing Presidio Béxar had been to protect Mission San Antonio de Valero from potential Apache attack. And, only two years after San Antonio's founding, the Apaches were committing depredations against convoys, missions, and the settlement. In the 1760s, Comanches joined the Apaches in making life hazardous in Béxar. Attracting new settlers and recruits under such conditions was extremely difficult. As early as 1724, the presidial commander complained that "it is necessary to seek [recruits] outside the province because here there is no population whatever; and some time is needed to court [recruits] and give them some aid in costs besides their salaries, because of the resignation with which they all come to this country." During periods of extensive violence some of the more faint hearted left Béxar with their families, and there were general threats of abandoning the province. Occupation of the countryside, which did not begin until the 1750s because of hostilities, was often interrupted by renewed depredations.

Despite these problems, population increases did occur. Much of San Antonio's growth during the eighteenth century was inspired by direct government action in response to strategic defensive needs. The Islanders' immigration was the first stage in an abortive scheme to create a large, populous buffer province against both European and Indian intruders. The forced abandonment of East Texas with the relocation of the population to San Antonio in 1773 was also triggered by the government's desire to promote Béxar's development as a strategic outpost. In between these two large additions, and as late as 1780, military reorganizations brought soldiers and their dependents to San Antonio as well. Béxar's population grew from approximately 200 in 1726, to 500 in 1750, to 1,350 in the mid-1770s, before stabilizing at about 1,600 in the 1790s. . . .

Economic opportunities had to be taken where found in remote Béxar. Isolation played a crucial role in sensitizing the population to any perceived threats to the presidio, the town's chief source of livelihood, for even without the Indian problem San Antonio would have been only marginally integrated into the colonial economic system. Although regular export of ranching products began in the 1750s, the traffic was of minor importance, and reliance on the presidial market remained overwhelming. In 1756, for instance, the town council accused the missionaries of wishing to destroy the settlement by moving the presidio, even though the friars knew the town was already isolated by distance and numerous rivers and hostile Indians. Complaints about one parish priest's demands to be paid in cash for services focused on the fact that there was little money in circulation and that there was "no place to find it, this being a solitary and commerceless frontier."

With no more than 1,600 inhabitants in the 1790s, San Antonio's people continued to know each other and continued to exercise a number of economic roles, just as they had in the earliest days. Those who had enough land or cattle to provide the local market sometimes became part-time merchants, converting their profits into goods that they sold out of their homes. Almost everyone did some farming, and even the wealthiest residents went into the field on roundups with their sons and hired hands. Presidial service formed an important economic opportunity for local men, although all residents were expected to contribute to the town's defense. Many residents came to San Antonio as soldiers, and their sons followed them into military service. . . .

Shared roles, kinship ties, and the frontier experience tied much of Béxar's population into a dynamic community. The proximity between presidio and town, and the interdependence between the two, slowly fostered a joint identity for many. The term "Canary Islander" passed from denoting a distinct ethnic group to providing an identifying label for much of the town's core population. While two or three of the Islander descendants called attention to their origins in carrying on personal conflicts, it is inaccurate to portray Béxar in the late eighteenth and early nineteenth centuries as beset by racial conflict. Labels used to divide the population into Islanders and original military settlers slowly fell into disuse. These were generally replaced by the interchangeable *primeros* and *principales pobladores,* that is, first and principal settlers. . . .

Eighteenth-century San Antonio was not the static society so often portrayed, neatly divided into an elite of wealthy Canary Islanders and a mass of mestizo peons. In effect, the hierarchy used to describe early divisions of local society must be modified in order to accommodate a new reality which emerged near the end of the eighteenth century. By 1800 one can distinguish in San Antonio two broad social groups. One group was formed by the mass of the population, made up of poor later arrivals, Hispanicized Indians, and poor relations. Above them stood the better-off members of the community, most of whom were descendants of Islanders and original settlers, but also including merchants and a few other later arrivals who climbed to success. From this second group were drawn the ranchers, large-scale farmers, merchants, and politically active townsmen. For most of these individuals, ancestry and relative economic well being combined to provide status within the community.

As a whole, San Antonio in the eighteenth century reflected, in some aspects in magnified form, social trends apparent in greater Spanish colonial society. Distinctions between Indians, mixed races, and whites in Béxar became increasingly difficult to sort out in the course of the century, just as they were in central New Spain. In the colony as a whole, a socio-economic hierarchy was well on its way to displacing increasingly outdated ethnic distinctions as the principal ingredient in social stratification.

This is not to suggest that Béxar's was a caste-blind or egalitarian society. However, distinctions in social position were based not so much on overarching colonial classifications but on considerations deemed important within the local context. In the absence of a large peninsular-Spanish population, the growing antagonisms between American and European Spaniards was absent. There was, however, a growing sense of separate identity, of being a distinct part of the Spanish world, and of having certain rights and prerogatives earned through constant sacrifice on the frontier. Danger, isolation, limited economic development, and strong kinship structures brought the people of San Antonio close together. The forces that demanded unity of action also worked to bring about a unity of society. The very labels used by individuals to identify themselves within local society attest to the forging of a common identity. As the group that could claim Canary Islander descent grew in the course of generations, that identity was subsumed under the broader concept of a Béxar community. In the town council's words, when it argued in 1793 against a governor who did not want to allow relatives to serve concurrently on the body: "Here [we] are all kin, so that if [we] fixed on that, it would not be possible to form a council."

❧ F U R T H E R   R E A D I N G

Felix D. Almaraz, *The San Antonio Missions and their System of Land Tenure* (1988)
Herbert E. Bolton, *Texas in the Middle Eighteenth Century: Studies in Spanish Colonial History and Administration* (1915)
Carlos Castañeda, *Our Catholic Heritage in Texas,* 7 vols., (1936–1958)
Donald E. Chapman, *Spanish Texas, 1519–1821* (1992)
Gilberto Hinojosa, *A Borderlands Town in Transition: Laredo, 1755–1870* (1983)
Jack Jackson, *Los Mesteños: Spanish Ranching in Texas, 1721–1821* (1986)
Gerald E. Poyo, *Tejano Journey, 1770–1860* (1996)
——— and Gilberto Hinjosa, "Spanish Texas and Borderlands Historiography in Transition," *Journal of American History* 75 (September 1988)
Sandra L. Myres, *The Ranch in Spanish Texas* (1969)
Jesús F. de la Teja, *San Antonio de Béxar: A Community on New Spain's Far Northern Frontier* (1995)
Robert S. Weddle, *San Juan Bautista: Gateway to Spanish Texas* (1968)
———, *The San Saba Mission: Spanish Pivot in Texas* (1964)
David J. Weber, *The Spanish Frontier in North America* (1992)

Populating Texas During the Late Spanish and Mexican Periods, 1810–1835

As Anglo Americans began to push westward across the continent in large numbers after their revolution against Great Britain, they began to look covetously at the broad expanse of land to the west owned by Spain. Although the term "Manifest Destiny" would not be coined until the mid-1840s, many Americans, particularly in the southern states, developed a firm ideology of territorial expansion by the early nineteenth century. The outbreak of Mexico's War for Independence in 1810 prompted many Americans to seek to exploit the vacuum of political authority in Spain's northern territories. Filibusters—privately financed and organized military expeditions—entered Texas in 1812 and 1819 with the goal of wresting Texas away from Spanish rule.

In an effort to fend off the aggressively expansionist United States, Spain initiated an immigration program designed to bring settlers to Texas. It embraced the principle that "to populate is to govern." The colonization policy, which Mexico continued after winning its independence from Spain in 1821, was designed to attract an international community consisting of Mexican, American, and European immigrants. During the 1820s, however, the overwhelming majority of emigrants to Texas were citizens of the United States who possessed the resources necessary to take advantage of Mexico's offer. Mexico, then, was obliged to resort to the dubious expedient of populating Texas with settlers from the very country whose territorial ambitions its land grant policy was designed to thwart.

Initially, the settlement program went forward smoothly as migrants established farming communities and became peaceful, law-abiding citizens of Mexico. The first signs of tensions came in 1825, when American empresario Haden Edwards attempted to remove from his East Texas land grant Mexican families who had inhabited the region for several decades. When the Mexican government rescinded his grant, Edwards declared the region in a state of rebellion and proclaimed the Fredonian Republic. The revolt proved short-lived, and Haden Edwards and his brother Benjamin soon fled to New Orleans. An investigation of conditions in Texas undertaken by Mexican official Mier y Teran soon afterward presented the government with a disturbing picture of a rapidly growing Anglo American popula-tion that displayed only nominal loyalty to Mexico. As a result, the Mexican govern-ment took steps to block further Anglo American settlement in Texas.

Were these problems the inevitable result of conflicting and utterly disparate cultures, or were they minor disputes that did not preclude the peaceful settlement of Anglos under the flag of Mexico? Clearly, the Mexican government and many Anglo settlers had widely divergent attitudes about the rights and obligations of citizenship. To what extent did race contribute to the problems that arose between the Anglo American community and Mexico? What role did differences of political and economic philosophy between Anglos and Hispanics play?

🖈 D O C U M E N T S

American filibusters, sometimes acting in concert with Mexican citizens, organized several expeditions into Texas during the early decades of the nineteenth century. Their activities did much to excite the Spanish government's suspicions of the United States. Document 1 is a proclamation issued in Nacogdoches by Bernardo Gutierrez, a Mexican revolutionary who, with Augustus Magee, a former U.S. Army officer, invaded Texas with an army of volunteers in 1812. Although written ostensibly to the soldiers under his command, the document was widely published throughout the southern United States. Its promise of land and other valuable property was undoubtedly intended as an inducement to attract new recruits to the revolutionary cause. The expedition sub-sequently seized San Antonio and declared Texas' independence, but was crushed by a Spanish army in the summer of 1813.

By the mid-1820s, the land grant policy implemented by a newly independent Mexico was beginning to show promising results. Document 2 outlines the terms of settlement in Stephen F. Austin's colony and reveals the empresario's concern that only individuals of upstanding moral character be allowed to settle in Texas. The $12.50 per one hundred acres which Austin charged for surveying and title fees was deemed exorbitant by many colonists, however, and was the cause of considerable grumbling. Document 3 is the Coahuila y Texas Land Colonization Law, which offered prospective settlers more than a league of land for a nominal fee, a highly attractive opportunity for American citizens. Life in Mexico's remote northern province was hard for early settlers, as illustrated in Document 4 by the account of Caroline von Hinueber, whose family purchased land in Austin's colony.

Early signs of friction between Anglos and the Mexican government can be de-tected in Document 5, in which the leaders of the Fredonian revolt state their reasons for insurrection. Employing the rhetoric of liberty reminiscent of the American Revolu-tion, the proclamation is a telling example of the way in which Anglo Americans of the early nineteenth century drew from their political heritage to justify their own economic interests. Although citizens of Mexico, the Fredonian rebels defend their actions on the basis of their rights as Americans.

The Mexican government's response to the Fredonian Rebellion is described in the next two documents. Document 6 is an excerpt from the report of Manuel de Mier y Teran, commandant general of Mexico's Eastern Interior Provinces, who undertook a fact-finding tour of Texas in 1828. Mier y Teran's concerns that Mexico was in danger of losing Texas prompted the Mexican Congress to pass the April 6 1830 law, cited in Document 7, which prohibited further immigration from the United States.

The law prompted a firestorm of protest, as might be expected, from Anglo American settlers and speculators, whose hopes for reaping rich profits from Texas lands were contingent upon the continued migration of Americans into the region. But these former citizens of the United States were not the only residents upset with the new law. As Document 8 reveals, tejano landowners were also anxious to find ways to promote economic development. Complaining of Indian depredations and prolonged neglect by the government in Mexico City, the San Antonio ayuntamiento also argued in favor of a liberal immigration policy in order to bring prosperity to the region.

1. Mexican Revolutionary Bernardo Gutierrez Promises Spoils of War to Army Volunteers at Nacogdoches, 1812

Fellow soldiers and volunteers in the Mexican cause.

I desire you to receive from me the tribute of my private feelings, and also as the agent of my Mexican brethren, my warmest and most sincere thanks for the activity, zeal, promptitude and courage that you have shewn in the obedience of those orders which you have received from your officers, acting under my command; and I flatter myself with the idea that the line of conduct which you have hitherto observed will be continued in, to the *discomfiture of tyrants,* to the *emancipation* of the *Mexicans,* and to the complete success of the enterprise you have undertaken, which will crown your exertions with glory, honor and fortune. The consolation of the justice of the cause which you support—of the fame and immortality which awaits your success—the idea that all the civilized nations of the world look on your actions with admiration and good will—the reflection that the future happiness or misery of a large portion of the habitable globe is now in your hands, will, I am certain prompt you on, and shew your enemies and the enemies of liberty, in every part of the world, that the spark which lighted the flame of independence in the northern part of America is not extinct in the bosoms of the descendants of those who fought, bled, and prevailed over tyrants; and will at the same time establish, beyond a possibility of doubt, your individual right to that liberty, for the attainment of which for others, you have volunteered your lives, your property, and sacrificed all your social connections.

You are now, fellow-soldiers, in peaceable possession of one of the out-posts established by European tyranny, the more effectually to enslave the oppressed Mexicans. This possession has been obtained without bloodshed on your part, from the consciousness in the minds of the cowardly instruments of tyranny, that they never can prevail in arms against the brave, free, and independent citizens of the United States of America.

This pusillanimity of conduct in the engines of despotism has left in your power, in a weak and defenceless state, all the citizens of the post which you have gained. Your conduct to those citizens has met my entire approbation. It has done honor to yourselves, as men and as soldiers; and if continued, will be more powerful than all the arms in the world—as it will conquer their minds and force them (should they ever feel a doubt) to declare that you are to them as friends, as brothers and as protectors against those who have held them enthralled for ages past, in bondage the most ignominious. From the information which I have received from different quarters, I flatter myself that your stay in this place will not be long—that

"Revolution in Mexico," *Niles' Weekly Register,* vol. III, 104, October 17, 1812.

your numbers will increase to a sufficient extent and enable you to seek the tyrants in their strong holds, and force them to acknowledge this long enslaved country as a free, sovereign and independent government. When this event takes place (and the time is not far distant) you are to look for the reward of your toils, dangers, sufferings and difficulties, in the enjoyment of all the rights of honored citizens of the Mexican republic, in the cultivation of those lands, which I pledge myself will be assigned to every individual among you, or in the pursuit of wealth and happiness, in such way as your inclinations may point out to you. To those who desire it, the right of working or disposing of any mines of gold, silver, or what nature soever, which you may find will be given. The right of taming and disposing of the wild horses and mules which roam unclaimed over an immense tract of country, within the limits of the Mexican republic, will be common to all of you.—The surplus of property confiscated, as belonging to those who are inimical to the republican cause after the expences of the expedition are paid, will be divided amongst you—and those powerful and almost inestimable services which you will render, will further be rewarded from the public treasury of that government which you will have so materially aided in erecting.

JOSE BERNARDO GUTIERREZ.

2. Stephen F. Austin Seeks Settlers of "Unblemished Character," 1823

The terms on which Settlers are admitted into the Colony forming by Stephen F. Austin in the Province of Texas are as follows—

No one will be received as a Settler, or even be permitted to remain in the country longer than is absolutely necessary to prepare for a removal who does not produce the most unequivocal and satisfactory evidence of unblemished character, good Morals, Sobriety, and industrious habits, and he must also have sufficient property to begin with either as a farmer or mechanic besides paying for his land—No frontiersman who has no other occupation than that of a hunter will be received—no drunkard, nor Gambler, nor profane swearer no idler, nor any man against whom there is even probable grounds of suspicion that he is a bad man, or even has been considered a bad or disorderly man will be received. Those who are rejected on the grounds of bad character will be immediately ordered out of the County and if the order is not obeyed they will be sent off under guard and their property seized and sold to pay the expences, and should forcible resistence be made by them, the guard will be ordered to fire on and kill them—

Those who are received as Settlers will get one league of land if so much is wanted, to be chosen by the emigrant, which land will cost at the rate of twelve Dollars and fifty cents p^r hundred acres payable in cash or Spanish Cattle or negros on receipt of title, which will be in full for surveying, title deeds, recording, and all other charges.

Terms of Settlement, Eugene Barker, ed., *Austin Papers,* Annual Report of the American Historical Association for the Year 1919, Volume 1, Part I, 705.

The above only applies to men of families—Single men will be examined as to character more particularly than men of families and ten of them must unite to form a family and they will be entitled to one League of land to be divided between them. An exception will be made to this rule in favor of single men who bring a considerable capital into the country all such will be ranked as a family and draw on League—

A person who brings in a large capital and who has a large family will draw more than a league should he wish it. The head of each family will be held personally responsible for the good conduct of every member of his family.

The Roman Catholic is the established religion of the Mexican nation and the law will not allow of any other in this Colony—October 30 1823—

3. The Coahuila y Texas Immigration Law of 1824

DECREE, No. 16.—The Congress, assembled for the purpose of forming the Constitution of the Sovereign and Independent State of Coahuila and Texas, desirous of augmenting by all possible means the population of its territory; of encouraging the cultivation of its fertile lands, the raising of stock, and the progress of arts and commerce, in exact conformity with the Act on which the Constitution is founded; with the federal Constitution; and the basis established by the Sovereign Decree of the general Congress, No. 72; decree as follows:—

Law of Colonization
OF
The State of Coahuila and Texas.

ART. 1.—All those foreigners who in virtue of the general law of the 18th August, 1824, by which security for their property and persons is offered in all the territory of the Mexican Nation, may be desirous of establishing themselves in any of the towns of Coahuila and Texas, are hereby permitted; that State invites and proposes to them so to do.

ART. 2.—Those who shall do so, far from being in any way molested, shall be secured by the local authorities of the above mentioned towns; which shall allow them full liberty to engage in whatever honest calling may suit them, as long as they duly obey the general laws of the nation, and the ordinances of the State.

ART. 3.—Whatever foreigner at present resident in Coahuila and Texas, may determine on settling there, shall make a declaration to that effect, addressed to the municipal authorities of the town in which he is desirous of fixing his residence. The municipal authorities then shall bind him by oath, which he shall make, to abide by and obey the general Constitution, and that of the State; to observe the Religion as stipulated by the former; and in a book (the register of foreigners) which shall be kept for that purpose, his name and those of the members of his family, if he has any, shall be set down; noting the country from whence he comes,

H. P. N. Gammel, ed., *Laws of Texas* (Austin: Gammel Book Co., 1898), 1822–1897, 1:99–105.

whether married or single, his employment; and he having taken the requisite oath, shall be considered thenceforward, and not before that time, a fellow-citizen.

ART. 4.—From the very day in which any foreigner becomes a citizen, agreeably to the preceding article, he may denounce any land belonging to the State, and the proper civil authority being under the obligation of passing to the government, for its approbation, the petition thus made on this subject, shall award it to him; as also to every native of the country, acting in conformity with the laws on that subject.

ART. 5.—The foreigners of any nation and the native Mexicans may undertake to form new settlements on lands belonging to the nation, and even if belonging to individuals under the circumstances stated in Art. 35; but the new settlers, who may demand admission into the nation, must prove, by certificate from the authorities of the place from whence they came, that they are Christians, and also the morality and propriety of their conduct.

ART. 6.—Whatever foreigners shall arrive at a period at which the sovereign general Congress shall have prohibited, as it may do after the year 1840, or previously as regards the natives of any one nation, shall not then be admitted; and all those who shall arrive within the time allowed them, agreeably to this article, shall, nevertheless, be subjected to such measures for the security of the federation as the supreme government may adopt, regarding them without prejudice to the object of this law.

ART. 7.—The government shall take care that no settlement be made within 20 leagues of the boundaries of the United States of North America, and 10 leagues along the coast of the Gulf of Mexico, except such as shall obtain the sanction of the Supreme Government of the Union: for which purpose it shall forward to it every petition on that head, made by Mexicans or foreigners, adding to it whatever remarks it may deem expedient.

ART. 8.—All projects for establishing colonies, on which one or more persons may offer to bring, at their own expense, 100 or more families, shall be presented to the government which, if it finds them agreeable to the law, shall approve of them, and immediately mark out to the projectors the lands which they are to occupy, and the number of years allowed them for presenting the number of families for which they have stipulated, under penalty of forfeiting the rights and benefits offered them in proportion to the number of families they shall omit to provide, and the grant shall be wholly annulled should they not present, at the least, 100 families.

ART. 9.—This law guarantees all contracts made between the projectors and the families brought at their expense, inasmuch as they are in conformity with its provisions. . . .

ART. 11.—A square of land, of which each side is one league of 5,000 yards, or, what is precisely the same, 25,000,000 yards of surface, shall be named a lot, and this shall be considered as the unity in counting one, two, or more lots: thus, also, the unity in counting one, two, or more subdivisions shall be 1,000,000 yards of surface, or a square of 1,000 yards each side, which is the measure of one subdivision: the yard used in these measurements shall be three geometrical feet.

ART. 12.—Supposing the quantity of land above stated to be the unity, and a division of the land being made, when distributed into grazing lands and those adapted for tillage by means of irrigation, or not requiring irrigation;—this law grants to such projector or the projectors of plans for colonization, for each 100 families which they convey, and establish in the State, 5 lots of grazing land, and 5 subdivisions, of which at least one-half shall be arable land, not requiring irrigation; but they shall only receive this premium for as many as 800 families, even if they should introduce a greater number; nor shall any fractional number, be it what it may, which does not amount to 100, give them a right to any recompense, even in proportion to its amount.

ART. 13.—If any one or more projectors shall, on account of the families they have conveyed, obtain, agreeably to the preceding article, more than 11 square leagues, the whole of the land shall be granted to them, but they shall be under the obligation of selling the surplus within 12 years; and should they neglect to do so, the proper civil authorities shall do it, selling it at public auction, and delivering to them the net proceeds, after deducting all the expenses attending the sale.

ART. 14.—To each of the families included in a project of colonization, whose sole occupation is the cultivation of the land, one division of land shall be given; should it also breed cattle, it shall receive also of grazing land a sufficient quantity to complete one lot; and if it only breeds cattle, it shall have of grazing land an extent of 24,000,000 superficial yards.

ART. 15.—Bachelors shall on marrying obtain a similar quantity, and those foreigners who marry Mexican women shall have one-fourth more; but all those who are alone, or forming a part of no family, whether they are Mexicans or foreigners, must content themselves with one-fourth part of the above-mentioned portions, nor will any greater quantity be allowed to them, and the allotments will be assigned to them in this proportion.

ART. 16.—The families, and single men, who having performed the journey at their own expense may wish to join any of the new settlements, shall be permitted to do so at any time; and their assignments of lands shall be to each individual the same as those mentioned in the preceding articles; but if they do so within the first 6 years of the establishment of the colony, one more subdivision shall be given to each family, and each bachelor, in lieu of the one-fourth which the 15th Article designates, shall receive one-third part. . . .

ART. 19.—The Indians of all the tribes on the confines of the States, as also those of the wandering tribes in it, shall be received in the markets without demanding of them any duties on account of the traffic which they carry on in the natural productions of the country; and, if thus induced by kindness and confidence any of them should be desirous (previously making a declaration in favor of the religion and institutions) to establish themselves in any of the settlements which may be formed, they shall be admitted, and obtain the same quantity of land as the settlers mentioned in Articles 14 and 15; the natives being always preferred to the Indians coming from a foreign country. . . .

ART. 22—The new colonist shall, as a species of acknowledgement, pay to the State for each lot of pasture land, 30 dollars; 2½ for each subdivision or arable land not irrigated, and 3½ dollars for each one of irrigated land, each in proportion to the kind and quantity of land which has been allotted to him; but the payment of those sums shall not be made in less than 6 years after their settlement, and in 3 equal installments, the first at the expiration of the fourth, the others at the expiration of the fifth and sixth years, under penalty of forfeiting their lands should they neglect the payment of any one of these instalments: but the projectors and military men, mentioned in the 10th Article, are excepted, with regard to those lands which the former have obtained as a recompense, and the latter agreeably to the documents given them by the government. . . .

ART. 24.—The government shall sell to the Mexicans, and only to them, the lands which they may be desirous of purchasing, but shall not allow more than eleven lots to fall into the hands of one individual, and under the express condition, that the purchaser must cultivate the lands which he obtains by these means within 6 years, under the penalty of losing them: the price of each lot, in conformity with the preceding Article, shall be 100 dollars for grazing, 150 for arable not watered, and 250 for irrigated lands.

ART. 25.—Until 6 years after the publication of this law, the Legislature of the State shall have no power to alter it, inasmuch as regards the measurement of lands, the price to be paid for them, the quantity and description of those which are to be granted to new settlers, and sold to Mexicans.

ART. 26.—It shall be considered, that the many settlers who within 6 years from the date of their grant have not cultivated or occupied according to its quality the land which has been granted to them, have renounced their rights, and the proper civil authority shall resume the grant and the title deeds.

ART. 27.—The projectors, and military men, of whom previous mention has been made, and those who have purchased lands, can sell their lands at any time, on condition that the purchaser oblige himself to cultivate them within the period in which the original possessor ought to do so, including also the time which they have been in his hands; the other settlers may sell theirs when they have cultivated them wholly, and not before that time.

ART. 28.—Every new settler from the very day of his settlement can dispose of his lands by will, made agreeably to the present or then existing law, even although he has not cultivated them; and if he should die intestate, the person or persons who inherit his property agreeably to the laws, shall succeed to them under the same obligations and conditions that he held them.

ART. 29.—The lands granted in virtue of this law can on no account be allowed to pass into the hands of religious communities.

ART. 30.—The new settler who shall determine on quitting the State, in order to establish himself in a foreign country, shall be allowed so to do, together with all his property, but in this case shall not retain his land, and if he has not previously sold it, or the sale been effected agreeably to the 27th Article, it shall be again considered as wholly belonging to the State.

ART. 31.—Those foreigners who agreeably to this law have obtained lands, and established themselves in these settlements, are considered from that moment as naturalized in the country, and should they marry Mexican women will be considered to have established a meritorious claim to obtain the rights of citizenship of the State, except, however, in both instances the cases provided for by the enactments of the Constitution of the State.

ART. 32.—During the first 10 years, counting from the day in which settlements are established, they shall be free from every contribution under whatever denomination, excepting such as in the event of the invasion of an enemy. . . .

ART. 33.—From the very day of their establishment the new settlers shall be at liberty to pursue every branch of industry, as well as to work mines of every description. . . .

ART. 34.—The towns shall be founded on the spots deemed by the government, or the person it names for that purpose, most fitting, and for each of them four leagues square shall be designated, which space shall be either of a regular or irregular shape, according to the locality. . . .

ART. 36.—The sites for houses in the new towns shall be given gratis to the projectors of them, as also to artizans of every description those which they may require for their workshops, and they shall be sold to the others at public auction, an estimate of the value being previously made, on condition of the price being paid in three equal instalments, the first in six months, the second in twelve, and the third in eighteen; but every possessor of sites, including projectors and artizans, shall pay yearly one dollar for each one that he holds, and this sum, as also the product of those sales, shall be collected by the municipalities, and applied to the purpose of erecting a church in the town. . . .

ART. 40.—As soon as at least 40 families are united, they shall proceed to the formal establishment of a new town, all binding themselves by oath, taken before the commissioner, to observe the general Constitution, and that of the State, and subsequently the commissioner presiding for this the first time, shall proceed to the election of the municipality.

ART. 41.—The new town whose population amounts to 200 inhabitants shall elect a corporate body, if there be no other established within the distance of 8 leagues, but if there be one it shall be added to its jurisdiction; the number of members of which the corporation is to be composed shall be regulated agreeably to the existing laws.

ART. 42.—A reservation being made in favour of all the enactments of the Constitution of the State, the foreign settlers are permitted to elect and be elected members of the municipal body. . . .

ART. 44.—The government shall send to the head of that department those individuals who in other parts of the State may be sentenced to hard labour as vagrants or for other crimes, in order that they may be employed in making and repairing the roads in Texas. These persons may also be employed in the services of individuals, who shall in that case pay them the requisite daily allowance, and at the expiration of the period for which they were condemned, they shall be allowed as settlers to join any of the new towns, and to obtain the due quantity of land, if by the improvement of their conduct they shall, in the opinion of the aforesaid chief of the civil department, have rendered themselves fit, but they shall not be admitted without his certificate.

ART. 45.—The government, agreeably to an arrangement with the proper ecclesiastical authorities, shall see that the new towns are provided with a proper number of clergy, and agreeably to an arrangement with the aforesaid authorities, shall propose to the Congress the salary which the new settlers are to pay them.

ART. 46.—As regards the introduction of slaves, the new settlers shall obey the laws already established, and which hereafter may be established on the subject.

4. Caroline von Hinueber Describes the Hardship of Life in Austin's Colony, 1832

When my father came to Texas, I was a child of eleven or twelve years. My father's name was Friedrich Ernst. He was by profession a bookkeeper, and emigrated from the duchy of Oldenburg. Shortly after landing in New York he fell in with Mr. Fordtran, a tanner and a countryman of his. A book by a Mr. Duhde, setting forth the advantages of the new State of Missouri, had come into their hands, and they determined to settle in that State. While in New Orleans, they heard that every settler who came to Texas with his family would receive a league and labor of land from the Mexican government. This information induced them to abandon their first intention.

We set sail for Texas in the schooner *Saltillo,* [with] Captain Haskins. Just as we were ready to start, a flatboat with a party of Kentuckians and their dogs was hitched on to our vessel, the Kentuckians coming aboard and leaving their dogs behind on the flatboat. The poor animals met a grievous fate. Whenever the wind arose and the waves swept over the boat, they would howl and whine most piteously. One night the line parted, and we never saw them again.

We were almost as uncomfortable as the dogs. The boat was jammed with passengers and their luggage so that you could hardly find a place on the floor to lie down at night. I firmly believe that a strong wind would have drowned us all. In the bayou, the schooner often grounded, and the men had to take the anchor on shore and pull her off. We landed at Harrisburg, which consisted at that time of about five or six log houses, on the 3d of April, 1831. Captain Harris had a sawmill, and there was a store or two, I believe. Here we remained five weeks, while Fordtran went ahead of us and entered a league, where now stands the town of Industry. While on our way to our new home, we stayed in San Felipe for several days at Whiteside Tavern. The courthouse was about a mile out of town, and here R. M. Williamson, who was the alcalde, had his office. I saw him several times while I was here, and remember how I wondered at his crutch and wooden leg. S. F. Austin was in Mexico at the time, and Sam Williams, his private secretary, gave my father a title to land which he had originally picked out for himself. My father had to kiss the Bible and promise, as soon as the priest should arrive, to become a Catholic. People were married by the alcalde, also, on the promise that they would have themselves reunited on the arrival of the priest. But no one ever became Catholic, though the priest, Father Muldoon, arrived promptly. The people of San Felipe made him drunk and sent him back home. . . .

After we had lived on Fordtran's place for six months, we moved into our own house. This was a miserable little hut, covered with straw and having six sides, which were made out of moss. The roof was by no means water-proof, and we often held an umbrella over our bed when it rained at night, while the cows came and ate the moss. Of course, we suffered a great deal in the winter. My father had tried to build a chimney and fireplace out of logs and clay, but we were afraid to

Caroline von Hinueber, "Life of German Pioneers in Early Texas," *Texas State Historical Quarterly,* vol. 2 (October 1898): 227–230.

light a fire because of the extreme combustibility of our dwelling. So we had to shiver. Our shoes gave out, and we had to go barefoot in winter, for we did not know how to make moccasins. Our supply of clothes was also insufficient, and we had no spinning wheel, nor did we know how to spin and weave like the Americans. It was twenty-eight miles to San Felipe, and, besides, we had no money. When we could buy things, my first calico dress cost 50 cents per yard. No one can imagine what a degree of want there was of the merest necessities of life, and it is difficult for me now to understand how we managed to live and get along under the circumstances. Yet we did so in some way. We were really better supplied than our neighbors with household and farm utensils, but they knew better how to help themselves. Sutherland used his razor for cutting kindling, killing pigs, and cutting leather for moccasins. My mother was once called to a neighbor's house, five miles from us, because one of the little children was very sick. My mother slept on a deer skin, without a pillow, on the floor. In the morning, the lady of the house poured water over my mother's hands and told her to dry her face on her bonnet. At first we had very little to eat. We ate nothing but corn bread at first. Later, we began to raise cow peas, and afterwards my father made a fine vegetable garden. My father always was a poor huntsman. At first, we grated our corn until my father hollowed out a log and we ground it, as in a mortar. We had no cooking-stove, of course, and baked our bread in the only skillet we possessed. The ripe corn was boiled until it was soft, then grated and baked. The nearest mill was thirty miles off.

As I have already said, the country was very thinly settled. Our three neighbors, Burnett, Dougherty, and Sutherland, lived in a radius of seven miles. San Felipe was twenty-eight miles off, and there were about two houses on the road thither.

5. Anglo Leaders of the Fredonian Revolt State Their Reasons for Insurrection Against Mexico, 1826

Nacogdoches December 25, 1826.

Fellow citizens!

Having assembled at the town of Nacogdoches under the flag of Independence, and consequently in open hostility towards the Mexican United States, we consider it to be due to you, fellow citizens! in common with all the Inhabitants of the Province of Texas, who are alike interested in the destiny of this our adopted country, to explain the motives and causes, which have impelled us to take this bold and determined stand, without first calling upon you to participate in this holy cause.

It was not from any want of respect and consideration for your character and feelings, it proceeded not from an unworthy suspicion of your patriotism and your sympathies for us. No, fellow citizens! We knew you were Americans, the sons of those long departed patriots, who, when their rights were invaded, nobly grasped their arms, and planted the standard of liberty and Independence in our native land.

"B. W. Edwards and H. B. Mayo to the Inhabitants of Pecan Point," December 25, 1826. Eugene Barker, ed., *Austin Papers, Annual Report of the American Historical Association for the Year 1919*, vol. II, Part 2 (Washington, D.C.: Government Printing Office, 1924): 1542–1545.

Having the same confidence in your patriotism and your valor, believing that the sons of America would never tarnish the proud glory of their fathers, even in a foreign land, and that as brothers far from our homes and removed to a land beyond the maternal protection of our native country, we could not doubt your sympathies for us. We could not question your feelings and your judgments in the present aspect of our political affairs. Placed in a situation peculiar to ourselves and impelled by the most serious necessity; our properties daily seized by violence and injustice, our persons violated, our liberties trampled under foot, and ourselves the destined and immediate victims of the Spanish or Mexican bayonets; we have sprung to arms for our safety.

No longer secure in our properties and our lives, and having long since ceased to hope for liberty and justice under this imbecile, this faithless and perfidious Government, we have planted the standard of liberty and Independence for our protection with a firm and solemn resolve to live or perish with it. Self preservation, the great law of nature, is our justification for planting it thus early, and before we could formally invite our fellow citizens to concur with us in this important matter. Not only the threats of those pretty [sic] tyrants here, who have so long trampled upon the rights of your brother Americans, but the official communications of the Government themselves, now in our possession, prove, that we were selected as the victims of destruction, and that a brutal soldiery were soon to be let loose upon us. . . .

Fellow citizens! We need not here recapitulate the lawless and repeated outrages, that too many of our citizens have had to endure. We were enticed from our native country under the promise of important advantages to our families, and by a guarantee of our rights and liberties. We have been basely deceived in all these promises, and we know not now, that we have a valid title to one foot of land in the province of Texas. Lands have been granted and taken away at the mere will and pleasure of a corrupt and prejudiced Governor without any regard to the forms of justice or the rights of the Judicial Department of the Government. Our slaves have been attempted to be taken from us, and even the most favorable issue of that subject, as is now anticipated, would be the ruin of our country and of our every hope and prospect in it.—Military despotism has been substituted for that liberty which was promised as our shield and protection. Our citizens have without notice of a charge against them, been seized by a brutal soldiery, bound hand and foot and dragged into exile or incarcerated in their dungeons at the will of a petty tyrant, and all these things sanctioned by the Government under which we live. Great God! Can you any longer hesitate, fellow citizens! what to do? Did our fathers, who are now no more, hesitate, what to do, when they were oppressed? No, their blood ran in willing torrents upon the altar of liberty, when their rights were invaded. Shall their sons do less? Forbid it Allmighty God!!! What have we to fear in such a contest? What have we to hope from such a corrupt and perfidious Government as this. Shall we sit with our arms folded in fatal security, untill we are bound in chains and slavery? No! fellow citizens! We have nothing to hope for but in our arms. They will guaranty rights, that will not be wrested from us. Let us then join heart and hand in the noble struggle for our liberties. We are the children of the same mother country. We are Americans in a foreign land, groaning under the galling yoke of injustice and oppression. Our fathers in their struggle for liberty contended against the giant of the world. We have to contend against a corrupt and imbecile Government, now tottering upon its own foundation, and ready to crumble into its former ruins.

We for ourselves have no fears of a speedy establishment of our Independence. We have now the means of making *this empire shake to its very centre.* We ask you not to risk your lives and properties with us in this enterprize, unless your own feelings and your own judgments sanction such a cause. The rights and properties of every American and Spaniard will be held sacred, unless he raises arms against us. We will not dictate to you what course you should pursue.—Should you think proper to leave the struggle to us alone, We are nevertheless willing to fight for your rights and security in common with our own. Should we secure the Independence of this country, of which we have not an earthly doubt, you will of course share its blessings with us. We have undertaken this glorious cause with a determination to be freemen or to perish under the flag of liberty. We at least are determined to live or to die like Americans and like the sons of freemen.

6. Mier y Teran Fears Mexico May Lose Texas, 1830

. . . As one covers the distance from Béjar to this town [Nacogdoches], he will note that Mexican influence is proportionately diminished until on arriving in this place he will see that it is almost nothing. And indeed, whence could such influence come? Hardly from superior numbers in population, since the ratio of Mexicans to foreigners is one to ten; certainly not from the superior character of the Mexican population, for exactly the opposite is true, the Mexicans of this town comprising what in all countries is called the lowest class—the very poor and very ignorant. The naturalized North Americans in the town maintain an English school, and send their children north for further education; the poor Mexicans not only do not have sufficient means to establish schools, but they are not of the type that take any thought for the improvement of its public institutions or the betterment of its degraded condition. Neither are there civil authorities or magistrates; one insignificant little man—not to say more—who is called an *alcalde,* and an *ayuntamiento* that does not convene once in a lifetime is the most that we have here at this important point on our frontier; yet, wherever I have looked, in the short time that I have been here, I have witnessed grave occurrences, both political and judicial. It would cause you the same chagrin that it has caused me to see the opinion that is held of our nation by these foreign colonists, since, with the exception of some few who have journeyed to our capital, they know no other Mexicans than the inhabitants about here, and excepting the authorities necessary to any form of society, the said inhabitants are the most ignorant of negroes and Indians, among whom I pass for a man of culture. Thus, I tell myself that it could not be otherwise than that from such a state of affairs should arise an antagonism between the Mexicans and foreigners, which is not the least of the smoldering fires which I have discovered. Therefore, I am warning you to take timely measures. Texas could throw the whole nation into revolution.

Allein Howren, "Causes and Origins of the Decree of April 6, 1830," *Southwestern Historical Quarterly,* vol. 16 (April 1913): 395–397.

The colonists murmur against the political disorganization of the frontier, and the Mexicans complain of the superiority and better education of the colonists; the colonists find it unendurable that they must go three hundred leagues to lodge a complaint against the petty pickpocketing that they suffer from a venal and ignorant *alcalde,* and the Mexicans with no knowledge of the laws of their own country, nor those regulating colonization, set themselves against the foreigners, deliberately setting nets to deprive them of the right of franchise and to exclude them from the *ayuntamiento.* Meanwhile, the incoming stream of new settlers is unceasing; the first news of these comes by discovering them on land already under cultivation, where they have been located for many months; the old inhabitants set up a claim to the property, basing their titles of doubtful priority, and for which there are no records, on a law of the Spanish government; and thus arises a lawsuit in which the *alcalde* has a chance to come out with some money. In this state of affairs, the town where there are no magistrates is the one in which lawsuits abound, and it is at once evident that in Nacogdoches and its vicinity, being most distant from the seat of the general government, the primitive order of things should take its course, which is to say that this section is being settled up without the consent of anybody.

The majority of the North Americans established here under the Spanish government—and these are few—are of two classes. First, those who are fugitives from our neighbor republic and bear the unmistakable earmarks of thieves and criminals; these are located between Nacogdoches and the Sabine, ready to cross and recross this river as they see the necessity of separating themselves from the country in which they have just committed some crime; however, some of these have reformed and settled down to an industrious life in the new country. The other class of early settlers are poor laborers who lack the four or five thousand dollars necessary to buy a *sitio* of land in the north, but having the ambition to become landholders—one of the strong virtues of our neighbors—have come to Texas. Of such as this latter class is Austin's colony composed. They are for the most part industrious and honest, and appreciate this country. Most of them own at least one or two slaves. Unfortunately the emigration of such is made under difficulties, because they lack the means of transportation, and to accomplish this emigration it has become necessary to do what was not necessary until lately: there are empresarios of wealth who advance them the means for their transportation and establishment.

The wealthy Americans of Louisiana and other western states are anxious to secure land in Texas for speculation, but they are restrained by the laws prohibiting slavery. If these laws should be repealed—which God forbid—in a few years Texas would be a powerful state which could compete in productions and wealth with Louisiana. The repeal of these laws is a point toward which the colonists are directing their efforts. They have already succeeded in getting from the Congress of Coahuila a law very favorable to their prosperity: the state government has declared that it will recognize contracts made with servants before coming to this country, and the colonists are thus assured of the employment of ample labor, which can be secured at a very low price in the United States. This law, according to the explanation made to me by several, is going to be interpreted as equivalent to permission to introduce slaves.

In spite of the enmity that usually exists between the Mexicans and the foreigners, there is a most evident uniformity of opinion on one point, namely the separation of Texas from Coahuila and its organization into a territory of the federal government. This idea, which was conceived by some of the colonists who are above the average, has become general among the people and does not fail to cause considerable discussion. . . .

. . . The whole population here is a mixture of strange and incoherent parts without parallel in our federation: numerous tribes of Indians, now at peace, but armed and at any moment ready for war, whose steps toward civilization should be taken under the close supervision of a strong and intelligent government; colonists of another people, more progressive and better informed than the Mexican inhabitants, but also more shrewd and unruly; among these foreigners are fugitives from justice, honest laborers, vagabonds and criminals, but honorable and dishonorable alike travel with their political constitution in their pockets, demanding the privileges, authority and officers which such a constitution guarantees.

7. Mexico Seeks to Block Anglo-American Immigration: The April 6, 1830 Law

The Decree of April 6, 1830

Article 1. Cotton goods excluded in the Law of May 22, 1829, may be introduced through the ports of the Republic until January 1, 1831, and through the ports of the South Sea until June 30, 1831.

Article 2. The duties received on the above mentioned goods shall be used to maintain the integrity of Mexican territory, to form a reserve fund against the event of Spanish invasion, and to promote the development of national industries in the branch of cotton manufacturers.

Article 3. The government is authorized to name one or more commissioners who shall visit the colonies of the frontier states and contract with the legislatures of said states for the purchase, in behalf of the federal government, of lands deemed suitable for the establishment of colonies of Mexicans and other nationalities; and the said commissioners shall make with the existing colonies whatever arrangements seem expedient for the security of the Republic. The said commissioners shall supervise the introduction of new colonists and the fulfilling of their contracts for settlement, and shall ascertain to what extent the existing contracts have been completed.

Article 4. The chief executive is authorized to take such lands as are deemed suitable for fortifications or arsenals and for the new colonies, indemnifying the states for same, in proportion to their assessments due the federal government.

Article 5. The government is authorized to transport the convict-soldiers destined for Vera Cruz and other points to the colonies, there to establish them as is deemed fit; the government will furnish free transportation to the families of the soldiers, should they desire to go.

Allein Howren, "Causes and Origins of the Decree of April 6, 1830," *Southwestern Historical Quarterly,* vol. 16 (April 1913): 415–417.

Article 6. The convict-soldiers shall be employed in constructing the fortifications, public works and roads which the commissioners may deem necessary, and when the time of their imprisonment is terminated, if they should desire to remain as colonists, they shall be given lands and agricultural implements, and their provisions shall be continued through the first year of their colonization.

Article 7. Mexican families who voluntarily express a desire to become colonists will be furnished transportation, maintained for one year, and assigned the best of agricultural lands.

Article 8. All the individuals above mentioned shall be subject to both the federal and state colonization laws.

Article 9. The introduction of foreigners across the northern frontier is prohibited under any pretext whatever, unless the said foreigners are provided with a passport issued by the agents of this Republic at the point whence the said foreigners set out.

Article 10. No change shall be made with respect to the slaves now in the states, but the federal government and the government of each state shall most strictly enforce the colonization laws and prevent the further introduction of slaves.

Article 11. In accordance with the right reserved by the general congress in the seventh article of the Law of August 18, 1824, it is prohibited that emigrants from nations bordering on this Republic shall settle in the states or territory adjacent to their own nation. Consequently, all contracts not already completed and not in harmony with this law are suspended.

8. The San Antonio Ayuntamiento Petitions the Mexican Government for a Liberal Immigration Policy, 1832

Honorable Congress

When illnesses occur, the treatment adopted should be proportionate to the gravity of the situation, and application should be immediate. Such is the only rule to be followed when the physical body is attacked by some severe illness. To be consistent, the same procedure should be followed when dealing with ailments of the social body. No doubt exists that ills, similar in nature, have afflicted each of the unfortunate towns of Texas from the very moment they were founded. So it is that some towns have been destroyed while the rest have been unable to attain, even for a single day, that peace or those other guarantees which should have insured population and other resources for their development under the paternal protection of their governments. This town of Béxar was established 140 years ago, La Bahía del Espíritu Santo and Nacogdoches 116 years ago, and the fort of San Sabá, the towns of Jaén, San Marcos, and Trinidad, were founded in the intervening years along with other military establishments on the Guadalupe, Colorado and Brazos rivers. These communities have disappeared entirely; in some of them the residents dying to the last man. One can discern the neglect they always experienced, just by

Conchita Hassell Winn, trans. and David Weber, ed. and trans., *Troubles in Texas, 1832* (Dallas: Wind River Press, 1982): 16–22. Copyright © 1983 DeGolyer Library, Southern Methodist University. Reprinted with permission.

examining the census of the current population of the first three communities, the only ones which still survive, and by retelling the unspeakable stories of the many types of suffering they endured even as they labored for their country. Many early settlers and their descendants have been sacrificed to the barbarians, and not a few others have died of hunger and pestilence, which have caused havoc in this part of the republic due to the inaction and apathy of those who govern. How sad that ninety-seven men have been murdered by Indians within the limits of this city [San Antonio], Bahía, and the new *villa* of González alone (not counting the veterans who perished in campaigns in all the years from 1821 to the present). It should be observed that these [Indian] enemies only waged war from 1825 to 1827, and that peace prevailed during the rest of the time. Other frontier communities, located toward the west have, perhaps, suffered much more, and every last one of us is probably threatened with total extermination by the new Comanche uprising. This very large and most warlike tribe renewed hostilities four months ago, just when the national forces were involved in bloody struggle stemming from the aberrations and Constitutional infractions committed on all sides—especially since the year 1828.

These disturbances have caused us to suffer absolute poverty. Since the troops protecting this part of the frontier have not received even one-tenth part of their salary during the entire past year, it has been necessary to put more than half of them at liberty so they would find means for their own subsistence. Today, in all of Texas, only seventy men are at arms. Their pay in arrears, these troops are a burden on the poor townspeople. To assure themselves that even this limited support will remain available, the poor townspeople are obliged to supply these men with grain and other essential articles from the already meager community resources. By advancing these sums to the troops, however, the settlers jeopardize their ability to hold on to this portion of their own small holdings, since past experience shows they have yet to be repaid for advances they made on several other occasions. . . .

Experience suggests that the first colonization law of this state contains many omissions and contradictions. These have paralyzed population growth in Texas and, because of them, elements of its territorial wealth have failed to develop. Article 26 of that law gives settlers six years to populate and cultivate the lands granted to them; article 27 of said law denies them the right to transfer or give away property that is not totally under cultivation. Who fails to observe, therefore, a contradiction in the spirit behind these two articles with respect to the increase of population? If possible, such rights should be applicable from the first year, be it to the grantee or to any other legally entitled person to whom these lands might be sold or transmitted by any other means.

On the other hand, what inducement, what incentives, or what privileges capable of attracting Mexicans have been written into that or any later law designed to encourage an increase in the population of Mexicans (who doubtless would be the most desirable citizens for Texas)? Not even one. On the contrary, the May 2, 1832 law establishes that lands in Texas are priced at from one to three hundred pesos, according to their quality, while those of Coahuila at only fifteen pesos. What an admirable measure! Principally it serves to keep the Mexican population at a greater distance from Texas, because people from the interior of the Republic have always resisted immigrating to these deserts which they greatly fear. Very few Mexican residents of Texas will be able to afford the indicated fees because of their limited capital. In extreme cases, even those who already acquired concessions of some lands are abstaining from asking for their respective properties. This is due as much to the aforesaid exorbitant price as to provisions in article 13 of the law that demands on quarter of the payment immediately.

And what shall we say concerning evils caused by the general law of April 6, 1830, which absolutely prohibits immigration by North Americans? The lack of troops and other officials capable of supervising it has made it impossible to enforce this law. On the other hand, the law prevents immigration of some capitalists and of some industrious and honorable men who have refrained from coming because of it, but has left the door open to wicked adventurers and others who constitute the dregs of society. Since they have nothing to lose, they have arrived furtively in large numbers and may cause incalculable harm.

The same is true of the numerous tribes of semicivilized Indians. Expelled from the United States of North America, they have crossed the Sabine River and, unchallenged, have established themselves in our territory. It will be very difficult to uproot them and even more so if we intend to make them observe our legal system. Yet, risking all kinds of dangers and inconveniences, North Americans reclaimed a considerable part of these lands from the desert prior to the passage of the law of April 6, 1830, and toiled assiduously to further agriculture and to introduce crafts unknown in these parts since the discovery of this land by the old Spanish government. They planted cotton and sugar cane, introduced the cotton gin, and imported machinery for the cultivation of sugar and sawmills to cut wood economically. We owe these advances to the efforts of these hard-working colonists, who have earned a comfortable living within seven or eight years. Theirs is not a precarious existence, the only kind known in Mexican towns, which depend solely upon the troops' payroll that circulates so slowly among us.

Although it grieves us to say so, we should state that the miserable manufacture of blankets, hats, and even shoes was never established in Texas towns. Lack of these articles has obliged us to beg them from foreigners or from the interior of the republic, two or three hundred leagues distant. The only known loom here is one brought to Béxar two year ago. Meanwhile, residents of La Bahía and Nacogdoches who have never left their communities have no idea of this very simple machine, or the way a hat is made. All these resources came to us with the North American colonists, but if their immigration is blocked who knows how long we will be denied such advances.

Immigration is, unquestionably, the most efficient, quick, and economical means we can employ to destroy the Indians and to populate lands they now occupy—directing the immigrants to the northern interior whenever possible. This goal can only be achieved by freely admitting these enthusiastic North Americans so they may live in this desert. They already are experienced in dealing with the barbarians in their native land, where they have done similar work. Not a single European nation that might be interested in colonizing offers their people similar advantages. Because they have been very regimented, the Europeans' transportation, climate, customs, and forms of government are very different from those of the neighboring republic and are not as suitable for Mexico.

The opening of roads going directly from Texas ports to New Mexico, Paso del Norte, or even Chihuahua, would place Texas at the rank it should occupy in the

Mexican federation. This achievement, too, is the result of the immigration of North American capitalists. They built these at least more economically and in less time than could be accomplished by any other nation and even by Mexico itself. The same is true of direct communication from all the far northern part of our republic with the state of Missouri of the neighboring nation, which is maintained today despite great risk and cost of freight. The population of those lands [between Texas and Missouri, and between Texas and New Mexico] would benefit Texas and would be the best barrier against the Indians. It would thrust population 200 leagues farther north than it is today, and protect the entire line of defense for Coahuila, Nuevo León and Tamaulipas, and even that of Chihuahua.

The advantages that would accrue to this part of the republic, if it could be populated without need of sacrifice by the public treasury or the state, are so numerous they are hard to imagine. Perhaps an entire volume would be insufficient to provide full and minute details of such a beautiful scene. And would not the inhabitants of Texas find it painful and even intolerable to continue envisioning how easily prosperity could be attained in this fertile land—with its mildness of climate, the plenty of its rivers, the abundance of its fish and game, which provides the most beautiful kinds of pelts—and for these settlers to realize that only the government's lack of knowledge and the mistaken measures it undertook to encourage population in this country increasingly separate us from the well-being to which nature invites us? This same apathy and the fatal arrow of the barbarians will probably deprive us of our existence as they did our forebears. Unquestionably, the lack of a government with special sensitivity to the needs of Texas, which would take the necessary and simple measures to increase Texas' population and promote its prosperity and growth in all branches, has been, is, and perhaps will continue to be the source of our suffering.

❧ E S S A Y S

The extent to which Anglos and Mexicans coexisted amicably during the years of early settlement is an issue of considerable importance for Texas historians, in view of the political developments that would lead to the separation of Texas from Mexico in the mid-1830s. In the first essay, Arnoldo de León, history professor at Angelo State University and author of several books on Mexican Texans, argues that deeply-rooted Anglo cultural prejudices predisposed settlers from the United States to view Tejanos with hostility. A long tradition of anti-Catholicism combined with a southern attitude that viewed all non-whites as racially inferior made Anglo immigrants incapable of living on a basis of equality with their new Tejano neighbors.

Gregg Cantrell, history professor at the University of North Texas, and the author of a prize-winning study of Stephen F. Austin, offers a very different view of Anglo-Mexican race relations in his analysis of the first empresario of Texas. Although Cantrell concedes that many Anglo Americans subscribed to a racialist ideology that provided a cultural context for political tensions, he cautions against viewing Austin strictly by some of his more inflammatory statements. Cantrell reminds us that, for fifteen years, Austin was an unflagging mediator between Anglo residents, Tejanos, and Mexican authorities; only Mexico's failure to establish effective republican institutions prompted him to reluctantly embrace the cause of independence.

Early Anglo Settlers View Mexicans with Hostility

ARNOLDO DE LEÓN

Most whites who first met Tejanos in the 1820s had never had prior experiences with Mexicans nor encountered them anywhere else. Yet their reaction to them upon contact was contemptuous, many thinking Mexicans abhorrent. What caused pioneers to feel this way? Why were their attitudes bigoted instead of neutral? What did they find in Mexicans that aroused xenophobic behavior, or what was it within themselves that generated that response?

According to one Texas historian, Anglo settlers who entered Texas accepted Mexicans on a basis of equality initially and did not react scornfully toward the native Tejanos until the Texas war for independence of 1836. Relationships before then, according to him, were characterized by a marked tolerance, lack of basic antipathy between the two races, and an almost total lack of friction traceable to racial problems. In the opinion of another student of Anglo attitudes during the period 1821–1845, white feelings toward Mexicans were very complex, at times contradictory, and constantly in flux.

The latest scholarship on the subject of racial and cultural attitudes, however, does not sustain these arguments. Americans moving to the west, recent studies indicate, had much more in mind than settling the land and creating prosperous communities. Cultural heirs to Elizabethans and Puritans, those moving into hinterlands sensed an "errand into the wilderness" and felt a compelling need to control all that was beastly—sexuality, vice, nature, and colored peoples. Order and discipline had to be rescued from the wilds in the name of civilization and Christianity. Moving westward with this mission uppermost in their minds, whites psychologically needed to subdue the external world—forests, beasts, and other peoples— for the rational had to be ever in command. Coming into constant encounter with peoples of color in wilderness settings, these sensitive whites struggled against noncivilization. To allow an inverse order and a concomitant surrender of themselves and their liberties to primitive things was to allow chaos to continue when God's will was to impose Christian order.

The desire to bring fields and Indians under submission did not emanate solely from religious passion but was also a product of the individual compulsion to repress instinctual urges. Within humanity were encased base impulses (e.g., sexuality, savagery) that were just as primitive and animalistic as the things of the forest which demanded domination. Killing, destruction, subordination, and appropriation of lands not only brought the external wilderness under control but also served as a form of release for the animal within. In prevailing over primitive things through violence, whites found regeneration, but their efforts also resulted in the uglier manifestations of racism. Therein lay the seed for the perverse responses toward Mexicanos in the first encounter.

Waves of Anglo settlers first entered Texas when the Mexican government in 1821 granted colonization rights in the province to a Missouri entrepreneur named

Arnoldo de León, *They Called Them Greasers: Anglo Attitudes Toward Mexicans, 1821–1900* (Austin: University of Texas Press, 1983), 1–9, 12. Copyright © 1983. By permission of the University of Texas Press.

Moses Austin. Hundreds more followed thereafter, coming to Mexican Texas under the aegis of Moses' son, Stephen, and other empresarios. Most were not radically different from the pre–nineteenth-century pioneers. Like them, they entertained a strong belief in themselves and the superiority of their way of life.

Why, asked the historian Samuel M. Lowrie in his study of culture conflict in Texas, were Americans as narrow and freedom loving as frontiersmen willing to settle in a country as religiously intolerant and undemocratic as Mexico? Perhaps because they felt it their duty to make order of what they perceived as chaos. Certainly they uttered such sentiments many times, though Lowrie did not discern it, given the state of scholarship in the 1930s when he wrote his study. As William H. Wharton, one of the more radical agitators for independence from Mexico, put it in an appeal for American support as the revolution went on in Texas,

> The justice and benevolence of God, will forbid that the delightful region of Texas should again become a howling wilderness, trod only by savages, or that it should be permanently benighted by the ignorance and superstition, the anarchy and rapine of Mexican misrule. The Anglo-American race are destined to be for ever the proprietors of this land of *promise* and *fulfilment. Their* laws will govern it, *their* learning will enlighten it, their enterprise will improve it. *Their* flocks will range its boundless pastures, for *them* its fertile lands will yield their luxuriant harvests: its beauteous rivers will waft the products of *their* industry and enterprise, and *their* latest posterity will here enjoy legacies of "price unspeakable," in the possession of homes fortified by the genius of liberty, and sanctified by the spirit of a beneficent and tolerant religion. This is inevitable, for the wilderness of Texas has been redeemed by Anglo-American blood and enterprise. The colonists have carried with them the language, the habits, and the lofty love of liberty, that has always characterized and distinguished their ancestors. They have identified them indissolubly with the country.

But none was more articulate than Stephen F. Austin, who several times before the war for independence confessed, almost stereotypically, that his intent was "to redeem Texas from the wilderness." In one of his most eloquent expressions, he averred: "My object, the sole and only desire of my ambitions since I first saw Texas, was to redeem it from the wilderness—to settle it with an intelligent honorable and interprising [*sic*] people."

To Austin, redemption could come by "whitening" Texas—or, phrased differently, by making it a cultural and racial copy of the United States. In August 1835, he wrote that the best interests of the nation required "that Texas should be effectually, and fully, Americanized—that is—settled by a population that will harmonize with their neighbors on the *East,* in language, political principles, common origin, sympathy, and even interest." It was well known, he continued, that his object had always been to fill up Texas with a North American population. "I wish a great immigration from Kentucky, Tennessee, *every where,* passports, or no passports, *any how.* For fourteen years I have had a hard time of it, but nothing shall daunt my courage or abate my exertions to complete the main object of my labors—to *Americanize Texas.* This fall, and winter, will fix our fate—a great immigration will settle the question."

At the national level, Americans had never been oblivious to the prospects of rescuing Texas from its alleged primitive status. At all times, there had been those in Washington who had similar thoughts and expressed them publicly. Among them was Henry Clay, who asked in 1821: "By what race should Texas be peopled?" Lest it be settled by others who would make it a "place of despotism and slaves, of the Inquisition and superstition," it should be taken over by settlers from the United States who would transplant to it the free institutions of Anglo-Americans. Should Texas then break off from the United States for some reason, Clay affirmed, at least it would have been rescued from a race alien to everything that Americans held dear.

Clay did not stop at rhetoric. While he was Secretary of State, he and President John Quincy Adams instructed Joel R. Poinsett, the United States Minister to Mexico, to attempt to purchase Texas. Mexico, which had never put Texas up for sale, squarely rejected the proposal, only to see it repeated. When Andrew Jackson assumed office in 1829, he urged Poinsett to renew his efforts, authorizing the minister to offer $5 million for whatever amount of Texas Mexico would surrender. Similar futile attempts at negotiating the purchase of Texas continued until the time of the revolution.

What whites refused to accept was a state of affairs in which chaos presided over them. But what exactly was it that they considered as disorder? Texas was already settled and under the rule of a government, heir to centuries of Spanish civilization. Something else disturbed them, for to them, a connection existed in the new land between the state of civilization and chaos. Thus all the discussion about rescuing Texas from primitivism. The newcomers saw the Tejanos as mongrels, uncivilized, and un-Christian—a part of the wilderness that must be subdued. Living in Mexico and Texas were a sort of people who threatened the march of white civilization.

Incontrovertibly, as far as whites were concerned, order and discipline were missing. For Anglo settlers who arrived in Texas imported certain ideas from the United States, which regarded the native Mexican population as less than civilized. These attitudes ranged from xenophobia against Catholics and Spaniards to racial prejudice against Indians and blacks. Thus Mexicanos were doubly suspect, as heirs to Catholicism and as descendants of Spaniards, Indians, and Africans.

In England, hostile feelings toward the Roman Church originated in the sixteenth century with Henry VIII's religious and political break with the Pope and were hardened by conflict with Catholic Spain. The English mind readily thought in terms of a Catholic-Spanish alliance, conjured by Satan himself, from which nothing less than demonic designs could be expected. Additionally, the English associated the Spanish with cruelty and brutality. Alleged Spanish tyranny in the Netherlands during the latter half of the sixteenth century as well as atrocities toward the Indians in Latin America produced an image of the Spaniard as heartless and genocidal. And, finally, the English saw the Spanish as an embodiment of racial impurity. For hundreds of years, racial mixing or *mestizaje* had occurred in the Iberian peninsula between Spaniards and Moors. At a time when Elizabethans were becoming more and more sensitive to the significance of color—equating whiteness with purity and Christianity and blackness with baseness and the devil—Spaniards came to be thought of as not much better than light-skinned Moors and Africans.

English immigrants to the North American colonies probably brought those ideas with them and were certainly exposed to them through anti-Catholic and anti-Spanish literature constantly arriving in the new society. Men of letters, ministers, and propagandists helped in disseminating such notions. Military clashes along the Georgia-Florida border in the eighteenth century only intensified the hatred.

As for the Mexican aborigines, the English conceived of them as degenerate creatures—un-Christian, uncivilized, and racially impure. From letters, histories, and travel narratives, English writers put together a portrait that turned the people of Mexico into a degraded humanity. The natives subscribed to heathenism, and witches and other devilish agents permeated their culture. They partook of unholy things like polygamy, sodomy, and incest and rejected Christianity outright. Furthermore, they practiced savage rituals like human sacrifice and cannibalism. Of all the Latin American inhabitants, the Mexican Indians seemed the most beastly, for though they were in many ways the most advanced of all the New World peoples, they exercised the grossest violation of civility by these practices. Stories of Aztec gods like Quetzalcoatl who were half man and half beast and accounts of exotic Aztec rites only convinced the English of the Indians' place on the fringes of humankind, with dubious claims to existence, civilization, and Christian salvation.

While such images of the Mexican natives may not have been as widespread as those held of Spaniards, they were nonetheless familiar to many colonists. In newspapers, recent histories, and re-editions of old propaganda materials, furthermore, colonists were able to read things about the origins of the Mexicans which perpetuated enriched images acquired from the mother country.

In addition to ideas that had been fashioned vicariously, there were those that arose from intimate contact with other peoples whom whites esteemed no more than the Mexican aborigines or the Spaniards. The long history of hostilities against North American Indians on the frontier and the institution of Afro-American slavery molded negative attitudes toward dark skin, "savagery," "vice," and interracial sex. The majority of those who responded to empresario calls most assuredly thought along those lines, for they came from the states west of the Appalachians and south of the Ohio River—Louisiana, Alabama, Arkansas, Tennessee, Missouri, Mississippi, Georgia, and Kentucky. A significant number were Eastern born, but had been part of the frontier movement before their transplantation into Texas. From the Southern and frontier-oriented culture they had acquired a certain repulsion for dark-skinned people and a distaste for miscegenation. Believing that the mores of their own provincial institutions should apply in the new frontier, they assumed a posture of superiority and condescension toward the natives. By conditioning, they were predisposed to react intolerantly to people they found different from themselves but similar to those they considered as enemies and as inferiors. Along with dislike for Spaniards and the Indians of Latin America, these perceptions produced a mode of thinking that set the contours of the primordial response.

And what particularly provoked this reaction? Most Tejanos were descendants of Tlascalan Indians and *mestizo* soldiers from Coahuila. Additionally, a few Nacogdoches were the offspring of people from Louisiana and reflected that area's racial amalgam, including Indians and blacks. Throughout the province, Tejanos had intermarried among themselves and with Christianized Indian women from local missions so that the colonists continued as a mixed-blood population. Their contrast to "white" and salient kindred to "black" and "red" made Mexicans subject to treatment commensurate with the odious connotations whites attached to colors, races, and cultures dissimilar to their own.

Manifestly, Americans who immigrated to Texas confronted the native Mexicans with certain preconceptions about their character. Whites believed that the inhabitants of the province had descended from a tradition of paganism, depravity, and primitivism. Mexicans were a type of folk that Americans should avoid becoming.

The fact of the matter was that whites had little contact with Tejanos up to 1836, for most of the Mexican population was concentrated in the San Antonio and La Bahía areas, quite a distance from the Anglo colonies. But whites knew what they would find in Texas before contact confirmed their convictions. They encountered biologically decadent and inferior people because their thoughts had been shaped by the aforementioned circumstances. Thus, Mexicans lived in ways that Anglos equated with an opprobrious condition. They inhabited primitive shelters. William F. Gray, a land agent from Virginia, comparing Mexicans with the black American culture he knew, pronounced some of the Mexican homes "miserable shabby *jacales*" scarcely equal in appearance to the Afro-American houses in the suburbs of his state. Mexicans adhered to a different religion: they were completely the "slaves of Popish superstitions and despotism" and religion was understood not as an affection of the heart and soul but as one requiring personal mortification in such superficialities as penances and other rituals. If Anglos and Mexicans were not inherently different peoples, editorialized the *Texian and Emigrant's Guide* in 1835, habit, education, and religion had made them essentially so.

Additionally, Texians thought that Mexicans' cultural habits clashed with American values, such as the work ethic. Mexicanos appeared a traditional, backward aggregate, an irresponsibly passive people dedicated to the present and resigned not to probe the universe about them. An American arriving in Nacogdoches in 1833 found the citizens there the most "lazy indolent poor Starved set of people as ever the Sun Shined upon." He could not comprehend their lethargy by day nor their inclination to play the violin and dance the entire night. J. C. Clopper of Ohio reasoned in 1828 that Mexicanos were "too ignorant and indolent for enterprises and too poor and *dependent* were they otherwise capacitated." Mexicanos habitually succumbed to indolence and ease and indulged themselves in smoking, music, dancing, horse-racing, and other sports, noted David Woodman, a promoter for a New York and Boston land company, while activity, industry, and frugality marched on in the new American settlements. "The vigor of the descendents of the sturdy north will never mix with the phlegm of the indolent Mexicans," Sam Houston (the future hero of the war for independence) argued in January 1835 in an address to the citizens of Texas, "no matter how long we may live among them." In contrast to the newcomers, Tejanos were chained by custom to complacency, and instead of committing themselves to progress, they preferred fun and frolic. Some three years after Mexico opened Texas to Anglo-American settlement, Anthony R. Clark complained that Spaniards in the District of Nacogdoches, "generally of the lower sort and illitterate [*sic*]," would rather "spend days in gambling to gain a few bits than to make a living by honest industry." William B. Dewees, who lived in San Antonio in the late 1820s, found Bexareños totally hedonistic. "Their whole study seems to be for enjoyment. Mirth and amusement occupy their whole time. If one is fond of balls and theatres, he can here have an opportunity of attending one every evening. Almost every species of dissipation is indulged in, except drinking." In Goliad, the Mexicans had such a strong predisposition for gaming that almost all the inhabitants in 1833 were gamblers and smugglers, said empresario Dr. John Charles Beales. And Alexander McCrae, touring Texas in 1835 under the auspices of the Wilmington

Emigrating Society, remarked in astonishment: "I for the first time saw females betting at a public gambling table; I do not suppose they were of respectable standing in society, from the company they kept; but I am told that it is not all uncommon for Mexican *ladies* to be seen gambling in public."

Acting further to stimulate negative attitudes was the racial composition of Tejanos, who, in the white mind, were closely identified with other colored peoples. For two hundred years, ideas that black men lusted for white women and notions that slaves were of a heathen or "savage" condition had played upon Americans' fantasies; the result had been the institutional debasement of blacks because of their race. Images of the Indian as fierce, hostile, and barbaric similarly affixed themselves in the thoughts of white settlers, and the constant confrontation over land led more to the reaffirmation of these images than to their dissolution. Consequently, when whites arrived in Texas, they unconsciously transferred onto the new "colored" folk they encountered a pseudo-scientific lore acquired from generations of interaction with blacks and Indians.

Travelers, who frequently came in contact with Tejanos, plainly discerned the Mexicans' relation to the black and red peoples. At no time did Americans hold up Frenchmen, or Germans, or themselves for that matter, as a people who physically resembled Mexicans—comparison invariably was with Indians and blacks. Several factors steered discussion in that direction: Anglos were not about to elevate Mexicans to the level of European whiteness; their own sense of superiority turned Tejanos into a people lesser than themselves; and obviously, in any comparison, Mexicans were going to resemble their progenitors. Thus, whites often likened Mexicans to Africans and Native Americans. When Clopper mentioned the complexion of the Tejanos, he thought it "a shade brighter than that of the aborigines of the country." On the other hand, the land agent Gray stamped Tejanos as a "swarthy looking people much resembling our mulattos, some of them nearly black." Sam Houston asked his compatriots (in the aforementioned address) if they "would bow under the yoke of these half-Indians," while abolitionist Benjamin Lundy, in Laredo in 1834, remarked that the Mexicans in the town looked like mulattoes. Even when commentators omitted drawing comparisons about color, they nonetheless made reference to the Mexicans' dark complexion. One traveler asserted that because of it they were "readily designated at first sight."

The same association with Indians and Africans was also apparent in caustic comments about the Mexicans' ancestors. A Texan identifying himself as "H. H." in a letter to the *New Orleans Bee* in 1834 pronounced the people of Mexico the most "degraded and vile; the unfortunate race of Spaniard, Indian and African, is so blended that the worst qualities of each predominate." Two years later, when the Texans were locked in a fateful struggle with the Mexican nation, leaders of the rebellion appealed to their comrades by reminding them that Mexicans were "the adulterate and degenerate brood of the once high-spirited Castilian."

In addition to all their other discoveries about Mexicans, whites in the period between 1821 and 1836 thought Tejanos lax in virtue. A number of aspects of Mexican morality bothered them, including the native *fandango*, a dance of a sinuous sort with sexually suggestive moves. George W. Smyth from Tennessee witnessed it in Nacogdoches upon his arrival in 1830, and was surprised "that the priest and all participated, so contrary to all my pre-conceived notions of propriety." Asahel

Langworthy, a New York lawyer and land speculator, found the dance somewhat uncivilized, identifying it with lack of culture and refinement. "I witnessed one afternoon," he wrote, "a Spanish *fandango* danced in the open air by a party of these people, evidently of a low class."

Because of the apparent revelry of such recreational forms, whites began early on to assume Mexicans had a defective morality, and Mexican attitudes toward sexuality strengthened the white image of Mexicans as sensuous and voluptuous. Despite the close supervision given unmarried girls to prevent intercourse with their male counterparts, Clopper alleged, "soon as married they are scarcely the same creatures—giving the freest indulgence to their naturally gay and enthusiastic dispositions, as if liberated from all moral restraints." To the Ohioan, Mexicans were not cut from the same moral fabric as Americans. . . .

What whites found in the Texas experience during these first fifteen years was that Mexicans were primitive beings who during a century of residence in Texas had failed to improve their status and environment. Mexicans were religious pagans, purposelessly indolent and carefree, sexually remiss, degenerate, depraved, and questionably human. The haunting prospect of being ruled by such people indefinitely explains in part the Texian movement for independence in 1836.

Stephen F. Austin: Political and Cultural Mediator

GREGG CANTRELL

The Anglo-American colonists who came to Mexican Texas brought with them some heavy cultural baggage. Most came from slaveholding states and subscribed to southern notions of white supremacy—notions that might easily be applied to dark-skinned Mexicans as well as to African Americans. Many undoubtedly embodied the other forms of ethnocentrism peculiar to the Jacksonian era, such as a strident prejudice against Catholics and an intense hatred of Indians. Moreover, few settlers would have questioned the basic tenets of the ideology that would someday be called "Manifest Destiny:" the belief that the United States would inevitably spread American-style democracy and cultural institutions westward across the continent. Given these realities, many recent scholars have viewed the Anglo settlement of Texas as little more than an American invasion, a racist land grab of Mexico's northern frontier in which Mexicans and Indians were the chief victims.

At first glance, the foremost leader of this "invasion" seems to sustain these interpretations. Stephen Fuller Austin was a Virginia native who had grown up mostly on the Missouri frontier, where he utilized slave labor on a large scale in his family's lead-mining operation. In Texas, he worked repeatedly to ensure that slavery would be protected by the government. He had also served in the Missouri militia during the War of 1812, participating in a military campaign that burned Indian villages in Illinois. His credentials as a white supremacist seemed secure.

The same might be said for his standing as a proponent of Manifest Destiny. In an Independence Day speech in 1818, he delivered an address extolling the virtues

Essay by Gregg Cantrell, written for this volume. Reprinted with permission of the author.

of American civilization and the Founding Fathers. Near the end of the oration, he alluded to Mexico's ongoing independence struggle:

> . . . the same spirit that unsheathed the sword of Washington and sacrificed servitude and slavery in the flames of the Revolution, will also flash across the Gulph of Mexico and over the western wilderness that separates independent America from the enslaved colonies of Spain, and darting the beams of intelligence into the benighted souls of their inhabitants awake them from the stupor of slaves to the energy of freemen, from the degradation of vassals to the dignity of sovereigns.

After emigrating to Texas, he frequently defined his mission as that of "[spreading] over it North American population, enterprise, and intelligence."

In addition to his racial beliefs and his pro-American chauvinism, Austin also seemed typically American in his attitudes toward Mexican Catholicism. On his first trip through the interior of Mexico, he wrote that "the people are bigoted and superstitious to an extreem, and indolence appears to be the general order of the day." And in another, oft-quoted passage, he added, "to be candid the majority of the people of the whole nation as far as I have seen them want nothing but tails to be more brutes than the apes. . . . Fanaticism reigns with a power that equally aston-ishes and grieves a man of common sense."

Austin's words and deeds seemed to confirm his ethnocentrism when Texas began to wage war against Mexico. Not only did he publicly advocate independence several months before the actual declaration, but he justified the revolution on the grounds that "A war of extermination is raging in Texas, a war of barbarism and of despotic principles, waged by the mongrel Spanish-Indian and Negro race, against civilization and the Anglo-American race." He recounted the fifteen years in which he had labored "like a slave to *Americanize Texas*" so that the southwestern frontier of the United States would be safe. "But the Anglo-American foundation, this nu-cleus of republicanism, is to broken up," he declared, "and its place supplied by a population of Indians, Mexicans, and renegadoes, all mixed together, and all the natural enemies of white men and civilization." In other statements he raised the cry of anti-Catholicism, claiming that the revolution was being fought for "religious liberty" and against the "banner of the inquisition." With such actions and state-ments coming from the man who initiated the Anglo-American colonization of Texas, who could doubt that racism, imperialism, cultural chauvinism, and greed were the main impulses behind the American occupation of Texas all along?

Despite all of this, the case of Stephen F. Austin—when considered in its en-tirety—actually tells a very different story. For the better part of fifteen years, the young Missourian served as a political and cultural mediator between Anglo Texans and Mexicans. When examined objectively, Austin's career demonstrates the very real potential for political, economic, and social cooperation across racial and cul-tural lines. The history leading up to the Texas Revolution emerges as a far more complex story than it appears.

When Austin received permission in 1821 to introduce 300 American families into the region between the Brazos and Colorado, his timing was perfect. The newly independent government of Mexico, as well as the local Tejano leadership of Texas, recognized the need to populate the sparsely settled province with hard-working, taxpaying citizens who would contribute to the economic development of northern Mexico, help fight hostile Indians, and hopefully prevent the loss of Texas to the rapidly expanding United States. Austin's title was *empresario,* which meant that he was responsible for recruiting settlers, surveying and issuing land titles, enforcing the laws, and acting as liaison between his colonists and the Mexican government. From the start, Austin labored tirelessly and took his responsibilities as empresario seriously.

One of the first indications of that seriousness was his approach to the language barrier. Austin spoke little or no Spanish when he first arrived in Texas, but he dedicated himself to learning the language not just passably but fluently. Most of this effort took place in 1822 when he was forced to travel to Mexico City to secure confirmation of his grant from the new government of Mexico. Within a few weeks of his arrival there, Austin was conducting business in Spanish and even acting as spokesman for other Americans in their business with the government.

We get a glimpse of Austin's attitudes toward the language issue in his letters to his younger brother, Brown Austin. Stephen had left Brown, who was only nineteen, behind in Texas when he went to Mexico City. But rather than leave Brown with Anglo friends in the new colony, he placed Brown in the household of the prominent Tejano citizen Erasmo Seguín of San Antonio with instructions to spend every waking moment studying Spanish and learning Mexican ways. "Remember," Stephen lectured Brown, "that all your hopes of rising in this country depend on lear[n]ing to speak and write the language correctly. Without that, you will do nothing," Ten years later he would take a similar course with his teenage nephew, Moses Austin Bryan.

By the time Austin returned to Texas in 1823, he could speak Spanish and was personally acquainted with a host of major Mexican leaders. Arriving home, he issued a proclamation reminding the settlers of their obligation to the government. He instructed them "to remember that the Roman Catholic is the religion of this nation" and urged them to "respect the Catholic religion with all that attention due to its sacredness and to the laws of the land." Two years later, when the new national constitution was published, he summoned the colonists to San Felipe for a grand celebration of the new system of government. There, in the village he had laid out in a traditional Spanish pattern with streets named for Mexican statesmen, Austin raised the Mexican flag, read the constitution, and administered the oath of allegiance. Good order prevailed the entire day, and the people expressed "general enthusiasm in favor of the Government of our adopted Country." Austin made the phrase "fidelity to Mexico" his motto and for years preached it like gospel to the colonists, frequently reminding them that they lived under "the most liberal and munificent government on earth to emigrants."

Austin soon formed harmonious working relationships with important Tejanos as well as Mexicans from the interior. When the national congress combined Texas with Coahuila to form one state, he succeeded in forging an effective three-pronged political coalition between Anglo colonists, Tejanos, and a group of powerful Coahuilan politicians/businessmen headed by the Viesca brothers of Parras. Together, they dominated the politics of the vast frontier state for more than a decade, finding common ground on a wide range of issues.

Prominent Tejano José Antonio Navarro of San Antonio was one of Austin's key allies in this coalition. Navarro represented Texas in the 1828 state legislature, at a time when Austin, along with other Anglo colonists, feared that the state was on the verge of enforcing its prohibitions on slavery. Navarro came to the rescue, quietly se-curing the passage of a bill that allowed Americans to continue to bring their slaves into Texas. Modern sensibilities will condemn the purpose of Navarro's labors, but the point here is to show the close cooperation and identification of mutual interests between these two men who came from such different cultural backgrounds.

Equally telling is the *personal* relationship that apparently developed between Austin and Navarro. Stephen F. Austin was not the sort who formed intimate friendships easily, and he tended to be a very private and reserved man, rarely men-tioning personal matters to business or political associates. But in 1829, he faced one of the greatest personal crises of his life when his beloved younger brother, Brown, suddenly died of yellow fever. The stress of this event triggered a severe attack of fever in Austin, who lingered near death for weeks. When he finally was able to sit up in bed and write a few letters, Navarro was one of the first people he contacted—and one of the few in whom he confided. Austin poured out his grief to his Tejano friend, poignantly writing of the "terrible blow" he had received. That Austin would share his anguish with Navarro (who would later sign the Texas Declaration of Independence) says much about the degree of trust and friendship that existed between the two men.

Similarly strong and enduring was Austin's relationship with the Seguín family. Erasmo Seguín was among a group of Tejanos who traveled to Louisiana in 1821 to escort Stephen F. Austin to the site of his grant. The men became friends, and Brown Austin apparently lived with the Seguíns for the entire year that Austin was gone. Several years later, Austin made efforts to purchase cotton ginning equipment for Erasmo in New Orleans because Erasmo had refused to accept any reimbursement for the time that Brown had boarded with him.

Like the Austin-Navarro relationship, the Austin-Seguín relationship extended into the period of the Revolution itself. In the fall of 1835, when Austin was com-manding Texan troops in the field, into the camp galloped Juan Seguín—Erasmo's son—along with a company of Tejano cavalrymen, volunteering their services in the Texas cause. Austin welcomed them into the ranks, commissioning Seguín as a lieutenant colonel. Austin would later praise the Tejano troops, saying that "They uniformly acquitted themselves to their credit as patriots and soldiers."

But Austin did not simply cooperate with Mexicans when they were willing to take the side of Anglos in some conflict. There were also times when he stood by the Mexican government in conflicts with other Anglos. Perhaps the most famous case involved the Fredonian Rebellion of 1826–27. In 1825, an Anglo-American, Haden Edwards, received an empresario contract from the state government to introduce 800 settlers into the Nacogdoches area. Edwards, a reckless and undiplo-matic man, soon angered both Anglo and Tejano settlers who had long predated him in the region, and finally the Mexican government canceled his contract and ordered him expelled from Texas. He responded by declaring the independence of the "Fredonian" republic, and he made an alliance with a portion of the local Cherokee Indian tribes who had failed in their attempts to gain land titles from the Mexican government. Political chief José Antonio Saucedo assembled Mexican troops from Goliad and San Antonio, marched to San Felipe where they were joined by Stephen F. Austin and his colony's militia, and together the mixed force marched to Nacogdoches and put down the rebellion with minimal difficulty.

In hindsight, the Fredonian rebellion resembles comic opera, but for those willing to read the lessons carefully, it indicates more about the real nature of the Texas frontier from 1821 to 1835 and of racial and ethnic relations than almost any other incident. The temptation is to look only at surface facts and to see the rebellion as a precursor of the 1836 revolution—a land grab by aggressive, ungrateful Anglos. But the realities are much more complex. Consider several points. Before the granting of the Edwards empresario contract, the Nacogdoches region was occupied by an incredibly diverse population of Tejanos and Anglos, with a sprinkling of other ethnic Europeans. The region was also home to a number of indigenous Texas Indian tribes, plus the semi-Europeanized Cherokees, who were themselves recent emigrants from the American southeast. Edwards's contract was granted by a state legislature in far-off Saltillo, by Mexican elites whose own financial interests depended on the economic development of Texas. Edwards antagonized both Anglos and Tejanos in Nacogdoches, and the actual fighting that took place there was by no means an Anglo vs. Mexican affair. When Austin learned of the revolt, he called the Fredonians "a party of infatuated madmen," and Austin's Anglo colonists turned out unhesitatingly to aid the Mexicans in putting down the rebellion. Furthermore, facts show that the Cherokees themselves were actually sharply divided over the affair, and a sizable portion of them repudiated their comrades who had sided with Edwards and instead aided the Tejanos and Anglos in opposing the rebels. When the revolt disintegrated, the Cherokee leaders who had joined with the Fredonians were condemned by a tribal council, hunted down, and executed by their own people. In the aftermath of the rebellion, Anastacio Bustamante, commandant general of Mexico's northern frontier states, wrote Stephen Austin a letter expressing his gratitude for Austin's colonists' support, saying he wanted personally to give Austin *"un Extrechisimo abrazo"*—a very strong embrace—for "the happy result of the Expedition to Nacogdoches."

Like so much Texas history during this period, the simple dichotomies break down. In the Fredonian episode, Austin and his Anglo colonists marched side by side with Mexican troops against other Anglo-Americans. Even the Indians were bitterly divided. At Austin's suggestion, the Mexicans later granted amnesty to all but the ringleaders of the revolt, and he remained in East Texas several weeks, traveling the region with the Mexican leaders to calm the fears of the inhabitants and restore peace and order. Brown Austin undoubtedly spoke for his brother when he wrote that the insurgents were "treated with a degree of lenity by the Mexicans they had no right to expect from the nature of their crimes—and which I vouchsafe would not have been shewn them in their native country for similar offences." The actions of Austin and his colonists, as well as the response of the Mexican authorities, suggest a degree of cooperation and identification of common interests that transcended cultural differences.

After the notorious Law of April 6, 1830 disrupted the empresario system and initiated a Mexican crackdown on Anglo Texas, Austin once again sought to act as mediator. Although he potentially had more to lose under the law than almost anyone else, he counseled calmness and continued loyalty toward Mexico, even pointing out to his colonists the beneficial aspects of the much-hated decree. Over the next four years, every time that Texans grew dissatisfied with the actions of the government in Mexico City, he tried to forge solidarity between the Tejanos and Anglos of Texas and to encourage the Tejanos to take the lead in petitioning the government for redress. Even after Austin's arrest and imprisonment in 1833, he continued to call for calm in Texas. Indeed, after four months in a dungeon, he was still asking friends in Texas to "Remember me to Ramón Músquíz [the Tejano political chief in San Antonio] particularly—I shall feel grateful to him as long as I live. . . ."

Austin's friendship and respect for a long list of Mexican and Tejano leaders never faltered. His efforts to build a society in Mexican Texas where enterprising men of Anglo and Hispanic backgrounds might live in harmony and prosperity remained constant for fifteen years prior to the outbreak of revolution. He tried to avoid warfare against Indians, and he even accepted a few free blacks as settlers in his colony.

Given these efforts, how are the seemingly bigoted statements that he occasionally uttered to be explained? Take, for example, his famous 1823 complaint about Mexicans being as being as uncivilized apes. It is easy to take such a statement out of context, but if one continues reading that same letter, Austin predicts optimistically that the Mexican nation would soon "assume her rights in full, and bursting the chains of superstition declare that *man has a right to think for himself.*" In other words, Austin directed his criticism at the Church itself and what he perceived as its oppression of the Mexican people, not at Mexicans for any inherent defect of character. In 1833, he was even more explicit on this theme, actually defending Roman Catholicism as "a religion whose foundation is perfect harmony, a union of principles, & of action." But he condemned the *type* of Catholicism then being practiced in Mexico, saying it was "in theory divine, in practice infernal." These were not the words of a knee-jerk nativist.

But what about the harsh racial invective that he employed in 1835–1836? What are we to make of his support for independence, his 1836 outburst about the "war of barbarism" being "waged by the mongrel Spanish-Indian race, against civilization and the Anglo-American race," and his declaration that the non-Anglos of Texas were "the natural enemies of white men and civilization?" Was this the chauvinistic American finally showing his true colors? How do we reconcile such statements with his actions during the previous fifteen years?

Again, context is everything, and placing Austin's racist-sounding comments in context reveals the great tragedy of Anglo-Tejano relations in the Texas Revolutionary period. Austin wrote these words at a point in the Revolution when he was desperately trying to arouse sympathy and support from citizens of the United States. His main audience was made up of Jacksonian Democrats—and *southern* Democrats at that. His rhetorical transformation of the Texian struggle into a war against racially inferior Mexicans was carefully calculated to stir the deepest fears and emotions of southerners. One of the tragic consequences of this war—and of almost all others in which the enemy is of a different race, ethnicity, or culture—is that such wars almost inevitably generate this sort of propaganda. Portray your enemies as somehow less than human, and killing them becomes much easier. Recall how Germans were portrayed in American propaganda during World War I, or the Japanese during World War II, and the genesis of Austin's words can be understood. Was he wrong to resort to racist appeals when his actions over a fifteen-year period clearly contradicted such sentiments? Of course he was. In this one instance, Austin sacrificed his principles in a desperate attempt to reverse the tide of a war that by all appearances was about to be lost. We may wish that he had possessed the superhuman strength of character needed to resist such a sellout, but in the end he was only human.

Returning to his beloved Texas in the critical summer of 1836, Austin reverted to his tried-and-true philosophy of seeking reconciliation and national unity. He never had the opportunity to visit his old Tejano friends in San Antonio, but there is no indication that he would have treated them any differently than before. The harsh rhetoric was never repeated at home. Nothing from his short, ill-fated presidential campaign against Sam Houston that September suggests that he would have changed his longstanding policy of working to build a Texas in which Anglos and Tejanos could honorably cooperate and coexist. And his willingness to accept a cabinet appointment from his rival, Sam Houston, and to support Houston in all broad policy matters, further suggests that he, like Houston, would have resisted the movement toward persecution and recrimination against Tejanos that grew in intensity over the coming years.

However, Stephen F. Austin was a man of his times in one important respect. He believed that American-style democracy—flawed though it may have been by the stain of slavery—was the best system of government yet devised. He only gave up on Mexico when he became convinced that his adopted country had utterly failed to secure the blessings of democracy for its people, Anglo and Hispanic. Having reached that determination, he was willing to employ whatever necessary means to win the Revolution and bring Texas under a better government. That decision—and those means—could give the appearance that he was motivated by an unthinking bigotry against all things not American. But to arrive at such a conclusion, based on a selective reading of the evidence, is to overlook the fifteen-year reality of Austin as a genuine political and cultural mediator.

❧ F U R T H E R   R E A D I N G

Eugene C. Barker, *The Life of Stephen F. Austin: Founder of Texas, 1793–1836* (1925)

Gregg Cantrell, *Stephen F. Austin, Empresario of Texas* (1999)

Julia Kathryn Garrett, *Green Flag Over Texas; A Story of the Last Years of Spain in Texas* (1939)

Margaret Swett Henson, *Juan Davis Bradburn: A Reappraisal of the Mexican Commander of Anahuac* (1982)

Malcolm D. Maclean, ed., *Papers Concerning Robertson's Colony in Texas,* 17 vols. (1974–1991)

Timothy Matovina, *Tejano Religion and Ethnicity: San Antonio, 1821–1860* (1994)

Manuel de Mier y Terán, *Texas by Teran: The Diary Kept by Manuel Mier y Terán on 1828 Inspection of Texas* (2000)

W. H. Oberste, *Texas Irish Empresarios and their Colonies* (1953)

Rebecca Lee Smith, *Mary Austin Holley: A Biography* (1962)

Noah Smithwick, *Evolution of a State, or Recollections of Old Texas Days* (1900, reprinted, 1995)

Andres Tijerina, *Tejanos and Texas Under the Mexican Flag, 1821–1836* (1994)

Harris Gaylord Warren, *The Sword Was their Passport: a History of American Filibustering in the Mexican Revolution* (1943)

David J. Weber, *The Mexican Frontier, 1821–1846: The American Southwest Under Mexico* (1982)

Revolutionary Texas,

1835–1836

The early 1830s proved to be years of relative political calm for Texas. Most Anglo Texans demonstrated a willingness to discuss their grievances through the procedures familiar to them as former citizens of the United States. However, a "war party" led by William Barret Travis lobbied for a more militant response to disagreements with local officials. For its part, the federalist government demonstrated a cautious willingness to discuss these issues. In 1834, it repealed the Law of April 6, 1830, which had proved largely unenforceable in any case, and promised to address many of the Texans' long-standing grievances.

Relations between Mexico and the communities of Texas deteriorated sharply in 1834, however, when Mexican president Antonio López de Santa Anna abolished the Constitution of 1824 and took steps to establish a centralist, authoritarian system of government. The so-called Plan of Cuernevaca threw the entire country into chaos, sparking federalist uprisings in the provinces of Zacatecas, Coahuila, the Yucatan, and Santa Fe. By October 1835, Santa Anna had moved to further consolidate his power, abolishing the state legislatures and replacing them with military districts. The long-simmering Texas problem now flared into open rebellion. Unlike the other uprisings against the new centralist government, the revolt in Texas drew its support largely from Anglo Americans, many of whom had only recently arrived in Texas.

The causes of the Revolution have provoked much debate among historians in both Mexico and the United States. Was the revolution the product of deep-seated cultural cleavages between Anglos and Mexicans, or was it a political crisis occasioned by the collapse of federalism and representative government in Mexico? Although some historians have emphasized the inconsistent and ultimately heavy-handed policies of the Mexican government, others have pointed to the fact that many Anglo Texans willfully disregarded the customs of the country which granted them citizenship. The Texas Revolution, they maintain, was a blatant land grab by Anglo Americans who were determined to wrest the territory from Mexican control by whatever means necessary. Still another question historians have asked is whether the conflict was an inevitable one. Could Anglo Americans have ever lived as dutiful citizens under Mexican rule, or was the conflict the result of short-term crises that could have been avoided had cooler heads prevailed on both sides?

❖ D O C U M E N T S

In 1835, there existed widespread disagreement among Anglo Americans about what course to pursue toward the government in Mexico City. As Gregg Cantrell states in Chapter 4, Stephen F. Austin had long been an effective advocate for conciliation. In 1833, however, Austin was arrested and imprisoned in Mexico City, and did not return to Texas until the fall of 1835. Austin's call for "a general consultation" in Document 1, at a dinner in his honor in Brazoria County, signalled a marked departure from the empresario's previous statements and moved Texas rapidly closer toward the armed resistance that would ultimately lead to independence. Less than a month after Austin delivered this address, Texans would clash with Mexican troops at Gonzales, sparking the Revolution. Document 2 is a map of Texas drafted by Stephen F. Austin when the conflict began. Although the map clearly shows the Nueces River as the southern boundary of Texas, by the end of the war Texans regarded the Rio Grande as the legitimate boundary with Mexico. The boundary dispute would remain unresolved in the years ahead, ultimately providing the pretext for the United States' declaration of war against Mexico in 1846.

The Texas declaration of independence is presented in Document 3. Clearly modeled after the document by which the United States asserted its own independence in 1776, the declaration was designed to inflame public opinion, justifying the Texas action by presenting the policies of the Mexican government in the worst possible light. A rebuttal to the declaration's charges is offered by Jose Maria Tornel, Mexico's Secretary of War in 1836, in Document 4.

The Alamo siege is the most famous episode in Texas history. In Document 5, commander of the Alamo garrison, William B. Travis, appeals for aid in the last of several letters written during the siege. Document 6 is an excerpt from the memoir of José Enrique de la Peña, an officer in the Mexican Army. De la Peña's memoir, which did not come to light until 1955, has been labeled a forgery by some historians and an invaluable eyewitness account of the siege by others. At the center of the debate are the circumstances of the death of former Tennessee congressman David Crockett.

News of the fall of the Alamo, as well as the subsequent capture and execution of another Texas army under Colonel James Fannin at Goliad in March threw Texans into panic and disarray. Document 7 is an account of the "Runaway Scrape," the exodus of Anglo Texans into Louisiana as Santa Anna's army advanced in the spring of 1836. The Texan forces also remained in a fractious frame of mind, and even a stunning victory over the Mexican army at San Jacinto on April 21 did not bring an end to the chaos and disorder of revolutionary upheaval. In Document 8, Mirabeau B. Lamar, who had been appointed commander of the Texas army after San Jacinto, complains in a letter to interim president David G. Burnet of the insubordination that reigned in the ranks in the summer of 1836. A want of discipline among Texas troops, coupled with the ambitions of a number of prominent military leaders, would continue to imperil the stability of the new nation in the years ahead.

Although the Revolution could not have been won without the aid of American volunteers, public opinion in the United States was deeply divided over the struggle for

Texas independence. In Document 9, the prominent American abolitionist Benjamin Lundy attributes the struggle in Texas to a Southern conspiracy bent on expanding the slave empire. This thesis was widely accepted by the Northern antislavery movement, which would furiously oppose any and all efforts to bring Texas into the Union in the years ahead.

1. Stephen F. Austin Declares His Support for Independence, 1835

I left Texas in April, 1833, as the public agent of the people, for the purpose of applying for the admission of this country into the Mexican confederation as a state separate from Coahuila. This application was based upon the constitutional and vested rights of Texas, and was sustained by me in the city of Mexico to the utmost of my abilities. No honorable means were spared to effect the objects of my mission and to oppose the forming of Texas into a territory, which was attempted. I rigidly adhered to the instructions and wishes of my constituents, so far as they were communicated to me. My efforts to serve Texas involved me in the labyrinth of Mexican politics. I was arrested, and have suffered a long persecution and imprisonment. I consider it my duty to give an account of these events to my constituents, and will therefore at this time merely observe that I have never, in any manner, agreed to any thing, or admitted any thing, that would compromise the constitutional or vested rights of Texas. These rights belong to the people, and can only be surrendered by them.

I fully hoped to have found Texas at peace and in tranquility, but regret to find it in commotion; all disorganized, all in anarchy, and threatened with immediate hostilities. This state of things is deeply to be lamented; it is a great misfortune, but it is one which has not been produced by any acts of the people of this country: on the contrary, it is the natural and inevitable consequence of the revolution that has spread all over Mexico, and of the imprudent and impolitic measures of both the general and state governments, with respect to Texas. The people here are not to blame, and cannot be justly censured. They are farmers, cultivators of the soil, and are pacific from interest, from occupation, and from inclination. They have uniformly endeavored to sustain the constitution and the public peace by pacific means, and have never deviated from their duty as Mexican citizens. If any acts of imprudence have been committed by individuals, they evidently resulted from the revolutionary state of the whole nation, the imprudent and censurable conduct of the state authorities, and the total want of a local government in Texas. It is, indeed, a source of surprise and creditable congratulation, that so few acts of this description have occurred under the peculiar circumstances of the times. It is, however, to be remembered that acts of this nature were not the acts of the people, nor is Texas responsible for them. They were, as I before observed, the natural consequences of the revolutionary state of the Mexican nation; and Texas certainly did

---

"Austin to the People of Texas," *The Austin Papers, October 1834–January 1837,* Eugene C. Barker, ed., vol. III (Austin: University of Texas Press), 116–119.

not originate the revolution, neither have the people, as a people, participated in it. The consciences and hands of the Texians are free from censure, and clean.

The revolution in Mexico is drawing to a close. The object is to change the form of government, destroy the federal constitution of 1824, and establish a central or consolidated government. The states are to be converted into provinces.

Whether the people of Texas ought or ought not to agree to this change, and relinquish all or part of their constitutional and vested rights under the constitution of 1824, is a question of the most vital importance; one that calls for the deliberate consideration of the people, and can only be decided by them, fairly convened for the purpose. As a citizen of Texas I have no other right, and pretend to no other. In the report which I consider it my duty to make my constituents, I intend to give my views on the present situation of the country, and especially as to the constitutional and national rights of Texas, and will, therefore, at this time, merely touch this subject.

Under the Spanish government, Texas was a separate and distinct local organization. It was one of the unities that composed the general mass of the nation, and as such participated in the war of the revolution, and was represented in the constituent congress of Mexico, that formed the constitution of 1824. This constituent congress, so far from destroying this unity, expressly recognized and confirmed it by the law of May 7th, 1824, which united Texas with Coahuila *provisionally,* under the especial guarantee of being made a state of the Mexican confederation, as soon as it possessed the necessary elements. That law and the federal constitution gave to Texas a specific political existence, and vested in its inhabitants special and defined rights, which can only be relinquished by the people of Texas, acting for themselves as a unity, and not as a part of Coahuila, for the reason that the union with Coahuila, was *limited,* and only gave power to the state of Coahuila and Texas to govern Texas for the time being, but *always subject to the vested rights of Texas.* The state, therefore, cannot relinquish those vested rights, by agreeing to the change of government, or by any other act, unless expressly authorized by the people of Texas to do so; neither can the general government of Mexico legally deprive Texas of them without the consent of this people. These are my opinions.

An important question now presents itself to the people of this country.

The federal constitution of 1824 is about to be destroyed, the system of government changed, and a central or consolidated one established. Will this act annihilate all the rights of Texas, and subject this country to the uncontrolled and unlimited dictation of the new government?

This is a subject of the most vital importance. I have no doubts the federal constitution will be destroyed, and a central government established, and that the people will soon be called upon to say whether they agree to this change or not. This matter requires the most calm discussion, the most mature deliberation, and the most perfect union. How is this to be had? I see but one way, and that is by a general consultation of the people by means of delegates elected for that purpose, with full powers to give such an answer, in the name of Texas, to this question, as they may deem best, and to adopt such measures as the tranquility and salvation of the country may require. . . .

It is also proper for me to state that, in all my conversation with the president and ministers and men of influence, I advised that no troops should be sent to Texas, and no cruisers along the coast. I gave it as my decided opinion, that the inevitable consequence of sending an armed force to this country would be war. I stated that there was a sound and correct moral principle in the people of Texas, that was abundantly sufficient to restrain or put down all turbulent or seditious movements, but that this moral principle could not, and would not unite with any armed force sent against this country; on the contrary, it would resist and repel it, and ought to do so. This point presents another strong reason why the people of Texas should meet in general consultation. This country is now in anarchy, threatened with hostilities; armed vessels are capturing every thing they can catch on the coast, and acts of piracy are said to be committed under cover of the Mexican flag. Can this state of things exist without precipitating the country into a war? I think it cannot, and therefore believe that it is our bounden and solemn duty as Mexicans, and as Texians, to represent the evils that are likely to result from this mistaken and most impolitic policy in the military movement.

My friends, I can truly say that no one has been, or is now, more anxious than myself to keep trouble away from this country. No one has been, or now is more faithful to his duty as a Mexican citizen, and no one has personally sacrificed or suffered more in the discharge of this duty. I have uniformly been opposed to have any thing to do with the family political quarrels of the Mexicans. Texas needs peace, and a local government: its inhabitants are farmers, and they need a calm and quiet life. But how can I, or any one, remain indifferent, when our rights, our all, appear to be in jeopardy, and when it is our duty, as well as our obligation as good Mexican citizens, to express our opinions on the present state of things, and to represent our situation to the government? It is impossible. The crisis is such as to bring it home to the judgment of every man that something must be done, and that without delay. The question will perhaps be asked, what are we to do? I have already indicated my opinion. Let all personalities, or divisions, or excitements, or passion, or violence, be banished from among us. Let a general consultation of the people of Texas be convened as speedily as possible, to be composed of the best, and most calm, and intelligent, and firm men in the country, and let them decide what representations ought to be made to the general government, and what ought to be done in future.

2. Map of Texas on the Eve of Revolution, 1835

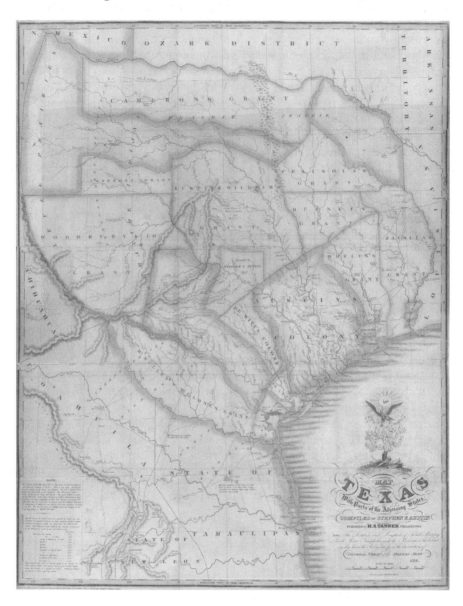

Map of Texas, with Part of Adjoining States (Philadelphia: Henry S. Tanner, 1836), University of Texas at Arlington Cartographic Collection.

3. Texas Declaration of Independence, March 2, 1836

When a government has ceased to protect the lives, liberty and property of the people, from whom its legitimate powers are derived, and for the advancement of whose happiness it was instituted; and so far from being a guarantee for their inestimable and inalienable rights, becomes an instrument in the hands of evil rulers for their oppression. When the federal republican constitution of their country, which they have sworn to support, no longer has a substantial existence, and the whole nature of their government has been forcibly changed, without their consent, from a restricted federative republic, composed of sovereign states, to a consolidated central military despotism, in which every interest is disregarded but that of the army and the priesthood, both the eternal enemies of civil liberty, the ever ready minions of power, and the usual instruments of tyrants. When, long after the spirit of the constitution has departed, moderation is at length so far lost by those in power, that even the semblance of freedom is removed, and the forms themselves of the constitution discontinued, and so far from their petitions and remonstrances being regarded, the agents who bear them are thrown into dungeons, and mercenary armies sent forth to enforce a new government upon them at the point of the bayonet.

When, in consequence of such acts of malfeasance and abduction on the part of the government, anarchy prevails, and civil society is dissolved into its original elements, in such a crisis, the first law of nature, the right of self-preservation, the inherent and inalienable right of the people to appeal to first principles, and take their political affairs into their own hands in extreme cases, enjoins it as a right towards themselves, and a sacred obligation to their posterity, to abolish such government, and create another in its stead, calculated to rescue them from impending dangers, and to secure their welfare and happiness.

Nations, as well as individuals, are amenable for their acts to the public opinion of mankind. A statement of a part of our grievances is therefore submitted to an impartial world, in justification of the hazardous but unavoidable step now taken, of severing our political connection with the Mexican people, and assuming an independent attitude among the nations of the earth.

The Mexican government, by its colonization laws, invited and induced the Anglo American population of Texas to colonize its wilderness under the pledged faith of a written constitution, that they should continue to enjoy that constitutional liberty and republican government to which they had been habituated in the land of their birth, the United States of America.

In this expectation they have been cruelly disappointed, inasmuch as the Mexican nation has acquiesced to the late changes made in the government by General Antonio Lopez de Santa Anna, who, having overturned the constitution of his country, now offers, as the cruel alternative, either to abandon our homes, acquired by so many privations, or submit to the most intolerable of all tyranny, the combined despotism of the sword and the priesthood.

"The Declaration of Independence Made by the Delegates of the People of Texas," H. P. N. Gammel, comp., *The Laws of Texas, 1822–1897* (Austin: Gammel Book Co., 1898), 1:1063–1066.

It hath sacrificed our welfare to the state of Coahuila, by which our interests have been continually depressed through a jealous and partial course of legislation, carried on at a far distant seat of government, by a hostile majority, in an unknown tongue, and this too, notwithstanding we have petitioned in the humblest terms for the establishment of a separate state government, and have, in accordance with the provisions of the national constitution, presented to the general congress a republican constitution, which was, without a just cause, contemptuously rejected.

It incarcerated in a dungeon, for a long time, one of our citizens, for no other cause but a zealous endeavor to procure the acceptance of our constitution, and the establishment of a state government.

It has failed and refused to secure, on a firm basis, the right of trial by jury, that palladium of civil liberty, and only safe guarantee for the life, liberty, and property of the citizen.

It has failed to establish any public system of education, although possessed of almost boundless resources, (the public domain,) and although it is an axiom in political science, that unless a people are educated and enlightened, it is idle to expect the continuance of civil liberty, or the capacity for self government.

It has suffered the military commandants, stationed among us, to exercise arbitrary acts of oppression and tyranny, thus trampling upon the most sacred rights of the citizen, and rendering the military superior to the civil power.

It has dissolved, by force of arms, the state congress of Coahuila and Texas, and obliged our representatives to fly for their lives from the seat of government, thus depriving us of the fundamental political right of representation.

It has demanded the surrender of a number of our citizens, and ordered military detachments to seize and carry them into the interior for trial, in contempt of the civil authorities, and in defiance of the laws and the constitution.

It has made piratical attacks upon our commerce, by commissioning foreign desperadoes, and authorizing them to seize our vessels, and convey the property of our citizens to far distant parts for confiscation.

It denies us the right of worshiping the Almighty according to the dictates of our own conscience, by the support of a national religion, calculated to promote the temporal interest of its human functionaries, rather than the glory of the true and living God.

It has demanded us to deliver up our arms, which are essential to our defence— the rightful property of freemen—and formidable only to tyrannical governments.

It has invaded our country both by sea and by land, with the intent to lay waste our territory, and drive us from our homes; and has now a large mercenary army advancing, to carry on against us a war of extermination.

It has, through its emissaries, incited the merciless savage, with the tomahawk and scalping knife, to massacre the inhabitants of our defenceless frontiers.

It has been, during the whole time of our connection with it, the contemptible sport and victim of successive military revolutions, and hath continually exhibited every characteristic of a weak, corrupt, and tryannical government.

These, and other grievances, were patiently borne by the people of Texas, until they reached that point at which forbearance ceases to be a virtue. We then took up arms in defence of the national constitution. We appealed to our Mexican brethren for assistance: our appeal has been made in vain; though months have elapsed, no sympathetic response has yet been heard from the interior. We are, therefore, forced to the melancholy conclusion, that the Mexican people have acquiesced in the destruction of their liberty, and the substitution therefor of a military government; that they are unfit to be free, and incapable of self government.

The necessity of self-preservation, therefore, now decrees our eternal political separation.

4. Mexico's Secretary of War José Maria Tornel Rebuts the Texan Reasons for Independence, 1836

Finally a day arrived when, seduced by the happy coincidence of a thousand unforeseen circumstances, the Texas colonists sundered all ties and openly declared themselves independent from the Mexican nation. Their delegates assembled in Washington, in the District of Brazoria, drew up a declaration of independence, March 2, 1836. This is but the admission of a fact and the carrying out of a plan long since recognized. An attempt is made, however, to support this action by an astonishing jumble of impostures. It is stated that the Texans were invited and admitted subject to the observance of a contract by which assurances were given to maintain the written constitution; that this having been annulled, all their obligations ceased. Our country, with ill-advised generosity, acceded to their requests and took them into our midst because they asked and desired to be taken in. We have observed that at the time when the first grants were made the government of the nation was a monarchy and that subsequently several changes have been effected in the government none of which justify them in refusing their obedience because no specific form of government was stipulated in the contracts. An insolent minority cannot arrogate to itself the right of determining the form of government of the republic in violation of the wishes of the great majority. If such a minority was not in accord with the changes effected it was free to leave the country whenever the obligations imposed upon it became too great a burden or a menace to its liberties.

The rebels allege as the principal complaint that they were not permitted to organize themselves as an independent state of the union, governed by a constitution framed and designed by themselves. Granting the stability of the federal system, it was still very questionable whether Texas already possessed the necessary elements and resources to be organized as an independent entity. Furthermore, we cannot ignore the natural distrust which such a forward step inevitably inspired, when we consider the well-known aim of all the petitions of the colonists. A change in the administration of the country having taken place, the Texans should have waited the results of the principal innovations planned, in view of the fact that congress had raised Texas to the rank of a department, separating it from Coahuila to that extent.

They accuse us of having neglected primary education in Texas. This charge clearly shows their bad faith. As is well known, education is left by our laws to the

"Jose Maria Tornel y Mendivil," Carlos Castaneda, trans. and ed., *The Mexican Side of the Texas Revolution* (Austin: Graphic Ideas, 1977), 355–357. Reprint made possible by Ayer Co. Publishers, 2001.

respective *ayuntamientos*. The city councils of Texas not only exercised all the prerogatives allowed them but assumed many that are foreign to such bodies. Why then did they not look after education if it interested them so deeply? Furthermore, the Texas *ayuntamientos* imposed taxes and used their revenues without the least interference on the part of Mexican officials. If they failed to use them for the education of their children, it was clearly their fault. The people of Texas were represented in the legislature of the state. It was there that they should have presented their demands regarding this subject as they did with regard to lands, the prime object of their desires, the obvious aim of their insatiable greed.

The colonists bitterly complain of their having been sacrificed to the interest of Coahuila. This is but a typical untruth. The officers of the state inclined rather to the opposite extreme, indiscreetly favoring the Texans by assenting to their endless petitions. In the course of the preceding pages, the grants of lands made to them have been noted. It is particularly noteworthy, however, that among the grantees there were only two or three citizens of Coahuila, whose grants were in general usurped by other empresarios. The colonists sometimes curse Coahuila for her supposed injustices to them, and at others they curse the nation for its arbitrary acts against Coahuila.

The charges of oppression and tyranny brought against our military officers are false and unfounded. Far from this, our soldiers have, on the contrary, been exposed to the same libelous charges as all our public officers. They have been disarmed and driven from their posts while holding them in the discharge of their duties. Every attempt made to enforce law has been pointed out by the colonists as an attack, while the repression of crime has been called an insult and classed as an attempt upon individual liberties in their newly invented dictionary. Even now they maintain that trade has been hampered by unheard-of restrictions and vexations. During the first seven years they were exempt from paying duties on all goods imported into Texas. After the expiration of this privilege, there has been nothing but contraband trade along the entire coast and the whole frontier.

The prohibition against the erection of places of worship and the practice of other cults than the Roman Catholic was the law of the land at the time when the colonists came and they agreed to conform to it. Why didn't they stay in their own country to raise temples in the vast solitudes of the west? Nations adopt or reject restrictions with regard to religious practices as they see fit. To pretend to force us to promulgate religious toleration is to assume the exercise of a right over us even superior to that of conquest, for the religion and the customs of a conquered country have always been respected.

Lastly, the rebels have tried to justify their criminal uprising before God and before man as the result of the adoption of necessary repressive measures by the easygoing Mexican government. The use of force to restrain the restless, to punish the rebellious, and to maintain obedience is an inherent right of the sovereignty of nations. What other right can the United States invoke in support of the troops sent to Florida to chastise the Seminoles and the Creeks? What is right for one nation should be right for all: The attributes of sovereignty are identical in all nations. The civilized world has already passed judgment upon the usurpations of the Texans, refusing to admit the reasons advanced in support of their declaration of independence.

5. Alamo Commander William B. Travis Appeals for Aid, March 3, 1836

Bejar, March 3, 1836.

Sir,—In the present confusion of the political authorities of the country, and in the absence of the commander-in-chief, I beg leave to communicate to you the situation of this garrison. You have doubtless already seen my official report of the action of the 25th ult., made on that day to Gen. Sam. Houston, together with the various communications heretofore sent by express. I shall therefore confine myself to what has transpired since that date.

From the 25th to the present date, the enemy have kept up a bombardment from two howitzers, (one a five and a half inch, and the other an eight inch,) and a heavy cannonade from two long nine pounders, mounted on a battery on the opposite side of the river, at the distance of four hundred yards from our walls. During this period the enemy have been busily employed in encircling us with entrenched encampments on all sides, at the following distances, to wit:—in Bejar, four hundred yards west; in Lavilleta, three hundred yards south; at the powder house, one thousand yards east by south; on the ditch, eight hundred yards northeast, and at the old mill, eight hundred yards north. Notwithstanding all this, a company of thirty-two men, from Gonzales, made their way into us on the morning of the 1st inst., at 3 o'clock, and Col. J. B. Bonham (a courier from Gonzales) got in this morning at 11 o'clock, without molestation. I have so fortified this place, that the walls are generally proof against cannon balls; and I still continue to intrench on the inside, and strengthen the walls by throwing up the dirt. At least two hundred shells have fallen inside of our works without having injured a single man: indeed, we have been so fortunate as not to lose a man from any cause; and we have killed many of the enemy. The spirits of my men are still high, although they have had much to depress them. We have contended for ten days against an enemy whose numbers are variously estimated at from fifteen hundred to six thousand men, with Gen. Ramirer Siesma and Col. Batres, the aids-de-camps of Santa Anna, at their head. A report was circulated that Santa Anna himself was with the enemy, but I think it was false. A reinforcement of about one thousand men is now entering Bejar from the west, and I think it more than probable that Santa Anna is now in town, from the rejoicing we hear. Col. Fannin is said to be on the march to this place with reinforcements; but I fear it is not true, as I have repeatedly sent to him for aid without receiving any. Colonel Bonham, my special messenger, arrived at La Bahia fourteen days ago, with a request for aid; and on the arrival of the enemy in Bejar ten days ago, I sent an express to Col. Fannin, which arrived at Goliad on the next day, urging him to send us reinforcements—*none have yet arrived.* I look to the *colonies alone* for aid: unless it arrives soon, I shall have to fight the enemy on his own terms. I will, however, do the best I can under the circumstances; and I feel confident that the determined valor, and desperate courage, heretofore evinced by my men, will not fail them in the last struggle: and although they may be sacrificed to the vengeance of a gothic enemy, the victory will cost the enemy so dear, that

Mary Austin Holley, *Texas* (Lexington, KY: J. Clarke & Co., 1836), 351–353.

it will be worse for him than a defeat. I hope your honourable body will hasten on reinforcements, ammunition, and provisions to our aid, as soon as possible. We have provisions for twenty days for the men we have—our supply of ammunition is limited. At least five hundred pounds of cannon powder, and two hundred rounds of six, nine, twelve, and eighteen pound balls—ten kegs of rifle powder, and a supply of lead, should be sent to this place without delay, under a sufficient guard.

If these things are promptly sent and large reinforcements are hastened to this frontier, this neighborhood will be the great and decisive battle ground. The power of Santa Anna is to be met here, or in the colonies; we had better meet them here, than to suffer a war of desolation to rage in our settlements. A blood red banner waves from the church of Bejar, and in the camp above us, in token that the war is one of vengeance against rebels: they have declared us as such, and demanded that we should surrender at discretion, or that this garrison should be put to the sword. Their threats have had no influence on me, or my men, but to make all fight with desperation, and that high souled courage which characterizes the patriot, who is willing to die in defence of his country's liberty and his own honor.

The citizens of this municipality are all our enemies except those who have joined us heretofore; we have but three Mexicans now in the fort; those who have not joined us in this extremity, should be declared public enemies, and their property should aid in paying the expenses of the war.

The bearer of this will give your honorable body, a statement more in detail, should he escape through the enemies lines—*God and Texas—Victory or Death!!*

Your obedient servant,

W. BARRETT TRAVIS

6. Mexican Lieutenant Colonel José Enrique de la Peña Describes the Fall of the Alamo, 1836

The columns advanced with as much speed as possible; shortly after beginning the march they were ordered to open fire while they were still out of range, but there were some officers who wisely disregarded the signal. Alerted to our attack by the given signal, which all columns answered, the enemy vigorously returned our fire, which had not even touched him but had retarded our advance. Travis, to compensate for the reduced number of the defenders, had placed three or four rifles by the side of each man, so that the initial fire was very rapid and deadly. Our columns left along their path a wide trail of blood, of wounded, and of dead. The bands from all the corps, gathered around our commander, sounded the charge; with a most vivid ardor and enthusiasm, we answered that call which electrifies the heart, elevates the soul, and makes others tremble. The second column, seized by this spirit, burst out in acclamations for the Republic and for the president-general. The officers were unable to repress this act of folly, which was paid for dearly. His attention drawn by this act, the enemy seized the opportunity, at the moment that light was beginning to

José Enrique de la Peña, *With Santa Anna in Texas: A Personal Narrative of the Revolution,* trans. and ed. Carmen Perry (College Station: Texas A&M University Press, 1975), 47–53. Reprinted by permission of Texas A&M University Press.

make objects discernible around us, to redouble the fire on this column, making it suffer the greatest blows. It could be observed that a single cannon volley did away with half the company of chasseurs from Toluca, which was advancing a few paces from the column; Captain José María Herrera, who commanded it, died a few moments later and Vences, its lieutenant, was also wounded. Another volley left many gaps among the ranks at the head, one of them being Colonel Duque, who was wounded in the thigh; there remained standing, not without surprise, one of the two aides to this commander, who marched immediately to his side, but the other one now cannot testify to this. Fate was kind on this occasion to the writer, who survived, though Don José María Macotela, captain from Toluca, was seriously wounded and died shortly after.

It has been observed what the plan of attack was, but various arrangements made to carry it out were for the most part omitted; the columns had been ordered to provide themselves with crow-bars, hatchets, and ladders, but not until the last moment did it become obvious that all this was insufficient and that the ladders were poorly put together.

The columns, bravely storming the fort in the midst of a terrible shower of bullets and cannon-fire, had reached the base of the walls, with the exception of the third, which had been sorely punished on its left flank by a battery of three cannon on a barbette that cut a serious breach in its ranks; since it was being attacked frontally at the same time from the height of a position, it was forced to seek a less bloody entrance, and thus changed its course toward the right angle of the north front. The few poor ladders that we were bringing had not arrived, because their bearers had either perished on the way or had escaped. Only one was seen of all those that were planned. General Cos, looking for a starting point from which to climb, had advanced frontally with his column to where the second and third were. All united at one point, mixing and forming a confused mass. Fortunately the wall reinforcement on this front was of lumber, its excavation was hardly begun, and the height of the parapet was eight or nine feet; there was therefore a starting point, and it could be climbed, though with some difficulty. But disorder had already begun; officers of all ranks shouted but were hardly heard. The most daring of our veterans tried to be the first to climb, which they accomplished, yelling wildly so that room could be made for them, at times climbing over their own comrades. Others, jammed together, made useless efforts, obstructing each other, getting in the way of the more agile ones and pushing down those who were about to carry out their courageous effort. A lively rifle fire coming from the roof of the barracks and other points caused painful havoc, increasing the confusion of our disorderly mass. The first to climb were thrown down by bayonets already waiting for them behind the parapet, or by pistol fire, but the courage of our soldiers was not diminished as they saw their comrades falling dead or wounded, and they hurried to occupy their places and to avenge them, climbing over their bleeding bodies. The sharp reports of the rifles, the whistling of bullets, the groans of the wounded, the cursing of the men, the sighs and anguished cries of the dying, the arrogant harangues of the officers, the noise of the instruments of war, and the inordinate shouts of the attackers, who climbed vigorously, bewildered all and made of this moment a tremendous and critical one. The shouting of those being attacked was no less loud and from the beginning had pierced our ears with desperate, terrible cries of alarm in a language we did not understand.

From his point of observation, General Santa Anna viewed with concern this horrible scene and, misled by the difficulties encountered in the climbing of the walls and by the maneuver executed by the third column, believed we were being repulsed; he therefore ordered Colonel Amat to move in with the rest of the reserves; the Sapper Battalion, already ordered to move their column of attack, arrived and began to climb at the same time. He then also ordered into battle his general staff and everyone at his side. This gallant reserve merely added to the noise and the victims, the more regrettable since there was no necessity for them to engage in the combat. Before the Sapper Battalion, advancing through a shower of bullets and volley of shrapnel, had a chance to reach the foot of the walls, half their officers had been wounded. Another one of these officers, young Torres, died within the fort at the very moment of taking a flag. He died at one blow without uttering a word, covered with glory and lamented by his comrades. Something unusual happened to this corps; it had as casualties four officers and twenty-one soldiers, but among these none of the sergeant class, well known to be more numerous than the former.

A quarter of an hour had elapsed, during which our soldiers remained in a terrible situation, wearing themselves out as they climbed in quest of a less obscure death than that visited on them, crowded in a single mass; later and after much effort, they were able in sufficient numbers to reach the parapet, without distinction of ranks. The terrified defenders withdrew at once into quarters placed to the right and the left of the small area that constituted their second line of defense. They had bolted and reinforced the doors, but in order to form trenches they had excavated some places inside that were now a hindrance to them. Not all of them took refuge, for some remained in the open, looking at us before firing, as if dumbfounded at our daring. Travis was seen to hesitate, but not about the death that he would choose. He would take a few steps and stop, turning his proud face toward us to discharge his shots; he fought like a true soldier. Finally he died, but he died after having traded his life very dearly. None of his men died with greater heroism, and they all died. Travis behaved as a hero; one must do him justice, for with a handful of men without discipline, he resolved to face men used to war and much superior in numbers, without supplies, with scarce munitions, and against the will of his subordinates. He was a handsome blond, with a physique as robust as his spirit was strong.

In the meantime Colonel Morelos with his chasseurs, having carried out instructions received, was just in front of us at a distance of a few paces, and, rightly fearing that our fire would hurt him, he had taken refuge in the trenches he had overrun trying to inflict damage on the enemy without harming us. It was a good thing that other columns could come together in a single front, for because of the small area the destruction among ourselves could be partially avoided; nevertheless, some of our men suffered the pain of falling from shots fired by their comrades, a grievous wound indeed, and a death even more lamentable. The soldiers had been overloaded with munition, for the reserves and all the select companies carried seven rounds apiece. It seems that the purpose of this was to convey the message to the soldier not to rely on his bayonet, which is the weapon generally employed in assault while some of the chasseurs support the attackers with their fire; however, there are always errors committed on these occasions, impossible to remedy. There remains no consolation other than regret for those responsible on this occasion, and there were many.

Our soldiers, some stimulated by courage and others by fury, burst into the quarters where the enemy had entrenched themselves, from which issued an infernal fire. Behind these came others, who, nearing the doors and blind with fury and smoke, fired their shots against friends and enemies alike, and in this way our losses were most grievous. On the other hand, they turned the enemy's own cannon to bring down the doors to the rooms or the rooms themselves; a horrible carnage took place, and some were trampled to death. The tumult was great, the disorder frightful; it seemed as if the furies had descended upon us; different groups of soldiers were firing in all directions, on their comrades and on their officers, so that one was as likely to die by a friendly hand as by an enemy's. In the midst of this thundering din, there was such confusion that orders could not be understood, although those in command would raise their voices when the opportunity occurred. Some may believe that this narrative is exaggerated, but those who were witnesses will confess that this is exact, and in truth, any moderation in relating it would fall short.

It was thus time to end the confusion that was increasing the number of our victims, and on my advice and at my insistence General Cos ordered the fire silenced; but the bugler Tamayo of the sappers blew his instrument in vain, for the fire did not cease until there was no one left to kill and around fifty thousand cartridges had been used up. Whoever doubts this, let him estimate for himself, as I have done, with data that I have given.

Among the defenders there were thirty or more colonists; the rest were pirates, used to defying danger and to disdaining death, and who for that reason fought courageously; their courage, to my way of thinking, merited them the mercy for which, toward the last, some of them pleaded; others, not knowing the language, were unable to do so. In fact, when these men noted the loss of their leader and saw that they were being attacked by superior forces, they faltered. Some, with an accent hardly intelligible, desperately cried, *Mercy, valiant Mexicans;* others poked the points of their bayonets through a hole or a door with a white cloth, the symbol of cease-fire, and some even used their socks. Our trusting soldiers, seeing these demonstrations, would confidently enter their quarters, but those among the enemy who had not pleaded for mercy, who had no thought of surrendering, and who relied on no other recourse than selling their lives dearly, would meet them with pistol shots and bayonets. Thus betrayed, our men rekindled their anger and at every moment fresh skirmishes broke out with renewed fury. The order had been given to spare no one but the women and this was carried out, but such carnage was useless and had we prevented it, we would have saved much blood on our part. Those of the enemy who tried to escape fell victims to the sabers of the cavalry, which had been drawn up for this purpose, but even as they fled they defended themselves. An unfortunate father with a young son in his arms was seen to hurl himself from a considerable height, both perishing at the same blow.

This scene of extermination went on for an hour before the curtain of death covered and ended it: shortly after six in the morning it was all finished; the corps were beginning to reassemble and to identify themselves, their sorrowful countenances revealing the losses in the thinned ranks of their officers and comrades, when the commander in chief appeared. He could see for himself the desolation among his battalions and that devastated area littered with corpses, with scattered limbs and bullets, with weapons and torn uniforms. Some of these were burning together with the corpses, which produced an unbearable and nauseating odor. The bodies, with their blackened and bloody faces disfigured by a desperate death, their hair and uniforms burning at once, presented a dreadful and truly hellish sight. . . .

The general then addressed his crippled battalions, lauding their courage and thanking them in the name of their country. But one hardly noticed in his words the magic that Napoleon expresses in his, which, Count Ségur assures us, was impossible to resist. The *vivas* were seconded icily, and silence would hardly have been broken if I, seized by one of those impulses triggered by enthusiasm or one formed to avoid reflection, which conceals the feelings, had not addressed myself to the valiant chasseurs of Aldama, hailing the Republic and them, an act which, carried out in the presence of the commander on whom so much unmerited honor had been bestowed, proved that I never flatter those in power.

Shortly before Santa Anna's speech, an unpleasant episode had taken place, which, since it occurred after the end of the skirmish, was looked upon as base murder and which contributed greatly to the coolness that was noted. Some seven men had survived the general carnage and, under the protection of General Castrillón, they were brought before Santa Anna. Among them was one of great stature, well proportioned, with regular features, in whose face there was the imprint of adversity, but in whom one also noticed a degree of resignation and nobility that did him honor. He was the naturalist David Crockett, well known in North America for his unusual adventures, who had undertaken to explore the country and who, finding himself in Béjar at the very moment of surprise, had taken refuge in the Alamo, fearing that his status as a foreigner might not be respected. Santa Anna answered Castrillón's intervention in Crockett's behalf with a gesture of indignation and, addressing himself to the sappers, the troops closest to him, ordered his execution. The commanders and officers were outraged at this action and did not support the order, hoping that once the fury of the moment had blown over these men would be spared; but several officers who were around the president and who, perhaps, had not been present during the moment of danger, became noteworthy by an infamous deed, surpassing the soldiers in cruelty. They thrust themselves forward, in order to flatter their commander, and with swords in hand, fell upon these unfortunate, defenseless men just as a tiger leaps upon his prey. Though tortured before they were killed, these unfortunates died without complaining and without humiliating themselves before their torturers.

7. Mrs. Dilue Harris Recounts the "Runaway Scrape," March 1836

On the 12th of March came the news of the fall of the Alamo. A courier brought a dispatch from General Houston for the people to leave. Colonel Travis and the men under his command had been slaughtered, the Texas army was retreating, and President Burnet's cabinet had gone to Harrisburg.

Then began the horrors of the "Runaway Scrape." We left home at sunset, hauling clothes, bedding, and provisions on the sleigh with one yoke of oxen. Mother

"The Reminiscences of Mrs. Dilue Harris," *Quarterly of the Texas State Historical Association,* vol. 4 (January, 1901): 162–164.

and I were walking, she with an infant in her arms. Brother drove the oxen, and my two little sisters rode in the sleigh. We were going ten miles to where we could be transferred to Mr. Bundick's cart. Father was helping with cattle, but he joined us after dark and brought a horse and saddle for brother. He sent him to help Mr. Stafford with the cattle. He was to go a different road with them and ford the San Jacinto. Mother and I then rode father's horse. . . .

We camped the first night near Harrisburg, about where the railroad depot now stands. Next day we crossed Vince's Bridge and arrived at the San Jacinto in the night. There were fully five thousand people at the ferry. The planters from Brazoria and Columbia with their slaves were crossing. We waited three days before we crossed. Our party consisted of five white families: father's, Mr. Dyer's, Mr. Bell's, Mr. Neal's, and Mr. Bundick's. Father and Mr. Bundick were the only white men in the party, the others being in the army. There were twenty or thirty negroes from Stafford's plantation. They had a large wagon with five yoke of oxen, and horses, and mules, and they were in charge of an old negro man called Uncle Ned. Altogether, black and white, there were about fifty of us. Every one was trying to cross first, and it was almost a riot.

We got over the third day, and after travelling a few miles came to a big prairie. It was about twelve miles further to the next timber and water, and some of our party wanted to camp; but others said that the Trinity river was rising, and if we delayed we might not get across. So we hurried on.

When we got about half across the prairie Uncle Ned's wagon bogged. The negro men driving the carts tried to go around the big wagon one at a time until the four carts were fast in the mud. Mother was the only white woman that rode in a cart; the others travelled on horseback. Mrs. Bell's four children, Mrs. Dyer's three, and mother's four rode in the carts. All that were on horseback had gone on to the timber to let their horses feed and get water. They supposed their families would get there by dark. The negro men put all the oxen to the wagon, but could not move it; so they had to stay there until morning without wood or water. Mother gathered the white children in our cart. They behaved very well and went to sleep, except one little boy, Eli Dyer, who kicked and cried for Uncle Ned and Aunt Dilue till Uncle Ned came and carried him to the wagon. He slept that night in Uncle Ned's arms.

Mother with all the negro women and children walked six miles to the timber and found our friends in trouble. Father and Mr. Bundick had gone to the river and helped with the ferry boat, but late in the evening the boat grounded on the east bank of the Trinity and didn't get back until morning. While they were gone the horses had strayed off and they had to find them before they could go to the wagons. Those that travelled on horseback were supplied with provisions by other campers. We that stayed in the prairie had to eat cold corn bread and cold boiled beef. The wagons and carts didn't get to the timber till night. They had to be unloaded and pulled out.

At the Trinity river men from the army began to join their families. I know they have been blamed for this, but what else could they have done? The Texas army was retreating and the Mexicans were crossing the Colorado, Col. Fannin and his men were prisoners, there were more negroes than whites among us and many of them were wild Africans, there was a large tribe of Indians on the Trinity as well as the Cherokee Indians in Eastern Texas at Nacogdoches, and there were tories, both Mexicans and Americans, in the country. It was the intention of our men to see their families across the Sabine river, and then to return and fight the Mexicans. I must say for the negroes that there was no insubordination among them; they were loyal to their owners.

8. Mirabeau B. Lamar Complains of Insubordination in the Ranks of the Texas Army, 1836

Head Quarters
17th July 1836

To His Excellency
President Burnet

Dear Sir—I have just recd several letters from you on various subjects, to none of which have I time to reply at present; I have but five minutes to dictate this note to let you know the dreadful state of affairs in the army. Every thing is in the utmost confusion and rebellion. On my arrival, I was informed that I could not be recognized as Commander in Chief. I proposed to speak to the Soldiers, and did so, but was answered by Rusk, Greene and Felix Houston who carried the popular currant against me. I had an open rupture with Genl. Rusk believing it to be the secret arrangmts of his to supplant me. Some hostile correspondence ensued; which, instead of leading to further difficulties has resulted in this arrangement, viz, that he is to recognise my orders in future; that the regulars and about 6 or 8 volunteer companies are to march to another encampment under my Command; where I shall issue my Orders as Commander in Chief to the balance of the army of Texas, and if Greene and Felix Houston still maintain their present attitude of rebellion to my authority, I shall punish them by Court Martial, if possible, & if not shall report them to Congress. You will perceive from this dreadful state of affairs the high & absolute necessity of Convening a Congress. Nothing else can save the Country from dreadful disorganization and anarchy. The general Officers all seem determined to defy the civil authority of the land; I stand alone in its defense, and in consequence am fast loosing my influence. I hope I shall be able to recall the old citizens of Texas to a sense of their rights and their duty; the volunteers are bent on supremacy. A Vote was taken a few days since on the question of Bringing Santa Anna to the army, which was deter[mi]ned in favor of the measure by a vast majority. They have sent after him. My present purpose is, when I shall take my position with the Regulars and a few companies of the volunteers, to stop him before he reaches the main army, and refer his fate to the Citizens of Texas instead of turning him over to the decision of Greene's soldiers. I believe he has forfeited his life & should die—that is my voice—but I want the Congress to pronounce it and not a rebellious mob of strangers who have been made such by an ambitious and weak General. If I am wrong in any matter, write me your views cordially as I wish to be ruled by the best

Mirabeau Lamar to David G. Burnet, July 17, 1836, *Papers of Mirabeau Lamar,* ed. Charles Adams Gulick (Austin: A. C. Baldwin, 1921–27), 1:417–418.

councils that can be had. I aim only at the interest and glory of my country and whenever it is deemed by the intelligence of that county that I stand in the way of its prosperity, I am ready to retire. I have a dreadful task and duties to perform here, & shall require the aid & support of every friend of Order and Civil government. . . .

Yours

M. B Lamar—

9. American Abolitionist Benjamin Lundy Sees a Southern Slave Conspiracy, 1836

The advocates of slavery, in our southern states and elsewhere, want more land on this continent suitable for the culture of sugar and cotton; and if Texas, with the adjoining portions of Tamaulipas, Coahuila, Chihuahua, and Santa Fe, east of the Rio Bravo del Norte, can be wrested from the Mexican government, room will be afforded for the redundant slave population in the United States, even to a remote period of time. . . .

The breeders of slaves, in those parts of the United States where slave labour has become unprofitable,—and also the traffickers in human flesh, whether American or foreign, desire an extended market, which Texas would afford if revolutionized, and governed as well as inhabited by those who are in favour of re-establishing the system of slavery in that section of country. The northern land speculators most cheerfully co-operate with the southern slave-holders, in the grand scheme of aggression, with the hope of immense gain; and the slave-merchants play into the hands of both, with the same heartless, avaricious feelings and views. The principal seat of operations, for the first, is New York,—though some active and regular agencies are established at New Orleans and Nashville, and minor agencies in other places. The second exercise their influence individually, without any particular organization: while the third cooperate with all, as opportunities present themselves. They have subsidized presses at command, ready to give extensive circulation to whatever they may wish to publish in furtherance of their views. And orators, legislators, and persons holding official stations under our Federal government, are deeply interested in their operations, and frequently willing instruments to promote their cause.

Such are the motives for action—such the combination of interests—such the organization, sources of influence, and foundation of authority, upon which the present *Texas Insurrection* rests. The resident colonists compose but a small fraction of the party concerned in it. The standard of revolt was raised as soon as it was clearly ascertained that slavery could not be perpetuated, nor the illegal speculations in land continued under the *government* of the Mexican Republic. The Mexican authorities were charged with acts of oppression, while the true causes of the revolt—the motives and designs of the insurgents—were studiously concealed from the public view. Influential slave-holders are contributing money, equipping troops, and marching to the scene of conflict. The land speculators are fitting out

---

Benjamin Lundy, *The Origin and True Causes of the Texas Insurrection* (Philadelphia, 1836), 30–31.

expeditions from New York and New Orleans, with men, munitions of war, provisions, &c., to promote the object. The Independence of Texas is declared, and the system of slavery, as well as the slave trade, (with the United States,) is fully recognised by constitutional regulation. Commissioners are sent from Texas to the United States, to make formal representations, enlist the sympathies of our citizens, and solicit aid in every way that it can be furnished. The subsidized presses are actively employed in magnifying the successes of the insurgents; misrepresenting the character and strength of the Mexican forces; and by inflammatory appeals urging forward the ignorant, the unsuspecting, the adventurous and the daring, to a participation in the struggle.

♣ E S S A Y S

In the first essay, Eugene Barker, an early twentieth-century scholar who had an enormous influence on the study of Texas history, presents the traditional interpretation of the Texas Revolution, arguing that the conflict had its roots in a clash between two opposing cultures. Barker gives special emphasis to the wholly disparate political systems of the United States and Mexico, one democratic, the other inclined toward greater centralized authority. Although Santa Anna's decision to abrogate the Constitution of 1824 provided the final rupture between the two sides, chronic political instability in Mexico City had already undermined Anglo American confidence in the national government. Jealously protective of their liberties, the American migrants to Texas, Barker suggests, were bound to resist any central authority that sought to undermine their political sovereignty.

In the second essay, David J. Weber, a professor at Southern Methodist University who has written widely on the American Southwest, offers a critique of Barker's cultural conflict thesis. Although Weber does not ignore deep-seated cultural tensions, he cautions against viewing the Revolution strictly as an upheaval pitting Anglos against Hispanics. Such an interpretation, he argues, serves not only to minimize the significant role that Tejanos played in the events of 1835–36, but has helped to perpetuate the myth that a morally superior Anglo Texan community triumphed over a degenerate Mexico.

Another challenge to the Barker thesis, though an indirect one, is suggested in the third essay by Paul Lack, an historian at McMurry University. Like Weber, Lack argues that the momentum for revolution did not crystallize until 1835, drawing attention to Anglo Texans' fears that the new central government in Mexico would now attempt to undermine slavery. Although the Mexican government did little to actually foment a rebellion in Texas, the widespread perception that it *might* do so, he argues, provided a powerful stimulus for insurrection. Lack's essay offers a valuable reminder that the traditional interpretation of the Revolution as a struggle for liberty against oppressive rule did not apply to Anglo Texans alone. Ironically, as Lack points out, African Americans were inclined to "identify with Mexico as a force of freedom." Lack's essay should also be examined in conjunction with Benjamin Lundy's assessment of slavery's role in the Revolution (see Document 9). Whereas Lundy maintained that slaveowners were engaged in a deliberate, long-term effort to expand the slave empire, Lack views the actions of Anglo-Texas slaveholders during the insurrection as defensive in nature, as an attempt to protect rather than to expand the "peculiar institution."

Mexico and Texas: A Collision of Two Cultures

EUGENE BARKER

On the one side was the Anglo-American immigrant, blunt, independent, efficient, a rebel against authority, a supreme individualist. On the other side was the Latin American master of the soil, sensitive, secretive, subtle and indirect in his ways, by training and temperament a worshiper of tradition and a creature of authority. With the political ascendancy of the two elements reversed the situation would have held no threatening aspects, but with the Mexicans in the political saddle conflict was certain.

In 1821, after three hundred years of subjection to Spain, Mexico gained its national independence. It was poorly prepared for self-government. In practice, even more than in theory and in law, the Spanish colonial system was rigidly centralized. The highest positions in army, church, and civil service were reserved for Spaniards. [Hubert H.] Bancroft declares, on the authority of Alaman, that from 1535 until 1813 only three creoles became viceroys of Mexico, and he says that out of seven hundred and fifty-four individuals who in the same period held the highest civil and military positions in all Spanish America only eighteen were born in the colonies.

Exclusion from the highest offices need have had little effect upon the political training of the Spanish-blood Mexicans had the subordinate administration been allowed a measure of independent development. But the duties of every officer, down to the *sindico* of the local *ayuntamiento,* were meticulously prescribed and regulated by the omnipotent Laws of the Indies.

In spite of their political incapacity—or perhaps because of it—the Mexicans, after several false starts, declared in 1823 for the most complex form of government ever devised by man, and the next year promulgated the federal republican constitution of 1824.

Greater contrast in the political experience of two peoples could scarcely be imagined than that presented by the Mexicans and their immigrants from the north. The English colonists came to America with a training in local self government already centuries old. Roots of the precinct, the county, and trial by jury go back beyond the dawn of English constitutional history. Parliament and the representative system were developed in all their essential characteristics before the great emigration to America in the seventeenth century. Once on this side, the English colonists settled down to more rather than less local independence and responsibility than they had had in England. Legally no civil office in America was closed to them, from the office of governor down to constable, and only in the royal colonies were they in common practice excluded from the governor's office.

The congregational organization of the churches in the North added its contribution to the political training of the colonists; and even in the South, where the English Episcopal Church was established, sparse population, widely extended parish boundaries, and difficulties of travel and communication combined to foster a high degree of local independence and responsibility in matters of the church.

Eugene Barker, *Mexico and Texas* (Dallas: P. L. Turner, 1928), 1–5, 143–146. Reprinted with the permission of Scribner, A Division of Simon & Schuster.

Generation after generation of thrusting their way through the American wilderness renewed and strengthened the self-reliance and efficiency of the English colonists. On every successive frontier adventurous pioneers re-enacted, with the necessary adaptations of time and circumstance, the experiences and the expedients of the original immigrants. Daniel Boone's colonists at Boonesborough were not less dependent upon their own resources than were Captain Smith's Englishmen at Jamestown. . . .

To men such as these democracy was the breath of political life. As they trudged westward and ever westward to new homes in the wilderness, they shed the property and religious restrictions of the tidewater states on the voting franchise and established manhood suffrage. With political equality went social equality, universally assumed in theory, and commonly conceded in practice. Withal was a rampant nationalism. America and Americans were the best. All foreigners were inferiors.

The causes of popular movements are rarely concrete and simple; on the contrary, they are diffuse and complex. It was so in the Texas revolution. In the end, it was the development of national politics, I think, which precipitated the Texas revolution. Not to mention local and state insurrections and isolated "plans" and pronunciamentoes touching national affairs, there were four major revolutions during the six years from 1829 to 1835. First, . . . the grim old warrior, Vicente Guerrero, overthrew the mild and liberal Pedraza and ruled for nine months, most of the time invested by Congress with the military power of a dictator. Second, General Bustamante succeeded Guerrero by the sword and gave his power a fictitious legality by the sanction of Congress. Third, the republican Santa Anna overthrew Bustamante and restored the accommodating Pedraza to the presidency—all with the approval of Congress—in order to gain time for his own formal election as the champion of liberalism and democracy. Finally, Santa Anna, the Liberal, yielded to Santa Anna, the reactionary Centralist, and a centralized dictatorship took the place of the so-called federal republic—again with the fictitious congressional sanction. The successive eruptions gave no indication of a tendency toward national political stability; quite the contrary—a fact which might be expected to have caused, and which did cause, uneasy reflections in Texas.

The really ominous fact, however, was that each successive change seemed to bring Texas more completely within the blighting sphere of the federal government's attention. Guerrero issued the emancipation decree of 1829; Bustamante approved the fateful Law of April 6, 1830, which, had it been enforced with its original design, would have paralyzed the development of Texas for many years; Santa Anna's Liberal revolt, by a fortuitous chain of circumstances, caused the abandonment of Austin's policy of aloofness and brought the Texans squarely into the national party convulsions that Austin had always tried to avoid; finally, the victory of Centralism threatened, as the Texans would have expressed it, to bring the country under the heel of military despotism.

There are many indications, only three of which can be mentioned now, that Santa Anna's about-face from Liberalism to Centralism was the last unbearable straw upon the proverbial camel's back.

In the first place, I think Santa Anna's overthrow of republican government determined Austin's attitude, and Austin's attitude was decisive. He could have disorganized the resistance of the colonists in the fall of 1835; instead, he organized and united their resistance.

In the second place, a Fourth of July address by R. M. Williamson explaining the circumstances that led to Travis's attack on Anahuac was directed entirely toward the end of convincing the Texans that they were in dire danger from Santa Anna's destruction of the federal system. Williamson was not a radical malcontent chronically bent upon stirring up agitation, but was a man of independent mind and generally of sound judgment. . . .

The third bit of evidence to be mentioned here indicating the importance which the Texans attached to the centralization of the government by Santa Anna is furnished by a set of resolutions drawn by David G. Burnet on August 8, 1835, and adopted by a public meeting on the San Jacinto River. Burnet was a man of judicious temperament, and wrote as a conservative and a pacifist. Assuming it to be true that the federal system was destroyed, he saw no reason, he said, why Texas should not be happy under another form of government. Names were the mere signification of things, he declared, and the people were not "so obstinately prejudiced in favor of the term, 'federal republic' as . . . to reject another government purely because it has assumed a different external sign or denomination."

But, although the overthrow of the nominal republic and the substitution of centralized oligarchy precipitated the revolution, its fundamental causes lie deeper. Always in the background was the fatal fact that the Mexicans distrusted and feared the Anglo-American settlers, while the settlers half despised the Mexicans. A permanent atmosphere of suspicion magnified and distorted mutual annoyances which might otherwise have been ignored or adjusted. The apparent determination of the United States to obtain Texas heightened Mexican apprehensions; and the chronic caprice and instability of state and federal politics and policies exhausted the patience of the Texans. At bottom the Texas revolution was the product of the racial and political inheritances of the two peoples.

Refighting the Alamo: Mythmaking and the Texas Revolution

DAVID J. WEBER

The lore surrounding the battle of the Alamo provides the clearest examples of how the Texas rebellion, like so many major events, has been romanticized to take on meanings that transcend the event itself and its principal characters reduced to caricature—to heroes and villains. In certain kinds of history, and in American popular culture, the Texas fight for independence has come to represent a triumph of Protestantism over Catholicism, of democracy over despotism, of a superior white race over a degenerate people of mixed blood, of the future over the past, of good over evil. Heroes of the Texas revolt are portrayed as committed republicans fighting for the noblest of motives (the blood of Davy Crockett, one historian has written, was shed upon "a holy altar"). The conflict over Texas has been reduced to nothing more than a conflict of two incompatible cultures. And the rebellion itself, which was a uniquely successful version of the separatist movements and rebellions that broke

"Refighting the Alamo, Mythmaking and the Texas Revolution," in *Myth and the History of the Hispanic Southwest: Essays,* David J. Weber (Albuquerque: University of New Mexico, 1988), 138–151. Reprinted with permission.

out all over Mexico at this time, has been elevated to the status of a "revolution"—a designation that few, if any, modern social scientists would apply to a revolt that did not seek a profound restructuring of society.

What are the sources of these exaggerated notions about the Texas rebellion? Certainly one source was wartime propaganda—myths invented to stir people to action during conflict. Writing just after the fighting ended, for example, Stephen Austin explained the conflict as "a war of barbarism and of despotic principles, waged by the mongrel Spanish-Indian and Negro race, against civilization and the Anglo-American race." That refrain echoed in nineteenth-century Romantic historiography, and its reverberations can be heard yet today in American popular history and popular culture. . . .

The simple fact that Texas became an independent nation as a result of the rebellion has given Texans enormous pride—perhaps too much pride. Historian T. R. Fehrenbach carried this idea to Texas-size proportions when he wrote, apparently without tongue in cheek: "The great difference between Texas and every other American state in the 20th century was that Texas had a history. Other American regions merely had records of development."

But it is more than a traditional big brag that has led Texans to exaggerate the events of 1836 and to make mortal men into heroes of mythological proportions. This certainly reflects a more universal tendency—the tendency to write pietistic history and to use the past as a kind of Rorschach test, seeing wistfully in the past what we wish to see about ourselves in the present. In the interest of creating a usable past, all peoples seem to engage in the making of myths and passing them off as historical fact. In this country, we begin at an early age to be exposed to such historical figures as Santa Claus, and to learn to tell the truth from the homily about George Washington and the cherry tree. No matter that this fabled episode of the cherry tree did not occur—that the story is a lie. No matter that our teachers lied to us in order to teach us to tell the truth. History was being employed toward good ends. So, in many respects, have the tales of the Alamo been exaggerated to serve particular ends.

Rather than trying to read our present-day concerns into the past, let us try to reconstruct the past and look briefly at the coming of the Texas rebellion as contemporaries might have seen it. What did it mean to them? Certainly there was less heroism, less altruism, less patriotism, less clarity of purpose, and less unity than most of us might imagine. Instead, much as today, events moved along more quickly than contemporaries could grasp them and most Anglo Americans and Mexicans in Texas pursued their private lives, wishing that the entire affair would go away.

Let us look first at the proposition that the Texas rebellion represented a clash of cultures, rendering it nearly inevitable. This line of argument was advanced by some Anglo Texans at the time of the revolt and has continued to receive the support of some scholars.

Certainly it is easy to view the revolt as an "ethnic" conflict, for in some respects it was. Between 1821, when Mexico became independent, and 1836 when the armed struggle between Mexico and Texas began, perhaps 35,000 Anglo Americans had flocked across the border and into Mexican Texas, outnumbering the

Mexican Texans, or tejanos, by a ratio of ten to one. The Anglo Americans, so the argument goes, could not adapt to Mexican culture. Historians have identified a number of sources of cultural friction.

First, Anglo Americans were required to become Catholics, and were not permitted to hold Protestant services.

Second, Anglo Americans, some 75 percent of whom were southerners, were shocked when Mexico prohibited slavery in 1829. Mexicans seemed to have little respect for private property.

Third, Anglo Americans could not tolerate the lack of a jury system and deplored the Mexican system of justice in which alcaldes made decisions on the merits of a case.

Fourth, Anglo Americans could not abide the lack of local autonomy in Texas— of home rule. Since 1824 Texas had been subservient to a larger and more populous state, Coahuila. Both Coahuila and Texas had been joined together as the single state of Coahuila y Texas. Control of state government rested squarely in the hands of officials in the distant state capital at Saltillo, and Coahuila's larger population assured that the state legislature would be controlled by representatives from Coahuila.

Fifth, many Anglo Americans could not abide Mexicans themselves. Stephen Austin, on visiting Mexico City in 1822–23, wrote in private correspondence that "the people are bigoted and superstitious to an extreem [*sic*], and indolence appears to be the order of the day." "To be candid the majority of the people of that whole nation as far as I have seen them want nothing but tails to be more brutes than apes." Many years after the bloody days at the Alamo and San Jacinto, one pioneer who had settled in Texas in 1827, Noah Smithwick, echoed Austin's sentiments. "I looked upon the Mexicans as scarce more than apes," Smithwick recalled.

Anglo Americans made no attempt to conceal their sense of superiority from Mexicans. In 1819, two years before Mexico won her independence from Spain, the Spanish minister who was negotiating with John Q. Adams what became the transcontinental treaty, characterized Americans as an "arrogant and audacious" people who believed themselves "superior to all the nations of Europe," and who were convinced "that their dominion is destined to extend. . . . to the isthmus of Panama, and hereafter, over all the regions of the New World." At the dawn of Mexican independence, in 1821, a Mexican Committee on Foreign Relations warned the government that unless Mexico could populate its northern borders, hordes of North Americans would descend on the fertile province of Texas "Just as the Goths, Ostrogoths, Alans, and other tribes [of barbarians] devastated the Roman empire." As this last statement suggests, many Mexicans believed themselves superior to the uncultured, brash, and barbaric Anglo Americans.

On the surface, then, the two cultures seemed incompatible and, even more important, the fact that some Anglo Texans *believed* the two cultures to be incompatible, contributed to Texas independence. Indeed, there seems little reason to doubt that profound cultural differences, including American racism, contributed to the Texas rebellion and gave it a special virulence.

Nonetheless, it would be easy to exaggerate the importance of cultural differences, incorrectly identifying them as the principal cause of the rebellion. *Within* Texas itself, relations between Mexicans from Texas and the Anglo-American newcomers were generally amicable. A few Anglo Americans had settled in the

Mexican communities of San Antonio and Goliad, where they became assimilated. In the main, however, the two groups lived essentially apart, separated by considerable distance. Most Anglo Americans lived in East Texas and most Mexicans in the area of San Antonio and Goliad. As a result, Anglo Americans enjoyed a good deal of autonomy. Differences in religion, philosophy, or what we have come to call "lifestyles," did not become major irritants.

The alleged "religious conflict" offers a case in point. Some writers have argued that Anglo Americans chaffed at the lack of religious freedom in Texas. In practice, the law requiring immigrants to become Catholics was never enforced. The Mexican government failed to send priests to minister to the Anglo-American colonists, as the Colonization Law of 1824 required, so the colonists were not obliged to practice Catholicism. Nor was the government ever so efficient that it investigated the private or quasi-public worship that went on in East Texas homes, where most Anglo Americans lived far from the watchful eye of Mexican officials.

Indeed, there is some evidence to suggest that Mexico's refusal to allow non-Catholics to worship openly (at least in theory) served as a screening device that kept the most devout or dogmatic Protestants out of Texas. Those who did filter through were less inclined to be irritated by strictures on their religious lives. Indeed, many of those early pioneers who entered Texas may have come precisely because of the lack of religious restraints and the absence of Protestant preachers.

Put simply, the Mexican government never forced Catholicism on the Anglo-American colonists in Texas. To the contrary, in 1834, two years before the revolt broke out, the state of Coahuila y Texas went so far as to guarantee that "no person shall be molested for political and religious opinions provided the public order is not disturbed." Freedom of worship never became an important issue among the foreigners in Mexican Texas and, notwithstanding Anglo-Texan wartime propaganda, the issue of freedom of worship did not directly cause the Texas revolt in 1836.

The idea that cultural conflict caused the Texas rebellion has contributed to the notion that the struggle itself was fought along ethnic lines, pitting *all* Mexicans against *all* Americans in Texas. This was decidedly not the case. Tejanos, for example, contributed substantially to the resistance against centralist forces in the fall of 1835, in the wave of hostilities that preceded Santa Anna's march into Texas. The Texas forces that laid siege to General Martín Perfecto de Cos in San Antonio in the fall of 1835 included as many as 160 *tejanos,* among them companies led by Colonel Juan Nepomuceno Seguín of San Antonio, Plácido Benavides of Victoria, and a group of rancheros from Goliad. The next spring, seven tejanos died inside the Alamo, fighting alongside Anglo Americans *against* Santa Anna. Colonel Seguín and the Second Company of Texas Volunteers, which he raised, performed valuable scouting services prior to the fall of the Alamo and contributed to the defeat of Santa Anna at San Jacinto. (Indeed, Seguín and one Antonio Cruz would have died defending the Alamo had they not been sent on a dangerous ride through enemy lines to seek help from Colonel James Fannin at Goliad.) Tejanos also participated in the famous "Consultation" at San Felipe on November 7 of 1835, which endorsed a conditional declaration of Texas independence. Four months later José Antonio Navarro and Francisco Ruiz, both Texas-born, signed the declaration of Texas independence at Washington-on-the-Brazos.

Thus, the sides did not divide up uniformly along ethnic lines. The issues that caused men to take to arms in 1835–36 may have had to do more with the culture of politics than with the politics of culture. And both tejanos and Anglos *within* Texas found much about politics with which they could agree. Let us look at some areas of agreement.

Elites in the predominantly *tejano* communities of San Antonio and Goliad had apparently *shared* Anglo-American concerns about the need to improve the system of justice and to achieve greater autonomy by separating Texas from Coahuila. Many *tejano* leaders even saw slavery as a necessary evil for Texas if the underpopulated and beleaguered province was going to prosper. Nor, it would appear, did the large influx of Anglo Americans into Texas trouble the tejanos as much as it did the Mexican government. For the tejano *elite,* Anglo-American immigrants meant economic growth. From the *local* perspective Anglo Americans were a necessary evil, and Mexican officials in Texas opposed national laws that would restrict the number of Anglo-American immigrants.

From a *national* perspective, however, officials in Mexico City saw Anglo Americans as aggressive and expansionistic, and as a clear and present danger to Texas. There was no doubt that the United States government wanted Texas. The United States had advanced the absurd claim that Texas was part of the Louisiana Purchase. When that claim could not be sustained, the United States had sought to purchase Texas. Mexico, of course, declined to sell the national patrimony, and Mexican statesman Lucas Alamán feared that the Americans' next strategy would be to take Texas from Mexico by peopling it with Americans. As Alamán wrote in 1830: "Where others send invading armies . . . [the North Americans] send their colonists."

As events would demonstrate, Alamán's fears were quite rational. If Mexican leaders *in Texas* shared those concerns, they subordinated them to their economic interests and called for more immigration to make Texas grow. Francisco Ruiz of San Antonio put it squarely when he wrote in 1830: "I cannot help seeing advantages which, to my way of thinking, would result if we admitted honest, hardworking people, regardless of what country they come from . . . even hell itself."

The evidence is scanty, but it appears that the Anglo Texans and the Mexican-Texan elite shared a number of common concerns. No matter how much mutual interests might tie them together, however, once the fighting began it must have been agonizing for tejanos to decide whether to remain loyal to Mexico or to join forces with Americans and take up arms against fellow Mexicans. Although they might agree with Anglo Texans on certain issues, the idea of separation from Coahuila, much less independence from Mexico came to hold less attraction for tejanos in the mid-1830s than it had in the 1820s. Anglo Americans, who vastly outnumbered tejanos by the early 1830s, would surely dominate the state and tejanos would become, to paraphrase Juan Seguín, "foreigners in their native land." When, however, Coahuila fell into anarchy in the mid-1830s and Santa Anna's centralist dictatorship replaced Mexico's federalist Republic, tejano leaders must have wrung their hands over their unhappy alternatives—domination by Anglo Americans or domination by the centralist dictatorship.

The hard choice must have divided some families. We know, for example, that Gregorio Esparza, who died fighting alongside Americans inside the walls of the

Alamo, had a brother, Francisco, who fought on the Mexican side. Most tejanos, however, probably responded like any residents of a war-torn land. They looked first to their families' welfare, fought on neither side, cooperated overtly with the group in charge at the moment, and hoped for an end to the nightmare.

The same may also be said for most Anglo Texans, who had no desire to fight over political issues until Mexican forces threatened their lives and property. Until autumn of 1835, Anglo Americans in Texas were divided between groups that had come to be called the "war party" and the "peace party." Both parties sought greater political autonomy for Texas in order to enable Texans to adopt measures that would make Texas more attractive to immigrants from the U.S.—measures such as more favorable tariffs, an improved judicial system, and the maintenance of slavery. While they agreed on the goals, the peace and war parties disagreed about the means to achieve them. The "peace party," of which the *empresario* Stephen Austin was the most influential representative, wanted Mexico to grant Texas a divorce from its unhappy and unequal marriage with Coahuila. The radical war party, led by ambitious and sometimes angry young men such as William Barret Travis (who a few years earlier had abandoned a wife and law practice in Alabama after killing a man), sought independence from Mexico itself.

Until the autumn of 1835, the "war party" remained a decided minority, its actions repudiated by most responsible Texans of both Anglo and Mexican background. Then, Mexico committed the blunder of sending troops into Texas under the direction of Santa Anna's brother-in-law, Martín Perfecto de Cos. In part, Mexico had been provoked into that action by the attack on a small Mexican garrison at Anahuac in June of 1835, led by Travis and thirty-some radicals. At first, Anglo-American communities throughout Texas repudiated that attack and professed loyalty to the government, but when Anglo Americans learned that Mexican troops would be sent to Texas, public opinion swung away from the "Tories," as Travis called the peace party, and over to the "war party." Even the foremost Texas "Tory," Stephen Austin, became convinced of the necessity of armed resistance. His private correspondence reveals that by the autumn of 1835 he had come to believe that Texas "must, and ought to become a part of the United States."

Although Anglo Americans in Texas achieved unity of purpose by the fall of 1835, that unity disappeared again after General Cos's forces were defeated in San Antonio. In the spring of 1836, Anglo Americans were in disarray once again, both before, during, and after the tragic events at Goliad and the Alamo.

Clearly, then, the Texas struggle for independence was not a simple conflict of Mexicans versus Anglos, of Mexican culture versus American culture, of democracy versus despotism, or of good versus evil. It was not a conflict in which issues were so clearly drawn that men of good will united readily to fight for principles greater than themselves. That such men existed, I have no reason to doubt, but it should be remembered that many Anglo Americans who came to Texas had more interest in fleeing the law than in changing the law; that they came to Texas for personal gain. Pragmatism rather than principle, self interest rather than political democracy, had driven a disproportionate share of Anglo Americans to Texas in search of opportunity. And the unbridled pursuit of self-interest on the part of some Anglo Americans, rather than the quest for liberty, may have helped to bring on the Texas rebellion. The story is a complicated one, but Professor Malcolm McLean has developed a strong case, in his monumental series, *Papers Concerning Robertson's Colony in Texas,* that land speculation by certain Anglo Americans, and their manipulation of the state government in Saltillo, helped win the wrath of the federal government, bring Mexican troops into Texas, and provoke the Texas revolt. . . .

. . . [I]n a historical event as complicated as the Texas struggle for independence, there are few heroes or villains, but rather men and women much like us, looking after their day-to-day interests and responding to a variety of impulses. By writing romanticized history that magnifies men and events, that simplifies a complicated story of a struggle for political and economic power into an ethnic conflict, and that makes Anglo Americans in the past more altruistic, courageous, patriotic, and united than they were, we not only distort the past, but we diminish ourselves. We come to believe that our own generation, when compared to the giants of yesteryear, is unprincipled and decadent.

Many of the giants of yesteryear—both heroes and villains—are, of course, creatures of our own making, invented to serve salutory ends. First, they provide us with a way to avoid abstractions and complicated issues and to focus instead on the personal, the concrete, the easily understood. As historian Michael Meyer, writing about the villain, has explained: "it is much easier to prepare a diatribe against an antihero than to fathom the actual dynamics of an age." Second, by conjuring heroes of mythic proportions and keeping their memories alive, we hope to offer lessons in morality to the young, or to inspire the young with patriotism and pride. And such lessons have been well learned. As one Texas-educated young man, Lyndon B. Johnson, wrote in his college newspaper, "Down with the debunking biographer. . . . Hero worship is a tremendous force in uplifting and strengthening . . . let us have our heroes. Let us continue to believe that some have been truly great."

Myths are, of course, important to a people. As historian William McNeill has reminded us in a recent essay, myths play an essential role in binding a people together and in serving as a basis for common action. The question, however, is whether a myth is useful or pernicious; whether it drives people to constructive common action or to collective foolishness or disgrace. Perhaps these two extremes are not mutually exclusive, but the mythology surrounding the Alamo has served as rationalization for aggressive behavior toward Mexico and Mexicans that runs counter to our finest national ideals. In the immediate aftermath of the Texas revolt, the enshrinement of the Alamo as a holy place and the popular sanctification of its defenders as martyrs helped reinforce and intensify two complementary articles of faith among Anglo Americans: belief in the moral superiority of Anglos and the degeneracy of Mexicans. From those antipodal myths, which ran strongest among Anglo residents of Texas, it followed that Mexico's conquest by its morally superior neighbor might redeem her benighted citizenry. Their faith affirmed by the windy rhetoric of their elders, young American men of the mid-1840s swallowed the myth of a holy war against Mexico. Entering a fantasy world of promised glory and heroism against a foe they believed to be inferior, many young Americans marched to the Halls of Montezuma. One out of eight never returned.

It may be that by *manufacturing* heroes from the past we do not necessarily "uplift and strengthen" the present generation, as young LBJ supposed, or add to patriotism and pride. Instead, we may only succeed in adding to our self-loathing and cynicism, for as mere human beings we cannot live up to the impossible standards that we set for ourselves when we invent heroes who are larger than life.

Slavery and the Texas Revolution

PAUL LACK

This study of slavery and the Texas Revolution concentrates on the impact of the 1835–36 struggle on both slaves and slaveholders. The conflict with Mexico raised before Anglos the spectre of slave revolt, created for blacks other avenues to freedom besides rebellion, generated forces that weakened the hold of masters over bondsmen, and placed the very survival of the institution in Texas on the success of Texas arms. In order to understand the events of these two years, some attention will also be given to the status of slavery in the earlier period of Mexican rule and to the difficult question of slavery as a factor leading to the Texas movement for independence.

This latter issue attracted attention as soon as war erupted between Mexico and Texas; antislavery zealots quickly attributed the Texas Revolution to a proslavery conspiracy. The most thoroughgoing of these denunciations, *The War in Texas* by Benjamin Lundy, appeared in 1836. Lundy's suspicions regarding the conflict grew out of a decade-old career as an antislavery writer and his visits in Brazoria, Bexar, and other Mexican provinces in 1833. Lundy viewed the origins of the Revolution as exactly opposite to those identified in public pronouncements in Texas, which stressed liberty and human rights. His historical narrative developed the theme that southern-born immigrants had evaded Mexican emancipation measures and had finally sought separate statehood in order to establish the institution on a firm constitutional basis. When foiled in this and other proslavery efforts, a "vast combination" of slaveholders in Texas, supported by land-jobbers, slave-breeders and dealers, and their political lackeys in the United States, implemented a "treasonable" "scheme" to divide Texas from Mexico and reestablish slavery. Like most abolitionists, Lundy placed blame on individual sin: the Texas war derived from "motives of personal aggrandizement, avaricious adventure, and unlimited, enduring oppression."

When historians like Eugene C. Barker challenged this conspiracy theory, they marshalled not so much new evidence as a new perspective. In fact, Barker acknowledged the southern, proslavery origins of many Anglo-Texans and their resistance in the name of progress to Mexican efforts to limit, exclude, or abolish slavery. He not only recognized other facts—the proslavery features of the constitution of the Republic of Texas, the military support that came from the southern United States, and the Texans' desire for annexation—but published evidence that, if known to Lundy, would have made the conspiracy theory seem irrefutable. On his way from Mexico to Texas in the summer of 1835, Stephen F. Austin had written to his cousin, "The best interests of the United States require that Texas shall be effectually, and fully, *Americanized. . . . Texas must be a slave country. It is no longer a matter of doubt.*" But like other "scientific" historians, Barker doubted the existence of a "slaveocracy" or the prevalence of proslavery crusading zeal among Texas revolutionaries. He asserted that the number of slaves and the frequency of

Paul Lack, "Slavery and the Texas Revolution, *Southwestern Historical Quarterly,* vol. 89 (October 1985): 182–202. Copyright Texas State Historical Association. Reprinted with permission.

Texan-Mexican disagreements over the status of slavery had both declined after 1830. Subsequent scholars have followed this lead so faithfully that they allude to the issue mostly to deride Lundy's theory. Barker's conclusion "that anxiety concerning the status of slavery [does not appear to have] played any appreciable part in producing the Texas revolution" has gone virtually unchallenged.

Whatever doubts they express about the significance of slavery as a causative factor in 1835–1836, historians have acknowledged that disputes over the institution served as a long-standing irritant in relations between Anglo settlers and Mexico. A sense of uncertainty had characterized the status of slavery from almost the beginning of North American colonization of Texas. Throughout the 1820s local authorities blunted repeated but indecisive antislavery measures enacted by the Mexican Congress. In 1822 and again in 1824 the Congress passed legislation to abolish the slave trade and gradually erode the institution. Anglo Texas leaders gained little legal relief by their arguments that these measures undermined economic progress, but they either muted the impact of these laws or simply ignored them. Even the state constitution, which recognized the legality of slavery, outlawed further importations and freed children born of slave parents. Texas memorials then persuaded the Coahuila legislature to sanction a bogus "contract" system allowing imports of bound labor. This apparently successful subterfuge evaporated suddenly on September 15, 1829, with the promulgation of a general emancipation decree by Mexican president Vicente Guerrero. An exemption for Texas was once again granted; however, the pattern of evasion by Texans created alarm regarding the governability of the province. On April 6 of the next year another decree ended all North American emigration to Texas, though it reconized the existence of slavery there.

The 1830s brought something of a respite from the barrage of antislavery measures of the previous decade, partly because of political instability in Mexico. Yet the status of the institution remained in doubt. In April, 1832, the legislature of Coahuila y Texas set a ten-year limitation on the length of labor contracts, thus jeopardizing the evasions of Texas slaveholders and indicating that abolitionist sentiment still prevailed among Mexican authorities. Realization of this fact helped spur a movement in Texas for separate statehood that originated in that year. Texans had blunted some of the effects of governmental hostility to slavery, but defense of the institution ultimately rested on sympathetic and weak local governments that failed to enforce antislavery measures. When a more powerful (authoritarian from the Texas perspective) government arose in Mexico, rebellion broke out. The immediate target of the resistance was John Davis Bradburn, commander at Anahuac. The insurgents included in their Declaration of Grievances a charge that he had encouraged and protected runaway slaves.

Clearly, critics like John Quincy Adams exaggerated in asserting that the Texas Revolution reestablished slavery "where it was abolished." Emigrants from the United States used the indenture system to bring forced labor into Texas, while masters bought, hired, and sold workers without regard for antislavery enactments. In no instance did bondsmen or women become free due to legal procedures. Mexican hostility toward slavery, however, did have some effect. Slaves in Texas had a measure of judicial privilege. Such as the right of petition. A knowledgeable observer like Mary Austin Holley believed that blacks were "invested with more liberty and [were] less liable to abuse" in Texas than in the United States. Flurries of antislavery legislation had other effects as well. The laws slowed the pace of American immigration and possibly the importation of blacks. An estimate from 1834 suggests that the number of slaves had grown at a slower rate than had the white population. Also, continual labor shortages lengthened the period of frontier conditions and retarded the growth of plantations, except for a few instances along the coast.

All things considered, however, Anglo immigrants seem not to have significantly modified their hopes or expectations of slavery, inhospitable laws and government disapprobation notwithstanding. Planters commonly considered their slaves "indispensable," as one traveler noted, and leaders of the province believed that cotton held the key to progress. When Anglo lawmakers came into power in places like Nacogdoches in the mid-1830s, the legal privilege conferred on bondsmen by Mexican law was quickly eroded. And Mexican inattention to slavery after 1830 allowed the institution to grow in at least one area: statistics for the Nacogdoches region reveal a spurt in the slave population between 1831 and 1835. . . .

As political tensions between Texas and the central government grew in the spring of 1835, Texans also began receiving warnings that traditional Mexican restraint with regard to slavery had come to an end. Francis W. Johnson sent a report from Monclova on May 6 concerning impending abolitionist legislation intended for application throughout the republic. "It does appear," he concluded, "that they will stop at nothing short of the ruin of Texas. . . ." William Barrett Travis considered this law as one of a series of "alarming circumstances" produced by "a plundering, robbing, autocratical, aristocratical, jumbled up govt which is in fact no govt at all. . . . There is no security for life, liberty, or property." News of Mexican military preparations created further fear that the expedition intended, in the words of Robert McAlpin Williamson, "to compel you to liberate your slaves" and accept other forms of dictatorial government. . . .

The approach of war was attended by more complaints about Mexican abolitionism and by heightened racial invective. A correspondent of the *Telegraph and Texas Register* pleaded for separation "from a people one half of whom are the most depraved of the different races of Indians, different in color" and inferior in character. From this it took but a short leap of imagination to transform the struggle into one between "Texian freemen" and slaves. "Will you now," John W. Hall asked the people of Texas, "suffer the *colored* hirelings of a cruel and faithless despot, to feast and revel, in your dearly purchased and cherished homes?" Lest any doubt remain about the racial and sexual nature of this reveling, Fannin called Texans to arms to prevent the prostitution of "the *Fair daughters* of chaste *white women.*" Given this view of the conflict as one between white and colored races, Anglo-Texans naturally feared slave insurrection. With "war now pending," William H. Wharton compiled a list of evidence of Mexican hostility toward Texas:

> With a sickly philanthropy worthy of the abolitionists of these United States, they have, contrary to justice, and to law, intermedled with our slave population, and have even impotently threatened . . . to emancipate them, and induce them to turn their arms against their masters.

The military events that soon transpired led many to fear that Mexican abolitionism was far from "impotent."

As early as 1828 the Mexican government had considered the relation between slave revolt and Texas independence. General Manuel de Mier y Terán, who believed that bondsmen experienced severe maltreatment and that they knew of the pro-emancipation intent of Mexican law, viewed the slaves as ripe for an uprising. But he argued against abolition, suggesting that the potential for a slave insurrection would restrain both the secession of Texas and the threat of invasion by the United States. Some subsequent officials believed that Mier y Terán had miscalculated. The government of Mexico dispatched Juan N. Almonte to Texas in 1833–34 with secret instructions to inform the slaves of their liberty under Mexican law and to promise them land as freedmen.

By the summer of 1835 many Anglo-Texans concluded that Mexico had acquired the will and power to implement an antislavery strategy. Reports circulated that Thomas M. Thompson, commander of the Mexican schooner of war *Correo,* had intended to impress and subsequently liberate "all the negro slaves in the country that he could get in his possession" when he sailed into Galveston Bay in late July. Even James H. C. Miller, a defender of the Mexican centralists who had believed the government's goals to be pacific, wrote to the people to warn of the Mexican invasion of Texas, which contemplated, among other evils, slave emancipation. More graphically, another Texan recently back from the interior of Mexico reported to the public that a large army had been dispatched. Its numerous oppressive policies included an intent to liberate the slaves and also to "let them loose upon their [the Anglo Texans'] families."

Benjamin R. Milam summarized the emerging consensus of opinion. He too warned that the troops headed for Texas to enforce the centralist constitution planned an unconventional warfare of recruiting Indians and attempting "if possible to get the slaves to revolt." Altogether these forces would "make a wilderness of Texas, and beggars of its inhabitants"; thus the constitutional quarrel had far-reaching implications. "If the Federal system is lost in Texas, what will be our situation? Worse than that of the most degraded slaves." As Milam noted, the political and military crisis posed by the triumph of Santa Anna and centralism in 1835 challenged more than the governmental theories of the Anglo Texans. Over the previous decade unpopular policies emanating from Mexico—whether on immigration, taxation, troop strength, or slavery—had been blunted by sympathetic local officials who ruled with considerable autonomy under the federalist system. This arrangement tacitly protected slavery, an institution that the central government had repeatedly, and officially, condemned. Despite the shroud of uncertainty that hung over it, slavery began to expand aggressively in the two or three years prior to 1835, as evidenced by the invigorated though illegal slave trade. From the Anglo Texan perspective the constitutional changes of that year once again threatened liberty and interrupted economic progress, their version of which included a system of slave labor. Texans took up arms in 1835 against a regime that apparently intended to undermine their political ideals, their emerging prosperity, and their understanding of social and racial peace. Clearly the challenge to slavery contributed to the Texas decision to resist the new order in Mexico. . . .

. . . [V]irtually all the preconditions for rebellion existed in Texas in 1835–1836. As frontiersmen, the slaves of this region had of necessity acquired skills with weapons that in this crisis could be turned against their masters. The slave ranks had recently grown in numbers with the importation of Africans, an element that frequently led uprisings throughout the Americas. The intellectual climate had filled with revolutionary rhetoric emphasizing freedom, rights, and liberty in the struggle against tyranny, despotism, and even slavery. Blacks had apparently acquired some familiarity with the emancipationist leanings of Mexico, which would have prepared them to embrace the invading force as an army of liberation. The internal divisions of the ruling authorities presented a real opportunity; only the whites' continued numerical superiority and success on the battlefield obstructed the chance for a more powerful black revolt.

Threats to slavery posed by political change in Mexico, military efforts to impose this new order, and the upheavals generated by war—these challenges dominated the thoughts of defenders of the institution during 1835 and 1836. Slaveowners also recognized the dangers represented by a growing international antislavery movement. Texas authorities acted quickly to discourage a northern "Abolition society" scheme to establish a free black colony in Texas in 1835, just as they had made their sentiments clear to Lundy on this matter two years earlier. Buoyed by this proslavery consensus, Texas law and constitution makers in 1835 and 1836 moved to the task of protecting property, including the ownership of human beings, while also emphasizing doctrines of freedom. Texas thus entered nationhood with a constitution that defined human rights in racial terms and also provided a long list of positive guarantees of slavery. In deference to world opinion and diplomatic necessity the document prohibited importation of blacks from places other than the United States. The African slave traffic had accelerated in 1835 and 1836, when at least eight vessels, carrying about 600 slaves from the West Indies, disembarked their cargoes at Gulf ports or river plantations. Those who debated the foreign slave trade considered it only as a problem of state; not a delegate expressed a trace of genuine humanitarian feeling for the slaves. The other racial question that drew the attention of the convention, the fate of free blacks, also grew out of concern for the protection of slavery. Texas masters believed that the presence of this class disrupted slave discipline and discouraged slaveholder migration. The constitution, by providing that "no free person of African descent. . . . shall be permitted to reside permanently in the republic, without the consent of Congress," gave the government a free hand to discourage any of this group from tampering with bondsmen.

The events of 1835 and 1836 had shaken slavery considerably, but in the end the Texas victory confirmed the institution. Furthermore, the pattern of race relations that emerged in this period persisted in subsequent years. Blacks continued to identify with Mexico as a force of freedom. Mexican military ventures in Texas and around the Rio Grande attracted the participation of former slaves. Runaways, especially those who fled in groups, still sought their liberty in Mexico in the years just after the Revolution. Troublesome as this outlet for freedom proved to be, white Texans also feared a far worse prospect—that abolitionists would provide financial support to Mexico for a renewal of the war along antislavery lines. . . .

The Texas movement for independence had a dual character in respect to slavery. Ideologically, the Texans displayed mostly reactionary impulses, despite their frequent and fervent identifications with the Spirit of '76. The practical-minded Anglo-Americans applied their version of liberty, equality, and democracy cautiously and only to themselves. This aspect of the Texas Revolution clearly owed a debt to the Great Reaction that swept the southern United States in the early 1830s. By then, radical worldwide abolitionism had also emerged, a development that fostered more reaction and thus reinforced the conservative emphasis on property, order, and white supremacy. However uncongenial in spirit toward black freedom, the Texas Revolution generated other forces—including armed conflict and internal dislocation—that temporarily challenged the slave-labor system and Anglo racial hegemony. Yet the brevity of the war and the sudden collapse of the Mexican invasion effort prevented the disintegration of slavery and allowed Texans three more decades to apply the doctrines of their southern heritage.

 F U R T H E R   R E A D I N G

Alwyn Barr, *Texans in Revolt: The Battle for San Antonio* (1990)
Holly Beacher Brear, *Inherit the Alamo: Myth and Ritual at an American Shrine* (1996)
William C. Davis, *Three Roads to the Alamo: The Lives of David Crockett, James Bowie, and William Barret Travis* (1998)
Ann Fears Crawford, ed., *Eagle: The Autobiography of Santa Anna* (1988)
Stephen Hardin, *Texian Iliad: A Military History of the Texas Revolution, 1835–1836* (1994)
Margaret Swett Henson, *Lorenzo de Zavala, the Pragmatic Idealist* (1996)
Paul D. Lack, *The Texas Revolutionary Experience: A Political and Social History, 1835–1836* (1992)
Jeff Long, *Duel of Eagles: The Mexican and U.S. Fight for the Alamo* (1990)
Timothy Matovina, *The Alamo Remembered: Tejano Accounts and Perspectives* (1995)
Mark E. Nackman, "The Making of the Texan Citizen-Soldier, 1835–1860," *Southwestern Historical Quarterly* 78 (January 1975)
Randy Roberts and James Olson, *A Line in the Sand: The Alamo in Blood and Memory* (2001)
Susan Schoelwer, *Alamo Images: Changing Perceptions of a Texas Experience* (1985)

CHAPTER
6

The Fragile Republic:
Building New Communities,
1836–1845

After the Battle of San Jacinto, most Anglo Texans assumed that Texas would be speedily annexed by the United States. By an overwhelming margin, Texas voters favored joining the Union in 1837, but the measure was defeated in the U.S. Congress by an antislavery faction that included former president John Quincy Adams. Texas was now obliged to make good on its claim as an independent, sovereign nation. Diplomatic recognition from the United States and the major powers of Europe soon followed. Mexico, on the other hand, continued to insist that Texas was a province in revolt, which it vowed to reconquer. Any attempt by the United States to annex Texas in the future, it warned, would be tantamount to a declaration of war.

During its brief, nine year existence, the fledgling nation was beset with problems. A worldwide depression that lasted into the 1840s severely limited the demand for cotton (the Republic's chief export), while the dire economic situation was aggravated by the government's inability to obtain foreign loans. Border hostilities with Mexico and the depredations of Indian tribes kept Texas's western frontier in a constant state of turmoil, discouraging immigration from the United States and Europe. Internal divisions within the Anglo Texan community also plagued the young republic, as the dissension which had characterized the revolutionary effort continued to undermine political stability and social order.

The challenges Texas faced as an independent nation—a prostrate economy, ethnic conflict, and political strife—all contributed to its reputation as a region where a frontier ethos of self-reliance prevailed. In the absence of well-established political and juridical institutions, according to this interpretation, Anglo Texans were obliged to fend for themselves, establishing a society characterized by a spirit of reckless, anti-authoritarian egalitarianism. Recently, however, some historians have been less inclined to view the Republic as a nation of unfettered individualism. For all their roughhewn qualities, Anglo Texans did not abandon Jacksonian cultural norms when they crossed the Sabine River, but continued to value social conformity and community obligation, much as they had done in the United

States. What effect, then, did frontier conditions have on the Jacksonian society that emerged in the nascent republic? How successfully did Anglo Texans recreate the world they had known in the United States? More broadly, does Texas deserve to be regarded as a legitimate experiment in nationhood—as Mark Nackman contends in his essay in Chapter One—or merely the westernmost fringe of an ever-expanding American empire?

✦ D O C U M E N T S

In the years immediately following the Revolution, the infant Republic seemed ripe with opportunity. In Document 1, an anonymous visitor to Texas in 1837 describes Houston City, a makeshift boom town that emerged almost overnight after the war along Buffalo Bayou. White settlers, lured by the prospect of cheap land, found an egalitarian culture characteristic of early nineteenth-century American frontier communities, one in which land scrip passed as legal tender and class formation had not yet occurred.

After the U. S. Congress rejected the Republic's overture of annexation in 1837, a number of Texas leaders argued that the new nation should now seek to carve a permanent niche for itself in the American southwest. The most prominent spokesman for Texas nationalism was Mirabeau Lamar, whose presidential inaugural address is excerpted in Document 2. Although the address does not refer specifically to the institution of slavery, Lamar, a slaveholder who had emigrated to Texas from Georgia, had become increasingly alarmed by the tenor of antislavery opinion in the Northern states, and the document should be read with this concern in mind. Lamar's call for an independent republic is consistent with the nationalist fervor in evidence in both the Americas and Europe during the mid-nineteenth century; many Anglo Texans, however, seem never to have abandoned their hope for annexation.

The Panic of 1837 dashed the hopes of an easy fortune for many, prompting the Texas Congress to pass the Homestead Exemption Act in 1839, presented in Document 2. One of the most progressive debtors' protection laws ever passed in North America, and widely copied by other states after Texas joined the Union, the Homestead Exemption Act reflected the egalitarian notion that debtors should be allowed the means to regain their financial independence despite economic hard times.

Anglo Texans sought to establish political hegemony over one of the most racially diverse populations in North America. Document 4 is an excerpt from the memoir of Noah Smithwick, who negotiated a treaty with the Comanche Indians in 1838 that was never ratified by the Texas Senate. In Document 5, Mary Maverick describes the pitched battle known as the Council House Fight that raged on the streets of San Antonio between Comanches and residents of the town in 1840, during which thirty-three Indians and seven townspeople were killed. Tejanos, unlike Native Americans, enjoyed basic rights of citizenship during the Republic period, but were frequently regarded with intense hostility by their Anglo neighbors. Continued clashes with Mexico did not improve the climate of racial suspicion. In the spring and fall of 1842, Mexican forces briefly captured San Antonio. Document 6, an excerpt from the memoir of San Antonio mayor Juan Seguin, reveals the problems many Tejanos faced in the aftermath of the Revolution. They now found themselves "foreigners in their native land."

The border war with Mexico prompted President Sam Houston to issue the bellicose proclamation presented in Document 7. Despite Houston's fiery rhetoric, many Texans believed that the president was lukewarm in his enthusiasm for an aggressive military campaign against Mexico, as illustrated by the poem penned by a Houston critic in Document 8. Opposition to Houston also intensified after his decision to remove the nation's capital from Austin to Houston City, as well as his public denunciations of Edwin Ward Moore, commander of the Texas fleet, who continued to prey on Mexican ships in 1843 even after he had been ordered to return to port.

1. An Anonymous Visitor Describes Land Speculation in Houston City, 1837

Houston, more properly called the city of Houston, as no place of less denomination exists in all Texas, is situated upon the south side of Buffalo Bayou, at least sixty feet above the water and about one hundred miles from the coast. The place stands upon the edge of a prairie which spreads out in a southerly direction to the timbers of the Brazos and on the east and west, after steering clear of the pines which flank the city in the shape of a crescent, to a great extent. The bayou immediately below the town assumes the most novel appearance. It does not exceed thirty yards in width but is very deep, with high steep banks covered with heavy dense timber, whose limbs interlock from the opposite sides, excluding the sun from its dark waters. It seems to wind its way under the earth until, encountering a high bluff immediately below the city, it divides off into two branches, fixing at the point of separation the head of all navigation. . . .

. . . The place was laid off during the winter and spring of 1837, as the future seat of government for at least four years to come, and when I arrived, in the latter part of March, the improvements consisted of a one story frame, two hundred feet or more in length, which had just been raised, intended by the enterprising proprietors for stores and public offices, several rough log cabins, two of which were occupied as taverns, a few linen tents which were used for groceries, together with three or four shanties made of poles set in the ground and covered and weatherboarded with rough split shingles. All, however, was bustle and animation. Hammers and axes were sounding in all directions, and I heard the trees falling around and saw some men engaged in laying the foundations of houses, others raising, and a number busily at work marking out the ground and preparing timber for a government house. I might say that here was concentrated all the energy and enterprise of Texas, for there were but few improvements making in any other portion of the Republic. Lots were selling at enormous prices, in some instances as high as four and five thousand dollars apiece. The spirit of speculation was afloat, which, as a false medium, distorted and displaced everything. . . .

. . . When the members of Congress saw the immense fortunes which were likely to be realized out of the sale of lots, they agitated the removal of the seat of government to some other part of the Republic. All concurred in the propriety of a change, but all disagreed from conflicting interests as to the place. Should Houston continue for any length of time to be the seat of government, it will be owing much to the fact that all the members of Congress cannot be accommodated in the change. The prospect of a removal will always operate to the disadvantage of the city, whether it ever took place or not, and that it is agitated at all is much owing to

---

Andrew Forest Muir, ed., *Texas in 1837, an Anonymous, Contemporary Narrative* (Austin: University of Texas Press, 1958), 26–36.

the course of the proprietors themselves. But notwithstanding all this, when I arrived, Houston was not only the center of most of the spirit and enterprise of Texas, but it seemed to be the focus of immigration from all directions, as it continued to be during the summer. Persons came pouring in until, in a short time, a floating population had collected of some four or five hundred people. Houses could not be built near as fast as required, so that quite a large number of linen tents were pitched in every direction over the prairie, which gave to the city the appearance of a Methodist camp-ground. Some of these tents, such as were used for groceries, were calculated to surprise one from their great size. A number of them measured more than a hundred feet each in circumference, with conical tops, thirty or forty feet in height supported by means of a pole in the center. . . .

During the summer, the money most in circulation was notes of the Louisiana and Mississippi banks and gold and silver. Notes upon most of the southern and middle states passed without difficulty. Bank paper was by no means scarce, as every person coming from the States, especially those who were called speculators, brought it with them in large quantities. But paper of all kinds vanished so soon as the great money embarrassments began to be seen and felt at home. Gold and silver too soon disappeared, being mostly gathered up by speculators to make their purchases of the Mexicans, who would receive no other money, or carried off by the gamblers. From such causes, money of all kinds became exceedingly scarce, which made the issue of shinplasters a matter of necessity. Congress has granted several bank charters, but as yet none has gone into operation, and from present appearances, none is likely soon to do so. A charter was created by the First Congress, with the most enormous powers, and which has been the subject of great excitement in Texas. I think there is little cause for alarm, however, as the act of incorporation requires that the bonus, *twenty thousand dollars,* should be paid within a limited time, which expired, if I have not forgotten, sometime in November last. From appearances in October, there was no probability that the money would be paid, notwithstanding the incorporators were composed of the most wealthy and influential men in the country, who made frequent attempts in person to negotiate for the amount in the United States. . . .

. . . I ought not to omit to mention the *modus operandi* of the speculator, who finds a fine field here for the exercise of his shrewdness and energies. Some were engaged in purchasing the discharges of the soldiers, each of whom is entitled, beyond his pay of eight dollars a month in government paper, to six hundred and forty acres of land for each six months' service and in proportion for a less period. For this he gets a certificate from the government. The discharged soldier comes to Houston, hungry and next to naked, with nothing but his claims upon the government, which his situation compels him to sell. If he gets ten per cent for his money scrip and fifty dollars for a six months' discharge, he receives quite as much as these claims were selling for during the summer. When the storm beaten soldier thus sees the reward of all his sufferings reduced to a few dollars, he has too much reason to lament over the time which he has worse than thrown away and often in despair gives himself up to total abandonment. Upon this subject I might say much, but as Texas may have need for more soldiers, it is well that I should be silent.

Another class of citizens were busy in buying what in the language of the country are called headrights. In order that the reader may understand what these are, I will add that the Constitution of Texas provides that all white males of a specified age who were in the country on the second of March, 1836, the date of the Declaration of Independence, provided such persons are married, shall be entitled to a league and labor of land and if single to one third of a league. As the land office has been closed since the commencement of the Revolution, these rights are nothing more than claims upon the government but are more valuable than soldiers' discharges or government land scrip, as the Constitution provides further that all such rights have a priority of location, for six months, when the office is opened. Such rights have been known to sell for twenty-five cents an acre and in some instances for much more. Those, however, who contracted to take such claims through all the legal steps necessary to procure a title from the government when the land office is opened, for the one half and pay all attendant expenses, made the safest and most profitable speculation.

2. Mirabeau Lamar Appeals to Texas Nationalism, November 10, 1838

There is . . . one question of the highest national concernment, on which I feel it a privilege and a duty to address myself to the great body of the people themselves. I mean the annexation of our country to the American union. Notwithstanding the almost undivided voice of my fellow-citizens at one time in favor of the measure, an[d] notwithstanding the decision of the national congress at its last session, inhibiting the chief magistrate from withdrawing the proposition at the cabinet of Washington, yet still I have never been able myself to perceive the policy of the desired connexion, or discover in it any advantage either c[i]vil, political or commercial, which could possibly result to Texas. But on the contrary a long train of consequences of the most appalling character and magnitude, have never failed to present themselves whenever I have entertained the subject, and forced upon my mind the unwelcome conviction, that the step once taken would produce a lasting regret, and ultimately prove as disastrous to our liberty and hopes, as the triumphant sword of the enemy. And I say this from no irreverence to the character and institutions of my native country, whose welfare I have ever desired, and do still desire above my individual happiness, but a deep and abiding gratitude to the people of Texas, as well as a fervent devotion to those sacred principles of government, whose defence invited me to this country, compel me to say that however strong be my attachment to the parent land, the land of my adoption must claim my highest allegiance and affection; her glory and happiness must be my paramount consideration, and I cannot allow myself to speak in any other than the language of freedom and frankness on all matters involving her safety, dignity and honor.

When I reflect upon the invaluable rights which Texas will have to yield up with the surrender of her Independence—the right of making either war or peace; the right of controlling the Indian tribes within her borders; the right of appropriating

---

Inaugural Address, November 10, 1838, Charles Gulick, ed., *The Papers of Mirabeau Lamar* (Austin: A. C. Baldwin; 1921–27), 2:319–321.

her public domain to purposes of education and internal improvements; of levying her own taxes; regulating her own commerce and forming her own alliances and treaties—when I view her divested of the most essential attributes of free government; reduced to the level of an unfelt fraction of a giant power; or peradventure divided into Territorial districts, with Governors and judges and excise men appointed from abroad to administer laws which she had no adequate voice in enacting, and to gather imposts for the benefit of those who levy them—when I look upon her, as she soon will be, the cornucopia of the world, pouring her abundant treasures into the lap of another people than her own; a tributary vassal to remote and uncongenial communities; communities as widely separated from her in pursuits as in distance, who are known to be opposed to her peculiar and essential interests, and who are daily sending forth their denunciations against her from the fire-side, the pulpit and the council chamber; and when I bear in mind that all this sacrifice of rights and dignity and character is to be made, for what! for the privilege of going into a union in which she carries wealth without proportional influence—for the glory of identifying her fortunes with a government in which a large portion of the inhabitants are alarmed for the safety of the very institution upon which her own hopes of happiness are based; a government embracing conflicting interests and irreconcilable prejudices with lasting causes of domestic quarrel, where Texas can hope for nothing but a participation in the strifes that distract the public councils, and [after] passing through many throes and convulsions be the means perhaps of producing or accelerating an awful catastrophe which none could be more ready to avert or sincerely deplore than herself—when I reflect upon these, the inevitable and fatal consequences of the proposed connection, and then turn from the dark and dreary picture to the contemplation of the high destiny that awaits our country; the great prosperity which lies within her attainment if sh[e] will but appreciate her natural advantages, and not part with the right of developing and controling her incalculable resources: when I view her vast extent of territory, stretching from the Sabine to the Pacific and away to the South West as far as the obstinacy of the enemy may render it necessary for the sword to make the boundary; embracing the most delightful climate and the richest soil in the world, and behold it all in the state of high cultivation and improvement—her mountains of minerals yielding their vast treasures to the touch of industry; her luxuriant pastures alive with flocks and herds, and her wide fields whitening with a staple commodity, in the production of which she can have no rival; with the whole world for her market; and then consider the noble purposes to which this immense and exhaustless wealth may be applied, in adorning and beautifying the country, providing for its safety and defence, endowing institutions for the spread of virtue, knowledge and the arts, and carrying to the door of every citizen of the Republic, peace, plenty, and protection—and when in addition to these glorious and grand results, I look still farther to the important improvements which she will be able to devise in government, and to the entire revolution which her example in free trade will effect in the commerce of other nations, emancipating it from the thralldom of tariff restrictions and placing it upon the high grounds of equitable reciprocity, all of which will as certainly flow from the maintainence of her present independent position as the sun courses the heavens. When I reflect upon these vast and momentous consequences, so fatal to liberty on the one hand and so fraught with happiness and glory on the other, I cannot regard the annexation of Texas to the American Union in any other light than as the grave of all her hopes of happiness and greatness; and if, contrary to the present aspect of affairs, the amalgamation shall ever hereafter take place, I shall feel that the blood of our ma[r]tyred heroes had been shed in vain—that we had riven the chains of Mexican despotism only to fetter our country with more indissoluble bonds, and that a young Republic just rising into high distinction among the nations of the earth, had been swallowed up and lost like a proud bark in a devouring vortex.

3. The Homestead Exemption Act Protects Debtors, January 26, 1839

AN ACT

Sec. 1. Be it enacted by the Senate and House of Representatives of the Republic of Texas in Congress assembled, That from and after the passage of this act, there shall be reserved to every citizen or head of a family in this Republic, free and independent of the power of a writ of fire facias, or other execution issuing from any court of competent jurisdiction whatever, fifty acres of land or one town lot, including his or her homestead, and improvements not exceeding five hundred dollars in value, all house hold and kitchen furniture, (provided it does not exceed in value two hundred dollars,) all implements of husbandry, (provided they shall not exceed fifty dollars in value,) all tools, apparatus and books belonging to the trade or profession of any citizen, five milch cows, one yoke of work oxen or one horse, twenty hogs, and one year's provisions.

4. Noah Smithwick Negotiates a Treaty with the Comanche Indians, 1838

The country [the Comanches] considered theirs by the right of inheritance; the game had been placed there for their food. In the true poetry of the simple child of the forest old Muguara said:

"We have set up our lodges in these groves and swung our children from these boughs from time immemorial. When game beats away from us we pull down our lodges and move away, leaving no trace to frighten it, and in a little while it comes back. But the white man comes and cuts down the trees, building houses and fences, and the buffalos get frightened and leave and never come back, and the Indians are left to starve, or, if we follow the game, we trespass on the hunting ground of other tribes and war ensues."

I suggested allotting them land and furnishing them with means to cultivate it like white men.

H. P. N. Gammel, comp., *The Laws of Texas, 1822–1897* (Austin: Gammel Book Co., 1898), 2:125–126.

Noah Smithwick, *Evolution of a State, or Recollections of Old Texas Days* (Austin: University of Texas Press, 1990), 134, 139, 151–154.

"No," said he emphatically, "the Indians were not made to work. If they build houses and try to live like white men they will all die. If the white men would draw a line defining their claims and keep on their side of it the red men would not molest them." . . .

We finally fixed up a treaty, the provisions of which I do not remember, nor is it essential since they were never complied with by either party. One article of the treaty stipulated that a trading post should be established on Brushy [Creek] at the site of the old Tumlinson block house, where the Indians could come and get supplies. They were fast becoming civilized in that respect, bartering buffalo robes and buckskins for blankets and clothing. . . .

Open hostilities ceased for a time, however, and gave the settlers a chance to quarrel among themselves. Dissensions arose, and, lulled by the fancied security, the more venturesome spirits pushed further out, exciting anew the distrust of the Indians. Then, when the time in which the trading post was to have been established passed, and they came in with their skins to trade and found no trading house, they came to call on me to know why the treaty had not been complied with. As there was no plausible excuse for the failure, they held me responsible, saying I had lied to them, which, of course, destroyed any influence I might have previously exercised over them, and the irrepressible conflict recommenced with redoubled vigor. . . .

In 1838 the land office was opened and speculators began flocking into the country, accompanied by surveyors, who at once began an aggressive movement upon the hunting grounds of the wild tribes, thereby provoking them to a more determined resistance to the encroachments of the settlers. Then, too, the Mexican government egged them on, furnishing them with arms and ammunition. It was the same old story of the troubles of the frontiersmen everywhere and destined to the same finale—the survival of the fittest.

True, the Indian mode of indiscriminate warfare was barbarous, but there were not wanting white men to follow their example. Extermination was the motto on both sides. That was President Lamar's avowed policy and Colonel Moore carried it out when he attacked their camp over on the Red fork of the Colorado in 1843. There was a man in Bastrop county whose family had been slaughtered by the Cherokees in the United States, for which he swore eternal vengeance on Indians in toto. He came to Texas and never let an opportunity pass to get a scalp, regardless of the consequences it might entail on others. He was several times apprehended for killing friendly Indians, but could never be convicted.

5. Mary Maverick Describes the Council House Fight Between Comanches and San Antonio Residents, 1840

On Tuesday, 19th of March, 1840, "dia de San Jose" sixty-five Comanches came into town to make a treaty of peace. They brought with them, and reluctantly gave up, Matilda Lockhart, whom they had captured with her younger sister in December 1838, after killing two other children of her family. The Indian chiefs and men met

Rena Maverick Green, ed., *Memoirs of Mary Maverick,* (Lincoln: University of Nebraska Press, 1989), 106–113.

in council at the Court House, with our city and military authorities. The calaboose or jail then occupied the corner formed by the east line of Main Plaza and the north line of Calabosa (now Market) Street, and the Court House was north of and adjoining the jail. The Court House yard, back of the Court House, was what is now the city market on Market Street. The Court House and jail were of stone, one story, flat roofed, and floored with dirt. Captain Tom Howard's Company was at first in the Court House yard, where the Indian women and boys came and remained during the pow-wow. The young Indians amused themselves shooting arrows at pieces of money put up by some of the Americans; and Mrs. Higginbotham and myself amused ourselves looking through the picket fence at them.

This was the third time these Indians had come for a talk, pretending to seek peace, and trying to get ransom money for their American and Mexican captives. Their proposition was that they should be paid a great price for Matilda Lockhart, and a Mexican they had just given up, and that traders be sent with paint, powder, flannel, blankets and such other articles as they should name, to ransom the other captives. This course had once before been asked and carried out, but the smallpox breaking out, the Indians killed the traders and kept the goods—believing the traders had made the smallpox to kill them. Now the Americans, mindful of the treachery of the Comanches, answered them as follows: "We will according to a former agreement, keep four or five of your chiefs, whilst the others of your people go to your nation and bring all the captives, and then we will pay all you ask for them. Meanwhile, these chiefs we hold we will treat as brothers and 'not one hair of their heads shall be injured.' This we have determined, and, if you try to fight, our soldiers will shoot you down."

This being interpreted, the Comanches instantly, with one accord raised a terrific war-whoop, drew their arrows, and commenced firing with deadly effect, at the same time making efforts to break out of the council hall. The order "fire" was given by Captain Howard, and the soldiers fired into the midst of the crowd, the first volley killing several Indians and two of our own people. All soon rushed out into the public square, the civilians to procure arms, the Indians to flee, and the soldiers in pursuit. The Indians generally made for the river—they ran up Soledad, east on Commerce Street and for the bend, now known as Bowen's, southeast, below the square. Citizens and soldiers pursued and overtook them at all points, shot some swimming in the river, had desperate fights in the streets—and hand to hand encounters after firearms had been exhausted. Some Indians took refuge in stone houses and fastened the doors. Not one of the sixty-five Indians escaped—thirty-three were killed and thirty-two were taken prisoners. . . .

When the deafening war-whoop sounded in the Court room, it was so loud, so shrill and so inexpressibly horrible and suddenly raised, that we women looking through the fence at the women's and boy's markmanship for a moment could not comprehend its purport. The Indians however knew the first note and instantly shot their arrows into the bodies of Judge Thompson and the other gentleman near by, instantly killing Judge Thompson. We fled into Mrs. Higginbotham's house and I, across the street to my Commerce Street door. Two Indians ran past me on the street and one reached my door as I got in. He turned to raise his hand to push it just as I beat down the heavy bar; then he ran on. I ran in the north room and saw my husband and brother Andrew sitting calmly at a table inspecting some plats of surveys—they had heard nothing. I soon gave them the alarm, and hurried on to look for my boys. Mr. Maverick and Andrew seized their arms, always ready—Mr. Maverick rushed into the street, and Andrew into the back yard where I was shouting at the top of my voice "Here are Indians!" "Here are Indians!" Three Indians had gotten in through the gate on Soledad street and were making direct for the river! One had paused near Jinny Anderson, our cook, who stood bravely in front of the children, mine and hers, with a great rock lifted in both hands above her head, and I heard her cry out to the Indian "If you don't go 'way from here I'll mash your head with this rock!" The Indian seemed regretful that he hadn't time to dispatch Jinny and her brood, but his time was short, and pausing but a moment, he dashed down the bank into the river. and struck out for the opposite shore.

As the Indian hurried down the bank and into the river Andrew shot and killed him, and shot another as he gained and rose on the opposite bank,—then he ran off up Soledad street looking for more Indians.

I housed my little ones, and then looked out of the Soledad Street door. Near by was stretched an Indian, wounded and dying. A large man, journey-apprentice to Mr. Higginbotham, came up just then and aimed a pistol at the Indian's head. I called out: "Oh, don't, he is dying," and the big American laughed and said: "To please you, I won't, but it would put him out of his misery." Then I saw two others lying dead near by.

Captain Lysander Wells, about this time, passed by riding north on Soledad Street. He was elegantly dressed and mounted on a gaily caparisoned Mexican horse with silver mounted saddle and bridle—which outfit he had secured to take back to his native state, on a visit to his mother. As he reached the Verimendi House, an Indian who had escaped detection, sprang up behind him, clasped Wells' arms in his and tried to catch hold of the bridle reins. Well was fearless and active. They struggled for some time, bent back and forward, swayed from side to side, till at last Wells held the Indian's wrists with his left hand, drew his pistol from the holster, partly turned, and fired into the Indian's body—a moment more and the Indian rolled off and dropped dead to the ground. Wells then put spurs to his horse which had stood almost still during the struggle, dashed up the street and did good service in the pursuit. I had become so fascinated by this struggle that I had gone into the street almost breathless, and wholly unconscious of where I was, till recalled by the voice of Lieutenant Chavallier who said: "Are you crazy? Go in or you will be killed." I went in but without feeling any fear, though the street was almost deserted and my husband and brother both gone in the fight. I then looked out on Commerce street and saw four or five dead Indians. I was just twenty-two then, and was endowed with a fair share of curiosity.

Not till dark did all our men get back, and I was grateful to God, indeed, to see my husband and brother back alive and not wounded.

Captain Mat Caldwell, or "Old Paint," as he was familiarly called, our guest from Gonzales, was an old and famous Indian fighter. He had gone from our house to the Council Hall unarmed. But when the fight began, he wrenched a gun from an Indian and killed him with it, and beat another to death with the butt end of the gun. He was shot through the right leg, wounded as he thought by the first volley of the soldiers. After breaking the gun, he then fought with rocks, with his back to the Court House wall. . . .

. . . Captain Caldwell was assisted back to our house and Dr. Weiderman came and cut off his boot and found the bullet had gone entirely through the leg, and lodged in the boot, where it was discovered. The wound, though not dangerous, was very painful, but the doughty Captain recovered rapidly and in a few days walked about with the aid of a stick.

After the captain had been cared for, I ran across to Mrs. Higginbotham's. Mr. Higginbotham, who was as peaceful as a Quaker to all appearances, had been in the fight and had received a slight wound. They could not go into their back yard, because two Indians had taken refuge in their kitchen, and refused to come out or surrender as prisoners when the interpreter had summoned them. A number of young men took counsel together that night, and agred upon a plan. Anton Lock-mar and another got on the roof, and, about two hours after midnight dropped a candlewick ball soaked in turpentine, and blazing, through a hole in the roof upon one Indian's head and so hurt him and frightened them both that they opened the door and rushed out—to their death. An axe split open the head of one of the In-dians before he was well out of the door, and the other was killed before he had gone many steps—thus the last of the sixty-five were taken.

6. Juan Seguín Flees to Mexico After the Vásquez Invasion, 1842

After the retreat of the Mexican army under Santa Anna, until Vásquez' invasion in 1842, the war between Texas and Mexico ceased to be carried on actively. Al-though open commercial intercourse did not exist, it was carried on by smuggling, at which the Mexican authorities used to wink provided it was not carried on so openly as to oblige them to notice it, or so extensively as to arouse their avarice.

In the beginning of this year I was elected mayor of San Antonio. Two years previously a gunsmith named James Goodman had taken possession of certain houses, situated on the Military Plaza, which were the property of the city. He used to shoe the horses of the volunteers who passed through San Antonio. Thus the Re-public owed him a debt, for the payment of which he applied to the president to give him possession of the buildings referred to, which had always been known as city property.

The board of aldermen passed a resolution to the effect that Goodman should be compelled to leave the premises. Goodman resisted, alleging that the houses had been given to him by the president, in payment for public services. The board could not, of course, acknowledge any power of the president to dispose of the city property and, consequently, directed me to carry the resolution into effect. My compliance with the instructions of the board caused Goodman to become my most bitter and inveterate enemy in the city.

Juan Seguín, *A Revolution Remembered: The Memoirs and Selected Correspondence of Juan Seguín.* Jesús de la Teja, ed. (Austin: State House Press, 1991), 73–74; 92–100. Edited version of the memoirs reprinted by permission of the editor, Jesús F. de la Teja.

The term for the mortgage, that Messrs. Ogden and Howard held on my property, had run out. In order to raise money and comply with my obligations, I determined to go to Mexico for a drove of sheep. But, fearful that this new trip would prove as fatal as the one already alluded to, I wrote to General Rafael Vásquez, who was then in command of the Mexican frontier, requesting him to give me a pass. The tenor of Vásquez' answer caused me to apprehend that an expedition against Texas was in preparation for the following month of March.

I called a session of the board of aldermen (of which the Hon. Samuel A. Maverick was a member) and laid before them the communication of General Vásquez, stating that according to my interpretation of the letter we might soon expect the approach of the Mexicans. A few days afterwards Don José María García, of Laredo, came to San Antonio. His report was so detailed as to preclude all possible doubts as to the imminent approach of Vásquez to San Antonio.

Notice of the impending danger was sent immediately to the government. In the various meetings held to devise means of defense, I expressed my candid opinion as to the impossibility of defending San Antonio. I observed that, for myself, I was going to the town of Seguin and advised everyone to do the same.

On leaving the city, I passed through a street where some men were making breastworks. I told them I was going to my rancho and thence to Seguin, in case the Mexican forces should take possession of San Antonio.

From the Nueces River, Vásquez forwarded a proclamation by Arista to the inhabitants of Texas. At my rancho I received a bundle of those proclamations, which I transmitted at once to the municipality of San Antonio.

As soon as Vásquez entered the city, those who had been determined to defend the place withdrew to Seguin. Among them were James Dunn and Chevallie, both of whom had succeeded in escaping from the Mexican hands into which they had fallen while on a reconnoitering expedition on the Medina River. . . .

On my return to San Antonio, several persons told me that the Mexican officers had declared that I was on their side. This rumor, and some threats uttered against me by Goodman, left me but little doubt that my enemies would try to ruin me.

Some of the citizens of San Antonio had taken up arms on the side of the enemy. Judge John Hemphill advised me to have them arrested and tried but, as I was starting out with the party that was to go in pursuit of the Mexicans, I could not follow his advice.

Having observed that Vásquez gained ground on us, we fell back on the Nueces River. When we came back to San Antonio, reports about my implausible treason were spreading widely. Captain Manuel Flores, Lieutenant Ambrosio Rodríguez, Matías Curbier and five or six other Mexicans joined me to find out the origin of the false rumors. I went out with several friends, leaving Curbier in my house. I had reached the Main Plaza when several persons came running to inform me that some Americans were murdering Curbier. We ran back to the house where we found poor Curbier covered with blood. On being asked who assaulted him he answered that the gunsmith Goodman, in company with several Americans, had struck him with a rifle. A few minutes later Goodman returned to my house with about thirty volunteers but, observing that we were prepared to meet them, they did not attempt to attack us. We went out of the house and then to Mr. Francois Guilbeau's, who offered me his protection. He went out into the street, pistol in hand, and succeeded in dispersing the mob which had formed in front of my house. Mr. John Twohig offered me a shelter for that night. The next morning, I went under disguise to Mr. Van Ness' house. Twohig, who recognized me in the street, warned me to "keep my eyes open." I remained one day at Mr. Van Ness'.

The next day General Edward Burleson arrived at San Antonio, commanding a respectable force of volunteers. I presented myself to him, asking for a court of inquiry. He answered that there were no grounds for such proceedings. In the evening I went to the camp and, jointly with Colonel William H. Patton, received a commission to forage for provisions in the lower ranchos. I complied with this assignment.

I remained, hiding from rancho to rancho for over fifteen days. All the parties of volunteers en route to San Antonio declared "they wanted to kill Seguín." I could no longer go from rancho to rancho, and determined to go to my own rancho and fortify it. Several of my relatives and friends joined me. Hardly a day elapsed without receiving notice that a party was preparing to attack me; we were constantly kept under arms. Several parties came in sight but, probably seeing that we were prepared to receive them, refrained from attacking. . . .

Matters being in this state, I saw that it was necessary to take some step which would place me in security and save my family from constant wretchedness. I had to leave Texas, abandon all for which I had fought and spent my fortune, to become a wanderer. The ingratitude of those who had assumed onto themselves the right of convicting me, their credulity in declaring me a traitor on the basis of mere rumors, the necessity to defend myself for the loyal patriotism with which I had always served Texas, wounded me deeply. . . .

. . . I sent in my resignation as mayor of the city to the municipality of San Antonio, stating to them that, unable any longer to suffer the persecutions of some ungrateful Americans who strove to murder me, I had determined to free my family and friends from their continual misery on my account, and go and live peaceably in Mexico. That for these reasons I resigned my office, with all my privileges and honors as a Texan.

I left Béxar with no obligation to Texas, my services repaid with persecutions. Exiled and deprived of my privileges as a Texan citizen, I was outside the pale of society in Texas. If Texas could not protect the rights of her citizens, they were privileged to seek protection elsewhere. I had been tried by a rabble, condemned without a hearing, and consequently was at liberty to provide for my own safety.

When I arrived at Laredo the military commander of that place put me in prison, stating that he could not do otherwise until he had consulted with General Arista, whom he advised of my arrest. Arista ordered that I be sent to Monterrey. When I arrived in that city, I earnestly prayed the general to allow me to retire to Saltillo, where I had several relatives who could aid me. General Arista answered that, as he had informed Santa Anna of my imprisonment, he could not comply with my request. Santa Anna directed that I be sent to the City of Mexico but Arista, sympathetic to my unfortunate position, interceded with him in my behalf to have the order revoked. The latter complied, but on condition that I should return to Texas with a company of explorers to attack its citizens and, by spilling my blood, vindicate myself.

Under the orders of General Arista, I proceeded to the Rio Grande to join General Woll, who told me that Santa Anna, at his request, had allowed me to go to Texas with Woll's expedition, but that I should receive no command until my services proved that I was worthy.

I set out with the expedition of General Woll. In the vicinity of San Antonio, on the 10th of September, I received an order to take a company of cavalry and block the exits from the city. By this order the city was blockaded and, consequently, it was difficult for any person to escape. When I returned from complying with this order, at dawn of day, the general determined to enter the city with the infantry and artillery. I was sent to the vanguard with orders to take possession of the Military Square despite all obstacles. I entered the square without opposition and, shortly afterwards, the firing commenced on the Main Square. John Hernández came out of Goodman's shop with a message from him to the effect that if I would pardon him for what he had done against me he would leave his place of concealment and deliver himself up. I sent him word that I had no rancor against him. He delivered himself up, and I placed him under the special charge of Captain Manuel Leal. Those who had made some show of resistance in the Main Square surrendered, and the whole city was in General Woll's possession.

The next day I was ordered, with two hundred men, to take the Gonzales road and approach that town. On the Cibolo I divided my forces, sending one detachment up the creek, another down the creek, and with the main body proceeded on the Gonzales road. The following day, these parties joined the main body. Lieutenant Manuel Carvajal, who commanded one of the parties, reported that he had killed three Texans who would not surrender in the Azufrosa [Sulphur Springs].

I returned to San Antonio. A party of Texans appeared by the Garita road and the troops were taken under arms. The general took one hundred infantry, the cavalry under Cayetano Montero, and one piece of artillery and proceeded towards the Salado. The general ordered one hundred *presidiales* [former garrison soldiers from Texas] to attack. The commander of those forces sent word that the enemy was in an advantageous position and that he required reinforcements. The answer of the general was to send me with orders "to attack at all costs." I obeyed. On the first charge I lost three killed and eight wounded, on the second seven killed and fifteen wounded. I was preparing for a third charge when Colonel José María Carrasco came to relieve me from my command. I returned to the side of the general and made my report, whereupon he ordered the firing to cease.

A new attack was in preparation when the attention of the general was called to some troops on our rear guard. The aides reported them to be enemies and near at hand. Colonel Montero was ordered to attack them with his cavalry. He called on them to surrender to the Mexican Government; they answered with scoffing and bantering. Montero formed his dragoons; the Texans commenced firing, killing two soldiers. Montero dismounted his troops, also began firing, and sent for more ammunition. The general angrily sent him a message asking whether his dragoons had no sabres or lances. Before Montero received this answer he had charged, sabre in hand, ending the engagement in a few minutes. Only some ten or fifteen Texans survived. During this time, I remained by the side of General Woll and was there when Montero made his report and brought in the prisoners. At dusk the troops received orders to return to San Antonio.

In accordance with his orders not to remain over a month on this side of the Rio Grande, General Woll began his retreat by the road he came. . . .

After General Woll's expedition I did not return to Texas until the treaty of Guadalupe Hidalgo.

7. Sam Houston Threatens Reprisals Against Mexico, March 21, 1842

To His Excellency Antonio Lopez de Santa Anna, President of Mexico:

. . . You touchingly invite Texas to "cover herself anew with the Mexican flag." You certainly intend this as a mockery. You denied us the enjoyment of the laws under which we came to the country. Her flag was never raised in our behalf nor has it been seen in Texas except when displayed in an attempt at our subjugation. We know your lenity—we know your mercy—we are ready again to test your power. You have threatened to plant your banner on the banks of the Sabine. Is this done to intimidate us? Is it done to alarm us? Or do you deem it the most successful mode of conquest? If the latter, it may do to amuse the people surrounding you. If to alarm us, it will amuse those conversant with the history of your last campaign. If to intimidate us, the threat is idle. We have desired peace. You have annoyed our frontier; you have harassed our citizens; you have incarcerated our traders, after your commissioners had been kindly received, and your citizens allowed the privilege of commerce in Texas without molestation. You continue aggression; you will not accord us peace. *We will have it.* You threaten to conquer Texas; we will war with Mexico. Your pretentions with ours you have referred to the social world, and to the God of battles. We refer to the same tribunals—the issue involves the fate of nations. Destiny must determine—its event is only known to the tribunal of heaven. If experience of the past will authorize speculations of the future, the attitude of Mexico is more problematical than that of Texas.

In the war which will be conducted by Texas against Mexico, our incentive will not be a love of conquest; it will be to disarm tyranny of its power. We will make no war upon Mexicans or their religion. Our efforts shall be made in behalf of the liberties of the people; and directed against the authorities of the country, and against your principles. We will exalt the condition of the people to representative freedom. They shall choose their own rulers—they shall possess their property in peace; and it shall not be taken from them to support an armed soldiery for the purpose of oppression. With these principles we will march across the Rio Grande, and, believe me, Sir, ere the banner of Mexico shall triumphantly float upon the banks of the Sabine, the Texian standard of the single star, borne by the Anglo-Saxon race, shall display its bright folds in Liberty's triumph, on the isthmus of Darien. . . .

Sam Houston.

Houston to Santa Anna, March 21, 1842, Eugene Barker and Amelia Williams, eds., *Houston Writings*, 2:513–527.

8. A Texan Mocks the Houston Administration's Military Record, 1843

Twelve months have passed, since the war blast,
Blown by Sam's threatening letter;
Whose valor found no resting ground,
This side of the Equator.

Then did he swear, that he would bear,
To Darien our Banner—
Yet his Religion, *now* takes in dudgeon
All war with Santa Anna.

Some say his courage cooled off like porridge
By oosing through his quill;
And some again, say that he can
Write like a hero still.

He's doubtless read, "Who wields the sword
Shall by the sword be slain."
But who by writing, does his fighting,
Shall live to fight again.

He counts the cost—the millions lost
Orphans and widows made—
And he found paper, and ink much cheaper
Than powder, steel and lead.

To doubt his force, in war, of course
Is wanton defamation,
Since he blockades, likewise invades
With many a *Proclamation.*

"Who arms dare wield, by flood or field
Are pirates and highwaymen."—
Such must prepare, to feel his ire
And hang as high as Haman.

Then let him spill by mouth and quill
The blood of all our foes,
And batter down each walled town
With overwhelming prose.

No fleet does he, require at sea—
No army on the shore,
But just to kill, our *Capital,*
And hang our gallant *Moore.*

Untitled Poem, *Morning Star* (Houston), June 6, 1843.

❦ E S S A Y S

In the first essay, the late historian William Ransom Hogan, writing in the 1940s, describes Anglo-Texan society during the Lone Star Republic as a bastion of frontier individualism. Borrowing from the triumphalist tradition of Walter Prescott Webb, Eugene Barker, and others, Hogan views the frontier as a space that liberated its white inhabitants from the constraints of established society, an inhospitable environment that forced them to rely on individual initiative and their own resources.

Sam Houston has often been viewed as one of the great exemplars of this frontier ethos. Yet in the second essay by Sam W. Haynes, associate professor at the University of Texas at Arlington, the famed hero of San Jacinto and twice-elected president of the Republic is viewed as a man at odds with the deeply felt community values of his era. The deep-seated, almost rabid hostility which his political enemies felt toward Houston, Haynes argues, is rooted in the Texan leader's penchant for self-aggrandizement. Later generations may have admired Houston's flamboyance, as well as his willingness to make unpopular decisions as both a military and a political leader, but his contemporaries often regarded these same qualities as character flaws. Thus, while Hogan emphasizes a spirit of individualism, Haynes suggests that historians have often failed to appreciate the social dynamics of the Jacksonian community, instead viewing the early years of Anglo Texan settlement by their own modern values.

Frontier Individualism and the Texas Republic

WILLIAM RANSOM HOGAN

In February, 1846, when Dr. Anson Jones performed his last official act as president of the Republic of Texas, an old settler could look back upon a decade of partial frustration and disillusion in his economic affairs. To be sure, many changes had occurred. The population of the country had more than quadrupled since 1836. Cotton production was perhaps ten times as great. The line of settlement had been pushed west of the modern cities of Dallas, Waco, Austin, and San Antonio in the face of possible Indian raids and Mexican invasions. Schools, newspapers, and incipient industries had been established. Striking contrasts between the crude and the luxurious had appeared in some of the towns. But these changes did not mean that the ordinary Texan had profited greatly. On the contrary, sound economic growth of his country had been seriously retarded first by a convulsion of speculation and then by the ravages of a devastating financial depression. Immediately following the end of the false boom in lands and townsites, both the government and its citizenry in 1840 had found themselves "land poor" and cruelly afflicted with a disorganized monetary system. The collapse of unsound real-estate values had coincided roughly with governmental issuance of large quantities of paper money, which promptly had undergone violent depreciation. Even in the towns there had been a widespread reversion to barter, which never had been wholly abandoned, as the method of exchange. In the summer of 1842 a leading newspaper had dolefully

William Ransom Hogan, *A Social and Economic History of the Republic of Texas* (Austin: University of Texas Press, 1969), 292–298. Copyright © University of Oklahoma Press. Reprinted with permission.

confessed: "A general gloom seems to rest over every section of the Republic, and doubt and sorrow are depicted on almost every brow."

Aside from dependence on selling land, the Republic's hopes for immediate economic salvation rested upon the exportation of cotton, some cattle, and a few hides. Texas was inescapably an agricultural country; the river valleys and the prairies contained very fertile cotton lands, and cattle were easily raised. But the expectations of most farmers were thwarted in several directions. Though the opinion was widely held that Negro slaves were needed for success in cotton culture, a large majority of Texas farmers were not able to buy even one. In addition to suffering the handicap of an inadequate labor force, they relearned the age-old lesson that farming was an uncertain undertaking which provided no assurance of reasonable returns; some Texas cotton drew the lowest prices in a low-price era because it was found difficult to prepare it properly for the market under frontier conditions, and in the early eighteen forties cotton and corn crops partially failed in two successive seasons. Finally, transporting the staple to shipping points was a time-consuming and onerous task.

Oxen still pulled a large part of Texas cotton to export centers through the mire of unimproved roads. A few steamboats and keelboats negotiated the often obstreperous, snag-blocked rivers, but the inland waterways were largely a failure as a medium of transportation. Although there was much talk of constructing highways, railroads, and canals, few internal improvements resulted. This failure to develop more advanced transportation facilities not only tended to accentuate sectional differences between the eastern and western counties but made stress upon cotton production almost inevitable. More perishable farm products could not have been as safely hauled and stored, and markets for them had not been developed.

Thus the Republic of Texas in the early eighteen forties was virtually impoverished. Its internal transportation system still was largely primitive. Many of its plans for achieving rapid economic maturity came to nothing. What, then, held it together?

Texans felt that their country had struck bottom during the depression years, that any buffeting that the future might bring could not be worse than what had gone before. Like frontiersmen everywhere, most of them were people of unhesitant faith, and their materialism was always tinged with visions of things hoped for in a world that was not only competitive but adventurous and quickly changing. Even new inventions, such as the Colt revolver, were reaching the frontier more rapidly than in an earlier day.

Meanwhile, settlers of both sexes were practicing the art of roughhewing civilization in a semiwooded wilderness, an art that had been almost perfected by past pioneer generations. Many of the women were vigorous products of one or more generations of frontier life, they had been trained from childhood to do their jobs, and they were able to bear hardships. The evidence is strong that most women were both busy and happy, and that they rarely voiced the complaints which some modern historians chivalrously assume that they often made. Even in an economic depression, participation in the process of creating a new country tended to produce resilient spirits and strong muscles.

The poverty of the frontier family undoubtedly differed from the abject poverty of the poorly paid urban artisan of the eastern seaboard. The possessions in a cabin might be few, but they had been fashioned on the adamantine anvil of experience, and they were cherished and owned in a very real sense. Shelter, food, and clothing could always be obtained. Life could be sustained regardless of the price of cotton, and hopes that the future would bring increased security and added value to land-holdings were never abandoned.

The broad distribution of land ownership—an inheritance from the liberal policy of the Mexican regime, reinforced by the typically Western demand for free land—did much to alleviate the pain of the depression years, because ownership of land in this period of American history was viewed as "the key to happiness." The chief source of agrarian discontent arose from uncertainty concerning land titles, and in this matter the government took vigorous steps to rectify an alarming situation.

Although professional speculators partially succeeded in withholding some of the best lands from immediate settlement, their activities in the Republic were hampered by several circumstances. Since the national government, which con-trolled the public domain, was close to the people, the antispeculation sentiment of the "real cultivators"—who constituted the mass of the electorate—was suffi-ciently strong not only to secure constitutional guarantees but also to force any politician to think twice before openly associating himself with a land-grabbing scheme. The antispeculation sections of the Republic's constitution, including one which specifically prohibited aliens from acquiring land titles except directly from the government, dealt a blow to rapacious moneyed interests in the United States who hoped to achieve extraordinary returns from unearned increment in Texas land ventures. Thereafter, any attempted land grab involving any group of politicians within the Republic also was subject to condemnation by an opposition group, al-though neither might be wholly blameless. Moreover, the monetary tightness of the early eighteen forties forced many of the resident "land sharks" to sell their lands. The depression also combined with antagonistic public opinion to cause the Texas Rail-Road, Navigation and Banking Company—considered "the biggest steal ever attempted in Texas" by one historian—to fold up before it began operations.

Large-scale land speculation, commonly condemned by historians of the Amer-ican West, was not an unmixed evil in the Republic of Texas. Although McKinney, Williams and Company of Galveston and the Allen brothers of Houston acquired thousands of acres of land, they also contributed largely to the development of two important towns, started industries, operated steamboats, set up credit facilities, and established channels for the inflow of productive capital. Matthew Cartwright of San Augustine eventually realized a fortune from land purchases, but he was also a prominent and highly respected merchant who supported many worthwhile local causes. Merchandise firms in nearly every town acquired land at the same time that they combined the functions of banker, shipper, middleman, and retailer. The Mills brothers of Brazoria carried on all of these activities and also became large-scale cotton producers, while members of two leading San Augustine firms, I. D. Thomas and Blount and Price, operated plantations. Regardless of the exten-sive land acquisitions of some of these firms, they constituted the backbone of the financial and commercial structure of the country.

The public-land system furnished one of the original mainsprings of the in-tense Texas nationalism that has never subsided. Whereas frontier titles elsewhere emanated from a distant federal government in Washington, free land was obtained in the Republic of Texas from a national government that was close at hand. Most citizens, moreover, were proud that their Republic had shown ability to maintain itself in the face of staggering obstacles, that their laboratory experiment in self-government was proving workable. A sense of participation in the task of "helping to rear up our infant republic" permeated the thinking of all classes. Whether the first professional theater was being opened or the first rail was being laid in a prospective railroad, the orator of the occasion or the local newspaper editor invariably dramatized the event in terms of historical beginnings. This was a popular note, for Texans believed that there was a certain admirable singularity about their frontier commonwealth and that they themselves were a part of history in the making.

While citizens of the Republic demanded that their government see that "all start fair," they were perfectly willing to maintain freedom on a competitive basis, and the pressures of potential insecurity were never so great that they drove the people to any form of collectivism or utopian experiment. On the other hand, cooperative action freely taken by individuals was common. Newly arrived immigrants were aided by houseraisings and similar neighborly frolics. When the Indians or Mexicans threatened, the exodus of volunteers who hurried to join the ranks left whole towns without able-bodied males. Local meetings occasionally expressed community sentiment in regard to political or economic questions, and important political decisions were made by conventions which were proving to be an effective cross between pure democracy and representative government. In the field of religion, camp meetings met both spiritual and social needs. Participation in all of these enterprises was entirely voluntary.

While distance from centers of traditional culture was a handicap, many persons found compensation in the simplicity and freedom of the social mechanism and in the prevailing equalitarian standards that tended to provide broad bases for future development. Cabins were reflections of the personalities of the builders—strong, angular, and open. Both food and clothing usually were rough; refinements in the latter were occasionally seen, but class distinctions in dress were tending to disappear. The chief amusements were square dancing, horse racing and gambling, carousing, practical joking, and yarn swapping—all reflections of a hardy civilization. Imaginative, exaggerative humor aided in withstanding the rigors of frontier life at the same time that malaria, an unbalanced diet, and economic misfortune made life burdensome. The leaders among the lawyers, the doctors, and the teachers were men of ability, but charlatans flourished in all of the professions and standards of apprentice training were low. In the field of education, two achievements that were not petty in a frontier society were recorded: Instruction rose above the secondary level in a few church "colleges," and the substructure of a future educational system for "the whole people" was firmly fixed both in law and in public opinion.

Methodist and "Old School" Presbyterian preachers took the lead in providing facilities for education, and the Methodists, Baptists, and Cumberland Presbyterians dominated the religious scene. In spite of the pertinacity of the indomitable circuit riders, not more than one-eighth of the population were enrolled as church members. Strong forces opposed to the spread of formal religion included postwar social ferment, the riotousness of boom towns, frontier resentment of dogmatic authority, and intradenominational struggles. The religious atmosphere of the Republic was congenial to the skeptics occasionally found among the doctors and lawyers, to those who sought their religion in the open spaces, and to the persons who were repelled by the emotionalism of camp meetings. But the churches were largely responsible for the maintenance of mass moral standards that were conservative in aim, if not always in practice.

Most heads of families were men who sought a productive farm and future comfort for themselves and their families. Every community also had young men who hoped to achieve a more rapid rise in the legal and medical professions and in politics than would be possible in older communities. The most successful among the lawyers and doctors tended to blend into the small planter class, while many others were versatile enough to shift from their professions to other occupations as the occasion demanded. In the larger towns the diversity of occupations was surprising for towns so recently established. On the streets of Houston and Galveston, farmers, small planters, slaves, doctors, and lawyers touched elbows with merchants, clerks, boat crews, actors, barbers, auctioneers, tanners, carpenters, blacksmiths, tailors, teamsters, an occasional friendly Indian, a long-haired scout or two, possibly a group of Germans, rowdies, and loafers.

A small segment of the population gave Texas a reputation for sharp dealing and lawlessness. In the last half of the eighteen thirties the frontier Republic attracted a number of adventure-craving Southern hotheads as well as canny, land-seeking gentlemen who were not overly particular concerning the methods they used to attain an estate. Land frauds by a handful of swindlers were the key factor in igniting the Regulator-Moderator War, which for a time transformed a region centering in Shelby County into an area of law defiance and bloodshed. Some immigrants were shiftless, others had come to Texas to avoid the consequences of discreditable actions, and a few had criminal records. Professional gamblers gravitated to the towns that offered opportunities for the exercise of their special talents. Communities which fortunately failed to attract large numbers of these elements were comparatively peaceful, but individuals everywhere were forced to maintain a hair-trigger regard for their "rights."

The period of the Texas Revolution and the republic which emerged from it bred a temper peculiarly Texan—or "Texian" as it was often spelled in those days. The defense of the Alamo, recently called "the high mark of all times for fearless behavior," the massacre at Goliad, and the subsequent defeat of the Mexicans at San Jacinto gave Texan men at arms rallying cries and a tradition that have persisted for a century. Their fighting spirit arose not alone from national compulsion but also from individual necessity. In the years immediately following the Texas Revolution, law enforcement agencies were still in the process of organization precisely at the time that the country was in a state of postwar unrest and in the grip of a paroxysm of speculation. Disputes between persons with upper-class backgrounds were settled by resort to the Code Duello, and men of all classes engaged in other forms of personal conflict. Indians, Mexicans, desperadoes, drunken ruffians, gamblers, trigger-quick duelists who sought to have their honor offended—any of these might assail normally peaceable citizens. Hence they learned to defend themselves and, if necessary, take the offensive. Their confidence in their ability to look any man in the eye gave them a feeling of strength in their own opinions.

In a society which required strength and self-reliance both in acquiring the necessities of life and in social relationships, everyone was inclined to be self-assertive and restive under restraint. Theoretically one man was as good as another on the frontier, and a feeling of equality prevailed. Although the energy and leadership of business and professional men generally enabled them to exercise dominance, they rarely assumed attitudes of social superiority. The plain people elected few demagogues to high office, but politics was a rough-and-tumble spectacle. In 1838 two candidates for president committed suicide, and the campaign of 1841 was featured by vituperative charges of cowardice, dishonesty, and habitual drunkenness against the candidates.

The Republic was fortunate in its choice of leaders. Houston, Austin, Travis, Lamar, Rusk, Hemphill, Burleson, Burnet, Jones, Ashbel Smith, the Whartons, Henderson—these names only top a long list. The repercussions of the revolution they led and the republic they helped establish have not yet spent themselves, for their actions have impressed themselves indelibly on the consciousness of every Texan to this day. Houston responded to his elevation to the presidency by rising in stature from his former position of speculation-minded adventurer to one of real statesmanship, while Lamar's interest in intellectual matters is still felt in Texas.

So there arose a Texan way of life that still exists, even in the face of all the mass promotion and standardization of machine civilization. Stamina, individualism, "go-ahead" initiative, pride in everything Texan—these were and still are, in varying degrees, among the ingredients of the Texas spirit. Bitter courage, wry or raucous laughter, and kindliness stood out amidst the drabness and coarseness of frontier life. An astonishing number of urbane and intelligent men found a satisfying freedom from compulsion. Indeed, the Republic of Texas worked a curious alchemy with its citizenry, educated and untutored alike. It took the sons and daughters of Tennessee, the Carolinas, Georgia, Mississippi, New York, France, and Germany and set its own ineffaceable stamp on their souls. The same process is still working in Texas today.

Sam Houston and His Antagonists

SAM W. HAYNES

By any standard, Sam Houston's career in Texas was a turbulent one. Public figures are rarely strangers to controversy, but few have provoked such deep-seated animosity or been the target of such bitter invective. Houston's appeal today, no doubt, owes much to the fact that for almost a quarter of a century he braved the scorn and vituperative attacks of his political enemies, who routinely denounced the hero of San Jacinto as a charlatan and a fraud. Though his popularity with the electorate remained high, at least until the twilight of his career, to his antagonists he was, in Mosely Baker's phrase, "an incubus upon the land."

Mudslinging and character assassination, of course, were staple features of nineteenth century American politics, and a thick skin was required of all political leaders in order to withstand the calumnies and abuse of campaign opponents. What

Sam W. Haynes, "Sam Houston and his Antagonists" (paper presented at meeting of Texas State Historical Association, Austin, March 1994). Reprinted with permission.

is notable about the attacks on Houston, however, is the dogged persistence of his detractors, some of whom harassed him with a zeal bordering on monomania. For David G. Burnet, Mirabeau Lamar, Thomas Jefferson Green and others, their campaign to discredit Houston became a lifelong preoccupation. Moreover, in contrast to political contests elsewhere, the rancor that characterized Texas politics was intensely personal in nature, creating a climate of contentiousness that was aggravated by, but ultimately extended well beyond, issues of policy or partisanship.

Given Houston's venerable reputation, it is tempting to dismiss such hostility as little more than mean-spirited envy. The hero of San Jacinto cast a long shadow over the landscape of early Anglo Texas, and it is not unreasonable to suppose that there were those who begrudged him his success. But this explanation seems woefully inadequate when one considers how many key military and political figures quarreled bitterly with Houston at one time or another during the course of his career. Nor is it enough to simply assert that nineteenth century Anglo Texans were an independent lot who were inherently averse to all forms of authority, and that some would have chafed under the leadership of any strong-willed individual. Houston's principal antagonists defy ready classification, but they all shared a strongly held belief that the most celebrated figure in Texas did not deserve the laurels bestowed upon him.

The antipathy which many prominent Texans felt toward Houston was due at least in part to the fact that the Republic acted as a magnet for ambitious men eager to make their mark in a frontier society that seemed ripe with opportunity. Although Houston's enemies attacked him on a whole range of issues, they were particularly alienated by his economic and military policies, policies that often had a direct bearing on their own careers. Houston's refusal to sanction an invasion of Matamoros in the fall of 1836 aroused a firestorm of protest from men like Felix Huston, who viewed continued hostilities with Mexico as a means to establish military reputations, a prerequisite for any politically ambitious Texan. Similarly, Houston's opposition to legislation creating a general land office and his stand against the Texas Railroad, Navigation and Banking Company antagonized many speculators and entrepreneurs, among them Branch T. Archer and Thomas Jefferson Green, who hoped to emerge as the country's economic elite. As the consistent advocate of caution and retrenchment, Houston invariably clashed with men who had gravitated to Texas to realize their loftiest ambitions.

Their failure to do so contributed in yet another way to the acrimony that surrounded Houston's leadership. Many had been drawn to Texas as a result of financial problems in the United States, and now experienced further setbacks in the new Republic. Plagued by doubts of self-worth, they often displayed an almost obsessive desire to defend their reputations as men of honor and good standing. In Texas, a young nation beset by economic difficulties, the esteem in which one was held by others in the community took on particular significance in the absence of more tangible determinants of status. To besmirch a man's reputation, to impugn his honor, was to rob him of everything he had.

As a consequence, Houston's enemies exhibited a prickly sensitivity to insult, which allowed arguments with the famous Texan to fester and become lifelong feuds. Duelling, which had once provided immediate satisfaction for injured parties, had fallen into disfavor by the late 1830s, the practice giving way to more democratic, nonviolent means of redress. Men who believed their reputations had been sullied now sought to vindicate themselves before the bar of public opinion, publishing pamphlets or writing open letters to sympathetic newspapers, in which they systematically and thoroughly rebutted each of the charges against them. Sidney Sherman, whose conduct on the eve of San Jacinto was censured by Houston; Thomas Jefferson Green, who Houston accused of leading Texas troops in the sack and pillage of Laredo in 1842; and Commodore Edwin Ward Moore, who was court-martialed by the Houston administration on charges of piracy in 1843, never forgave Houston for the damage they believed had been done to their reputations, and were still defending themselves in blistering attacks against him many years later. For his part, Houston also felt obliged to speak out to protect his "good name," which invariably led to a new round of charges and countercharges. Some of his longest and most impassioned speeches in the United States Senate had nothing to do with national policy or Texas affairs, but were devoted instead to answering allegations that his enemies had been making against him for more than twenty years. His last major address to that body in 1859 was one of several speeches he delivered in response to charges that he was guilty of cowardice and vacillation during the Texas Revolution.

Houston's antagonists may have had personal or self-serving motives for repudiating his leadership, but their implacable opposition was also rooted in a firm antipathy to the man himself. A complete list of the failings ascribed to him by his critics would be too numerous to mention here. Some were little more than scurrilous fabrications—that he deliberately planned the deaths of Travis and Fannin because he saw them as rivals to his command of the Texas army, for example—and do not merit our serious attention. Houston's critics were on much firmer ground, however, when they confined their attacks to questions of character. The hero of San Jacinto, they alleged, was inordinately vain, fond of praise, and eager to take credit for the accomplishments of others. They decried Houston's legendary dissipation, which on occasion rendered him incapable of performing the duties of his office. Above all, they abhorred the utter want of candor, the predilection for artifice and intrigue, that were the hallmarks of Houston's statecraft and which, they maintained, revealed a blatant disregard for the sovereign will of the people.

All of these allegations have been duly noted by students of Houston's career, but they have done little to tarnish his reputation; indeed, such character traits have added luster and color to a persona that has often been described—to use a tired and shopworn cliché—as "larger than life." Still, the fact remains that to many who knew him, Houston was not larger than life, nor was he heroic in stature, and to arrive at a full understanding of the man some effort to account for this discrepancy must be made. The answer lies, I think, not in the kind of man he was, but in the significance we attach to his failings. Whereas later generations have taken, on the whole, a rather charitable view of Houston's foibles, to his contemporary critics such defects of personality were nothing less than unpardonable sins that utterly disqualified him from high office.

If this verdict seems unreasonably harsh to us, it may well be because Houston's enemies judged him by standards with which our own generation is largely unfamiliar. Cultural values are never static, and any attempt to impose the attitudes of one era upon another inevitably leads to fundamental misunderstanding. The need for caution is particularly advisable when dealing with the Jacksonian era, a transitional period in our history which sought to distance itself, with varying degrees of success, from the epoch that preceded it. Any examination of Houston's controversial career must not lose sight of this volatile and uncertain cultural context.

By the early decades of the nineteenth century, Americans had largely rejected the hierarchical, deferential social order of the Revolutionary era in favor of a stridently democratic, egalitarian one. Inevitably, this break with the past was not as easily accomplished as Americans were wont to believe, for it required each citizen to redefine his or her own place within a broad matrix of social relationships. Unfettered by rank, privilege or social pedigree, Americans could now rise or fall according to their innate abilities—or so they believed. But such freedom, as Alexis de Tocqueville noted, was an intimidating prospect for many Americans. Even as they wholeheartedly embraced a brave new competitive world, they also sought refuge from it in a myriad number of voluntary associations, from mass-based political parties to evangelical Christianity to volunteer militia regiments to fraternal brotherhoods. While the opportunities for such institutional networks were necessarily circumscribed by frontier conditions, Texans sought, much as they had done in the United States, to reconcile their new-found freedom as self-directed individuals with their traditional role as members of a larger community.

Houston, it is clear, adapted much more readily to the new ethos of individualism than did many of his counterparts. In both his public and private life, Houston stood alone, shunning the voluntary associations that his generation considered to be the very sinews of a civilized society. His sojourns among the Cherokee Indians are only the most striking examples of Houston's desire to distance himself from the fellowship of his own community. During the course of a long career of public service he formed remarkably few friendships. He does not appear to have been a particularly active Freemason, and only late in life did he seek church membership.

Even his political allegiances were tenuous in nature. Despite his claim to be a "Democrat of the Old School," Houston did not worship at the "shrine of party" as did most stalwart Jacksonians. Although Houston made much of his connections with Andrew Jackson, he proved to be a somewhat fractious protege, and their relationship was not one which he felt required his total candor or cooperation. Houston's decision to run for a second term as Tennessee governor in 1829 against the popular Jackson intimate William Carroll was hardly conducive to party harmony, and indeed caused a rupture in the Tennessee Democracy, at least until the scandal following his estrangement from Eliza Allen cut short his reelection bid. When Texas gained admittance to the Union in 1846, President Polk was unsure if Houston would take his place in the Senate as a Democrat or a Whig. He chose the former, but once seated, Houston showed little inclination to tow the party line if it did not suit him. As the two-party system began to crumble under the weight of the sectional crisis in the 1850s, he was quick to cast about for political support elsewhere, embracing briefly the agendas of two short-lived third parties, and ultimately entertaining the fanciful, if not bizarre notion that he could offer himself in the 1860 presidential campaign as a "People's Candidate," an idea which showed, if nothing else, a fundamental ignorance of the deep-seated attachments which many Americans still felt for the party of their choice.

It was the absence of these ties that enabled Houston to develop the attributes for which he has become celebrated: his pragmatism, his independence, his stubborn determination to follow the dictates of his own conscience. But such qualities were not held in the highest regard in a political culture that placed a premium on institutional and parochial loyalties. Like their revolutionary forebears, Jacksonian Americans tended to view the common good as immutable and absolute. It followed, then, that those who aspired to represent the public interest be men of fixed and unyielding principles. As president of the Republic, however, Houston frequently pursued a wayward course, sending out mixed signals that confounded his friends and enemies alike. During his second term, he pushed for annexation to the United States, even as he sought British aid to ensure that Texas would remain an independent, sovereign state, prompting historians to wonder whether Houston was indecisive, pursuing a master strategy known only to himself, or just keeping his options open. Houston's contemporary critics, on the other hand, viewed his inconsistency in an altogether different light. They condemned his erratic behavior, but not, as one might expect, because it was evidence of a lack of resolve. Rather, in their minds Houston was governed by expediency, which suggested a sinister willingness to subordinate the common good to his own selfish purposes.

Of all the indictments against him, perhaps the most serious was Houston's overweening egotism, a far more damning character flaw in the mid-nineteenth century than it is today. But if Houston's enemies were men of driving ambition, engaged in a relentless pursuit of their own self-interest, why then were they so quick to condemn him for exhibiting similar characteristics? Once again, the answer lies in the fact that Jacksonian Americans were engaged in a process of cultural reorientation, one which pitted conventional values emphasizing public duty against a more permissive, modern set of attitudes that condoned self-aggrandizement. The era has often been described—correctly—as one in which the "anxious pursuit of gain" was universal and all-consuming. To be sure, Americans were engaged in a frenzied pursuit of wealth and distinction, but they nonetheless remained attached to a Jeffersonian political tradition that had imbued the values of republican virtue and social obligation with a sanctity that could not be ignored.

Many remained uncomfortable with the new professionalism which had become a part of American political life. For this reason, aspirants to high office often assumed a pose of passive indifference, allowing their friends and supporters to advance their candidacies on their behalf. No doubt most politicians hungered for the status, power, and honor that were the rewards of high office, but any display of naked ambition was certain to offend republican sensibilities. Similarly, some officeholders felt obliged to step aside and retire—at least temporarily—from public life, thereby offering irrefutable evidence of their lack of ambition. At various points in their careers, Thomas Jefferson Rusk, David G. Burnet, Mirabeau Lamar, Anson Jones, and James Pinckney Henderson either declined to run for office or refused the opportunity to serve second terms.

Houston, on the other hand, was not one to set aside his love of the spotlight for the sake of appearances. The perennial candidate, he pursued high office with an enthusiasm and energy that his detractors found indecorous, to say the least. Try as he might, Houston could not convincingly portray himself as an American

Cincinnatus, who humbly served when called upon, all the while longing to return to simple, agrarian pursuits. One suspects that even his wife Margaret must have come to realize at some point that his repeated promises to retire from public life were less than sincere.

Houston's enemies castigated him not only for the way he sought power but for the way he wielded it. To his critics he seemed more demagogue than democrat; seeking always to manipulate public opinion, but rarely guided by it. Insisting instead on complete control of the decision-making process, Houston made little effort to establish a public consensus for his policy objectives, and as a result some of the most notable achievements of his career failed to receive the widespread approbation one might have expected. Much of the abuse heaped upon him in the wake of the battle at San Jacinto might well have been avoided had he established a dialogue with his subordinate officers. Instead, he held but one council of war, shortly before the battle began. It is, of course, highly unlikely that Houston could have silenced all his critics, given the querulous nature of the citizen-soldier armies of Texas during this period and the resentment many officers felt when he garnered the lion's share of credit for the victory. Nonetheless, the bitter debate over Houston's role in the campaign was fueled by his refusal to divulge his plans to either the provisional government or the officers under his command. "I held no councils of war," Houston wrote in his famous letter to Thomas Jefferson Rusk, "if I err, the blame is mine alone." This statement has often been cited as an example of Houston's stern resolve, but it is also indicative of a brand of leadership that was high-handed and imperious. Said Jess Billingley: "Houston is the basest of all men, as he has, by willfully lying, attempted to rob that little band of men of their well-earned honors on the battlefield of San Jacinto. He has assumed to himself credit that was due others."

Houston's personal conduct also belied his Jacksonian credentials. At a time when even the most aristocratic Whigs found it politically advantageous to promote themselves as models of republican simplicity, Houston cultivated the image of the eccentric showman, flouting conventional forms of behavior. Houston's compulsive desire for attention manifested itself most notably in his manner of dress. While Houston's fondness for flowing capes, garish waistcoats, and enormous rings has often been seen by later generations as evidence of his irrepressible personality, during his own lifetime it was the subject of a great deal of unfavorable comment. His lavish Indian costumes not only earned him a rebuke from John C. Calhoun when he appeared in Washington in 1818, but were ridiculed at the council meetings of the Cherokees themselves. Eccentric behavior could be tolerated in public figures, of course, but only if it reinforced and exemplified acceptable normative values. Houston's antics, however, drew attention to the man, not to the virtues of a larger constituency. His appearance at Mirabeau Lamar's inauguration in a powdered wig and, equally incongruously, as a buckskin-clad frontiersman at the swearing-in ceremony of his second presidential term, were viewed as evidence of Houston's monumental vanity, and thus his desire to set himself apart from, and above, other men.

Nor can the severe criticism heaped upon Houston for his dissipation be lightly dismissed as the feigned outrage of political rivals. To be sure, heavy drinking was endemic in Jacksonian America, and politicians were expected to imbibe freely with the voters as a sign of their "common touch," and to treat their constituents at campaign rallies. Nonetheless, elected officials, then as now, were frequently held to a higher code of behavior than the general public. Leadership carried with it certain responsibilities; and public figures were expected to adhere to standards of probity and decorum as guardians of the people's trust. While Houston was not the only Texas public servant who found such standards too demanding, there is no reason to think that the indignation his opponents expressed at such conduct was mere hypocritical cant. Among the most outspoken critics of Houston's habitual drunkenness were David G. Burnet and *Telegraph and Texas Register* publisher Francis Moore, both of whom were well-known advocates of the fast-growing temperance movement in Texas. That Houston had the temerity to address temperance groups on the evils of alcoholism long before he had made a serious effort to curb his own drinking habits only added to his opponents' ire.

In short, Houston was viewed as an illegitimate leader by some because he lacked the requisite qualities of leadership in a democratic age. Houston's enemies could not deny that he possessed enormous personal charisma, which accounted in large measure for his extraordinary political success. But popular appeal alone did not qualify him to serve as an agent of the people. Like Ralph Waldo Emerson, his critics subscribed to the ideal of the "representative man:" the mantle of leadership could only be worn by one who personified the values of society at large.

The hero of San Jacinto lacked this spirit, his antagonists maintained. Frustrated by his popularity, they never gave up hope that the people would ultimately come to share their opinion of him. In 1854 Mirabeau Lamar wrote wistfully: "His name is now in the transition state; and will, as the light of truth dawns with increasing force upon it, pass from the . . . famous to the notoriously infamous, where it will rest, covered by the dust of oblivion."

Lamar proved to be a poor prophet, for history has been more than kind to the hero of San Jacinto. With few exceptions, students of Houston's career have been inclined to applaud his unwavering faith in his own judgment, his steadfast determination to swim against the tide of public opinion. But this verdict ignores the fact that Houston's independence of thought and action, though undeniably virtues by our own standards, seemed to many of his contemporaries inimical to the precepts of good republican government. Houston's antagonists cannot, therefore, be simply dismissed as reckless firebrands or crankish malcontents. Their furious opposition reminds us that our own admiration for Houston is framed by a modern cultural perspective, one that allows us to be more tolerant of Houston's self-indulgent excesses, his disdain for convention, his talent for self-promotion and relentless pursuit of his own celebrity, than were many members of his own generation.

 F U R T H E R   R E A D I N G

Randolph B. Campbell, *Sam Houston and the American Southwest* (1993)
Jesús F. De la Teja, "Discovering the Tejano Community in 'Early' Texas," *Journal of the Early Republic* 18 (1998)
Llerena Friend, *Sam Houston, The Great Designer* (1954)
Herbert P. Gambrell, *Mirabeau Buonparte Lamar, Troubador and Crusader* (1934)

————, *Anson Jones* (1948)

Sam W. Haynes, *Soldiers of Misfortune: The Somervell and Mier Expeditions* (1990)

Margaret Swett Henson, *Samuel May Williams; Early Texas Entrepreneur* (1976)

Jim Dan Hill, *The Texas Navy* (1937)

John S. Jenkins and Kenneth Keselus, *Edward Burleson: Texas Frontier Leader* (1990)

Andreas Reichstein, *Rise of the Lone Star: The Making of Texas* (1989)

Andreas Resendez, "National Identity in a Shifting Border: Texas and New Mexico in the
Age of Transition, 1821–1848," *Journal of American History* 86 (1999)

Stanley Siegel, *The Political History of the Texas Republic, 1836–1845* (1956)

Walter Struve, *Germans and Texans: Commerce, Migration, and Culture in the Days of the
Lone Star Republic* (1996)

Elgin Williams, *The Animating Pursuits of Speculation; Land Traffic in the Annexation of
Texas* (1949)

John Hoyt Williams, *Sam Houston: A Biography of the Father of Texas* (1993)

Texas Joins the Union: Changing Roles for Tejanos and Women in the New State, 1845–1860

By 1845, the inability of the Lone Star republic to stand alone as an independent nation-state had become apparent even to the most prominent spokesmen for Texas nationalism. Rumors that Texans might turn for aid to Great Britain had become the subject of great concern in the United States. These reports were particularly alarming to Southern slaveholders, who had always coveted Texas and feared the interference of British abolitionists in the area. Although Northern antislavery forces remained staunchly opposed to annexation, in the spring of 1845 Congress passed by a slim margin a joint resolution offering to admit Texas into the Union as the twenty-eighth state. In July, Texans voted overwhelmingly to accept the annexation offer. Mexico, however, still unreconciled to the loss of Texas, warned the United States that annexation would lead to war. Relations between the two countries continued to deteriorate over the Texas question until the spring of 1846, when a clash between U.S. and Mexican troops along the Rio Grande prompted Washington to declare war against Mexico.

Texans who had voted for annexation in the hope that statehood would improve the region's economic climate were not disappointed. Access to American capital, as well as a steady flow of immigrants from the United States and Central Europe following the U.S.-Mexican War ushered in an era of burgeoning prosperity unknown during the Republic period. But the state's integration into the economy of the United States was not immediate, nor did it benefit all citizens. For many men and women, life in Texas remained one of considerable hardship and privation. How did these challenges vary, according to one's socioeconomic status and ethnicity? What impact did frontier conditions have on gender roles?

In the south, Tejanos found themselves in an even more precarious position after the war with Mexico. Denied access to U.S. capital investment and unfamiliar *with the American legal system, Tejano ranchers were often unable to compete with the large-scale business practices implemented by their Anglo counterparts. How did the Tejano community adapt to the rapidly changing power structure in South Texas? What methods did Tejano elites employ to retain their ebbing social and economic status?*

✦ D O C U M E N T S

By the mid-1840s, the annexation of Texas had become nothing less than a holy grail for Americans who envisioned their nation as a continental empire. Although some writers of the period waxed poetic about the United States' "mission" to expand westward, the phenomenon known as Manifest Destiny had little to do with lofty idealism. In Document 1, Texas politician and adventurer Thomas Jefferson Green calls upon the United States not only to annex Texas, but to push its boundaries to the Pacific Ocean and as far south as the Sierra Madres. Green's utter disregard for Mexican sovereignty, deep-seated feelings of Anglo-Saxon racial superiority, and unabashed sense of entitlement toward the region's economic resources were shared by many Americans, and helped set the stage for conflict between the United States and Mexico. Document 2 is the Brown resolution, passed by the U.S. Congress by a narrow margin in 1845, offering to admit Texas as the twenty-eighth state. Despite the provision to adjust "all questions of boundary that may arise with other Governments," the resolution promptly sparked a boundary dispute with Mexico, providing a pretext for the U.S. declaration of war in 1846.

In the next three documents, the rise of an agricultural capitalist economy and its attendant problems for Tejanos are examined. Document 3 chronicles the rise of the mercantile and cattle empire in South Texas founded by entrepreneurs Richard King and Mifflin Kenedy. In Document 4, Frederick Law Olmsted describes the racial strife that characterized Anglo-Mexican relations in Texas after annexation. The social and economic tensions that Texans experienced during this new era in its history sometimes flared into violence. In 1859, a dispute between a ranchero, Juan Nepomuceno Cortina, and the marshal of Brownsville erupted into a series of skirmishes between the Mexican community on both sides of the Rio Grande and the Texas Rangers. In Document 5, two proclamations issued by Cortina state his reason for leading a revolt against Anglo Texas authority.

In the last two documents, two women give accounts of the sickness, hardships, and absence of creature comforts that were part of daily life for women who immigrated to Texas. In Document 6, Lucadia Pease, a Connecticut native who moved to Brazoria in 1850, writes to her sister after a severe bout of influenza. Her husband, Elisha Marshall Pease, would serve as governor from 1853 to 1857. In Document 7, Ottilie Fuchs Goeth recalls her childhood as a German immigrant in Central Texas.

1. Thomas Jefferson Green Dreams of Empire, 1845

All history teaches that the general course of conquest has been from north to south. It was so in the days of Tamerlane, of the Goths and Vandals, and, from the best evidence upon the subject, it has been so already with Mexico herself. Physiology also instructs us, as a general law, that animals are more daring and ferocious in high

---

Thomas Jefferson Green, *Journal of the Texian Expedition Against Mier,* Sam W. Haynes, ed. (repr., Austin: W. Thomas Taylor, 1993), 185–186, 194–195, 198–200.

than in low latitudes; that as the cold climate makes it the more difficult of subsistence, it nerves the system to an energy commensurate to the want; that while the perpetual produce of the warm climate renders such energy unnecessary, it enervates the system and debases the mind. Nothing can be more true, and a knowledge of the people of the United States and Mexico is strikingly illustrative of the fact. . . .

Two nations so contiguous, so opposite in their policy, and every way so unlike each other, can never live in friendship with a border which invites both to its advantages. The Rio Grande, from its head to its source, from the forty-second to the twenty-fifth degree of north latitude, is capable of maintaining many millions of population, with a variety of product which no river upon the north continent can boast. This river, once settled with the enterprise and intelligence of the English race, will yearly send forth an agricultural export which it will require hundreds of steamers to transport to its delta, while its hides, wool, and metals may be increased to an estimate which would now appear chimerical.

If annexation of Texas to the United States of the North succeeds, this boundary can exist but for a short period; and though there seems to me to be a destiny in the womb of time which marks her southern boundary at the extremity of the north continent, where the two great oceans of the world will unite under a genial sun and a smooth navigation, yet her more *immediate* southern boundary must extend to the *Sierra Madre,* that great Chinese wall which separates the people of the Rio Grande from those of the more southern tablelands. Can this be considered a greedy desire upon the part of the mighty northern nation, when her facilities of communication with those people from her capital in twelve days are superior to their present means of communication with the capital of Mexico in thirty? We say not. This age has merged distance in time, and the people of the Rio Grande at present are as near neighbours to the capital of the United States as Boston was to Philadelphia at the promulgation of President Washington's inaugural message to the first Congress. . . .

The most desirable portion of this continent lies between the 28th and 42d degrees of north latitude upon the Pacific. It presents more than a thousand miles of seacoast, with the important ports of Guaymas, San Diego, San Gabriel, Monterey, San Francisco, and many others, with a soil and climate of unsurpassed capability for grazing and agriculture, and a mineral wealth supposed to be equal, if not superior, to any in the world. This vast country of more than one million of square miles, lying due west of the settled portion of the United States, between the frozen regions of the north and the vertical sun of the south, between the gentle influences of the Pacific Ocean and the great backbone of the continent, capable of giving wealth and happiness to a hundred millions of souls, is now in possession of roaming tribes of unhoused Indians, and a few settlements of less than two hundred thousand Mexican subjects.

If Oregon is important to the United States, this country is a thousand times more so. The extreme northern lines of the states of Pennsylvania, Connecticut, and Rhode Island only reach to the 42d degree of north latitude: that latitude cuts in two the states of Massachusetts and New-York, and Lake Erie and Michigan, while the 28th degree is north of the United States settlements in Florida, and nearly three degrees north of Texas, at the mouth of the Rio Grande. While it is due to the United States that she should not permit this important country to fall into

European hands, it is equally due to her that she should possess it by any and every means necessary thereto.

Let the United States apply, if necessary, the usufruct doctrine of her possession of this country, which Old England and Old Spain practised towards the aborigines upon the discovery of this continent—a doctrine of common sense and sound reason—of human necessity and justice. If the Author of the universe intended the earth for the support of the few, to the exclusion of the greater number, the reverse of this doctrine is true, and then it is right and proper that a very few should hold this country, of which they can make no adequate use, to the exclusion of many millions in other portions of the earth, who may be dying for the want of space to live in. When Spain claimed title and possession to this vast tract of country under this doctrine, that the aborigines had no title in the soil, but only a temporary right to the use and occupancy thereof, such only as the buffalo enjoys, she was justified in such possession only by applying it to a better use. Three hundred years have passed, and neither herself nor those claiming under her have applied it to that better use, and she holds it without such ability so to apply it, to the exclusion of others who have, and whose necessities require it. England, France, or any other nation, whose population is greater than her means of subsistence, has a right, derived directly from the Maker of the earth, to occupy it with her redundant people; and it alone is a question of policy or power whether its present claimants or nearest neighbour will permit it. This era, so marked in the improvements of agriculture, machinery, and navigation—in the knowledge of geography, and the increased necessity of the case, will not allow a perversion of the use of this country. For many wise reasons, the United States should extend her settlements over it; but should she, by a different policy, fail to do so, the all-seeing eye of Great Britain will not let slip such a golden opportunity in possessing herself of this desirable middle ground between home and her vast Eastern possessions. Besides, if the Oregon settlement is important to the United States, without a harbour sufficient for the entrance of her smallest vessels of war, the port of San Francisco, or some other port in the south, is absolutely necessary for her.

It may, however, well be questioned whether either Spain or the present government of Mexico has ever had any other than a nominal possession of this vast region; for only here and there, in a very few isolated spots, has she had a few people in real possession, and those few shut in by fortifications as protection against the aboriginal occupants. If, therefore, she has no power of absolutely possessing herself of this country, her declaration of ownership to it was arbitrary, and the act not justified by her means; and with the same propriety she might have claimed, to illimitable extent, that which she neither had the use of nor power of using, depriving millions of the earth's population of support and the proper uses thereof.

While I hold that it is both just and proper that any nation with an overgrown population may settle these vast wastes with her redundant people, I repeat again that it would be short-sighted policy in the United States to permit it. That nation, with her twenty millions of people, in the ordinary course of events, in fifty years, will have eighty to provide for, and a large country will be necessary for so many within the lifetime of numbers now busy in the politics of that country. With such an acquisition, the United States would not be larger than Brazil with her six millions of people, and about one third of the size of the present British dominions. With such an acquisition, the United States would contain but a fraction over three millions of square miles, and without Texas that would be cut nearly in twain by a narrow slip extending to the 42d degree of north latitude, which is the parallel of Boston. If it be wise policy, and the United States extends her dominions to the 28th degree upon the Pacific, then Texas becomes absolutely necessary to her. Then the *Texas wedge,* making into the centre of her square and compact surface, will appear obviously wrong. It would be a severance of her entirety, which few would be willing to reconcile; and without a union of the two countries, a conflict of interest would inevitably grow up between the separate nations, detrimental certainly to one, and probably to both. This conflict would beget countervailing laws, such as are at present in the bud, and would produce estrangement to the advantage of European powers, which would profit by the quarrel.

2. The United States Annexes Texas, March 1845

"Resolved by the Senate and House of Representatives of the United States of America in Congress assembled, That Congress doth consent that the territory properly included within and rightly belonging to the Republic of Texas may be erected into a new State, to be called the State of Texas, with a Republican form of Government, to be adopted by the people of said Republic, by deputies in Convention assembled, with the consent of the existing Government, in order that the same may be admitted as one of the States of this Union.

"2. And be it further Resolved, That the foregoing consent of Congress is given upon the following conditions, and with the following guarantees, to wit.

"First. Said State to be formed subject to the adjustment by this Government of all questions of boundary that may arise with other Governments, and the Constitution thereof, with the proper evidence of its adoption, by the people of said Republic of Texas, shall be transmitted to the President of the United States, to be laid before Congress for its final action, on or before the first day of January, one thousand eight hundred and forty six.

"Second. Said State when admitted into the Union, after ceding to the United States all public edifices, fortifications, barracks, ports and harbors, navy and navy-yards, docks, magazines, arms, armaments and all other property and means pertaining to the public defence belonging to the said Republic of Texas; shall retain all the public funds, debts, taxes, and dues of every kind which may belong to or be due and owing said Republic; and shall also retain all the vacant and unappropriated lands lying within its limits, to be applied to the payment of debts and liabilities of said Republic of Texas, and the residue of said debts and liabilities, to be disposed of as said State may direct; but in no event are said debts and liabilities to become a charge upon the Government of the United States.

"Third, New States of convenient size, not exceeding four in number, in addition to said State of Texas, and having a sufficient population, may hereafter, by the consent of said State, be formed, out of the territory thereof, which shall be entitled to admission under the provisions of the Federal Constitution. And such States as

---

H. P. N. Gammel, ed., *Laws of Texas* (Austin: Gammel Book Co., 1898), 2:1303–1304.

may be formed out of that portion of said territory lying south of thirty six degrees thirty minutes north latitude, commonly known as the Missouri compromise line, shall be admitted into the Union, with or without slavery, as the people of each State asking admission may desire. And in such State or States as shall be formed out of said territory north of said Missouri compromise line, slavery or involuntary servitude (except for crime) shall be prohibited."

3. Entrepreneurs Richard King and Mifflin Kenedy Build a Mercantile and Cattle Empire, 1850

Mifflin Kenedy came to the lower Río Grande in 1846. He was then the commander of the *Corvette,* a steamboat belonging to the United States Quartermaster Department. She was plying between the mouth of the Río Grande and Camargo and Mier. Captain Kenedy had brought her from Pittsburgh, where she had been built. It is needless to say that he did his duty well and that he acquired the confidence and the esteem of all with whom he had transactions.

In the year 1847 Captain Richard King arrived on the Río Grande. He was employed as pilot on the *Corvette.* In this manner the names of these two gentlemen became associated. They remained associated until the close of the war between Mexico and the United States. They had won honor and the confidence of men who controlled affairs. They had won the confidence of the public.

In the year 1850 a company was formed. It was known as M. Kenedy & Co. and consisted of M. Kenedy, Richard King, Charles Stillman, and James O'Donnell. In 1852 Captain Kenedy purchased O'Donnell's interest. This firm continued in existence for about fifteen years. It was the main reliance for navigation from the port of Brazos Santiago to Roma, the center of navigation on the Río Grande in those days.

In 1850 the company had two boats on the Rio Grande—the *Comanche* and the *Grampus.* Captain King and Captain Kenedy each commanded a boat. Whatever could be effected by prudence, foresight, and good management was done. Annually, millions of dollars worth of merchandise entered the customhouse of Brazos Santiago on Point Isabel. The merchandise was transported to Brownsville, Matamoros, Río Grande City, and other points along the river. A large proportion of it was carried into the northeastern States of Mexico. The carrying trade of the Río Grande was extremely lucrative, and those engaged in it soon amassed fortunes. Men possessing capacity, energy, and wealth were not likely to remain silent spectators of events they might control. M. Kenedy & Co. soon became an important factor in the affairs of the lower Río Grande. The firm possessed the requirements calculated to produce good results. It encouraged every enterprise calculated to promote the development of the natural resources of the country.

It must be remembered that in 1850 there was only a single family living on the road made by General Taylor from Corpus Christi to Brownsville—a distance of about one hundred and sixty-five miles. The country was infested with companies of Mexicans who frequently united the business of corralling wild mustangs and murdering and robbing travellers. The Comanches made descents into this district

John Salmon Ford, Stephen B. Oates, eds., *Rip Ford's Texas* (Austin: University of Texas, 1963), 457–463. By permission of the University of Texas Press.

ostensibly to capture horses to ride and to eat, but really to kill the men and to make mistresses and slaves of women and children. In 1850 troops were stationed at various points to give protection to the settlers in the valleys of the Río Grande and the Nueces and to those engaged in mercantile pursuits. The writer has spoken of this matter elsewhere.

Life on the border of Texas was wild, rough, and dangerous. There were few points on the border where a family could locate without incurring dangers from which the boldest would recoil. The operations of the troops had inspired a degree of confidence, yet it remained to be seen who would be the first to make the venture to cast his fortunes in a district where life was menaced almost continuously and where property had no security beyond the range of the rifle and the six-shooter. It was Captain Richard King who made the first move in the matter of settling between the Río Grande and the Nueces. He came to the lands of the Santa Gertrudis and became one of the pioneers of that country. . . .

In 1852 Captain Richard King, in company with Captain G.K. Lewis, better known as "Legs" Lewis, established a cattle ranch on the Santa Gertrudis Creek. They made their headquarters near where Captain Ford's old camp stood in 1849. This cattle camp became a stopping-place for wayfarers, a sort of city of refuge for all classes, the timorous and the hungry. The men who held it were of no ordinary mould. They had come to stay. It was no easy matter to scare them. The Indians still made descents upon the country. The regular troops were operating against them. In many of the fights the red men appeared to have been victorious. They fought in a manner at variance with that in which the drilled troops of the United States had been taught to fight. The savages had the advantage in numbers and in movement. But all this had no effect on the brave men who held the ranch of Santa Gertrudis. They had determined to make a ranch on the Santa Gertrudis or leave their bones to tell of their failure.

The company at Brownsville pursued the even tenor of its way. M. Kenedy & Co. aided enterprising men, encouraged the industrious, and was open-handed to the unfortunate and the afflicted. Kenedy and partners had extensive relations with Mexico and were always on the side of those who were struggling against the intolerable oppressions set on foot by the agents of a centralized military despotism, whose instincts and practices were prompted by unmitigated tyranny. On many occasions they took an active part in elections. In State and Federal campaigns they made it a rule to support the Democratic party. It was a difficult matter to be successful against them. They were zealously in favor of advancing the interests of the Río Grande region. . . .

In 1852 Captain Kenedy established a cattle ranch at Valenio on the Nueces River. In 1854 he became the owner of another ranch at San Salvador del Tule, which was one of the first ranches in that country. It was destroyed by General Juan N. Cortina in 1859, when he made war upon the people of the United States and wreaked a bloody vengeance upon Americans whom he could not subjugate.

In 1856 Captain King moved his family from Brownsville to the ranch of Santa Gertrudis. It was an undertaking of great danger. The country between his residence and the Río Grande was thinly settled. The intervening country was raided by Indians. The Mexicans had not acknowledged the supremacy of the Americans. They expected to reconquer the country. For an American to carry his family into the wild country and settle fifty miles from Corpus Christi and one hundred and ten or twenty miles from the Río Grande was looked upon in those days as an act of extreme audacity. . . .

The raids of Cortina caused considerable loss to Captain Kenedy. His ranch of Tula was almost ruined. George and Mr. Cornelius Stillman suffered by the robbers. So did numerous others. Captain King promptly furnished all the supplies and all the intelligence needed by the United States and Texas troops. At that time there were some settlements on the road from King's ranch to Brownsville. It was strongly suspected that many Mexicans employed at the ranches were in collusion with Cortina.

After the Cortina War the vessels of M. Kenedy & Co. attained very respectable proportions. They transported vast quantities of merchandise from Brazos de Santiago to Brownsville and Matamoros and to all the places from the mouth of the Río Grande to Camargo on the San Juan River as well as to Roma on the Río Grande. For a long while Captain Kenedy and Captain King commanded steamboats themselves. Each boat had a full complement of officers and men. All the business of each boat was transacted on board. In process of time the number of boats in their service precluded this manner of transacting business; then it was done to a great extent in Brownsville.

In 1860 Captain Kenedy purchased an equal interest with Captain King in the ranch of Santa Gertrudis. Captain Walworth had an interest of 160 acres which the other partners bought and thus became full owners of the ranch. The firm name was Richard King & Co. The hospitalities extended to travellers and sightseers were undiminished. As genuine a welcome was extended to them as in the days gone by. The ranch on the broad bosom of the prairie maintained its celebrity as the resting place of the weary and as an asylum for the needy and distressed. It had won fairly the confidence and the esteem of the public, and has retained the respect of all classes up to date.

4. Frederick Law Olmsted Describes Tejano and Anglo Conflicts in the New State, 1859

The Mexicans were treated for a while after annexation like a conquered people. Ignorant of their rights, and of the new language, they allowed themselves to be imposed upon by the new comers, who seized their lands and property without shadow of claim, and drove hundreds of them homeless across the Rio Grande. They now, as they get gradually better informed, come straggling back, and often their claims give rise to litigation, usually settled by a compromise.

A friend told us, that, wishing, when he built, to square a corner of his lot, after making diligent inquiry he was unable to hear of any owner for the adjoining piece. He took the responsibility, and moved his fence over it. Not long after, he was waited upon by a Mexican woman, in a towering passion. He carried her to a Spanish acquaintance, and explained the transaction. She was immediately appeased, told him he was welcome to the land, and has since been on the most neighborly terms, calling him always her "amigo."

Frederick Law Olmsted, *Journey Through Texas, Or a Saddle-Trip on the Southwestern Frontier* (New York: Dix, Edwards, 1857), 163–165.

Most adult Mexicans are voters by the organic law; but few take measures to make use of the right. Should they do so, they might probably, in San Antonio, have elected a government of their own. Such a step would be followed, however, by a summary revolution. They are regarded by slaveholders with great contempt and suspicion, for their intimacy with slaves, and their competition with plantation labor.

Americans, in speaking of them, constantly distinguish themselves as "white folks." I once heard a new comer informing another American, that he had seen a Mexican with a revolver. "I shouldn't think they ought to be allowed to carry fire-arms. It might be dangerous." "It would be difficult to prevent it," the other replied; "Oh, they think themselves just as good as white men."

From several counties they have been driven out altogether. At Austin, in the spring of 1853, a meeting was held, at which the citizens resolved, on the plea that Mexicans were *horse-thieves,* that they must quit the county. About twenty families were thus driven from their homes, and dispersed over the western counties. Deprived of their means of livelihood, and rendered furious by such wholesale injustice, it is no wonder if they should take to the very crimes with which they are charged.

A similar occurrence took place at Seguin, in 1854; and in 1855, a few families, who had returned to Austin, were again driven out.

Even at San Antonio, there had been talk of such a razzia. A Mexican, caught in an attempt to steal a horse, had been hung by a Lynching party, on the spot, for an example. His friends happened to be numerous, and were much excited, threatening violence in return. Under pretext of subduing an intended riot, the sheriff issued a call for an armed posse of 500 men, with the idea of dispersing and driving from the neighborhood a large part of the Mexican population. But the Germans, who include among them the great majority of young men suitable for such duty, did not volunteer as had been expected, and the scheme was abandoned. They were of the opinion, one of them said to me, that this was not the right and republican way. If the laws were justly and energetically administered, no other remedy would be needed. One of them, who lived on the Medina, in the vicinity of the place of the occurrence, told us he had no complaint to make of the Mexicans; they never stole his property, or troubled him in any way.

5. Ranchero Juan Nepomuceno Cortina States His Reasons for Revolt Against Texas, 1859

30 September 1859

An event of grave importance, in which it has fallen to my lot to figure as the principal actor since the morning of the 28th instant, doubtless keeps you in suspense with regard to the progress of its consequences. There is no need of fear. Orderly people and honest citizens are inviolable to us in their persons and interests. Our object as you have seen, has been to chastise the villainy of our enemies, which heretofore has gone unpunished. These have connived with each other, and form, so to speak, a perfidious inquisitorial lodge to persecute and rob us, without any cause, and for no

---

Jerry D. Thompson, ed., *Juan Cortina and the Texas-Mexico Frontier, 1859–1877* (El Paso: Texas Western Press, 1994), 14–18, 27–28.

other crime on our part than that of being of Mexican origin; considering us, doubt-less, destitute of those gifts which they themselves do not possess.

To defend ourselves, and making use of the sacred right of self-preservation, we have assembled in a popular meeting with a view of discussing a means by which to put an end to our misfortunes.

Our identity of origin, our relationship, and the community of our sufferings, has been, as it appears, the cause of our embracing, directly, the proposed object which led us to enter your beautiful city, clothed with the imposing aspect of our exasperation.

The assembly organized, and headed by your humble servant, (thanks to the confidence which he inspired as one of the most aggrieved), we have careered over the streets of the city in search of our adversaries, inasmuch as justice, being ad-ministered by their own hands, the supremacy of the law has failed to accomplish its object.

Some of them, rashly remiss in complying with our demand, have perished for having sought to carry their animosity beyond the time limits allowed by their pre-carious position. Three of them have died—all criminal, wicked men, notorious among the people for their misdeeds. The others, still more unworthy and wretched, dragged themselves through the mire to escape our anger, and now, perhaps, with their usual bravado, pretend to be the cause of an infinity of evils, which might have been avoided but for their cowardice. They concealed themselves, and we were loth to attack them within the dwellings of others, fearing that their cause might be con-founded with that of respectable persons, as at last, to our sorrow, did happen. On the other hand, it behooves us to maintain that it was unjust to give the affair such a terrible aspect, and to represent it as of a character foreboding evil; some having carried their blindness so far as to implore the aid of Mexico, alleging as a reason that their persons and property were exposed to vandalism. Were any outrages committed by us during the time we had possession of the city, when we had it in our power to become the arbiters of its fate? Will our enemies be so blind, base, or unthinking, as to deny the evidence of facts? Will there be one to say that he was molested, or that his house was robbed or burned down? . . .

These, as we have said, form, with a multitude of lawyers, a secret conclave, with all its ramifications, for the sole purpose of despoiling the Mexicans of their lands and usurp[ing] them afterwards. This is clearly proven by the conduct of one Adolph Glavecke, who, invested with the character of deputy sheriff, and in collu-sion with the said lawyers, has spread terror among the unwary, making them be-lieve that he will hang the Mexicans and burn their ranchos, etc., that by this means he might compel them to abandon the country, and thus accomplish their object. . . .

All truce between them and us is at an end, from the fact alone of our holding upon this soil our interests and property. And how can it be otherwise, when the ills that weigh upon the unfortunate republic of Mexico have obliged us for many heart-touching causes to abandon it and our possessions in it, or else become the victims of our principles or of the indigence to which its intestine disturbances had reduced us since the treaty of Guadalupe? When, ever diligent and industrious, and desirous of enjoying the longed for boon of liberty within the classic country of its origin, we were induced to naturalize ourselves in it and form a part of the Confederacy, flattered by the bright and peaceful prospect of living therein and inculcate in the bosoms of our children a feeling of gratitude towards a country beneath whose aegis we would have wrought their felicity and contributed with our conduct to give evidence to the whole world that all the aspirations of the Mexicans are confined to one only—*that of being freemen;* and that, having secured this ourselves, those of the old country, notwithstanding their misfortunes, might have nothing to regret save the loss of a section of territory, but with the sweet satisfaction that their old fellow citizens lived therein, enjoying tranquility, as if Providence had so ordained to set them an example of the advantages to be derived from public peace and quietude; when, in fine, all has been but the baseless fabric of a dream, and our hopes having been defrauded in the most cruel manner in which disappointment can strike, there can be found no other solution to our problem than to make one effort, and at one blow destroy the obstacles to our prosperity.

It is necessary: the hour has arrived. Our oppressors number but six or eight. Hospitality and other noble sentiments shield them at present from our wrath, and such, as you have seen, are inviolable to us.

Innocent persons shall not suffer, no; but, if necessary, we will lead a wandering life, awaiting our opportunity to purge society of men so base that they degrade it with their opprobrium. Our families have returned as strangers to their old country to beg for an asylum. Our lands, if they are to be sacrificed to the avaricious covetousness of our enemies, will be rather so on account of our own vicissitudes. As to land, nature will always grant us sufficient to support our frames, and we accept the consequences that may arise. Further, *our personal enemies shall not possess our lands until they have fattened it (sic) with their own gore.*

We cherish the hope, however, that the government, for the sake of its own dignity, and in obsequiousness to justice, will accede to our demand, by prosecuting those men and bringing them to trial or leave them to become subject to the consequences of our immutable resolve.

It remains for me to say that, separated as we are, by accident alone, from the other citizens of the city, and not having renounced our rights as North American citizens, we disapprove, and energetically protest, against the act of having caused a force of the National Guards from Mexico to cross unto this side to ingraft themselves in a question so foreign to their country that there is no excusing such weakness on the part of those who implored their aid. . . .

[November 23, 1859]

Mexicans! My part is taken; the voice of revelation whispers to me that to me is entrusted the work of breaking the chains of your slavery, and that the Lord will enable me with powerful arm to fight against our enemies, in compliance with the requirements of that Sovereign Majesty, who from this day forward, will hold us under His protection. On my part, I am ready to offer myself as a sacrifice for your happiness; and counting upon the means necessary for the discharge of my ministry, you may count upon my cooperation, should no cowardly attempt put an end to my days.

This undertaking will be sustained of the following bases:

FIRST. A society is organized in the State of Texas, which devotes itself sleeplessly, until the work is crowned with success, to the improvement of the unhappy condition of those Mexicans residents therein; exterminating their tyrants, to which end those which compose it are ready to shed their blood and suffer the death of martyrs.

SECOND. As this society contains within itself the elements necessary to accomplish the great end of its labors, the veil of impenetrable secrecy covers "The Great Book" in which the articles of its constitution are written; while so delicate are the difficulties which must be overcome that no honorable man can have cause for alarm if imperious exigencies require them to act without reserve.

THIRD. The Mexicans of Texas repose their lot under the good sentiments of the governor elect of the State, General Houston, and trust that upon his elevation to power he will begin with care to give us legal protection within the limits of his powers.

Mexicans! Peace be with you! Good inhabitants of State of Texas, look on them as brothers, and keep in mind that which the Holy Spirit saith: "Thou shalt not be the friend of the passionate man; nor join thyself to the madman, lest thou learn his mode of work and scandalize thy soul."

6. Lucadia Pease Recovers from Influenza, 1852

My Dear Sister Augusta,

I have had a long and severe sickness and am now only able to sit up part of the day—I think it is five or six weeks ago, tho' time seems so long to me that it appears like as many months, since I was taken with Influenza, which has been very prevalent here, which settled in my breast, which became very much inflamed and swollen, and at times most excruciatingly painful—The Dr thought it advisable to scatter the tumors and made many applications which caused me great pain in his desire to avoid the necessity of lancing—I had a very high fever for some days, but at length got better except my breast, and as there chanced to arrive, in this remote town, that much desired by us personage a traveling Daguereau Artist, it seemed to me almost like a special providence, for little Carrie's benefit, and we determined to have him try to take her pic—We thought it might be necessary for her to be taken in my arms, and I made the effort, and went to the Court House with her (the Artists room) On my return I went on the bed, which I have scarcely left since, now nearly three weeks—I had so much fever we were compelled to wean little Carrie, who was so much grieved, that she learned to speak at once, most distinctly and piteously ma ma ma ma. Among my other ailments I had the nettle rash, something like the Erysipelas tho not as dangerous, but most exceedingly painful—Marshall is a most excellent nurse, and I know not what I should have done had he not been, as it is not possible here to hire any one to take care of the sick—The baby was kept on the gallery, and away from my room as much as possible. As the weather was very mild they kept her in the open air most of the time, and one night she was taken with all the symptoms of the croup. Her papa gave her all the remedies which we have before tried, but she grew worse so fast, he went in the night for the Doctor, who administered emetics and by morning she was much better—She is not yet

Katherine Hart and Elizabeth Kemp, eds., *Lucadia Pease and the Governor, Letter, 1850–1857* (Austin: Encino Press, 1974), 68–70.

well, has a severe cold, and is very fretful, quite unlike what she has ever been before—Last week Marshall was compelled to go to Galveston to attend Court, having postponed it as long as possible. He will stay only about a week instead of the month which we remained last year—We had made our plans early in winter to go with him, which are now so sadly frustrated. Baby slept with her Aunt Carrie last night, who is now nurse for us both—My breast was finally lanced in three places, and is now I trust getting well, only those who have had a similar one can know how much one suffers—Marshall has writted once since I have been sick, directed to Poquonock where I suppose Maria now is—I was very sorry to hear that Mr Moore's health has failed him, wish he could be induced to stay at Poquonock this year, and leave preaching altogether—We had a short visit from a gent—n from Janesville, who is an invalid, and passing the winter at Galveston for the benefit of his health—he likes the mild weather here much, tho' I think he has the consumption and will not probably be much better—

7. German Pioneer Ottilie Fuchs Goeth Recalls the Hardships of Life in Central Texas, 1859

How tedious and time consuming life was in those earlier days as compared with present. How wonderfully easy things are today when it is possible to buy practically all clothing ready-made, both for grownups and children. How many jackets I had to make for my brothers, as well as for my husband and children. Even a dressmaker could not have had more sewing to do. And as for the kitchen: When one wanted to bake bread, one had first to hand grind corn on a steel mill fitted with two handles. Even then it was more like groats rather than flour. Cooking and baking in an open fireplace was extremely difficult, and one had to watch carefully that baked goods did not burn. Practical as they are now, the first cooking stoves were not completely satisfactory, although they did make things a little easier than before. Food was simple, but wholesome.

We did not have many dishes in our home, and thus there were not many dishes to wash. Our parents had brought along a complete set of pewter dishes from Bremen. It was a terrible job to keep these at least fairly well polished. An American who had dinner at our home related everywhere that at the Pastor Fox house they eat on silver plates. We were very happy when after some years we were able to replace the "silver" plates for porcelain ones. The old pewter plates and dishes were as heavy as lead, and if one did not constantly clean them with soap and lye they turned quite black. We also had an iron stove from Germany which could be used for cooking, but was not usable for baking. This had to be done in the coals in the fireplace. Later the old stove still served as a means of heating.

We had all kinds of meat, such as venison, turkey, lamb, and beef, as well as quantities of fish. There was no lack of milk and butter, so our table was always rather well supplied with food. Guests were always welcome. Flour was more of a problem. It had to be brought from Houston by wagon. This took fourteen days.

Ottilie Fuchs Goeth, *Memoirs of a Texas Pioneer Grandmother* (Austin: Eakin Press, 1982), 61–63.

If we did not wish to sit in the dark at night, we had to make our own candles, having no kerosene or lamps. We prepared a mixture of wax and tallow which was poured into candle moulds. Unfortunately the light was so weak that any reading or fine needlework ruined one's eyes. Probably as a result of the poor light of those days, Father was unable to read anything handwritten when he was old. We did not have any lamps until after the Civil War. After that we even obtained a sewing machine, a very important event!

Not enjoying the luxury of ready-made soap, we had to fabricate our own. Lye balls, which merely have to be dropped into water in order to obtain a solution of lye, were fully unknown. Lye had to be produced in the most cumbersome manner. First one had to build a wooden hopper in which ashes were collected. Then just sufficient boiling water was added to make the lye drip out at the bottom. When it was possible to float an egg on top, fat was added and the mixture was boiled as long as necessary, sometimes taking days until one hit upon the right mixture. Our home-made product turned out very well, for our log cabin was always spick and span.

Fence-building was the most tedious job for the men. Fences were made of split logs, usually set up in zigzag fashion. Wire became available much later. Rock walls were also in use, but building these was even more time-consuming. On the other hand, broken window panes were no problem. This was for obvious reasons, for the log houses had only a few, and these were as carefully guarded as our own eyes.

Wagons were scarce. Everyone rode horseback. Large ox-drawn wagons were used to transport freight as well as passengers, stage coaches in a way, but the postillion unfortunately was less romantic, driving the oxen with his whip, and completely forgetting to sound the post horn. Also women and children were usually seen traveling on horseback. The scene often resembled the movement of a Germanic tribe of ancient times. One woman I saw had made two large pockets, resembling sacks, which she laid across the back of her horse, carrying a child in each one and a third child in her lap as she rode along.

Once to attend a celebration in Cat Spring, Mother, having difficulty in walking, rode on a sled decorated with green branches. The sled was drawn by a large white horse, and it glided smoothly through the tall grass, much as it might have done on the ice in the old country, only there were no accompanying sleigh bells. Instead there was much joking and laughing. In spite of all the hardships, most of the time morale was high, because everyone firmly believed that a better future was in store. This thought made the many hardships easier to endure.

❦ E S S A Y S

The first two essays in this chapter examine some of the problems Mexican Americans faced in the years after statehood, as Texas was rapidly transformed from an isolated frontier region into an integral part of the U.S. market economy. The first selection is excerpted from a prize-winning study of Anglo Tejano relations by David Montejano of the University of Texas at Austin. Montejano describes the process by which an Anglo minority managed to establish economic and political control over the tejano majority in the southern part of the state. Although violent clashes between the two ethnic groups periodically occurred, Anglo and Tejano elites often worked together to preserve social order. The emergence of an Anglo-male dominated society in South Texas had a particularly profound impact on the lives of many Mexican women. In the second essay, Jane Dysart, an historian at the University of West Florida, examines the process by which many Tejanas became assimilated into a new American culture through intermarriage. Facing severe economic pressures (which Montejano describes below), some prominent Tejano families viewed the marriage of daughters to Anglo males as a means of maintaining their upper-class status. Such unions, however, did little to prevent the rise of a distinctly Anglo American cultural and economic elite.

In the final essay, Ann Patton Malone, formerly a professor at Illinois State University, studies the Texas frontier from the perspective of Anglo American women. The hardships and primitive conditions of frontier life, she suggests, may have been particularly difficult for women of high social standing, who had been conditioned in the United States to aspire to a Victorian ideal of feminity. Unlike immigrants of central Europe, these well-to-do Anglo American women experienced a "psychic crisis" when confronted with a frontier existence so starkly at odds with the world they had known.

Anglos Establish Authority over Mexicans in South Texas

DAVID MONTEJANO

Although the Rio Grande settlements south and west of San Antonio were not directly affected by the Texian struggles for independence, these wars depopulated the coastal areas close to the Nueces River, the boundary between the Mexican states of Texas and Tamaulipas. The livestock industry in this area was completely disrupted as Mexican settlers fled from their *ranchos* to the protected towns of the Rio Grande. As a measure of retribution, the Texas Republic had declared Mexican livestock to be public property, prompting many Texan veterans to conduct stock raids below the Nueces. These "reckless young fellows," according to one old-timer, were the first to be given the name of "cowboys." In short, between 1836 and 1846 the strip between the Nueces and the Rio Grande constituted a veritable "no-man's land," claimed by the Republics of Texas and Mexico but actually controlled by Indian tribes.

Military occupation in 1846 and subsequent annexation replicated, in some respects, the experience above the Nueces after Texas independence. On the one hand, the fate of Mexican property rights was uncertain. Squatters and adventurers were everywhere; tales of fraud and chicanery were common; and deliberations in the Texas Legislature and in Texas courts all suggested an eventual confiscation of Mexican-owned property. The considerable expense of legal proceedings to defend old Spanish and Mexican titles, together with the uncertainty of the outcome, prompted many owners to sell to interested American parties at low prices.

On the other hand, as had happened with the Texas Revolution, there was considerable repatriation after the Mexican War. Mexican refugees moved across the Rio Grande and settled among the old established towns of Paso del Norte, Guerrero, Mier, Camargo, Reynosa, and Matamoros. Other refugees established new towns,

David Montejano, *Anglos and Mexicans in the Making of Texas, 1836–1986* (Austin: University of Texas Press, 1987), 30–40. Copyright © 1987. By permission of the University of Texas Press.

such as Nuevo Monterrey (now Nuevo Laredo) opposite Laredo and Mesilla and Guadalupe, both near El Paso del Norte. Despite these refugee movements, Texas south and west of the Nueces River remained predominantly Mexican in population.

Unlike Texas above the Nueces, where the Mexican population had soon found itself outnumbered, the length of the Rio Grande region remained isolated until the turn of the century. Following the initial Anglo settlement after the Mexican War, there was no continued influx. The only exception was the Civil War period when another layer of ex-soldiers and merchant–camp followers was added to the communities of the Upper and Lower Rio Grande valleys. El Paso served as an important stop for travelers and merchants, but permanent Anglo settlement remained small until the arrival of the railroad in 1881. In South Texas, Laredo and Brownsville were completely away from the westward land movements and no free land existed. As in the case of El Paso, the few Anglo settlers who came were merchants, lawyers, or professionals whose occupation was tied with the northern Mexican trade or the new land business of the border region. . . .

According to the best estimates . . . in 1850 there were 25,000 Mexicans in the state. Approximately 7,000 were concentrated in the region above the Nueces (around San Antonio and Goliad), 5,500 were below the Nueces (Laredo and the lower Rio Grande), 8,500 were in West Texas (El Paso and Presidio), and 4,000 were "floating about" the state. Comparable estimates for the Anglo population were 120,000 above the Nueces and 2,500 south and west of the Nueces. In other words, in 1850 the population beyond the Nueces consisted approximately of 2,500 Anglos and probably 18,000 Mexicans.

In the immediate postwar period, this demographic mix made for an unstable situation. As had occurred earlier (in the 1830s) with the San Antonio and Victoria settlements, the Rio Grande settlements attracted the worst elements among the Anglo pioneers. In Laredo, as José María Rodríguez recalled in his memoirs, some Americans "began a movement to clean out the Mexicans. They would rant at public meetings and declare that this was an American country and the Mexicans ought to be run out." In the Lower Valley, Abbé Emanuel Domenech, who ministered to the religious needs of the Brownsville area from 1849 to 1855, was blunt in his appraisal of the Americans: "The Americans of the Texian frontiers are, for the most part, the very scum of society—bankrupts, escaped criminals, old volunteers, who after the Treaty of Guadalupe Hidalgo, came into a country protected by nothing that could be called a judicial authority, to seek adventure and illicit gains." The *abbé* had especially harsh words about the Texas Rangers and ex-army volunteers in the area, describing them as "the very dregs of society, and the most degraded of human creatures." The Abbé Domenech was equally frank in his judgment of Mexicans: "I could never comprehend the Mexican's submission, supporting, as he did, at once the cruelty and the contempt of a nation which he sovereignly detested, had I not been so often the witness of his incredible *nonchalance* and imperturbable meekness. In these badly-organized regions, the Mexican might have an easy vengeance on his persecutors, who are quite the minority on the Texan frontiers; but vengeance is not in his heart; he would rather forget an injury than take the trouble of avenging it." Notwithstanding the *abbé*'s assessment, the situation along the Rio Grande proved to be extremely volatile. All that was lacking for the emergence of a movement of resistance and retribution was a precipitating gesture or act of defiance. The first Cortina War, which exploded a few years after Domenech had returned to France, had such origins.

According to the well-embossed story, Juan Nepomuceno Cortina, scion of a wealthy landowning family in the Lower Valley, came to the defense of a drunk *ranchero* and former servant from the beating of Brownsville Marshal Bob Shears. Cortina shot the marshal in the arm in self-defense and carried the *ranchero* off to his ranch. Charges of attempted murder were filed, the Brownsville authorities refusing to compromise with Cortina. In response, Cortina and his supporters raided and captured Brownsville, the initial blow of a six-month-long war. . . . Within a month, Cortina had organized an irregular force of five to six hundred men. Many of those involved in the Cortina War, according to a federal report on the matter, were *rancheros* who had been "driven away from the Nueces." Cortina defeated the Brownsville Rifles and Tobin's Rangers from San Antonio, maintaining control of the region until the U.S. Army sent troops in December 1859.

The results of the Cortina War, according to the army commandant, were the depopulation and laying to waste of the whole country from Brownsville to Rio Grande City, 120 miles. Business as far up as Laredo, 240 miles, had been interrupted and suspended for five months. There remained no property belonging to Americans that had not been destroyed. And those *ranchos* spared by Cortina's men had been burned by the Texans.

At the other end of Texas, attempts to assert ownership over several large salt deposits in the mid-1870s ignited a confrontation known as the "Salt War." Anglo merchants and politicians had shown interest in the salt lakes at the foot of the Guadalupe Mountains since annexation, and conflict over various schemes to tax the salt had constituted a volatile element in El Paso politics. For a hundred years or more the residents of Yselta, San Elizario, and other towns along the Upper Rio Grande had hauled salt from the lakes freely. The lakes had created in these towns a group of merchants who plied salt throughout northern Mexico. In 1877 Judge Charles Howard attempted to make the lakes into "a money-making proposition," but his actions, including the public murder of Louis Cardis, the leader of the Mexican opposition, aroused a "mob" to seek revenge. Howard and two of his associates were killed, and the relief troop of Texas Rangers was defeated before order was restored.

Thus, along the border, overt land dispossession, expulsions, and other repressive measures were not safe options. The Anglo pioneers were quite conscious of their small numbers in the region. After the Cortina rebellion, the threat of an uprising formed an important undercurrent in their psychology, a fear that perhaps motivated the practice of benevolent *patronismo* on their part. The "Cortina Wars" of 1859–60 and later of 1873–75 and the El Paso "Salt War" of 1877 were examples of what could happen. In all three episodes, competing claims to land or livestock precipitated a state of virtual warfare, with a mobilized Mexican element matching arms with the local constabulary and the Texas Rangers. The losers in these conflicts were usually the uninvolved civilian population, who bore the brunt of escalating and indiscriminate retaliation and counterretaliation. Indeed, the Nueces Strip of South Texas and the Trans-Pecos region of West Texas remained "untamed" for nearly fifty years after annexation. A frontier battalion of Texas Rangers, stationed in the border zone until 1920, represented the armed force of the Anglo-Texas order. A military unit during the Mexican War, the Texas Rangers functioned as the military police of occupation, waging sporadic warfare whenever the need arose.

Profits and stability, however, could not be maintained under such volatile circumstances. Peace and everyday governance required a more secure arrangement.

Structure of Peace

The changes brought about by Texas independence and later American annexation were clear: a new political authority, new markets, and new land laws, to mention the most sweeping. A highly conspicuous elite of Anglo merchants, lawyers, army officers, and office-holders now controlled the trade and politics of the annexed Mexican settlements. Whether they lived together above San Pedro Springs in San Antonio, on the bluff overlooking the bay of Corpus Christi, or around Franklin's store opposite El Paso del Norte, the clique of Anglo merchants, military officers, and lawyer politicians constituted a self-conscious foreign enclave. How did they govern?

In the case of the Texas-Mexican border region and generally in the annexed Southwest, the ability to govern in the immediate postwar period was secured through an accommodation between the victorious Anglos and the defeated Mexican elite, with the latter in command of the Mexican communities. In sociological terms, this accommodation was essentially a "peace structure."

By "peace structure" I refer to a general postwar arrangement that allows the victors to maintain law and order without the constant use of force. The concept focuses on the manner in which victors are able to exercise and establish authority over the defeated. In the Texas-Mexican region, such a peace structure was characterized by two major aspects: one, the subordination of Mexicans to Anglos in matters of politics and authority; and two, the accommodation between new and old elites.

The Fabric of Peace.   Although the American presence generally represented a new class in an old Mexican society, it did not completely transform the traditional authority structure. On the contrary, the American merchants and lawyers merely affixed themselves atop the Mexican hierarchy. In some cases, they intermarried and became an extension of the old elite. For individual families of the Mexican elite, intermarriage was a convenient way of containing the effects of Anglo military victory on their status, authority, and class position. For the ambitious Anglo merchant and soldier with little capital, it was an easy way of acquiring land. The social basis for postwar governance, in other words, rested on the class character of the Mexican settlements. . . .

The Rio Grande settlements south and west of San Antonio differed little in their social structure. At the time of American occupation in the mid–nineteenth century, there were four major strata: the landed elite; the *arrimados,* or landless relatives of the elite; the *rancheros* and *vaqueros;* and the *pastores.* The society of the time has been described as a "patriarchal" one where the landlord acted as the head and the *vaqueros* and *pastores* acted as "faithful" subjects.

Of the Rio Grande settlements, Laredo represented the peace structure at its best. Although Laredo had suffered from the depredations of "East Texas outlaws" and many families had resettled across the river (thus founding Nuevo Laredo), much of the strife prevailing in the Texas interior had been avoided. To a large extent, the confirmation of twenty land grant titles by the Texas Legislature in the 1850s was responsible for the peace. The wealth and power of landed elite were generally left undisturbed, and considerable intermarriage bound the old and new elites. Thus, in the postannexation politics of the area, ethnic divisions were secondary to those of class. Ordinances were published in both English and Spanish, American and Mexican holidays celebrated, and political offices divided equally; Mexicans ran the city while Anglos ran the county. Likewise, there was a tacit division of labor; Mexicans ranched and farmed while Anglos commerced.

In the Lower Valley, the conservative upper class, fearful of outright confiscation of their property, was divided in their response to the Anglo presence. According to a well-informed source, some landed families "learned to get along with Americans by overlooking whatever misfortunes fell on the lower class of Mexicans." Retaining their property and benefiting from the American presence, the established families had little cause for complaint. Their loyalties were subjected to a difficult test with Cortina's rebellion in 1859. Some lent the "war" quiet approval while others organized the repression of the "uprising." Unwavering support for the Anglo military forces—the Brownsville Rifles, the Texas Rangers, U.S. Army troops, and, later, Confederate troops—came from the Laredo elite in the form of a company of Mexican *rancheros* led by Santos Benavides, grandson of Don Tomás Sánchez, founder of Laredo.

As in San Antonio and Laredo, the accommodation between the old and incoming elites in the Lower Valley manifested itself in tactical marriages. It was customary among the Mexican elite, as Jovita González has noted, that daughters were "married at an early age, and not for love, but for family connections and considerations." On the other hand, for the Anglo settler, marrying a Mexican with property interests made it possible to amass a good-sized stock ranch without considerable expense. The Americans and the European immigrants, most of whom were single men, married the daughters of the leading Spanish-Mexican families and made Rio Grande City "a cosmopolitan little town." Among those who claimed the Spanish language as their own were families with such surnames as Lacaze, Laborde, Lafargue, Decker, Marx, Block, Monroe, Nix, Stuart, and Ellert. As one Texas Mexican from this upper class recalled: "There were neither racial nor social distinctions between Americans and Mexicans, we were just one family. This was due to the fact that so many of us of that generation had a Mexican mother and an American or European father." . . .

For the Anglo settlers, some degree of "Mexicanization" was necessary for the most basic communication in this region, given the overwhelming number of Mexicans. But such acculturation meant far more than the learning of a language and a proper etiquette; it represented a way of acquiring influence and even a tenuous legitimacy in the annexed Mexican settlements. From participation in religious rituals and other communal activities to "becoming family" through godparenthood or marriage—such a range of ties served to create an effective everyday authority, a type that Ranger or army guns alone could not secure.

Occupation Politics. The military occupation established the pattern and climate for civilian rule. This meant that the interim military government of the Mexican settlements of the Upper and Lower Rio Grande valleys did not allow the defeated Mexicans to rule over the victorious American soldiers, however lowly in rank. This applied, by extension, to the American quartermaster employees and merchants accompanying the army of occupation. Mexican civilian leadership may have continued administrative functions but military personnel were under distinct military jurisdiction. Thus in 1850 a sizable fraction of the Anglo population in the Mexican settlements was essentially immune from the acts of civilian authorities. In San Antonio nearly half of the American population was part of the military presence, either as enlisted personnel or as wagon surveyors working for the military. Another 9 percent were merchants or clerks. In the occupied Lower Rio Grande Valley, nearly 40 percent of the American population were army personnel or employees and 15 percent were merchants or clerks.

Once martial law was lifted and troops withdrawn or discharged Americans and Mexicans, former enemies, maintained their distinct statuses in the courts, in the political parties, and in the town administrations of the old settlements. Two questions had to be settled. One concerned the status of Mexican property in the state. Since Texas had, under the terms of statehood in 1845, retained jurisdiction over all the land within its borders, it claimed to be exempted from the Treaty of Guadalupe Hidalgo. Thus the former republic carried out its own deliberations concerning the status of the annexed Mexicans and their land grants.

To adjudicate the matter of land grants, Governor Peter H. Bell appointed William Bourland and James Miller to investigate the validity of Spanish and Mexican titles. In Webb County, site of the first hearings, the Bourland-Miller Commission encountered opposition from Mexican landowners, who believed that the investigation was out to destroy rather than protect their rights. The impartiality of the proceedings and the prompt confirmation by the legislature of the commission's recommendations removed "this unfounded prejudice" and secured the loyalty of the landed elite of the Laredo area to the new order. Other landowners beyond the Nueces were not as fortunate and thus not as loyal as the Laredo grantees. In the Chihuahua Secession, only seven of the fourteen land grants were recognized. Of approximately 350 cases in the Tamaulipas and Coahuila secessions, "some two hundred" were confirmed by the legislature in 1852, and another 50 were subsequently confirmed by 1901. Of course, many of the grants confirmed were already owned, in part or whole, by Anglos.

The second question requiring immediate attention was the political status of the Mexican in Texas. One of the liveliest debates in the Texas Constitutional Convention (1845) concerned whether or not the Mexican should be allowed the right to vote. The debate centered on whether the qualifying adjective "white" should be retained in the constitutional provisions that described the voters of the state. The Harris County representative argued that the qualifier "white" should be kept, not because he feared the Spaniard; he welcomed them as he welcomed any portion of the Caucasian race that desired to settle in Texas. Rather he feared the mass immigration of "hordes of Mexican Indians": "Silently they will come moving in; they will come back in thousands to Bexar, in thousands to Goliad, perhaps to Nacogdoches, and what will be the consequence? Ten, twenty, thirty, forty, fifty thousand may come in here, and vanquish you at the ballot box though you are invincible in arms. This is no idle dream; no bugbear; it is the truth." The proposal failed, however, because of opposition by several Anglo-Texan allies and protectors of the Texas Mexican elite (like Col. Henry Kinney of Corpus Christi). José Antonio Navarro of San Antonio, the only Texas Mexican (and the only native-born Texan) at the Constitutional Convention, argued eloquently against the proposal.

In spite of the formal defeat of disfranchisement at the convention, Mexicans in certain districts were denied the vote or allowed only limited participation. Corpus Christi merchant Henry Kinney observed that in several counties the practice immediately after independence had been to withhold the franchise from Mexicans, even though they may have fought against a people "of their own race." Traveler Frederick Olmsted observed that, if the Mexicans in San Antonio voted, they could elect a government of their own; "such a step would be followed, however, by a summary revolution." Where Mexicans did have the right to vote, protests and threats from Anglo-Americans were constant reminders of a fragile franchise.

A typical protest was exemplified by a hotly contested election for state representative from Nueces and Webb counties in 1863, where S. Kinney of Corpus Christi lost to Charles Callaghan of Laredo by a margin of thirty-five votes. The *Corpus Christi Ranchero* noted that Kinney was the choice of fifteen or sixteen voters where the English language was spoken and that "American men in an American country should have a fair showing in shaping the destinies of the country." The *Fort Brown Flag* of Brownsville joined in the protest, editorializing that "we are opposed to allowing an ignorant crowd of Mexicans to determine the political questions in this country, where a man is supposed to vote knowingly and thoughtfully." Disfranchisement was the usual sentiment of disgruntled losers in electoral politics.

Where Texas Mexicans constituted a significant portion of the male vote, the politicians among the American settlers proceeded to instruct and organize the new voters. A common pattern was the controlled franchise, where Mexicans voted according to the dictates of the local *patrón,* or boss. Since these political machines delivered sizable blocs of votes in state and national elections, the Anglo *patrones* acquired influence far beyond that usually accorded "backwater" county politicians.

Generally, the lesser bosses were members of the wealthy Mexican families who had entered the political arena to maintain and defend their traditional status, as in the "subrings" of Brownsville, San Antonio, and El Paso. But in all these instances, including places where Mexicans controlled most offices, as in Starr and Zapata counties, the figure of an Anglo boss legitimized Mexican political involvement. In the 1850s, the specific arrangements varied. Cameron County in the Lower Valley showed a nearly equal division of county commissioner positions. In Webb County, Anglos ran the county while Mexicans ran the city of Laredo. In El Paso County, the pattern was reversed, and Anglos ran the city while Mexicans ran the county.

The role of the Mexican elite as influential politicians was contingent, of course, on the presence of a large Mexican electorate. In San Antonio, where the Mexican population increasingly declined through the nineteenth century, Mexican representation on the city aldermanic council fell at an exponential rate after 1836. In 1837, for example, all but one of the forty-one candidates running for city elections were of Spanish-Mexican descent; a decade later there were only five.

Table 1.   San Antonio Aldermen by Ethnicity, 1837–1904

PERIOD	NON-SPANISH-SURNAMED	SPANISH-SURNAMED
1837–1847	31	57
1848–1857	82	17
1858–1866	82	11
1867–1874	55	4
1875–1884	67	2
1885–1894	72	1
1895–1904	60	0

Source: Based on listing in August Santleban, *A Texas Pioneer,* pp. 314–321.

Between 1848 and 1866 each aldermanic council included one or two Mexican representatives; after 1866, however, even token representation was rare. Mexican political clubs remained active but constituted minor actors in the city's affairs. Through the early 1900s, the Mexican voice in city politics was symbolically represented by Anglo officials with familial ties to the Mexican upper class—the Lockwoods, Tobins, and Callaghans, for example. The tabulation in Table 1, with city administrations organized roughly in periods of seven to ten years, gives a clear indication of the decline in power of the Mexican elite in San Antonio during the late nineteenth century.

The principle that in all matters of authority the Anglo stood over the Mexican was most evident in the area of law enforcement. Afer the 1840s, for example, there were no Mexican county sheriffs or city marshals in San Antonio but quite a few—again, generally members of the older wealthy families—were deputy sheriffs and assistant marshals. With some exceptions along the border counties, this division of authority was the pattern in the Mexican region of Texas.

Mexican Women and the Process of Cultural Assimilation

JANE DYSART

During the course of European expansion, social contact between different ethnic, racial, and national groups initiated a process of assimilation. In those instances where widespread intermarriage occurred, cultural, ethnic, and even racial distinctions were blurred as the two groups incorporated in a common culture. Where prevailing attitudes assuming cultural or racial superiority prevented extensive intermarriage, the assimilation process was only partially complete. Such attitudes on the part of Anglo-Americans inhibited large-scale marriage with Mexicans, and the celebrated frontier melting pot failed to absorb the majority of Mexicans in the southwestern United States.

Jane Dysart, "Mexican Women in San Antonio, 1830–1860: The Assimilation Process," *Western Historical Quarterly* (October, 1976): 365–375. Copyright © 1976 by The Western Historical Quarterly. Reprinted with permission.

The continuing existence of a culturally and visibly distinct Mexican minority in the Southwest can be partially explained by a historical analysis of the relationship between Mexican women and Anglo men. Following the pattern of settlement and conquest in other frontier regions, Anglo immigration into the southwestern frontier was preponderantly male; consequently, intermarriage as well as informal sexual unions almost exclusively involved Mexican women and Anglo men. Focusing this study upon the Mexican women rather than describing male attitudes toward them provides insights into the nature of the assimilation process and delineates more clearly the active role of the women. . . .

Frontier conditions forced limited modifications in traditional sex roles for both Anglo-American and Hispanic societies. When men were absent for extended periods of time—hunting, fighting, or conducting business in distant cities—women had to assume responsibility for managing family and business affairs. . . .

Despite certain liberating tendencies of the frontier, which might have enhanced or modified women's economic and social status, both Anglo and Hispanic cultures remained basically masculine in orientation. They shared a common belief in the subordination of women, and both societies restricted women's political, legal, social, and economic activities. While men dominated business and politics, women's sphere was home and family. In customs and manners the two cultures were markedly different, but an exaggeratedly masculine style of behavior was just as evident among Anglo males as *machismo* among Mexicans. Hero of the Alamo, William Barret Travis, for example, carefully noted in his diary his frequent sexual affairs with young women, both Anglo and Mexican. A double standard of sexual morality enjoined chastity and legal marriage on women but applauded sexual prowess and experience in men. Frontiersmen resolved this dualistic attitude by shielding certain women behind an elaborate code of chivalry while regarding others, especially those with darker skins, as suitable partners in casual sexual relations. Thus, both societies defined appropriate female roles as either wife and mother or mistress. Passive acceptance of such roles was expected, and research to date has not presented evidence that Mexican women in San Antonio deviated from role expectations to any significant degree.

During the 1840s and 1850s American frontiersmen apparently delighted in recounting tales of the passionate and pleasure-loving senoritas of San Antonio. Wishful thinking probably prompted many Anglo males to exaggerate the promiscuity of Mexican women. Different ideas about proper behavior and appropriate dress also accounted for reports of moral laxity. American travelers found the Mexicans' practice of nude public bathing offensive, though judging from their detailed descriptions, few left the scene quickly. Nor did they refrain from attending fandangos, public dances which were held almost nightly in San Antonio, but most expressed shock at the sensuous movements of the Mexican women. (The fandangos, in fact, were taxed by the municipal government and provided the largest single source of public revenue in 1847.) Anglos also regarded the native women's low-cut dresses as provocative and their uncorseted figures immodest. In most instances they did acknowledge that female immorality was largely confined to the lower classes. Fair skin and wealth apparently protected a woman from criticism as well as from unwelcome sexual advances. . . .

Before the outbreak of hostilities in the mid-1830s, upper class Tejanos often identified their own political liberalism with Anglo American ideals and welcomed newcomers from the United States into their homes. In this manner James Bowie met and later wed Ursula Veramendi, daughter of the liberal Mexican governor of Texas. After 1836 it was politically advantageous for Texas Mexicans, often indiscriminately regarded as enemies, to establish family connections with the dominant Anglo group. Several marriages, in fact, united Anglo political influence with Mexican landed wealth. For example, one daughter of José Antonio Navarro married the adjutant general of the state, while one of the De la Garzas married the county clerk, and her sister wed the sheriff. The political benefits of such familial alliances, however, were not entirely one-sided; for although the number of Spanish-surnamed office holders declined after 1840, the Mexican vote remained a significant factor in San Antonio elections. Anglo men with family ties in the Mexican community consistently won election to city office during the 1840s and 1850s.

Mexican *ricos* more than likely regarded retention of political influence an economic necessity. Unfamiliar with American legal practices and suspected of disloyalty to the American cause, many of the wealthy Tejanos undoubtedly viewed an Anglo son-in-law as a protection from the loss of their extensive landholdings. Several of the wealthiest families did indeed marry one or more of their daughters to Anglo men, thereby reinforcing their political as well as economic position. Included among them were the Seguíns, whose family holdings according to the 1840 tax rolls totaled almost twenty thousand acres; the Navarros, who held title to more than twenty thousand acres in addition to fifteen town lots; and the Cassianos with almost twenty-three thousand acres of land and twelve town lots.

The prospect of marrying a Mexican woman from one of the wealthy families was all the more attractive to an enterprising Anglo male, since daughters customarily inherited property, often on an equal basis with sons. Through his marriage to Margarita de la Garza, James Trueheart, a San Antonio politician, acquired a large tract of valuable land, formerly part of the Mission Espada. There he lived in the style of a *patrón* with a number of peon families who maintained his farming operations. Several other Anglo men like Trueheart advanced their own economic position considerably by marrying the daughters of land-rich Tejanos.

Frequent social contacts coupled with a surplus male population promoted intermarriage between Mexican women and Anglo men. During the 1840s and 1850s dances and parties in San Antonio included leading families from both Anglo and Hispanic groups. José María Rodríguez, whose family was counted among the aristocracy, recalled that he was "kept busy acting as an escort" for his sisters, three of whom did marry Anglos. A young soldier stationed in San Antonio during the 1850s reported attending a dance where "two or three of the bloods of Castile were present." Their land-rich parents, he added, were determined that the girls must wed "genuine Americans."

For the upper-class Mexican woman, marriage to an Anglo after 1830 initiated a process of assimilation and acculturation which in the vast majority of cases led to the americanization of their children. This pattern represented a divergence from past experiences and differed markedly from the process which occurred in rural areas of Texas even during the midnineteenth century. The paternal ancestors of the Navarros had emigrated from Corsica and those of the Cassianos from Italy, but both of these prominent San Antonio families were thoroughly hispanicized by 1830. Among the isolated ranchos of the lower Rio Grande Valley, descendants of

Americans who married Mexican wives in the 1850s attended schools in Mexico and were, in fact, thoroughly mexicanized. After 1840, however, San Antonio became a commercial and military center dominated economically, politically, and socially by Anglos.

The trend toward americanization of Anglo-Mexican families in San Antonio developed in spite of certain factors which seemed to lend greater support to a hispanicization process. The familial ties of the men who married upper-class Mexican women were generally weak and their cultural backgrounds diverse. Few of the men who chose high status Mexican brides between 1830 and 1860 had relatives living in San Antonio. Only seven were born in nearby states of the lower South, and judging by their surnames three of those men were of French extraction. Approximately one-third, however, came from the upper South or the North. Europeans were also well represented in these mixed marriages, including five German husbands, two Irish, two French, and one each from England and Scotland. In contrast to the women who maintained close familial ties and whose cultural background was homogeneous, the men seemingly lacked strong reinforcements for americanization of their families. . . .

Nevertheless, the vast majority of these upper-class children of mixed marriages established identity with their father's ethnic group rather than that of their mother. Since the well-to-do Tejano and Anglo-Mexican families did not live in separate residential districts, they had frequent contacts with their American neighbors. School attendance also aided the assimilation process, for according to the 1850 census all of these children between the ages of six and fifteen were attending school. A few children from affluent families were sent to boarding schools and colleges in other states—some as far away as New Jersey, Kentucky, and Virginia. By the time they became adults, the majority had anglicized their given names. At least three families even joined Protestant churches, while five others affiliated with the English-speaking Roman Catholic parish. With rare exceptions both sons and daughters married non-Mexicans. In short, the second generation became assimilated into Anglo-American society.

The pressures urging Anglo conformity on upper-class Mexican women and their children were indeed intense. In addition to the nativist movement of the 1850s, which exacerbated hostilities against non-Anglo-Saxon and Catholic groups, Anglo Texans forced upon the Mexicans an onus of guilt for the Alamo and Goliad. At the root of discrimination and violence, however, was the Anglo's sense of racial and cultural superiority. They considered Mexicans as innately inferior and as obstacles to economic and political progress. Even the high-status Tejanos felt the sting of cultural, if not racial, prejudice. Thus, the majority of Mexicans in San Antonio, even if they desired to become americanized, found that Anglos had erected almost insurmountable obstacles to assimilation. Only the women and children with Anglo surnames, light skins, and wealth had a reasonable chance to escape the stigma attached to their Mexican ancestry. Judging from their actions, many of them considered it important, perhaps even necessary to do so.

Mexican women were not in a position to direct the course of social change that occurred in San Antonio during the midnineteenth century. The male-oriented frontier society limited female role alternatives to either wife and mother or mistress and at the same time determined the racial and class criteria which shaped the nature of relationships between Anglo men and Mexican women. Given the patriarchal family structure of both ethnic groups, the wife's function was child care and home management, while the husband assumed primary responsibility for making decisions affecting the family's relationship to the society. Because the assimilation process in San Antonio demanded conformity to Anglo social and cultural patterns, those few Mexican women whom Anglo men found acceptable as wives lost their own distinctive ethnic identity, and in many cases their children rejected the rich cultural legacy of their Mexican ancestry.

Victorian Womanhood on the Texas Frontier

ANN PATTON MALONE

Ironically, the women on the Texas frontier with the greatest social and economic advantages suffered a dislocation and incongruity with their social system which other women were generally spared. The Anglo American woman of the mid-nineteenth century matured within a Victorian society with prescribed feminine roles and expectations. Whenever feasible, they were expected to fulfill the ideals of the "womanly woman." Upper and middle-class women's lives were dictated by these expectations; lower and working-class women also aspired to them and accepted the "womanly woman" as a role model. The strong Southern heritage of most Texas settlers and the scarcity of women on the frontier reinforced the Victorian ideals of womanhood. However, frontier conditions made it nearly impossible for women to achieve them.

According to the Victorian social system, the proper model for men was the "manly man;" for women, the "womanly woman." These two ideals mutually reinforced each other. The "manly man" was aggressive, expansive, and worldly; the entire scope of human endeavors was his sphere. He was actor, leader, defender, and discoverer. Since his primary function was economic, he was forced into the marketplace where he must be strong-willed, rational, inquiring, and occasionally ruthless. The competitiveness, violence, and persistent conflicts of the world made men hard and insensitive. The Victorian code decreed that women should be protected from these hardening influences, and that they should help mitigate such influences for their men. The home served a vital function for the Victorian male. It was a place where he could express himself freely, be soothed, softened, strengthened, cheered, and comforted by domestic tranquility. One of the primary objectives for the "womanly woman" was to assure this peace for her husband; her other primary role was to bear his children.

The ideal Victorian woman was passive, childlike, unreflective, self-sacrificing, and dependent. Whereas men were to be self-possessed, women were to submit to the control of others, principally to their husbands, fathers, and brothers. Above all, women were to be adaptable, able to mold themselves to their husband's expectations and desires. In a Victorian marriage, potential conflict was removed through

Ann Patton Malone, *Women on the Texas Frontier: A Cross-Cultural Perspective* (El Paso: Texas Western Press, 1983), 14–19. Reprinted with permission of the author.

constant wifely adjustment, and this submission sometimes included accompanying husbands to remote frontier regions such as Texas regardless of the wives' personal inclinations.

Since motherhood and wifehood were equally glorified, the Victorian woman was expected to bear children not only dutifully but joyfully. Yet she was to be passionless and submissive in sexual matters. Home and family were her only worlds. She was neither trained nor thought suited for anything else. Even in the sacred spheres of home and family, however, she did not reign as "Queen of the Household" as did women of other cultures on the Texas frontier. Even in household matters the Anglo American woman was expected to defer to her husband or father. Her training from childhood was designed to fulfill the roles prescribed by society. According to the code, female education ceased or was neglected after the age of fifteen because intellectual or opinionated women were considered unwomanly. Her training was almost exclusively in the domestic arts after that point. She learned how to run a household frugally and to direct servants efficiently while performing little of the actual labor herself. She was expected to be charming and pleasing to family and guests, and to this end she was taught a smattering of music, literature, drawing, dancing, and the "art of light conversation." Such skills were generally of little use to the elite women who removed to the Texas frontier.

The mid-nineteenth century Victorian code for female behavior both glorified and oppressed, protected and controlled. Most women, especially in the South, submitted to the code, and some enjoyed the view from the pedestal, but an undercurrent of discontent did exist. An anonymous widely sung Southern rural folk tune of the period, "The Wagoner's Lad," expressed a common attitude among women:

> Hard is the fortune of all womankind,
> They are always controlled,
> They are always confined,
> Controlled by their family until they are wives,
> Then slaves to their husbands
> The rest of their lives.

Women found ways to circumvent some of the male authority. Particularly in the South, women often made a weapon of their womanhood, using coquetry to gain their way. In some cases they could mitigate their husband's authority by appealing to conscience or religion since even husbands could not dictate on such matters. They could gain support by appealing to a formidable array of female kin, the Victorian woman's most constant companions. But on the frontier, the domination of the Anglo woman was almost complete. Coquetry was out of place, organized religion was weak, and supportive kinship networks were removed or dispersed in many cases. If the woman had inherited wealth, she might exercise some independent judgment, but she did so rarely. In Texas a woman's wealth was often absorbed into her husband's estate even if it remained technically in her name.

The Victorian social system was powerful and reached even into the frontier regions. But frontier experiences created challenges to the code, and incongruities developed. The women who had been inculcated from infancy with the feminine ideals of the Victorian code and then found many of the precepts obsolete or inappropriate on the Texas frontier were often torn and bewildered—even traumatized—

by the experience. They were separated from kin, community, and what they considered civilization. Many felt totally inadequate to perform the tasks required of them in their new circumstances, as did Rebecca Pilsbury, a New Englander who accompanied her husband to Brazoria, Texas, in 1848. On November 17, she wrote, "I felt totally incapacitated. I was to perform the duties of chargé d'affaires to slaves." And several days later she confessed that "I am inclined to think that I was not designed for a worker, surely no one ever put their hand to plow more willingly than I. Attempted to preserve some pumpkin today, and surely no one ever met a more total failure."

Even a cursory examination of the voluminous published and unpublished literature of these first-generation frontier women reveals their conflict. A pathetic stream of letters to family and kin plead for more correspondence, any word from "home." They desperately attempted to preserve what they associated with civilized society despite its inappropriateness in the wilderness. It was no accident that frontier wife Harriet Ames wore a black silk dress on the Runaway Scape. And the elite women who were wives of leading colonists dressed in silks, brocades, and diamonds for parties in Columbia and Matagorda Bay. Travelers frequently commented upon the stark contrasts they encountered in Texas, such as fine furniture in crude log cabins, libraries in the wilderness, and elegantly attired and graciously mannered women in remote settlements.

Woman of all social and economic classes accompanied their husbands and families to the frontier during the expansionistic thirties, forties, and fifties, but more is known about the elite women since they left more records. These daughters and wives of planters, merchants, professionals, and army officers had previously performed little physical labor. On the frontier, they had to perform unaccustomed and often untraditional tasks. Although they did not customarily work in the clearing, building, or planting processes, they had to undertake much of the cooking, spinning, gardening, and nursing duties which had been relegated to servants in their distant homes. In addition to their own familial responsibilities, frontier women were frequently expected to care for slaves and neighbors in times of sickness, death, or other crises.

Understandably, the elite women found it difficult or impossible to run a smooth-functioning household on the frontier and to provide what they considered a proper Christian upbringing for their children. Concern for the physical well-being of their families is the most persistent theme in the letters women wrote to relatives. Health, a precarious matter anywhere in the nineteenth century, was especially hazardous on the Texas frontier. Frequent outbreaks of cholera and fevers, frontier lawlessness, wars with Indians and Mexicans, accidents, and childbirth all took a frightful toll on frontier women and their families.

Anglo American women who migrated to the Texas frontier underwent a psychic crisis which their Texas-born daughters could scarcely appreciate. The second generation matured in a new environment, with different expectations and models and with their support groups intact. Lucadia Pease, later the wife of a Texas governor, shortly after leaving her family home to accompany her husband to Texas wrote her sister, "I cannot tell you how sad I felt after parting from you, the last member of our own family, with the prospect of so long a journey before me, and its termination placing me so far from home . . . ." Another homesick transplanted wife wrote that she spent a few hours sewing the garment "wetted by my tears." These first-generation pioneering women, ill equipped for the tasks expected of them, suffered a profound sense of alienation in their new homeland because of the nature of Anglo settlement which tended to be nuclear and scattered rather than organized by family groups, communities, or presidios. Women who had matured while surrounded by relatives and servants found the isolation difficult. Anna Maria Campbell Reynolds recalled that "the first night's camp on the prairies was horrible to me. . . . There was no sound to greet my ears but the howling of wolves. . . . I was frightfully blue." Many women left reminiscences which express feelings of utter loneliness, even terror, in their little cabin homes, miles from the closest neighbors. Considering the frequency of male absences, the unstable and sometimes hostile relations with the Indians, and the general lawlessness of the Texas frontier, the concerns and fears expressed by these women were well founded.

When a social system develops stresses and finally gives way to another, a great burden is placed upon the traditional generation. On the Texas frontier, numerous adjustments were required of these elite women. Some adjusted in a single generation and emerged stronger, more self-reliant than they would have become under less trying circumstances. Mary Austin Holley, a perceptive observer, wrote concerning her 1836 visit to Texas: "Delicate ladies find that they can be useful and need not be vain. . . . Many latent faculties are developed." Other women, however, were unable to satisfactorialy adjust but bore children who faced less conflict with their environment. A few never adjusted and quietly mourned themselves into early graves or returned to their distant familial homes. The latter groups rarely left reminscences of their bitter experiences, hence we have a rather one-sided and glorified record written by the women who persevered. These accounts unconsciously present a stereotype of pioneer women of unbelievable character—stoic, brave, adventuresome, and ladylike. Their chronicles include confrontations with Indians, runaway slaves, invading Mexican armies, wild animals, and the elements, but they generally avoid comment on confrontations they had with loved ones and themselves. These women who persevered and left records may not have been, in fact, extraordinarily courageous, but they had successfully developed powerful survival mechanisms. Paradoxically, the Victorian social system in some ways prepared these women for the adaptations required of them. The system had conditioned them to develop the traits of patience, acceptance, submission, stoicism, and above all, adaptability. The keen-honing of such traits might explain why supposedly helpless women could defend their cabins with guns and axes against marauding Indians, or could very ably manage businesses, farms, or plantations in their husbands' absences. Since their survival mechanisms had developed within a Victorian framework, the increasingly self-reliant and independent frontier women were also willing, even anxious, to abdicate their authority upon their husbands' return or when the crisis had passed. The submissiveness of the elite women often puzzled foreign visitors. Eugene Maissin, a Frenchman who visited many Texas plantations, observed that the men "talk rarely to the women, and only if they have nothing else to do. The women appear quite accustomed to this neglect and seem astonished if one attempts to converse with them."

In summary, Victorian daughters, wives, and mothers of the first generation became embroiled in social ambiguity on the frontier. Separated from their family and traditional society, they went through multiple migrations and uprootings. They became preoccupied with their health and that of their children and were insecure about their ability to provide a genteel home. Their inculcated instincts told them that the physical and spiritual well-being of their families was foremost, literally their raison d'être. The risks to both were great on the frontier, and the sources of assistance—whether institutional, communal, or familial—were fewer. Because of the absence of community, extended families, and churches, the first generation women came to view themselves as civilizers and felt obligated to bring gentility, culture, and beauty to the raw life of the frontier. In some ways the primitive nature of frontier life inspired a creativity in all women which was expressed in their quilts, pottery, basketry, beadwork, weaving, flower gardens, garments, and in a myriad of other ways.

The elite women of the Texas frontier rose to its many challenges, but at considerable costs. Frequently they submitted to the new demands, attempted to combine old roles with new, and found surprising strength and resolve within themselves. But when reading the diaries, reminiscences, and journals of the pioneer women of Texas, elite or otherwise, one is urged to look for what Lillian Schlissel calls the obscure or hidden patterns. One finds, between the lines, signs of tortured ambiguity. The daughters were less in conflict. They, and the yeoman class women were the self-sufficient Anglo women often commented upon. However, it was not these hardy young women of the soil who were the most remarkable. It may have been instead the first generation elite women—the most reluctant pioneers of all—who made their peace with a hostile world in spite of their fears, conflicts, and insecurities.

The elite woman, or "refined lady" as many nineteenth-century observers called her, eventually achieved a somewhat more liberalized relationship with men on the frontier. The frontier simply precluded the existence of a class of purely ornamental or decorative women. Even planters' wives ultimately became involved in plantation affairs. Immigrant women and Anglo American middle class women developed even stronger economic roles, much like women in Indian society. These hard-working females were much admired by their contemporaries.

Women of varied ethnic groups migrated with their families to the Texas frontier in the thirties, forties, and fifties, and in even larger numbers after the Civil War. Migrants from the German states, from Moravia and Bohemia (areas which later became Czechoslovakia), England, France, Ireland, and Scotland were among the most numerous. They encountered the same basic problems of other newcomers, but their responses to the Texas environment were often as varied as the cultures and circumstances from which they originated. Some generalizations can be extracted from their experiences, however. Separations from homeland, family, kin, and other support groups and institutions were generally acknowledged by immigrating groups to be permanent, thus making the initial adjustment to the frontier doubly trying. Scholars of the immigration process have suggested that immigrants are severely and permanently affected by the loss of community, regardless of any resultant economic or social improvement. Immigrants did attempt to recreate that which was good and familiar from the world they had left, but the motivations behind their migration to a new world were generally much more compelling and concrete than the vague urges of manifest destiny and frontier impulses which propelled Americans to the area. Although they had nostalgia and affection for much of the world they left behind, most migrants had very urgent political, ideological, economic, or religious reasons for leaving. They were not reluctant pioneers, for the most part, as were so many elite Anglo women. Observers frequently commented upon the optimistic demeanor of the immigrants, most of whom were determined to make a new life and to adjust quickly. Mrs. Jesse Houstoun described in 1843 the disembarkment of 115 French settlers in Galveston. She said that they were a "motley group" but "one and all" looked "cheerful and happy." She seemed to think that they were well suited for the frontier experience, commenting upon their "extreme fitness . . . to cope with the inconveniences of a new country, such as Texas. They are more light of heart, and less easily depressed than the British settler . . . (and) their wants are fewer and more easily supplied."

In some ways the immigrant woman did have a psychological advantage over her English and Anglo American counterpart for she was better accustomed to a strong economic role. The peasant or agricultural societies from which many European immigrant women came prepared them well for the hard labor and role adjustments they would encounter in Texas. For example, German women worked in the fields of south-central Texas along with their husbands and servants with no sense of shame or loss of status, since they had worked similarly in their homeland. Furthermore, although the men ruled the family rather autocratically among most European immigrant groups represented on the Texas frontier, the women ruled their households in a like fashion, exercising considerable authority and control in their own realm.

While cultural differences such as language barriers and a lack of frontier know-how presented unique difficulties for the immigrant pioneers, the absence of certain Anglo American cultural biases sometimes resulted in better relations with the Indians, Mexicans, and Blacks on the frontier.

Many immigrants suffered greatly during their first year or so on the Texas frontier. Among them, childbearing women, the elderly, and small children suffered most. Immigration propaganda circulated in Europe had misled many, especially those who came early without an established ethnic community to welcome and advise them. Consequently, most lacked any real understanding of the area, geographically or culturally. Mortality schedules in the leading immigrant areas often contain the notation that most of the dead were infants or new immigrants who had settled in the fever-ridden river bottoms. Once the dangerous period of initial adjustment had passed, the immigrant woman generally thrived on the frontier. Practical, industrious women with few pretensions or grandiose expectations, they contributed much to the development of the region.

Akin to the immigrant woman and between the elite and the poor white woman was a large group of females who were socially and economically of the middle rank. These were the wives, daughters, and other kin of yeomen farmers, small slaveholders, craftsmen, and tradesmen. They were probably more comfortable on the frontier than any other groups of Anglo women. Like the elite women, they, too, were strongly influenced by the feminine role expectations of the Victorian code. It provided them with a sense of duty, loyalty, determination, adaptiveness, and submissiveness, all helpful in adjusting to frontier conditions. But these women also had the advantage of a broader work experience. Because their prior lives had not been ones of either luxury or abject poverty but of hard work and activity, these yeoman-class women were better prepared to fulfill their expected roles on the frontier. Unlike the poor white women, they viewed reversals as temporary and were able to accept hardship with relative equanimity. While the Victorian code made them feel uncomfortable in strictly defined male-related work, they knew how to garden, sew, spin, weave, cook, and raise children without a retinue of servants or kin to assist. And they were accustomed to a division of labor which included demanding economic and familial duties. They were confronted with the same problems as the elite and other women on the frontier. Since these yeomen-class women were generally in a more exposed position on the frontier rather than in a plantation setting, they probably experienced even greater difficulties. They were, however, better prepared by training and experience to meet the challenges, and they developed into strong independent, resourceful, and self-reliant women. Some parallels can be drawn between the yeomen-class frontier Anglo women and Indian women. Both had strong economic roles in addition to their familial roles, acting with their husbands as partners in production. Also, like Indian women, they tended to internalize certain elements of the dominant male culture. These women could not be protected and segregated from worldly events by a secure impenetrable circle of home and family. On the frontier, they witnessed aggression, danger, greed, violence, and death. They experienced fear, undertook varied responsibilities, accomplished new tasks; in short, they were exposed to the whole range of human activities and emotions. But the milieu to which they were exposed was aggressively male-oriented. Males set the goals, provided the criterion for success, and received the rewards. Like the Indian women the yeoman woman adopted some of the characteristics of the dominant male culture. She was, in some respects, masculinized by the frontier experience. . . . Stoic, fatalistic, taciturn, the women who participated most fully in the frontier experience were hardened as well as strengthened by it. Such women could wield a hoe or a rifle nearly as well as their husbands. Such were the women who defended their homes and children against Indian attack with hatchets and guns rather than with feminine appeals for mercy. Such also was the woman who demanded the right to unflinchingly view her scalped son's corpse, or who wept at the birth of a daughter, who urged her sons and husband into battle against the Indians, Mexicans and Yankees, regretting that she couldn't go herself. Frontier men admired her greatly, even though she departed from the prevalent feminine ideal, because she displayed so many of the attributes which they admired in themselves. Yet she rarely failed to defer to her menfolk. The yeoman-class woman was the prototype of the Texas pioneer woman to her contemporaries. . . .

In addition to the genteel and middle-rank yeoman women, a third group which has received little scholarly attention also resided on the Texas frontier. These were the poor white women whose existence was at best marginal. Not much is known about them and their families, but they were occasionally observed and described by travelers and in reminiscences. Most settlers had to endure temporary hard times, but not a debilitating and seemingly hopeless poverty which passed down through the generations. Such poverty was present on every Texas frontier despite abundant natural resources and opportunities. . . .

The experiences of Anglo women on the Texas frontier varied widely according to their backgrounds and circumstances. Some, such as the elite women, were better equipped economically to benefit from the opportunities offered by a developing region. Others, such as the immigrant and second-generation women, were better prepared psychologically for the pioneering experience.

✦ *F U R T H E R   R E A D I N G*

Armando Alonzo, *Tejano Legacy: Rancheros and Settlers in in South Texas, 1734–1900* (1998)

Ty Cashion, *A Texas Frontier: The Clear Fork Country and Fort Griffin, 1849–1887* (1996)

Arnoldo De León, *Tejano Community, 1836–1890* (1982)

Fane Downs, "Tryels and Trubbles: Women in Early Nineteenth Century Texas," *Southwestern Historical Quarterly,* 90, 564–570.

John Salmon Ford, Stephen B. Oates, eds. *Rip Ford's Texas* (1963)

Joe S. Graham, *El Rancho in South Texas: Continuity and Change from 1750* (1994)

Terry Jordan, *North American Cattle-Ranching Frontiers: Origins, Diffusion, and Differentiation* (1993)

Paula Mitchell Marks, *Hands to the Spindle; Texas Women and Home Textile Production, 1822–1880* (1998)

Timothy Matovina, *Tejano Religion and Ethnicity: San Antonio, 1821–1860* (1995)

Frederick Merk, *Slavery and the Annexation of Texas* (1972)

David E. Narrett, "A Choice of Destiny: Immigration Policy, Slavery, and the Annexation of Texas," *Southwestern Historical Quarterly,* 100, 271–302

David Pletcher, *The Diplomacy of Annexation: Texas, Oregon, and the Mexican War* (1973)

Justin H. Smith, *The Annexation of Texas* (1911)

Thomas T. Smith, *The U.S. Army and the Texas Frontier Economy, 1845–1900* (1999)

Paul N. Spellman, *Hugh McLeod, Forgotten Texas Leader: Hugh McLeod and the Texas Santa Fe Expedition* (1999)

Mark J. Stegner, *Texas, New Mexico and the Compromise of 1850; Boundary Dispute and Sectional Crisis* (1996)

CHAPTER
8

Secession and Civil War,

1861–1865

When Texans joined the Union by virtual acclamation in 1845, it seemed inconceivable that they would vote to leave it a mere sixteen years later. In addition to the manifold economic advantages of annexation, Anglo Texans in the western regions of the state relied upon the U.S. Army to protect them from the tribal bands of Plains Indians. In terms of ethnic composition, too, the population of Texas, with its sizable enclaves of Hispanics and German immigrants, bore little similarity to the other southern states that joined the Confederacy in 1861. Some of its leading public figures, most notably Sam Houston, remained steadfast adherents of Union even as public support grew in the late 1850s for the secessionist cause. Yet for all its unique characteristics, Texas displayed many of the same cultural chromosomes that defined the Lower South. The rich, alluvial soil of east Texas, the most densely populated area of the state, nourished a plantation economy based on cotton and slaves, binding it firmly to the interests of its southern neighbors. In the end, the dominance of the cotton culture led Texans to follow the path of disunion and Civil War.

The extent to which Texas shared in the broader regional identity that made secession possible is an issue that has long intrigued historians, for it calls into question the state's vaunted claim to uniqueness. Some historians have argued that the bitter experience of Civil War prompted Texans in later years to downplay their southern roots. In a subconscious effort to disassociate Texas from the trauma of the "Lost Cause," they tailored their historical memory to give greater emphasis to the state's frontier heritage. In so doing, they laid claim to an artificial brand of exceptionalism, constructing an elaborate and ennobling mythology around the exploits of Anglo Texans in their struggles against Mexico and Native Americans. While this interpretation may not be shared by all historians, Texas' decision to join the Confederacy must be viewed as a significant marker in the formation of the state's identity. In 1861, to be sure, Texas was a state of many competing and disparate identities. What factors contributed to the ascendancy of a distinctly southern perspective? Was the system of slave labor the key ingredient in making Texas a southern state? To what extent did political conditions play a role in convincing Texans that they should take the momentous step of severing their ties to the Union?

In the first two documents, two former Texas slaves recall their lives before emancipation. Both were among the hundreds of former slaves interviewed in the late 1930s as part of an ambitious oral history project conducted by the federal government. Andy J. Anderson was ninety-four years old when interviewed. Lulu Wilson moved to Texas from Kentucky during the Civil War. She was interviewed when she was ninety-seven.

The secession crisis is the focus of the next two documents. In Document 3, the delegates of the state's secession convention present their case for disunion. This document reveals the importance of slavery to the secessionist cause as well as its fear that Lincoln's election would now put the institution in jeopardy. Sam Houston, more fearful that secession would lead to a bloody and destructive war, refused to swear allegiance to the Confederacy and was promptly ousted as governor by a secession convention called by the legislature. Document 4 is an excerpt from Houston's speech at Brenham shortly after his removal, one of the last he gave during a remarkable public career in Texas spanning more than a quarter of a century.

Document 5 is an eyewitness account of the "Great Hanging," which occurred in Gainesville, Cooke County. Although rumors of a unionist conspiracy appear to have been greatly exaggerated, a large non-slaveholding population had voted against secession in Cooke and surrounding counties, creating a climate of intense suspicion in North Texas that culminated in the lynching of 42 individuals in October 1862.

Although most of the fighting between North and South took place in other parts of the United States, the conflict had a wrenching and sometimes violent impact on the civilian population of Texas. In Document 6, Rebecca Ann Adams writes to her husband, a physician serving in the Confederate army. For many Anglo Texas women, the absence of husbands during the war required them to assume new and unfamiliar roles. Accustomed to caring for nine children—a tenth, Robert, was serving with her husband—Rebecca Ann was obliged to take on the added responsibility of running a large East Texas plantation of fifty slaves.

1. Andy J. Anderson, Former Slave, Recalls Life During the Civil War, n.d.

The war broke out, and that made the big change on the master's place. He joined the army and hired a man named Delbridge for overseer. After that, the hell started to pop, because the first thing Delbridge did was cut the rations. He weighed out the meat, three pounds for the week, and he measured a peck of meal. And that wasn't enough. He half starved us niggers, and he wanted more work, and he started the whipping. I guess he started to educate them. I guess that Delbridge went to hell when he died, but I don't see how the devil could stand him.

We were not used to such, and some ran off. When they were caught, there was a whipping at the stake. But that Delbridge, he sold me to Massa House in Blanco County. I was sure glad when I was sold, but it was short of gladness, because here was another man that hell was too good for. He gave me the whipping, and the scars are still on my arms and my back, too. I'll carry them to my grave. He sent

Ronnie Tyler and Lawrence Murphy, eds., *Slave Narratives of Texas* (Austin: State House Press, 1974), 98, 126. Copyright © State House Press. Reprinted with permission.

me for firewood, and when I got it loaded, the wheel hit a stump, and the team jerked, and that broke the whippletree. So he tied me to the stake, and every half hour for four hours, they laid ten lashes on my back. For the first couple of hours the pain was awful. I've never forgot it. Then I'd stood so much pain that I did not feel so much, and when they took me loose, I was just about half dead. I laid in the bunk for two days, getting over that whipping, getting over it in the body but not the heart. No, sir, I have that in the heart till this day.

After that whipping I didn't have the heart to work for the massa. If I saw the cattle in the cornfield, I turned them back, instead of chasing them out. I guess that's the reason the massa sold me to his brother, Massa John. And he was good like my first massa; he never whipped me. . . .

Then surrender was announced and master told us we were free. When that took place, it was about one o'clock by sun. I said to myself, I won't be here long. But I had not realized what I was in for till after I'd started, but I couldn't turn back, for that meant whipping or danger from the patrollers. There I was and kept on going. No nigger was supposed to be off the master's place without a pass, so I traveled at night and hid out during the day. I stayed in the brush and got water from the creeks, but didn't get much to eat. Twice I was sure those patrollers were passing while I was hiding.

I was 21 years old then, but it was the first time I'd gone any place except to the neighbors, so I was worried about the right way to Master Haley's place. But the morning of the third day I came to the place, and I was so hungry and tired and scared for fear Master Haley was not home from the army yet. So I found my pappy, and he hid me in his cabin till a week passed, and then luck came to me when Master Haley came home. He came at night and the next morning that Delbridge [the overseer] was sent off the place, because Master Haley saw the niggers were all gaunt and lots had run off, and the fields were not plowed right, and only half the sheep and everything was left. So master said to that Delbridge, "There are no words that can explain what you've done. Get off my place before I smash you."

Then I could come out from my pappy's cabin, and the old master was glad to see me, and he let me stay till freedom was ordered. That was the happiest time in my life, when I got back to Master Haley.

2. Lulu Wilson, Former Slave, Describes the Hardships of Slavery, 1938

'Course I was born in slavery, ageable as I am. I am a old time slavery woman and the way I been through the hackles I got plenty to say about slavery. . . .

My paw wan't no slave. He was free man 'cause his mammy was a full blood Creek Indian. Now I ain't saying what his paw was 'cause I ain't knowing. All I know is what my mammy told me and I ain't never seed my paw but one time.

My maw says she was born in slavery to Wash Hodges' paw. He gave her to Wash Hodges when he married. That was the only woman slave he had. He had one man slave, a young buck. My maw says she took with my paw and I was born but

"Lulu Wilson," *The American Slave: A Composite Autobiography,* Supplement, Series 2, vol. 10, Part 9, Texas Narratives (Westport: Greenwood Press, 1979), 191–198.

some time passed and didn't no more younguns come and so they said my paw was too old and wore out for breedin' and they wanted her to take with this here other buck. So the Hodges set the nigger hounds on my paw and run him away from the place and maw said he went to the free state. So she took with my step paw and they must of pleased the white folks that wanted niggers to breed like livestock 'cause she birthed nineteen children. Two died, one when it was a young baby and one when it was a yearling baby. [About one year old.] . . .

Now when I was little chap they was the hardest times. They nearly beat us to death. They took me from my mammy out'n the little house built on to their house and I had to sleep in a bed by Missus Hodges. I cried for my maw but I had to work and wash and iron and clean the house and milk cows when I was so little.

The Hodges had three chilluns. The olderest one they was mean to 'cause she was a gal and so thick headed. She couldn't learn nothing out'n a book but she was kinder and more friendly like than the rest of the lot.

Wash Hodges was mean pore trash and he was a bad actor and a bad manager. He never could make any money and he starved it out'n the niggers. For years all I could get was one little slice of sowbelly, a puny little piece of bread and a tater. I never had enough to stave the hongriness out'n my belly.

My maw would have to cook in the house sometimes and she was a clink. [Cline, best of its kind.] She could cuss and she wan't afeared. Wash Hodges would try to whip her with a cow hide and she would knock him down and bloody him up. Then he would go down to some of his neighbor kin and try to get them to come help him whup her. But they would say, "I don't want to go up there and let Chloe Ann beat me up." Leastways, I heared him tell his wife that they said that.

My step paw used to sit on the rail fence by the yard and hear my maw in a tantrum in the kitchen and wouldn't partialize with her but jest set there laughin' and say, "Chloe Ann is a clink."

My maw did tell me that she was a 'ligious woman and she b'lieved that the time would come when the niggers wouldn't have to be slave to the white folks. She told me to pray for it. She told me she seed a old man what the nigger dogs chased and et the legs nearly off him. She said she was chased by them bloody hounds and she just picked up a club and layed they skull open. She said they had hired her out and they had sold her twice but they brung her back to Wash Hodges.

Now Mrs. Hodges studied 'bout meanness more than Wash done. She was mean to anybody she could lay her hands to, but special mean to me. She beat me and she used to tie my hands and make me lie flat on the floor and she put snuff in my eyes. I b'lieve I ain't lyin' before God when I say that I knows why I went blind. I did see white folks sometimes that spoke right friendly and kindly to me.

I gits to thinkin' now how Wash Hodges would sell off my maws chilluns. He would sell them and have the folks come for them when my maw was in the fields. When she would come back she would raise a rukus. Then many the times I seen her plop right down to a settin' and cry 'bout it. But she 'lowed there wan't nothing could be done 'cause it was the slavery law. She said, "Oh lord let me see the end of it 'fore I die and I'll quit my cussin' and fightin' and rarin'." My maw claimed to me she was part Indian and 'twas 'countable for her ways.

One day they truckled us all down in a covered wagon and started out with the family and my maw and step paw and five of us chilluns. I know I was past twelve year old. We come a long way and we passed through a free state. (Probably Missouri) Some places we drove for miles in the woods instead of the big road and when we come near to folks they hid us down in the bed of the wagon.

We passed through a little place and my maw told me to look and I saw a man going up some steps toting a bucket of water. She said, "Lulu, that man is your paw. He aint such a youngish man but he was good to me and good for me." I ain't never think she was as considible of my step paw as she was of my paw and she gave me to think as much. My step paw never did like me but he was a fool for his own younguns. 'Cause at the end of the wars when they set the niggers free he tramped over half the world gathering up them younguns that they had sold away.

He went to a place called Wadefield (Texas) and settled for some short passing of time and they was a Missionary Baptist church next to the house. When we was there Mrs. Hodges let me go twice and I was fancified with the singing and the preaching. They sang something 'bout the Glory Road. I set it in my mind that some day I'd jine with them and I spoke it over with my maw.

We went on to Chatfield Point. (Navarro County, Texas) Wash Hodges built a log house and covered it with weather boarding and built my maw and paw quarters to live in. They turned to raising corn, taters and hogs. I had to work like a dog. I hoed and I milked ten cows twice a day.

Missus told me I had ought to marry. She told me if I would marry she would togger me up in a white dress and give me a weddin' supper. She made the dress and Wash Hodges married me out'n the Bible to a nigger b'longing to a nephew of his'n. I was bout thirteen or fourteen. I know that it wan't long after that when Missus Hodges got a doctor to me. The doctor told me that less'n I had a baby, old as I was and married, I'd start in on spasms. So it twan't long 'til I had a baby.

In b'twixt that time Wash Hodges started laying out in the woods and swamps all the time. I heared that he was hidin' out from the war and that he was sposin' to go 'cause he had been a volunteer in the first war they didn't have back in Kentucky.

One night when we was all asleep some folks whooped and woke us all up. Two sojers came in and they left more outside. They found Wash Hodges and they said it was midnight. They said to get them something to eat. They 'et and then some more came in an 'et. They tied Wash's hands and made me hold the lamp in the door for them to see by. They had some more men in the wagon with their hands tied. They driv' away and in a minute I heared the reports of the guns three or four times. The next day I heared that they was civil sojers and that they done shot some conscripts in the bottoms back of our place.

Wash Hodges was gone away four years and Missus Hodges was meaner than the devil all the time. Seems like she just hates us worser than ever. She said blobber mouf niggers done cause a war.

Well now things just kind of drift along for a spell and then Wash Hodges come back and he said, "Well now we done whupped the hell out'n them blue bellies and that will teach them a lesson to leave us alone.

Then my step paw done told him that he seen some Federal sojers. I seen them too. They drifted by in droves of fifty and a hundred. My step paw 'lowed as how the Federals told him they ain't no more slavery and he tried to pint it out to Wash Hodges. Now Wash says thats a new ruling but the ruling is that the growed up niggers is free but the chilluns have to stay with the masters 'til they is of age. I have to stay with them but my maw and step paw 'low they ain't. My step paw went out to hunt for his younguns. . . .

I don't never recall just like the real passing of time. I know that I had my little old boy youngun' and he growed up but after he was born I left the Hodges and felt like it was a fine good riddance.

3. Texans State Their Reasons for Secession, 1861

A declaration of the causes which impel the State of Texas to secede from the Federal Union.

The government of the United States, by certain joint resolutions, bearing date the 1st day of March, in the year A.D. 1845, proposed to the Republic of Texas, then *a free, sovereign and independent nation,* the annexation of the latter to the former, as one of the co-equal States thereof. . . .

But what has been the course of the government of the United States, and of the people and authorities of the non-slave-holding States, since our connection with them?

The controlling majority of the Federal Government, under various pretences and disguises, has so administered the same as to exclude the citizens of the Southern States, unless under odious and unconstitutional restrictions, from all the immense territory owned in common by all the States on the Pacific Ocean, for the avowed purpose of acquiring sufficient power in the common government to use it as a means of destroying the institutions of Texas and her sister slaveholding States.

By the disloyalty of the Northern States and their citizens and the imbecility of the Federal Government, infamous combinations of incendiaries and outlaws have been permitted in those States and the common territory of Kansas to trample upon the federal laws, to war upon the lives and property of Southern citizens in that territory, and finally, by violence and mob law, to usurp the possession of the same as exclusively the property of the Northern States.

The Federal Government, while but partially under the control of these our unnatural and sectional enemies, has for years almost entirely failed to protect the lives and property of the people of Texas against the Indian savages on our border, and more recently against the murderous forays of banditti from the neighboring territory of Mexico; and when our State government has expended large amounts for such purpose, the Federal Government has refused reimbursement therefor, thus rendering our condition more insecure and harrassing than it was during the existence of the Republic of Texas.

These and other wrongs we have patiently borne in the vain hope that a returning sense of justice and humanity would induce a different course of administration. . . .

In all the non-slave-holding States, in violation of that good faith and comity which should exist between entirely distinct nations, the people have formed themselves into a great sectional party, now strong enough in numbers to control the affairs of each of those States, based upon the unnatural feeling of hostility to these

"Declaration of Causes which Impel the State of Texas to Secede from the Federal Union," Ernest Winkler, ed., *Journal of the Secession Convention of Texas* (Austin: Austin Printing Company, 1912), 61–65.

Southern States and their beneficent and patriarchal system of African slavery, proclaiming the debasing doctrine of the equality of all men, irrespective of race or color—a doctrine at war with nature, in opposition to the experience of mankind, and in violation of the plainest revelations of the Divine Law. They demand the abolition of negro slavery throughout the confederacy, the recognition of political equality between the white and the negro races, and avow their determination to press on their crusade against us, so long as a negro slave remains in these States.

For years past this abolition organization has been actively sowing the seeds of discord through the Union, and has rendered the federal congress the arena for spreading firebrands and hatred between the slave-holding and non-slave-holding States.

By consolidating their strength, they have placed the slave-holding States in a hopeless minority in the federal congress, and rendered representation of no avail in protecting Southern rights against their exactions and encroachments.

They have proclaimed, and at the ballot box sustained, the revolutionary doctrine that there is a "higher law" than the constitution and laws of our Federal Union, and virtually that they will disregard their oaths and trample upon our rights.

They have for years past encouraged and sustained lawless organizations to steal our slaves and prevent their recapture, and have repeatedly murdered Southern citizens while lawfully seeking their rendition.

They have invaded Southern soil and murdered unoffending citizens, and through the press their leading men and a fanatical pulpit have bestowed praise upon the actors and assassins in these crimes, while the governors of several of their States have refused to deliver parties implicated and indicted for participation in such offences, upon the legal demands of the States aggrieved.

They have, through the mails and hired emissaries, sent seditious pamphlets and papers among us to stir up servile insurrection and bring blood and carnage to our firesides

They have sent hired emissaries among us to burn our towns and distribute arms and poison to our slaves for the same purpose.

They have impoverished the slave-holding States by unequal and partial legislation, thereby enriching themselves by draining our substance.

They have refused to vote appropriations for protecting Texas against ruthless savages, for the sole reason that she is a slave-holding State.

And, finally, by the combined sectional vote of the seventeen non-slave-holding States, they have elected as president and vice-president of the whole confederacy two men whose chief claims to such high positions are their approval of these long continued wrongs, and their pledges to continue them to the final consummation of these schemes for the ruin of the slave-holding States.

In view of these and many other facts, it is meet that our own views should be distinctly proclaimed.

We hold as undeniable truths that the governments of the various States, and of the confederacy itself, were established exclusively by the white race, for themselves and their posterity; that the African race had no agency in their establishment; that they were rightfully held and regarded as an inferior and dependent race, and in that condition only could their existence in this country be rendered beneficial or tolerable.

That in this free government *all white men are equal and of right ought to be entitled to equal civil and political rights;* that the servitude of the African race, as existing in these States, is mutually beneficial to both bond and free, and is abundantly authorized and justified by the experience of mankind, and the revealed will of the Almighty Creator, as recognized by all Christian nations; while the destruction of the existing relations between the two races, as advocated by our sectional enemies, would bring inevitable calamities upon both and desolation upon the fifteen slave-holding States.

By the secession of six of the slave-holding States, and the certainty that others will speedily do likewise, Texas has no alternative but to remain in an isolated connection with the North, or unite her destinies with the South.

4. Sam Houston Opposes Secession, 1861

Fellow-Citizens: It was not my purpose or desire to address you today upon the great issues now confronting our common country, but old soldier comrades who fought with me at San Jacinto, and other dear friends, insist that I shall explain the reason why I refuse to take the oath of allegiance to the Confederate Government, and why I have been deposed from the Governorship of our beloved State. The earnest solicitations of my old soldier comrades outweigh my desire to remain silent until the whirlwind of passion and popular clamor have subsided and the voice of reason can be fairly heard.

I shall, therefore, speak my honest sentiments and convictions and I now submit to you the reasons why I could not take the oath of allegiance to the so-called Confederate Government, and thereby violate the oath of allegiance I took to the Federal Government when I entered upon the duties of the Chief Magistracy of Texas. It has always been the invariable rule of my life never to form an opinion or verdict upon any great public question until I have first carefully and impartially heard and considered all the evidence and facts upon both sides, and when I have thus formed my verdict, no fear of popular condemnation can induce me to modify or change such verdict. I have never permitted popular clamor, passion, prejudice nor selfish ambition to induce me to change an opinion or verdict which my conscience and judgment has once formed and tells me is right. My only desire is to be right, and for this reason I can not nor will not sacrifice what my conscience and judgment tells me is right. I love the plaudits of my fellow citizens, but will never sacrifice the principle of right and justice for public favor or commendation.

The Vox Populi is not always the voice of God, for when demagogues and selfish political leaders succeed in arousing public prejudice and stilling the voice of reason, then on every hand can be heard the popular cry of "Crucify him, crucify him." The Vox Populi then becomes the voice of the devil, and the hiss of mobs warns all patriots that peace and good government are in peril. I have heard the hiss of mobs upon the streets of Austin, and also heard the hiss of mobs upon the streets of Brenham, and friends have warned me that my life was in great peril if I expressed my honest sentiments and convictions.

"Speech at Brenham," March 31, 1861, Eugene Barker and Amelia Williams, eds., *The Writings of Sam Houston* (Austin: Jenkins, 1970), 8: 295–299.

But the hiss of the mob and the howls of their jackal leaders can not deter me nor compel me to take the oath of allegiance to a so-called Confederate Government. I protest against surrendering the Federal Constitution, its Government and its glorious flag to the Northern abolition leaders and to accept in its stead a so-called Confederate Government whose constitution contains the germs and seeds of decay which must and will lead to its speedy ruin and dismemberment if it can ever secure any real existence. Its seeds of ruin and decay are the principle of secession which permits any one or more of the Confederate States to secede from the parent Confederate Government and to establish separate governments. Can any well-informed man doubt that the time will soon come when several of the Confederate States will secede and establish separate governments? Why will such results follow in the event the Confederate Government is established? Because in all the Confederate States there are ambitious secession leaders who will be aspirants for the Presidency of the Confederacy and to exercise controlling influence in its government and in all cases where their ambitions are frustrated these leaders will cause their respective States to secede and form separate governments wherein they may be able to realize their selfish political hopes. Within ten years we would have ten or more separate Confederate Governments, which would in time fall an easy prey to foreign Governments. The increase of secession leaders will be rapid and large in all the Confederate States and their contests against each other for political leadership will lead to discord, promoting continual conspiracies and revolutions, which will produce many Count Julians, or traitors, who will call to their aid foreign Governments to despoil the people who refuse to help them gratify their selfish ambitions.

Never will I consent to give up our Federal Constitution and our union of States for a Confederate constitution and government whose foundation principles of secession must and will prevent its successful establishment; or if it should triumph, its triumph would be only temporary and its short-lived existence end in revolution and utter ruin.

The Federal Constitution, the Federal Government and its starry flag are glorious heritages bequeathed to the South and all sections of our common country by the valor and patriotism of Washington, and all the brave revolutionary soldiers, who fought for and won American independence. Our galaxy of Southern Presidents—Washington, Jefferson, Monroe, Jackson, Taylor, Tyler, and Polk cemented the bonds of union between all the States which can never be broken. Washington declared for an indivisible union and Jackson made the secession of South Carolina and of other States impossible. Jefferson by the Louisiana purchase added a vast empire of country to our union, and Polk followed his example by further extending our Union to embrace Texas, New Mexico, Arizona, Colorado, and California. Monroe established the Monroe Doctrine which for all time preserves and safeguards the Governments of the Western Hemisphere against foreign conquest. All our Northern Presidents have been equally patriotic and just to the South. Not a single Southern right has been violated by any President or by any Federal Administration. President Lincoln has been elected, because the secession Democratic leaders divided the Democratic party and caused the nomination of two separate Presidential Democratic tickets and nominees.

Both branches of Congress are Democratic; therefore it will be impossible for President Lincoln's administration to enact or enforce any laws or measures that can injure Southern rights. But grant for the sake of the argument that the time may come when both branches of Congress are Republican and laws are enacted and enforced which will injure or destroy Southern rights what shall we then do? I answer that sufficient unto the day is the evil thereof, nor would there be the least danger of the Republican party ever controlling both branches of Congress and all branches of the Federal Government if the secession leaders would permit the Democratic party to remain a solid indivisible party.

But if the day should ever come when Southern rights are ruthlessly violated or injured by the Republican party, we of the South will then fight for our rights under the Stars and Stripes and with the Federal Constitution in one hand and the sword in the other we shall march on to victory.

I believe a large majority of our Southern people are opposed to secession, and if the secession leaders would permit our people to take ample time to consider secession and then hold fair elections the secession movement would be defeated by an overwhelming majority. But the secession leaders declare that secession has already been peaceably accomplished and the Confederate Government independence and sovereignty will soon be acknowledged by all foreign governments. They tell us that the Confederate Government will thus be permanently established without bloodshed. They might with equal truth declare that the fountains of the great deep blue seas can be broken up without disturbing their surface waters, as to tell us that the best Government that ever existed for men can be broken up without bloodshed.

The secession leaders also tell us if war should come that European Nations will speedily come to our relief, and aid us to win our independence because cotton is King and European commerce and civilization can not long exist without cotton, therefore they must help us maintain and perpetuate our Confederate Government. Gentlemen who use such false and misleading statements forget or else are ignorant of the facts that commerce and civilization existed a long period of time before cotton was generally known and used.

They also forget or else are ignorant of the fact that the best sentiment of Europe is opposed to our systems of negro slavery. They also tell us if war comes that the superior courage of our people with their experience of the use of firearms, will enable us to triumph in battle over ten times our number of Northern forces. Never was a more false or absurd statement ever made by designing demagogues. I declare that Civil War is inevitable and is near at hand. When it comes the descendants of the heroes of Lexington and Bunker Hill will be found equal in patriotism, courage and heroic endurance with descendants of the heroes of Cowpens and Yorktown. For this reason I predict that the civil war which is now near at hand will be stubborn and of long duration. We are sadly divided among ourselves, while the North and West are united. Not only will we have to contend against a united and harmonious North, but we will also have to battle against tens of thousands of our own people, who will never desert the Stars and Stripes nor surrender the union of states for a Southern Confederacy of states, whose principles of secession must inevitably lead to discord, conspiracy and revolution, and at last anarchy and utter ruin. When the tug of war comes, it will indeed be the Greek meeting Greek. Then, oh my fellow countrymen, the fearful conflict will fill our fair land with untold suffering, misfortune and disaster. The soil of our beloved South will drink deep the precious blood of our sons and brethren. In earnest prayer to our Heavenly Father, I have daily petitioned him to cast out from my mind the dark foreboding of the coming conflict. My prayers have caused the light of reason to cast the baleful shadows of the coming events before me. I cannot, nor will I close my eyes against the light and voice of reason. The die has been cast by your secession leaders, whom you have permitted to sow and broadcast the seeds of secession, and you must ere long reap the fearful harvest of conspiracy and revolution.

5. Dr. Thomas Barrett Describes the Gainesville Lynching, 1862

The arresting continued for about thirteen days and nights. How many were arrested, I have no means of knowing, having kept no account at the time, but I suppose there was not less than one hundred and fifty, and perhaps more.

There was a good many arrested who had connection with the organization.

There were squads of men in every part of the country, and they arrested every man that they suspicioned, and in this way a good many innocent men were arrested.

When I arrived near town, there were crowds in sight in every direction, armed, pressing forward prisoners under guard. The deepest and most intense excitement that I ever saw prevailed. Reason had left its throne. The mind of almost every man I saw seemd to be unhinged, and wild excitement reigned supreme. When I arrived on the square, there were perhaps three or four hundred armed men in town and in sight.

These with the unarmed, constituted a crowd whose words and actions seemed to indicate an upheaving of the most dangerous character, because it was known that the members of that clan were sworn to go to the assistance of any member who was arrested. . . .

Soon after I arrived on the square I heard hanging spoken of. I found the tree had been selected, that same old historic elm, with its long and bending limbs, which was afterwards used for that purpose.

The crowd seemed to be settling down on beginning to hang.

I opposed it with all the power within me. Others also opposed it, and about the time we were in the heat of contention, the church bell rang for a meeting of the crowd for consultation. The ringing of this bell put an end to all plans, in order to see what would be the result of that meeting. This was a military move, sanctioned by soldiers and citizens.

The meeting was called to order and a chairman appointed. A motion was made and carried for the chair to appoint five men to select a jury to decide upon the course to be pursued with these men. This committee selected twelve men, and my name was reported as one of them. My first thought was, not to serve as one of them, when I took the situation under consideration; I at once saw that unless there was considerable influence in that jury against extreme violence, there was great danger of awful work, so I consented to serve, intending to oppose all extreme violence, which I did. And here I will state the excitement was so great that every man found it necessary to exercise much caution in reference to what he said or did. This condition of things had its influence with me in deciding this question.

Thomas Barrett, *The Great Hanging at Gainesville* (Austin: Texas State Historical Association, 1961), 7–9, 13–14, 16–18, 20–21.

The jury was instructed to go into a fair examination and bring accused and witnesses face to face and decide, and they would abide by their decision.

The meeting adjourned, and the jury met and organized, and night came on. The militia and others had been coming in all day, and after dark they continued to come.

Squads of men were sent to different parts of the county to ascertain what was going on, for an attack was expected, which would cause desperate fighting. A double line of sentinels were put around the town. . . .

About fifteen or twenty men had gone about half a mile from the square to stay all night; I was one of the men. We were ordered to the square. When we got there I walked around and to see how the thing was going on. The soldiers were in line of battle and some in the houses making cartridges, others moving to and fro as is always the case in times of great excitement, everyone expecting a desperate fight before morning, for the clan was supposed to be stronger than they were. . . .

After seeing how everything was going on, and not having a gun and not having any desire to be in the fight, I went into a friend's house and asked the lady for a pillow and turning a chair down on the carpet slept til morning. There was no attack, consequently no fighting. . . .

While the multitude did not at this time know the full intention of the clan, enough was known to give the idea that if the clan carried out its designs, the country would be thrown into a bloody war, with neighbor against neighbor, and in some cases the brother against brother, and in some cases the father against the son and the son against the father, and a man's foes would be of his own household.

The second day dawned and no attack being made, the jury met. . . .

The jury met and passed an order that a majority should rule. I opposed this, and wanted it unanimous, or at any rate, two-thirds, but the majority rule was adopted. As far as could be done the leaders were tried first. . . .

The excitement had increased. It was terrible with the crowd outside, and no less so in the jury-room. One man, known to be a leader, was brought in and proven to be guilty. . . . This man was condemned and hung; another was brought and was disposed of the same way, and this was continued till seven were doomed to die likewise. A number of others and I were opposing it with all our powers; I did all the speaking (nearly) but had as well tried to build a dam across Red River in a time of high water with straw, as to resist and control the excitement in the jury-room, and the crowd of soldiers on duty pushed on by influential men. There were eight hundred or a thousand armed men in town by the time the jury condemned seven men.

The crowd were threatening to take the prisoners out and kill all of them. There was a trial made to have me taken off of the jury, because I took the lead in opposing these violent measures. We who opposed hanging insisted to turn the men over to the civil or military authorities instead of hanging, and those not very deep in the thing, to set them at liberty.

The eighth man was tried; he was only slightly in it, but the excitement was so great that he was condemned as readily as the others.

When this was done I concluded that I would stand it no longer; I was determined that I would have a change or leave the jury-room. I rose to my feet and addressed the jury as near as I can recollect as follows: Gentlemen: You are as reckless of human life as though it was a matter of little importance. I am not acquainted with this man, I never saw him till I saw him in the jury-room, consequently my course is not influenced by any particular feelings of partiality. But if you intend to hang all who are no further in this thing than this man is, it is not necessary to do more than bring a man before you and prove him to be slightly connected with this organization and hang him, so you had better pass sentence of death on every man in the prison, for if you continue to carry out the course you have pursued since you came into this jury-room, you will hang all, so you had better dispatch them at once and adjourn. . . .

As soon as I was seated, one of the jurors who had stood shoulder to shoulder with me in opposing the hanging of these men, rose to his feet, took up his hat, and said, he was no longer a member of the jury, and said good bye, and started to the head of the stairs, (we were in an upper room). At this instant two men came rushing to me, one of them caught me by both arms and gave me one of those honest and friendly shakes, which is an indication of deep interest. When this took place the man who had bid the jury good bye, halted. The man who had me by the arms said, for God sake don't break this jury. I asked him why. He said if you break this jury, every man in that prison will be killed before the setting of the sun. The other man who came with him sanctioned what he said. He went on to state that the only chance to save these men, was for the jury to save them, and said he, you can save some. . . .

I perhaps did as much thinking and planning in a few seconds as I ever did. I knew that if a general slaughter was gone into, unless I made good use of my legs I would go up with the rest, as my course in opposing this wholesale hanging had given great offence. The excitement in the jury-room was of that still and deep character which some times takes place every one waiting in silence to see what would be done.

I said to the two men that approached me: Gentlemen, I yield to your judgment, I will try and arrange this thing.

I then went to the man who had told the jury good bye, and told him what these men had told me, and after a short consultation, we agreed to go back and if the jury would adopt the two-thirds rule, we would act with them, but unless the two-thirds was adopted we would leave. The jury readily adopted the two-thirds rule.

We then gave the man who had been condemned to hang, the benefit of the two-third rule and reversed the sentence of death, by deciding to turn him over to the military authority. . . .

Seven had been hung. When we commenced under the two-thirds rule, we had considerable contention till it was found that this rule would prevent hanging. After that was ascertained we got along quietly and speedily till we got through with all the prisoners on hand, and turned some of them over to the military authorities, the rest being set at liberty.

This brought Saturday evening, and the soldiers were beginning to leave. As the excitement had greatly moderated in the jury-room, we thought it was moderating the same outside, and in order to give it time to moderate still more, we agreed to adjourn for a week and come together the next Saturday and let our decision be known, and I was to make a speech to the people to influence them to abide by our decision, for we were fearful of a mob. Our decision was to be kept secret till the next Saturday. Secrecy was enjoined on all, and we were ready to adjourn.

Some person betrayed us, and told the crowd outside of our decision, and a mob rose and sent two men into the jury-room with word that if we did not give up twenty more to be hung, they would kill every man in the prison.

When this demand came, one of the jurors who acted with me, asked what will you do now? I said the Lord only knows what I ought to do; I have risked my life for six or eight days, and gone as far as I dared to go to prevent hanging. I could contend in the jury-room as I pleased, but cannot war against a regiment of men. I oppose it, but if they take them, they will have to do so, I am not going to say a word.

When I failed to oppose the taking of the men, there was no objection.

I thought when the military failed to protect us and suffered a mob to rise and take these men and hang them, contrary to the decision of the jury, I say, when I thought all this over, I concluded that it was in vain for me to raise my voice against it, so I remained silent. I knew my doom if wholesale killing commenced.

One of these men called for a list of the names of the prisoners. Our clerk handed it to him, and he went over it; took such men as he chose and wrote their names down, then handed the list back to the clerk, and called over the names he had and our clerk marked them out. He then counted his names and he had fourteen. He said as he rose from his seat: I reckon this will satisfy them.

These two men went into the prison, called these fourteen men out, put them in a separate room, and notified them that they must hang next day, which was Sunday.

As soon as these men were gone, I said to the jury: Delay, breeds danger if we undertake to send these men to the headquarters of the military they will not get there, they will be killed. I propose that we meet next Saturday to set all the remaining prisoners at liberty. I told them I did not believe that they would be molested, as we had set a good many at liberty, and none of them had been molested.

To this they readily agreed, and passed an order to that effect. I was to make a speech to influence the people to abide by our decision. The jury then adjourned, to meet the next Saturday morning.

I went home that evening, having been absent twelve days and nights. When I arrived at home my wife met me at the gate and asked the news. I attempted to tell her, but my feelings overcame me so, that I choked up and commenced crying. I said I would tell her after I became quiet. And here I will say that no tongue can tell or pen detail what I suffered during those twelve days and nights just closed; not that I had any sympathy for the plans and designs of the organization, for I abhorred and detested their designs. But I considered that it was war times, and as the organization was broken up, all that was necessary was to send them to the military, as the jury at Sherman did, and the county would be relieved. . . .

During this week of adjournment, I went to town every day, and the excitement was moderating, and everything bidding fair for a favorable condition on the next Saturday, the day the jury was to meet.

About the middle of the week, when I got into town I was met with the startling news that a man by the name of Dickson, who was a citizen of Gainesville, had been killed in the brakes of Red River by a squad of men belonging to that organization. This revived the excitement to a flame. I walked in amongst the soldiers; I could hear threats of clearing up the prison that night.

Several, including myself, commenced pursuading them not to do that, for there were men in the prison that were only slightly in this thing, and we continued to pursuade all day, but seemingly to little effect. Late in the evening the talk was that they would clear the prison that night.

I went home that evening with a gloomy feeling, and during the night when I awoke, I listened for the report of guns, but heard none. I was up next morning very early, and went to town, and learned that the prisoners had not been interrupted, but heard the horrible news that Col. Young had been killed by that clan.

The excitement was fearful. Men were swearing they would kill every man in the prison that night. I availed myself of every opportunity that presented itself to pursuade them not to murder the prisoners, but I was compelled to be very humble, in order to effect anything, and finally came down to hard begging.

Late that evening I went home, feeling the prisoners would be murdered that night, and I expected any minute to hear the horrifying report of the death warning guns, but that awful sound failed to reach my ears. When I arrived in town next morning, learned to my great satisfaction, that the prisoners had not been molested.

Saturday morning came, the day for the jury to meet, and when the roll was called, two of the jurors who had opposed the hanging were absent, and their places filled with men who failed to act on the moderate side.

The first thing the jury did, was to reconsider the decision of the jury to set these men at liberty when they met this morning.

This decision was rejected, which placed the prisoners on trial the same as though they had not been tried.

The excitement had reached the jury-room. I and a few others saw the situation at once. The testimony against the men on which they had been tried was all written down, consequently there was nothing to be done but read it, and take the vote. One was put on trial the vote taken and he condemned to hang; a second was disposed of in the same manner. I made a trial to stop the course of things, but I saw that it was useless to make any attempt to save the men by a vote. I then proposed a compromise: I proposed to allow them to select six of the worst ones and hang them, and set the rest at liberty. I saw they were going to hang a good many more than that, and I was striving to save as many as possible, but the jury rejected my proposition. When they rejected it, hope fled, and I took my seat to watch the course of events. I sat sad and silent till six were condemned and not one set at liberty, for it was hang or set at liberty.

The seventh one was put on trial, his was quite a moderate case, and some defended him. While they were talking on his case, they would look at me as though they wanted to say: help us. I thought now is the time to effect something.

I rose to my feet and addressed the jury about in these words: Gentlemen, I have remained silent, and suffered you to take your own course without interruption, but in this moderate case, I would with due respect, ask the question, if it would not be better to set these moderate cases at liberty, and if you must have blood, take the worst cases? We took the vote and set the man at liberty.

I saw that a reaction, to some extent, was taking place in the minds of some of the jury, and right here the day's fight commenced.

I did all I could to save the men, and those with whom I voted came up nobly to the work, and our side gained regularly. After we commenced setting some at liberty, we succeeded in saving about two-thirds.

This was the hardest day's work I ever did, or ever saw done. A portion of the men with whom I acted, contended manfully against all hanging, while others sometimes voted against the men.

This condition of things caused the fight to be fierce, each party striving to get those who sometimes voted for the men, who held the balance of power, and the party that got them, carried their point.

The present condition of things was well calculated to cause the contention to be of the fiercest character. Everything was done and said by each party that it was thought would cause them to succeed. As for myself, I know that I never exerted myself to the same extent as I did that day.

In speaking against the hanging, I said everything I could think of, that I thought would prevent hanging.

I can give substantially any speeches that day. I told the jury what I had often said to them before, that they were laboring under an excitement which had unhinged their minds. You think you are doing right, but said I, when the war closes and the excitement passes away, and you calmly look back on the course you are now pursuing, for you are bound to come to these sober hours of reflection, you will be astonished that you were so excited as to think that you were doing right. When you come to this, you will then say Barrett was right. All of those jurors that I talked with afterwards came to this sober conclusion. . . .

There were nineteen men condemned to be hung; the balance, about fifty or sixty, were set at liberty.

These nineteen men were hung in consequence of the killing of Dickson and Young. If they had not been killed, all of these men would have been set at liberty that Saturday morning.

The prisoners condemned, were notified that they were to hang next day. . . .

The hanging did not commence very early, and when the last one was hung, the sun was low.

When I started home, my nearest way was to go so as to pass within twenty feet of the tree on which the men were hung, but I took the next street north, to keep from seeing any man hanging.

This day closed this thing, which had caused such an upheaving and excitement for the last twenty or twenty-five days.

There were forty hung, and two who broke from the guard were shot and killed, making forty-two deaths.

6. Rebecca Ann Adams Writes to Her Husband About Life on the Home Front, 1863

December 7th, 1863

My Dear Husband,

I received a long letter from you Saturday morning written from Waldeck. I know your visit there this time would have been pleasant if you had only been well enough to enjoy it. I was in hopes from what you wrote in your last letter about your good health that you would not be troubled with chills again. You can cure others, why not cure yourself. I hope you may succeed in breaking them up before you leave that part of the country. How fortunate that you are camped so near Pa's. I wish very much that you could remain there at least during the winter months. How pleasant it would be if I and the children were there to enjoy your many visits

Jo Ella Powell Exley, ed., *Texas Tears and Texas Sunshine, Voices of Frontier Women* (College Station: Texas A&M University Press, 1990), 132–136.

to that place but I know it is best for us to remain at home and try to feel submissive to all privations caused by this cruel war. I think living at this place away from relations and friends has been a kind school for me. It has taught me to submit more willingly to inconveniences and privations of all kinds. A lesson which you know I very much needed. I feel that I am entirely a changed being in that respect. My daily prayer now is that you may be protected during this war and spared to return to your family. It is true I would like above all things to have you here at home with us, but I know it is a duty you owe your country. I submit.

You complain of not receiving letters from home. I acknowledge that I have not written as often as I should, but at the time you mentioned I was in bed suffering with severe pain in my face and head. Julia wrote to you that week. This is my fifth letter, but I know your great anxiety to hear from home often. I will try and do better in the future. . . .

I frequently caution the negroes about saving the corn and not wasting it. They have used about half a crib of corn. I sold thirteen bushels of corn, two dollars and a half per bushel. I have sold nothing else since you left home. George hauled ninety-nine loads of corn, putting nine in the government pen. They had twenty sacks of fodder; used all of one sack. Jack is using a good deal of corn to fatten the hogs in the pen, he put them up last week. You said nothing about fattening the hogs on the corn. Not knowing what you intended, I have waited this long expecting you would write. I walked down to see them a few days after he put them up, they are looking very well. I will have some killed the next change in weather. Jack has fifty-three in the pen, says he had three more to put in, leaving just seventy-five year and half old hogs for another year. I write you just as he tells me. Col. Moreland has bought a great many hogs expects to bacon them up for sale. He bought six pair of cards, will pay for them in bacon. I am needing some wool cards, but there is none in the country. The cotton cards that I have been using for wool are nearly ruined. The teeth are pulled nearly straight. The negro women are needing yarn sacks this winter. I have the wood but I don't want to ruin another pair of cotton cards. Mr. Caldwell has returned I hear, he has cards for sale with a good many other goods. Mrs. Garrett went in to see them, she says he has the highest price for everything. It is generally believed that he and Miss Sarah Moreland will marry soon. He brought a great many goods for that family. Amelia was here yesterday morning. It has been some time since Mary had done any weaving, she has a severe bone felon on her finger, but I think it now is getting well. Grayson cut it open twice. I have had Souvenia spinning for some time. Jane cooks in her place four days in the week, she spins faster than any of the others. George thinks he will get through sowing the grain tomorrow or the next day. Fed was badly hurt by one of the oxen. I thought one time it would kill him, but we nursed him well and he finally got over it. Old Black died last week. She was very poor, I think she died with old age. You say you will leave the employment of Mrs. Garrett entirely to me. I must say that I don't feel that I am a competent judge of such a matter, the proper education of our children is very important. It is true I have been with her and ought to know what she is competent to teach. I think she is a good teacher for children beginning. The other children have learned but little, Julia almost nothing. But one thing I do know they have learned no wicked sayings. I think it has been of great service to David to be entirely with his sisters. Julia's great anxiety to go to college has kept her from learning what she might have learned. I don't think Mrs. Garrett can teach her anything but Smith's Grammer. Mrs.Garrett is a *very plain* not neat but I think a well meaning woman. She would like to remain here if she could go to town every Saturday. If I don't hear from *you* before she closes her school I shall employ her another term but I had rather you would decide what is best to be done. I have been very busy lately knitting you some gloves, the thread was spun of mule eared rabbit furs with a little wool. I think the gloves will be warm, pleasant feeling to the skin. David and Old Allen caught the rabbits. Are you wearing your old gloves, or have you bought new ones? Are you or Robert needing anything in the way of clothing? You must let me know in time so I can have them ready. Jennie had another chill yesterday, her skin is yellow, I think her body is swollen. She has been calling for you at night in her sleep. Little Fannie has not looked well since Pa was here.

The children all send love to PaPa and Buddie. Mrs. G. sends respect. Write as often as you can and I hope you will not be sent from that section of the country. Your wife with much love,

R.A.

E S S A Y S

In the first essay, Randolph Campbell, an authority on Texas slavery at the University of North Texas, provides an overview of the state's "peculiar institution." The slave labor system that emerged in Texas, Campbell argues, differed little from the institution that existed throughout the Lower South. Slaveholders were a privileged minority, enjoying a disproportionate share of economic and political power in the state.

In the second essay, Texas A&M University professor Walter Buenger examines the reasons that prompted Texans to secede from the union. Buenger emphasizes the complex and paradoxical nature of the secessionist movement, in which Texans were torn by conflicting allegiances to their region and the nation. Buenger reminds us that for many Texans, as for many southerners, the decision to secede was not easy nor simple. In the final analysis, however, the state's connections with the Lower South were of paramount importance in the formation of the state's identity, an identity which, most Texans had decided by 1861, was incompatible with Unionism. Thus, both authors view the state's southern heritage as a uniquely formative one.

An Empire for Slavery

RANDOLPH B. CAMPBELL

Negro slavery became important in Texas with the arrival of Anglo-American colonists during the 1820s. Most of these settlers came from the Old South and believed that Texas' fertile lands could best be populated and brought into cultivation with the aid of an institution that they knew well. Mexican governments, both federal and state, resisted the development of slavery in Texas and probably retarded its

Randolph B. Campbell. *Empire for Slavery* (Baton Rouge: Louisiana State University Press, 1989), 252–259. Copyright © 1989 by Louisiana State University Press. Reprinted by permission of Louisiana State University Press.

growth during the colonial period. Official opposition was limited and vacillating, however, in the face of insistence by Anglo settlers, led by Stephen F. Austin, that slavery was an economic necessity in Texas. Mexican leaders made concessions that allowed the institution to gain a significant, albeit not completely secure, foothold in the province by 1835.

Slavery constituted one underlying factor in the general clash of Anglo-American and Hispanic cultural traditions that culminated in the Texas Revolution during 1835–36. Had Mexico won the war, slavery almost certainly would have been abolished. As it was, the conflict seriously disturbed slavery in Texas and allowed some bondsmen to escape. Sam Houston's army won the Battle of San Jacinto, however, and Texans succeeded in establishing their new republic with a constitution that guaranteed slavery. The revolution did not begin primarily as a movement to protect the Peculiar Institution, but certainly one major result was, in the words of Justice Abner S. Lipscomb of the Texas Supreme Court, the removal of "all doubt and uneasiness among the citizens of Texas in regard to the tenure by which they held dominion over their slaves."

Slavery expanded rapidly, both numerically and geographically, through the republic and statehood periods from 1836 to 1861. As bondsmen poured into Texas, arriving primarily with immigrant owners, their total population increased from approximately five thousand in 1836 to more than thirty thousand in 1846, when the republic became a state. By 1861, when Texas seceded and joined the Confederacy, the slave population, which had grown more rapidly than the free, was approaching two hundred thousand. Bondsmen lived in largest numbers along Texas' major rivers—the Red in the northeast, the Sabine and Trinity in the east, and the Brazos and Colorado in the south-central region down to the Gulf Coast. By 1860, however, blacks constituted at least 25 percent of the population in all settled portions of the state, except the north-central area centering on Dallas and the southwestern plains extending from the San Antonio River to the Rio Grande.

Perhaps slavery faced, as Charles Ramsdell argued, a barrier to expansion once it reached the semiarid plains of western Texas and the areas within easy reach of the Mexican border, but those limits were not reached by 1861. Slavery was still growing everywhere in the state, and the blackland prairie/Grand Prairie region of north-central Texas offered a vast expanse of suitable acreage relatively untouched by slaveholders and their bondsmen. To open that area, only transportation was needed, and the railroad would have provided that. Texas constituted a virtual empire for slavery, and on the eve of secession Texans talked with buoyant optimism of the millions of bondsmen who would build the state's future.

Slavery existed in antebellum Texas primarily as an economic institution. Those who purchased bondsmen to supply labor on farms and plantations generally found their investments profitable. Slaves produced larger and larger cotton crops, reproduced themselves, and appreciated in value through the late antebellum years. They also produced enough corn and other food crops to provide self-sufficiency in the state's agricultural economy. Finally, slavery was very flexible and highly functional, as witnessed, for example, by the hire system, so that it was economically advantageous in ways that did not appear on a profit-and-loss balance sheet. The institution may have contributed to Texas' relative backwardness in commercialization and industrialization, but there were no important demands that it be ended in order to promote diversification. Slavery flourished in Texas throughout the late antebellum period and was never in danger of failing from its own economic weakness.

Between 1836 and 1861, Texas legislators and judges developed a slave code for the Lone Star state based largely on practices elsewhere in the Old South. The law assured slaveowners of their right to own, buy, and sell bondsmen while protecting their property against criminal interference by others. It regulated the conduct of slaves and prescribed rules for the capture and return of runaways. The legal status accorded free blacks made it clear that, no matter how few, they were an unwelcome minority who would frequently be equated with slaves. Lawmakers and judges recognized that slaves were human and therefore a very special form of property. The weight of the law, however, usually rested with protection of the masters' property rights rather than concern for the slaves' humanity.

Most Texas slaves lived on farms and plantations and worked long hours clearing land, cultivating crops, and taking care of innumerable chores. Many had Saturday afternoons free from labor, but only Sundays, July 4, and Christmas week were regarded virtually without exception as days off. A minority of bondsmen, perhaps 10 to 20 percent of the total, worked as skilled craftsmen or house servants or lived in Texas' towns and few fledgling cities. Compared to agricultural workers, these slaves were less exposed to the elements and performed labor that was less burdensome physically. Some, especially the house servants, may have had longer hours, but few, it seems, wanted to change places with field workers. Slaves frequently were given positions of considerable responsibility as, for example, "drivers" and teamsters. Some had the opportunity, although the practice was illegal for most of the antebellum period, to hire their own time and seek profitable employment for themselves. Many earned at least a little money of their own, especially by working small patches of cotton and food crops.

The state of Texas had constitutional and statutory provisions concerning the material conditions of slaves' lives and the physical treatment accorded them by their masters. In all but the most extreme cases, however, these matters were left, in the words of Justice James H. Bell of the Texas Supreme Court, "to the master's judgment, discretion, and humanity." Texas bondsmen generally had food adequate to provide the energy for work and the nutrition, by the standards of that era, for health. Their housing was usually uncomfortable at best and inadequate for winter weather. Clothing and shoes were made of cheap, rough materials, and slaves found them a source of considerable discomfort. When bondsmen suffered, as they often did, from diseases and accidents, masters generally provided doctors' care. Slaves were, after all, a valuable form of property. Unfortunately, medical science in mid-nineteenth-century Texas could not deal effectively with many of the diseases and injuries that afflicted slaves. Masters, in exercising their right to obedience and submission from their bondsmen, inflicted a variety of punishments, particularly whippings. Any whipping was a fearsome prospect, and all slaves lived with the knowledge that it could happen to them, largely at the whim of their master. At times, punishments became cruel treatment and even murder, but Texas courts were extremely reluctant to interfere with the master-slave relationship. Regardless of the law, slaves' material conditions and physical treatment depended largely upon their individual masters.

Texas slaves endured the psychological pressures of bondage with the aid of strength that came from their families, their religion, and their music. The great majority of bondsmen experienced family ties, and in spite of constant threats and numerous disruptions, depended on those relationships for identity, support, and a sense of worth. Families appear to have been the focal point for survival. Thousands of Texas slaves drew strength too from religion. They listened to white ministers emphasize the virtues of loyal and honest servants, but they heard the underlying message, often brought to them by black preachers, of salvation for all and perhaps even deliverance. Music provided psychological strength also because it served as a means of expression, communication, and protest.

Behavior patterns among Texas slaves varied widely. At one extreme was the loyal servant who apparently loved and identified with his master; at the other was the rebel who resisted bondage at every opportunity, especially by running away. Most common, however, were the bondsmen who, in the words of one woman, did "the best we could." Neither loyal servants nor rebels, they recognized the limitations of their situation and sought to endure on the best terms possible. Such slaves expected certain types of treatment and became rebellious if they did not receive it. Regardless of their behavioral adjustments, the vast majority of blacks wanted freedom, and everyone knew it. In short, the enslaved blacks were simply human. They employed their intelligence and their moral and spiritual resources to survive in an attempt to influence the world in which they found themselves. Some were capable and strong; others were incapable and weak. In any case, the enslaved blacks were not an inherently inferior part of the human race, and slavery was no school for civilization.

A minority of Texans owned slaves, and only a handful achieved elite status as planters. Slaveholders generally found the institution to be a source of tension in their lives. Slaves proved so difficult to manage that owners, while they enjoyed picturing themselves as benevolent paternalists, spent a good deal more time discussing means of punishing effectively. Masters did not labor, it seems, under a great burden of guilt, but constant criticism from outside the South also created tension. Texas slaveholders thus found the institution troublesome and unsettling, but, at the same time, it benefited them to the extent that they would attempt a revolution to keep it.

Slaveholders dominated economic, political, and social life in antebellum Texas. They produced 90 percent of the state's cotton, dominated officeholding at all levels of government, and by virtue of their wealth occupied the top rungs of the social ladder. Not surprisingly under these circumstances, most articulate Texans such as newspaper editors and ministers defended slavery with every imaginable argument, and the vast majority of the state's people either supported or quietly acquiesced in the institution. A few German immigrants found it unworthy of a democratic, liberal nation, but most had no serious objections.

In spite of the proslavery consensus that had no significant opposition anywhere in the state, antebellum Texans often demonstrated the fear and intolerance typical of a society under siege. They struck hard at anyone suspected of preaching abolitionism or fomenting insurrection and were only slightly less tolerant of individuals or groups who did not support the system enthusiastically. As the Galveston *Weekly News* expressed it, "Those who are not for us, must be against us." The potential for terror inherent in this attitude was realized most fully during the summer of 1860, when a series of disastrous fires in north-central counties led to a widespread panic called the "Texas Troubles." Vigilante action to deal with the supposed abolitionist-inspired insurrection plot signaled by the fires claimed an undetermined number of victims, white as well as black. Within a year, "the voice of reason," as Governor Sam Houston termed it, was stilled entirely as Texas seceded and joined the Confederate States of America. The decision for secession involved a variety of considerations for Texans depending on their backgrounds and their circumstances in the Lone Star state, but the fundamental reason for having to decide at all was absolutely clear—it was Negro slavery.

During the Civil War, slavery remained less disturbed in Texas than in other areas of the Confederacy because Federal troops did not invade the state's interior. The most significant disruptions resulted from the impressment of bondsmen to serve Confederate authorities in building fortifications and, to a lesser extent, from the arrival of thousands of "refugeed" slaves fleeing Federal invaders in other states. Most slaves were aware of the war and its implications for their future freedom. They hoped for a Union victory but were in no position to contribute to it or to hinder the Confederate military effort. When the day of jubilee, June 19, 1865, finally came with the arrival of General Gordon Granger at Galveston and the reading of the Emancipation Proclamation, most Texas slaves celebrated their freedom as the answer to a lifelong prayer.

Slavery in Texas did not differ in any fundamental way from the institution as it existed elsewhere in the United States. Claims that somehow Negro bondage was "milder" or "worse" in the Lone Star state are morally pointless and historically inaccurate. Material conditions and physical treatment had nothing to do with making slavery right or wrong. Even if it could be demonstrated convincingly, for example, that Texas slaves had a better diet, worked fewer hours in a milder climate, and were whipped less often than bondsmen elsewhere, the moral nature of a system that held humans as property would remain the same. It was still wrong.

On a day-to-day basis, of course, material conditions and physical treatment were of great importance to Texas slaves themselves. Studies of the institution in other states, however, provide no basis for claiming that it was generally "milder" or "worse" in the Lone Star state. Bondsmen in older southern states were subject to essentially the same laws and, except in very special areas, lived under relatively similar circumstances in terms of work, material conditions, discipline and punishment, formation and preservation of families, religion, and so on. This should be expected. After all, the immigrants who brought slavery to Texas learned its ways in the Old South. They were not likely to change significantly once they reached a new home unless the area was dramatically different from any previously experienced. Granted that Texas constituted a frontier region during the antebellum period, those portions of the state having large numbers of slaves by the 1840s and 1850s were not so different in terms of climate and topography or so wild and unsettled as to change common patterns of labor and management. Slavery in Texas was simply American Negro slavery; nothing about the Lone Star state led or forced slaveholders there to accord their bondsmen appreciably different treatment than the variations common from master to master across the South.

Far from being unimportant, slavery played a vital role in shaping antebellum Texas and determining its future. The state could not have grown as it did without the labor of its slave population. Secession and participation in the tragedy of civil war resulted primarily from the desire to preserve an institution that was flourishing and had seemingly unlimited potential in 1861.

The Roots of Texas Secession

WALTER L. BUENGER

Secession remains a mystifying puzzle, a puzzle whose solution in 1861 was a bloody civil war and a puzzle whose solution in our time still defies rational explanation. From the end of the American Revolution until the start of the Civil War, the United States survived a series of intensely bitter internal disputes. Yet within the span of a few months in the winter of 1860–1861 the nation split apart, and a civil war soon began that resulted in over one million casualties. In Texas, secession seemed all the more improbable. Texans had continually asked to become part of the Union from 1836 to 1845. Their precarious position on the southwestern frontier reminded them daily of the value of belonging to a large and powerful nation. Prosperity seemed to preclude a political upheaval in 1860. The burgeoning trade in cotton, hides, and sugar flowing out of the commercial centers of Texas gave promise of making it one of the richest states in the Union. Slavery, while a major part of the social and economic life in some regions of Texas, was almost absent in other regions, and, except for Tennessee and Arkansas, Texas slaves made up the smallest percentage of the total population of any state in the Confederacy. Reflecting its position on the border of the South, politics in Texas on the eve of secession was dominated not by militant secessionists or unionists but by more moderate folk, who wanted to preserve the Union and the status quo if the costs of such action were not too high. At no time before 1860 did these moderates, who comprised a clear majority of the electorate, more persistently and urgently away from their comfortable middle ground. Nonetheless, before the firing on Fort Sumter changed the political question to either defending one's home or defecting to the enemy in defense of principle, Texans voted to secede by a three-to-one margin. . . .

Secession in Texas was part of the central conflict of the nineteenth century, a conflict between forces that encouraged the splintering of the United States into smaller social, political, and economic units and forces that bound the nation more tightly together. Secession, however, was not simply the triumph of localism over nationalism. Nor did it reflect some Hegelian dialectic in which the thesis of localism and the antitheses of nationalism were resolved in the synthesis of secession. Localism and nationalism were the reflex of each other. Factors that nourished localism could also stimulate nationalism. Moreover, a factor that encouraged localism or nationalism could often strengthen both a commitment to the Union and a belief in the necessity of secession. Slavery, for example, was the most prominent feature separating the South from the rest of the nation. Yet its

---

Walter L. Buenger, "Texas and the Riddle of Secession," *Southwestern Historical Quarterly*, 87 (October 1983), 151–182. Copyright Texas State Historical Association. Reprinted with permission.

slave/cotton economy tied the South to northern merchants and northern mills. The need to defend slavery was one argument for secession. As late as 1861, however, some Texans insisted that in the long run slavery was safer inside the Union than in a smaller more vulnerable southern Confederacy. Thus slavery was both localistic and nationalistic in its implications and could create an impetus toward either secession or preservation of the Union. In a conceptual sense, the secession crisis in Texas involved a struggle among all those elements within Texas society that, like slavery, strengthened unionism or strengthened secession sentiment. What was curious about this struggle was that the two opposing concepts were surprisingly alike. In fact, it was the similarities between the forces behind unionism and secession as much as their differences that accounts for the success of the secession movement in Texas.

If indeed the secession crisis in Texas had two interdependent dimensions, then understanding the cause of secession and the Civil War requires more than understanding the role of individuals, ideology, parochial interests, or instinctual fears. Understanding secession requires envisioning the nature of unionist and secessionist sentiment, and how in the end the imbalance between these two made secession possible.

Though opposite in intent, sentiments for secession and unionism never existed without each other. This dualism grew out of the interlaced nature of localism and nationalism in antebellum Texas. Localism and nationalism coexisted in individual Texans as well as in the collective value system of the state. Texans accomplished this sleight of hand by either compartmentalizing nationalism and localism within nonconflicting spheres of thought and action, or by temporarily subordinating one set of values to the other. Local values related to slavery offer the clearest example of compartmentalization. Texans voted for a unionist ticket in 1859 and at the same time adamantly defended slavery. As long as local notions about slavery or any other divergent point of view were confined within a framework that did not impinge directly upon nationalism, both nationalism and localism existed together. This explains how the La Grange *True Issue* in the midst of the secession crisis ran on its masthead: "Our Country, Our State, the South and the Union."

Texans, however, seldom achieved an exact equilibrium between localism and nationalism. From 1846 to 1848, spurred on by the euphoria of annexation and the Mexican War, Texans were more nationalistic. From 1849 through mid-1850, because of antipathy for President Zachary Taylor and the dispute over the Texas claim to eastern New Mexico, Texans were more localistic. From the closing months of 1850 up until 1854, encouraged by economic growth and stable borders, Texans elevated the Union above their sectional concerns. Then from 1854 through 1857, aroused by the controversy over slavery in Kansas and influenced by a steady influx of people from the plantation South, Texans became more localistic. Worried by the excesses of southern militants, from 1858 until mid-1860 the bulk of the Texas population moved once again toward the Union. About mid-1860 the move toward sectionalism began once more and continued until Texas seceded. In every case, except for the secession crisis, the development of either nationalism or localism was balanced by the resurgence of its countervailing force. This did not happen in the winter of 1860–1861 because of the conflicting and also surprisingly complementary appeal of the Union and secession. . . .

Self-interest, the influence of powerful personalities, ideological conceptions and beliefs, party politics, and certain cultural and regional biases within Texas all combined in 1858 and 1859 to produce a stunning revival of unionism. The force that tended to break the Union into smaller component parts, however, did not disappear from the body politic. Localism was instead only temporarily submerged. It, too, fed upon cultural biases, party politics, ideology, articulate spokesmen, and self-interest. Connecting and intertwining all of these facets of localism was slavery.

Just as Texans from the Upper South seemed to have a cultural bias in favor of the Union, Texans from the Lower South more easily accepted secession. Until 1850, the largest percentage of Anglo immigrants came from the Upper South—primarily from Tennessee, Kentucky, and Missouri. Beginning in 1836, however, people from the Lower South—primarily from Georgia, Alabama, and Mississippi—came to Texas in increasing numbers. By 1860 Texans from the Lower South comprised the largest cultural group in the state. Moreover, these Texans were not equally dispersed among all regions of Texas but were concentrated in specific areas. Not only was the total number of people from the Lower South growing in Texas, but, because their numbers were relatively undiluted by peoples from other groups, their cultural voice remained clear. It would be a voice that would speak ardently for secession in 1860 and 1861.

Slavery and the plantation system were the most distinct features of the Lower South. Texans from the Upper South certainly owned slaves, as did a few Germans. Still, taken as a whole, farm size, crop selection, and lack of capital limited the impact of slavery on both these non-Lower South groups. Germans, while they might raise cotton, farmed less land more intensively, and they usually lacked the capital to buy slaves, or else preferred to invest their limited capital in other things considered more necessary for the efficient operation of their farms. Texans from the Upper South owned cotton plantations. This was especially true if they lived in East Texas, which was ideal for cotton and contained many former residents of the Lower South. If they lived in regions not dominated by lower southerners, however, they typically concentrated on corn, wheat, or livestock. They therefore needed fewer slaves and by habit, and perhaps by preference, were less inclined to acquire more slaves and expand heavily into the production of cotton. A Texas farmer from Alabama, on the other hand, grew cotton by habit and often aspired to the ownership of large numbers of slaves. It was not surprising that Texans from the Lower South who had the most to lose both at the time and in the future by any challenge from the North to slavery increasingly viewed the world from a local and not a national perspective.

Significantly, this local perspective surfaced most clearly in lower southerners, the most dynamic of the four primary cultural groups in Texas. Texas in 1860 was not yet like Alabama, but the future seemed to hold promise that one day it would be so. Counties between Lower South-dominated East Texas, Upper South- or German-dominated North and West Texas, and Mexican-dominated South Texas—counties with a population drawn not only from the Lower South but the other primary source areas as well—seemed to be undergoing a process by which the fecund Lower South culture dominated the entire county. Over a period of years the agricultural and slaveholding habits that distinguished cultures in Texas began to merge into a culture much like that of the Lower South. Perceiving this ascendancy, visionaries talked of a better life tied to slavery, the plantation system, and Lower South culture. Not only the present reality of this culture but also its dynamic characteristic gave secession a strong cultural base.

By 1857 the cultural transformation occurring in Texas society was reflected in the state Democratic party's increasing alliance with the Democratic parties of the Lower South. By 1858 ardent southerners who would be quick to resort to secession at any provocation controlled the apex of the state structure. By 1859 almost all moderate Democrats who had served as party functionaries and who had helped defeat and destroy the Know-Nothings from 1855 to 1858 had left the party and joined the newly formed Opposition party. As an institution the Democratic party was much stronger than the Opposition. Texans supported it out of loyalty and habit. Germans and Mexicans supported the party because it had defended them against the nativist Know-Nothings. Democrats like John H. Reagan still supported the party in 1859 because they hoped to reform its sectional character and revitalize its national heritage. Nor were the Democrats decimated by their losses in August of 1859. The party rapidly bounced back with the election of party war horse Louis T. Wigfall to the U.S. Senate by the Democratic-controlled legislature. Democratic editors continued to dominate the newspapers of the state and to place sectional writings into the hands of the public. All in all, the Democratic party was a powerful force—a force that was harnessed in 1860 and 1861 by its state and local leaders to the cause of secession.

One reason that the Democratic party became an important force in the secession movement was that to a slight but noticeable degree its ideology always stressed the functional nature of the Union and emphasized that local customs and personal liberty must be defended. That is, the Union was a means to an end and not wholly a valuable thing in itself. For Democrats the Union was a means of fulfilling the American destiny. Thus it was that Democrats tended to be moderate secessionists and Whigs moderate unionists. Whigs certainly viewed the Union as necessary for social stability, law and order, and economic prosperity. Yet Whigs, in whatever group they later belonged, stressed more heavily the sacred nature of the Union and spoke in reverential terms of their devotion to the nation. Such sentiments were not absent among Democrats, but they were not as dominant. Thus when Democrats became convinced that the Union threatened the very functions it was meant to achieve, they were more willing to leave behind the old church and seek a new vehicle to achieve salvation.

Here, then, was a perfect example of goals that had once made men unionists converting them to secessionists. Secessionists wanted to change the form of their nation in 1860, but they did not want to change what they interpreted to be the meaning and purpose of a nation of Americans. Indeed, secessionist ideology gained power after November of 1860 because it stressed the dangers that remaining in the United States posed to the traditional purposes of that Union. For secessionists the Republican party symbolized the corruption and decay of their nation. As the presidential elections of 1856 and 1860 proved, it was purely sectional and not a national party. For Texans this sectionalism meant the poisoning of the governmental system whenever Republicans gained control of any branch of government. Texas secessionists had only to point to the chaos generated by the race for Speaker of the U.S. House of Representatives in 1859 or to the failure of the House to allocate money for the defense of the Texas frontier as proof of their arguments. Republicans were also depicted as threats to the nation's role as preserver of law and order and guarantor of social stability. Time and time again secessionists shouted that Republican state governments broke statute law and the dictates of the Constitution when they passed personal-liberty laws that prevented the return of fugitive slaves. They argued persistently that the Republicans' reliance upon some higher moral or divine code was a threat to the very nature of law because it could be interpreted capriciously with no regard for minority rights. Secessionists insisted as well that Republican control of the federal government would eventually destroy slavery in the states where it already existed or would seriously impair the ability of white southerners to control their black slaves. The result of this would be anarchy and chaos. As John Reagan saw it, Texans faced a difficult choice: "The sad alternative is now submitted to us of the unconditional submission to Black Republican principles, and ultimately to free negro equality, and a government of mongrels or war of races on the one hand, or secession and the formation of a Southern Confederacy and a bloody war on the other." . . .

. . . This accelerating movement toward dissolution was not braked by a re-awakened awareness of the pragmatic value of the Union, by the influence of Unionist leaders, by the resurgence of nationalist ideology, by the expression of this ideology in a political party, and by the inherent unionist tendencies of some Texas subcultures. Lincoln's election and the ascendancy of the Republican party made Texans question as nothing had before the ability of the United States to function as an American nation should function. After November of 1860 the Union seemed both unbeneficial and an unfit carrier of nationalist dreams. This perception was reinforced and the balance between attachment to the Union and to region was further endangered when a consensus in favor of secession virtually ended all debate on the matter in many parts of Texas. Still, even so powerful a force as consensus in a democracy could not submerge nationalism. Instead this nationalism caused Texans to focus on the Confederacy as the new hope for the fulfillment of old dreams and needs.

By late 1860 many Texans had come to perceive Republican power in the national government and in the North as eroding both the ideological and pragmatic functions of the Union. Secessionists portrayed the Union as now incapable of providing stabilizing law, social harmony, military protection, and a guarantee of individual rights to its southern citizens. The question of secession became not simply a choice between defending slavery or defending the sanctity of the nation. The point of the secession debate in Texas was what Lincoln's election that November told and foretold about the nature of the Union. The argument that the Union had decayed, backed up by the specific examples of northern attitudes toward slavery, Republican neglect of the frontier, Republican disregard for the law, and Republican fomenting of social discord, weakened attachments to the nation based upon its role as a preserver of order, a promoter of future prosperity, and a keeper of such traditional values as a respect for the law. Thus the impact of parties and people moved by unionist ideology or a rational assessment of the Union's benefits was undercut.

Unionism, however, did not cease to exist either within individuals or within groups, and habit, together with the emotional side of unionist ideology, would have created stronger opposition to secession in 1861 if it had not been for the force of consensus. Human societies, when threatened by an external enemy, have a tendency to require conformity of their members. In the winter of 1860–1861, in regions of Texas with substantial slave populations, a closing off of debate occurred. In that part of Texas most like the Lower South, which was roughly everything east of the Brazos River below a line running from Waco to Texarkana, secessionists, using the apparatus of the Democratic party and the Democratic press, spread their arguments into every hamlet. Meanwhile unionists were disorganized and silent. They lacked the strength of an institutional framework like the Democratic party. The unionists' silence sprang as well from a tactical decision to boycott all discussions of secession and hope that nearsighted visions of the Union would soon be replaced with a healthy nationalism. To an immeasurable degree, however, the silence of unionists arose from various forms of intimidation. Many times this intimidation was direct and overt. Newspaper editors who stridently opposed secession, like Ferdinand Flake of the German- and English-language *Union,* had their presses smashed. In other areas paramilitary groups, such as the minutemen of Harrison County or the Knights of the Golden Circle to which Newcomb took such exception, might have taken part in organized repression of unionist spokesmen and influenced voting. It is a fact, in any case, that secessionists used force to seize the federal government's property in Texas before the statewide referendum on secession, and that they occasionally tried to overtly intimidate or disrupt unionist spokesmen. Unionists also contended that fair election procedures in both the selection of Secession Convention delegates in January, 1861, and in the secession referendum of February 23, 1861, were not used. In such an atmosphere, physical intimidation might have forced some voters to favor secession despite reservations or to simply stay home.

It seems probable, however, that more subtle forms of intimidation and persuasion were primarily responsible for the growing consensus in favor of secession in January and February of 1861. Since even most unionists agreed that secession was legal, the question before the public was whether it was justified. The answer came back a sure and emotion-packed "YES" from the secessionists and a rather timid "perhaps not" from the unionists. The secessionists were aided by their assured and direct approach, and the offering of a simple solution to a universally perceived problem. . . . In the end, either overtly or covertly, unionists were induced to stay home during public discussions and on election day, or they were convinced to quietly support secession.

In some sense the triumph of the secessionists and the existence of a bellicose Confederate States of America for five years was a victory for localism. Texans first began to accept the idea of secession because their local institution of slavery was challenged by the North and by the Republican party. When they came to believe that the Union's proper character would be subverted by the hegemony of the Republican party, Texans moved toward secession. Secessionist propagandizing by the regular Democratic party, the emergence of pragmatic local reasons for supporting secession, the identification of traditional local leaders with secession, the forced consensus in some cultural regions of the state, and the particular ideology of Texas secessionists all had a parochial nature. Even the decision made by many unionists to support the Confederacy was in large measure the result of their realization that their community, their county, their state, or their region was more their physical emotional, and psychological home than the nation as a whole.

To describe the force of localism in creating secession and sustaining the Confederacy in its early days, however, does not negate the existence of nationalism at any time after 1860. Secessionists displayed a widely held assumption that it was only as part of a large and stable nation that Americans could achieve their individual and corporate goals. Almost from the beginning Texas secessionists were nation builders as well as destroyers of the Union. Texans toyed with the notion of restoring the Republic of Texas, but when they made their decision to secede it was clear that Texas would be part of the Confederacy. Six states had left the Union by February, 1861. While some of these states hesitated to leave the Union without a guarantee of cooperation from other southern states, Texans knew they would not be alone. As early as January, 1861, propagandists of secession in Texas began to argue that separate state secession, since it would be the fastest means of removing their state from the Union and uniting it with the other states of the cotton-growing South, was in effect the most efficient form of cooperating in the building of a new nation. In essence, the secession movement did not kill nationalism in Texas, but redirected it toward the Confederate States of America.

Texans did not move toward secession in a straight and simple line. Perhaps only through imagery, then, can secession be reduced to the understandable. If so, the image of Texas and Texans that emerged in 1860–1861 was like the Roman god Janus. Two almost identical faces looking in opposite directions on the same head, secession and the Union, drew sustenance from the same body. Within their common brain secessionists and unionists were localists and nationalists at the same time. Janus, though, evokes an image of balance and inertia—an image that was untrue of Texas in 1861. Commitment to the United States began to evaporate when Abraham Lincoln and the Republican party achieved hegemony within the North and the national government. This event signalled to Texans, as none had done before, the irreparable decay of the Union. All the things that the nation had once done or Texans hoped the nation would do—preventing anarchy, protecting the frontier, insuring the protection of constitutional and legal rights—a Republican-dominated nation promised not to do. In fact, Republicans were perceived as anarchists, as attackers of the frontier as well as all other portions of Texas, and as law breakers. Even so, the pull of the Union was strong, and most Texans might have been willing to give the Republicans a chance to prove themselves worthy of their trust if the momentum of the secession movement had not been constantly accelerated by a growing consensus in favor of secession which ended all debate over its wisdom in many parts of Texas. A greater attachment to one's state and region rather than the nation prompted even secession's critics to accept the dismembering of the Union. In a way that is difficult to measure, however, what made secession acceptable was the realization by most Texans that secessionists were nation builders as well as destroyers. Here again secession was intertwined with notions about the Union. Secession was a continuation of the past, not a radical departure from the past. Its purpose was not simply to tear apart the Union, but to dismantle it in order to construct a purer type of union which would achieve all the goals and purposes of a nation of Americans. Texans did not lose their nationalism in 1861, nor did they cease to define that nationalism in an American fashion. They refocused that nationalism on the Confederacy instead of the United States.

 F U R T H E R   R E A D I N G

Alwyn Barr, *Black Texans: A History of African-Americans in Texas, 1528–1995* (1996)

Dale Baum, *The Shattering of Texas Unionism: Politics in the Lone Star State During the Civil War Era* (1998)

Walter L. Buenger, *Secession and the Union in Texas* (1984)

Randolph B. Campbell and Richard Lowe, *Wealth and Power in Antebellum Texas* (1977)

Donald Frazier, *Blood and Treasure: Confederate Empire in the Southwest* (1995)

B. P. Galloway, ed., *Texas, the Dark Corner of the Confederacy: Contemporary Accounts of the Lone Star State in the Civil War* (1994)

Paul A. Levengood, "In the Absence of Scarcity," *Southwestern Historical Quarterly* 101 (April 1998)

James Marten, *Texas Divided: Loyalty and Dissent in the Lone Star State* (1990)

Richard McCaslin, *Tainted Breeze* (1994)

David Pickering and Judy Falls, *Brush Men with Vigilantes: Civil War Dissent in Texas* (2000)

Ralph Wooster, *Texas and Texans in the Civil War* (1996)

CHAPTER
9

Race, Politics, and

Reconstruction,

1865–1875

The single most important struggle of the Reconstruction era in Texas focused on defining the role of the state's newly freed African Americans. Freedom, the efforts of blacks to assert their legitimate political and civil rights, and the white backlash against social change provided the foundation for race relations in Texas for the next century. The actors in this drama are well known. Ex-Confederates, now generally identified as conservative Democrats, attempted to regain the political power they had wielded before the war and to restore the social order that the war and emancipation had disrupted. White Texas Unionists, who made up the core of the Republican Party, felt that political power was their due in compensation for their sufferings during the war, even if it required denying the ex-confederates their political rights and extending these rights to the freedmen. Northerners, some genuinely concerned about the need to preserve the Union and prevent a resumption of war, others seeking retribution against southern rebels for the violence and destruction they unleashed, were determined to impose a loyal (and Republican-dominated) government on the defeated South. And African Americans, mostly freed slaves, were in the middle of this conflict, as victims and pawns of political interests, to be sure, but also as active players, pursuing their individual and group interests as they sought to define their role in post-Civil War Texas.

Violence existed in Reconstruction Texas, and African Americans were more often the victims of this violence than were whites. And many who avoided becoming victims of racial violence became victims of economic oppression and poverty. However, opportunity also existed and for a time, successful African Americans achieved prominence in politics, and to a lesser extent business and agriculture. In truth, the Reconstruction experience differed, person to person and community to community. Questions remain, however. How pervasive was the violence and to what degree did it undermine efforts of the freedmen to reconstruct their lives after slavery? How real was the opportunity for freedmen to assume positions of leadership, or even to secure a life free from want and fear?

❖ D O C U M E N T S

Document 1 is a section of the Juneteenth Proclamation which dealt with slavery.
These orders were issued by General Gordon Granger when he landed in Galveston
with federal troops on June 19, 1865 to begin the occupation of Texas following the
Civil War. General Granger emancipated all Texas slaves under the terms of President
Lincoln's Emancipation Proclamation. The fact that federal troops did not reach
Texas until June 19 delayed both emancipation and the organization of civil govern-
ment. It also underscored the fact that Texas was unoccupied when the war ended.
Document 2 consists of three accounts of emancipation as remembered by African
Americans more than seventy years later. They are from the collection of interviews
with former slaves conducted by the Federal Writers' Project in 1937 and 1938.
General Granger's terse announcement on June 19, 1865 set in motion a process
that radically altered the lives of Texas' African American population. However, as
these slave narratives reveal, a common emancipation experience did not exist, either
for whites or blacks.

Emancipation led to a debate over the civil and social status of the former slaves
in Texas. This debate affected politics and frequently provoked violence. White Texans
were deeply divided over the issue of political and civil rights for African Americans,
while blacks, and for the most part the North, were determined to guarantee the rights
of the freedmen. In Document 3, John L. Reagan, in an open letter to the people of
Texas, advised his neighbors about the need to accept civil and political rights for
blacks. Reagan's perspective is unique. He had been an opponent of secession, but
had supported the Confederacy loyally, ultimately serving in President Davis's cabinet. After the war, he was briefly imprisoned, along with other members of the Confederate government. Consequently, he was aware of northern expectations on these
issues. Documents 4 and 5 chronicle the break down of order and the rise of racial
violence. Document 4 is an editorial written by John L. Haynes, a pro-Republican
San Antonio newspaper editor who attacks Governor Throckmorton and his administration for their failure to protect the freedmen from the rampant violence. Governor
Throckmorton was removed from office by federal miliary authorities four months
later, as military authorities under the authority of the Reconstruction Act of 1867,
moved to establish governments in the former Confederate states that would enforce
the laws and protect the rights of the freedmen. Document 5 consists of two monthly
reports filed by Freedmen's Bureau agents, one in Mount Pleasant and the other in
Houston, for November 1867. These reports assess the status of freedmen in their
respective communities and reveal differences both from one community to another,
and from one agent to another.

Documents 6 and 7 reflect the range of feeling among whites. Document 6 is a
poem, written by an "unreconstructed" southerner. Its author is unknown, as is its
exact date of publication. It appeared in newspapers around the state in the early years
of Reconstruction. Document 7 is an excerpt from a handwritten history of Austin
county during Reconstruction by Martin M. Kenney. It underscores that conditions
varied from community to community, and that some areas experienced the war and
postwar period with relatively little disruption. Most residents, black and white, concentrated on efforts to carry on with life after the war.

Under the Reconstruction Act of 1867 and the Texas Constitution of 1869 that
followed, the political and civil rights of African Americans were guaranteed, and law
and order were restored. However, the political reign of the Republicans in Texas
(including their black political allies) was short-lived. By 1873, conservative Democrats were on the verge of regaining political power. The final Document in this

collection illustrates the political agenda of African Americans during the last years of Reconstruction. Document 8 was part of a presentation made in Brenham in July 1874 during a "Colored Men's Convention" of leading African American politicians. It expressed the political concerns of African Americans at a time when Republican rule in Texas was beginning to unravel.

1. General Gordon Granger Frees All Texas Slaves, June 19, 1865

GALVESTON; June 20th, 1865.

ED. NEWS:—The following are the first five orders issued under the new Administration:

[Official.]

HEADQUARTERS DISTRICT OF TEXAS,
GALVESTON TEXAS, June 19 1865.

General Orders, No. 3.

The people are informed that, in accordance with a proclamation from the Executive of the United States, all slaves are free. This involves an absolute equality of personal rights and rights of property, between former masters and slaves, and the connection heretofore existing between them, becomes that between employer and hired labor.—The Freedmen are advised to remain at their present homes, and work for wages. They are informed that they will not be allowed to collect at military posts; and that they will not be supported in idleness either there or elsewhere.   By order of
                                                      Major General GRANGER.
(Signed,)   F. W. EMERY, Maj. & A. A. G.

2. Three Slaves Remember Emancipation (1865), 1937–1938

Annie Hawkins: *Age 90 Years*

We was the happiest folks in the world when we knowed we was free. We couldn't realize it at first but how we did shout and cry for joy when we did realize it. We was afraid to leave the place at first for fear old Mistress would bring us back or the pateroller would git us. Old Mistress died soon after the War and we didn't care either. She didn't never do nothing to make us love her. We was jest as glad as

Major-General [Gordon] Granger, "General Orders, No. 3," *Galveston Daily News,* 21 June 1865.

T. Lindsay Baker and Julie P. Baker, eds., *Till Freedom Cried Out: Memories of Texas Slave Life* (College Station: Texas A&M University Press, 1997), 32–33, 41–42; 76–77. Reprinted by permission of the Texas A&M University Press.

when old Master died. I don't know what become of the three gals. They was about grown.

We moved away jest as far away as we could and I married soon after. My husband died and I married again. I been married four times and all my husbands died. The last time I married it was to a man that belonged to a Indian man, Sam Love. He was a good owner and was one of the best men that ever lived. My husband never did move far away from him and he loved him like a father. He always looked after him till he died. My husband has been dead five years.

Phyllis Petite: *Age 83 Years*

I was born in Rusk County, Texas, on a plantation about eight miles east of Belleview [Bellview]. There wasn't no town where I was born, but they had a church. . . .

Mammy say we was down in Texas to get away from the War, but I didn't see any war and any soldiers. But one day old Master stay after he eat breakfast and when us negroes come in to eat he say: "After today I ain't your master any more. You all as free as I am." We just stand and look and don't know what to say about it.

After while pappy got a wagon and some oxen to drive for a white man who was coming to the Cherokee Nation because he had folks here. His name was Dave Mounts and he had a boy named John.

We come with them and stopped at Fort Gibson where my own grand mammy was cooking for the soldiers at the garrison. Her name was Phyllis Brewer and I was named after her. She had a good Cherokee master. My mammy was born on his place.

We stayed with her about a week and then we moved out on Four Mile Creek to live. She died on Fourteen-Mile Creek about a year later.

When we first went to Four Mile Creek I seen negro women chopping wood and asked them who they work for and I found out they didn't know they was free yet.

Lewis Jenkins: *Age 93 Years*

That war that freed the niggers started in 1861. I had two young Masters to go. It lasted 4 years. They was figuring on taking me that very next year, and it was so fixed that the war ended. We had a big drought during the war, which made it bad on the soldiers. I never seen the Yankees only when they was passing 'long the road. One day whilst we was eating our dinner, our Master said, "All you, young and old, when you git through come out on the gallery, I got something to tell you." When we got through we all trooped out and he said, "This is military law, but I am forced to tell you." He says, "This law says free the nigger, so now you is jest as free as me by this law. I can't make you all stay wid me 'less you want to, therefore you can go any place you want to." That was about laying-by crop time in June. It was on June 19th an' we still celebrates 'at day in Texas, 'at is "Nigger Day" down there. He say, "I'd lak for you to stay till the crops is laid by iffen you will.["] Iffen it hadn't been for his wife maybe we would've stayed on, but she jest kept bossing the nigger women and we jest didn't lak it and that's what brung on the scatter. I left my old Master and went wid one of my young Masters, which was my uncle.

3. Confederate Unionist John H. Reagan Advocates Civil and Political Rights for Blacks, 1865

IN PRISON, FORT WARREN,
BOSTON HARBOR, August 11 1865.

TO THE PEOPLE OF TEXAS:

The condition of the country is such as to awaken the anxious solicitude of every citizen. Portions of you have honored me with your confidence on many occasions. I have tried to repay that confidence by sincere efforts for your good, and by faithful service. Though now a prisoner, in solitary confinement, and far from you, without knowing when, if ever, I shall be permitted to mingle with you again, and my children and relatives and friends among you, my anxiety for their and your welfare induces me to ask the permission of the Government to send you this communication. . . . I need not assure you of my sympathy with you, and I trust I need not doubt your confidence that I would advise you to no course which I did not think best for you. . . .

The State occupies the condition of a conquered nation. State government and State sovereignty are in abeyance, and will be so held until you adopt a government and policy acceptable to the conquerors. A refusal to accede to these conditions would only result in a prolongation of the time during which you will be deprived of a civil government of your own choice. . . .

. . . In order to secure to yourselves again the blessings of local self-government, and to avoid military rule, and the danger of running into military despotism, you must agree:

First, to recognize the supreme authority of the Government of the United States, within the sphere of its power, and its right to protect itself against disintegration by the secession of the States.

And, second, you must recognize the abolition of slavery, and the rights of those who have been slaves to the privileges and protection of the laws of the land.

From what I can see this much will be required as the least that would likely satisfy the Government, and secure to you the benefits of civil government, and the admission of your members into the Congress of the United States.

But even this may fail of the attainment of those ends, unless provision shall be made, by the new State government, for conferring the elective franchise on the former slaves. And present appearances indicate that this will be required by Northern public opinion and by Congress. . . . If you can do this, and secure to yourselves liberty, the protection of the Constitution and laws of the United States,

---

"To The People of Texas," [John H. Reagan's letter from prison, August 11, 1865] reprinted in *John H. Reagan, Memoirs: with Special Reference to Secession and the Civil War* (New York: The Neale Publishing Company, 1906), 286–295.

and the right of local self-government, you will be more fortunate than many conquered peoples have been. . . .

The adoption of these measures . . . would secure your protection against other great and pending evils, and is, I am persuaded, of the greatest consequence to your future peace, prosperity and happiness. And for these reasons:

First, it would remove all just grounds of antagonism between the white and black races. Unless this is done, endless strife and bitterness of feeling must characterize their relations, and, as all history and human experience teach us, must sooner or later result in a war of races. . . .

Second, this course would disarm and put an end to interstate, sectional, political agitation on this subject at least, which has been the special curse of our country for so many years, and which was the cause of the unnumbered woes we have recently experienced and still suffer, by depriving the agitators of a subject on which to keep up such agitation, and of the means of producing jealousy, animosity, and hatred between the different parts of the country, and between the different races. . . .

With these two lines of policy adopted, I think, notwithstanding all your recent misfortunes, you might look with hope and confidence to the future. The negroes will, it is hoped, gradually diffuse themselves among the greatly preponderating numbers of the whites, in the different States and Territories; many of them will probably go to Mexico, and other countries, in search of social equality, and few or none of their race will be added to their numbers by accessions from other countries. While the steady rapid influx of great numbers of the white races, from other countries, will gradually increase the disproportion in numbers between them and the whites, and so render this new element in society and government innocuous, or at least powerless for evil, if they should be so inclined. But from the general docility of their dispositions we may expect the most of them to be orderly, and many of them industrious and useful citizens. But to secure these desirable ends, it must not be forgotten that it is an essential prerequisite to confer on them their reasonable and necessary rights, and to adopt a policy which will prevent them from becoming an element of political agitation, and strife and danger. And we must bury past animosities with those of our fellow-citizens with whom we have been at war, and cultivate with them feelings of mutual charity and fraternal good will. And it will be greatly to your advantage, in many ways which I cannot trespass upon you to mention now, to hold out inducements to them and to emigrants from other countries, to come and settle among you, with their labor, and skill, and capital, to assist in the diffusion of employments, the increase of your population, and the development of your vast resources into new creations of wealth and power.

Time, and patience, and wisdom, and justice, mingled with the holy precepts in the New Testament, are necessary to enable you to secure these great and beneficent ends. That you may by the means I have indicated or others secure these results, shall have my constant hopes and prayers.

Very truly and respectfully,
JOHN H. REAGAN.

4. Republican Newspaper Editor John L. Haynes Berates the Democrats for Failure to Protect Freedman, 1867

San Antonio Express, **Saturday, March 30, 1867**

Governor Throckmorton

No one of the Governors of the Rebel States elected under the auspices of the President's reconstruction policy had so fair a chance as Governor Throckmorton of winning the golden opinions of all men and establishing for himself a national reputation. He had worked and spoken against the Ordinance of Secession. In opposing that measure as a Constitutional remedy he was in accord with a large majority of the people of the State who accepted it finally as simply a revolutionary act. When this occurred Governor Throckmorton gave way to local influences, deserted the principles of his whole life, and joined in the rebellion. As a candidate for Governor his former conscience made him acceptable to many Union men, whilst his service as an officer in the Rebel army gave him claim to the confidence of the disloyal. Thus his record was such as to enable him to appeal to both parties, and by moderate and wise action, after his election, he might have had a controlling voice in directing public opinion for the good of the whole people.

But, unfortunately, the Governor had not the capacity and grasp of mind to realize the situation and grapple with a question of such magnitude as that of reconstruction. . . . He is a man of narrow mind, of limited information, and with no fixed political principles. He gravitates to the local majority with the unerring certainty of instinct. He has not the moral courage to face popular clamor. . . .

To throw dust in the eyes of the country and withdraw attention from the lawlessness and anarchy prevalent in the State, Governor Throckmorton has ordered all the judges in the frontier counties to make reports of Indian depredations, which reports are being published weekly in his Austin organ. This is well. But we have no such reports of the hundreds of cases of crime in the interior counties of the State which call as loudly for protection and punishment. For every ten killed on the Frontier, a hundred in other parts of the State are murdered in cold blood by ruffians as ruthless as the Comanche with his tomahawk and scalping-knife. Of these crimes the governor is as silent as the murdered dead.

We have no report from the Judge of Grayson County of the murders and outrages in that county which have proved so many and so atrocious, . . . without any effort on the part of said judge and other civil servants to suppress them, that General Griffin has placed the county practically under martial law. We have no paper from his judge in Red river, or in Lamar county of a Rebel organization in those

Editorial, "Governor Throckmorton," *San Antonio Express,* Saturday, 30 March [1867] in Colonel John L. Haynes, Scrapbook, 2J144, The Center for American History, University of Texas at Austin.

and adjoining counties generally known as the "Black Brigade" (from their blackened faces and blacker deeds), whose object is to shoot, flog, or otherwise maltreat Negroes in order to control their labor by terror. . . .

We have no report from Collin County of the outrages upon the freedmen, the stoning and shooting of a quiet gathering of colored Christians by the Governor's immediate neighbors. . . .

The judge of Travis County, the Capital county, and the present residence of the Governor, tells us nothing through the columns of the organ of the several murders in his county, nor whether the "notoriously disloyal" John Ireland has yet found a Union man who might be hung as an example.

Judge Cowan of Caldwell County is so busily engaged in the business of holding public meetings "upon the suggestion of the Governor," that he has no time to report the murder of the freedmen at Prairie Lea, and other outrages upon that class of people, which have caused a garrison to be placed there to protect them. . . .

Victoria county sends no report of the several murders in that county, nor of the fact that three men were killed in one day, it is supposed, by the same man, one of them a Mexican, having been shot, it is said, "just to see how he would kick." . . .

It is not too much to say that the newspapers of the state have reported, since the inauguration of Governor Throckmorton, at least five hundred cases of murder and felony. And many crimes are committed which are unheralded to the world.

These facts cannot be unknown to the Governor, yet he has the audacity to write about them as "occasional" acts of lawlessness. . . .

Nowhere in the state do the civil authorities seem to make any attempt to execute the criminal laws except against the freedmen. For them alone there is speedy trial and swift condemnation. True we had one conviction of a white man in Fayette County for the brutal murder of a freedman, but the governor interposed his Executive pardon, and the criminal goes unwhipt of justice.

The Governor of the state and the editors of the rebel press are justly chargeable, at least, with dereliction of duty in not making some attempt to stem this tide of crime, even if they are not responsible at the bar of public opinion as encouragers and promoters of disorders. They continually cry aloud that peace and law exist when there is no peace and the courts are farces. They denounce those who wish to put an end to this lawlessness as manufacturing northern opinion for our punishment. In his letter to Judge Cowen, the governor says "you are aware that our enemies charge upon us that we do not attempt to protect the lives of freedmen or those who were Union men. *I know these things are false and I have sought every occasion to announce it.*" . . .

Now that the northern elections have passed and the reconstruction policies of Congress have been settled, when there is no necessity for misrepresenting facts and denouncing Union men because they wish to see the laws enforced, let Governor Throckmorton go to work in his appropriate duty of seeing that the laws are fully and impartially executed. If he cannot do this, then we hope to see him set aside, and an Executive appointed who will perform his duty.

5. Freedmen's Bureau Agents Report on the Status of Freedmen, 1867

Report from Freedmen's Bureau Agent, Houston, Texas, December 2, 1867 for the month of November 1867

Criminal Offenses

Date	Name and Race of Criminal	Name and Race of Person Injured	Nature of Offense, Statement of Circumstances, Action taken by Courts and Bureau, etc., etc.
Nov 11th	James Potter, fm	Col'd Congregation of the New Zion Church	Swindling—Obtaining money to be applied to the use of said church and using the same for his own personal use, and giving no satisfactory account of the same.
Nov. 29th	Albert George, fm	Caroline Doud, fm	Stealing $9 corn. Found guilty of theft by his own acknowledgment.
			Verdict in both cases: Guilty. Sentenced each to be confined in Camp Guard House for the period of one month.

"Report the disposition and feeling of the white people towards the freed people as expressed by words and actions."

The disposition of the white people is of mixed character, the owners of property and citizens who are educated except violent politicians and partisans entertain a friendly disposition, but I find among the ex-confederate soldiers and the younger part of the community a deep and violent hatred both in actions and words, and only the presence of a military force prevents them from many acts of violence.

Education

"Report the feeling upon the subject of education; what steps have been taken to promote the same; what efforts the freed people are making in that direction and in what manner they may be assisted, etc., etc."

The freed people are deeply solicitous upon the education of themselves and children, but are too poor, owing to the failure of the cotton crop, being made to obtain work they are barely able to earn sufficient to procure the actual necessities of life. The county officials and citizens entertain no desire to assist in the education of

---

"Report from the Freedmen's Bureau Agent, Houston, Texas, December 2, 1867 for the month of November 1867" and "Report from the Freedmen's Bureau Agent, Mount Pleasant, Texas, December 3, 1867 for the month of November 1867" in Record Group 105, The Records of the Bureau of Refugees, Freedmen, and Abandoned Lands, The National Archives.

either colored or white children, until Teachers are maintained by the government and suitable buildings furnished, I fear that little progress will be made in advancing the cause of education. A few night schools will probably be commenced during the month of December.

Report from Freedmen's Bureau Agent, Mount Pleasant, Texas, December 3, 1867 for the month of November 1867

Criminal Offenses

Date	Name and Race of Criminal	Name and Race of Person Injured	Nature of offense, Statement of circumstances, Action taken by Courts and Bureau, etc., etc.
Nov 5th	Stephen Shiray, w	Wilson Peppers, fm	Horse stealing. Absconded
6th	Gor. Carter, fm	Church members	Disturbing Public worship, fined five dollars
16th	Tmas. Johnson, w Nancy Johnson, w	John Whitley, fm	Threats of violence, case dismissed
16th	Henderson Hall, w	Marios S, w	Assault & battery. Arrested. Complaint trifling, dismissed
20th	G.S. Irons, w	J. Baldwin, fm	Threats of violence. Not arrested
20th	G.S. Irons, w	Roda Baldwin, fw	Threat to kill. Not arrested
21st	H. Gay, w	C. Hancock, fm	Threat to kill. Dismissed
23rd	Wm. Dodd, w	Green Clay & wife, ff	Threats of violence and false imprisonment. Both parties to blame. Mutual apologies
26th	Luke Carter, fm	Maria Scott	Assault & battery. Committed to jail
28th	Chas. Sheeler, w	R.A. Pleasants, fw	Adultery and obtaining money under false pretenses. Not arrested
29th	M. Hervey, w	G. Saunders, fm	Assault & battery. Trifling, dismissed

"Report the disposition and feeling of the white people towards the freed people as expressed by words and actions."

The feeling is growing worse. The freed people are continually saying, after making complaints that they are afraid to go back to old neighborhood.

Education

"Report the feeling upon the subject of education; what steps have been taken to promote the same; what efforts the freed people are making in that direction and in what manner they may be assisted, etc., etc."

The feeling is unfavorably. I have recommended the establishment of a school at this place and Mount German. At the last place surveyed the freed people have subscribed a small sum for a school which they propose paying toward its support.

"Give a statement of the official business transacted during the month; its nature and your method of disposing of the same. State your office hours; the number of days absent from office, if any, and occasion for the same."

Office hours all hours of the day.

"State the number of Troops at your Post and the necessity for the same; whether or not the freed people would be secure if they were removed; in other words will the civil authorities protect them and give them justice, etc., etc."

No change since last report. To remove the troops is death to the freed people. Hundreds of crimes are committed against them that they dare not report. They should be emigrated by the government. That is the only way to save them from slaughter.

6. An "Unreconstructed" Rebel Laments His Cause (poem), c. 1865

The Unreconstructed Texan

I am a good old rebel:
    Now that's just what I am,
For this great land of freedom
    I do not care a d—n.
I'm glad I fit agin it,
    I only wish I won,
And I don't ax no parding
    For anything I dun.

I hates the Constitution
    This glorious Union too;
I hates the Freedmen's Bureau
    And everything in blue;
I hates the American Eagle
    With all his bran and fuss
And the lyin', cheatin Yankees,
    I hate them wuss and wuss.

I followed Massa Robert
    For four years nigh about,
Got wounded in three places
    And starved at Point Lookout;
I cotched the rheuma-tis-em
    A campin' in the snow

"Poem—Author Unknown—Veteran of the Confed. Army, 1865" in Colonel John L. Haynes, Scrapbook, 2J144, "The Unreconstructed Texan," Colonel John L. Haynes, Scrapbook, 2J144, The Center for American History, University of Texas at Austin.

But I killed a sight of Yankees—
    I'd like to kill some mo'.

Three hundred thousand Yankees
    Is buried in our dust;
We got three hundred thousand
    Before they conquered us.
They died of southern fever,
    And southern shell and shot;
I wish it was three millions
    Instead of what we got.

I can't take up my musket
    And fight 'em now no more;
But I ain't a-goin' to love 'em,
    And that is sartin sure
And I don't ax no parding,
    For what I was I am
And I won't be reconstructed,
    If I do—may I be d—d.

7. White Southerner Martin M. Kenney Describes Reconstruction in Austin County, n.d.

The result of the war removed all value from the law and all rural fields of the river valley to the uplands. The river plantations were not abandoned, but greatly depreciated, the small farms in the prairie took a higher value than before the war. The sudden turning loose of so many Negroes did not produce any disturbance. They wandered around for a while in an aimless manner but were soon obliged by want of food to go to work which they performed more inefficiently than before but better than was expected. The fanatical part of the conquering party were much disappointed that the Negroes did not perpetrate brutal outrages on the whites and emissaries came and made speeches at Hempstead and other points designed to incite outrages but the Negroes had the sense or apathy to let good enough alone, or their masters had raised them to better principles. No ill feeling has sprung up between the whites and blacks. The enormity termed reconstruction affected this county less than almost any other which had a considerable Negro population. The military commandant Capt. Whitney proved to be rather an American than a partisan. No exactions were made beyond what was levied in the State at large to secure the election of radical officers. A sufficient number of the opposite party were prohibited from voting. But no false count was effected. Beyond the heavy and unnecessary taxes none graver evils have been complained of attributable to the conquering party than neglect to keep the public roads in repair.

Martin M. Kenney, Literary Production, Austin County History—Untitled ZE290, The Center for American History, University of Texas at Austin.

8. African American Platform Expresses Concerns About the End of Republican Rule, 1873

Colored Men's Convention, 1873

BRENHAM, July 3 and 4

Officers: President, N. W. Cuney. Vice-Presidents, Mathew Gaines, Richard Allen, and John Reed. Secretaries, John N. Coss, and J. H. Washington.

Committee on Address: W. C. Richer, W. A. Price, Jacob Freeman, G. T. Ruby, J. J. Hamilton, John DeBruhl, B. F. Williams, P. J. Moore, Cooke Jenkins, L. A. Clope, J. J. Webb. Walter Riptoe, N. W. Cuney, W. H. Holland, J. H. Washington, and Richard Allen, chairman.

ADDRESS

We, the undersigned members of the committee on address, do most respectfully, by leave, report as follows:

That we consider one of the prime objects of our assemblage to be the promotion of good feelings between ourselves and our white fellow-citizens of the State, without whose earnest and sincere efforts in cooperation with our own, to effect our elevation, our progress must be slow and constrained. . . .

. . . It must be borne in mind that the mass of the colored people are in a lamentable state of ignorance, the result of that wicked system of bondage, which shut them out from the acquisition of all knowledge of letters and made it a penal offense to teach them to read the Word of God. They must also remember that they have from the day of the acquisition of our liberty set their faces in steadfast opposition to our political, educational, and social progress, with a blind spirit of malignant opposition not calculated to inspire us with either confidence or affection. . . .

. . . It becomes our duty here to define clearly what is understood by us as civil rights in contradistinction to social privileges. . . . We know perfectly well that a man's social relations cannot be made by legislative enactments. We have no disposition to intrude ourselves upon them, and would *resent as an indignity any intrusion upon ourselves.* But we do demand our Civil Rights Bill of the Hon. Charles Sumner, and shall agitate the question of their concession with unabated ardor until we can celebrate their acquisition. . . .

It is a misfortune for both races that the Southern white men seem determined to leave their colored fellow-citizens nothing to be grateful for, as every right we enjoy has been forced from their grasp, in face of stern opposition and openly expressed hatred. . . . With stolid obstinacy they have clung to their prejudices. Yet we do not despair and feel our duty to ourselves and them render it imperative for us to hold out the olive branch, and express a willingness to cooperate with them in any measure for the advancement of the interests of our State and the welfare of its citizens. We appeal to them to meet us with the free concession of our civil rights in

---

"Colored Men's Convention, 1873," in *Platforms of Political Parties in Texas,* ed. Ernest William Winkler (Austin: Bulletin of the University of Texas, 1916), 148–151.

their hands, and will thus become a truly homogeneous people, animated by one common purpose, and that purpose the prosperity of the State. . . .

"With charity for all, and malice toward none" of our fellow-citizens, we appeal to the law-abiding and honest people of Texas, of whatever political party, to join with us in deprecating the outrages and wrongs perpetrated upon the colored people in various sections of our State, because of our new relations as freemen and citizens, and we ask that all acts of violence towards us, from whatever source, shall be condemned by the public sentiment of the community in such unequivocal terms as that law and order shall be enforced.

We also recommend to our people the acquisition of land and homesteads, and that they do not support for office any man or set of men who are likely to place obstacles in the way of their success in this direction.

We also urgently recommend to them that they refuse to support for any office whatever any man who is not pledged against repudiation in all its forms. We are not to consider how the State has been brought into debt, or the means by which its obligations were incurred; we only are to consider how we can earliest pay them, and we pledge ourselves to use our humble efforts to the payment of the State obligations, to the last dollar in the treasury, and we will cheerfully submit to any amount of taxation to accomplish that object.

We also express ourselves as being decidedly in favor of internal improvements.

This we also consider an appropriate occasion to disabuse the minds of our fellow-citizens of foreign birth, of the desire that has been attributed to us to lay obstacles in the way of the immigration of their brethren in Europe to this State. We indignantly deny that we cherish any so unworthy or selfish feeling. We look on the Americans as the trustees of this soil for the oppressed of all nations, and we welcome the downtrodden immigrant from wherever he may come with open arms.

We cannot close this address without the strongest expression of our confidence in, and regard for President Grant and reiterate our thanks to him for his efforts to ameliorate our condition and obtain our civil rights.

We also express our confidence in the Federal government and reaffirm our allegiance to the National Republican party.

In conclusion, we tender our grateful thanks to Chas. Sumner for his constant and unwearied efforts for our acquisition of civil rights, and earnestly trust that his existence be so prolonged to win the completed result of his lifelong labors. And we confidently hope and believe that our future will justify his past.

❧ E S S A Y S

These two essays examine African Americans, both as victims of Reconstruction era violence and as effective politicians. Texas experienced more than its share of violence in the months and years that followed the Civil War. Some of this violence was simply the crime and lawlessness that followed the collapse of the Confederacy and the collapse of the frontier. Texas, a relatively sparsely settled region on the southwestern frontier of the Confederacy, was particularly vulnerable due to the lack of an effective police force when civil government vanished in the late spring of 1865. This violence continued because insufficient numbers of federal troops were available to police the Lone Star state.

Although all Texans suffered from the epidemic of postwar violence, African Americans were disproportionately victims. In the first essay by Barry Crouch, of Gallaudet College, two Reconstruction-era reports on crime and violence are used to document, both statistically and narratively, the extent and the nature of the racial violence in Texas. In the second essay, Carl H. Moneyhon of the University of Arkansas in Little Rock explores African American political power through the career of George T. Ruby. Ruby was a "carpetbagger," a northern-born African American who moved South, first to Louisiana, then to Texas, where he initially worked with the Freedman's Bureau. Moneyhon critically examines Ruby's efforts to build a political power base during the turbulent period following the Civil War, as well as his political successes and failures.

White Violence in Reconstruction Texas

BARRY A. CROUCH

Southern history, though rich and compelling, is stained by the theme of violence. Both before the Civil War and long after violence was an accepted facet of southern society. Reconstruction, however, may have been that region's most violent era. Blacks and whites struggled to redefine their roles within an atmosphere of bitterness, frustration, and resentment. Racial tensions, always an important characteristic of southern life, reached new extremes that appalled even contemporaries. From Paris, Texas, a year after emancipation, Mrs. L. E. Potts, a native Tennesseean, implored President Andrew Johnson to do something about the plight of the "*poor negro*" and "their persecution." Just a few months out of slavery, she wrote, "their masters are so angry to loose [sic] them that they are trying to persecute them back into slavery." Killing black people was not considered a crime, she continued, and "they are often run down by blood hounds, and shot because they do not do precisely as the white man says." Black Texans needed federal protection, for the area "savors of rebellion." When blacks did work, Potts concluded, they "scarcely get any pay, and what are they to do [?]."

Violence was a major component of postwar race relations. . . . Leon Litwack has been especially forceful in accentuating the role of Reconstruction violence and dramatically portraying some of its effects and results. The number of blacks, "beaten, flogged, mutilated, and murdered in the first years of emancipation," he maintains, "will never be known." . . .

Litwack's graphic description of white violence against blacks is useful in calling attention to this issue, but it has not led to an examination of individual acts of violence. . . . No one has attempted to assess the different aspects of white violence in the immediate postwar era, to analyze the whites who perpetrated it, to ascertain its rationale, or to determine in what social and geographical context the violence occurred. Nor have statistical compilations been undertaken comparing white and black violence, the numbers killed, and the percentage of a specific black population murdered.

Barry A. Crouch, "A Spirit of Lawlessness: White Violence; Texas Blacks, 1865–1868," *Journal of Social History,* 18 (Winter 1984): 217–232. Copyright © 1984 Carnegie-Mellon University Press. Reprinted with permission.

Fortunately, some of these issues can be explored in the case of Texas. Two extant sets of evidence related to the Lone Star state permit a detailed look at white violence against blacks for the years from mid-1865 until mid-1868. The first is the conclusions reached by a special committee on lawlessness and violence established by the 1868 Texas Constitutional Convention. The second is the violence register compiled by the Texas Freedmen's Bureau.

These records reflect certain limitations and biases and must be used with caution. Republican sentiment inspired both documents, and recorders probably stressed rather than minimized white violence against blacks. In addition, the state committee only recorded homicide totals, thus hindering the detection of any statistical errors. Often the Bureau sources provide only minimal background material. Frequently, age and sex statistics of the black victims are missing and have to be inferred. The information about the whites and their backgrounds is sketchy at best. Although the type of assault they committed is included, recurrently the motivation for the crime is ignored. Furthermore, local Bureau agents depended upon various sources for their data, as they did not witness all the violence themselves. Officials throughout the districts submitted reports collected in varying fashion. Surely, some were hearsay and distorted thus skewing the figures.

Another critical difficulty with violence records is that many events were never recorded, so both documents must be weighed against possible omissions. . . . In spite of these problems, these documents represent a rich source of information for the Presidential Reconstruction years. . . .

The special committee's report is less comprehensive than the Bureau's record. Dealing only with homicides, the committee gathered data from state department records (comprising about forty counties) where indictments had been found, Freedman's Bureau materials for approximately sixty counties, and sworn statements of witnesses throughout the state. The committee recognized this was a "very imperfect view of the actual violence and disorder in the State."

According to the committee, the homicide figures reveal a "frightful story of blood." During the three year period from June 1865 to June 1868 Texans killed 939 people. Of this total, 373 were blacks murdered by whites, but only 10 were whites killed by blacks. Additionally, the committee reported 8 blacks killed by unknown assailants. The committee also indicated another 40 homicides where the victim's race was not specified. It concluded that the "great disparity between the numbers of the two races killed, the one by the other, shows conclusively that 'the war of races' is all on the part of the whites against the blacks."

The Texas Freedmen's Bureau compiled the second, and more important, violence record. . . .

The statistical breakdown of the 2,225 offenses catalogued by the Texas Bureau not only corroborates the special committee reports on lawlessness and violence, but reveals much more. The Bureau attempted to describe all physical acts of violence, not simply homicides. Even though there are some minor discrepancies between the state committee's death statistics and those of the Bureau, what should command attention is the high death rate caused by white males killing primarily black males.

More to the point is the meaning of the number of deaths in relation to the Texas black population from June 1865 to June 1868. According to the 1870 census,

253,475 blacks lived in the Lone Star state. Thus, the annual death rate for blacks from white inflicted outrages for these years averaged 65.4 per 100,000. If this same ration is projected to only the 126,278 black males, the violence-specific death rate rises to 131.5 per 100,000. If this ratio is further extended to males in the 15–49 year age range, the rate would be 290.4 per 100,000. This means that a number equal to approximately *one percent* of the black male population between 15 and 49 years old was killed in the early years of Reconstruction. . . .

Of all the southern states at the close of the war, Texas had three distinctive factors that may have affected its violence record: the state's relative immunity from the devastation of the war, location on the frontier, and low population density. Texas is so large that the eastern half of the state is the combined size of Mississippi and Alabama, yet in 1870 only 818,579 citizens resided in the state. Thus, the Army had a difficult responsibility trying to enforce order and protect the ex-slaves, and the Bureau never had more than 100 agents. Moreover, most of the Army's troops were stationed on the vast frontier, not in the heavily populated areas where they could have protected the freedpeople. That Texas was never invaded successfully, and therefore did not accept defeat easily, also helped produce conditions for individual and group attacks by whites against blacks.

The Lone Star state's vast size permitted individuals or groups to elude the law and justice, even when local officials did not connive to aid them in escaping punishment. By 1868 there were 5,000 pending homicide indictments in Texas. Yet from the end of the war until the fall of 1868 only one legal execution occurred in the state, ironically a Houston freedman. . . . Geography, the frontier, a lax system of law enforcement, and inadequate support from the Army or the Bureau all conspired to make rural blacks general targets for white violence.

Did whites commit the violence individually or in groups (a group being defined as two or more people)? Litwack argues that "much of the violence inflicted on the freedmen had been well organized, with bands of white men meting out extra-legal 'justice' and anticipating the Klan-type groups that would operate so effectively during Radical Reconstruction." Texas does not bear out Litwack's argument. Of the 1,524 total attacks or threats on blacks during 1865 to 1868, 1,037 (or 68 percent) were perpetrated by individuals. Blacks were terrorized by groups in 301 cases, mostly by desperadoes, some bandits, or in a few instances by the Ku Klux Klan, making its first appearance in early 1868. In 186 actions, the party or parties were unknown. In many of these unsolved outrages the black person was found dead, and no identification of the attacker could be made. Black families were enumerated in only 35 altercations.

White violence against Texas blacks took many forms and resulted from a variety of causes that are difficult to pinpoint precisely. It was, for example, sometimes related to political or labor activities, to social relations and mores. Sometimes it was directed at women and children or institutions such as schools and churches, and, at times by gangs that preyed upon the freepeople. . . .

Two questions might be raised about violence against blacks in the years covered by the sources. First, were certain types of violence more frequently committed by groups of whites or by individuals? Second, were some classes of whites more prone to use group or mob violence than others? Some kinds of violent attacks, or course, were committed by both individuals and groups, but patterns might be established for specific motivations. The question of which classes were likely to commit violence is much more difficult, and a complete answer will need further supporting studies.

In past writings about Reconstruction, historians have too often narrowly focused on politically motivated violence against blacks. This was certainly a central part of the violence equation. There were, to be sure, many other reasons for outrages, ending in injury or death for blacks. At work or play, while drinking, in an institutional setting, or in circumstances when refusing to sanction old social mores, blacks were the subject of numerous outrages. Although black Texans are seen largely as victims in this essay (a concept not without evident pitfalls), the major conclusion to be drawn is that whites used violence in different guises to control blacks politically, economically, and socially. Texas whites resented black political equality, a free labor ideology, or more equitable social relations. Blacks most assuredly responded to white violence and committed individual acts against whites. But the [data] substantiate the judgment that black violence was minimal compared to what whites were doing to them. Obviously not all whites were participants in the outrages, even abhorring the incidents, but the high number of incidents suggest there was little concerted action to stop them. . . .

Once blacks organized, met politically, and were enfranchised, they became sources of potential and real conflict in the political arena. The rise in the death rate of Texas blacks, besides being more carefully tallied, coincides precisely with the Congressional Republicans' struggle to control the Reconstruction process and with the emergence of local blacks as voters, community leaders, registrars, and Union Leaguers. From 1866 to 1867, when freedmen won the right to vote, the total number of blacks slain by whites rose twofold. But worse lay ahead. According to the state committee, sixty-nine percent of the blacks murdered by whites died during 1867 and 1868. Republicans, both black and white, states Otto Olsen, "provoked a hatred from their opponents so intense that it soon turned Reconstruction into an age of violence and terror." White Texans, as one historian has noted, perceived political rights for blacks as a temporary aberration, which "could be taken back by the state after it was readmitted to the Union." Thus, violence, terror, and intimidation became acceptable standards for the destruction of black political equality.

The case of George E. Brooks, a politically active minister from Millican, Texas, is instructive. His decomposing body was found following a racial clash between Millican's blacks and whites in mid-1868. The incident originated after a black man was murdered near the sheriff's residence, the culprit not arrested for two days, and then released on his own recognizance. When blacks protested this lenient treatment, the Ku Klux Klan entered the affray, inciting a racial imbroglio, which resulted in the killing of prominent members of Millican's black community. In the Millican affair, it seems likely that whites, with substantial economic and political interests in the community, were concerned about blacks banding together, asserting their rights, and demanding justice. The killing of Brooks, who was a prominent local politician, registrar, and Union League member, one observer wrote, was a "deliberate murder" and one of a "most outrageous character."

Even if Texas blacks simply wished to learn more about their rights they risked danger. While on his way to hear the Bureau Assistant Commissioner speak, James

Cole of Walker County was beseiged by a mob of "white rowdies," assaulted and pistol whipped. The same thing happened in Harrison County, only the whites involved in that incident were described as "civil officers" and the "disloyal." Where politics motivated violence, whites used both individual and group tactics, depending upon whether blacks had organized and protested denial of rights, served a political function, or attended meetings. The evidence suggests that all classes of whites participated in the attacks, especially where blacks emerged as a vocal segment of the body politic.

Violence associated with labor-related behavior was prevalent in the postwar years. Activities such as contracting, working, moving for better jobs, securing rations, arranging credit bills, seeking wages and dividing shares, or being driven off the land without compensation led to violence. Because of the refusal of blacks to work in gangs, and the dominating presence of sharecropping, much of the violence was committed on individuals. Whites perpetrating the attacks were property-holders, the Bureau records suggest, probably former planters with varying size acreages, who were concerned about maintaining a reliable, dependent, and available labor pool. . . .

Disciplining blacks to the "new" labor relations was another component of white violence. When Texas blacks decided to control their own labor and make the best arrangements with whom and where they worked, their actions provoked physical assaults, injuries, and even death. Again, this type of violence was largely individual. There were rare instances, such as in Davis County, where a gang of white men (perhaps hired by the planters) generally whipped blacks who refused to sign new contracts. Those who controlled the land after the war liberally used the lash to suppress any notions of independence that blacks may have perceived. But not all blacks were only whipped for seeking a new work environment: some were killed, as were a mother and her baby in 1868 in Rusk County when she left her employer. Others were murdered when they refused to return to their "masters."

Allowing Texas blacks total freedom of movement brought indignation from those concerned about a stable labor force. Blacks were not permitted to look for better jobs, or more advantageous share arrangements, and leaving the farm without permission was certainly a transgression of the old pass system. A few owners went to great lengths to find and punish blacks who departed without consent. In Fort Bend and Walker Counties whites used dogs to chase two blackmen (one was shot at twice) because they failed to check with the farm owner before leaving. A Fort Bend County freedman, named Shade, was confined two days in the "calaboose" for attempting to move. Families had to be careful about allowing their offspring freedom of movement. Stephen Bryant and his wife, Liberty County freedpeople, were handcuffed, whipped, and beaten because two of their sons left the farm without asking the owner's permission.

White violence against black Texans, however, involved more than just the contracting process or movement away from the confines of the plantation. It lurked over the freedpeople's everyday working life. Texas blacks were beaten and wounded for being too sick to work, for taking too long to eat breakfast, for being too late coming to work, for hoeing too slowly (100 lashes), for incompetence, laziness, carelessness, or for paying too much attention to an ailing relative. One freedman appeared at the Freedmen's Bureau office in Seguin covered with large scabs and scars. He informed the agent that because he was too sick to pick cotton he had been whipped with a strap that has a two-inch iron buckle. Miles, a Fort Bend Country freedman, told a similar story. His employer beat him over the head and back with a heavy walking stick. Much of this ill-treatment was parcelled out by owners themselves or their hired foremen and managers.

Labor related violence often surfaced at the end of the contracting year or following the harvesting of crops when it was time to collect wages or, more commonly, divide shares. The complaint books of the Texas Freedmen's Bureau contain a large number of cases indicating the role of planters in violence against blacks. Laborers deluged the Bureau with grievances asserting they received too little or no compensation whatsoever from their employers. According to Texas freedpeople, they were shot, struck with pistols, cut with hatchets or knives, whipped, beaten with clubs and chains, assaulted with monkey wrenches, stabbed, or threatened with shotguns and pistols. If a freedperson actually was able to get his/her employer before a Bureau court for non-payment, retaliation was too often the result. Oliver, a Montgomery County freedman, was killed for bringing his employer before the Bureau, while an Anderson County black man, Henry Jones, was waylaid and murdered by his boss because Jones sued him for seven dollars. . . .

Still, anti-black violence was not prompted solely be economics and labor relations. In social relations, whether implementing or maintaining acceptable social mores or monitoring the social activities of blacks, white Texans followed antebellum patterns. Black Texans could not make insulting noises, speak disrespectfully or out of turn, talk back, dispute the word of whites, or disobey a command. Further, they had to stand at attention when whites passed, step aside when white women were on the sidewalk, properly address whites, and remove their hats in their presence. "Improper actions" by blacks resulted in swift retaliation. Although outrages of this sort were not common, the ones that did occur demonstrated to black Texans that social intercourse was still imbued with prescribed rules. . . .

Texas whites who attempted to guard and maintain the old social mores generally did so individually, though there were a few exceptions. Whites who attacked blacks at dances, parties, or social functions did so in groups, apparently angered that blacks found ways to enjoy themselves. These "gangs," as the Bureau referred to them entered a Palestine saloon where local blacks were dancing and threw several of them through the upper story windows. A similar occurrence in Panola County in 1868 ended with three black men dead and four wounded. The white ringleader was the county sheriff. Freedmen were also murdered at celebrations.

Texas whites did not respect sex when committing outrages. Whites victimized black women in 183 incidents, according to a tabulation of the Bureau records. Too often in discussions of anti-black violence following the Civil War, males are the major focus. The rather significant number of offenses perpetrated on black women strongly indicates that there was a deep rage underlying many of the attacks and that much of the violence was purposeless, almost elemental and irrational. In addition to this violence, black women at times received gruesome treatment. A Limestone County freedwoman, Jo Brooks, had her ears cut off and her arms burned to a crisp, for no stated provocation. Others, if not so horribly violated, were nonetheless brutalized beyond rationality. These attacks, when women were not engaged in a specific activity such as labor, were perpetrated by individuals, who, the sources suggest, had little economic standing in communities and were of a desperate, socially irresponsible class.

Nor were children immune from white violence. They suffered as did adults from whipping, flogging, beating, assaults, castration, and murder. Much violence against children seems to have a random quality, with whites motivated by nothing more than a deep rage. This may lead to the surmise that whites who brutalized black children were from the lower economic echelon and thus presumably more frustrated than wealthier persons, but this conclusion is not entirely valid. For example, three prominent citizens of McLennan and Bosque Counties, two of whom were doctors, committed what a Bureau agent called one of the "most atrocious deeds in the annals of barbarity," castrating a freedboy. Perhaps in the same social strata was the planter who shot a freedchild because the mother left his employ. However, child assault instigated by influential whites remained rare. Most of the other recorded outrages were as brutal, but there is nothing to indicate that those who performed them were of the same class as those who castrated the boy or the planter who shot a child because of a labor incident. Children were whipped and kicked, stabbed to death, shot at, and had turpentine placed on their "fundaments" in a random pattern of violence. In the fall of 1866, a Bosque County black boy was whipped to death, while a seven year old girl, Dolla Jackson, suffered an attempted rape and was robbed of twenty-five cents. The Bureau viewed the whites who precipitated these cases as characters of a desperate and mean sort, with no established economic or community standing.

Two treasured institutions of the black community, schools and churches, also were the objects of white violence. In Anderson County, with an almost equal black and white population, a white mob stoned the black church, twice broke the windows, and threatened the minister. In Washington County congregation members were beaten. A white mob attacked a Harris County Baptist Church in September 1868. The whites assaulted the former minister, an "old man," his son, and daughter-in-law, brutally kicking, mauling, and mangling them, nearly killing the elderly preacher and his daughter-in-law. Teachers and schools suffered the same fate. The former were driven from counties or killed. The latter were trashed and burned. Northern white soldiers, apparently not immune to the deep racial hatred of Texas whites, fired on a school on their way to the outer frontier, leading to a "regular skirmish" between the two races with four wounded, two on each side. Whites also entered schools with drawn pistols, disrupting classes.

Although individual acts of violence accounted for over two-thirds of the total, white desperadoes committed the most destructive forms of group violence against blacks. In the immediate postwar years these bandits robbed, plundered, harassed, and murdered blacks who lived in Northeastern Texas and along the Arkansas border. Marauding bands, composed of ex-Confederate soldiers and other economically dispossessed social elements, hated both blacks and Yankees. Blaming the war and Northern invaders for their depressed plight and bleak circumstances, their attacks bordered on the fanatical. . . . Many of these desperadoes, as one contemporary observed, would kill a freedman for seventy-five cents and boast of the deed as a "laudable one to high minded chivalry." . . .

Texas whites often killed blacks for no obvious reason other than racial hatred or the satisfaction of sadistic fantasies. Some reportedly shot freedmen to "see a d———d nigger kick" or because they just wanted to shoot a "damned nigger." Others shot them, apparently, to test their skills as marksmen. The very presence of free blacks led to murders. In Grayson County, for instance, where blacks comprised only eighteen percent of the population and therefore were not a political threat, three whites murdered three freedmen because, they said, they felt a need to "thin the niggers out and drive them to their holes."

Texas anti-black violence, in the years 1865 to 1868, was significant because of its high yearly death toll and the percentage of the population affected. . . .

Probably due to the size of the state and the isolation of many sections, more than any other factors, white attacks on blacks were largely individual and only partially by groups. Certain patterns emerge, however, in relation to the motivations behind the various categories of white violence.

Politically motivated white violence had a varied background, with three distinct patterns. The one major group confrontation occurred at Millican involving a cross-section of both the white and black communities. Much of the political violence was perpetrated by individuals or by quite small groups that harassed, intimidated, and sometimes murdered black Texans who participated in some fashion in politics or simply desired to live a free life. Those blacks directly involved in politics, such as registrars, were subjected to the violence of small groups, described as bullies and rowdies. The nature of the particular circumstances dictated which whites engaged in this type of violence. Prominent members of the community were apparently part of the Millican affray, and perhaps where blacks were attacked when they held some official position.

Labor violence, or its related categories, was largely individual, perpetrated by planters. The constant references in the source to former "owners" and "masters" suggest this clearly. In this struggle of economic independence versus continued dependence, with racial and class overtones, whites could not hope to emerge victorious without the complete subordination of blacks. Although this cannot be definitely ascertained from the records, there are indications that those who perpetrated much of the labor-related violence were landowners of some type. Indeed, almost all may have been previous slaveholders. Occasionally there were attacks on working blacks that can be classified as random, but most were purposeful. Whipping was still widely practiced as a means of discipline and punishment, but other ingenious ways of using violence to keep blacks working and tied to the land were found.

Anti-black violence directed against persons who violated prewar social relations or mores is much more difficult to classify. Those whites who committed outrages against blacks for violating the "old" ways seem to have been from a different economic strata than those who attacked blacks who were enjoying themselves socially. Another difference is that the former were performed largely by individuals, while "gangs" accounted for the latter, according to the sources. When attacks focused on schools and churches, lower class white crowds or mobs were the villains. Desperadoes were the final element in the violence equation, and they wreaked havoc upon individual blacks and communities. . . .

During the early years of Texas Reconstruction conditions were " 'anomalous, singular, and unsatisfactory,' " according to General Philip H. Sheridan. He also reputedly remarked that if he had owned both Texas and hell he would have rented out Texas and moved to hell because of Lone Star state terror. Texas was all this and more, particularly for blacks who tried to take advantage of their supposed freedom. Clearly more studies of violence in other Southern states are necessary before we can conclude, as does James M. Smallwood, that an "examination of sources" suggests "there was little difference in the degree of harassment suffered by Texas blacks and those of other states." If the remainder of the old Confederacy had a scale of violence similar to Texas, then the Southern black populace faced an even more desperate situation than earlier assumed. All this serves as a reminder that Reconstruction elicited remarkable and wrenching experiences. Texas blacks needed extraordinary resilience because their potential social, economic, and political losses surpassed even the fetters of slavery.

George T. Ruby and African American Politics During Reconstruction

CARL H. MONEYHON

In the post–Civil War era no black man in Texas exercised more political power than did George Thompson Ruby. An astute politician, Ruby built a base of power in the black community of Galveston, then used that support to make himself a major force in the state at large. He was a forceful advocate of civil and political rights for his race, but he knew when to compromise to gain his larger goals, and he moved carefully among hostile white politicians in his efforts to expand opportunities for black people. In the context of his time and place, his goals were radical, but he was hardly a political fanatic. His entire career demonstrated responsibility and moderation. In the end his work failed and he left Texas for a more favorable environment, but rather than any personal character flaws or lack of depth in his vision, forces outside his control undercut his efforts. The refusal of whites to compromise on racial matters, the white majority of the state, and Ruby's steadfast willingness to adhere to democratic politics prevented his attaining the goals he sought. His career is instructive, not only in that it shows how at least one black politician gained power during Reconstruction, but also because it indicates the problems that beset both Ruby and the southern Republican movement in their efforts to establish a viable political alternative to the white-dominated Democratic party.

Ruby was not a native Texan, but arrived in the state after the Civil War. . . .

In September 1866, . . . Ruby joined the Freedmen's Bureau schools in Texas. . . . He received an appointment as school organizer and operated in Galveston and the surrounding counties. This job placed him in the heart of the black belt of Texas and helped him establish contacts with the local black community. During this time he gained a reputation, even among whites, as a man of integrity. A Unionist newspaper cited him as "a colored man of education, character, and ability, and . . . an honest man." One local Democratic newspaper begrudgingly viewed him as a

Carl H. Moneyhon, "George T. Ruby and the Politics of Expediency in Texas," in *Southern Black Leaders of the Reconstruction Era*, ed. Howard N. Rabinowitz (Urbana: University of Illinois Press, 1982), 363–392. Reprinted with permission of the author.

good fellow among a bad lot. General Charles Griffin, assistant commissioner of the Freedmen's Bureau in Texas, wrote of his agent, "He is an energetic man and has great influence among his people." At this time Ruby began to build the base for his later political activities.

In spring 1867 Ruby turned from education to politics. . . . The introduction of black people into the political process [through the Reconstruction Act of 1867] meant that successful politicians would have to attract their votes. Ruby, who had emerged as an individual with contacts throughout the black belt, proved an excellent intermediary between the freedmen and ambitious white politicians.

Ruby's first office was president of the Galveston chapter of the Union League, and the league would thereafter remain the center of his power. . . . The league was a secret organization with elaborate rituals—mechanisms that allowed freedmen to be instructed in patriotism toward the Union and the Republican party, marched to the polls, and protected from outside white interference.

At the beginning Ruby appears to have been little more than an instrument used by the Unionists and other white politicians. . . . His relationship with political leaders in Galveston during the period affirms this. . . . These men, although they publicly supported the doctrine of political and civil equality of blacks, hardly carried out these ideas in practice. With few exceptions they did not approve of black officeholding and did not see blacks as filling leadership roles even within the party. . . .

While Ruby probably realized the incongruity of his friends' public and practical positions, he defended them nonetheless, leading to accusations that he was nothing more than "a yellow negro, a tool." He may have been just that, but at that time his political power lay with the white Republicans, no matter how insincere they may have been, and he remained loyal. He faithfully turned out the league for party rallies and conventions.

Eventually he began to receive rewards, although modest. At the first state Republican convention, in July, he received an honorary vice-presidency. Later he solicited and obtained an appointment as a notary public for Galveston. . . . Although the beginnings were small, Ruby had shown that he could organize black voters, and he had been rewarded. The offices, as minor as they were, in turn showed blacks that he had access to white political leaders, and this bolstered his support among them.

The composition of the electorate following the initiation of Congressional Reconstruction added to Ruby's importance to white politicians. The required registration of voters proceeded through the spring and summer of 1867 and certified over a thousand blacks in Galveston. Potential white registrants outnumbered blacks, but restrictions imposed by the Reconstruction Act passed March 23 and the refusal of many, who were otherwise qualified, to swear to the oath provided by that law, limited the number of those actually registered to about two-thirds of the blacks. To be elected required the support of black voters; therefore, the man who could deliver that support possessed political power.

As Ruby used his bureau position to organize local Union leagues around the Galveston area in preparation for the convention election, he became less satisfied with his role as a spokesman for white interests. In autumn 1867 he finally announced that he intended to run for one of Galveston's seats in the convention. His associates argued against a black man representing such an important county, suggesting that if he ran, the men in business and industry whom they hoped to attract to their party would be dissuaded from joining. Ruby countered that he was the only true representative of the great majority of loyal men in Galveston, and it was his right to run and their right to have him run. He refused to back out of the race and, thus, precipitated a vitriolic fight between himself and his friends in the Galveston Republican Association.

To minimize Ruby's threat and undercut his power, association leaders immediately attempted to broaden white participation in the organization's activities by bringing in individuals not yet eligible to vote. When Colonel A. P. Wiley, a "father of secession," applied for membership [they] . . . heartily endorsed his admission and called for the acceptance of all converts to the Republican cause. If enough such men came in, black power would be severely reduced. Ruby, along with B. Rush Plumly, who . . . considered himself a protector of blacks, fought the move. . . . When the association admitted Wiley anyway, Ruby resigned and charged that the association's leaders had sold out to the rebels.

Cut out of the Republican association, Ruby determined to run for the convention without its backing. He believed that the Union League actually controlled black voters, and he knew that he controlled the league; therefore, he believed that he could win the election despite the opposition of white Republicans. He obtained some white support. Plumly continued to work with him, and a convert to his cause was Dr. Robert K. "Revenue" Smith of the customhouse. On December 21, 1867, the Galveston Union League met to decide whom it would support for the convention election. Ruby demanded that it endorse him, whereas association leaders desperately tried to prevent such a move. However, Ruby showed that he controlled this group when the members announced that their choices for the convention were he and Smith.

But the nominee was not satisfied simply with the league's endorsement; he quickly moved to take over the rest of the machinery of the local Republican party. He and Smith called a meeting of the Galveston Republican Association to ratify the league nominations. . . . Over opposition of the white leadership, the association joined with the league and approved Ruby and Smith as the convention nominees.

The campaign that followed was relatively quiet, with the election of Ruby a foregone conclusion. . . .

Ruby had run for constitutional convention as a candidate of the black community. When he arrived at Austin, most people believed he was a radical politician who was primarily interested in securing equal rights and suffrage for blacks. His actions proved him a strong advocate of both of these goals, but he did not turn out to be the firebrand that whites had expected. He was an active participant in debate, a forceful behind-the-scenes manipulator, yet an acute observer of the political situation and a spokesman for moderation. His work in the convention made him an important figure in the state Republican political scene for the next five years and marked his transformation to the state level of leadership. . . .

The Constitutional Convention of 1868 provides the first opportunity to examine Ruby's ideas concerning the problems of blacks and the ways to rectify them. He envisioned a comprehensive program of education, economic development, and legal protection. Perhaps because of his background in education, he placed the development of a system of public schools at the center of his program. In this he was typical of others, of both the North and the South, who believed that education was the panacea that would help blacks climb out of the darkness of slavery. After the convention's committees had already been named, he solicited an appointment as an additional member of the Committee on Education, and he helped draft the constitutional mandate for a public-school system for the children of all races.

Yet Ruby was not content to rely solely upon education. He supported provisions to make available public lands for homesteading, which would give blacks an opportunity to become landowners. Understanding from personal experience how artificial and legal barriers could be built to exclude blacks from full participation in the community, he also worked to prevent legal or other kinds of discrimination. Just prior to the convention he had been denied first-class passage on a steamship to New Orleans. Now he obtained a place on the Committee on General Provisions and helped draft a section that would have made the exclusion of blacks from public conveyances, places of public business, and businesses licensed by the state illegal. That committee also produced a section that called for equal rights for all free men, with no man or set of men entitled to exclusive separate offices or privileges.

On the convention floor, Ruby also repeatedly supported investigations of violence and favored all measures to suppress these less subtle actions against blacks. While he believed in democratic political processes, he thought the restoration of former Confederates to their civil rights would lead inevitably to the imposition of limits on his own race; consequently, he argued that their continued exclusion from the franchise and officeholding was necessary and proper as punishment for their treason. With some modification, Ruby worked for these goals in 1868 and continued to pursue them through the rest of his career.

Given the fact that in the convention eighty of the ninety delegates were white, Ruby had little chance to secure the provisions he sought. Unable to carry out his plan in full, Ruby's major accomplishment in the convention was working for a coalition with whites that would aid him in carrying out as much of it as possible. He demonstrated in this effort mature political abilities, successfully exploiting for his own ends the factionalism among the white members of his own party. . . .

The factionalism of the white Republicans . . . provided an avenue along which Ruby could move to greater power. Two events aided him in this rise—his unexpected takeover of the state Union League on June 15, 1868, only two weeks after the beginning of the constitutional convention, and the formal split of the white Republicans into two parties in the state convention in August.

Under the leadership of white Unionist politicians, the state Union League had never been particularly responsive to the aspirations of its black members. Following the removal of Governor Throckmorton in 1867 and his replacement with E. M. Pease, these unionists had been even less interested in the blacks and went about their business distributing offices among white loyalists. Pease's administration and, consequently, the state league under the direction of Pease's associate Bell lost popularity among blacks because of its reluctance to give public offices to blacks, its weak stand on civil rights, and its hesitation in prosecuting white terrorists. This discontent provided the background for the annual league convention at Austin in 1868, where Ruby became the spokesman for those wanting change.

When Ruby discovered the extent of the unrest, he announced his candidacy for Bell's office. The action caught administration supporters by surprise and, unaware of Ruby's potential challenge, they were unprepared to beat him back. White leaders tried to restrain the black delegates and managed to hold many in line; but by a vote of 91 to 90, Ruby took over the state league organization. . . .

The regular party leadership realized too late the extent of Ruby's power and the importance of his league presidency. In an effort to rectify the situation, they attempted, after the party convention adjourned, to undermine his base of power at Galveston. Smith, Ruby's running mate the previous spring, led the attack, returning to Galveston, where he accused his colleague of corruption and selling out his black constituents. Ruby denied the accusations and appealed to league members for support. Smith quickly found himself in the midst of outraged blacks who refused to believe the charges and, when called upon to affirm the course of their leader at Austin, overwhelmingly voted their approval. . . . He had easily survived the first attack upon his base of power.

The constitutional convention continued despite the Republican party's collapse. . . . The regulars controlled the convention; therefore, the document they produced reflected their interests. . . . Rather than Ruby's proposals for a clear statement on the extent of an individual's civil rights, the draft incorporated a general resolution recognizing the equality of all persons before the law. A proposal by blacks to include a resolution that would not require mandatory segregation . . . was not included. Most portentous for blacks, the proposed constitution included a provision allowing all adult males to vote, except those explicitly disqualified by the United States Constitution. Given the white majority in Texas, this section paved the way for the ultimate failure of Ruby and his program.

Ruby, who considered the draft constitution a disaster for blacks, joined with twenty-two other convention delegates who opposed it on other grounds. . . . He urged league leaders to instruct members to vote against the constitution but to select candidates in legislative races who favored the Radical cause in the event a majority of voters ratified the document. As president, Ruby issued new league charters and harangued members throughout the state to reorganize, meet regularly, and prepare for an active campaign.

A major task was to break away any residual black support from Pease and Hamilton. Hamilton became the focus of Ruby's attacks upon the administration's forces after he announced his intention of running for governor. Ruby characterized Jack Hamilton as the archetypal white man who could be anything he wanted to be, rebel or loyalist, a man without principles and totally untrustworthy. In a speech at Galveston, Ruby warned blacks that they could never vote for a politician who had tried to convince Congress that no Negroes were being killed in Texas. . . .

By spring of 1869 the ground upon which Ruby was fighting was quicksand. Ruby discovered, as he warmed to the fight, that political conditions were rapidly changing. Through the Galveston Republican Association, Ruby had helped to plan a convention of bolting Republicans for May 11, 1869. He supported Morgan Hamilton, brother of Jack, who urged that the Radicals organize to oppose the constitution but make no nominations for public office until the president called for an election. . . .

Within the Radical group, however, a strong movement had emerged . . . to accept the constitution and bring about a compromise between the two factions. The middle-road movement had strong support, including General Joseph J. Reynolds, commander of the Fifth Military District, and, implicitly, Reynolds's close friend, President Grant. Grant appears to have tired of the internal squabbles within the southern-state party organizations and, unable to decide which group to back, began to pressure them to cooperate. . . .

Ruby realized that a shift was taking place. If General Reynolds and the president wanted compromise, to stick with Morgan Hamilton opened up the possibility of being left isolated. As a result, Ruby attended the middle-party convention and backed its nomination of E. J. Davis for governor, and its decision no longer to oppose the constitution. Ruby indicated that he believed united action was now necessary to settle the local political situation, and he was willing to compromise. "Whenever unnecessary," he wrote to Morgan Hamilton, "I do not believe in open force among those claiming to be with us, *at this time.*" . . .

Having joined the middle-party movement, Ruby was at the center of activity after President Grant, in midsummer, ordered the Texas election for the following November. Ruby quickly found that mobilizing the Union League was a task of considerable difficulty and encountered a problem that plagued the Republican organization throughout its early history. At the heart of the problem was inadequate financing. . . . Ruby sought alternative funding in the North, but found Republicans there reluctant to help. He called upon the national council of the league, claiming that the perpetuation of freedom in Texas depended upon their willingness to give money; but the support did not come. . . . Without financing, organization was practically impossible, and Ruby would discover that the league was always more efficient in its reputation among its antagonists than it was in actuality.

In addition to handling league work, Ruby decided to run for a seat in the Senate from the Twelfth District. The Twelfth consisted of Galveston, Brazoria, and Matagorda counties; and while Galveston did not contain a large black population upon which to draw support, the other two were old black-belt counties with large black majorities. Ruby faced the same arguments he had encountered in his run for the convention, in particular that the time had not come for black men to put themselves forward for public office. Even friends who had urged him to take over the state league and to run for the constitutional convention now opposed him. . . .

Although facing strong opposition, Ruby responded vigorously and refused to abandon the race. Accusing his opponents of being motivated by their own thwarted ambition, he effectively manipulated league chapters in his district to keep voters in line behind him. His candidacy created an excited response throughout the black community. . . . Ruby's campaign raised fears among whites, who complained that throughout the district blacks had become more defiant.

The chances of success for Ruby appeared good, but the campaign of the middle-party languished through the summer of 1869. Ruby possessed good possibilities for election to the state Senate, but unless the Davis ticket did well throughout the state he would be in the minority. The middle-party movement received a major boost in September, when President Grant . . . finally gave his open support to it.

Grant's decision to back Davis worked immediately to Ruby's advantage. At Galveston the Treasury replaced the pro-Hamilton collector of customs with a Davis man, Nathan Patten, who had worked with Ruby in the constitutional convention; and Patten appointed the senatorial candidate a special deputy collector. For the next four years Ruby would be the chief arbiter of appointments to positions as clerks, inspectors, weighers, watchmen, and messengers in the customhouse. The president's recognition of the middle-party group placed in Ruby's hands the ability to provide tangible rewards to his supporters and thus gave him another powerful tool to promote party loyalty. . . .

Ruby still faced a difficult election campaign and the candidate had to adjust to changing political realities if he hoped to maintain power. Whites who had been reluctant to register and vote in 1867 were returning to the polls. While black voters still outnumbered white voters in adjacent counties, last minute registration in Galveston placed more whites than blacks on the lists. . . . When the returns came in, Ruby's opponent carried Galveston County, 1,597 to 1,554; but Ruby's majority in Brazoria and Matagorda insured him the seat he sought. Despite the victory, the election of 1869 indicated that politics based solely on black power was no longer possible in the Twelfth District and that Ruby would have to adjust his politics to meet the new situation. . . .

When the state Senate met at Austin in a special session, George Ruby faced a difficult problem. He had to work for measures that would insure his continued control over his black constituency but at the same time act to make inroads among white voters. As senator from the Twelfth District, Ruby would work to develop a new image, one of a conservative politician who looked after not only the interests of blacks, but also whites in his community. During his four- year term he worked to tie himself and his constituents closer to the white business interests of Galveston in particular, seeking an alliance that would benefit all three.

Ruby tried several new approaches and techniques in rearranging his base of power. A major goal was to decrease his reliance upon the Union League. Whites did not like the organization because they saw it as a somewhat corrupt institution in which they could have little say. . . . He began efforts to weld blacks in his district into an organization that whites could not ignore and would have to deal with politically and economically—a labor union. He believed that if he could create a situation of mutual economic interdependence between blacks and white businessmen blacks would have a greater chance to maintain political power. In his effort the urban nature of his district was important; black workers in an urban economy could make demands that unskilled and unorganized workers in rural areas could not. Dependence on organized black labor would, theoretically, force white businessmen and industrialists to help maintain black political rights.

Ruby turned to the docks in his efforts to organize blacks. Whites had dominated the work on the Galveston wharf prior to the war, but in the postwar period large numbers of blacks moved into these jobs. If he could control this labor force, he would obtain power that even the most grudging white politician would have to recognize. . . .

Ruby's organizational activities unified black workers on the docks, but the philosophy of the local union movement limited its effectiveness. Ruby did not see the union as a device for confrontation, but rather as an institution to make possible an alliance with Galveston's white businessmen. The Galveston union denied the need for strikes but argued, rather, that the union provided capital with an organized work force. Politically, the union suffered from many of the charges of corruption and political manipulation that plagued the league, charges that worked against the alliance Ruby envisioned. Information about black activities on the wharf during this period is practically nonexistent, but at least one former dock worker remembered how he was used politically. On election days, leaders appeared and took the workers to picnics, gave them whisky, cigars, and marked ballots, then took them to cast their votes. . . . Despite his hopes, Ruby never used the union effectively to support his own political power. The work he accomplished, however, would provide a base for his young protégé, N. Wright Cuney, who would dominate the wharf in the 1880s and 1890s.

In addition to seeking economic interdependence that would link blacks and whites, Ruby tried to build his ties to whites by establishing himself as a power broker between them and the newly installed Davis administration. While Davis was in power, Ruby was the intermediary between the state government and the local community, providing direct access to Governor Davis when appealed to. Ruby also oversaw the appointment of local officials and worked tirelessly to insure that they acted in the party's interest. Unfortunately, rather than strengthening his position, this role worked against him, for it irritated many whites who complained of having to rely upon a black man. . . . Another weakness of his particular approach to the local businessmen was that it required continuation of the Davis administration to remain effective. . . .

Ruby also attempted to improve his connections with white business interests by working for them in the legislature. He held major assignments on committees concerned with the judiciary, militia, and public lands. He was assiduous in his efforts in behalf of railroads, banks, and insurance companies connected with Galveston. . . .

While trying to establish some sort of working relationship with the economic leaders of Galveston, Ruby had few illusions about the benevolence of these or any other white Texans. He made concessions on such issues as railroads, but he remained a strong advocate of measures designed to protect blacks in their civil rights and to provide equal opportunities. With Matthew Gaines, the other black member of the Senate, and backing from the Davis administration, Ruby helped pass bills that created a state militia, the state police, and a public-school system. He never believed these were enough to protect blacks, but he found whites unwilling to go further. When he attempted to pass a bill that would have enforced the compliance of public carriers with constitutional provisions that demanded equal access by all peoples, he found that his most ardent white supporters were not interested in helping. Ruby worked this bill through the Judiciary Committee and saw it reported to the floor, but the bill never even came up for a vote. Thus, while he was willing to compromise with whites, he did not forget his black constituents and pushed as far as he could in trying to protect them.

But in spite of his work for blacks, as Ruby tried to appease the white community his position among blacks became less secure. The interests of a landless agrarian, and urban work force, which comprised the bulk of Ruby's backing, were inimicable to the interests of the planter and merchant groups Ruby had to approach for support. The education and self-help programs Ruby sought for his black constituents were hardly in the interest of the whites, since they would serve to make the former slaves more independent. The state aid for railroads and public improvements demanded by white business men, on the other hand, took away money needed to support the programs intended to aid blacks. Funding to support the interests of both groups was not possible, since the tax base in the state was too narrow. Ruby was forced to make concessions; and as he provided support for white interests, he sacrificed some of the goals of his black constituents, who were denied educational opportunities, office, and greater economic freedom. As a result, his position drew fire from blacks. Compromise gained him little from whites also; for no matter what he did, businessmen continued to view him as an upstart and a threat. . . .

Ruby also appropriated a new mechanism for political purposes, the newly created public-school system. This activity greatly offended whites, who feared Ruby's increased power. The school system was a potentially important political tool because of the valuable patronage associated with it. The supervisor of schools in each district appointed local school boards that had tremendous power—they chose teachers, leased buildings, and made contracts for books and construction. At Ruby's request, Davis appointed Captain William H. Griffin supervisor of education at Galveston because he was a party loyalist, in addition to being a good school officer. When Griffin arrived at Galveston, he joined Cuney's chapter of the Union League, legitimizing its official status, and appointed a proadministration school board: Ruby; George Lawrence, a Union League organizer; Nathan Patten of the customhouse; N. Wright Cuney; and F. C. Mosebach, a German Republican businessman. From this position Ruby used school patronage to party advantage. Already hostile to the costs of public education, white businessmen were further alienated by Ruby's blatant use of the schools for political ends. Ruby managed to hang onto power, but he also undid work that was aimed at pacifying local whites. . . .

Despite his efforts . . . the changing electorate threatened Ruby. . . . The growing white majority turned the election [of 1871] into a Republican debacle. . . . When all the returns were in, the Democrat[s] had won by a narrow margin. . . . In Galveston County, intimidation and black distrust of Clark had cut into the number of Republican votes, decreasing the party poll from nearly one thousand in 1869 to only 304. Other counties made the election close, but the Galveston returns indicated approaching disaster for Ruby. Despite what he had done for Galveston's business leaders, they were not coming into the Republican party and he could not count on them for votes. It was also apparent that he could no longer muster black voters in full strength. While he would continue to be an important figure in state politics until 1874, the election of 1871 marked the collapse of his independent power. His political base had been eroded, both in real numbers and in the importance of the black vote relative to the total electorate.

After 1871 Ruby's power depended increasingly upon his connections with the national Republican leadership and with the Davis administration. In his continued bid for power, he now turned to Washington and Austin rather than to activity in the local community. . . .

However, neither Grant nor Davis could protect Ruby's office in his predominantly white district. From members of his own party, pressure increased for the senator to step aside in 1873 for a white candidate in the general election. A group of German Republicans, who demanded that the party recognize their claims to office, advocated that Judge Chauncey B. Sabin be put up for the Senate instead of Ruby. Because Ruby himself realized the unlikelihood of his reelection and thought that Sabin might have a chance, he refused to stand for renomination. . . .

In the general election of 1873, Texans voted Davis out of office. Sabin lost despite Republican hopes that the judge was attractive enough to be elected. The Democratic administration of Richard Coke set about dismantling much of the Republican administration's programs, including the final dismemberment of the police force that had been introduced to protect black voters. Under Coke, Texas was not a promising place for a former black senator. . . .

[In 1874], Ruby moved to New Orleans, where he found conditions more congenial to his efforts in behalf of blacks. He received an appointment in the customhouse, perhaps a reward from Grant for his prior services; but he spent most of his time working on newspapers in behalf of Republican and black causes. . . .

The Exoduster Movement of the later 1870s occupied must of Ruby's time. He became a prominent figure in the promotion of black migration from Louisiana to Kansas. In his newspaper, at public meetings, and before Congress he argued that the only way for blacks to obtain complete freedom was to leave the South. . . . Clearly, by 1880 Ruby had come to see improvement in the social relations of races in the South as hinging on increased respect of whites for black economic power. . . .

Ruby's work in New Orleans continued the fight that had occupied him from his youth—for economic opportunities and civil rights for black people. His politics were those of expediency; the men he supported and the course he pursued changed with shifting conditions. But his political opportunism always aimed at securing goals to which he remained dedicated. Alliances changed, but the ends changed very little. Unfortunately the people he had to work with were not as willing to compromise. In 1882, at forty-one years of age, Ruby promised to be a prominent leader among blacks for many years to come, a man who could lead, a model of educated and astute political ability. That promise would never be fulfilled, however, for on October 31, 1882, after a short attack of malaria, Ruby died in his home at 125 Euterpe Street.

✦ F U R T H E R   R E A D I N G

Alwyn Barr, *Black Texans: A History of African Americans in Texas, 1528–1995* (1996)

Randolph B. Campbell, "Carpetbagger Rule in Reconstruction Texas, *Southwestern Historical Quarterly,* 97 (1994)

———, *Grass-Roots Reconstruction in Texas, 1865–1880* (1997)

Gregg Cantrell, "Racial Violence and Reconstruction Politics in Texas, 1867–1868" *Southwestern Historical Quarterly,* 89 (1986)

Paul D. Casdorph, *A History of the Republican Party in Texas, 1865–1965* (1965)

Barry Crouch, "'All the Vile Passions': The Texas Black Code of 1866," *Southwestern Historical Quarterly,* 97 (1993)

———, *The Freedmen's Bureau and Black Texans* (1992)

———, "'Unmanacling' Texas Reconstruction: A Twenty Year Perspective," *Southwestern Historical Quarterly,* 98 (1995)

Carl Moneyhon, "Public Education and Texas Reconstruction Politics, 1871–1874"
    Southwestern Historical Quarterly, 89 (1986)
———, *Republicanism in Reconstruction Texas* (1980)
William C. Nunn, *Texas Under the Carpetbaggers* (1962)
Merline Pitre, *Through Many Dangers, Toils and Snares: Black Leadership in Texas,
    1870–1890* (1997)
Charles W. Ramsdell, *Reconstruction in Texas* (1910)
Williams L. Richter, *The Army in Texas During Reconstruction, 1865–1879* (1987)
———, *Overreached on All Sides: The Freedmen's Bureau Administrators in Texas,
    1865–1868* (1991)
James M. Smallwood, *Time of Hope, Time of Despair: Black Texans During Reconstruction*
    (1981)
Ernest Wallace, *The Howling of the Coyotes: Reconstruction Efforts to Divide Texas* (1979)

C H A P T E R
10

Conquering and Populating

the Frontiers,

1860–1890

What Texas experienced during Reconstruction was not unlike that of other southern states; however, its frontier experience in the late nineteenth century linked it to the west. Like other western states in the late nineteenth century, Texas was defined more by the pacification and settlement of the frontier than by efforts to define and create a "New South." In this process the black-white racial dichotomy of Reconstruction gave way to a far more complex blending of race and gender on the frontier. Furthermore, the Texas frontier was more complex than that of many other western states. It consisted of a western frontier and a southern frontier, and the last decades of the nineteenth century witnessed the conquest, settlement, and economic exploitation of both. On each frontier, men and women endured danger and hardship as they settled and developed new lands. Settlement also involved conflict with other inhabitants of the new lands—Mexicans and Mexican Americans in South Texas, and Native Americans in the West.

    Traditionally, historians have focused on the settlement of the western frontier. Two waves of settlers, cattlemen who moved north from South Texas and farmers who moved west from the East, spread into the western areas of the state in the 1870s, 1880s, and 1890s. More recently, historians have modified this interpretation, noting that the process of settlement was far more complex, that it involved issues of gender as well as the complex interaction of diverse peoples and cultures, and that it must be understood through the stories of individuals and families as well as through the conflict of classes and races. The traditional outline, though, remains relatively unchanged. When the Civil War ended, the frontier line extended from the Red River north of Dallas southwestward past Waco to the hill country west of Austin and San Antonio, and then southeast to the Nueces River and into South Texas. Post-Civil War expansion involved the subjugation of Tejano and Mexican settlers in South Texas and the removal of Native Americans. The cattle industry moved into the plains of the west and northwest in the post-Civil War period. Hundreds of thousands of farm families followed, spreading west of the 100th meridian as the century came to a close.

The process of frontier settlement raises issues of conquest and racial dominance as well as questions about the nature of the conquest and settlement of the Texas frontier. Was the Texas frontier experience dominated by the westward extension of southern culture and mores, or did other forces define it? What role did men and women play in this process, and how were they changed by it? What was the interaction of African Americans, Mexican Americans, Anglo Americans, and Native Americans?

DOCUMENTS

In 1870 Hugh Harmon McElvy moved his family from southwest Georgia to Collin County, Texas. McElvy was one of thousands of southerners who abandoned war-ravaged areas of the former Confederacy for the promise of wealth and opportunity on the Texas frontier. Document 1 describes McElvy's impressions of Texas and indicates that the promise of Texas was not always realized. In Document 2, Emily K. Andrews, presents her first impression of West Texas as she traveled with her new husband from Austin to Fort Davis in the late summer of 1874. Andrews was accompanying her husband Colonel George Lippitt Andrews to his post as commander of Fort Davis. Her diary chronicles her impression of the land, its scattered settlements, and its people. Especially compelling is the sense of emptiness, stark beauty, and ever-present danger.

The next three documents consist of the recollections of three "cowboys" who describe their lives and their work. Document 3 is the story of Will Crittendon, an African American, who was introduced to the life by his father, who came to Texas after emancipation to start a horse ranch. Crittenden took up the cowboy life at the age of five and set out on his own at the age of fifteen. Document 4 tells the story of Elario Cardova, a descendent of a family that began farming and ranching in the Nacogdoches area during the Spanish colonial period. At the age of ten, Cardova left home to find work in South Texas as a ranch hand where he experienced the turmoil and conflicts that characterized that region in the post-Civil War period. Lastly, in Document 5, Mrs. Ben Miskimon tells of entering the cattle business when she was a child. After her marriage she ran the family cattle business and directed the move west from Jack county in North Central Texas to Tom Green county near San Angelo. Each of these selections de-romanticizes the cattle business, focusing on it as work.

Document 6 satirizes the myths about Texas and its cowboys and Indians. Alexander Sweet was a late-nineteenth-century Texas humorist who describes a "Wild West Show" that he witnessed in the Polo Grounds, in the heart of New York City in 1884. The central feature of this show was a mock-battle between cowboys and Indians. Document 7 vividly describes the last battle between the Apache and the Texas Rangers. In 1880 Apaches attacked the Overland Stage in Southwest Texas near Eagle Springs. Captain George Wythe Baylor of the Texas Rangers commanded the posse sent out to track the Indians and deliver punishment. Here the conflict between whites and Indians is presented unadorned by myth.

1. Hugh Harmon McElvy, a Georgia Farmer, Reports on the Hardships Farmers Faced on the Texas Frontier, 1871

Sunday Evenig August 27th 1871
Collin Co Texas

Well Lawson your letter reached us yesterday being out just as long again as it Should have bin. I have nothing much to write you. We are all well & our country burned up with drouth. We have not had any rain Since the 28th of May. We had on that day a ground Soker & it lasted tell a bout the 4th of July. Since then we have suffered beyond any thing I ever new in the way of drouth. There is maney places the ground is cracked open tell it is daingrous to ride through the grass. Your horses feete can if he happens to Strike one of thoes cracks fall in to his belly. Our forward corn is maid a bout half crop whare it was will tilled. Late corn & half tended corn will yeald from 10 to 15 bushels per acre. Cotton is no go. There was verry little planted & what was has maid a flash. It grew up verry rapid full of sapp & had just commenced to fruite when the drouth set in & it threw of[f] the forms & the boles that stuck has swiveled & opened. The lint is short & nearly all pickd out now. . . .

You ask me a bout Maj Hines. I do not no any thing of the Maj. When he got here last winter the Maj was out of funds & he could not git in business & he was in a tite. So he engaged to drive a 6 mule gin which he did for 20 dollars per month. He drove tell he got money enoug to leave on & he left for the frontier. He never has written back but once & then said he had an offer to drive stock to Kansas. Whether [he] acceped it or not we do not no. I would not be surprised if the Indiens got his scalp. He left heare with two other Georgians, young men from Mitchell County, Eavans & Willingham. We have not heard from none of the party. They were verry much dissatisfied with this part of the State. If they got a birth to drive stock to cansis citty they will not git back to Texas soon.

You ask me to give you the report of the country at Waco. We Set out the 3rd day of this Inst. & travel down to the edge of the plain which is a bout 60 miles wide, one etarnal pariar [prairie]; no water only in wells & it worth or cost 10 cents a bucket full for our stock; the grass all dried up & nothing mid [made] only in the valley of the Brases [Brazos] River. We met Sitizens from that sexion & they told us it was a fine country all up and down the Brases but it was subject to this drouths. It is a wheete country & the winter rains make the wheete. Corn there is 2.00 dollars per bushel at the railroad 40 miles from Waco and as we have all maid corn a plenty to do us an other year & one dollar is all we can git for it we con-cluded we would turn our cours & look for a more plesent portion of country & rent one more year. . . .

There is one thing I can Say for the Sitizens of Texas. They are a longs ways a head of the Sitizens of Ga in Schools. Evry kneighborhood I Saw they had large fine Schools & churches houses & the School rooms ware all occupied. Thes frontier

---

"'I Am Tired of Writing,' A Georgia Farmer Reports on Texas in 1871," ed. William Warren Rogers, *Southern Historical Quarterly* 87 (October 1983): 185–188.

counties we traveld in are nearly all Settle up from the old States mostly from Kentucky, Tennessee & Missourea & a good chance of north Georgians. Some fiew from South Carolina & a fiew from North C.

I am tired writeing & will Close.

I remain as Ever
H. H. McElvy

Send this letter to your farther.
It will Save me a long letter to him.

2. Army Wife Emily K. Andrews Gives a Woman's View of the Texas Frontier, 1874

Our Trip from Austin to Fort Davis Texas

'Sunrise'
"Dripping Springs"
'In Camp' Augt. 11 1874

My Dear Father,

Feeling sure that some little account of our trip through Texas would be entertaining to you, I have tried to note down each days doings, and herewith send them to you. . . .

"Half way House" "Adams Creek"
Wednesday evening, Augt 12th

We have now arrived at our second camping ground, and while the tents are being pitched I am waiting in a real Texan house.

It is made of logs, with daylight peeping in at the many crevices. The chairs are covered with skins, while the rest of the furniture is primitive in the extreme. Hens and chickens are running in and out the doors, and the pigs in the yard would I think be quite as friendly were it not for the old darkie who sits at the door and keeps away all such intruders. . . .

Friday Morning, Augt 14th

A good bath, plenty of sound sleep, a breakfast of rabbit and squirrel, and we are ready to start again—I find . . . a good deal of pleasure in this out of door life, and I often wish you could see us in camp especially at night. The men who are marched carefully, are never to weary to dance and sing about their camp fires. Their voices are many of them, so rich and full of melody that I am very glad if I can hear them as I go to sleep—. . .

"A Women's View of the Texas Frontier, 1874: The Diary of Emily K. Andrews," ed. and annotated by Sandra L. Meyers, *Southwestern Historical Quarterly* 86 (July 1982): 49–80.

"Seven Mile Creek" Friday Evening 14th

Fredericksburg is a small German town filled with Lager beer saloons, and beer gardens, with more blue eyed round faced fraüleins about, than anything else—

At the only Hotel in the place we had a real German dinner, highly seasoned with herbs and onions, but our appetites were sharp enough to enjoy anything. . . .

Peg Leg Station, Monday evening Augt 17th

This morning we broke camp at half past six and were soon "en route" again. . . .

After traveling about twelve miles we came to "Rock Springs Station", where an old man 75 years old with his wife and one child, live all by themselves, certainly it was the most broken down, and homeless looking place. However they were so kind as to give us plenty of delicious milk. Just before reaching this place we espied a body of horsemen descending the hill in front of us, I must say I was a little frightened, but we soon discovered by their dress, that they were a band of Rangers under command of Major Jones, with two Tonqua [*sic*] Indians, acting as guides. As the Col. desired it I went forward and looked at the brave red man, but knowing their desire for light haired scalps I kept a good distance from them. . . .

Kickapoo Springs Wednesday evening, 19th, Aug.

After a breakfast of Rabbit as we were off at an early hour this morning. We started just before the Cavalry and with their wagon train and ours made quite an imposing sight—. . .

The troops are all to move early in the morning over the same road as we do, so if possible we start by half past four, to avoid the dust. Last night, 12 Indians made a raid on a train encamped here, and captured 17 mules. As soon as the troops arrived this morning a company was detailed to recapture them, but the Indians having 12 hours the start there is not much chance for the soldiers success. . . .

Thursday Evening, August 20th
"Fort Concho"

This morning we were all up at half past three and at half past four after a hasty cup of coffee, taken by starlight . . . we were ready to move—

Just as we were starting Col. Anderson sent word to our Camp, that he feared the Indians were nearer than he supposed as one of his men had been chased the evening before. So we had to creep along using extra precautions. . . .

We lunched at rather a poor looking place, called Lipan Springs, with not a very inviting looking house, so we preferred making an eating house of our ambulance. The woman here tried to make me believe that if I walked far from the house I should be carried off, but as I have not found many persons in this country who really tell the truth, I paid very little attention to her, and walked as I liked. . . .

Friday evening, Augt 21st
Johnson's Station—

The ride of today has been much pleasanter [sic] than that of yesterday. The country has mountains, with very beautiful interval lands, while the grass and trees were very green. . . . We met an immense Mexican train today going to Concho, there were 15 teams each 8 or ten yoke of oxen. These carts are similar to our tip carts only very much heavier carrying 3500 pounds each. . . .

We have just heard that a Mexican was killed here last night by an Indian, not very pleasant news, and I, for one shall sleep with one eye open, not withstanding we are to have a special guard round our tent. I does seem strange to think that in this beautiful country where every thing is apparently so peaceful, each man sleeping or waking must have his carbine loaded just at hand. . . .

Central Station, Stake [*sic*] Plains
Augt. 23rd. 10.45 P.M. *Full moon*

Ten hours ago we left the head of the Concho, and entered at once the dense Chaparral. In any other country I should have enjoyed this ride very much, for the road was very beautiful and the moon at its full, but these thickets are such dangerous places, so well fitted for an ambush, that I was not sorry when we struck out on the famous Staked Plains. . . . [W]e arrived here at the "Central Station", where we are resting and taking a bit of lunch—This is a queer house, looking more like a small fortress than anything else. Standing here alone in the midst of this great Desert. Nothing to break the view as far as the eye can see. We are rather a strange looking party as we stand or sit, taking our midnight cup of tea, while in the back ground are the keeper and guard of the house who have come out of their beds to see us pass—But I am sure it is impossible to give you any correct idea of the scene—

Leon Hole's, Sunset
September 5th

Now after a week or so of garrison life [at Ft Stockton] we are again in Camp, and sitting at my tent door, just at sunset enjoying the luxury of out of door freedom.

I must tell you a little of Stockton. To me it is not as pleasantly situated as Concho. The lack of shade and the want of grass, on the Parade make a glare as you look upon it almost intolerable, and we found many of the officers suffering from the effect of it on the eye. They, and also their wives I found the most agreeable, cultivated people, hospitable in the extreme. They reminded me very much of home people, and sitting chatting in their pleasant parlors, I could easily fancy myself in Boston again. . . .

Fort Davis
Tuesday Evening Sept. 8. 1874

Every body was stirring bright and early this morning, and in the best of spirits while trying to make the travel worn harnesses and carriages presentable to drive into the Post. . . .

About two miles from the Post, near the Station House we were met by three of the officers, who had come out to receive their Colonel, and very heartily they did it. From here we had a good view of the cleanly cut mountain known as "Mitre Peak," and which on a clear day can be easily seen from Stockton.

In less than an hour, we dashed into the garrison where officers and men were eagerly waiting to welcome us. So here I am safe and sound and so ends my pleasant camp life, to which I shall ever look back as one of the happiest epochs in my life, and as I sit here in my homelike quarters, I cannot but be thankful to that Kind Providence, that has brought us in safety to our Journey's end.

Affec yr daughter
Emily K Andrews—

3. Will Crittenden, an African American Cowboy, Describes Life on the Range, 1870s–1880s

Do I know anything about the range? Why, man, I made a trail drive right through Fort Worth when it wasn't even a whistle-stop and I was only nine years old! I learned to ride a hoss on my pap's stock farm at Cedar Grove, Texas. I was born on December 12, 1868, right after Pap came to Texas from Alabama, where he was a slave of Governor Crittendon.

It was while he was a slave that he got his love of good hoss flesh from the governor. He always had a good surrey team and used Pap to drive it. When freedom came, one of the governor's sons had already taught Pap to read and write, so he came to Texas to start a hoss ranch and to get himself a school to teach. We did all right about the school by getting one at Cedar Grove. He was the first teacher in the county at that time. He didn't do so well about the hoss ranch. He only got around twenty to thirty head and forty to a hundred cattle critters at a time. . . .

When I got to be fifteen, I'd got fifty mules together and set out to make my fortune. I traded those mules around and busted hosses on the side. Among the places I busted hosses was the Tom King ranch at Greenville, Texas. Tom King had thousands of critters. Jim Harris, a banker at Terrell, Texas, had a ranch in West Texas but bought his hosses at Terrell and always had me bust them for him. . . . The Manning hoss ranch had me bust all his hosses. His place was close to Terrell, and I'd contract to bust forty at a time. Many a time I'd have the money gambled off before I'd busted half of what I'd contracted for. . . .

The last man I worked for busting hosses was Lindsey, at Elmo, Texas. He was a big hoss man and ran a regular hoss ranch. He'd gotten a big order for so many head of hosses, and I was hired to round them up for him. Well, I rounded his hosses up for him, but I cut back a few for myself, and after the sale was made, I went back and got the stuff and took it to Abilene, Texas, and sold it.

4. Elario Cardova, a Mexican American Cowboy, Remembers Working as a Ranch Hand in South Texas, 1870s–1880s

I was born on November 3, 1861, at my father's farm seven miles east of Nacogdoches County. . . .

The Spanish government made a grant of land to my grandmother, Rachel de los Santos Coez, and her three brothers. The grant consisted of eleven leagues of land in the Nacogdoches section. . . .

Jim Lanning and Judy Lanning, eds., *Texas Cowboys: Memories of the Early Days* (College Station: Texas A&M University Press, 1994): 169–75.

Jim Lanning and Judy Lanning, eds., *Texas Cowboys: Memories of the Early Days* (College Station: Texas A&M University Press, 1994): 177–182.

Our farm consisted of about fifty acres under cultivation and about fifty acres in pasture for our milk cows and work stock. In addition to our farming, we owned longhorn cattle which ranged on the unsettled land. Farms were all fenced and were situated far apart, leaving great tracts of land for the cattle to graze on. . . . We didn't give the cattle any attention. The cattle bred and multiplied at their will and found their own living on the range where it suited their taste. All we did to hold the herd was to provide salt licks in the section we desired the animals to make their bedding ground. When we needed a little beef or made a sale, we held a little roundup and cut out the critters desired. . . .

As part of our farm work we raised hogs, using the same method we employed raising the cattle. The hogs bred, ranged, and obtained their living in the woods. . . .

. . . My mother married the second time when I was ten years old, and then I left home to make my own living. That I have done ever since.

The cattle range was about the only place a young farm boy could secure employment. Consequently, I went to the open-range country where large ranches were established, and I chose Goliad County as the place to find work. I was successful and was given work on a ranch owned by the Hughes brothers. That was in 1871. . . .

My career on the range was during the period when there was a great deal of conflict among the ranchers of the Goliad range territory. I happened to secure a job with an outfit which was not only called rustlers, but were classed as one of the leaders of the rustlers. However, they maintained that they were defending the rights of the small ranchers against the impositions of the large ranchers [Pures]. . . .

During the Civil War and for a period after the war ceased, branding was neglected by many cattlemen. Also, very few cattle were sent to market, because the market was cut off from Texas. The lack of sales resulted in a large increase of cattle. Therefore, the two conditions produced thousands of cattle which were unbranded.

A few years after the war ceased, railroads extended west into Kansas, and markets were established within driving distance of Texas. Then the prices went up which resulted in a scramble to brand those cattle without a brand. Naturally, ranchers maintained they had a superior claim to the unbranded cattle within the section which they called their home range, and any unbranded cattle grazing with the cattle carrying their brand. This claim was generally accepted as proper, but there were some folks who did not confine their branding strictly within their territory. Branding cattle in territory claimed by some other rancher led to trouble and many killings. The conflict developed two contending parties.

The small fellows claimed that the Pures were claiming too much territory, for the purpose of excluding the small ranchers and to take undue advantage with the unbranded cattle. The small ranches, and some people who never had a herd, ignored the Pures' claims to territory and branded cattle where found. . . . These conditions started arguments, which progressed into quarrels and ended in many shootings and killings.

The Pures organized vigilante committees which operated secretly and set out to clean out the rustlers. In the section were some thieves, but when the vigilantes began to operate, they classed many cattle branders as rustlers, and many men were run out of the country who were not real thieves.

5. Mrs. Ben Miskimon, a Woman on the Range, Recounts Her Experiences Running the Family Cattle Business in Texas, 1874

When I was nineteen years old I married W. A. Miskimon. I had property and cattle, too. We lived in Jack County seventeen miles below Jacksboro. We had a mighty hard time, loss of cattle, and dry weather. My husband wasn't no cowman; I tried to teach him about cows, but he never could learn, not even to feed one. At last God gave me a boy. We would have to stay by ourselves on many instances. Once my husband went to Missouri on business. The severe drouth had caused all the water holes to sink and all wells to dry up. I strapped the baby on my back, papoose style, and would walk a mile or two for water. The wild hogs rooted in the low places, and water would come up in small holes. With my baby on my back and a teacup in my hand I would dip water here and there until I filled my buckets and carried the weary load home. . . . I didn't stay out of the saddle long. I began riding the range again when my baby (papoose, I called him) was quite small.

We started to Tom Green County on September 1, 1889. We had about one thousand head of cattle and three hundred head of horses. I had five cowboys to help; as I've said, my husband was no cowman, couldn't ride nor cut out cattle, so he wasn't much help. . . . When we neared the Brazos River, . . . I sent my husband on with the horses, and he crossed and put them in the corral. Me and the boys were to hold the cattle. We drove them down to the river and camped with intentions of pushing them across the next morning. The cowboys were from the malarial country, and when they got cold and wet they took chills. I got on my horse and logged the wood up, built a fire for the sick boys and made blankets down, the poor boys with high fever and me with the cattle. That was one awful night, trying to hold the cattle all alone, with wolves howling and panthers screaming and boys sick. I stayed on my horse, rounding the cattle, keeping them down. The boys were better next morning, and we pushed the bellowing herd across the swollen stream. . . . We continued our journey on to Tom Green County, which was comprised of several counties then. We came to Red Creek, which looked very desirable for camping. There was plenty of water and fresh fall grass. . . .

We herded the cattle on that area until the fence was built and ranching started. In the later part of 1889 we built the old ranch house that now stands on the corner of Randolph and First Street. I traded a little old red bull for that lot.

Jim Lanning and Judy Lanning, eds., *Texas Cowboys: Memories of the Early Days* (College Station: Texas A&M University Press, 1994): 200–201.

6. Texas Humorist Alexander Sweet Scoffs at the Images in an Eastern "Wild West Show," 1884

November 15, 1884

New York City
To Big Foot Wallace,
Chacon Creek, Texas

Those who dwell in the busy haunts of men are tormented with a morbid curiosity to know all about the habits of their fellowman in his savage state. It is this that stimulated the manufacture of dime novels. . . . Buffalo Bill reproduces the wild nomadic life of the border, using real Texas cowboys and *bona fide* Indians, both of whom look as true to nature as if they had never seen the inside of a barber shop, much less that of a wash basin, and who furnish their own hair.

The most refined and cultured people attend these performances. I, myself, attended several of them. It is pleasant to sit in perfect safety and observe the pale-face cowboys murder the poor Indian in cold blood with blank cartridges. . . .

One of the most surprising features of the performances is the utterly unexpected attack by wild Indians, on the log cabin of a sturdy pioneer, who had established himself right in the midst of the Polo Grounds, far beyond the confines of civilization. . . .

. . . In this wild, lonesome spot, near Harlem, lived the heroic backwoodsman, with his solitary wife and fearless boy, exposed to the ravages of confidence men, in constant danger of policemen and other wild animals that prowl at nights around the jungles of New York. . . . The opening scene is supposed to occur at the peep of day. A large audience, who have just dined, are seated on the benches. The door of the cabin opens, just as the peanut boy walks around among the audience and offers three cents worth of peanuts for a dime. The wife of the frontiersman, who does not wear any bustle, now emerges from the cabin, and shading her eyes with her hand, looks at the roofs of the distant tenement houses for Indian signs. . . .

A distant rifle shot is heard in the corner of the Polo Grounds near Gimpel's beer saloon. . . .

The solitary hunter comes galloping up on a pony. Tied behind his saddle is a big fat buck, which, if it is not stuffed, must have fallen before his unerring rifle at the provision store opposite Gimpel's saloon. The wife and boy assist the hunter in hanging up the fat buck. The huntsman then performs his ablutions, several of them, in a tin wash basin. The boy stakes out the pony to graze. . . . The pony, however, is not staked out to graze. He is staked out to tempt the redskins to steal him. Even now two dusky forms can be seen emerging from their hiding places near Gimpel's saloon. . . .

The stealthy redmen of the forest have got near the pony. A man in the audience, perceiving that the horse is about to be stolen calls out "Police! Police!" The audience laughs vociferously, but, owing to Gimpel's beer, the Indians do not hear the racket.

"Alexander Edwin Sweet and the Wild West Show," ed. Virginia Eisenhour, *Southwestern Historical Quarterly* 93 (October 1989) 199–207.

At last the Indian seizes the rope. He knows the ropes. He looks at the roof of the tenement house to see if the frontiersman is watching. Not seeing him there, the Indian is about to go off with the horse, when the boy seizes a pistol and fires at the Indian. The husband takes a pop, and even the old woman blazes away as if it was a regular Fourth of July celebration. The Indian drops dead, and kicks about on the ground, like a decapitated chicken. The other Indian climbs up on the roof of the cabin, probably to see if there is another horse staked out to graze.

Thirty red devils, mounted on ponies, emerge from the vicinity of Gimpel's saloon. . . . The white family and the redskins exchange several tons of imaginary lead. The fight looks as if it were a real one. . . .

Now is the time for Buffalo Bill and his cowboys to take part in the canvass. Here they come, brandishing their revolvers, as fierce as so many United States deputy marshals. The first thing they do is to exchange a few thousand shots with the illegal voters—that is, the Indians who are not allowed to vote. Buffalo Bill kills a number of Indians single handed. Several Indians send in their resignations. The rest seek safety in flight, closely pursued by the cowboys. The hunter and his family are saved from a fate worse than death. The Indians did not even get away with the venison.

"Darned funny sort of a log cabin," said a rough looking customer behind me: "No chickens and no dogs about the place, and only one boy. All the log cabins I ever seen had about forty chickens, the same number of dogs and more'n a dozen children of different sizes. Maybe the Injuns stole 'em," he added philosophically.

Yours,
Alex E. Sweet

7. Captain George Wythe Baylor, Texas Ranger, Gives a Stark Account of the Last Battle Between the Apache and the Rangers, 1880

The writer having been promoted captain of Company A, Frontier Battalion [of the Texas Rangers], in October 1880, the strength of the company was increased to twenty men, stationed at Ysleta. The Overland Stage, then carrying United States mail and passengers between San Antonio and El Paso, was attacked in Quitman Canyon, between Eagle Springs and the Rio Grande. . . .

[John] Ford at the time, with a few of the ranchmen and Overland employees, went out to look for the stage when it failed to show up at the proper time, feeling pretty sure the Apaches had either captured or killed the driver and passengers. The searchers found the stage . . . the mailbags cut open and mail scattered over the ground, a leather boot cut up and carried off, but did not find the bodies of the men. Examining the signs, Ford believed there were only four Indians, and they had left the road and gone off southwest toward the river. The party took it for granted the

George Wythe Baylor, *Into the Far, Wild Country: True Tales of the Old Southwest,* ed., Jerry D. Thompson (El Paso: Texas Western Press, 1996): 304–322 driver and passenger had been taken prisoners and carried off to be tortured, and followed five or six miles, expecting to find their bodies.

Ford wrote to me, and Rangers were soon on the road. I had twelve of my men and three Pueblo Indians, making our force sixteen, quite small enough. . . .

By sunrise we were off and took a trail that left the river and wound through some rough hills. Coming in below again, we struck the trail where the Indians had come from the southeast, and picked up a small, handsome fur-tipped [red] glove, and our conjecture was it had been dropped by the passenger for the benefit of pursuers, and gave us hopes that both the men were alive. The trail showed one fresh shod mule, which had been taken by the Apaches from a colored soldier who was repairing the telegraph wire in Quitman Canyon. I once overheard him relating the affair to an admiring crowd on a San Antonio street. He was up the telegraph pole and did not see the Indians until they had him treed and were getting ready to shoot him like a 'coon, when the Rangers charged and saved his life, but he lost his mule. . . .

On reaching the river pretty well supplied with water, we followed a ledge of rocks crossing diagonally and making a splendid ford, and followed the trail down the river, they taking the old trail used by the Mexican customhouse guards. Where this leaves and strikes the rough hills we found the first camp of the Apaches after the murder in the canyon. . . .

Following the trail, we came to a wide gravely stream that came from the mountains to our right, and the trail led to the west, but when we struck the creek bed we found a fresh trail going east of some fourteen unshod ponies and knew in reason they were the game we were after, and we followed the fresh sign. We had with us old Bernardo Olguín, Domingo Olguín, his son, and Aniceto Durán, a nephew of the old Pueblo chief.

Bernardo, [who] had for a long while been acting as scout and trailer for the United States troops, was familiar with the whole county, brave, sober and reliable, and could read wood signs like a book. . . .

The three Pueblos had a score to settle with these same Apaches, as Simón Olguín, a brother of Bernardo and noted guide for the United States Army, was killed at Ojo Viejo when a company of Pueblos under a Lieutenant Bell was ambushed, or rather surprised, in a camp that Simón begged the Lieutenant not to stop at. But to go back to our trail. . . .

The chase was now becoming very exciting. The signs showed the Mescaleros had left that morning and were traveling slowly and carelessly, having come to the conclusion their last murders would be unavenged. We passed plenty of deer and antelope, but orders not to shoot anything but an Indian were positive. The Pueblos rode ahead a quarter of a mile, and often were strung up to highest pitch. Every coyote, antelope or moving thing seen was eagerly scanned.

In the evening we came to their camp, and an examination of the ashes showed that live coals of fire were still burning. In hunting large game, as the pleasure of the chase is in proportion to the danger, so we felt all the eagerness of tiger or lion hunter, but I doubt much if either comes up to the Apache warrior with his Winchester and fierceness and cunning.

Rushing ahead, by sunset we had covered a good deal of ground. . . .

Taking Old Bernardo and a couple of men with me we went up to where the trail crossed the crest of the mountains and with our glass scanned the hills in front of us, but no head of ponies, smoke, nor Indian could be seen. Whil'st we were standing there a flock of doves came sweeping by our heads and I said: "Boys, where those are going to water we will find the Indians in the morning." No fire could be seen from our front, so we cooked and were soon asleep, the sentinel instructed to waken us before day-break.

We were good tired and it seemed I had hardly been asleep an hour until we were awakened and had a hasty breakfast and were off on the trail. It was bitterly cold, so we walked and led our horses. . . . Old Bernardo was ahead and I and Lieutenant Nevill just behind, and just as day began to dawn, the Old Pueblo squatted down and said: *"Hay, están los Indios,* captain," and looking in the direction he pointed we distinguished two camp fires burning up brightly.

Luckily we were just on the crest of a hill and turning back, were soon out of sight. . . .

. . . My squad by following in Indian file and stooping as low as possible got within a hundred yards of the eastern camp. Here we came to a swag or low place between us and the Indians, who were huddled up around their fires cooking breakfast and not conscious of a Ranger being within a hundred miles. One was just coming to the fire with some wood and looked as big as a skinned horse, having an army cape on taken from some Negro soldiers killed at Hot Springs on the Rio Grande. It proved to be a little girl not over five years old, and goes to show how easily one can let his imagination run away with him. I was afraid if we passed down this swag some of the Apaches would see us and being just on the crest of the hill with a deep canyon beyond a few jumps would take them out of sight. So I kneeled down and motioned to the men to fall into line on my right and passed the word down the line when I fired to turn loose.

Old Bernardo's eyes were glistening like a panther's at the chance of getting even with the murderers of his brothers, his son and nephew by his side. . . . It was a complete surprise to the Indians, and there was plenty of blood all around their camp fire, showing some of us had good aim. Sergeant Carruthers got three at the other fire. Nearly all the men had Winchester carbines and rifles, but I used a Springfield rifle with hair trigger such as the United States officers used and I doubt if a better army gun was ever made for reliability.

We only had a few shots when the Apaches broke over the hill like a herd of deer and we charged the camp, as did the other squad, and when we got where we could see, the Indians were making two-forty time down the steep canyon. . . . The Apaches ran, some to the west and some east down the deep canyon and one warrior went up the opposite side of the canyon.

He bore along the hill in full view and drew the fire of every one and occasionally would turn around and shoot back at us. All we could do was to hold our breath until he shot, not knowing which one was his target. I took five pops at him myself. Frank De Jarnette and another Ranger followed his trail for over a mile and said he was bleeding like a beef, but still making big jumps toward the Tularosa Agency. . . .

Finding we could make no further progress in that direction, and the firing in the canyon ceasing, we turned back to the arroyo, and soon saw Sergeant Carruthers and a squad of Rangers coming up the bed of the arroyo with two squaws and a child, prisoners. . . .

. . . [Sam] Graham came up, and he was perfectly wild with rage at the sight of them, for this same band had . . . shot his brother, making him a cripple and killing his sister-in-law, . . . and killed an old man named [James] Grant. . . .

Of course, young Graham, a hot headed boy, wanted to kill the women. The prisoners soon took in the situation and cowered behind me as they saw his angry face and hostile attitude, but I told him I could never agree to killing women, crying and begging for their lives, but would go with him after the warriors willingly. . . . We started up the arroyo, and soon heard such a roar of Winchesters we thought the Apaches must have rallied and returned to their camp. We were pretty badly scattered, for the Indians went in every direction and the Rangers after them, but as we were afoot we were not in it in a race with fleet-footed Apaches, especially as they were running for dear life, assisted by a lively fusillade of Winchester bullets. . . .

We found in their camp women and children's clothing, showing we had struck the band that murdered Mrs. [Margaret] Graham and robbed their wagons. We found five United States cavalry saddles, showing that they had killed the six colored soldiers at the Hot Springs below Fort Quitman. We found the tops of old Morgan's boots which, no doubt, would have been used to make moccasins, and the pants of the passenger who was on the stage. They had cut them off at the body and above the knees and made them into sacks filled with tobacco and such little trinkets as delight the Indians. We had got the identical Indians that had killed ten people we knew of within a few months. . . .

We put the squaw on her horse and the little girl produced her saddle, quirt and army cape and selected her pony, and appeared as contented as if with her own people. We strung out and by 11 o'clock that night were back at Victorio's tank, pretty well tired out, thankful that none of the men were hurt, and satisfied we had given the Apaches a lesson that they would remember; in fact, they never committed another murder in Texas.

🌟 *E S S A Y S*

In the first essay, geographer Terry Jordan of the University of Texas at Austin uses migration patterns and other social data to challenge the traditional argument that the Texas and U.S. cattle industry was born in South Texas and was based on Spanish/Mexican cattle raising practices. Instead Jordan argues that the cattle industry originated in South Carolina, was influenced by British, African, and Spanish herding techniques, and spread westward into east and southeast Texas in the early nineteenth century. Spanish influences were absorbed primarily in the southeast and in Louisiana, not in Texas. In the second essay, historian Arnoldo De León and sociologist Kenneth Stewart, both of Angelo State University, analyze employment data and economic data to assess the clash between Hispanics and Anglos in South Texas. They argue that Anglo settlers relied on their domination of the political process and the presence of American military force to wrest control of South Texas from Mexicans and Mexican Americans. Both groups migrated to South Texas for economic opportunity. Historical racial and cultural antagonisms resulted in one group succeeding at the expense of the other. In the third essay, Jacqueline Reinier, Professor Emeritus at California State University at Sacramento, examines in detail the experience of forty women who migrated to the plains of the Panhandle and northwest Texas. She concludes that these women did not challenge existing social or political mores, but served primarily to transplant institutions and domestic practices to the Texas frontier.

Southern Origins of the Texas Cattle Industry

TERRY G. JORDAN

The continued westward expansion by herders following Texas statehood in 1845 created, as early as 1860, the first two clusters of Anglo cattle ranching within the Great Plains. One of these clusters lay in the Coastal Bend area, along and between the lower courses of the Guadalupe, San Antonio, and Nueces rivers, a region that formed the northeastern part of the South Texas "diamond." In the process the Anglos overran, not for the first time in their spread westward from Carolina, a formerly important Hispanic ranching region. The Coastal Bend had been the scene of a thriving Spanish cattle industry, particularly in the 1700s, and some vestiges remained in the middle nineteenth century. The Anglos, like the Hispanos before them, found the prairies and brush country *chaparral* of the northeastern diamond well suited to cattle raising. . . . By 1870, Anglos had expanded up the Nueces and San Antonio valleys, enlarging this South Texas ranching region to include, roughly, the northern half of the diamond area. In that year, the northern diamond housed fully one-third of the cattle population of Texas, a total of well over one million head.

By contrast, the southern half of the diamond, which remained an Hispano stronghold, did not witness an increase in cattle ranching during these decades. Instead, the purest Mexican-American counties, those lining the Rio Grande, formed a sheep-ranching district. . . .

The second major new cattle-ranching cluster by 1860 lay on the central-western frontier of Texas, in a block of rolling to hilly counties drained by the middle courses of the Brazos and Colorado rivers, a region including a northern part known in the vernacular as the Cross Timbers and a southern section called the Heart of Texas. . . . Cultural geographer D. W. Meinig and historian R. N. Richardson designated the Cross Timbers-Heart of Texas as a "main source region" of the western cattle industry, noting that it produced "more notable cattlemen than any other region of equal size in America." At the same time, the region formed one of the purest southern Anglo-American districts in Texas, lacking as it did any significant numbers of blacks, Hispanos, or European immigrants. . . .

The two major cattle-ranching regions implanted within the southeastern margin of the Great Plains between 1850 and 1870 were created by cattlemen migrating from eastern Texas, from the three areas where Anglo herding had developed during the first half of the nineteenth century. The Coastal Prairie corridor played a key role in this westward thrust.

Diffusion from the Coastal Prairie of Southeast Texas

The creolized herding culture rooted in the Texas Coastal Prairie east of the Guadalupe or Lavaca rivers before 1845 subsequently made a significant contribution to the rise of ranching in the Great Plains. In the last decade and a half of the antebellum era, these lower southerners were largely responsible for developing the Coastal Bend ranching area in the South Texas diamond. . . .

Terry G. Jordan, *Trails to Texas: Southern Roots of Western Cattle Ranching* (Lincoln: University of Nebraska Press, 1981), 125–157. Reprinted by permission of the University of Nebraska Press. Copyright © 1983 by the University of Nebraska Press.

When Anglo herders began entering the trans-Guadalupe country in the 1840s, they found a war-ravaged land from which most of the former Mexican ranchers had fled. Remaining behind were numerous longhorn cattle, as well as a relatively small population of *vaqueros,* some Irish-born ranchers, and a few Hispanic *rancheros,* such as the Navarro and de León families. The cattle industry of the Coastal Bend was all but dead. . . . Between 1850, and 1860, Anglos from the Coastal Prairie corridor rebuilt the cattle industry of the trans-Guadalupe country, elevating it to a magnitude previously unknown. By the time of the Civil War, Coastal Prairie settlers had created the cattle-ranching focus in the Coastal Bend. . . .

Even beyond the Guadalupe River, Anglo cattlemen in the South Texas diamond did not forget their traditional lower-southern markets. New Orleans remained their chief goal as late as the Civil War, and drives to Louisiana continued even in postbellum times. The Crescent City's hold on the receding coastal cattle frontier strengthened with the advent of steamship cattle transport, and the port town of Indianola thrived as the major handler of Texas cattle shipped by sea to New Orleans. Other cattle drives from the Guadalupe and San Antonio river valleys in the 1860s and early 1870s reached Mobile, Natchez, Shreveport, and Woodville in Mississippi. . . .

Continuing Diffusion after 1870

Many Anglos paused only briefly in South Texas and the Cross Timbers-Heart of Texas areas before continuing their migration. From these two clearly defined bases in the margins of the Great Plains, they spread rapidly westward and northward after 1870. In the wake of the decimation of the Plains Indians and the bison herds, Anglo herders, continuing the thrust that had long before brought their genealogical and cultural ancestors out of Carolina, surged through much of the Great Plains.

In this expansion, cattlemen from the two regions followed different paths westward. The primary goal of ranchers emigrating from South Texas was the trans-Pecos country, including the Davis Mountains and Big Bend. These inheritors of the coastal cattle tradition rarely ventured north of the thirty-second parallel, clinging instead to counties on or near the Mexican border. In South Texas and the Coastal Prairie, many of them had become accustomed to using Mexican *vaqueros,* a dependence which may help explain their migration pattern. In semiarid Southwest Texas, near the border, they could continue to ranch in the manner they had known in the valleys of the Guadalupe, San Antonio and Nueces rivers. Theirs remained a far southern, creolized herding culture, and they were not major participants in the spread of ranching through the Great Plains.

Instead, the Cross Timbers-Heart of Texas cattlemen provided the main westward and northward movement after 1870. The spread of ranching into the Texas South Plains and Panhandle was largely their work, as was a major thrust up the Concho Valley, across a low divide to the Pecos River, and northward along that stream into eastern New Mexico. Many soon expanded their ranching operations into states north of Texas, carrying the Anglo herding system through the Great Plains. . . . West Texas, in very considerable measure, was colonized from East and Central Texas, a pattern initially established by cattlemen from the Cross Timbers-Heart of

Texas. More than that, these sons of the Piney Woods and Upper South were chiefly responsible for bringing Carolina to the Great Plains.

Anglo Herding Traits in the West

As Anglo cattle herders spread westward after mid-century, they did not forsake the Carolina heritage. Rather, they introduced elements of their cattle tradition, passing on to descendants in the west many ancestral herding traits from the southeastern seaboard. They remained, in goodly measure, Carolina's children.

One typically Anglo custom imported to the west was the use of herder dogs. Tilden, the county seat of McMullen in the South Texas diamond, was called Dog Town in the 1870s, due to the local ranchers' habit of using packs of dogs to round up cattle in the surrounding brush country. Even the Mexican *vaqueros* on the famous King Ranch in South Texas had herder dogs by the 1940s, using them to find cattle that strayed into brush thickets. To the north, also, in the Cross Timbers-Heart of Texas ranching region, leopard dogs were common. Their use declined to the west, on the open grasslands, and relatively few major ranches in West Texas kept such canines. One late nineteenth-century rancher in the Texas Panhandle did own a pack of seventy-five "greyhounds," but their job was to protect his cattle from wolves and coyotes rather than to herd stock. These hounds lived in a low, elongated "mush house," and the man in charge of them was called a "mush-pot wrangler."

Black cowboys made a more effective transition to the west. Famous Cross Timbers cattlemen such as Dan Waggoner and Oliver Loving used black cowhands before and after the Civil War. On his Wichita County ranch in 1880, Waggoner employed thirty-one Anglos, one black, and one Mexican as cowboys. Even in the South Texas diamond, where *vaquero* labor was common, black cowboys were occasionally found. For example, C. C. Cox, a rancher in Live Oak County in the Coastal Bend area, used Negro help in the late 1850s. Blacks accompanied the Anglo rancher migration to West Texas, where sixty-eight of them worked as cowboys by 1880. While these blacks made up only 4 percent of the cowboy work force, a far lower proportion than claimed by some historians, their presence in West Texas is undeniable. . . . Eventually, a few blacks even became ranch owners in West Texas, and Negro cowhands continued to find employment on ranches there into the present century. . . .

Hispanic-derived longhorns, according to the commonly accepted account, provided the livestock for the early cattle industry of West Texas and the Great Plains. Only later, after the advent of barbed wire, were improved breeds introduced to displace the longhorn, goes the traditional argument. My evidence suggests, on the contrary, that West Texas cattle were not pureblood longhorns in the pre-fence era and that bloodlines derived from the Anglo-American East were always present. Dan Waggoner's experience in the Cross Timbers region is illustrative. . . . Waggoner began as a cattle raiser in the Blackland Prairie corridor of Northeast Texas, then moved his herds to the Cross Timbers of Wise County in the 1850s. About 1865 he became aware of a "slow change in appearance" in his cattle from one year to the next. Seeking the cause of this change, Waggoner finally located a single feral longhorn bull among his stock. This bull fought and defeated Waggoner's smaller bulls, presumably of British origin, and collected a sizable entourage of cows. Supposedly,

Waggoner's uninvited longhorn was the first of his breed to appear as far north as Wise County. Thus, on the very eve of the surge by Anglo ranchers onto the Great Plains, one of the legendary cattle kings noticed the first appearance of longhorn traits in his herd. It seems very likely that other cattle introduced to the Cross Timbers from Northeast Texas, such as the herd brought from Fannin to Palo Pinto County about 1858, were also dominantly British.

Nor were the cattle trailed west from the Piney Woods of unmixed Hispanic ancestry—and the East Texas area remained a major source of western cattle throughout the nineteenth century. In the 1880s cattlemen from West Texas came to the southern Piney Woods looking for herd replacements, and one East Texas resident recalled that "every once in a while somebody would go along the big road" in front of his house, "with a small herd of cattle, drifting them west to grass and prairie country."

Further diluting the longhorn parentage of early West Texas herds were cattle introduced directly from eastern states. One early rancher in the Cross Timbers had come from Alabama with some nonlonghorn stock, and Lum Slaughter, the cattle baron of Palo Pinto County in the Cross Timbers, imported shorthorn bulls from Kentucky as early as 1871 to improve his herd. It may well be true that Texas ranchers sent their purer longhorn animals north to stock the Great Plains ranges between 1870 and 1890, keeping the superior, part-British cattle to restock their own ranges. In this way, Texas cattle could have gotten the reputation in the north of being longhorns, even though the actual makeup of the herds reflected a mixture of Spanish and British stock. At any rate, the claim that pure longhorn cattle prevailed on the West Texas ranges between 1870 and 1890 deserves to be challenged. Not even the crucial Coastal Prairie corridor, the southernmost of the Anglo routes westward, was stocked with pure longhorns. . . .

Carolina, then, was abundantly represented in the Great Plains cattle industry. But so, too, was Latin America. Western ranching vocabulary abounded with Spanish loanwords such as "corral," "ranch" "remuda," "morral," "lariat," "bronc," and "pinto," and various other aspects of nonmaterial and material herding culture on the Great Plains reflected Hispanic influence. Traditionally, the South Texas diamond has been designated as the primary scene of Hispanicization.

It is not my intent to deny the Hispanos a role in the evolution of Great Plains ranching. Rather, the argument presented here . . . is (1) that the role of the South Texas diamond as an arena of Hispanicization has been greatly overemphasized and (2) that the case for Hispanic influence in the Great Plains has been consistently overstated.

Absorption of Spanish herding traits by lower southern Anglos began in the late eighteenth century, far to the east along the creole coast. . . . Hispanicization began in earnest in southern Louisiana and the Natchez area of Mississippi, and the process continued in the Coastal Prairie corridor of Southeast Texas, where Anglos employed Mexican herders and used lariats by 1830. Census marshals working the Coastal Prairie counties of Southeast Texas in 1850 found additional evidence that Hispanicization was well advanced there. They listed the profession of a Fort Bend County Anglo as "owner of ranch," while in nearby Jackson County one of the nine Mexican-American inhabitants declared himself to be a 'becero' (*vaquero*). The creolized herding culture carried west of the Guadalupe River by Anglos after

1845 or 1850 probably differed only in minor respects from the remnant Hispanic system already rooted there.

Moreover, the Mexican rancheros of the South Texas diamond had very nearly disappeared before 1850. In the Guadalupe, San Antonio, and Nueces river valleys—the crucial Coastal Bend area in the northeastern part of the diamond—only 10 persons of Spanish surname owned 100 or more cattle at mid-century, and the total number of resident Hispanic "herdsmen' was but 181, of whom 92 lived south of the Nueces River. In the most purely Mexican portion of South Texas—the Rio Grande Valley between Laredo and the Gulf—only 12 Spanish-surnamed persons owned as many as 100 cattle in 1850, and this southern part of the diamond remained inconsequential as a cattle-ranching region. Moreover, banditry, lasting from the 1850s through the middle 1870s, made cattle ranching in the district between the Nueces River and the Rio Grande next to impossible for Hispanos and Anglos alike.

A culture in rapid decline, such as that of the South Texas Hispanic rancheros between 1840 and 1880, is unlikely to exert much shaping influence on a vital, expanding neighbor culture. It is therefore more appropriate to regard the cattle industry that thrived in the northern part of the diamond area by 1860 and 1870 as mainly an Anglo-American achievement, as a successor of the creolized lower-southern herder culture. The diamond was the westernmost in a succession of arenas where coastal Anglos met Hispanos, and not demonstrably the most important.

The overemphasis on South Texas as a scene of Hispanicization has, in turn, led to an incorrect view of that region as the "cradle" of the Texas and Great Plains cattle industry. In fact, a better argument can be made for the South Texas diamond as a cradle of Texas sheep ranching. The combination of sheep and cattle on the same range, a combination in which sheep not infrequently exceeded cattle in importance, was typical of Hispanic-American ranching. In the southern half of the South Texas diamond, exactly such a situation existed in the middle nineteenth-century, as was suggested earlier. One result, perhaps, was that some Anglo ranchers in the northern half of the diamond, by 1870, combined cattle and sheep raising. Sheep outnumbered swine almost two to one in the northern diamond, a major departure from coastal southern Anglo tradition. Perhaps the sheep-ranching industry which developed in the Edwards Plateau region by 1880 can be traced to this experience gained in the South Texas diamond.

The principal Hispanic-American contribution to western cattle ranching lay in horsemanship and related paraphernalia and vocabulary. Anglos thereby acquired equestrian techniques well suited to open grassland country. Most likely, this acquisition began far to the east, perhaps even in Florida and South Georgia, and was largely completed in the Coastal Prairie of southern Louisiana and Southeast Texas. When Anglo and Hispano ranchers met again in the trans-Guadalupe country, both were mounted herdsmen.

Not only has South Texas been falsely designated as the cradle of the western cattle kingdom and overrated as a scene of Hispanicization, but also (and perhaps consequently) the extent of Spanish influence in the Great Plains ranching industry has been overestimated. The incorrect assumption that Anglos were neophytes who adopted intact the Hispanic herding system has led scholars of that school of thought to look for a Mexican behind every sagebrush. A good example of such overstatement is Sandra Myres's claim that the *mesta,* an Hispanic stockraisers' guild traceable to medieval Spain, was the forerunner of such Anglo cattlemen's organizations as the Panhandle Stockmen's Association, established in 1880, and the Texas and Southwestern Cattle Raisers Association, founded in the Cross Timbers area in 1877. This extravagant claim has no documented factual basis. The Cross Timbers-Heart of Texas was the less Hispanicized of the two major cattle-ranching districts of Texas by 1870, and yet it produced the first Anglo stockmen's organization. It is more logical to seek the origin of such associations in the traditional communalism of the Anglo frontier, the same communalism that produced claim clubs, house raisings, wagon trains, and home-guard militia. . . .

Still, as suggested earlier, Hispanic influence existed in the Great Plains, most notably in horsemanship. Agents and routes of diffusion must be found to account for the presence of these Spanish traits. Since Anglos ranching in the South Texas diamond were more thoroughly Hispanicized than any others, as a result of their long experience on the creole coast, they would seem to provide the key. Closer inspection, however, reveals several apparent problems with this diffusion model. First, a number of Hispanic traits failed to spread northward from the diamond area. Among these was the "Mexican plan" of herding, adopted by some Anglos in the Nueces Valley of South Texas in the 1850s. It involved a roundup or *rodeo* "once a week or oftener," instead of only once or twice each year, as was the Anglo custom.

Nor did large-scale sheep raising or the use of Mexican *vaqueros* spread notably north of the thirty-second parallel. Only 2 percent of the cowhands employed north of that parallel in 1880 were Hispanos. In fact, when Anglo ranchers in the Texas Panhandle were confronted by Hispano sheepmen from another source—New Mexico—in the late 1870s and early 1880s, Anglo-Texas ranchers stuck by their cattle and rejected the opportunity to give sheep a major place in their range operation. The Panhandle's Hispano *pastores,* who numbered 358 in 1880, had recently arrived from New Mexico. Though they accounted in that year for 22 percent of the Panhandle's total population—70 percent in the four western border counties—the Hispanos were quickly shunted out and their sheep replaced by Anglo cattle. They left behind only some place names.

Another problem with accepting South Texas Anglos as a major source of Hispanic traits lies in their migration routes. As we have seen, their principal path in the latter part of the nineteenth century led westward to the trans-Pecos country, not north into the Great Plains proper. Relocation diffusion in the form of migration from South Texas cannot explain the spread of Hispanic traits, since migration routes ran at right angles to the presumed direction of trait diffusion.

This apparent problem is resolved by a consideration of marketing routes. After the Civil War, South Texas Anglo cattlemen broke their longstanding allegiance to New Orleans as a market and began trailing herds northward to Missouri and Kansas, following the earlier example of ranchers in northern and central Texas. The principal cattle trails serving South Texas led directly north, through the Cross Timbers-Heart of Texas region (fig. 10A). Hispanic horsemanship skills, with the related items of material culture and vocabulary as well as the word "ranch," appear to have diffused northward along the cattle trails and to have been implanted in the Cross Timbers-Heart of Texas. Another potent force in the northward diffusion of Hispanic herding traits was the Mexican War of 1846–48, in which numerous Texans from the northern and central portions of the state saw action in the south. These

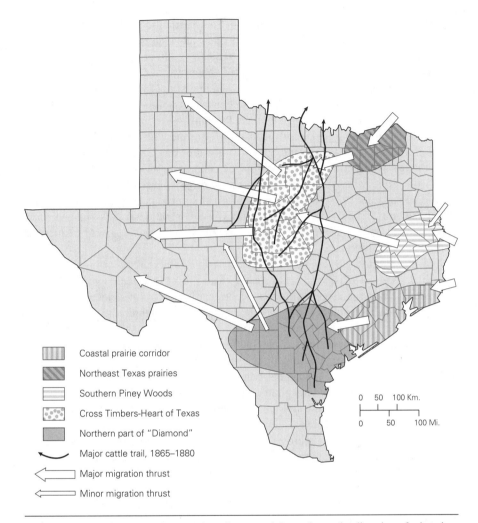

Coastal prairie corridor

Northeast Texas prairies

Southern Piney Woods

Cross Timbers-Heart of Texas

Northern part of "Diamond"

Major cattle trail, 1865–1880

Major migration thrust

Minor migration thrust

Fig. 10A   The major postbellum cattle trails ran at right angles to the direction of migration, encouraging south-to-north cultural diffusion.

contacts with South Texas were renewed during the Civil War, when the blockade of Texan ports forced a variety of goods to be shipped out through Mexican ports. So, while migration routes ran east to west, important north-south avenues of communication were opened by two wars and a new marketing pattern. These avenues brought selected Hispanic traits and huge numbers of longhorn cattle north without noticeably influencing migration. Principally in this manner, the techniques of the Creole coast cowmen reached the Great Plains.

Conclusion

Great Plains cattle ranching in the open-range era during the latter part of the nineteenth century contained an important Anglo-American component, a component that derived ultimately from seventeenth-century South Carolina. A spatial and temporal continuity between the colonial South Atlantic seaboard and western Texas has been demonstrated. Great Plains open-range cattle ranchers belonged in part among South Carolina children, both genealogically and culturally.

Geographer Donald Meinig enumerated "about twenty" nuclei of colonization on the Atlantic coast of North America in which distinct local cultures developed, later to spread westward and contribute to the shaping of the United States. Boston and its environs, for example, gave us the Puritan work ethic; the Delaware Valley provided the log cabin and family-operated farm; the Chesapeake Tidewater was the source of the plantation. Among the twenty, too, was Charleston and its hinterland, though its importance has generally been underestimated. Henceforth, colonial South Carolina, whose legacy reached the grassy expanses of the Great Plains, should be regarded as a cultural hearth of great significance to the evolution and understanding of both the South and the West. It should take its rightful place alongside the other major colonial nuclei as one of the major shapers of American culture and institutions. . . .

In ethnic terms, western ranching reflects a unique mixture of groups, a blending of British, African, Hispanic, and probably also French, German, and Amerindian influences. The crucial early mixing occurred in one confined locality, lowland South Carolina, the southern fringe of the English colonial empire in North America, where a favorable juxtaposition of Britons and West Africans occurred. Westward along the creole coast of the Lower South, as far as the Nueces Valley of Texas, vigorous ethnic blending continued for two centuries.

Environmentally, a subtropical belt of pine barrens better suited to grazing than cultivation provided a hospitable, though certainly not determinant, physical setting for the incubation of Carolina cattle herding. The same pine barrens, together with canebrakes, small prairies, and grassland corridors, offered suitable pathways to the west. Ultimately, ranching reached the greatest stretch of grassland on the North American continent, an environment that encouraged expansion of herding on a scale previously unknown.

Frontier conditions, most notably a shortage of labor, contributed to the rise of ranching in South Carolina, but large-scale cattle herding was not typical of other English colonial frontiers in America. Often, but not always, in the areas where it was implanted, ranching was confined to a pioneer stage and disappeared with the passing of the Anglo frontier. While helpful in certain instances, the concept of cattle herding as an occupance stage is not universally applicable in the westward diffusion to the Great Plains.

A desire to participate in the market of the Thünenian World City, coupled with the difficulty of access typical of frontier areas, helps explain the viability of an extensive form of land-use such as livestock ranching. The market, emanating initially from western Europe through the West Indian plantations, was essential to the rise and spread of open-range herding. But in the final analysis, the market model cannot explain the precise character of a frontier economy.

In sum, western ranching was the product of ethnic creolization occuring in a frontier setting and a suitable physical environment, under favorable market conditions. Had any one of these elements—culture, contact, remoteness, environment, or market—been fundamentally different, western ranching would also have been different, or quite possibly would not have come to exist at all. Indeed, when one element—remoteness—was broken down by railroads and the industrial age around the turn of the present century, traditional open-range cattle ranching quickly disappeared. Carolina's reign on the western grasslands was short, limited to the brief, pleasant interlude between the arrival of the first cattlemen and the coming of the machine age.

Power Struggle in the Valley:
Mexicans and Anglos in South Texas, 1850–1900

ARNOLDO DE LÉON AND KENNETH L. STEWART

The history of Spanish Texas is now well documented. First outlined by the pioneer Borderlands historian Herbert E. Bolton and advanced by Carlos E. Castañeda, the story takes up much space in Texana collections. . . .

Less well known is the story of Spanish-Americans in Texas following the arrival of Anglo settlers from the United States in 1821. The dissertations of James E. Crisp, Arnoldo De León, Fane Downs, Andrew A. Tijerina, Gilberto M. Hinojosa, and Mario T. García, however, have broadened historical understanding of social attitudes toward Tejanos and of Mexican-American demographic patterns in the Lone Star State during its formative decades in the nineteenth century. Many more works are in progress among them a comprehensive quantitative analysis of social life among Mexican Americans in Texas between 1850 and 1900.

This analysis of immigration into south Texas during the last half of the nineteenth century comes from that larger study. It attempts to trace the destiny of two immigrant groups—one from Mexico, the other from the United States and Europe—as they arrived in south Texas following the Mexican War. It seeks to describe how the two peoples fared, considering the fact that they came to south Texas bent upon making something of themselves in a frontier region that promised them an equal start. In explaining the eventual inequalities that developed, the study probes into the historical forces that determined the destiny of the two groups.

Understanding the fate of immigrant groups descending upon south Texas in the last half of the nineteenth century requires much more than grasping the dynamics of local historical forces. The fact is that the experience of newcomers to the region was determined by a host of patterns and events far beyond the section's immediate surroundings and reaching far back into time. Thus, the context inherited by the population ingressing into the region during the latter nineteenth century is outlined in the first part of the article.

Spain first took an interest in the northern part of Tamaulipas (or modern-day south Texas) in the 1740s, some thirty or forty years after establishing permanent settlements at Nacogdoches in east Texas and San Antonio and Goliad in central Texas. . . .

Arnoldo De Léon and Kenneth L. Stewart, "Lost Dreams and Found Fortunes: Mexican and Anglo Immigrants in South Texas, 1850–1900," *Western Historical Quarterly* 14 (July 1983): 291–309. Copyright © 1983 by The Western Historical Quarterly. Reprinted by permission.

Though hot and dry and unfriendly to farmers, the region proved beneficial to settlers with a penchant for raising livestock. Its topography offered an abundance of grazing land for cattle and mustangs, and ranching activities soon provided the bounty that made the Escandón settlements permanent. As the region became an active livestock center, it took on the features of other Hispanic enclaves. . . . By the dawn of the nineteenth century, . . . the settlements in the Rio Grande Valley were "on the threshold of an upward thrust from the Rio Grande to the Nueces River."

What signaled an incipient change for all of Texas was the arrival of Stephen F. Austin in 1821. Implementation of colonization plans for Anglo-Americans produced a wave of immigration from the United States that dramatically altered the social and cultural fabric of the entire state. By 1835, the demography of the region east of the Hispanic settlements in San Antonio and Goliad was radically different from before. The Anglo-American population centered in this eastern region numbered some 35,000, far more than the estimated 4,000 Hispanos located primarily in the central Texas area.

Though the influx of Anglo-Americans created a different kind of world for the Nacogdoches, Béxar, and Goliad areas, northern Tamaulipas, or what is present-day south Texas, was touched only peripherally. The Tamaulipecos took little interest in the changes occurring to the northeast. In fact, the region experienced a brisk expansion between 1821 and 1835. The settlements originally concentrated in a wedge of land along the Rio Grande extended outward. . . . The region now consisted mainly of ranching communities, including approximately 350 rancherías where settlers carried on a customary way of life and identified with the familiar institutions of the Spanish-Mexican tradition. . . .

Until the 1840s, residents of the section lived remotely from American influences as Mexico's claim to the region discouraged Anglo-Americans from entering. Within a few years, however, it became an area where immigrants from both Mexico and the United States came to mold their destinies. . . .

Americans came to the region with a decided edge, however. To begin with, troops came along with them to secure the area for the United States. Anglo appreciation for this military presence remained constant even after the end of the Mexican War when it was seen as crucial to their prosperity. . . .

Encouraged by the military fortifications and the support they could count on from Austin, Anglos scoured the territory in efforts to acquire lands held by the former Tamaulipecos. In Nueces County, where some land was acquired by Anglos while the war raged, original grants to Mexicans were displaced through a combination of methods including litigation, chicanery, robbery, fraud, and threat. . . .

Along the lower border, similar mechanisms were used. . . . In part, such indiscreet misuses of power incited the Juan Cortina "revolt" of 1859. One of Cortina's major grievances during the rebellion was that no justice existed for Tejanos in south Texas.

. . . By various means, then, Anglos transformed the formerly isolated south Texas region, and by 1860 it had become a part of Texas where the Mexican-American majority was militarily and politically subordinated to the Anglo-American minorities. Once the pattern was established, it held for the rest of the century.

The military and political advantages enjoyed by Anglo-Americans as they arrived in south Texas ultimately led to a new regional economic arrangement.

Within just twelve years after the Treaty of Guadalupe Hidalgo, large tracts of the most valued real estate in the region had been acquired by a few Anglo immigrants. Estimates based on the Census of 1860 show that immigrants, including those from Mexico, Europe, and the United States, comprised about 64 percent of the nonslave population in that year. Newcomers also held about 95 percent of the assessed real estate value of south Texas. . . .

What these figures show is that Anglo-American immigrants to south Texas rapidly appropriated not just lands but the foundation of the region's economy. Through the transfer of land ownership from Mexicans, they gained economic control of an area where persons rooted in the older Spanish-Mexican heritage comprised at least 73 percent of the total population through the last half of the nineteenth century. Moreover, it was military and political power, not entrepreneurial opportunities created by the transformation in agriculture during the 1870s and 1880s, that was responsible for the takeover of the means of production. The region remained almost exclusively a ranching area without adequate access to commercial markets during the 1850s and 1860s, and not until the decades following 1870 did it make the transition to commercialized farming and ranching. By the time the agricultural transformation reached the southern portion of Texas, both the economic and political processes were solidly held by the Anglo-American minority, which could reach out and reap its benefits.

Another aspect of post-Mexican War economic change in south Texas was the appearance of a complex process of occupational differentiation. Two contrasting patterns of diversification occurred simultaneously during the time the region came under the domination of Anglo-Americans and commenced the transition to a commercial agricultural base. First, economic and political conditions wrought changes in the demand for labor, and all gainful workers felt this impact regardless of their ethnic heritage. Second, ethnic cleavages became deeply drawn, with ominous consequences for both immigrants from Mexico and Mexican Americans born in Texas.

. . . The spread of the railroads and the growth of commercial farming operations meant improved technologies and greater mechanization, and the labor force as a whole paid the price for these developments in the form of job displacement. The proportion of workers specializing in agricultural pursuits, for example, decreased from nearly 30 percent in 1850 to only 17 percent in 1900. Declines also occurred in specialized trade, transportation, manufacturing, and mechanical employment. Only one category of workers—unspecialized laborers—increased rapidly between 1850 and 1900. An insignificant segment of the labor force in 1850, this group multiplied to over 40 percent of all workers in south Texas by 1900. The total effect of the agricultural transition was to reduce the degree of specialization required of the largest number of workers. Levels of skill among south Texas workers declined in accordance. . . .

As these dramatic changes took place in the overall labor force, a second pattern of more direct consequence for Mexicans was manifest. Divergent roles in the economic process developed in close correspondence to varying national origins of the region's immigrants, and an ethnic division of labor emerged. Subsequently, the stream of *inmigrantes* (immigrants from Mexico) crossing into the area faced distressing employment prospects, and their hopes for a better life in Texas were thwarted. . . .

In 1850 Mexican immigrants, together with native Tejanos, literally served as the backbone of the labor force. Over half (54.2 percent) of the immigrants were engaged in specialized agricultural pursuits, and the same was true of the native population, nine out of ten of whom were of Mexican descent. Together, the indigenous Tejanos and the *inmigrantes* comprised about 90 percent of the entire agricultural labor force of 1850. Only 4.6 percent of the Anglo-American immigrants were similarly employed, and they constituted less than 5 percent of the total workers specialized in agriculture.

A similar labor arrangement also held true in the area of manufacturing and craftsmanship. Over 40 percent of both the *inmigrantes* and Tejanos were involved in manufacturing and mechanical occupations in 1850, and the two groups together made up about two-thirds of this labor sector. The incoming Anglo-Americans, in contrast, were employed in manufacturing and mechanical endeavors at a rate of 17.4 percent, and they comprised only about 16 percent of all workers in the category. . . .

. . . The most notable change in the ethnic composition of labor between 1850 and 1900 was an extensive decline in the percentage of *inmigrantes* and indigenous Tejanos committed to agricultural labor. As noted, the agricultural segment of the total labor force dwindled from 29.8 percent in 1850 to just 17 percent in 1900. As the overall decline set in, however, the percent of Anglo-Americans entering south Texas to take up agricultural pursuits increased from less than 5 percent to 17.6 percent. Consequently, the reduction in the proportion of *inmigrantes* involved in agriculture was extreme. Where 54.2 percent of them were engaged in this labor segment in 1850, only 18.4 percent performed specialized agricultural tasks in 1900. Of course, a similar trend occurred among the indigenous workers, about 85 percent of whom were Mexican Americans in 1900.

Manufacturing and mechanical occupations also formed a waning sector of the total labor force of south Texas. This group dwindled from 33 percent to 11.6 percent of the working population in the years between 1850 and 1900, and once again, those coming from Mexico experienced a more radical decline than those from the United States. The proportion of *inmigrantes* pursuing manufacturing and mechanical employments decreased by 30 percent. The decline among Anglo-American immigrants, in contrast, was only 2 percent. The fact that Tejanos, who comprised a large majority of the indigenous Texans, underwent a reduction paralleling that of the incoming Mexicans makes the overall pattern of shifting labor in south Texas tellingly clear.

The labor displacement, associated intrinsically with the transition to commercial agriculture, focused primarily on the commodity production sectors of the economy. Agriculture and manufacturing and mechanical occupations, all with heavy concentrations of Mexican immigrant and native Tejano workers in 1850, were especially reduced. The result was a movement of *inmigrantes* and Tejanos into the general mass of unspecialized laborers. Over 40 percent of all Mexican and Tejano workers were confined to the general labor pool by 1900, and together they made up about 99 percent of its members. Meanwhile, immigrants from the United States continued to stream into service, trade, and transportation endeavors and even increased their participation in the declining commodity production segments of the labor force. The Mexicans and Tejanos, then, suffered a severe downturn in occupational standing during the agricultural transition, while opportunities for immigrants from the United States were apparently enhanced.

Such an ethnically stratified occupational structure obviously affected the personal and collective lives of Mexicanos in the lower strata. The jobs they came to have surely touched on their personal well-being, for certainly a nexus exists between vocation and standard of living. Given the correlation between ethnicity and labor that emerged in south Texas between 1850 and 1900, it should be expected that Mexican immigrants suffered not only in terms of occupational status but in terms of wage and wealth benefits as well. Indications are that this was the case exactly. . . .

Estimates of personal wealth in the south Texas area show that in the years between 1850 and 1870 the standard of living among the workers who arrived from Mexico fluctuated violently in comparison to that of Anglo-American immigrants. The proportion of Mexicans who reported possession of personal wealth totaled 2.6 percent in 1850. The number increased to 16.4 percent in 1860, but declined by more than 10 percent by 1870. A similar pattern of wealth ownership took place among the American immigrants, but the number reporting assets was not less than 16 percent in any one year. Thus, the relative percentage of the American immigrant population that was able to accrue some degree of wealth consistently surpassed that of the *inmigrantes.*

In addition, the relative amount of personal wealth concentrated in the hands of the Anglo-Americans remained constant over the years. Anglos controlled about 31 percent of all personal wealth in the region, though they composed only about 9 percent of the population. Wealth owned by *inmigrantes,* on the other hand, amounted to only 10.4 percent of the regional total in 1850, increasing to 37.1 percent in 1860, and then dropping sharply to 18.2 percent in 1870. At the same time, the Mexicans composed 31 percent of the region's population in 1850, and by 1870 they made up 50 percent. Hence, while immigrants from Mexico composed the fastest growing single ethnic group in the region, they were the ones most habitually consigned to a marginal level of existence or less. It cannot be argued, moreover, that the *inmigrantes* were unwilling to work hard toward personal betterment. Their participation in the labor force increased consistently, even as their standard of living, as reflected in wealth statistics, remained unstable. In 1850 the percentage of Mexican immigrants over the age of twenty pursuing gainful employment was 23.1 percent. This increased to 52.7 percent by 1870 and to 56.5 percent by 1900. As in the case of other immigrant groups streaming into the developing territory of nineteenth-century south Texas, they undertook work as a way of realizing their aspirations. An improved standard of living, however, was not a dependable outcome for them. Dreams for a better life in Texas escaped them.

During the twentieth century, numerous academicians and government policy makers concerned with the effects of migration from Mexico to the United States have tried to profile the essential characteristics and qualities of the *inmigrantes.* . . .

Since the earliest efforts to construct profiles of the character of the Mexicans coming to the United States, American scholars and public officials have been guided by the fundamental assumption that "Mexican" culture somehow does not mix well with "American" culture. . . .

. . . [T]he presumption of antipathy between Mexican and American cultures has been forged into a more sophisticated technical rhetoric by more recent scholars and bureaucrats, but the notion nonetheless remains. . . . Only in the last two decades, since the resurgence of interest in Mexican-American historical studies, have viewpoints impugning this belief in cultural antipathy been cultivated.

Rodolfo Acuña's book, *Occupied America,* serves as an excellent illustration of the kind of challenge being advanced in the more recent works of Chicano historians. As Acuña sees it, Mexico since the 1870s has been a sort of colony of the United States, and Mexican workers have been transformed into "migrants" by the push and pull of fluctuating labor demands in the powerful American economy. Inconvenient as it may be from the American perspective, the challenging connotations of Acuña's views are self-evident. Less apparent, however, is the lesson in methodology or historiography to be drawn from Acuña's observations. Where earlier approaches explained conditions among immigrants from Mexico in terms of the *internal nature of their culture and personalities,* Acuña explains them in terms of their *relations to American social and economic patterns.* Instead of looking only inside the lifeways of Mexican Americans, Acuña explores the relationships between Mexican-American and Anglo-American behaviors.

This study falls within the fold of the . . . revisionist understanding of the Mexican-American heritage introduced by Acuña and others. Committed to a comparative analysis of the destinies of both Mexican and American immigrants to south Texas, it points to several things that Texas historians have long suspected but neglected to document. Perhaps most important among these is the speculation that "Mexican" workers provided the massive amounts of general and unskilled labor required by the switch to commercial agriculture that eventually sent south Texas into the twentieth-century industrial age. *Inmigrantes* and indigenous Tejanos made up the largest part of the swelling, unspecialized labor pool in south Texas between 1850 and 1900. They supplied work demanding only general skills in large quantities to the agricultural sector and the burgeoning manufacturing and personal service sectors of the regional labor force, while the incoming Anglo-Americans streamed more frequently into the more skill-intensive areas of trade, transportation, and civil service. Corresponding to these differences in the occupational endeavors of the *inmigrantes* and Tejanos on the one hand and the Anglo-American immigrants on the other were inequalities of wealth and living standards.

Though support for long-standing speculation about labor patterns and standards of living in south Texas is important per se, such documentation does not constitute the most significant aspect of this study. Of greater importance is the understanding it makes possible of the sequence of historical events that determined the destinies of Mexicans and Anglos in the former region of Tamaulipas. South Texas, as indicated, was a relatively isolated territory steeped in at least one hundred years of Spanish-Mexican heritage before mid-nineteenth century when immigrants from the United States and Europe first arrived. Its institutional patterns were forged in that heritage, and its people identified with that legacy. In this tradition, the foundations of politics and economy in south Texas rested.

With the coming of Anglo-Americans, however, a veritable revolution in the social structure of the region occurred. The transformation was not so much the product of the Anglo-American influx; whites were, after all, relatively few in number and never comprised a majority of the region's population in the nineteenth century. Rather, it was the military, political, and economic ambitions and traditions pursued by Anglo-American newcomers that created the alteration of society in south Texas. Anglos showed too little regard for the rights and property of Mexicans and Tejanos, and they usurped control of both the political process and the means of production within a decade after their arrival. It was, in effect, a continuing conquest extending the legacy of the Mexican War over the remaining decades of the century.

This confrontation, . . . fostered the rise of an ethnic division of labor and subsequent impoverishment of the *inmigrantes*. For by the 1870s and 1880s Anglos were in a position to reap the benefits of the change to commercial agriculture and to insulate themselves from the transformation's less advantageous effects. The Mexican population, having lost control of the political and economic base in the 1850s and 1860s, became vulnerable to the negative effects of the transition. In comparison to Anglos, Mexicanos found themselves crippled in their ability to secure benefits from the new order. This vulnerability was more the result of displacement of control over crucial economic and political resources at an earlier period than it was from the tyranny of a ruling Anglo-American economic class of the time of the economic transition.

Women on the Texas Frontier

JACQUELINE S. REINIER

Definitions of "domesticity" and "the woman's sphere" in nineteenth-century America have been the subject of recent scholarly scrutiny. Nancy Cott has discovered that prescriptive literature published early in the century described woman's proper "sphere" as the domestic setting where her superior moral influence could restrain the vices of her husband and mold the character of future citizens, her children. Although most areas of public life were closed to nineteenth-century women, their "sphere" did include the church, the schoolroom and the religious or benevolent voluntary association. Katherine Kish Sklar's biography of Catherine Beecher has explained how Beecher elaborated these role definitions and extended them to single women by exalting the American mothers and schoolteachers who would play a special role in transmitting cultural values to the rapidly expanding Western frontier. Anne Firor Scott has demonstrated how the institution of slavery made acceptance of "woman's sphere" particularly urgent for Southern women. During and after the Civil War, Southern women were forced by necessity to extend their "sphere" beyond the domestic setting; some worked for wages, some enjoyed widened opportunities for education, and others participated actively in women's clubs and organizations. Nevertheless, even those who advocated female suffrage did not significantly challenge nineteenth-century definitions of femininity, arguing that women could use the vote to enhance their role as wives, mothers, and the nation's moral guardians.

Recent studies in women's history have investigated whether emigrating nineteenth-century women followed, altered, or abandoned these definitions of "woman's sphere" under the pressures of migrating and building new homes on the

Jacqueline S. Reinier, "Concepts of Domesticity on the Southern Plains Agricultural Frontier, 1870–1920," in *At Home on the Range: Essays on the History of Western Social and Domestic Life.* (Westport, CT: Greenwood Press, 1985), 57–68. Copyright © 1985 by John R. Wunder. Abridged and reprinted with permission.

frontier. In his study of midwestern farm families who crossed the plains on the Overland Trail to the Pacific Northwest, John Mack Faragher described "woman's sphere" in the rural setting, suggesting that feminine ideology that filtered into the Midwest essentially reinforced traditional agricultural sex roles and division of labor. Even on the trail, he found that sex roles did not change but were transferred to the new agricultural environment. . . .

Other historians, however, have suggested that the experience of women who settled the Great Plains might present a special case. Some time ago, Walter Prescott Webb argued that settlers who ventured into the "level, timberless, and semiarid" region west of the ninety-eighth meridian "were thrown by Mother Necessity into the clutch of new circumstances." Women, he conjectured, who left the humid regions they had known and were forced to cope with the isolation of the vast, empty prairie, the lack of wood and water, and problems caused by excessive dust and wind, found the Plains "peculiarly appalling." Mary Hargreaves has emphasized the loneliness and the domestic hardship experienced by women who settled the northern plains. And, disagreeing with the conclusions of Faragher and Jeffery, Christine Stansill has argued that plains women, who lived in sod huts and dugouts and lacked cultural supports, "failed to reinstate their own sphere" because of "the duration as well as the severity of cultural disruption" that they experienced. . . .

This case study is based on materials left by forty women who participated in the agriculturalization of one of the United States' later frontiers, the high Southern plains. It seeks to examine whether this plains environment did so disrupt the lives of women that they found establishment of conventional female culture especially difficult. These forty women lived in twenty-five Texas and three New Mexico counties which constitute a level, treeless, semi-arid plains region that the Spanish labeled the Llano Estacado. They were born or arrived during the years when this last frontier was being settled, largely between 1880 and 1910. Only two of the forty women migrated in the late 1870s; ten arrived in the 1880s, eight in the 1890s, eleven in the first decade of the twentieth century, and only one after 1910. Although their birthdates ranged from 1840 to 1903, most of the women were born between 1860 and 1890, with the largest number of their birthdates clustered between 1869 and 1878. Three of the women were born in Europe, three in the northeastern United States, and three in neighboring plains states; but most of them, the remaining thirty-one, came from east or central Texas, the border states, or the South.

Twenty-one of the women were wives and daughters in what could be called "ranching" families; their husbands or fathers were owners of large or small ranches or workers in the cattle industry. Ten of these "ranching" women married cowboys. Eleven of the forty were wives and daughters of "homesteaders"; two briefly had been homesteaders themselves before they married. These families generally engaged in a combination of stock farming and production of a small cotton crop. The remaining eight women best could described as "townswomen"; their husbands or fathers were merchants, lawyers, judges, or town founders.

Eight of the forty women were born in or set up housekeeping in a dugout, and only one, from Kansas, in a sod house. After an initial period of living in either a tent or a covered wagon, the rest of them lived in wooden houses of one or two rooms. Several of them were educated; five had been schoolteachers and one had been a governess. Of the forty, only one never married and only three gave up pioneering on the southern plains and returned "home." Unfortunately, the sources do not provide enough information to determine numbers of children and their birth intervals.

The experience of these forty pioneer women certainly was influenced by the plains environment they sought to settle. Once they climbed the escarpment of the Llano Estacado, they encountered a vast, empty grassland, with few rivers, sparse rainfall, and almost no trees, that was swept by hot dry winds in summer, blizzards in winter, and dust storms in the spring. However, this late frontier was opened when Eastern technology already was well advanced. By the late 1880s, railroads reached Amarillo in the north, and Colorado City in the south; many of these pioneering families began their trek west by rail. Technology could provide not only barbed wire and windmills, but also canned goods and sewing machines. Families could order manufactured items from mail-order catalogues. By 1910, the automobile brought relief from rural isolation. Mary Perritt Blankenship arrived in Hockley County in 1902; ten years later her life changed dramatically when her family purchased their first Ford. By 1910, the "frontier" period was essentially over in West Texas, although it lingered into the 1920's in eastern New Mexico. These forty women, then, were pioneers under unique circumstances. Largely of Southern background, they attempted to build homes under the difficult conditions created by a plains environment, at a late date when industrialization was of some help.

Southern plains women worked long and hard to recreate in their new homes the values of the particular cultural setting in which they had been socialized. Technology aided them, when they could make use of it, and temporary modifications were made to cope with the plains environment. The better educated pioneer women tended to focus on their role as educators rather than as experts in domestic production. One of the three women from the northeastern United States made a deliberate and conscious attempt to transplant northeastern feminine ideology. Margaret Adams McCollum Mooar was born in New York state and, according to her daughter, Lydia Louise, was "a highly educated lady both academically and musically" before she married John W. Mooar, a buffalo hunter who settled down to become a prominent rancher in Scurry County.

Margaret Mooar chose to spend much of her time at her town home in Colorado City, Mitchell County, where she became an active club woman. In 1892, she helped organize the "Up-to-Date History Club", which attempted to keep abreast of national issues concerning women. Members of the Up-to-Date Club were proud of being the first federated women's club in West Texas. They felt their spirits ennobled by their plains environment, those "vast prairies . . . in whose lap this child club of the West has been rocked and nourished—broadminded, full souled, big and generous hearted." Euphemistically, they considered themselves "as active in body, mind, and soul as the gentle zephyrs" that blew through their West Texas town. Catherine Beecher would have lauded Mooar's civic emphasis on molding citizens through motherhood rather than seeking the vote: "In this day when we hear so much of woman's sphere," wrote Mooar, "let us not forget that it is eminently her [concern] to teach her sons and daughters to be patriots." Members of the Up-to-Date Club gave reports on English and American history, on activities of the Texas Federation of Women's Clubs, and on eminent nineteenth-century women such as Margaret Fuller. On George Washington's birthday, they dressed up in colonial costumes and made speeches praising Washington's mother whose good influence clearly had molded his noble character.

Although less up-to-date on northeastern feminine ideology, West Texas pioneer women born in Europe worked as diligently to transmit learned cultural values to their new homes. Constance Aldous arrived from England in 1901 with a side saddle, a Singer sewing machine, and a tin bathtub, to keep house for her brother who had been herding sheep in Collingsworth County since 1887. A year later, she married a second English sheep herder, Albert Manby, fourteen years her junior. Constance Aldous Manby was a well-educated English "lady" who learned her limited domestic skills from her new husband. Throughout her years on their Elm Creek cattle ranch, she endeavored to instruct her only daughter, Mary, in English culture and values. In 1911, a governess came from England to occupy Mary with mornings of rigorous lessons and afternoons of reading and needlework. When this first teacher went to Canada to marry a cowboy in 1913, a replacement was quickly sent for from England.

Juliana McGregor, born in Munich, came to live on her American husband's Haskell County ranch in 1904. Dismayed by the hot, dry West Texas environment, she sought to beautify it according to European standards. Her daughter commented: "Julie so loved things to be pretty that she took a wheelbarrow down into the canyons where she gathered up the lace-like white caliche rocks and built 'rockeries' in which she planted flowers so that they looked like fountains. She also lined the walk-ways around the house with the rocks and made flower beds. . . . She drew the well dry, bucketfull by bucketfull [sic] carrying water to her garden."

Educated women of Southern and border state background, although less conscious than Margaret Mooar of feminine ideology, also worked diligently to transmit learned cultural values, especially to their children. Mollie Wylie Abernathy came to Lubbock County in 1902 with her husband, James Jarrott, who sought to settle twenty-five families on a strip of land missed in the early surveys. After Jarrott's murder by a paid assassin, Mollie stayed, living on her four sections of land, eventually increasing them to eighteen, and building a thriving cattle ranch. Mollie's strength was not in domestic skills: "I never did any hard house work," she said, "I never did wash and iron, scrub and scour, but I cooked a little bit." Nevertheless, she prided herself on providing an education for her three children. Although not a Catholic, she sent them to a convent school in Stanton, Texas. "It was the nearest place I could find that would take my children and take care of them," she said; "they stayed there four years and they got wonderful training and a fine start in school." Mollie had attended Add-Ran College near Fort Worth; "I come from an educated place," she declared, and "I educated my children."

After her marriage to Monroe Abernathy in 1905, Mollie lived part-time in the town of Lubbock where she became an active businesswoman in real estate and development, and a charter member of Lubbock's Business and Professional Women's Club. Like most of the forty women, she favored prohibition, but was unusual not only in her business career, but also in her advocacy of female suffrage. Her support of her beliefs neatly summarized the entire nineteenth- and early twentieth-century suffrage argument: "I was born a suffrager and almost a prohibitionist," she said. "When we were born, we were born equal. Women got as much sense as men. May not be the same kind, but its usually a better kind." And she acted on her views by organizing Lubbock chapters of the Women's Christian Temperance Union, and later, the League of Women Voters.

Other educated women born in Southern and border states also saw themselves essentially as educators. Texas-born Margaret Collins had been trained in a New York City conservatory of music. Shortly after she came to Cochran County as a governess at the Byrd Bar N Bar Ranch in 1905, she met and married Hiley T. Boyd, foreman on the nearby Slaughter Ranch. Her son later commented that single schoolteachers in West Texas generally married cowboys: "I . . . can't remember but one . . . or two at least that ever escaped some cowpuncher for the next twenty years." Margaret Collins Boyd was deeply concerned about the health, diet, and education of her three children in the isolated conditions of their ranch life. She put up hundreds of gallons of canned peaches, cherries, and plums in order that her children would have a proper diet even in drought years. Realizing that she was too busy with domestic chores to educate her children properly herself, she arranged for a "slight tax" in her area, hired and boarded a teacher, and set up a school in her front yard.

Julia Sutton taught school for thirteen years in Oklahoma before she homesteaded as a single woman in Curry County, New Mexico, in 1907. Within a year, she married U. S. Land Commissioner, Thomas Carter. While raising five children and helping with the family's "trading post" after their move to DeBaca County, she organized an interracial, interdenominational Sunday school. Her daughter explained: "Julia always had been a teacher at heart. Here in this even further west location, she extended herself into bringing some form of culture to her community." In her later years, Julia was postmistress of her town and Democratic chairperson of her county while her husband served as Republican county chair.

Yet, what of the southern Plains pioneer women less educated than these fortunate few? What cultural values did they endeavor to transmit? These women were not unlike the midwestern farm women described by John Mack Faragher; although they exhibited scant consciousness of feminine ideology, they were well trained in methods of domestic production and profoundly versed in traditional feminine lore. An excellent example would be Winnie Harris Rush, who carefully described the medical treatments, food processing, soap making, laundry procedures, and cloth production that she had learned during her Arkansas girlhood in the 1890s. Although her mother had a sewing machine, this introduction of technology followed a pattern frequently found in this group of forty women. It was the only such machine in the neighborhood and women came from miles around to use it: "People from all over the country would bring their sewing and sew all day, which was a little irritating. Some would bring their children to run the treadle."

After her father's death in 1909, Winnie, her mother, and her brothers homesteaded in Curry County, New Mexico. The two women valiantly transmitted their rich domestic knowledge to the new environment. On the plains, they made some interesting temporary domestic adaptations. Winnie's mother worked hard to make their dugout more comfortable. She put wagon sheets over joists to create a ceiling, "covered the dirt walls with gunny sacks," and then "papered over that with remnants of wall paper that she had brought along. She brought some cement and plastered the whole floor completely." Winnie later marveled, "it is still a mystery to me where she got all the stuff to work with."

Mrs. Arthur Duncan, one of the first women to come to Floyd County in 1884, lived with her husband and children in an abandoned sheep herder's dugout for seven years. She, too, attempted to make her new home "attractive and livable" by nailing towsacks covered with newspapers to the walls and building a partition that would divide her home into a kitchen and a "bedroom-parlor." She even managed to smile when a steer's leg penetrated the dug-out roof and spoiled the first meal for company she had prepared in three years. When the family moved to a two-room wooden house in Floydada in 1891, Mrs. Duncan was ecstatic: "A queen in all the splendor of her palaces," she said, "could not have glorified in her riches as much as I did in that home."

Other Plains women in the Llano Estacado environment followed a similar pattern, working diligently to transplant domestic values and procedures, yet being forced by circumstances to make temporary adaptations. For example, on the West Texas homestead, the windmill became an important focus for women. Mary Perritt Blankenship, who came to Hockley County in 1902, climbed the windmill tower when her husband was away, hoping for a glimpse of company. She hung a lantern on the windmill to direct her husband home, hung a towel to signal dinner for field hands, used the windmill tank for a cooler for milk, and the tower as a place to hang and dry beef. Before a church was built in her area, baptism took place in the windmill tank. Emma B. Russell was born in a dugout in Dickens County in 1890. Her mother attempted to use the power generated by the windmill to churn butter, attaching the dash of the churn to the windmill rod. She had trouble, however, controlling the wind.

Child care in the plains environment could be difficult for these busy pioneer women, and they evolved ingenious methods to make their task easier. Jane Lowe Quillan came to Hale County in 1888 when she was two. After her mother's death, she was raised by an aunt who insisted that Jane wear a bright red sunbonnet with two holes cut out for her braids so that she could not take it off. Then, whether Jane was in her playhouse by the cow lot or sailing homemade wooden boats in the pond in the pasture, her aunt could climb the windmill tower and spot her. Nanny Jowell came to West Texas with her cattleman husband in 1886 and moved with him from place to place, frequently living in a tent, while he sought pasture land unsettled by homesteaders. Her great worry in caring for her young children was the constant presence of snakes; finally she hit on the solution of using a mule for a babysitter. With her two toddlers high on the mule's back, she could concentrate on her domestic chores. Later, she said, "Old Jen was a dandy. She raised all the kids. That's a fact."

Another woman who practiced traditional domestic skills in an unusual way was Mrs. J. P. McDonald, wife of the foreman of the XIT Ranch, which covered ten counties in northwestern Texas. In 1904, she lived at the ranch headquarters, Las Escarbadas, where she cooked for the cowboys and measured out supplies for the line camps. McDonald was delighted with her domestic arrangements at XIT headquarters; later she commented: "I loved living in that house. It was cool in the summer and warm in the winter. . . . That was the nicest little ranch place that I've ever been in . . . everything was convenient." She lovingly described her 500 chickens, her splendid big black cookstove, her neat bins to keep supplies with the biscuit-rolling board that covered them, and her butter churn on a frame in which she made ten to fifteen pounds of butter a day. The cowboys helped her by clearing the table, and she, too, worked out arrangements for child care. While she cooked, either her husband cared for the children or three-year-old Raymond pulled baby Mary around the ranch yard in a little red wagon. Mrs. McDonald had learned home medical remedies, domestic skills, and methods of maintaining family harmony from her Southern mother-in-law. "We have always had harmony," she said, "I know people can live together without fussing."

These frontier women worked diligently to transmit learned cultural values and methods of domestic production to their new arid environment. Although they discovered ingenious ways of coping with the isolation of the empty prairie, the lack of wood and water, and the weather, their goal was always reestablishment of the conventions of female culture they had known. Although advanced technology was available to them, only a few with sufficient means were able to use it prior to 1910. A sewing machine mentioned in a memoir always was the only one in the county; women came from miles around to share in its use. Canned goods were considered a luxury and were not included in lists of supplies brought by wagon every six months. Some women thought that only cowboys and bachelors used store-bought canned goods; others were convinced that such provisions were unhealthy.

With the exceptions of Mollie Abernathy, businesswoman; Julia Carter, homesteader and postmistress; and Martha Killough Conaway of Mitchell County, who managed the family ranch after her husband's death, these women did not venture from nineteenth-century definitions of "woman's sphere." Although only Margaret Mooar consciously transplanted feminine ideology, most of the women implicitly followed it. Educated women of southern background concentrated on transmitting values and knowledge to children, as mothers and as schoolteachers. Less educated Southern women diligently transplanted their complicated methods of domestic production and their rich medical lore. Only three of the forty women even mentioned female suffrage. Instead of creating new gender definitions, they concentrated on recreating the world they had known. With the men who accompanied them, in a short span of thirty years, defying heat, wind, snakes, and dust storms, they transformed the vast and empty Llano Estacado into an extension of mainstream Anglo-American rural culture.

❧ *F U R T H E R   R E A D I N G*

Armando C. Alonzo, *Tejano Legacy: Rancheros and Settlers in South Texas, 1734–1900* (1998)

T. Lindsay Baker and Billy R. Harrison, *Adobe Walls: The History and Archeology of the 1874 Trading Post* (1986)

Arnoldo De León and Kenneth L. Stewart, *Not Room Enough: Mexicans, Anglos, and Socioeconomic Change in Texas, 1850–1900* (1993)

——, *Tejanos and the Numbers Game: A Socio-Historical Interpretation from the Federal Censuses, 1850–1900* (1989)

Jo Ella Powell Exley, ed., *Texas Tears and Texas Sunshine: Voices of Frontier Women* (1985)

Neil Foley, *The White Scourge: Mexicans, Blacks, and Poor Whites in Texas Cotton Culture* (1997)

Joe S. Graham, *El Rancho in South Texas: Continuity and Change from 1750* (1994)

William T. Hagan, *United States-Comanche Relations: The Reservation Years* (1976)

Theodore D. Harris, ed., *Black Frontiersman: The Memoirs of Henry O. Flipper* (1997)

Jack Jackson, *Los Mesteñeros: Spanish Ranching in Texas, 1721–1821* (1986)

Terry G. Jordan, *North American Cattle Ranching Frontiers* (1993)

Sara R. Massey, ed., *Black Cowboys of Texas* (2000)

Sandra Meyers, *Westering Women and the Frontier Experience* (1982)

Sandra L. Myres, ed., *Cavalry Wife: The Diary of Eveline M. Alexander, 1866–1867* (1977)

Charles M. Robinson, III, *Satanta: The Life and Death of a War Chief* (1998)

Robert Wooster, "The Army and the Politics of Expansion: Texas and the Southwestern Borderlands, 1870–1886, *"Southwestern Historical Quarterly* 93 (1989): 151–167

———, *Soldiers, Sulters, and Settlers: Garrison Life on the Texas Frontier* (1987)

CHAPTER

11

Suffrage and Beyond:

Texas Women and Reform,

1885–1925

During the last decade of the nineteenth century and the first two decades of the
twentieth century, social, political, and economic reform movements addressed
the problems that Texans confronted as the state moved from a frontier, agricultural society to an urban, industrial one. The immediate political result of these
reform movements brought an end to the series of conservative Democratic administrations that had controlled Texas government since the end of Reconstruction.
Discontent and protest among the rural population led to organizations such as
the Grange and the Greenback party in the 1870s. By the late 1880s the Farmers'
Alliance had become the primary vehicle for agrarian protest. The election of
James Stephen Hogg in 1890 and the emergence of the People's party (or the
Populist party) reflected the strength of reform sentiment. In the mid-1890s the
Farmers Alliance and populism gave way to the progressive movement. While
progressives in Texas were still deeply rooted in the issues of rural communities,
they also addressed the issues of the rapidly growing urban communities. Issues
such as good government, increased social services, regulation of child labor and
women's labor, and prison reform, were added to the earlier agenda of regulation
of big business and the railroads, extension of democracy, and banking and currency reform. Reformers from both movements addressed the issues of women's
suffrage and prohibition.

One aspect of the reform movements of the late-nineteenth and early twentieth
centuries was the increasing role of women both in reform movements and in politics.
The role of women in the Texas reform process is complex. Women undoubtedly
supported reform—especially when it addressed moral issues such as prohibition or
issues related to traditional women's concerns, such as education and the welfare of
children. The extent to which Texas women pushed into mainstream reform issues,
even the extent of the suffrage movement in Texas, are more complex issues. In the
past three decades historians have developed a deeper understanding of the role

*women played in these movements. At the national level women unquestionably
were active in, and occasionally in the forefront of, the agrarian unrest that
preceded the Populist uprising. Women's organizations also played a major role
in defining the social agenda of the progressive movement, and without question
women took the leadership in the crusades for prohibition and women's suffrage.
What is less clear is the role that women played in reform at the local level. Specific
questions remain about the relationship of women to reform movements. How
effectively did they function within male-dominated organizations? What was the
impact of women's clubs and other women's organizations? What were the origins
and the impact of the suffrage movement in Texas?*

🔖 D O C U M E N T S

The Farmers' Alliance and its journal, the *Southern Mercury*, introduced many Texas
women to the political arena. Document 1 is an example of the correspondence that
filled this journal during the late 1880s. This letter to the *Mercury* from Ann Other
of Ennis, Texas, illustrates the growing concern of these women with the suffrage
issue. The next three documents reveal the importance of the women's clubs. Document 2 is a poem about the virtues and utility of "The Club" that appeared *The Club
Monthly* of Tyler, Texas in 1897. In Document 3, Pauline Periwinkle (Isadore Miner
Callaway) uses her column in the *Dallas Morning News* to encourage the transformation of women's clubs from social clubs to organizations for civic improvement and reform. Calloway transformed her newspaper column from one devoted to
fashion to one that advocated political and social activism. She also was active in the
suffrage movement and in other women's political causes. Document 4 describes the
involvement of the Texas division of the General Federation of Women's Clubs in
environmental work. By 1914 women had transformed their clubs into effective
forces for reform.

Eventually the struggle for suffrage overshadowed all other women's reform
issues. The next four documents trace the final stage of the struggle for the right to
vote, and also illustrate the political sophistication of the suffrage movement and
the connection of suffrage to other political issues. In Document 5, Texas suffrage
organizer Jane McCallum describes a detour in the suffrage campaign—the rally for
the impeachment of Governor James Ferguson, an absolute opponent of women's
suffrage. Following Ferguson's impeachment, women achieved a partial victory in
their campaign when Texas allowed women to vote in primary elections. By the
early twentieth century, Mrs. Percy V. Pennybacker, founder of the Tyler Women's
Club in 1894, had become active in the women's club and suffrage movement at
both the state and national levels. In Document 6 she lobbies fellow Texan, Colonel
Edward M. House, a key advisor in the Wilson White House, on the political implications of loosing the vote in Congress for the suffrage amendment. In Document 7
she explains to national suffrage leader Carrie Chapman Catt the danger to the suffrage movement of ex-Governor Ferguson's efforts to resurrect his political career.
In this letter to Catt and again in Document 8 from fellow Texas suffragist Minnie
Fisher Cunningham, Pennybacker begins planning for political activity in the post-
suffrage era.

1. Texas Pioneer Ann Other Describes Women's Political Interests in the Farmer's Revolt, 1888

May 31, 1888. Ennis, Texas. Ann Other.

EDITOR MERCURY: As we are searching for facts on this subject, and I sincerely believe that none of us are writing for argument's sake, let us look candidly on the matter and sift each point, and try to give fair and unprejudiced opinion on the arguments. . . . Now, Sister Rebeca . . .

You class the decline of patriotism with the rise of the popularity of universal suffrage and "woman neglecting her duty in her proper sphere." Now will someone kindly tell me what is her proper sphere? I have always heard the expression, but have failed to locate it by any series of studies I have taken up. I am obliged to conclude it is whatever the state of society dictates to her.

Men have intruded and wrestled from her what were formerly her legitimate occupations. And her present effort is only to recover a useful sphere in life by those who have become weary for others to do that which God intended she should do for herself.

Women used to be our bakers, brewers, dry-salters, butter-makers, cooks, dressmakers, cheese-makers, confectioners, jam and jelly makers, pickle makers, soap makers, spinners, weavers, sock makers, lace makers, embroiders, and midwives. Thus crowded out of her old fields of labor by men's intrusion and invention, she must either accept a life of idleness, and be satisfied with such as her brothers see proper to give her, or she must demand a more useful and energetic life. The woman in idleness naturally loses the bright vigor of her mind, and a "scheming mama" must look for an "eligible partie" for her daughters, for society in its present state has so limited her sphere of usefulness in life that there is nothing left for her to do but marry, and the mother knowing there is no comfort or happiness in the married life without an eligible partie, naturally aspires to that.

But when society becomes enough advanced in marking the bounds of woman's sphere to give her the untrammeled right to write her name as high on the book of fame in any sphere her tastes dictate, as her brothers, then we will see mothers having higher aspirations for their daughters than marriage only as it may come by the dictates of their own lofty sentiments.

Yes, I am aware that the W.C.T.U. has the suffrage plank a movable plank, but when our leaders are boldly advocating it, what effect will those who cling to their shirts and cry against it have but to slightly impede its progress in that one direction?

Have you not seen Frances E. Willard's address before the senate committee? For fear you have not, I will quote a little from it: "I suppose these honorable gentlemen think that we women want the earth, when we only want one half of it. Our brethren have encroached upon the sphere of women. They have very definitely marked out that sphere and then they have proceeded with their incursions by the power of invention, so that we women, full of vigor and full of desire to be active

Ann Other, Ennis, Texas, letter to the *Southern Mercury,* May 31, 1888, in *Women in the Texas Populist Movement: Letters to the Southern Mercury* (College Station: Texas A&M University Press, 1997); 108–111.

and useful and to react upon the world around us, finding our industries largely gone, have been obliged to seek out new territory and to preempt from the sphere of our brothers, as it was popularly supposed to be, some of the territory that they have hitherto considered their own. So we think it will be very desirable indeed that you should let us lend a hand in their affairs of government." It is said that if women are given the right to vote, it will prevent their being womanly; how it is a sentiment of chivalry in some good men that hinders them from giving us the ballot. They think we should not be lacking in womanliness of character, which we most certainly wish to preserve but we believe that history proves they have retained that womanliness, and if we can only make men believe that, the ballot will just come along sailing like a ship with the wind beating every sail.

Again see her [Willard's] letter in *Union Signal* to the Kansas women urging them to let no false modesty keep them from registering and voting, as now the eyes of the world were upon them, to see if women would exercise the right of franchise if they had it.

"It is inconceivable to me why some women, simply because they do not wish to vote, should clamor so loud against giving the right to those who do, as there would be nothing compelling any to vote who did not think they could benefit the laws by doing so."

You "fear that men will lose their respect for women who assemble with them at the ballot box." Now I think those men who could think less of a woman because she took a judicious interest in the laws of her country would not be worth the while to mourn over; whether they respected her or not they would be obliged to respect her laws. When you hear men talking of women losing men's esteem by using the highest and most sacred right of an American citizen, you can rest assured that his esteem is not worth having. . . . If you are obliged to associate with all whom you meet at the polls, do not go there, for your soul is just as liable to be contaminated as mine.

I have written these few thoughts from a sick-bed. I do not think anyone can do justice to their subject when the physical machinery is out of repair but I do hope you will candidly consider the few thoughts I have tried to sketch out for you. Your loving friend,

2. Tyler Women's Club Presents the Virtues of the Club in a Poem from *The Club Monthly,* 1897

The Club

[With apologies to Edgar Allen Poe and everyone else]

> Hear the kick against "the club"
> Literary club:
> For solid information I guess it is the "hub."

"The Club," in *The Club Monthly,* published by a Tyler, Texas women's club for the new Texas Federation of Women's Clubs 1 (November 1897): 15 in Austin American History Club Papers, Austin History Collection, Austin Public Library.

How they study, study, study,
Intricacies of the day!
How the mind so strong and ruddy,
Clears the stream that's deep and muddy,
Fades the mysteries all away:
Like a dream, dream, dream.
Like a sudden spurt
From a teapot on the table just before you eat
    your grub,
Is the club, club, club,
Club, club, club,
When you're yearning for learning, see the club.

Hear the literary club,
Woman's club:
The men are quite forgot—and "there's the rub"
'Till the balmy air of night,
They must rock the cradle quiet,
They must pay two promised notes
    Very soon.
And unless a woman votes,
The world will go to thunder—and she dotes
    On the moon,
Oh, that man could take a club
And fight forbidden usage—compel his wife to rub!
And to scrub
For her grub
Then the erstwhile "dearest hub"
Would be called Beelzebub,
For the bringing and the swinging
    Of the club, club, club,
Of the club, club, club, club,
Club, club, club.
For the buying and applying of the "club."

"There are others"—
Real Clubs,
And the women call them wicked, with
    irreverential "dubs"
In the silent of the night
These clubs are "out-er-sight."
But they take the Men away—that is wrong:
His place, you know, is Home—
But a Woman, she can roam.
Doing "clubwork"—off a clubbing all
    day long.

3. Newspaper Columnist Pauline Periwinkle Celebrates Transforming Social Clubs into Civic Reform Organizations, 1904

It almost takes one's breath to contemplate the evolution of the Texas federation. Seven years ago the word "culture" comprehended its broadest meaning, and a book was its symbol. One would imagine that society had no ailment, spiritual or moral, that could not be relieved by a good strong dose of culture, administered in book capsule. Dooley's vision of Carnegie handing out a library to a starving man on his back doorstep, would have served as a pen-portrait of the club idea. Do you remember the "yard of roses," "yard of pansies," et al.—those popular gift lithographs that once cemented the friendship of women for their favorite journal? Well, the papers read at those old-time club occasions were like that—sentimentally rounded periods interspersed with flowery quotations, and set in formal rows, a yard, yes, two or more tiresome yards in length.

Now the federation counts its philanthropies by the scores—libraries and scholarships, kindergartens and civic betterment, music and art for the enjoyment of those unable to supply their own. Aesthetic science, patriotic endeavor, work for home and schools, and for that unfortunate element that has known the influences of neither good homes nor schools. The federation has awakened to the fact that the progress of the world does not depend on the acquirement of a little more culture on the part of a limited number of fairly well-educated women, but on the amount of leavening those women are enabled to impart to the masses.

As for prosy papers and flowery reports, the convention will have none of them. "Cut the papers and give the time to discussion" is the cry. When the presiding officer of the northeastern division presented the work for her division, the federation listened with eager attention to a concise statement of what each club in the district had accomplished, and I could but recall the listless interest once exhibited in the long, rambling reports that evaded the issue in the attempt to achieve literary distinction. And whereas great stress was always laid on the social side of club gatherings, one long instance of where "eatables and wearables" got the best of "thinkables and doables" raised a smile of toleration. Verily, we are coming on.

4. Mrs. R. W. Simpson, Chairman of the Texas General Federation of Women's Clubs, Presents the Federation's Environmental Agenda, 1914

The aim of the department representing the conservation of our national resources, has been to include forests, waters, birds, soils, ores, and minerals and the vital resources.

During the past two years the committee has tried to leave no stone unturned that would impress upon the people of Texas the importance of this great question. Personally, beside sending telegrams and writing letters, I have addressed 1400

Pauline Periwinkle [Isadore Miner Callaway], *Dallas Morning News,* November 28, 1904 in *Pauline Periwinkle and Progressive Reform in Dallas* (College Station: Texas A&M University Press, 1998), 73–74.

General Federation of Women's Clubs, Reports of State Chairmen of Conservation, 1912–1914: Texas: 54–57. Center for American History, University of Texas (2L505).

circular letters, including a few postcards, each letter containing condensed leaflets and other enclosures. . . .

While the inspiration of our state convention of 1912 at Fort Worth was still warm in the hearts of Texas women, a hasty call to arms came from our beloved National Conservation Chairman, Mrs. Crocker. Preparations were being made by a clique of politicians, representing selfish interests, to introduce into Congress bills under the guise of "States rights," which asked that the Federal government turn over to state control parts of our national forests. At once, the efforts of our committee were directed to prove that if such bills should pass, the whole system of conservation would be weakened and the national forests themselves would soon be frittered away; that the functions and uses of the forest extend far beyond state lines and involve the welfare of many people exterior of the state, for often they cover the headwaters of streams in one state, thus protecting the riverflow in another. . . . Circular letters, with resolution models, protesting against these measures, were mailed to every club in Texas, requesting that copies of these resolutions be sent to our representatives in congress. . . . We felt assured that we merited some credit in the battle that caused the authors of this proposed legislation to back down.

Requests were mailed to all clubs in the state to observe Arbor Day. Arbor Day programs, including birds and waterways as well as forestry and tree-planting, were sent to clubs requesting them. . . . Members of the legislature were interested in the project of introducing a bill to arrange the date of Arbor Day to suit the varied climate of our state. . . .

When the summons came to me from Mrs. Crocker to work for the revision of Schedule N so that it would mean protection to the birds all over the country, letters earnestly beseeching this revision were at once rushed to Washington to our representatives on the Ways and Means Committee. I also wrote to Hon. Oscar W. Underwood of Alabama, chairman of the committee; his courteous reply was reassuring. . . . After Schedule N was revised as conservationists desired, your chairman wrote to every Texas congressman asking that they use their influence to keep the desired revision, because it was loudly whispered that the National Millinery Association was preparing to have it stricken out. After the battle was won, we were happy to think of the memorable hour which soon afterward came, when President Wilson placed his signature to the new tariff bill.

There is a steady interest among children in the building of Jenny Wren bungalows, a pattern of which I sent to all Texas clubs last year, for the winter protection of birds. Pilot Point school children constructed fifty bungalows at one time. . . .

From the first our plea for cooperation has been given hearty response from Texas club women. Some have adopted a study course on national forest reservation and all other phases of conservation. Many clubs have placed conservation programs in yearbooks. Local conservation committees write articles for their city newspapers and report conservation items monthly to their respective clubs. School faculties have been asked that children be taught the importance of conservation. . . .

Resolutions urging that beautiful Palo Duro Canyon in the Texas Panhandle become a national park, endorsing the Lever Agricultural Bill, praising the action of custom officials in enforcing the new Federal law in regard to plumage and pleading for the protection of Hetch Hetchy, offered by this committee, have been adopted by the State Federation. . . .

In the controversy over Hetch Hetchy, Texas women worked valiantly to aid in preserving the natural beauty of this wonderful valley. I telegraphed to Senators Sheppard and Culberson asking them to vote against granting the valley to San Francisco for a reservoir. Pleas were mailed to every Texas club to write letters of protest to Washington and numerous were the letters thus sent from Texas women. Resolutions of protest were sent from the San Antonio City Federation. Similar resolutions and telegrams went from our state convention to the two senators and to President Wilson. This fight, though lost, leaves an influence gratifying to all conservationists.

The three hundred and fifty circular letters which our committee sent to Texas clubs in October, 1913, were accompanied by the same number of forest-fire circulars, showing how the careless tossing of a match or cigarette into a forest begins a flame which not only destroys all young trees and wild flowers, nuts, berries, and fruits, but all the wee birds in their nests and all young animal life.

The people of Texas have resources of enormous value in fruits and nuts, which should be planted along our highways emphasizing the growth of the already famous Texas pecan.

At the November state convention at Corpus Christi, 1913, I requested that the pecan tree be adopted as the Texas Federation Tree, to be planted henceforth at our annual meetings. . . .

We also urge the sowing of flower seeds along our watercourses and by the highways. This would add a glow of beauty, even to Nature's profusion of blossoms in Texas, where the blue bonnets grow.

5. Texas Suffrage Organizer Jane Y. McCallum Describes the Impeachment Rally Against James Ferguson, July 28, 1917

Friends of higher education rushed to the capital city in response to the clarion call. Ferguson looked to rural residents for his chief support. In the midst of preliminaries to the legislative session called for "impeachment purposes," a "Farmer's Institute" attended by over two thousand farmers and their families assembled in the capitol.

The times were very exciting. In addition to the residential population, there were the senators and representatives, members of the tribunal before which the offending governor would have to give an account of his stewardship; hot-headed University students milling about, and kept in bounds only by calmer ex-students gathered in Austin by the hundreds . . . —and everywhere . . . were towering figures, shod with cowboy boots, covered with "Texas Stetson," and armed with honest-to-goodness guns. They were Texas rangers; said to have been summoned by the governor from the border and the "badlands" for his "protection."

In the midst of this perfervid, chaotic situation, women, who were friends of the State University and not particularly sympathetic toward the gentleman whose record was up for discussion, decided to take a hand.

Led by their State president, Mrs. Minnie Fisher Cunningham, the members of the Equal Suffrage Association had during preceding years built up a State-wide

Jane Y. McCallum, "A Texas Suffragist" in *Texas Democracy,* 474–476. Reprinted in Janet G. Humphrey, ed., *A Texas Suffragist: Diaries and Writings of Jane Y. McCallum* (Austin: Ellen C. Temple, 1988), 89–91.

organization which was a marvel of efficiency. Ferguson probably had another name for it, in the light of later events and the remark of the expert stage-driver that "a fly is a fly, and a leaf is a leaf, but a hornet's nest is an organization." By whatever name, this machine, which included in its files the background of every lawmaker in the State capital, was brought to Austin and placed at the disposal of the committee, along with the services of a Woman's Committee.

"If only we might have an opportunity of placing the facts before the farmers they would never support Ferguson," was the committee's cry when the Farmers' Institute referred to was assembling.

It was when they were denied this opportunity, after announcement that "Farmer Jim" would address the farmers, that an ingenious method was devised by the women political leaders, joined by women patriotic organization leaders, of placing the facts before the public, especially the farmers whom Ferguson was using all of his wits to prejudice against their State school. . . .

When morning dawned of the day "Farmer (?) Jim" was to address the Institute in the afternoon, early arrivals on Congress Avenue at 13th Street stared in wonderment. They rubbed their eyes and looked again. *"Women of Texas Protest."* It was no optical illusion. There it loomed on the corner of the city's main thoroughfare, right in front of the capital grounds and flanked on the West by a State Park.

The words blazed from two orange colored banners, eight feet long, that were attached to scaffolding on either side of a large dray, further embellished with orange and white bunting, colors of Texas University.

Continued observation disclosed a unique procedure: without intermission except for brief introductions by a feminine presiding officer, one man and woman after another climbed on the dray and made a speech; not perfunctory talks, but addresses that were earnest, able, and in many instances impassioned. . . .

The gathering crowds pushed nearer to within sound of the voices of the speakers in their eagerness to learn what it was all about. They were not kept in doubt. . . . The farmers got the facts, and the crowd[,] because [the surrounding streets were] so dense with traffic[,] was blocked despite the commodious park to the side, and the "continuous protest" had to cease long enough to adjourn to the city's largest park where shortly before midnight it came to a rousing close with a speech by "fighting Bob Shuler," the well-known Methodist evangelist.

6. Mrs. Percy V. Pennybacker, Texas Suffrage Organizer, Writes About Political Implications of Losing the Suffrage Amendment in Congress, 1918

January 31st, 1918.

Dear Mr. House:–

For the good of the cause, may I take a few moments of your time?

I returned last night from Washington. While there, in a conference with Mrs. Carrie Chapman Catt, she told me that there was special need of making sure of

Mrs. Percy V. Pennybacker to Edward M. House, January 31, 1918. Center for American History, University of Texas (2M12).

Senator Culberson on the question of the Federal Amendment for Suffrage. Remembering the great influence of Mrs. Culberson over her husband, as I was to lunch with her the next day, I promised Mrs. Catt to ascertain how Mrs. Culberson stood. To my delight, I found that she was unequivocally in favor of Woman Suffrage, but was a bit uneasy as to the effect of the negro women as to suffrage and the Federal Amendment. I tried as best I could to show her how to-day the suffrage question was a war measure and how the vote of the negro woman was no more to be feared than the vote of the negro man. Aside from my earnest desire to see justice done us by means of the Federal Amendment, I am made each day more cognisant of the danger to our Democratic Party if this Amendment fails to pass, owing to the opposition of Democratic Senators. During the last two weeks I have heard from at least twenty sources, of work that is being socially done by Republican leaders to imbue the mind of women all over the country with the fact that if the Amendment is defeated, it will be the Democrats who defeat it. I can but feel that a word from you to Senator Culberson would bring about the result for which thousands and thousands of women are earnestly praying. Mrs. Catt spoke with deep appreciation of the attitude you and Mrs. House held towards the Suffrage Cause.

Apropos of the work of our Republican friends, I happened to learn a few days ago that certain Republican leaders are watching closely as to the reappointment of certain high naval and military officers. A group was discussing the reappointment of Gen. George Barnett, Commandant of the Marine Corps. It was universally conceded that his ability was beyond all question and that he was especially needed in his present position during these times of danger. The point was made that if the Secretary of the Navy should fail to reappoint him, it would throw superb campaign materials for the Republicans. Knowing what happened four years ago, I am venturing to call this matter to your attention in the hope that even in the midst of your busy life, you will find time to see about to it that the man who has so eminently filled the position as Commandant be continued in his post.

> With kindest regards to you and Mrs. House, I am,
> Ever cordially yours.

7. Mrs. Percy V. Pennybacker Explains the Dangers of Fergusonism to the Suffrage Movement, 1918

June 13th, 1918

Dear Mrs. Catt:

It seems a crime to ask your time to read a single letter, but this matter is urgent and so I must ask your indulgence.

Texas has never been in a more critical position. Mr. Ferguson and his cohorts are waging a most vigorous campaign and while you and I cannot realize how sane, sensible people can dream of supporting him, yet he has succeeded, by his half-truths

Mrs. Percy V. Pennybacker to Carrie Chapman Catt, June 13, 1918. Center for American History, University of Texas (2M12).

and whole falsehoods in arousing such bitter class, and town versus country prejudice, that there is no telling what the results may be. If he is elected his candidates
for the Legislature and his candidates for the Supreme Court will also be elected.
This will mean the repeal of the Primary Suffrage law. Mrs. Cunningham wisely
feels that the State Suffrage Assn. cannot work under any party name, but the Texas
suffragists are organizing "Good Government Clubs" over the State and getting in
excellent work. Really, however,—and here is the crux of the situation—we are
sadly hampered by lack of means. We came near losing Mrs. Cunningham as President at the State meeting in Austin. One of the main reasons was the fact that the
load of finances has always been laid upon her shoulders; that she has had to give as
security her own personal property. The Association was in debt $2700.00. Some
of us pledged ourselves to raise this indebtedness but this leaves Mrs. Cunningham
with virtually nothing for expenses and you know the work she is capable of doing
cannot be performed without money.

Now since the suffrage cause is in jeopardy, could you, as President of the
Leslie Commission, help out? I believe it is true that few states have ever financed
a suffrage campaign without some outside assistance. Were we to lose Mrs. Cunningham, I would look upon it as a calamity. Unless some definite budget can be
offered her there is no telling what may happen. Please let me hear from you as
soon as possible.

Your telegram was most welcome. Mr. Baster had written that he was hoping
to secure you for Saturday, July 20th. If you are engaged from Saturday, I am hoping that you could come the day before so we could have the privilege of you and
Dr. Shaw sharing the Women's Club hour and giving us the greatest session we
have ever had in all the history of the Club.

Ever yours,

8. Suffragist Minnie Fisher Cunningham
Begins Planning Political Activity in
Texas in the Postsuffrage Era, 1918

July 4, 1918.

My Dear Mrs. Pennybacker:

Yours of the 29th of June, with enclosures, to hand. Since you are so good as
to ask me to make suggestions, I offer a very radical one for the Club program. It is
that they take the book, "The Brewers and Texas Politics" as their text and around
it "gather current articles and thus make it very present day and practical." Such a
course of study adopted by the clubwomen if this state could and would revolution-
ize conditions in Texas, now that the women have the vote as a safe and sane
method of making their information effective. And there are a number of available

Minnie Fisher Cunningham to Mrs. Percy V. Pennybacker, July 4, 1918. Center for American History,
University of Texas (2M12).

lecturers who could supplement the book work, Gen. M. M. Crane, for instance. You, of course, realize that to have the vote is not enough if good men continue to refuse to stand for election to office, and corrupt men continue to wield the power and influence of the party machinery. We are going to have to devise some way of changing this situation, and letting the light of publicity in on it is at least a step in that direction. I feel quite certain that it would strike horror to the hearts of our friend, the enemy, if they knew the women were sitting down in cold blood to ex- amine into their past record and study the conditions which permitted them to flourish and grow fat off the state's resources, with a view to "doing something about it." Cannot you put some such idea before the State Federation convention this fall and get a state program adopted?

Mrs Bass's letter is interesting. . . . I was especially interested to learn that in none of the Suffrage states, except Colorado, have the women really been taken into the party organization. You know, I am opposed to the separate organi- zation plan, and hope to see the women of Texas go right into our Democratic party organization and "take over as a war measure" a reasonable number of party offices and a reasonable proportion of party power; only so can we be ad- vised as to the machinations within the party, and only so can we hope to defeat them, as I see it. . . .

Very truly yours,
Minnie Fisher Cunningham
President.

✦ E S S A Y S

The Farmers' Alliance, initially organized in Texas in 1875, evolved into the most important national voice of agrarian discontent in the late 1880s and was instrumental in the organization of the Populist party in 1892. Women played an important role in the movement, first by encouraging the involvement of their husbands, but more significantly as members in their own right with their own perspective on the reform program. Marion Barthelme, a journalist, historian, and independent scholar from Houston, documents the evolution of the political agenda of these women through the letters they wrote to the *Southern Mercury*, the official organ of the Farmers' Alliance. Through this outlet, a community of women emerged who developed a sophisticated analysis of the economic and political issues confronting the farmer. They also expanded their sense of the role of women in addressing these problems.

Following the collapse of the Farmers' Alliance and the Populist party in the mid-1890s, progressive reformers defined reform politics in Texas. Although many of the issues they addressed reflected the continued dominance of rural interests in the state, progressives were also well organized in the state's urban centers. Progressives tended to be more politically moderate than the Populists, but women in the progressive movement were more aggressive and assertive than their Populist sisters, especially as they pushed for prohibition and suffrage. Another historian and independent scholar, Betty Chapman, examines the evolution of women's clubs as a vehicle for the reform efforts of urban women during the progressive era.

Texas Women and the Farmers' Alliance

MARION K. BARTHELME

To most Americans, industrialization was a painful process. In the last quarter of the nineteenth century, many of the nation's groups developed alternatives to the emerging design of American industrial society. The farmers' effort—the brief but powerful Populist movement—was the largest and most significant endeavor of the era. It originated on the Texas farming frontier in 1877, as farmers, trying to improve their lot through cooperation and education, created the Southern Farmers' Alliance. In 1892, they turned to politics and formed the Populist party. The movement had peaked by 1896, but not before it had swept like wildfire through the South and West and out into the Great Plains, igniting the hopes of followers one to three million strong. . . .

Alliance and Populist Women

In pioneer agricultural states such as Texas, women often worked alongside men as equals in the business of farming, shouldering burdens traditionally deemed unwomanly. The Alliance recognized this and offered membership to white rural women over sixteen years of age. . . . Significant numbers of women, perhaps as many as 25 percent of its membership, joined the Farmers' Alliance and later supported the Populist party. . . .

At the heart of this reform press . . . was the sixteen-page *Southern Mercury,* a Dallas-based weekly under various editors and publishers. . . . The paper was published between 1884 and 1907. It became the official organ of the state Southern Farmers' Alliance in 1886. . . . [F]rom 1890 to 1892—its peak years—the paper had a circulation of twenty-six to thirty thousand. Although most subscribers lived in Texas, the large number of letters from elsewhere indicates that the *Mercury* had a sizable readership in other states. It cost one dollar a year.

From 1886 to 1907, with varying intensity and dedication, the *Mercury* singled out correspondence from women by devoting one page (usually the second page) of each weekly issue to their letters and concerns. . . .

A prodigious amount has been written about the Farmers' Alliance and the Populist party, but until recently historians have neglected the part played by women in the agrarian movement. . . .

In the 1960s, a handful of historians began to take a look at old records, creating a "new history" of Southern women. It was a "brave beginning," said historian Anne Firor Scott, yet on the subject of women and rural reform in the 1880s and 1890s, this sort of brave new work consists for the most part of a few biographical studies, two essays, one doctoral dissertation, and a master's thesis. . . .

The women of Texas, among the Southern states, were the most active and influential Alliance participants. A number of them—such as Fannie Moss of Cleburne;

Marion K. Barthelme, "An Introduction" in *Women in the Texas Populist Movement: Letters to the Southern Mercury,* ed. Marion K. Bartheleme (College Station: Texas A&M University Press, 1997), 3–76. Reprinted by permission of Texas A&M University Press.

Fannie Leak, a physician in Austin; and Mary Clardy of Sulphur Springs—held offices in the order. Bettie Gay of Columbus and Ellen Dabbs, a physician also from Sulphur Springs, represented the state at national conventions, while Bessie Dwyer from San Antonio was a staff writer for the *National Economist.* . . . But the Alliance movement was a mass movement, a grassroots effort, made by rank-and-file "plain" people. These people were marginal farmers and their families—tenants, landowners, teachers, preachers, and doctors operating farms in economically depressed sections of the country. Among them were ordinary women. . . .

Women's letters to the *Southern Mercury* . . . provide a rare look into the thoughts and daily life of rural Texas women. One comes away from a reading of the letters with a greater understanding of rural Populist women and a tremendous appreciation of their resilience, their attention to detail and duty, their light humor, their strong convictions, their compassion, and their growth. . . .

Over the six years in which the women correspond, they undergo political and personal growth, due in part to their participation in the movement and in part to the act of writing and communicating in the *Southern Mercury.* The letters suggest that many of the women emerge from the experience with a stronger sense of self. Their individual and collective self-esteem is augmented by the act of writing and by the mutual reading of each other's written words. The letters also reveal, among "conservative" rural women, far greater enthusiasm for suffrage than generally has been attributed to them. Scholars looking for the roots of the suffrage movement in Texas have overlooked suffrage sentiment in the countryside and have theorized that urbanization was an essential precursor. . . .

The Alliance's stated expectation that women would join as equal members did much to bring these women into public life, even while they remained linked to a domestic setting. They entered the public arena as representatives of private life, bringing private-life concerns such as education, morality, and temperance; but they also entered with broader public-life issues, such as equal representation and the fairer division of the young nation's resources. . . . Women in these associations and reform movements were expected to practice the basic skills of public life—to speak and to listen, to analyze issues in relation to structures of power, and to develop agendas and strategies for action.

Southern Farmers' Alliance

In the 1870s, caravans of beleaguered farmers—almost 100,000 each year—migrated across plank roads and rutted trails into Texas in search of fresh farmland and a better life. From 1870 to 1890, close to 1,500,000 newcomers flocked in, some from Germany and Mexico but most from Alabama, Arkansas, Louisiana, Mississippi, Missouri, and Tennesse. . . .

Women who joined the Alliance formed part of this amalgam. In carving homesteads and farms from the unsettled forests and prairies, they and their families faced the vicissitudes of uncertain rainfall, primitive housing, vicious feuds, cattle rustling, loneliness, and economic dislocation. . . .

Beginning in 1870, the price of cotton—the farmers' economic mainstay—began to drop steadily in price. Many cash-strapped farmers turned to the crop-lien method of financing, by which a furnishing merchant or landlord would advance supplies and goods to the farmer in return for a lien on the future crop. . . . The effect of the crop-lien system was to establish a condition of peonage, for women as well as men. Appreciating money and diminishing returns, drought, depression, or northers often meant loss of ownership, and the number of landless tenant farmers began to rise. Even those who fared well enough to avoid lien financing and debt complained bitterly about the agricultural depression. Some farmers formed organizations of economic self-help, such as the National Grange of the Patrons of Husbandry, a secret society that officially eschewed partisan politics but called for cooperative endeavor and state railroad regulation. Other farmers pioneered new political institutions, such as the Greenback Party or the Union Labor Party.

The Farmers' Alliance originated in Lampasas County, Texas, in 1877, to thwart cattle rustling. In 1880, it was moved to Parker County and chartered as the nonprofit Farmers State Alliance organization. . . . By 1885, it had been forged into a cohesive system of approximately two hundred thousand members in more than two hundred suballiances. . . .

In 1886, the Alliance recruited in Louisiana. The next year, representatives from Texas and Louisiana organized alliances throughout the South. . . . The movement expanded into Kansas and in 1889 merged with strong state agrarian organizations in North Dakota and South Dakota. . . . In December 1889, farmers' organizations met in St. Louis to constitute a truly national alliance called the National Farmers' Alliance and Industrial Union. In the next four years, it attained a strength of between one and three million members.

Throughout its lifetime, the Alliance struggled with the issue of political insurgency versus nonpartisanship. As early as 1886, a series of political demands was formulated, then modified by conservatives who hoped to avoid political divisions and promote harmony. These were the Cleburne Demands, and they became the agrarian gospel that organizers preached throughout the nation. They included calls for: legislation against alien land ownership, laws to prevent trading in agricultural futures, the immediate forfeiture of railroad lands, the removal of illegal fences from public lands, tax reforms on corporate holdings, unlimited coinage of both gold and silver, an expanded money supply based on legal tender notes issued by the federal government, passage of an interstate commerce act, and abolition of convict labor. . . .

In many ways, the Alliance was an ideal movement for women. "No other movement in history—not even the antislavery cause—appealed to the women like [Populism]," wrote novelist Hamlin Garland. The doctrine of "separate spheres" gave women responsibility for morality and a higher purpose in life, a leitmotif clearly sketched in and by the order's teachings concerning sobriety, morality, benevolence, and cooperation. Its constitution announced the need "to develop a better state, mentally, morally, socially and financially," and placed much stress on the moral conduct of its members. Protection of the family was another goal. Women were a valuable component of these aims. Harry Tracy, a national lecturer, told Alliance members: "The ladies eligible must join the order before we can succeed." . . .

It was disconcerting at first for these early letter writers to have their words and names appear in public print. Nineteenth-century middle-class American society was based upon widespread acceptance of a particular image of the "ideal lady"— modest, submissive, educated in the genteel and domestic arts, supportive of her husband's efforts, physically weaker, probably mentally inferior but morally superior to men, uncomplaining, a perfect wife and mother, and, most certainly, private and never public. Good women were not to be seen or heard outside the sacred confines of the family circle. But the traditional view of the submissive, virtuous Southern lady, set apart in her "woman's sphere," had begun to crumble under the impact of the traumatic Civil War and post-Civil War conditions. As well, these were farm women who, for the common good, often were required to undertake tasks outside the circumscribed sphere of woman's place. Despite literature produced in the East, which promoted the woman's sphere, many farm women continued to work in the fields and pastures and to exchange their domestic produce for essential goods. Doing so created contradictions for them, and their letters reveal their struggles to reconcile their actual roles with the feminine ideal. Paradoxically, the separate sphere also gave them a special identification with Alliance goals.

Initially the women were hesitant to appear in public. Some used pen names. Again and again, they apologized for their correspondence, their presumption of a place in the public eye, but they clearly felt that it was a duty required by the Alliance. . . .

As time passed, the women became less timid and less self-effacing. The painful apologies ceased, and confidence in their public stance grew. Their increasing numbers fortified them. . . .

As farm women began to see themselves as part of a class, they expressed concern for urban working people and organizations such as the Knights of Labor. The Knights encouraged the participation of women in its own ranks and supported women's suffrage in ways not unlike the practices of the Alliance. The women were aware of the activities of the labor movement and its demand for an eight-hour day and national events such as the 1884 Haymarket Square Riot in Chicago and the Great Southwest Strike of 1886. Some were radicalized and spoke of the brighter future that could be created by an organized working class. "I hope the day is not far distant when the downtrodden farmer can look back and say, we have gained the victory at last, for if any class of people have been slaves it is the farmers. If ever there was a time when the farming and labor elements should stick together it is now," wrote Ida Jones from Mansfield in May 1888. . . .

At first the Texas Alliance focused on economic strategies of protest. It attempted local trade agreements with merchants, local cotton bulking, and local cooperative stores which could lower the costs of goods to the farmer. In 1887, when Alliance President Charles W. Macune realized that such disjointed efforts would not improve the position of the farmer in the market, he proposed the Exchange, a statewide Alliance-owned cooperative, based in Dallas, in which farmers would unite to buy supplies, store their crops in giant warehouses, and send them to market when the price was right. The exchange was to have the dual effect of increasing the supply of money at harvest time, when it usually was scarce, and granting the farmer credit at a low rate of interest, thereby breaking the grasp of crop-lien. . . .

Women's Concerns

Alliance leaders believed American democracy to be in moral and political decay, corrupted by the professional politician and slick financier. The farmer was the last repository of the true values—the very humanity—of American culture. Education was needed not only to bolster agrarian self-esteem and to protect the unschooled farmer against merchandising fraud; it also was central to an understanding of urban, financial, and industrial capitalism and to the creation of a sophisticated political movement based upon unity, cooperation, and independence. . . .

Education also was a logical extension of women's traditional roles as child rearers and as moral and cultural guardians. Children constituted the next generation of voters and politicians, and they needed to be trained at the earliest age. Women were expected to shield home and family from the rapidly changing values of an increasingly materialistic society. Alliance and Populist platform demands included a uniform, inexpensive system of textbooks and free public schools. . . .

In the April 19, 1888, issue of the *Mercury,* "A Country Girl" from Belton wrote that there was one thing farmers "could go into debt for if we cannot obtain it otherwise, that is an education. Knowledge is power. . . . Educate your girls that they may be independent. Educate your boys that they may perform the work assigned them through life with intelligence and then our country homes will be a paradise surrounded by the beauties of nature and enlightened sons and daughters of toil and prosperity." . . .

The women discussed the propriety of working in the fields, an activity that conflicted with the notions of woman's sphere. In April 1889, Frankie Bradford of Luna Vista had written:

> . . . I am not ashamed to confess that I work on the farm, for I am sure it is no discredit to do so; and whoever thinks so, have some lack of knowledge. I believe a girl can work in the field and be so full of grace as one that dwells in a palace. . . . Let those who say it is a disgrace to a girl to work in the field take heed. . . .

Times got rougher as the currency contracted. Among other things, the dollar continued to appreciate, its value rising steadily, while prices for agricultural products, especially cotton, declined. The farming community, noted for its hard work and industry, worked harder. The women urged each other to economize, to be more frugal. "We can be the most independent people in the world if we will only try," said Eddie, from the Round Pound Alliance. "First, we must economize. If we want to accomplish anything, raise everything that we can at home, wear old clothes and keep out of debt." . . .

In June 1888, Bettie Gay from Columbus suggested boycotting coffee until the price fell, something she had done during the Civil War. She had a blunt response to a contributor's suggestion that women return to the spinning wheel and loom. "I am in sympathy with every economical move," she said, but

> . . . It will take three days to weave one yard of cloth; at twenty-five cents per day, it would cost seventy-five cents per yard to spin and weave a yard, besides the expense of the machinery, so you see there is no economy. It would be more healthful to raise a cotton patch, work in the open air and buy calico or muslin for five cents per yard. . . .

The Cleburne Demands of 1886 and later Alliance and Populist platforms were disseminated widely among the Alliance membership. Moreover, after 1888 the Alliance's educational campaign efforts intensified, and the many reform journals and suballiances embraced new roles as schools for education. Alliance newspapers carried voluminous eighteen- to twenty-part series on the history of democracy or on the economic theories of Ricardo, Mills, and Smith. Long and capable—if somewhat mythological—letters, such as Ann Other's earnest two-column synopsis of civilization's development, reflect a reading of Macune's similar multi-part educational accounts of history. . . . She went on to trace the arrival and decline of the Greeks and Romans, the development of family and government, as well as the growth of vast corporations. . . .

Some of the letters were sophisticated and explicit, and writers asked important, thoughtful questions. Other opinions were abstract, as indeed the whole Populist theme could be, again with the discussion of economic issues cast in moral or Christian terms and expressed in statements filled with Old Testament imagery and Christian metaphor. To some, the "money power" indicated particular individuals—for example, the legislators who had passed the bill for the demonetization of silver. For others, the phrase loosely denoted not only politicians on the wrong side but also all wealthy men and corporations—Wall Street brokers, bankers (American and British), small and large business owners, railroads, mortgage companies, mine owners, and landlords. . . . Always the letter writers urged the farmers on in the struggle.

The land belonged to the farmer—not the government, the speculator, the banker, the London financier, or the railroad magnate. "It is good to discuss the why's and wherefore's of the exceeding scarcity of money but there is another question of great magnitude," advised Mary of Limestone County. "Why is it that there are so many homeless men and women, men who would till the soil for a living, and yet there are thousands of acres of land lying idle. Why did our state officials give the railroads so much of the people's land, and compel the poor to rent? Why did they give so much land to build a state house? Would it have not been better policy to have given that 3,000,000 acres of land to the poor renting farmer and built a less palatial house by direct taxation?"

The women articulated economic theories and financial legislation well, but in their personal analyses and final conclusions, they emphasized the human aspects of poverty among all classes and its effects upon the family and home. They never doubted that impersonal industrial capitalism caused family poverty and the poverty of single women. . . .

Bettie Gay

In many ways, Bettie Gay epitomizes the ordinary Alliance woman—the stolid, independent, strong-willed, resourceful Texas farmer who heard the challenges of the Alliance and embraced its promises. In other ways, she is different, representing a smaller group of women who were radicalized first by the movement and then by its failure to deliver on its promises. . . .

Her first appearance in the pages of the *Mercury* may have been June 14, 1888, and signed "B. G." She was urging people to boycott coffee. In June 1889, she and Mrs. Shaw proposed that the Alliance women sell poultry and dairy items for money to save the Exchange. In 1891, she angrily complained about the decline of women's letters in the *Mercury*. When Nelson Dunning published his history of the Farmers' Alliance that same year, he included a chapter by Gay on "The Influence of Women in the Alliance," which summed up the status of women. It has been interpreted by McMath, among other historians, as accepting women's conventional roles, because in it Gay speaks of woman as man's companion and helpmeet. However, she did not marry again after her husband died, choosing not to become someone's "helpmeet." Read from a different perspective, her essay seems strongly feminist, almost revolutionary. "Nature has endowed women with brains," she wrote. "Why should she not think . . . why not act? If allowed to act, what privilege should men enjoy of which she should be deprived?" She looked to the Alliance to redeem woman from her "enslaved condition," insisting that "what we need is a better womanhood . . . acknowledging no master and accepting no compromise." Bettie Gay strongly espoused suffrage and eventually became a Socialist.

Historians of Alliance and Populist women have found that, despite the movement's official support of expanded roles for women, the meaning of equality was constricted by and to the organization's major goal of reviving Southern agriculture. It has been understood that political rights within the Alliance were not seen by women as the first step toward political rights outside the Alliance. . . . Despite the equality of membership in the Alliance and its promise of democracy, Alliance and Populist women were not able to convert the party—or even each other—to unequivocal support for suffrage. . . .

Success, however, is not the only criterion of importance. If an accelerated transformation of consciousness among a group of oppressed people was vital to the formation of the Alliance movement, it was to the suffrage movement as well. . . .

It is precisely this movement of awakening consciousness that these rural Texas letters illustrate. . . . Very possibly these letters about suffrage represent the first articulation of feminist consciousness for many rural women. Ann Other, one of the most frequent letter writers, confessed that "when I began to study suffrage . . . I thought women's only ambition should be to read the latest novels, work green dogs with pink eyes on cardboard and other ornamental work, keep her house and children clean and healthy and 'always meet your husband with a smile' but now I am satisfied that with suffrage, she can benefit her country, keep her own womanly traits and have more just laws for herself and better protection for her children."

Between April 19, 1888, and April 18, 1889, women were stirred to write to the *Mercury* about suffrage and women's rights, more than about any other topic. Fifteen percent of the women's letters focused on female suffrage or women's rights. Of the Texas letters, 56 percent were in favor of suffrage, while 44 percent were against it. . . .

Widespread support for prohibition existed among Populist women and was linked with suffrage sentiment, pro and con. "I have been reading sister Ann Other's letters and I think they're splendid," said Mary M. of Greer County in another letter published on June 28. "I can't understand why some are so opposed to us ladies voting. One good sister thinks it would be a downfall to the female sex to go there among so many grades of people. Well, have we not got all kinds of people in our country and do we have to stop and shake hands with them and tell them we are on their side? No Sir. . . . . Where would whiskey have gone if women had been allowed to vote? There would not have been a drop of whisky now in existence."

Eva J. Sims of Sault Creek Alliance, Indian Territory, also blamed the failure to pass prohibition on women's inability to vote. . . .

The June *Mercury* was full of interesting letters, including a heated antisuffrage message from Rebecca of Jefferson, Texas. "Please withhold your vials of wrath while I reassert that there are corrupt women as well as men," she wrote, in defiance of the traditional view of female perfection. . . . "Lady Macbeth whose unholy ambition (I think she wanted female suffrage) caused her to suggest and help execute the murder of her king, and which finally resulted in the ruin of herself and the overthrow of her family. Thus it is often the case when a woman obtrudes herself beyond her legitimate sphere." . . .

For Dianecia Jones of Dallas County, the discussion had gone on long enough. "Women's rights!" she exploded. "Now sisters, let that question rest. As for my part I don't think it would improve things for the ladies to vote. Let us allow the men to make laws. We can certainly live by their laws if they can. As to woman's suffrage, that is something we will never get in this world. I say look up and trust for our rights in a better world."

Despite Jones's weary surfeit, the Alliance and the Populist party awakened in other women the powerful drive to participate in the more formal realm of politics through suffrage, and aroused a discontent with purely private identities and definitions of femininity. . . . Women took their voting privileges seriously and looked to the Alliance to increase their political understanding. Through the order, women were able to practice the arts of participation and experience themselves as visible and effective. . . .

The Alliance Begins to Decline

The number of women's letters peaked during the fall of 1888 and declined swiftly thereafter. Several issues during the following few months of that year contained no letters at all from women, although a woman's page still existed. . . .

Some students of the agrarian movement have suggested that, as the Alliance became politicized, its social function declined in importance. . . . As things got tougher, the resilience and dedication of Alliance women became even more necessary to the order, if not to the *Mercury*. This suggests that the women's contribution had assumed an importance far beyond the social arena: the women had become a vital nexus of the organization, an essential segment of its spiritual backbone, a component, possibly, of its very survival. . . .

The *Mercury,* as well as the Alliance, was in crisis over the Exchange. A cryptic paragraph from the editors in an October issue said, "A great many of our readers are holding back the money they have saved to renew their subscription to the *Mercury* until everything was clear to them, or until the executive committee secured control of the paper. As the latter has been accomplished, all should renew at once." The reference is to the charge that Macune and other Exchange directors were incompetent, an accusation that had replaced the original explanation—merchant-banker opposition—for the failure of the Exchange. Alliance members had been warned not to put their hard-earned money into the doomed venture. The *Southern Mercury,* . . . took up this idea and, by the late summer of 1888, was taking a definite anti-Exchange stance, lambasting Macune and other Alliance leaders. . . .

An investigatory committee fully vindicated Macune and the Exchange of any wrongdoing, and Macune in turned accused the *Mercury* of betraying the Alliance to avoid losing advertising patronage. The reaction of the rank-and-file Alliance members to the controversy was bitter, however, and the consequences devastating. Local alliances began reporting immediate declines in membership. Although control of the *Mercury* passed into the hands of the state Alliance, the new editors never reversed the editorial position of the ousted editors. . . .

. . . Women's issues no longer appeared on the front pages of the *Nonconformist,* for example, and the remaining women's columns devoted themselves to fashions and cooking, rather than women's rights and politics. . . .

The failure of the Exchange led Macune to develop the most significant proposal in Alliance history: the subtreasury plan. The plan called for the establishment of locally situated federal subtreasuries, along with warehouses and elevators in which farmers could store certain nonperishable commodities. The government would provide short-term credit at low interest, giving the farmer more independence in marketing his crop. As projected, the system would end the deflationary glut of commodities on the market at harvest time and create an expanded, flexible currency that would reverse the decline of farm prices.

The proposal was a watershed for the Alliance. It brought the order directly into party politics, a move that, as many had predicted and feared, generated friction and divided the Texas Alliance. It precipitated the final protest strategy of the Alliance movement—the Populist party. The party siphoned off Alliance energy and led to the movement's demise. Then the party itself fused with the Democrats in the 1896 presidential election, lost the support of Texas Populists who refused to fuse, and eventually died out. . . .

Before the Populist conventions [in 1892], women had been excited about the potential of a new party—a party which included them, which might give them suffrage, which recognized the importance of home and family and woman's central role, which might support prohibition, and which would solve the economic problems of the farmers. . . .

However, in an opening speech in St. Louis, Ben Terrell of Texas urged delegates to consider only questions of "economic" reforms. "Moral reforms" should be put off until a later date, while other differences between Northern and Southern elements in the movement were bridged. . . . Many Democrats whom the Populists were wooing opposed women's suffrage; it was considered a fatally divisive issue that should be sacrificed for the Populist cause. The other major moral reform, prohibition, also was lost. . . .

The official platform was drawn up later that summer, on the Fourth of July, at the national nominating convention in Omaha, Nebraska. . . . It did not include women's suffrage or temperance. . . .

The Populists did not fare well in the 1892 presidential election against Republican Benjamin Harrison and Democrat Grover Cleveland. In only five Southern states did the total Populist vote amount to more than one half of the Alliance's potential voting strength at its peak. In Texas, the order was split, as many moderate Alliancemen remained loyal to the Democratic party and looked to the popular young governor, James S. Hogg, for leadership. . . .

. . . In 1896, the Democrats co-opted the free-silver issue and nominated Nebraska's William Jennings Bryan for president. The national party fused with the Democrats; the Texas Populists preferred to stay in "the middle of the road" between the major parties. Neither strategy worked. Bryan lost the election to William McKinley, although he received more popular votes than Grover Cleveland had garnered in 1892. It was essentially the end of the party. The Alliance already had died.

Strong urban agitation for suffrage had begun in Texas in 1893, when the Texas Equal Rights Association (TERA), an auxiliary of the National American Woman Suffrage Association, was formed. It is not surprising that Bettie Gay was among the rural women who moved from the Alliance into TERA. Joining her were Alliance sisters Grace Danforth, Ellen Dabbs, and Margaret Watson. Nor is it surprising that the rhetoric of TERA tended to be more radical on the redefinition of sex roles than that put forth two decades later by the suffrage organizations that resuscitated the movement after TERA had died. . . .

Lawrence Goodwyn has suggested that the most important contribution of the agrarian revolt was to create "the visible evidence of community that gave meaning and substance to all lesser individuals." Politically, women were among those lesser individuals. But the Populist movement challenged the status quo; with the help of the *Southern Mercury,* it provided many women with community, meaning, and a stronger sense of self. . . . Rural women's participation in the Alliance and the Populist party undoubtedly helped break the ground for later social legislation, including that for women's suffrage.

Women's Clubs as Vehicles for Reform in Houston, 1885–1918

BETTY T. CHAPMAN

During the latter decades of the nineteenth century and the early years of the twentieth, the lives of middle-class Southern women changed significantly. Before then they had existed in a separate sphere, described by historian Barbara Welter as the "cult of true womanhood," which had kept them confined mostly to the home. Piety, purity, submissiveness, and domesticity were considered the most desirable feminine attributes. Events outside the home were, however, sowing seeds for change.

Exigencies of the Civil War had moved women beyond the domestic realm and had exposed them to new experiences, which in turn had made them eager for more knowledge and a broader education. Increased industrialization eased the burden of homemaking and resulted in more leisure time for middle-class women. A rapidly urbanizing society raised new concerns and caused unrest among citizens of growing cities and towns. Women were confronted with the new challenge of escaping from their separate sphere into a broad new world. These trends were evident not only nationally, but also in Houston.

How did these women move from their Victorian parlors into the public arena where they would become full-fledged instruments of change and civic reform? One channel through which this extraordinary journey occurred was provided by female organizations that offered women opportunities to shape their ideas within

Betty T. Chapman, "From the Parlor to the Public: New Roles for Women in Houston, 1885–1918," *Houston Review* 15 (1993), 31–44. Copyright © 1993 University of Houston. Reprinted with permission.

the safe confines of a sisterhood and to expand them into the broader framework of the community.

In February 1885, nine women concerned about their need for greater knowledge and for female companionship met in Houston and announced that "the name of this Association shall be The Ladies' History Class and its object shall be intellectual and social culture." Two months later, their membership having grown to 24, they drafted a constitution, changed their name to the Ladies' Reading Club, and adopted a plan for study.

Before that time, Houston had offered few forums for women to collectively voice their opinions and to act on their convictions. Organized female activity was almost entirely within the churches. Most noticeably, two groups—the Ladies' Parish Association of Christ Episcopal Church and the Ladies' Association of First Presbyterian Church—had recognized the needs of their congregations and had acted to meet those needs. Records of Christ Episcopal Church show that in 1875 the Ladies' Parish Association succeeded in raising enough money to purchase an organ and to initiate a fund to erect a larger church building. Similarly, the Presbyterian ladies decided in 1880 that a dwelling was needed for their minister and his family. After securing a charter enabling them to hold property, they bought three lots and erected a manse at a cost of approximately $8,000. This is not to imply that women had any official voice in the transactions of the church body. Indeed, Presbyterians had been cautioned by their General Assembly that "It is not proper for girls and young women to preside over a meeting of a society or to make an address or to lead in prayer." However, it is apparent that these women, acting within their own organizations, had achieved a marked degree of independence and were making significant contributions to the entire congregation.

Interestingly, over half of the charter members of the Ladies' Reading Club were from these two congregations. Soon after their organization, however, it was apparent that their bond was more than just religious. Several had brought daughters and sisters into the group, most had husbands prominent within the business community, and many were descendants of Houston's first families. Though most were matrons, they welcomed unmarried women, declaring that "the new thoughts, strong sympathies, wider views, and the expression of mind and character . . . would be a gain for all women." While little is known of their schooling, it appears that most had had the advantage of a more extensive and formal education than many of their contemporaries. Several were employed as teachers.

The Ladies' Reading Club uniformly and firmly believed—as stated by their first president, Adele Briscoe Looscan—that a woman should be "one whose mind shall be trained to form her own opinions, to organize her own household and, if need be, to make her own living." At one of the meetings the topic for debate was "Resolved: That the education of our daughters for an independent career will unfit them for the duties of wife and mother." Club minutes show that this view was soundly defeated.

Chroniclers of the nineteenth-century women's club movement have stated that one of its more far-reaching results was that it stimulated women to think and gave them the opportunity to articulate their views. The substance of this statement can be seen in the Ladies' Reading Club, which pursued in-depth studies of subjects such as "The Progress of Art During the Reign of the Four Georges" and "The Cause of Spain's Low Rank in the Fields of Science and Philosophy." All members were required to participate; they presented carefully researched papers, engaged in lively debates, and prepared informative statements on assigned topics with which to answer roll call. It was an opportunity to teach and to be taught. This mutual exchange gave every woman in the club equal consideration and respect. While the meetings may not have produced avid scholars, careerists, or social critics, they did provide a means for the members to view themselves as something more than moral guardians of their homes. This club attracted intelligent women for whom turning from the realm of abstract thought to the arena of practical action was a natural progression.

In March 1887, four members of this club—Adele Briscoe Looscan, Harriet Fitzgerald, Eva McIlhenny, and Julia Huston—helped establish the Woman's Exchange, which advertised that it was the only organization in Houston assisting females. The Exchange secured employment for women who were forced to earn their own livings and served as a commission house selling goods produced by women. Though it frequently suffered financial problems, it managed to stay open with funds derived from the 25-cent monthly dues paid by its members, the commissions on sales of goods, periodic entertainments, and donations from local businessmen. It stated in its first annual report that it had 161 members 14 honorary members—males who had made donations—and 37 persons with goods for sale. Records for the next year indicated that the number of consignors had doubled, 23 women had been placed in jobs, and a sewing class for young girls was being successfully conducted. In spite of criticism, which they felt was unjustified, the Women's Exchange continued to offer a dignified means of support to women in need.

The Woman's Exchange and other female-related groups were supported by *The Ladies' Messenger,* a local publication begun in 1887. It proclaimed itself to be "the exponent of woman's thought and woman's work." While the publication did contain the usual amount of domestic advice, it also advocated equal educational opportunities for females and touted the advantages of calisthenics for young women in defiance of those who insisted that the female brain was smaller than the male and the female physique was frail. It encouraged the formation of women's literary clubs and offered to publicize and promote their causes. The Ladies' Reading Club accepted the offer and published its President's Annual Report in *The Ladies' Messenger.*

This support became less visible in 1890 when the name of *The Ladies's Messenger* was changed to *The Gulf Messenger.* The female editor explained the change by saying that the publication would be "no less devoted to women but the name change will give us a wider field and more readers, for many men still have a silly prejudice that a journal devoted to women has nothing in it pertaining to 'the grand thoughts that shape mankind.'" Despite the editor's stated intent, the paper became an organ divided between sentimental literary offerings and promotional information for males in the business community. Though the women of Houston had lost a strong voice in the public arena, they did not become invisible.

In an address to the Ladies' Reading Club on its tenth anniversary in 1895, Adele Looscan admonished its members, "Do we exercise . . . influence as largely as we might? Are we not inclined to be too conservative? . . . Ladies, failing to recognize a responsibility does not lessen the reality of a duty, which, from the very nature of our organization, becomes ours."

One of the greatest concerns of Mrs. Looscan and her fellow club members was that Houston had no public library. In 1894, they had requested that the books of the Houston Lyceum, a private, predominantly male literary organization, be made available to nonmembers and that its library be moved from the Market House to a location more accessible to the women of the community. Though the first request was granted, and a woman was hired as librarian, the Lyceum library remained where it had been. The ladies continued their campaign for new quarters, and finally in September 1897—almost three years after the initial request—the Lyceum allowed its library to be relocated. The Ladies' Reading Club paid for the move. To build a treasury for the new facility, each member of the club became a monthly subscriber, the club donated its magazine files and its own collection of 150 books, and they voted to give the library five dollars worth of new books each month. This provided the nucleus of the library, but it soon became apparent—at least to the women of the city—that a more substantial base was essential. When the city council reneged on its promise to include in its 1899 budget a provision for stocking and maintaining the library, the women used the strategy of both appeasing and chiding the male officials of the city. They invited them to an entertainment where they served refreshments, politely reminded them of their pledge, and then pointed to the empty bookshelves. The following week Mamie Ewing, one of the two club members who had personally invited the officials, recorded in the club minutes that she "believed the embarrassment of meeting an army of women re-solved itself into a pleasure to all of them . . . because the Mayor admitted he would deem it an honor to be the first mayor to recommend an appropriation for the library." Whether he felt it an honor or an obligation may never be known; one alderman was heard to comment that women would not have time to read books if they took care of their homes and families. Nevertheless, a monthly appropriation of $200 was made, and a free public reading room became a reality.

Encouraged by this victory but still dissatisfied with what they considered an inadequate facility, the ladies deluged the mayor with letters. Perseverance, though, seemed to accomplish little until two members of the Woman's Club, Belle Kendall and Mamie Gearing, wrote to Andrew Carnegie. In response to their solic-itation, he agreed to furnish money for a building if the city would provide a site. To support the city in this undertaking and "to give aid to the material welfare of the community," representatives of five women's clubs—the Ladies' Reading Club, the Woman's Club, the Current Literature Club, the Ladies' Shakespeare Club, and the Mansfield Dramatic Club—met in January 1900 to form the City Federation of Women's Clubs. The new federation joined with the Lyceum to coordinate their efforts to raise funds for the library site. Lectures, ice cream socials, musicales, bazaars, and a "home circus" produced funds that were applied to the $7,880 cost of the proposed site on Travis and McKinney streets. On May 1, 1902, the women of Houston could feel a real sense of accomplishment when the first brick was laid; the Houston Lyceum and Carnegie Library would soon be available to residents of the city.

The organization of the City Federation led to the formation of other groups. In March 1900, Emma Richardson Cherry was instrumental in founding the Public School Art League. Drawing its membership primarily from clubwomen and public school teachers, the group endeavored to encourage art education in the schools.

Still working within the accepted realm of home and family, they took as their inspiration these lines from the poem "Mother to a Child":

> For the sake of my child I must hasten to save
> All children on earth from the jail and the grave.

Convinced that one way to accomplish this was by introducing the children to great
works of art, they began to acquire reproductions of art masterpieces, which they
presented to the public schools. They were instrumental in having art courses
added to the curriculum, and they brought noted artists to the city to lecture. While
the children were receptive—five thousand students attended one lecture at the
City Auditorium—the adult citizens, from whom the League had hoped to receive
funding, showed little interest. To combat this indifference, the women of the Public
School Art League resorted to creative means of raising money. They first solicited
the help of a prominent businessman who provided a building where they could hold
art exhibits to which they would charge admission. Then each school was allotted
certain days on which it would sponsor attendance and sell artwork created by its
own students. Thus, by creating a friendly rivalry within a coalition of students,
parents, and teachers, they were soon able to raise the needed funds.

Not every attempt to promote art was so favorably received. When the Public
School Art League ordered a replica of the Venus de Milo to place in one of the
schools, it was rejected by the school administration for fear that it might adversely
affect the morals of the children. Not to be deterred, the League gave the statue to
the public library where its presence 89 years later attests to the determination of
these women. Houston's Museum of Fine Arts, which evolved from the Public
School Art League, further attests to their vision.

Affirming the values of art and literature led to more aggressive female-
inspired programs. By 1900, Houston's population was approaching 45,000 and
the city was experiencing rapid growth. This growth brought problems that would
only intensify during the next two decades. Public health, education, and city services continued to be addressed only sporadically by the city government. In 1901,
Margaret Hadley Foster published a call for action imploring clubwomen throughout
the city to put aside their petty rivalries and to join forces in an effort aimed toward
"improving and advancing the city." Realizing that men would still be essential to
their efforts, she invited their participation. "Men," she declared, "are very useful—
at times—and if they could only be stirred up to do something for the beauty and
cleanliness of the city, what a world of good they could do!" Though they still realized that males made policy and controlled purse strings, women were becoming
bolder about prodding men into action. Mrs. Foster then appealed to a broader segment of the female population. The strategy for implementing improvements was
to organize a civic club in each of Houston's six wards. Each ward club would, in
turn, determine the needs of its own neighborhood.

One of the first concerns of the Houston Civic Club was the scarcity of parks
and playgrounds in Houston. The city's first park had been established in 1899 after
a group of women, led by Elizabeth Ring, had flouted convention and appeared in a
body at City Hall to request that land be purchased for a park. Using this as a precedent, the women in the ward clubs succeeded in placing parks in several neighborhoods. Then they purchased playground equipment, sponsored free concerts, and

beautified the grounds of public buildings throughout the city. Operating in essence as a city recreation department, the women assumed the responsibility for establishing and maintaining parks but continually reproached city officials for their failure to do so.

Sanitation was another grave concern of the Houston Civic Club. In a 1906 report, they credit their group with the successful passage of two city ordinances: the anti-expectoration ordinance and the uniform garbage can law. Clearing trash and debris from the streets became an ongoing project of these energetic women. Though they insisted that "they had carefully abstained from meddling in politics," it is obvious that they were constantly reminding city officials that public services were less than adequate and that action was needed.

The increased population, which now included a growing number of immigrants, changed the demographics of many neighborhoods. This was especially true of the Second Ward where former residents had moved into the newly developed South End neighborhoods and had been replaced by immigrant families. Houses were divided into cramped apartments; poverty was readily apparent. Believing strongly that the expansion of educational opportunities was one of the keys to improving the lives of Second Ward citizens, the 26 members of the Woman's Club, under the leadership of Mamie Gearing, opened a free kindergarten in the neighborhood in 1902. The first quarters, a lean-to shed, were quickly outgrown. The club members rented land, solicited building materials from local businesses, and secured volunteer labor to erect a larger facility. With limited income at their disposal, the Woman's Club instituted an innovative system of securing the needed personnel to assist the one paid teacher. They opened a training school for volunteer teachers, thereby laying the foundation for future community volunteerism. Five years later, the program was expanded when the local school board gave the club permission to open a kindergarten in a newly constructed public school. These women steadfastly believed that a significant step in educating the city's young had been taken.

In 1907, as the Second Ward became increasingly crowded and impoverished, 12 women, recognizing a critical need for health and education in that area, organized the Houston Settlement Association. Alice Baker was selected to head the Association and, as one account states, she brought to this endeavor "intelligence, vision, and a tenacity of purpose." The women's first task was the inevitable one of raising funds. Their bylaws stated that "Monthly dues shall not be stipulated, each member subscribing as her pleasure dictates." This encouraged liberal giving from the more economically privileged members. It is also evident that these women tapped resources that were familiar to them. Their first outside donation was from the Ladies' Association of First Presbyterian Church, of which Mrs. Baker was a member.

Feeling strongly that the neighborhood should work for its own improvement instead of merely accepting charity from others, the Houston Settlement Association established the Second Ward Women's Club. This created a unique opportunity for cross-class cooperation, as members of the ward club, sustained by the experienced and affluent clubwomen, now provided volunteers and at least some financial support for its projects. These included assuming responsibility for the Woman's Club kindergarten and establishing a visiting nurses program. The Settlement Association focused its attention on the needs of children with a new intensity, but also broadened its horizons to include adult education classes, programs for the deaf and dumb, Houston's first branch library, community-sponsored manual training and domestic science programs, and a school for delinquent boys.

By first establishing programs through its own initiatives and then keeping them before the public, the Settlement Association was able to realize the creation of permanent institutions by 1918. Its visiting nurses program had been integrated into the city's newly organized Public Health Department. The Association's work with delinquent boys had led to the Seabrook School for Boys in Clear Lake. The Association had lobbied successfully to establish a City Recreation Department to oversee parks and playgrounds across the entire city. The Settlement Association believed that a neighborhood approach that depended on "the philanthropic whim of the individual giver" was not the most efficient one and they continued to work for the development of permanent agencies.

Clubwomen, who by now had become crusaders for their causes, realized that it was critical to their success to keep the public informed of what they viewed as the city's needs. Since the demise of *The Ladies' Messenger* in 1890, women's activities, other then those of a purely social nature, had received little attention from the press. This lack of publicity had not at first displeased the organized women's groups. The Ladies' Reading Club had even declared in their minutes of October 13, 1896, that "the *Post* may contain the exercises of the Ladies' Reading Club but the names may not be given." Club members had been acutely sensitive to the ridicule which had resulted from the less-than-serious articles printed about them in their formative years. By 1906, however, they realized that they needed a public voice; and Stella Christian brought together 11 women with a dual interest in literary writing and community improvements. Thus was born the Houston Pen Women, who took it as their objective "to proclaim the glory and sublimity of righteousness." If righteousness can be defined as combating poverty, ignorance, disease, indifference, and exploitation, these female writers achieved their goal; they regularly submitted articles to Houston publications and sponsored a weekly column by Mrs. Christian in the *Houston Post*. They were no longer reluctant to be mentioned in print.

Clubwomen realized that legislation was ultimately the key to ensuring permanent reforms in the community. Through the networking of the City Federation of Women's Clubs and its allied group, the Texas Federation of Women's Clubs, they kept issues before the appropriate legislative bodies. As a result, local storekeepers were required to shorten working hours and to provide seats for their clerks during breaks, a women's restroom was maintained in the Market House, and matrons were placed in both the jail and the railroad station for the protection of women. More kindergartens were opened and traveling libraries were sent into rural areas. Additionally, the need for pure food and milk laws was publicized and a municipal livestock fencing ordinance was enacted. Between 1909 and 1917, women's groups across the state came together to form powerful coalitions. These determined women lobbied successfully for legislation including a state child welfare commission, child labor laws, a juvenile court system, public kindergartens, compulsory school attendance laws, pure food inspection, and a state library commission. Always concerned about the quality of life, women broadened their role as guardians of the home to include being caretakers of the community.

What were the necessary components for the journey these women made in moving out of the narrow sphere of home and family into the real and troubled world around them? In order to succeed it was essential that they gain public acceptance, acquire financial support, and establish strong leadership. At the same time they had to operate within the bounds of propriety, never forgetting their roles as homemakers.

While they faced some opposition, not only from men but also from women who felt that too much public exposure would lead to a deterioration of home and family, it is apparent that many of the women were strongly supported by male family members, who contributed not only financially, but also through their influence within the business and political communities. Although most women's clubs avoided controversial issues that might overshadow their own more immediate goals, certainly some of their members individually supported the woman suffrage movement and strongly agreed with their fellow clubwoman, Elizabeth Ring, that "we could all do this work much better and quicker with less loss of time and dignity and self-respect by casting our vote as full-fledged citizens. It is not pleasant to have to wheedle and cajole or flatter men to give us these sensible and practical things. It takes too much of our time and energy and it makes us think less of ourselves and them." Though they might deplore it, they understood the necessity of having the support and approval of the male population, and they became experts at the art of persuasion. In a broader sense they appealed to middle-class society by emphasizing their goals and their spirit of service to the community in an attractive and, perhaps more importantly, nonthreatening way.

While the Ladies' Reading Club had firmly declared in their minutes of November 8, 1895, that they did not wish to become ticket sellers, clubwomen soon realized that the need for funds would be a perpetual reality and they became persistent and innovative money raisers. They entertained, decorously of course. They begged, always appealing to the goodness and generosity of the hoped-for benefactor. And they taught, feeling that funds would more readily come from an educated citizenry. Eventually they realized that by reproaching those in authority, they could persuade government to assume financial responsibility for improving the quality of life within the city.

Leadership, of course, was the ultimate key to success. Women like Adele Looscan, Elizabeth Ring, Emma Cherry, Margaret Foster, Alice Baker, and Mamie Gearing, who began with the desire for self-improvement, came to the realization that community improvement could enhance the general welfare. Though they lacked power in the conventional sense, they combined perseverance, intelligence, and an astute sense of timing to effect coalitions that would actively work for the good of the entire population.

From our late-twentieth-century perspective, these clubwomen may have acted conservatively, addressed a narrow segment of the population, and failed to achieve true equality. Within the ideological and political framework of the time, however, they helped to lay the foundation for the feminist expression of the future. The club movement provided a socially acceptable way for many women to begin moving out of the domestic realm and gain a public voice, without taking on the public notoriety that was attached to the crusading feminists of the time. Through their clubs, women learned the importance of joining together to effect change. In them, women found the strength to become autonomous persons.

⭐ *F U R T H E R   R E A D I N G*

Evan Anders, *Boss Rule in South Texas: The Progressive Era* (1982)

Donna K. Barnes, *Farmers in Rebellion: The Rise and Fall of the Southern Farmers'
    Alliance and the People's Party in Texas* (1984)

Alwyn Barr, *Reconstruction to Reform: Texas Politics, 1876–1906* (1971)

Marion K. Barthelme, ed., *Women in the Texas Populist Movement: Letters to the* Southern
    Mercury (1997)

Debbie Mauldin Cottrell, *Pioneer Woman Educator: Annie Webb Blanton* (1993)

Elizabeth York Enstam, *Women and the Creation of Urban Life, Dallas, Texas, 1843–1920*
    (1998)

James R. Green, "Tenant Farmer Discontent and Socialist Protest in Texas, 1901–1917,"
    Southwestern Historical Quarterly 81 (1977): 133–154

Patricia E. Hill, "Women's Groups and the Extension of City Services in Early Twentieth
    Century Dallas," *East Texas Historical Review* 30 (1992): 3–10.

Janet G. Humphrey, ed, *A Texas Suffragist: Diaries and Writings of Jane Y. McCallum*
    (1988)

James D. Ivy, "The Lone Star State Surrenders to a Lone Woman: Frances Willard's
    Forgotten 1882 Texas Temperance Tour," *Southwestern Historical Quarterly* 102
    (1998): 44–61

Judith N. MacArthur, *Creating the New Woman: The Rise of Southern Women's Progressive
    Culture in Texas, 1893–1919* (1998)

Jacquelyn Masur McElhaney, *Pauline Periwinkle and Progressive Reform in Dallas* (1998)

Elizabeth Hayes Turner, *Women, Culture and Community: Religion and Reform in Galveston,
    1880–1920* (1997)

CHAPTER
12

Oil, Industrialization, and Urbanization, 1900–1940

In the twentieth century, the traditional Texas of farms and ranches, cotton and cattle, gave way to an increasingly urban and industrialized Texas. Although urban growth in Texas has been spectacular, the change from rural to urban did not occur as soon or as quickly as it sometimes appears. In 1900 Texas was still 83 percent rural. In 1940 the state was approaching an even split between its rural and urban population, but it remained 54 percent rural. The balance of power between urban and rural shifted permanently in the decade of the 1940s. Not only did a majority (63 percent) of Texans in 1950 reside in urban areas for the first time, but rural population actually declined during the 1940s and has continued to decline ever since. Urban population growth can also be measured in the growth of individual cities, especially the growth of the state's two major metropolises, Houston and Dallas. At the turn of the century, San Antonio (population 53,321) was the state's largest city, followed by Houston (44,633), Dallas (42,638), and Galveston (37,788). By 1930 Houston (292,352) and Dallas (262,475) had emerged as the state's two largest cities.

Urban growth in Texas was directly related to the state's industrialization. Simply put, Spindletop and the resulting oil boom triggered unprecedented economic and urban growth. Before the end of the 1920s, industrial output had replaced agricultural output as the main source of the state's wealth. World War II created a second economic boom as aircraft manufacturing, shipbuilding, steel, chemicals, and electronics broadened the industrial base and accelerated the state's transition from rural to urban.

While many Texans embraced the boom times brought by oil, industry, and urban growth, others were concerned by the challenges that these developments introduced. Urbanization and industrialization shifted political power from rural areas and rural concerns to the cities and towns and their concerns. Urbanization increased the need for services and infrastructure to accommodate rapid population *growth. In addition, it raised questions about the adequacy of traditional political structures and policies. Racial and ethnic conflict often followed rapid population shifts to the cities, and overall social change led to efforts to preserve traditional social and racial mores, law and order, and standards of moral behavior.*

What Texas experienced with urbanization and industrialization has raised questions. First, what triggered urban growth? Was it solely the result of economic factors and economic advantage or did it arise from wise leadership and careful planning? Was rapid urbanization a blessing or a curse? Could the traditional image of Texas individualism survive the pressures of an urban society? How would the state deal with the problems that surfaced with economic growth and urbanization?

🤘 D O C U M E N T S

Industrialization and the Texas oil industry began to slowly develop in the last quarter of the nineteenth century, but it was the Spindletop discovery in 1901 that transformed Texas unlike any other economic event. The first two documents attest to the almost mythic aspects of Spindletop. Document 1 illustrates how this event was reported in Dallas, which along with Houston, most successfully reaped the economic benefits of the oil boom. Document 2 presents the worker's perspective on this event. It consists of the oral history testimony of two of the three men who were on the oil platform the day that the Spindletop gusher came in.

Interest in urban planning blossomed during the first quarter of the twentieth century as a logical outgrowth of the Progressive era reform philosophy. Both Houston and Dallas initially flirted with planning during the years immediately preceding the First World War. In Document 3 the *Dallas Morning News* reports favorably on the plan that a Kansas City urban designer, George Kessler, developed for the City of Dallas. The Kessler Plan would serve as the basis for Dallas planning efforts for the next twenty years. Three years later, Arthur Comey, a Boston city planner, provided Houston with its first city plan as Document 4 presents. Both of these plans were developed by national planning firms and reflect the approach to urban planning typical of the Progressive Era. Neither plan was fully implemented.

The next three documents address the racial and social conflicts that accompanied early twentieth-century urbanization. Document 5 presents the initial reports of the worst race riot in Houston history, the 1917 mutiny of African American troops stationed in the city. The revived Ku Klux Klan enjoyed considerable power and influence in Texas cities in the early 1920s. Document 6 attempts to explain the nature of the Klan and its popularity. Document 7 presents an African American perspective on urban promise and problems. In 1928 Houston proponents of urban planning established a magazine to promote a new city plan. Clifford F. Richardson, an African American newspaper publisher, businessman, and civil rights activist, was asked to contribute an article on the state of "Negro Houston." Richardson's contribution mixed a combination of black Houston "boosterism" with a fairly accurate assessment of the needs of black neighborhoods.

The final document, 8, details the growth of the Texas oil industry and its connection to the growth and prosperity of Houston. It was written by John R. Suman, a vice president of Humble Oil and Refining Company, and published in the magazine of the Houston Chamber of Commerce.

1. The *Dallas Morning News* Reports a Big Oil Discovery at Spindletop, January 11, 1901

A BIG OIL GEYSER
STREAM SIX INCHES IN DIAMETER SHOOTING **100** FEET
INTO THE AIR NEAR BEAUMONT.

ALL RECORDS BROKEN
IT IS ESTIMATED THAT ITS DAILY OUTPUT
IS ABOUT FIVE THOUSAND BARRELS.

BEAUMONT IN TRANSPORTS
**Road to the Well Is Lined with Vehicles
Carrying Delighted Citizens.**

Beaumont, Tex., Jan. 10.—A stream of oil six inches in diameter is shooting over 100 feet into the air from a well located about three miles south of the city and the people of Beaumont, of every sort and condition, are in a feverish state of excitement. Nothing in point of general interest ever before so wrought up the population of this city. The throng on the streets appears to be childishly happy and grown men are going about smiling and bowing to each other like school girls and oil geyser is the sole topic of conversation among men, women and children. . . .

The well was sunk by Capt. A. F. Lucas of Washington, D.C., who has been operating for oil in this territory for more than a year. It was dug by Hammil Bros. of Corsicana, professional oilwell men, and one of these gentlemen told the correspondent of The News this afternoon that he has not in all his experience seen a well that equaled this one. He said Corsicana's wells were insignificant compared with this well, if the size and force of the flow are indications of its value.

Capt. Lucas is fairly delighted. To the correspondent, who called upon him, he said he hardly knew what to say. "We've struck oil, is about all I know to tell you," said he. "You can see the well yourself and except for my experience; you can tell almost as much about it as I can tell you. I have had experience in nearly every oil field in the United States, and I never saw a well to equal this. It is a larger geyser than I ever saw in West Virginia or Pennsylvania, and I believe it is the strongest stream ever found in the United States. Our first step now will be to anchor the well by process familiar in all fields. I have two large well rigs on the road here now and will at once sink other wells."

2. Oil Workers Al Hamill and Curt Hamill Give Eyewitness Accounts of the Spindletop Gusher, 1901

Al Hamill: We put it on and was running this string of drill pipe back in, at about seven hundred feet or a little over in, when the drilling mud commenced to boil up through the rotary. And it got higher and higher and higher up through the top of

---

"A Big Oil Geyser," *Dallas Morning News,* 11 January 1901.

Mody C. Boatright and William A. Owens, *Tales from the Derrick Floor: A People's History of the Oil Industry* (Garden City: Doubleday, 1970): 40–42.

the derrick and with such pressure, why, the drill pipe commenced to move up. It moved up and started to going out through the top of the derrick. . . . The pipe went up through the derrick, then would break off in sections of three and four lengths at a time and fall over. Course, after that got out of the way, why, the rocks began to come out and gas to beat the cars.

It didn't last so awful long, but it died down very gradually. Well, we three boys then sneaked back down to the well after it quieted down and surveyed the situation, and I don't think I'm exaggerating to say that the mud was six inches deep on the derrick floor. And I had turned around to get a shovel to start to clean up, get some of that off the floor. And all of a sudden, a chunk of mud came out of the six-inch hole, full-size, with an explosion just like a cannon popping off. And that blew up with a little blue gas following it for a little bit, and then it quieted down, ceased altogether again.

. . . I walked over and looked down in the hole there. I heard—sort of hear something kind of bubbling just a little bit and looked down there, and here this frothy oil was starting up. It was just breathing like, you know, coming up and sinking back with the gas pressure. And it kept coming up and over the rotary table and each flow a little higher and a little higher and a little higher. Finally it came up with such momentum that it just shot up clear through the top of the derrick.

Curt Hamill: I was in the derrick at this time, and I couldn't tell you how I got down, but when I got down the driller had left the clutch in the draw works, and I got down in time to kick the clutch out. And by this time the pipe was going out the top of the derrick. And the other men had run and got out of the way, and, of course, I did the same thing. I ran as hard as I could and got away from the falling pipe, and no one was hurt from any of the blowout or the falling pipe.

Al: At first when we went down there to see all that mud and our drill pipe ruined—it was Mr. Galey's drill pipe, Guffey and Galey's, but it was our responsibility—we didn't know how much of the hole was ruined or what was in it. I rather expect that I was pretty disgusted. Of course, after the oil came in then and kept flowing and flowing we sent Peck on the run down to Mr. Lucas again. . . . And he immediately jumped in his old buckboard with his old horse and beat it for Spindletop. . . . Well, when he got so close, why, he just—well, . . . the old horse stopped, and Cap fell out and ran up. Of course, he was very heavy, you see, and by time he got up to me he was just about out of breath.

And he says, "Al! Al! What is it?"

And when I says, "Why, it's oil, Captain," well, he just grabbed me and says, "Thank God, thank God."

I daresay it wasn't over an hour, maybe, till people began to come. Some heard it, you see. You could hear this roar. And that afternoon they came in all kinds of conveyances. Lot of them walked. Young fellows walked out there from town and come on horseback and wagons and buggies. Practically everybody came from town because from where we were for miles and miles there wasn't another dwelling. That afternoon, there was a big crowd there.

3. The *Dallas Morning News* Praises Urban Planning for the City of Dallas, 1910

FEASIBILITY OF CITY REVISION
MR. KESSLER'S TENTATIVE PLANS
PRESENT HUGE, BUT
POSSIBLE TASK.

BENEFITS EXCEED OUTLAY
Thought Is to Help All Sections,
Citizens and Interests—What Seattle
Has Done.

When we were merely looking forward to the presentation of a city plan by Mr. Kessler, the landscape artist, there were many people in Dallas who expected it to be something in the nature of an Utopian dream, something impractical, a scheme merely of beautification, adornment and ornamentation. Now that Mr. Kessler has made his preliminary announcement and has given the Dallas public a glimpse of the studies thus far worked out, changes of opinion have come. For one thing, it is seen that Mr. Kessler has begun with two intensely practical ideas—facilitation of the traffic of the city, ordinary vehicular, traction, steam rail and boat, and the protection of the city's lower levels from overflow—and with them he has carried along the idea of converting unsightly places into scenes of beauty. . . .

Mr. Kessler's Suggestions.

1. The removal of the steam railroad lines which now cross the city in many directions.
2. The creation of a belt railroad, encircling the city beyond its boundaries, but affording access to the railroads along the river front only. The provision of passenger terminals along the river front: of a union passenger station in the vicinity of the Dallas County court house, creating in that district one of the civic centers of the city, the same to include besides the passenger station, the county court house main postoffice building, public library, City Hall and a large plaza. It is contemplated that local freight yards shall be placed in the territory contiguous to the river front and south of Commerce street, and transfer yards on the belt line outside the city. . . .
3. To protect the city from overflow and at the same time to provide room for the railroads and for rail and steamboat terminals along the river front, Mr. Kessler has tentatively planned the creation of a new, straight and broad channel for the Trinity River further west than the present channel and in the neighborhood of the foot of the bluffs on the west side and the keeping open of the bottoms on the west side.

Tom Finty, Jr., "Feasibility of City Revision," *Dallas Morning News,* 16 October 1910.

Parks and Boulevards.

4. A boulevard and park system, the main features of which are as follows:

   (1) A parkway along Turtle Creek, with a driveway on either bank, starting from a park which is to be created from the grounds of the present City Hospital, the grounds surrounding the present waterworks station and possibly some other land which may be acquired, and extending through Oak Lawn and Highland Park, taking in Oak Lawn Park.

   (2) A boulevard running south from the lower end of Turtle Creek parkway, through a territory between Maple avenue and the river bottoms to Masten street, thence along that street, St. Paul street, Evergreen street and Harwood street to some point in Colonial Hill, say South Boulevard or Pennsylvania avenue; thence east to Fair Park; thence, north, say along Carroll avenue, to a connection with the Turtle Creek parkway. It is contemplated that this boulevard shall be 100 feet wide and eleven miles long.

   (3) A cross boulevard of the same width, starting at the west from the Masten street boulevard and extending along Ross avenue to the city limits and thence to the White Rock reservoir, where it is planned to create the city's chief park, completely surrounding the reservoir with a driveway and beautiful grounds.

5. The widening of certain streets, the cutting of other streets through one or more blocks which now bar them, and the extension of others so as to produce needed diagonal ways, freer and shorter cuts than are now available. . . .

Mr. Kessler's tentative plans contemplate two things, basically: Revision to overcome existing defects; planning ahead to avoid defects in the future. . . .

. . . There are very few places such as Washington, which were planned as cities from the jump. Most of our cities started as villages and grew more or less illogically.

Dallas is of that class. It was not planned as a city; instead it began as a "settlement," and evolved through hamlet, village and town stages into the city class, bearing the marks of each. The bonds fastened upon it in its youth chafe and hamper it now. They ought to be removed; everybody admits that. The feasibility of removing them can scarcely be doubted by any one who contemplated the Titanic tasks performed by the people in scores of American cities.

4. Boston City Planner Arthur Comey Presents a Plan for the Development of Houston, 1913

The twentieth century is an age of cities. In thirty years from 1880 to 1910 the proportion of urban population in the United States has risen from 29.5 to 46.3 per cent. . . .

People live in the city primarily because it offers better facilities for trade and industry, . . . and, secondarily, because it provides better opportunities for enjoying the amenities of life. Trade and industry are dependent mainly upon a market and

Arthur Coleman Comey, *Houston: Tentative Plans for Its Development: Report to the Houston Park Commission* (Boston: Press of Geo. H. Ellis, Co., 1913): 5–8 facilities for communication with that market. Therefore, the cities which have grown most rapidly are those with the largest tributary areas and the most efficient means of transportation, where possible utilizing both water and rail. These fundamental causes for growth have frequently been supplemented by others, such as . . . the adoption of progressive measures in civic development.

In Houston we find all these and many other agencies combining to create a great city. The territory for the marketing of its commodities is vast in area and increasing in population at a rapid rate. Its radiating railroad lines give ready access to all this territory; and upon completion of its ship channel it will have a combination of rail and water facilities second to none in the State of Texas. Strategically considered, Houston's location assures it of becoming the metropolis of the great South-west. Its steady, rapid increase in population in the past indicates a keen appreciation of this fact.

With the growth of cities there has come a great increase in the mutual interdependence of their inhabitants. Whether we believe in socialistic doctrines or not, we all recognize the value of commercial activity in a great variety of directions, such as preserving law and order, safety from fire, provision for pavements, sewerage, and the other usual municipal departments. But it is only recently that any thought has been given toward correlating these activities and planning on broad lines in advance to secure the greatest public good, as would be done by a private corporation.

This, then, is city planning,—to study and determine in advance the physical needs of the growing city, and lay out a scheme of development in such a way that each improvement will dovetail into the next, thus gradually forming an organically related whole. The complex activities of a city demand an equally complex plan for development, so that each of its functions may be fulfilled without undue interference with any other. . . .

In the co-ordinated development of a city plan the underlying framework must be its means of communication. First the waterways must be determined, as they are rather rigidly fixed by the topography. Then the railroads, which are also located in large measure by existing grades, must be so planned as to best serve the needs of passengers and freight. . . . Finally, the thoroughfares must be laid out,—the net of traffic streets that will give access by foot, vehicle, or electric car to every portion of the city. . . .

Given such a plan, the next concern will be for the provision of homes and places to work. . . . A certain type of street plan is best adapted to factories, another to office buildings, and a third to workingmen's homes. If the class of building is determined in advance, great economies will result from this differentiation, and each section will benefit by having its special plan. The improvement of the working places and homes themselves should next be considered, for they constitute the normal environment of most of the city dwellers. Industrial welfare and housing are each in themselves subjects demanding exhaustive study.

The intense activity of city life and the increasingly artificial conditions under which its citizens live make more and more essential the introduction into daily life of recreation. . . . Such recreation facilities are for the most part to be provided by the city's park system, though school centres, public baths, and other agencies may contribute no small share of the opportunities for play.

Finally there will be needed in the modern city a large number of administrative and other public and quasi-public buildings, such as the city hall, post-office, railway station, institutional buildings, and the like, over whose design and location more or less direct control can be exercised.

The architectural treatment of individual buildings has recently been raised to a high standard in the United States. But the opportunity for an immeasurably enhanced effect due to the grouping of several buildings is as yet seldom availed of, despite the numerous reports lately issued in various cities urging this principle. In a rapidly growing city such as Houston . . . if these occasions are utilized to erect buildings on locations conforming to prearranged plans, in a few years monumental civic centres will be produced . . . in place of the usual haphazard "spotting" of public building about the city.

. . . In the case of Houston great increase in size is so assured that plans can be drawn along very broad lines. . . . Houston's problems can now be dealt with before the serious mistakes are made which have hampered so many American cities.

5. The *Houston Post* Reports the Mutiny of African American Troops, 1917

MARTIAL LAW DECLARED
Result of riot started by negro regulars who mutinied,
fired upon their officers and left camp, slaying 13,
wounding 19. One officer of Illinois regiment slain
and seven policemen are dead or wounded.

As a result of a riot which began early in the evening at the camp of the negro regulars of the Twenty-fourth infantry, Houston and its environs are today under martial law with Brigadier General John A. Hulen in command. This action was taken by Governor Ferguson, upon request by acting Mayor D. M. Moody, at about 12:30 this morning; and this was later followed with an order by General James Parker naming General Hulen as the officer in command.

General Hulen at once gave orders for the dispersing of the crowds who still thronged the streets at that hour, for the prompt arrest of such of the negro soldiers as were not in the camp under guard, for the closing of all saloons and drinking places until such time as he may direct.

Crowds are not to be permitted and incendiary oratory will be promptly suppressed.

Men bearing arms will be arrested.

Sheriff Frank Hammond hurried to the city from his home at Seabrook and has summoned a posse of citizens. This posse is to see to the suppression of excitement among the citizens. There are rumors that a great number of people from other counties are hurrying to Houston—and they are not wanted. If they come to Houston bearing arms they will be promptly arrested and put in jail. . . .

"Martial Law Declared," *Houston Post,* 24 August 1917.

THE DEAD.

At C. J. Wright's Morgue.

IRA D. RAINEY, mounted police officer.
RUFE DANIELS, mounted police officer.
MIDDLE AGED MAN NAMED SMITH.
S. SATTON, barber, 1207 Rusk.

At Wall & Stabe's Morgue.

CAPTAIN J. W. MATTES, battery A, Second Illinois Field artillery.
E. J. MEINEKE, police officer.

At Westheimer's Morgue.

EARL FINLEY.
A. R. CARSTEN, painter.
MANUEL GARREDO, 4903 Washington.
FRED E. WINKLER, 3910 Lillian street.
BRYANT WATTSON, negro soldier, company K, Twenty-fourth infantry.

Dead at Hospitals.

M. D. EVERTON, battery E, a local company.
C. W. WRIGHT, 3701 Wood street.

THE WOUNDED.

William J. Drucks, 4910 Lillian street, shot in right arm, amputation necessary; very low from loss of blood and surgical shock.

W. H. Burkett, Runnells streets, shot in left side, sprinkled on side and back with shotgun shot; condition serious.

E. A. Thompson of Hempstead. Gunshot in right leg; condition serious.

J. E. Richardson, 1203 Waverly street, shot in the head with rifle by negro soldier; condition not serious.

Asa Bland of Park Place, shot over left eye; injury slight.

Wylie Strong, negro private, company I, Twenty-fourth negro infantry, shot in right side accidentally by another soldier of his company; condition not serious.

Horace Moody, mounted police officer, wounded in left leg.

D. R. Patton, mounted police officer, received five or six wounds in hip, thigh, leg and shoulder.

Sammie Foreman of Livingston, company F, Fifth Texas infantry, shot in leg; not serious.

James Edwin Lyon, 4427 Walker street, employe of Cotton Belt office, shot in leg and arm.

Unidentified negro trooper, shot through abdomen

Unidentified negro trooper, shot in leg with buckshot.

G. W. Butcher, Cottage Grove, shot in left chest and right loin; seriously wounded.

W. A. Thompson, shot through right hip; condition serious.

Wiley Strong, negro soldier, Twenty-fourth infantry, wounded.

City Detective T. A. Binford, shot in the knee.

Sam Salensky, 105 Hamilton, badly hurt in auto accident going to camp.

Alma Reichert, white girl, 8001 Washington avenue, shot in stomach.

George Beavens, negro soldier, wounded in leg.

————————

Thirteen known dead and 19 wounded make the toll of race troubles that reached a climax Thursday night when negro soldiers of the Twenty-fourth infantry raided through West End.

The riot got its starting spark from trouble Thursday afternoon between negro soldiers and city police. That it had been brewing for several days is the general belief.

That the list of dead and wounded will grow with the coming of daylight is highly possible. . . .

All citizens will remain in their homes or usual places of business at once.

No citizen not an officer will appear on the streets with arms.

Parties will not assemble on the streets.

Saloons will not be permitted to open.

Places of business where arms and ammunition are sold, kept or stored will remain closed.

[General] Hulen.

————————

I call upon every citizen of Houston, white and colored, to preserve the peace, to go quietly about their business and to rest assured that there is going to be full inquiry and proper punishment for the crimes which have been committed.

It is time for coolness and for careful avoidance of further trouble.

It is no time for further excitement.

The city is under martial law, a condition which is most regrettable; but it is necessary.

There will be no further trouble if every citizen will carefully see to his own conduct. Incendiary speech is of no avail.

The situation is well in hand—unless there be studied effort to cause more trouble.

Dan M. Moody, Acting Mayor

6. Texans Tell Reporter Edward T. Devine That Some of "the Best People" Belong to the Klan, 1922

The New York World is quoted by the Searchlight of Atlanta as "chortling" to the effect that "now that the mask has been torn from the Ku Klux Klan, it has ceased to be a menace." In this county seat in the interior of Texas where I have been spending a week the Klan seems to be considered a very serious menace indeed—to evildoers.

————————

Edward T. Devine, "The Klan in Texas," *The Survey* 48 (April 1, 1922): 10–11; "More About the Klan," *The Survey* 48 (April 8, 1922): 42–43.

I am still rubbing my eyes and questioning my ears. This is surely not the same fantastic embodiment of anti-Catholic, anti-Jewish, anti-Negro, anti-labor prejudice which I have read about, the masked hundred percenters who are so free with whips and tar and feathers, or worse, whose lawless methods have become proverbial. . . .

. . . My next jolt came when a student in this Texas town . . . came to my room for a long evening talk, in the course of which he launched into a warm eulogy of the Ku Klux Klan. He is not a member, but that is only because a certain girl whose opinions are important to him had vetoed it. . . .

The Klan, this ardent college youth insists, is not against Negroes but in their interest, not against Catholics but only for Protestantism—as the Knights of Columbus are for their religion. It is for one hundred per cent Americanism, for law and order, and for white supremacy. He admitted that it sometimes upholds law and order by extra-legal means. He knew of the cases in Houston; for example, the tarring of a doctor who was known to be guilty of criminal practices. What the boy insisted upon was that the doctor was guilty, that he was a menace, and that the Klan rid the city of his presence and his practices when the authorities by their milder measures had failed to do so. . . .

It began to seem to me important to understand the point of view of this southern community. I therefore sounded next the Methodist minister. "I understand," I remarked casually, "that some very good people get into the Ku Klux Klan in these parts." "The very best people get into it," he replied emphatically. The good doctor who said this is not a bigot. . . . He is active in the inter-racial commission. He neither condemned nor advocated the Klan, but with discrimination expressed both his doubts and his appreciation of some of their acts. He is deeply distressed by the lawlessness of the time. He thinks that the intention of the Klan is to combat lawlessness and that . . . its ordinary method is to try to secure the election of capable and honest officials and to cooperate with them in furnishing evidence of criminal acts. . . .

I had a whole afternoon of serious talk with half a dozen men of the faculty of a school for the training of teachers. We talked about the race question and the Ku Klux Klan. All these men are southern in ancestry, birth, education and life-long residence. They are in sympathy with efforts to improve racial cooperation. They are taking part in them persistently. They would no doubt subscribe to the shibboleth of white supremacy, but they would narrow its meaning in practice in such a way as to make it comparatively unobjectionable to self-respecting Negroes. They are for equal justice in the courts and in economic relations; for better schools, for the colored, for better accommodations on railways. . . .

What these gentlemen, . . . had to say about the mysterious organization is no doubt as fair an estimate as one will find. They are confident that stories of lawless acts by the Klan published in northern newspapers are exaggerated; that hereabouts, at least, it does not represent anti-Jewish prejudice nor anti-Catholic bigotry nor antagonism to Negroes; that it is not hostile to labor; . . . that its main purpose, however, is to inculcate a wholesome respect for law and order. . . .

I had, finally, an interview with one representative business man, who was so well informed and so outspoken in his advocacy as to leave little doubt of his active membership. In his eyes it is a righteous crusade. It makes no mistakes. It will use whatever means are necessary. . . .

It is easy to laugh at the absurdities of the Klan, its childish follies, its illiterate nomenclature, its fallacious conception of law and order. But it is not easily laughed out of existence. Close at hand it is serious. It has a certain dignity of purpose. It is not sheer bigotry or stupidity or charlatanry or fraud. Perhaps it may be short-lived. I hope so; for the evils which it professes to attack are certainly for the most part to be overcome only by very different means.

More About the Klan

I have been hearing more about the Ku Klux Klan in Texas towns. . . .

I notice that there is rather more anti-Catholic sentiment in the complex than appeared to be the case in the first community studied. . . .

On the other hand, further evidence confirms my first impressions that the Ku Klux movement hereabouts is not conspicuously anti-Negro. . . .

Everywhere I hear, as I heard in my first Texas town, that "the best people" are among the Klansmen. . . .

Notwithstanding the repeated assurance that "the best people" join, it may not be entirely without significance that in fact only one of all the "best people" whom I have happened to meet appears actually to have done so. . . . With the one exception all have taken pains to make it clear that they are not members, though several of them have expressed strong sympathy with the purposes of the Klan and some had given serious consideration to an invitation to join. What has deterred them in the last analysis is the mask, and the resort to what are politely called "extra-legal methods of upholding law and order" when the ordinary processes do not avail, or are not sufficiently prompt and drastic.

7. African American Activist Clifford Richardson Assesses the Needs of Black Neighborhoods in Houston, 1928

With the largest colored population of any city in Texas—variously estimated from 55,000 to 60,000—"Heavenly Houston" can rightfully boast of as intelligent, thrifty, substantial, upstanding, law-abiding and patriotic a group of colored citizens as can be found in any other city in America, without regard to geographical lines or location. This is as it should be, for the progress, peace, growth and well-being in this community are indissolubly linked and intertwined with the black race. . . .

A recent survey of colored business enterprises in twenty Southern cities . . . reveals that Houston tops the list with business concerns owned and operated by members of the colored race. . . .

According to available statistics, more colored citizens own or are acquiring homes in Houston than in any other purely Southern city. It is further estimated that Houston's colored population has approximately $7,000,000 deposited with local banks and financial houses. . . .

Clifford F. Richardson, "Houston's Colored Citizens: Activities and Conditions Among the Negro Population," *Civics for Houston* 1 (August 1928): 5, 14, 29–30.

The residential sections inhabited by colored citizens, which, during the last two or three years, have received considerable civic consideration and physical improvement are still lacking (many of them) in the permanent type of improvements so essential to the moral, physical, civic and aesthetic welfare of the community. Rent houses are built in such close proximity to each other that one can stand in one house and hear the inmate in the adjacent house change his mind. . . .

If the City of Houston has an ordinance on its statute books regulating and prohibiting this method of building houses for tenants, the law is neither invoked nor enforced when it comes to rent houses for colored citizens. Surface privies are still ubiquitous in many sections occupied by colored residents, while drainage is extremely bad in most of these colored sections, with cess-pools and ponds of stagnant water which seldom dry up between rains.

Street lights are few and far between, and the resultant darkness obtaining in these colored neighborhoods becomes a[n] . . . incubator of crime and criminals. . . . These districts have very little fire and police protection, and it is becoming increasingly difficult for colored Houstonians to get much fire insurance upon their homes and household effects. . . .

In the face of such unhealthy and unsavory living conditions the death rate among colored Houstonians is alarmingly high. . . .

Emancipation Park, located at Dowling, Tuam and Elgin, Third Ward, which the colored citizens of the community bought years ago and turned over to the city . . . is the only colored park in the city; and, though under municipal management and control, the city has done very little towards beautifying and improving this park. . . .

Civic improvement associations are being fostered in some of the populous colored residential sections and, though rather sporadic in their activities, they are doing much to inspire the race along the lines of civic beautification, health, hygiene and sanitation.

Houston has three colored senior high schools (something that no other city in America possesses) . . . and the only municipally owned and operated colored junior college in the entire world. . . .

Houston offers the colored group the greatest opportunity of any Southern city for industrial employment and commercial and professional activity. . . .

Additional parks should be provided in the Fourth and Fifth wards for colored citizens, and the colored residents of the Heights should have a park. There is no swimming pool provided for our colored population, although playground activities are being conducted at two or three of the ward public schools.

Housing and living conditions among the colored residents of Houston should be surveyed and studied in the immediate future, and the findings made a basis for a well-defined program for the amelioration of these shameful, shocking and startling conditions under which thousands of colored Houstonians are forced to live and eke out a bare existence.

Additional colored patrolmen should be added to the local police force to patrol colored districts on all beats, and thus minimize the danger of clashes between minions of the law and colored citizens.

With its extremely large colored population and their various and varied activities and achievements, it is next to impossible to give a free and full account in such an article as this, but the writer has endeavored to give the readers of this magazine a graphic cross-section of Houston's colored citizenry, who constitute an important and integral part of our heterogeneous and polyglot population.

8. Humble Oil Vice President John Suman Relates Prosperity in Houston to the Growth of the Texas Oil Industry, 1940

Since Houston has become recognized as the oil capital of the world, in spite of the dying claims of cities in neighboring states, a brief discussion of the importance of world-wide, national, and state activities in petroleum will also be indicative of the importance of petroleum to Houston.

It has been estimated that the United States has produced over 21,000,000,000 barrels of the 33,200,000,000 barrels of oil produced for the entire world. To produce this volume of oil, investments amounting to $14,500,000,000 have been made, which consist principally . . . in crude-oil-producing properties, . . . in pipe lines, . . . in refineries, and . . . in marketing and transportation facilities. Although the industry is 80 years old, the principal activities in petroleum and consumption of products have extended over the past two decades. . . . Although the population of the United States is only 6.5 percent of the world population, it accounted for 55 percent of the total consumption. Also, it produced 61 percent of the world production and supplied 13 percent of the requirements of the remainder of the world. . . .

The world reserves of petroleum at present are placed at approximately 34,000,000,000 barrels and the American Petroleum Institute placed the reserves of the United States at 17,348,146,000 barrels as of January 1, 1939, or approximately 51 percent of the total reserve. . . . At the present rate of consumption, our reserves will not supply demand beyond a 15-year period. . . . Keeping reserves ahead of demand has largely been accomplished through intensive application of science and technology to oil production. When it is understood that such a large percentage of our population is directly or indirectly dependent on the oil industry for a livelihood and that a good percentage of governmental activities is supported through taxation of the oil industry, it will readily be agreed that the high standards of living in this country were considerably aided by developments in petroleum.

Although the petroleum industry is among the top-ranking industries in the United States, it occupies a position of greater significance in the state of Texas. Since the discovery of oil in Texas at Nacogdoches in 1866, shortly after the first discovery of oil in the United States, Texas has produced five and one-half billion barrels of the 21 billion barrels of crude produced in the United States. . . .

Petroleum is now considered to be the most valuable mineral resource of the state and petroleum refining holds the distinction of being the largest manufacturing industry, with its products accounting for over 40 per cent of all manufactured

From John R. Suman, Vice President, Humble Oil and Refining Company, "Importance of Oil and Gas Industry to Houston," *Houston* 11 (April 1940): 52–54. Copyright © 1940. Reprinted with permission of the Greater Houston Partnership.

products. This is somewhat in contrast to the former conception of Texas being principally an agricultural state. . . . Texas produced . . . during 1938, 40 percent of the total crude produced by the United States. . . . The petroleum income provides a livelihood directly or indirectly for approximately 1,000,000 people in Texas, 175,000 of which are employed directly in the production, transportation and refining branches of the industry. . . . In spite of large production in the past, Texas offers one of the most fertile fields of oil exploration and possesses, according to the American Petroleum Institute, 9,447,764,000 barrels of the 17,348,146,000 barrels of reserve in the United States as of January 1, 1939, or more than 54 percent of the national reserve. With this picture of reserve and prospective fields for development in the state, it can be seen that the industry will continue to occupy a position of great importance in the business of the state for many years to come.

You have probably wondered why Houston has been designated the oil capital of the world. This came about due principally to three main reasons as follows: (1) the location of Houston in regard to shipping facilities; (2) the location of Houston in regard to petroleum activities; and (3) the location of Houston in relation to future prospective petroleum activities. Due to the strategic location of Houston, a large number of companies interested in every phase of the petroleum industry have located here. Included among these are oil and gas producing, refining, transportation, marketing companies, and manufacturing plants supplying oil-field equipment. Houston is the largest concentration point in the world for oil field supply companies. The oil industry furnishes a means of livelihood to more than one-half the population of the city with something like 50,000 people being employed directly. The petroleum industry is by far the biggest customer of incoming and outgoing freight to railroads, and. . . . approximately 81½ per cent of all the tonnage handled through the port, and this amounts to 30½ per cent of all the oil produced in Texas. Oil is delivered by pipe lines to Houston from the states of New Mexico, Oklahoma, Kansas, Arkansas, and Louisiana, and there is also considerable tank car traffic. Tank steamers from California, Mexico, and other foreign countries bring special grades of crude for refining and blending and crude to be processed for consumption in the markets of the world. Besides serving the coastal area and Texas, Houston is rapidly becoming the center of oil equipment distribution for a considerable portion of the Mid-Continent area.

The reserves of oil have been maintained during the past 30 years principally by exploring structures of progressively greater depths, and geologists now agree that the Gulf Coast area in which Houston is located is one of the most promising areas in the United States for future development of crude reserves.

The desirable location of Houston for the oil industry has, in turn, been greatly enhanced for other industries by the petroleum industry through development of gas reserves within the near-by area. The gas available . . . within 50 miles of Houston . . . is adequate to supply the area with low-cost industrial fuel . . . for over 130 years. Additional large reserves of gas are located beyond the 50-mile radius from Houston and within distance for supplying cheap industrial fuel gas.

There is no other large city in the world that possesses the combined desirable transportation and fuel facilities so favorable to industrial growth. This should go a long way to insure the continued progress and growth of our city.

🔸 E S S A Y S

The two essays focus on different aspects of urbanization in Texas and reflect different approaches to this issue that historians have taken. The historian Bruce Beauboeuf examines the factors that transformed Houston into a rapidly growing industrial city. Like many urban historians he stresses the city's natural economic advantages and its transportation system. However, he also argues that World War I and the needs and policies of the federal government were the catalysts that transformed Houston into a major industrial center and placed the city with it's two major industries, cotton and oil, into the international economic arena. In the second essay, Robert Fairbanks of the University of Texas at Arlington addresses a different aspect of urbanization. He examines the efforts of Dallas business, political, and civic leaders to use planning to mold their city into a major urban center. He argues that economic advantage must be matched with enlightened civic leadership to create a great city.

World War I and Houston's Emergence as an Industrial City

BRUCE ANDRE BEAUBOEUF

The economic mobilization of the First World War . . . propelled the economy of the city of Houston into its modern position within the international community. . . . The war effort provided a . . . window of opportunity through which local business greatly accelerated the process of industrialization. Cotton and oil, both vital to the war effort, spurred Houston's economic growth during and after the war. The demand for these items during the war meant immediate profits, but that demand also brought about fundamental structural changes in the local cotton and oil industries, including expansion of operations and an unprecedented degree of cooperation between business and government at both state and federal levels. The renewed commitment to improve the Houston Ship Channel was a key aspect of this federal-local alliance, as was the federal government's encouragement of the merchant marine, whose vessels were instrumental in bringing international cotton trade to the Port of Houston. In both instances, and in many others, these economic trans-formations resulted from the process of mobilization during the First World War. This then set the stage for Houston's economic growth in the 1920s, enabling the city to become the model of the New South sought by Southern modernization proponents since Reconstruction. . . .

Initially, the war created an economic crisis in the United States, especially in the South. With the disruption of international trade caused by the war, national export trade decreased by over 58 million dollars. The country lost vital markets in Europe, and surplus amounts of cotton, oil, and other products grew, with prices falling sharply. . . . Bales of cotton piled up in the streets of Houston and many other Southern cities, and the price of cotton fell from 12 cents to under 7 cents per pound. . . .

While domestic attempts to alleviate the "cotton crisis" availed little, the foreign policy of the federal government, regarding the nations at war, proved to be very beneficial. The decision of the Wilson administration to forgo strict neutrality and assume a de facto . . . alliance with Great Britain and France, would revive international trade and bring a return of prosperity from the economic recession of late 1914 and early 1915.

Cotton was crucial to a modern war effort for its value in making smokeless powder, as well as military clothing, medical supplies, tenting for encampments, and a myriad of other uses. As the United States became economically tied to the Allied war effort, the cotton economy of Houston and the South rebounded dramatically. . . . Cotton prices grew from their low of under 7 cents per pound to over 35 cents per pound by 1919, increasing more than five times in price.

. . . This dramatic price increase, then, unchecked by ceilings, resurrected the Southern cotton economy. In turn, these new profits enabled Houston cotton merchants to expand their operations in significant and lasting ways.

With regard to cotton, the war placed renewed emphasis on improving the Port of Houston in two important ways. First, the economic recession of late 1914 to early 1915 made Houston cotton merchants realize the need to improve storage and compress facilities on the Ship Channel for surplus cotton. Second, the congestion of the railroad system because of the war effort made clear the need to use the nation's waterways as an alternative route for the transportation of goods. . . .

To fund this expansion, cotton merchants were able to take advantage of new investment assets as Allied purchases of U.S. goods and supplies transformed the United States from a debtor to a creditor nation. The Wilson administration's decision to allow U.S. industries to trade with the Allies brought a historic reversal to the U.S.-European financial relationship. Through Allied war purchases, bank deposits in the United States and in Houston increased dramatically. . . . Bank deposits in Houston grew from $32 million in 1915 to $50 million in 1916. With U.S. entrance into the war, Houston bank deposits reached $61 million in 1917, and were over $94 million by 1919.

This new financial backing also allowed Houston cotton merchants to increase the vertical integration of their operations and thus gain greater efficiency and stability. During and after the First World War, Houston cotton merchants such as Anderson, Clayton & Company, George McFadden & Company, and Alexander Sprunt & Sons developed closer ties to the growing, ginning, and milling of cotton. Of even greater importance was that this influx of capital to Houston banks enabled Houston cotton merchants to expand their cotton compresses, storage, and wharf facilities along the Ship Channel, making Houston more attractive as a seaport. A growing alliance between Houston banks and local cotton merchants provided the latter with the capital they needed to expand their operations along the Ship Channel continually during the period 1916 to 1930.

In 1916, Ship Channel warehouses could store roughly 400,000 bales of cotton, and at least 13 cotton merchants had facilities in the Port of Houston. . . . By 1920, there were 80 cotton merchant firms in the city, there were 9 cotton compresses along the Ship Channel, and storage capacity had increased to 600,000 bales. Houston emerged from the war as the largest spot cotton market in the world, and the largest inland seaport in the nation.

Seizing the opportunity, Anderson, Clayton & Company moved its head-quarters from Oklahoma City to Houston in 1916, and designated the Houston Ship Channel as its primary clearinghouse for all the cotton it dealt with. William Clayton later explained the move, stating that "Houston was the little end of the funnel that drained all of the Texas and Oklahoma territory . . . we were at the back door, and we wanted to be at the front door."

The Anderson, Clayton company's commitment to the burgeoning Port of Houston at this time was a sign that Houston's cotton economy and port activity were not only reviving; they were undergoing fundamental structural change. This economic expansion fostered a growth in Houston's cotton trade that played a large role in driving Houston's economy during the 1920s. Exports of cotton bales increased dramatically in that decade, growing from 45,000 bales in 1920 to just over 1,000,000 in 1924. By 1929, exports of bales of cotton were approximately 2.3 million; they stayed high into the 1930s.

Port facilities expanded to handle the increased traffic. Use of the city's public terminals and facilities increased 97.6 percent from 1921 to 1924. A number of firms built private facilities for cotton shipping during the 1920s. In 1922 and 1923, Alexander Sprunt & Son established the Ship Channel Compress Company; the following year, the Houston Compress Company, owned by Anderson, Clayton & Company, built the "Long Reach" facility that remained the largest cotton terminal and warehouse system on the channel for decades. In 1928, Joseph W. Evans completed the Manchester Terminal, with a storage capacity of 250,000 bales; by that year, Ship Channel facilities could hold 1,250,000 bales of cotton. By 1930, warehousing facilities along the Ship Channel could hold 2,000,000 bales of cotton, equal to 40 percent of all cotton produced annually in Texas.

With this tremendous growth in cotton facilities along the Ship Channel during the 1920s, net receipts of cotton—meaning cotton actually handled, compressed, and stored by Houston merchants, as opposed to being merely en route to Galveston and therefore not profiting Houston firms—increased significantly. As a percentage of gross receipts, net receipts of cotton increased from 27 percent at the beginning of the war to . . . 54 percent by 1919–20. . . . By the 1926–27 season, net receipts of cotton were over 3.5 million bales, equal to 99 percent of all the cotton that entered Houston to be exported. Now nearly all the cotton that entered Houston was exported from the Ship Channel; now Houston was a port in its own right, no longer merely a transition point to Galveston.

In addition, the void created by World War I allowed Houston cotton merchants to fill the role that European import firms had once held. During the war, the Anderson, Clayton company established its own selling organizations in such traditional European markets as Liverpool and Le Havre, as well as in other Allied countries: Russia, China, and Japan. The federal government worked with the nation's shipping interests to promote trade and expansion of U.S. shipping into foreign markets during and after the war. To this end, the government increased the size of the merchant marine, which had declined since the Civil War. With the passage of the Shipping Act of 1916, Congress created the United States Shipping Board, an agency designed to promote the development, construction, and regulation of the merchant marine. . . .

At the end of the war, Daniel Ripley saw a need to make the Port of Houston more widely known to shipping interests. Through contacts made by his business, the Ripley Steamship Company, he lobbied the Shipping Board to direct trade to the port. Ripley's efforts paid off when he was able to charter the Shipping Board vessel *Merry Mount,* which came into the port in November 1919 and sailed away with 23,319 bales of cotton destined for Liverpool. With the navigability of the waterway thus proven, the *West Chetac,* the *Bethlehem Ridge,* and the *Montgomery* soon followed, all under the authorization of the United States Shipping Board, carrying over 46,000 bales of cotton to Liverpool. Under the aegis of the Shipping Board, Ripley also expanded his own shipping concerns into such foreign markets as Liverpool, Le Havre, Bremen, and Barcelona in 1920. In this way, federal aid helped accelerate the growth of the cotton trade in the Port of Houston and enabled the city to significantly increase its ties to international ports. . . .

The Lykes Brothers Steamship company, which began operations as a charter shipping concern in Galveston in 1906 and in the Port of Houston in 1920, also became involved in the war-shipping effort. Lykes, abandoning its former practice of chartering foreign vessels, was the first Gulf Coast shipping company to charter the newly built Shipping Board vessels in the war effort. In 1922, Lykes purchased its first five vessels—ships that had been built as part of the federal government's wartime economic expansion. In 1923, Lykes transferred the bulk of its Texas Gulf Coast operations from Galveston to Houston, tangibly symbolizing the emerging Port of Houston overtaking the Port of Galveston.

After the war, Anderson, Clayton & Company renewed its connections with Bremen, Germany, and established ties to the newly formed nation of Czechoslovakia. The firm also bought a 40 percent share of a Liverpool importing firm, D. F. Pennefather & Co., which would later become a controlling 60 percent interest. As the owners of this firm, Anderson, Clayton dealt directly with the cotton spinners in Great Britain and the European mainland, effectively avoiding the overseas middlemen. Addressing the interrelated growth of shipping and the cotton trade in the postwar Port of Houston, Fleming commented that the transfer of wealth from Europe to the United States had "called for the assumption by American cotton interests of a much broader role than before in merchandising, storing, carrying, financing, and retail distribution to the ultimate consumer."

Assessing the overall expansion and transformation of Houston's cotton economy, Fleming stated that the Houston cotton merchants found that "at the close of the war . . . the previous handicaps of American cotton firms, with respect to banking, storing and handling surpluses, had been replaced by advantages." With federal support of the cotton trade in these ways, due to the war effort, merchant firms in Houston and throughout the region found themselves with opportunities for expansion of operations that would transform their industry.

The war effort also transformed the Texas oil industry. A modern, mechanized military depended heavily upon petroleum products. . . . [D]emand for petroleum products increased dramatically. . . .

As with the cotton industry, the initial disruption of trade and economic recession brought on by the war affected the oil industry. . . . Although exports of petroleum from the Port of Houston did not suffer significantly, this was largely because the Ship Channel was not yet the major petroleum port it would become. . . . Yet the Gulf Coast oil industry did suffer, as the price of crude oil fell from 95 cents per barrel in 1913 to 64 cents in 1914, before finally bottoming out at 48 cents in 1915. . . .

Yet after the U.S. economy became tied to the Allied war effort, exports and oil prices improved swiftly. In 1917, the United Stated exported 65.4 million barrels, with Great Britain and France the principal buyers. Shipments of petroleum products from the Port of Houston, both foreign and coastwise, grew dramatically from 31,584 short tons in 1915 to 293,400 in 1916. During the war, Houston oil concerns used their own ships to reach northeastern U.S. ports to supply the navy; in 1917, 288,503 short tons of crude oil were shipped coastwise from the Port of Houston.

With the war-related increase in demand, Gulf Coast oil prices rose from 48 cents per barrel in 1915 to 75 cents in 1916, and in some areas along the Texas Gulf Coast prices were even higher. . . . Will C. Hogg, writing to Cullinan and Thomas P. Lee (all three were involved with Cullinan's Farmer's Petroleum Company), announced: "Dollar oil has arrived." . . . By March 1917, the price of crude oil at Goose Creek, an increasingly productive field located along the banks of the Ship Channel, had reached $1.25 per barrel. By 1919, Gulf Coast oil prices had risen to $1.70 per barrel of crude oil.

The oil industry, like the cotton industry, also benefited from an absence of federally mandated price ceilings throughout the war. Again, the federal government allowed this inflation to spur production, and increasing prices did stimulate oil production in the Houston area. At the Goose Creek field, where the newly formed Humble Oil and Refining Company was predominant, production increased from 397,000 barrels of crude oil in 1916 to over 7,000,000 in 1917; then to nearly 9,000,000 by 1918; and continued at around the 6,000,000 barrel mark annually into the middle of the 1920s. Production at the Humble field, just north of Houston, spurred on by Farmers Petroleum Company, increased from roughly 3,000,000 barrels in 1914 to over 11,000,000 by 1916; annual production there varied from 6,000,000 to 10,000,000 barrels for the rest of the war. . . .

The oil industry acquired power as well as profits during the wartime era, particularly in its governmental relationships. The war effort, highly dependent upon the production of oil, meant that the oil industry dealt from a position of strength in its cooperative wartime relationship with the federal government. Furthermore, unlike coal, price hikes or shortages of oil brought relatively little public protest. Coal was the primary domestic consumption fuel; oil was more important to the army and navy. This helped to strengthen the oil industry's bargaining leverage with the federal government and allowed Houston-area oil companies to deal with their concerns of efficiency, stability, and integrated operations without the threats of either adverse public opinion or government sanctions.

Labor-management relations were to be a key example of the oil industry's new political muscle, as was manifest in the Gulf Coast oil strike of 1917. As oil field production, oil prices, corporate profits, and inflation all began to soar in 1916–17, oil field workers in Texas and Louisiana seized the opportunity to demand improvements in working conditions. The Houston-Goose Creek area oil concerns, however, such as the Producer's Oil Company, the Gulf Production Company, and the newly incorporated Humble Oil and Refining Company, all refused to recognize the oil workers' union or their demands. When 10,000 oil field workers in Texas and Louisiana went on strike on November 1, 1917, the local oil companies remained intransigent. . . .

A number of factors would work in favor of local oil management. One critical fact was that management could readily keep the refining process going by using the vast reserves of crude oil already pumped and stored, in large part a result of the high levels of production that had recently been attained. . . . Oil management also found it easy to replace the strikers, as many low-wage farm workers from Texas and Oklahoma were only too willing to accept the comparatively high-wage oil field work.

Local business and civic leaders stressed the danger of a reduction in oil production to the federal government. . . . With the rumor of local activities by the Industrial Workers of the World (IWW), with its incendiary ideology, state and local government leaders requested the War Department to send federal troops to Gulf Coast oil fields on November 2, after the strike was only one day old. The War Department quickly responded, deploying more than 2,000 federal troops at Goose Creek and other Houston-area oil fields.

Due to the perceived threat of "radical" and "disloyal" labor unions, local oil concerns were able to exploit both the federal government's need for oil and the general public opprobrium toward strikers during a war effort. The deployment of federal troops into the Gulf Coast oil fields to protect corporate assets, and strike-breakers, from rumored threats of sabotage by "alien enemies" was one of the more dramatic examples of wartime cooperation between business and government. The full impact of federal military influence was evident when, after a violent clash between union and nonunion men, martial law was declared in Houston on November 21.

The strike, however, had faded before that episode. . . . As oil field workers began to return to their jobs, the Department of Labor announced that it had no intention of intervening in the dispute, since the operators had convinced them production would be unaffected.

The presence of federal troops in this Gulf Coast labor-management dispute helped resolve the crisis into an unmitigated victory for local oil concerns. It resolved the immediate crisis in favor of the local oil industry; it symbolized the power relationship between the oil interests and the federal government; and, by suppressing the nascent oil field workers' union, it set the tone for the management-controlled labor relations of the 1920s.

During and because of the war effort, Gulf Coast oil companies were able to take full advantage of those aspects of the federal intervention that they valued, such as federal demand for oil products and federal troops to protect their operations, while they effectively ignored other aspects that tended to work against them, as with federal attempts to arbitrate the oil field workers' demands. Oil companies on the Gulf Coast and throughout the nation were also able to take advantage of the wartime emphasis upon production to free themselves from previous government restraints on establishing vertically integrated operations.

Antitrust policy was perhaps one of the first casualties of the war. The antitrust policies that had existed at the federal and state levels and in public sentiment before the war were of secondary importance to maintaining consistent and sufficient production levels. Vertically integrated operations, for petroleum concerns, meant consolidating production in the fields, the refining process, transportation, and the marketing of the ultimate product, such as gasoline. Corporate desires for consolidation were heightened by the economic recession of late 1914 and early 1915, since such integrated operations were seen as necessary to achieve stability and efficiency in times of economic disruption. As the economy began to improve in 1915–18, a desire to benefit from the wartime federal contracts was also an important motivation for consolidated operations.

At the federal level, the Fuel Administration allowed for and even encouraged ostensibly collusive activities. For example, the Oil Division of the Fuel Administration, in order to ensure adequate supply at a "fair price," encouraged the pooling of oil reserves. In early 1918, the Oil Division also suppressed an attempt by the Federal Trade Commission to begin litigation against Standard Oil-Indiana for violation of the Clayton Antitrust Act.

In February 1917, the Texas legislature passed a law allowing for the operations of production, refining, and marketing within one firm. The Texas Company, in an effort to legitimize its close relationship with smaller production companies, was the primary proponent of the bill. . . . Just a few months later, the Producers Oil Company was openly dissolved and absorbed into the Texas Company. Also in 1917, the Texas Company incorporated the Texas Pipeline Company as a wholly owned subsidiary. The company that Cullinan had founded (but had left in 1913) was becoming a fully vertically integrated petroleum concern. Standard Oil of New Jersey, no longer afraid of Texas antitrust statutes that they had suffered from in the past, in 1919 bought a 50 percent share of interest in the Humble Oil and Refining Company. . . .

Increased tax relief at the federal level was also made available as a spur to production. The Revenue Acts of 1916 and 1918 increased the "oil depletion allowance," a tax deduction which allowed the oil industry to recover production and discovery costs. Thus the war effort had reversed earlier antitrust policy, and had fostered a new era of conciliation and cooperation between business and government, a cooperation that facilitated the economic expansion of the 1920s.

With this expansion of the oil industry, oil-related industries grew and flourished in Houston during and after the war. The highly profitable tool company owned by Howard Hughes had existed at least a decade before the war, but the wartime expansion of the Gulf Coast petroleum industry greatly accelerated the growth of the oil-tool industry in Houston. For example, in 1916, Texas Iron Works established operations in the Goose Creek field. Also in 1916, the Reed Roller Bit Company and the Howard Smith Company were founded in Houston. In 1919, WKM Manufacturers began operations in Houston; in 1920, the Oil Well Supply Company, then the largest manufacturer of oil tool supplies in the world, established operations in Houston. Cameron Iron Works, which would become one of the world's largest producers of oil tool supplies, began operations in Houston that same year. The Lucey Manufacturing Company and the Mack Manufacturing Company had operations in Houston by 1920. In January 1921, the Wilson Supply Company was founded in Houston. In 1927, the Penick brothers, Arthur and Kirby, founded the Oil Tool Company in Houston; in 1928, the Houston Oil Field Material Company was established, adding to the growing list of oil-tool supply concerns in the city. In addition, in 1925 and 1926, the Houston Gulf Gas Company, owned by the Moody-Seagraves interests of Galveston, and the Houston Pipeline Company, a subsidiary of the Houston Oil Company, began to build extensive pipelines and supply natural gas to the Houston area.

Oil interests also expanded their operations along the Ship Channel in a period of fervent activity during and shortly after the war. The Texas Company, the Farmer's Petroleum Company, and the Merchants and Planters Oil Company had existed along the channel before the war, but during and immediately after the war oil companies greatly expanded their operations or established new ones. In 1916, the Gulf Oil Company transferred its offices to Houston and built a refinery along the Ship Channel. . . . By 1927, there were 8 oil refineries with a daily capacity of 125,000 barrels of crude oil located along the Ship Channel. Throughout the 1920s, the Shell Petroleum Corporation, Humble Oil, the Texas Company, the Gulf Refining Company, and virtually all the oil interests in southeast Texas expanded their facilities in the Port of Houston.

The growth of petroleum exports from Houston after the war was meteoric. While estimates vary, official Port of Houston figures showed 1,789 short tons of oil and oil products exported during 1919. Exports of petroleum products from the Port of Houston in 1925 were 1,044,824 short tons. By 1930, 27 tanker lines had operations in the port, and petroleum exports had risen dramatically to 3,918,927 short tons. The growth of the oil industry during the war brought the process of industrialization to Houston in the 1920s.

Indeed, the Port . . . would play an even larger role in the future economic growth of the area. The federal-local alliance to dredge and improve the Ship Channel was renewed during the war, and the rationale of aiding the war effort gave the business and civic leaders of Houston—the "boosters"—an added credibility, enabling them to overcome congressional opposition to funding "pork barrel" projects.

Starting in 1915, J. S. Cullinan led the efforts of Houston "boosters" to obtain federal funding for renewed Ship Channel improvement projects. Cullinan, other members of Chamber of Commerce, congressmen from Texas, and local oil men such as Ross Sterling of Humble Oil, were frequently in Washington lobbying Congress and writing letters to the United States Corps of Engineers for federal aid to channel improvement projects. . . .Cullinan emphasized that improving the Houston Ship Channel would aid the shipment of petroleum to France; that the channel's 25 foot depth, unable to accommodate the growing number of ships that drew 27 to 30 feet of water, hindered the war effort. . . .

The efforts of Cullinan and other boosters of Houston finally paid off with the Rivers and Harbors Act, passed by Congress in March 1919. The federal government had increased its role with the promotion of the merchant marine; now it also expanded its cooperative role in the development of the nation's waterways. With the Rivers and Harbors Act of 1919, Congress designated . . . the Houston Ship Channel to be dredged to 30 feet, among other improvements. [Federal funding] was to be matched by local funds. . . . By 1925, the Houston Ship Channel boasted a depth of 30 feet.

Port of Houston freight activity, just over 1,000,000 short tons in 1920, increased to over 9,000,000 short tons by 1926, after the Ship Channel had achieved its new depth. By 1930, activity in the Port of Houston increased to nearly 15,000,000 short tons; by 1940, freight tonnage in the port was over 27,000,000. This cooperative relationship between the federal government and the local leaders of Houston, increased by the war effort, continued afterwards and enabled the Houston Ship Channel to become a first-class port, facilitating the growth of the economy of Houston into the 1920s and beyond.

The . . . alliance of the United States with Great Britain and France created an almost limitless demand for U.S. products, including Houston cotton and oil. As part of the war effort's need for economic expansion, the government promoted centralization and integration of business operations while relaxing antitrust statutes, emphasized production over labor demands, and cooperated with the private sector to expand shipping and trade. These decisions left several important postwar legacies: a federal-municipal relationship committed to economic growth, which continued in infrastructure projects such as waterways; the transformation of structural relationships within and between businesses; and the facilities and expertise needed for business to serve a wider international market.

These legacies set the stage for Houston's astonishing economic growth in the 1920s, and indeed became the foundation of its economy for many decades. Cotton continued to be a mainstay of the city's trade through the 1930s, while oil became the catalyst of Houston's economy throughout most of the twentieth century. The growing oil economy, now geared to industrial production as well as simple shipping, generated an increasing number of related industries in Houston. The process would be further stimulated by another war effort, but the groundwork was laid during the First World War by the federal government's alliance with the business and civic leaders of Houston. This national and civic commitment to economic mobilization and expansion enabled the city to increase its importance as a commercial trading center for the mid-continent interior of the United States, hasten the process of industrialization, and follow the model of the New South that Southern modernization proponents had sought since Reconstruction.

Boosterism, Reform, and Planning in Dallas in the 1920s and 1930s

ROBERT B. FAIRBANKS

Despite its location in a largely rural and agricultural state, Dallas experienced rapid growth in the early twentieth century and approached problems associated with that growth in ways compatible with approaches embraced by cities in the more urbanized north. Undeniably committed to growing their city as much as Texas farmers were to raising cotton, Dallas boosters probably shared more in common with civic leaders in St. Louis or Chicago than they did with their county cousins. Dallas leaders also looked outside of Dallas for help in responding to perceived urban needs. Moreover, their changing definition and response to urban problems from the 1900s to the 1920s appears to reflect a national trend. By the 1920s, notions about the city emphasized the inextricable linkage of its parts and the need for comprehensive and coordinated solutions to urban problems.

Dallas's rapid development in the first three decades of the twentieth century mirrored the growth typical of Texas cities of this time. In 1900 the North Texas city had a population of 42,638, but by 1920 census takers there found 158,976 residents. That growth wetted the city's appetite for more and Dallas experienced another

Robert B. Fairbanks, "Dallas Confronts the Twenties: Boosterism, Reform, and the Urban Network," original essay drawn from Robert B. Fairbanks, *For the City as a Whole: Politics and the Public Interest in Dallas, Texas, 1900–1965* (Columbus: Ohio State University Press, 1998), especially pp. 37–72. Copyright © 1998 by Ohio State University Press. Reprinted with permission.

surge of population to 260,475 during the 1920s. Such an increase in population can be explained in part by the city's new dominant retail and wholesale position in North Texas. Connected to national markets through its rail system which also brought migrants to North Texas and helped establish it as a regional financial center, Dallas experienced spectacular growth. Oil and the textile industry also fed the city's growth at this time.

The city's expansion was neither accidental nor inevitable. City boosters, mainly businessmen working through their organizations, promoted Dallas to the region and the nation. For instance, one of the most active bodies in the first decade of the new century was the 150,000 club, committed to securing the city a population of 150,000 by 1910, a figure railroad magnet Jay Gould in 1887 predicted that Dallas would reach in his lifetime. Other businessmen-led organizations, such as the Chamber of Commerce established in 1909, also promoted the city with great zeal and commitment.

Not content with merely publicizing the city, turn-of-the-century civic leaders also embraced the Progressive era reform movements of city planning and governmental reform to further encourage the city's development. And they regularly participated in a variety of associations committed to improving the cities throughout the nation. However, Dallas leaders were selective in regard to the kinds of movements they embraced and participated most enthusiastically in efforts that promised to further encourage the city's rapid growth and development.

Growth, of course, accelerated a variety of urban problems and tensions that demanded attention. When the earlier solutions of the Progressive era did not satisfactorily meet the city's needs, civic leaders rethought the problems and searched for better solutions. The 1920s were a particularly critical time in the city's history. Not only did Dallas's population continue to mushroom, but its physical size more than doubled from 23 square miles to 45 square miles. Such expansion heightened local government's inability to provide adequate paved streets, sanitary and drainage sewers, as well as needed water, fire, and police protection. For example, the National Fire Protection Association found that among its survey of twenty-five of the nation's cities, Dallas experienced the highest per capita loss of all cities examined between 1922 and 1926. An undermanned police force made to patrol the much larger city of the 1920s also helps explain why Dallas suffered a particularly nasty wave of crime in 1927.

Growth also encouraged a variety of social problems as the large number of newcomers and the city's changing social geography seemed to threaten the old timers' sense of community. In addition, increasing numbers of blacks attracted to the city's economic opportunities found little adequate housing, and the expanding pockets of black dwellings created real serious racial tension in the city by the 1920s. The textile industries and their low wages also expanded the rolls of people near or below the poverty level in the city. Fearful that the city's increasing diversity, as well as the widening gulf between the haves and have-nots threatened to undermine the civic order, civic leaders turned to a growing volume of expert advice from outside of Dallas on how to operate that city. Indeed, how Dallasites responded to these challenges in the 1920s ultimately reminds us that Dallas and other Texas cities, despite their unique Texas qualities, were part of a larger urban network that defined and responded to problems in similar ways.

Unfortunately, many Dallas citizens chose not to embrace a reform strategy and followed the guidance of another national movement in the early 1920s, the Ku Klux Klan. Organized in late 1920 by Hiram Wesley Evans, a local dentist, and Z. E. Marvin, an owner of a chain of drug stores, the Dallas Klan enrolled approximately 13,000 members and dominated city and county government in the early 1920s. The Klan preached "one hundred percent Americanism" and focused its animus on Catholics, Jews, African Americans, and immigrants as well as transgressors of traditional morality. The organization had special appeal to working class Dallasites overwhelmed by the rapid changes in the city and unhinged by the growing new morality associated with city life in the 1920s. The Klan also offered sanctuary to Dallasites uprooted by neighborhood transformations and insecurity in the workplace, who confronted a growing, more heterogeneous population than ever before and the accompanying perceived loss of community. It responded to that loss by campaigning for a more homogeneous Dallas and promoting intolerance of those who were different. Although some leading businessmen and established politicians initially supported the Klan, this group's vigilante efforts throughout the city alienated many Dallas civic leaders who organized the Dallas County Citizens League in opposition. Their efforts, as well as some statewide political defeats, ultimately seriously weakened the Klan in 1924 and led to the waning of its influence.

If the Klan proved one type of response to rapid growth and change, not only in Dallas, but in the rest of urban America during the 1920s, civic leaders took a different tact. Dallas leaders in the 1920s consulted urban professionals and national associations to maintain the city on its course of proper growth and development. Two areas that illustrate this new commitment in the 1920s were city planning and governmental reform. Frustrated by the city's haphazard physical growth, as well as its inadequate streets, parks, and constant threat of flooding, Dallas leaders renewed their commitment to physical planning, yet went about it differently than they had earlier. Unhappy with the way city government seemed unable to respond effectively to a host of urban needs, civic leaders also embraced structural reform of their government promoting a more efficient and coordinated city hall that would better govern the city as a whole. Neither concerns were entirely new to the 1920s but the specific approach taken that decade mirrored an urgency in Dallas and elsewhere for a more comprehensive and better coordinated approach to the larger city. The rhetoric and emphasis of the new movements also reminds us how closely tied Dallas was to the national network of cities and the pronouncements of national planning and government improvement associations created to address modern urban problems.

Dallas had embraced planning since at least the first decade of the twentieth century when unhappiness with a variety of physical problems led to the development of the Kessler Plan published in 1911. George Dealey of the *Dallas News,* later tabbed "the father of planning in the southwest," played the most critical role in securing the plan. At first Dealey was interested in merely improving the city's surface sanitation, but after corresponding with J. Horace McFarland of the American Civic Association, the newspaperman became committed to planning and employed the *Dallas News* and the Chamber of Commerce to promote enthusiasm for planning in the city. The result of his efforts was the Kessler Plan, a document that proposed nine improvements including a Union railroad station, a levee system for the Trinity River, and a comprehensive system of parks and parkways.

The plan, then, focused on providing a variety of public works for the city but offered no systematic strategy to carry out a coordinated program. In a single paragraph, it discussed financing. Kessler warned against relying too much on bonds and called for special assessments and local improvement districts to fund most of his recommendations. Some projects rallied citywide support, such as the Union railroad station completed in 1916, but others languished because of the lack of such support, including the levee/reclamation project. The lack of clarity on how to proceed with planning along with the distraction of World War I stalled local enthusiasm for carrying out the Kessler Plan.

Frustrated by the delay in public improvements that would affect their property holdings, businessmen in the west end of downtown Dallas decided to reinvigorate planning after the war with special emphasis on the needs of their area. As a result, in 1919 they created a new organization, the Dallas Property Owners' Association (DPOA), and brought in Kessler to revise his earlier plan with more attention given to harnessing the nearby Trinity River with levees and reclaiming the foul-smelling bottoms. Uptown businessmen responded by organizing the Central Improvement Association which promoted Kessler Plan improvements for their eastern section of the central business district. The two groups saw little accomplished but did manage to stir up sectional animosity.

Soon these groups came to the conclusion that such piecemeal planning was not adequate for the demands of the new city, so they joined forces and created several new planning bodies including in 1919 the Dallas Metropolitan Development Association (DMDA), a Dallas Chamber of Commerce, and the Kessler Plan Association, a citywide planning body established in 1924 by the efforts of the DPOA. The DMDA helped engineer the establishment of a permanent City Plan Commission as part of city government, and together the two bodies worked diligently to develop the city's comprehensive zoning ordinance modeled on those written for New York City and Saint Louis. In order to produce the best zoning ordinance possible, the DMDA employed not only George Kessler but also prominent zoning consultant Robert Whitten for such a task. These actions, prompted by civic leaders and urban boosters, acknowledged that even in individualistic Texas, land use regulation was needed to order the city better. After Kessler's death in 1924, the city also sought, though never successfully hired (until 1943), a planner of national reputation to develop another plan for the city. Although court decisions delayed zoning, Dallas did finally secure its first comprehensive zoning ordinance in 1929. Unlike earlier efforts which were more limited in scope, the planning movement of the 1920s both in Dallas and elsewhere emphasized the inextricable linkage of all the parts to the whole and underscored the need to coordinate and plan for the entire city, both private and public lands. Earlier planning had focused on the comprehensive planning of public works but now with the addition of zoning, emphasis shifted toward managing all of the city's land.

The Kessler Plan Association (KPA) proved to be the other significant planning body to appear in the 1920s. At first, it seemed to be just another arm of the business community to secure support for planning projects and bond issues. Established in 1924 by the efforts of the DPOA after that group realized it could never get citywide support for its west end improvement projects, the KPA was the most ambitious effort yet to overcome the petty sectional jealousies that seemed to dominate the city at the time. This organization under the able leadership of John Surratt not only tried to secure support for projects such as the levee district and street openings in downtown, but it also attempted to educate the community to identify with the city as a whole rather than with neighborhoods. Its initial goal was to secure the completion of the Kessler Plan, but it quickly concluded this could be achieved only after educating the city of the interconnectedness of the city's parts. Borrowing freely from citizen planning movements in Chicago, Los Angeles, and St. Louis, the KPA focused on educating the public about the benefits of planning. Toward that end, it brought in nationally known speakers, such as J.C. Nichols of Kansas City and E. M. Bassett of New York, and it secured the prestigious National Conference on City Planning for Dallas in 1928.

Even more important, it developed a school textbook. *Our City Dallas—A Community Civics* focused on promoting a heightened sense of civic consciousness within the city and on educating readers how an improvement in one area of the city benefited the entire city. Written by former school superintendent Justin F. Kimball, this book, adopted for the city's seventh graders, examined not only the Kessler Plan but a variety of other civic issues including government, education, and even public utilities. The book also retold Dallas history and emphasized the importance of cooperative and civic-minded citizens in the city's development. Such an effort attempted to instill in the children a sense of civic pride and loyalty so that they could support and serve the city. Indeed, a flyer promoting the book called it "a guide to citizenship."

In order to secure citywide support for planning, the KPA sought to be the most representative civic body in Dallas. Unlike the Klan, which wanted to eradicate the city's diversity, the KPA embraced it and helped both black and white neighborhoods, rich and poor. Indeed, the association's board of directors included representatives from 115 civic groups such as labor unions, manufacturing associations, and mother's clubs. The KPA also provided a forum that allowed various neighborhood groups in the city to bring their planning concerns to civic leaders. In addition, the KPA acted as a resource for those groups and helped them to improve their neighborhood. First KPA president, Dr. E. H. Cary, was probably not off the mark when he claimed his organization was "the most democratic in Dallas."

The efforts of the KPA apparently paid off when citizens approved a $23.9 million bond package as part of the Ulrickson Program in 1927. That comprehensive program of long-range financial planning modeled after one developed by St. Louis attempted to not only complete the Kessler Plan but develop other projects such as a municipal airport, a library, and improved water purification. Not a traditional plan with maps and predictions of future growth patterns, the Ulrickson Program called the city to develop "mature, scientific and orderly plans." The comprehensive nature of the proposals, as well as the document's emphasis linking all these urban needs together, illustrates the prominent focus of comprehensive planning in Dallas in the 1920s, a strategy that civic leaders thought would guarantee the city's continuous growth.

Not only did the Ulrickson report identify and offer solutions to many of the city's physical needs, but it proposed charter amendments to give Dallas adequate "legal and financial power to plan, prosecute and complete the entire program in an orderly and connected way." With the help of massive support from the Kessler Plan

Association, voters on December 15, 1927 approved the program's fifteen bond proposals and the thirty-two amendments to the city's charter needed to implement the bond program and other planning strategies, such as comprehensive zoning.

During the time of the Ulrickson program and the culmination of the city's commitment to comprehensive planning in the 1920s, another movement occurred that also emphasized a comprehensive approach. Many of the same motives behind the efforts for comprehensive planning and zoning also help to explain the city's new interest in council-manager government. In an earlier reform movement to secure more effective government, Dallas citizens in 1907 had approved a city commission government. Under it, five commissioners were elected by the voters, each given a specific responsibility. One would be a commissioner of police and fire, another commissioner of streets and public property, a third would serve as waterworks and sewage commissioner, while a fourth would serve as commissioner of finance and revenue. The mayor would serve as the fifth commissioner. Together these five had both legislative and executive powers over city government.

Despite the implementation of the city commission government, and the nearly complete domination of businessmen's slates associated with the Citizens Association for the next eleven years, supporters of "good government" criticized both its form and its personnel. As early as 1918, a *Dallas Morning News* planning reporter complained to Dealey that an ineffective government hampered the completion of the Kessler Plan. Others criticized the politicization of a government structure based on administrative function. Instead of looking out for the city as a whole, commissioners were usually too busy looking out for their departments. Instead of focusing on long-term projects, commissioners were caught up in the day-to-day grind of administering their departments and taking care of their workers.

City government, then, paralleled pre-1920s planning. As we have seen, the Kessler Plan also had been a type of comprehensive citywide planning approach, but its execution focused on certain planning needs and/or city districts and failed to treat adequately the city as a whole. Only in the 1920s did civic leaders embrace more comprehensive strategies for the physical city through comprehensive zoning and a comprehensive bond package to ensure coordinated planning for the entire city.

The city commission form of government had centralized government over the fragmented and apparently impotent council/mayor form of government Dallas previously experienced. Yet its functionally divided treatment of the whole proved unsatisfactory to a growing number of people by 1920 because it appeared not to be working the way supporters had hoped. As a result, in the very year that the Ulrickson Program was proposed, civic leaders also initiated a movement to better city government.

The decision to alter government, then, did not stem from an attempt to destroy a political machine, or even to rid the city of incompetent public officials. Nor was it an attempt to weaken neighborhood influence through the destruction of wards—that had been achieved in 1907. Rather, the movement, which was widely publicized by the National Municipal League, focused on creating a more efficient and comprehensively administered government through structural change—a government capable of action on immediate problems and long-term planning for a healthy future. Toward this end, local leaders embraced the council-manager government as the best hope for the city. During the 1920s the popularity of this form of government soared as the emphasis turned from accountability and the ability to get things done to efficiency and comprehensive treatment. Indeed, by 1926, Cleveland, Cincinnati, and Kansas City had adopted city manager government. The government structure provided administrative powers to the city manager, and legislative powers to a city council elected at large without partisan labels.

In his textbook *Municipal Government,* Harvard Professor William Bennett Munro emphasized that council-government established "a real pivot of administrative authority," and it placed "this under expert control." Munro also argued that the city manager plan improved upon the commission form of government because it provided "a better basis for cooperation and harmony," another concern of Dallas leaders. Indeed, the rhetoric of the city manager supporters suggested that politics in city government caused fragmentation, and if politics were eliminated (as the city manager government promised to do), then fragmentation would decline.

The momentum for city government reform slowed as civic leaders decided to focus on securing charter amendments for the Ulrickson Program in 1927. After that election, however, it resumed when the city's mayor named a twenty-member Charter Committee to "make a systematic study of the charter of the city . . . and evolve a document consistent with a population of 300,000 instead of 90,000." Because under the state constitution cities could amend their charters once every two years, no charter election could be held until December 16, 1929, giving the committee ample time to do its job. The committee issued a report on March 5, 1929 that recommended Dallas adopt a nine member council-manager government. The charter committee advised that all councilman should be elected at large rather than just by wards "to eliminate the possibility of sectional jealousies and so-called log-rolling."

On October 10, 1930, 13,179 voters turned out for the election and approved the new government by a 2-1 margin (8,962–4,217). Supporters of the city manager movement, calling themselves the Citizens Charter Association (CCA), also offered a list of candidates to run the new government. Dallas voters endorsed the entire CCA slate in the first city manager election in 1931. The council selected John Edy as its inaugural city manager. The former president of the International City Managers Association had held a similar post in Flint, Michigan and Berkeley, California.

Edy and the council-manager government promoted a better coordinated and more professional government than earlier, something civic leaders believed critical for the city's continued health. Unhappy with the ineffectiveness of the city's fire and police departments, Edy consulted outside experts to improve them. He also implemented changes in the budgetary procedures, including the development of a budget office with budgetary control, that led to more efficiency and coordination. And unlike the commission form of government, where each commissioner fought for allocations for his department and often traded votes for budgetary favors, the council had no particular incentive to protect specific departments. Even more important, the city manager "brought all expenditures of the city together in one place and considered them as a whole." The procedure reflected the new emphasis on governing the city as a whole.

Not only did Edy try to coordinate better the city's finances, but he did the same for the staff. The city manager held bi-weekly meetings primarily to keep department heads informed of what others were doing. This simple act, according to one observer, marked "the first time in the history of Dallas that department heads were brought together to attack problems concertedly."

Those CCA sponsored councils operating under a new charter governed differently than the city commissioners. The city commissioners seemed more interested in protecting their little fiefdom, the department that they oversaw, than in governing for the city as a whole. For the most part, the commissioners acted as politicians and attempted to increase their power within the city. The new council, composed of prestigious businessmen and professionals, saw their entry into government as a service rather than a career, and did not, according to one outside observer, seek to reward their friends with the petty favors and special services as the commissioners had. The new system, on paper, set up procedures to treat all areas of the city equally, so no one had to depend on the influence of individual councilmen. Unlike earlier governments, the city now had, according to a 1939 report by Committee on Public Administration of the Social Science Research Council, "an administrative staff that was prepared to present a well-rounded program of municipal policy for its consideration and to produce on short notice information relating to all departments without favoring or neglecting the interests of any of them." As a result, the report concluded that: "For the first time the affairs of the city were determined by a deliberate body that considered municipal policy as a whole rather than in relation to the needs of individual administrative departments or minority pressure groups."

Although this system was clearly not without defects, and the administrative reality of government and planning never treated everyone equally, the rhetoric behind these programs suggests that changing assumptions about the city altered the nature of planning and government reform from that of the turn of the century. Efficiency replaced responsiveness and comprehensiveness overshadowed specificity.

The rhetoric of the 1920s emphasized comprehensive treatment of the city and called for a new civic consciousness emphasizing the city-as-a-whole. Manifestations of this included a new planning emphasis that called on coordinated planning for both public and private land and structural reform in government that attempted to better coordinate and administer government while at the same time de-politicizing it. The last goal proved particularly difficult due to a major dispute between civic leaders over the city's role in the Trinity River reclamation/levee project as approved by the Ulrickson bond program. Despite the implementation of a new form of government, and despite voter approval of a comprehensive bond program to better coordinate the development of Dallas, tensions developed among Dallasites about policy priorities. A conflict over the timing of the city's contribution to the Trinity River levee/reclamation program, authorized by the Ulrickson bond program, badly divided the city's civic leadership.

Ever since the Kessler Plan of 1911, there had been interest in leveeing the unpredictable Trinity River and reclaiming the nearby bottoms land. In 1926 a group of 1,300 property owners of the Trinity River bottoms organized the City and County Dallas Levee Improvement District for such a task. It worked out a coordinated program with the city, county, and utilities company for an ambitious undertaking costing more than $21 million to rechannel and levee the river. The city agreed to help and provide storm sewers, water mains, and other infrastructure for the district. Based on that agreement and similar arrangements with the county and the utilities, the reclamation district broke ground on July 24, 1928 for a project that would move the Trinity River three and one-half miles from its current course and salvage more than 10,000 acres of smelly, overgrown river bottoms.

However, controversy over the city's role in this project erupted during the Great Depression when the levee district insisted that their needs be taken care of first even though other parts of the city needed the infrastructure supported by the bonds. And when flamboyant Mayor J. Waddy Tate, the last mayor under the commission form of government, announced in 1930 that he would have to raise taxes to cover debt service on the bonds sold for drainage sewer development in the reclaimed land, outraged citizens protested. Among those opposed to the immediate funding of the levee were leading members of the Kessler Plan Association including president E. H. Cary, board member Karl Hoblitzelle, and executive secretary John Surratt. They argued that the Kessler Plan Association had supported the reclamation plan as part of a broader comprehensive package of improvements, but now it feared that reclamation was being singled out for special attention while other populated areas in south and east Dallas, in desperate need of sewers, were being ignored. Kessler Plan officials also reminded city officials that the Ulrickson Plan called for a comprehensive sewer system plan before any money was allocated and noted that it simply had not been done.

Proponents of the levee/reclamation, including newspaperman George Dealey, countered that that not only would the project bring needed flood protection to Dallas but launch significant economic expansion that would ultimately help the entire city. Such a response was unsatisfactory to opponents and by 1930, bad feelings about the reclamation project had polarized the city. One side viewed the excessive preoccupation with it as damaging to the development of the rest of the city while the other side saw the project as the key to more rapid development of Dallas. What is significant about this conflict is that the KPA became the leading opponent of the levee district, standing as an advocate for the needs of neighborhoods who would suffer if the city proceeded with using the bond money for the levee district.

Unable to resolve the problem, both sides agreed to wait and let the new council-manager government resolve the dispute. City manager John Edy proceeded cautiously and this alienated him from the levee supporters who wanted the city to immediately commit the funds to finish the levee/reclamation project. What the city council eventually did was to bring in an outside consultant from St. Louis, W. W. Horner, to develop a general plan for the city's drainage sewers. Only after that project was completed, did the city provide money for the reclamation drainage sewers. By that time the depression as well as the erosion of the levees stalled efforts to develop the area as an industrial district, and it remained undeveloped until after World War II.

Representing the neighborhoods of the working classes, the Kessler Plan Association had successfully stood up to some powerful business interests and persuaded them to protect the neighborhoods. But the KPA's involvement in the controversial issue proved costly, as its membership and financial support declined. Although the civic organization continued its work of helping neighborhood organizations and promoting planning in Dallas, it never regained the presence it had in the 1920s.

The levee/reclamation controversy reminds us that despite the rhetoric of both planning advocates and governmental reformers in Dallas during the 1920s, which stressed developing public policy for the entire city as opposed to special privileges for factions and special interests, a new age of urban consensus did not emerge. Even though Dallas leaders turned to the guidance of national bodies such as the National Conference on City Planning and the National Municipal League, and brought in an assortment of experts to help solve knotty problems, such a new commitment to professionalism and outside expert guidance did not eliminate controversy within the city. Different groups in Dallas continued to hold different notions of what constituted the public interest. The supporters of the levee/reclamation district argued that their massive project would not only protect much of the city from floods, but make access to the downtown from neighborhoods in Oak Cliff, on the other side of the Trinity River, much easier. In addition, they believed that the levee would salvage thousands of acres for industrial use at a time that the city desperately wanted more industry for its tax base. On the other hand, the Kessler Plan Association argued that the development of vacant land should not be taken at the expense of neighborhood needs for drainage sewers and adequate water. For that group, the quality of life for those already in Dallas took precedent over the promise of future growth offered by the levee advocates.

For many, the new structural changes in local government that promoted efficiency and coordination proved problematic even though the actions of the council-manager government sided with neighborhood interests in the levee controversy. Quite simply, council members elected at-large came primarily from business and professional backgrounds and adopted city booster notions of the public interest emphasizing pro-growth policies. With the city's strongest advocate of neighborhood interests, the Kessler Plan Association, greatly weakened by the levee fight, no strong voice was heard in Dallas during the 1930s to provide an interpretation of the public interest different from the city's boosters. Although neighborhood unhappiness with the CCA council did contribute to the defeat of that body in 1935, only four years after charter reform took place, that would prove to be the last gasp of neighborhood power in Dallas for a long time. When that CCA returned to power in 1939, it developed an even closer relationship to the city's business interests after the establishment of the Dallas Citizens Council. Meanwhile, many of the voices for neighborhood interests were quieted. As a result, Dallas experienced both the best and worst results from the planning and governmental reform movements of the 1920s. It received a more effectively administered city with a new commitment to professionally overseen comprehensive planning. But it also inherited a governmental structure increasingly occupied by professionals rather than representatives of the people, and a political ethos directed toward growth rather than quality of life issues.

❧ *F U R T H E R   R E A D I N G*

Charles C. Alexander, *Crusade for Conformity: The Ku Klux Klan in Texas, 1920–1930* (1962)

Mody C. Boatright and William A. Owens, *Tales from the Derrick Floor: A People's History of the Oil Industry* (1970)

Norman D. Brown, *Hood Bonnet, and Little Brown Jug: Texas Politics, 1921–1928* (1984)

Garna Christian, *Black Soldiers in Jim Crow Texas, 1899–1917* (1995)

Robert B. Fairbanks, *For the City as a Whole: Planning, Politics and the Public Interest in Dallas, Texas, 1900–1965* (1998)

Robert V. Haynes, *A Night of Violence: The Houston Riot of 1917* (1976)

Michael V Hazel, *Dallas: A History of "Big D"* (1997)

Patricia Evridge Hill, *Dallas: The Making of a Modern City* (1996)

Shawn Lay, ed., *The Invisible Empire in the West: Toward a New Appraisal of The Ku Klux Klan in the 1920s* (1992)

David G. McComb, *Houston: A History* (1981)

Char Millar and Heywood Sanders, eds., *Urban Texas: Politics and Development* (1990)

Harold L. Platt, *City Building in the New South: The Growth of Public Services in Houston, Texas, 1830–1915* (1983)

Marlyn Sibley, *The Port of Houston* (1968)

Johm Stricklin Spratt, *The Road to Spindletop: Economic Change in Texas, 1875–1901* (1955)

Defining Mexican American Identity in Texas, 1910–1950

Relations between Anglo Americans and Mexicans and Mexican Americans have been one of the defining elements in Texas history. The first half of the nineteenth century witnessed first the demographic, then the military conquest of Texas by immigrants from the United States. In the second half of the century, the border-lands of South Texas remained sparsely populated and culturally dominated by Texans of Mexican descent, many of whom were descendents of families who settled there during the Spanish period. Anglo migration to the region threatened the economic and social dominance of the Mexican residents. The clash of cultures in the borderlands left a legacy of suspicion, hostility, and violence.

In the early twentieth century, the demographics of Texas began to change as Mexican immigrants began to move northward in large numbers. The immigrants were an economic resource and valued as a cheap and supposedly docile work force for the fields, railroads, and growing industry of the region. As the Mexican American population grew, racial and ethnic tensions also increased. Mexican Americans suffered as victims of racial and ethnic prejudice, and political and economic oppression.

As Mexican Americans attempted to define their identity and assert their rights in Texas during the first half of the twentieth century, they faced a number of political and ideological options as well as pressures from the left and the right. The Mexican Revolution, which precipitated large-scale migration northward, also instilled a sense of nationalism and political radicalism in the Mexican and Mexican American population. Likewise, in the years around the First World War the International Workers of the World attempted to bring their radical labor movement to the largely Mexican and Mexican American agricultural and industrial workers of the southwest. The Red Scare that followed World War I contributed to the wave of anti-radicalism and nativism that lingered throughout the 1920s, deepening the historical antipathy towards Mexican Americans. The economic growth of the region led to increasing urbanization and the emergence of a Mexican American middle class that sought respect and equal rights, but rejected the extreme nationalism and radicalism of the lower classes.

The political ferment within the Mexican American community led to a variety of approaches to their social and political problems. On one extreme nationalists dreamed of reconquering the Southwest. Moderates sought assimilation and civil rights. Workers and labor organizers struggled to improve the economic plight of the Mexican American worker, and perhaps build a workers' paradise in the process. In the midst of the social, political, intellectual, and international upheaval that characterized this place and time, how did Mexican Americans define themselves and envision their role in this turbulent land? How did they organize and struggle for their rights?

🌟 D O C U M E N T S

As the revolutionary struggles in Mexico spread across the Rio Grande during the first two decades of the twentieth century, Mexican Americans in South Texas became caught up in the turbulence of this period. Document 1 is a recruiting poster for the "Plan of San Diego," a plot that surfaced in 1915 among extreme nationalists who proposed to separate Texas and the other border states from the United States and create an independent Republic. While this plan had little chance of success, it was associated with a brief but intense period of extreme violence and reprisal that spread fear through the South Texas borderlands. Document 2 maps the areas in northern Mexico where Americans were murdered and also notes the incursions of Mexican revolutionaries into Texas and New Mexico. Document 3 presents another perspective on this nationalist perspective. This brief excerpt from Lionel G. Garcia's 1987 novel, *A Shroud in the Family,* sets up a radically altered vision of key elements in Texas mythology—the Alamo, San Jacinto, the heroes of the Texas Revolution. This "fantasy" of early-twentieth-century South Texas Mexican Americans redefines the history of the 1836 clash between Mexicans and Anglos in Texas.

The next two documents reflect more traditional expressions of political activity among the growing Mexican American middle class. Document 4 presents two state-ments of the League of United Latin American Citizens (LULAC) beliefs: "Objectos y Fines de la Liga De Cuidadanos Unidos Latin-Americanos" (Objectives and Goals of LULAC) from 1932 and "The LULAC Code" from 1933. Document 5 lists the political concerns of the Chapultepec Club, a Mexican American women's club in Houston. This particular letter of grievances was likely inspired by the June 1937 acquittal of two Houston policemen charged with the death of a Mexican national. It may also be a reaction against the resurgence of Texas nationalism stimulated by the Texas Centennial celebrations the previous year.

Document 6 presents a more traditionally leftist/labor perspective on the Mexican American struggle for equal rights. Emma Tenayuca and Homer Brooks, respectively the chair and the secretary of the Texas Communist Party, outline their vision of a "move-ment for Mexican unification," a worker-led movement of equal rights and economic justice in Texas and the southwest. This manifesto appeared a short time after Emma Tenayuca won fame for her leadership in the San Antonio Pecan Shellers' Strike and confirmed her association with the Communist Party. In Document 7, the poet Américo Paredes Manzano presents his vision of the Mexican Texan, reviled and oppressed on both sides of the Rio Grande. The last document in this chapter, Document 8, presents the purpose of the American G.I. Forum, a civil rights organization created by Mexi-can American World War II veterans. The G.I. Forum took the leadership in the Mexican American struggle for civil rights in the immediate postwar period.

1. Mexican American Nationalists Call for a Separate Republic in the Southwest, 1915

To Our Fellow-Citizens
Mexicans in Texas

A cry of genuine indignation and rage has sprung from the very depths of our souls at the sight of the crimes and assaults committed on a daily basis against the defenseless women, old people, and children of our race by the bandits and contemptible Texas Rangers who patrol the banks of the Río Grande.

A righteous and just indignation inflames the blood which circulates in our veins. That rage drives us, no, compels us to punish—with all the energy we can muster—the pack of savages who would put even a starving tiger or a disgusting hyena to shame.

How could one remain calm and indifferent in the face of such criminal attacks? Who could permit such offenses to be inflicted on our race? Perhaps the feeling of humanity and patriotism has died out among us? No! It might be asleep, but it is easy enough to wake up.

Enough of tolerance, enough of suffering insults and derogatory remarks. We are men conscious of our actions; we know how to think as well as the "gringos" do; we could be free and we will be. We are sufficiently educated and strong to be capable of electing our own public authorities and we will do so.

The moment has arrived. It is necessary that all good patriotic Mexicans, all those who still have a sense of shame and self esteem, it is necessary, I repeat, that we resort to our weapons and to the cry of "Long live the Independence of the states of Texas, New Mexico, California, Arizona, and parts of the states of Mississippi and Oklahoma, which from today forward will be called the "Republic of Texas." We join our comrades in arms who are already waging the battle, proving their valor and patriotism.

Long Live Independence!
Land and Liberty
General Barracks at San Antonio, Texas

First Chief of Operations   Second Chief of the General Staff
Luis de la Rosa   Aniceto Pizaña

Handbill, 1915, from David Montejano, *Anglos and Mexicans in the Making of Texas, 1836–1986* (Austin: University of Texas Press): 154. Translated by Francine Cronshaw. Copyright © 1987. By permission of the University of Texas Press.

2. Map Showing Where Americans Were Killed in Ethnic Violence in Northern Mexico, Texas, and New Mexico, 1910–1919

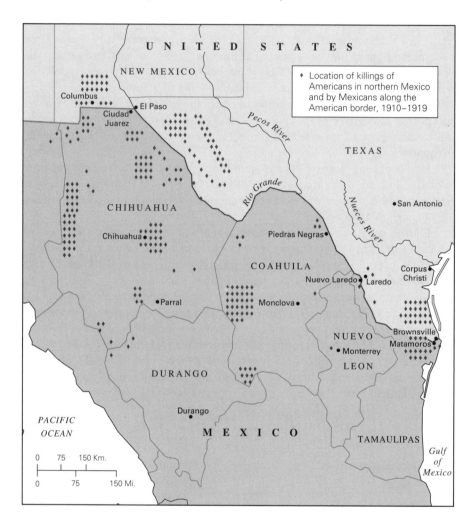

From "Map depicting killings of Americans in northern Mexico and South Texas and New Mexico, 1910–1919" in David Montejano, *Anglos and Mexicans in the Making of Texas, 1836–1986* (Austin: University of Texas Press): 124. [Based on "Murder Map of Mexico," U.S. Congress, Senate, *Investigation of Mexican Affairs,* Document 285, 66th Congress, 2nd Session, 1920, 1: 845]

3. Novelist Lionel G. Garcia Presents the Battle of the Alamo and San Jacinto from a Fictional Twentieth-Century Perspective, 1987

Father Procopio, early into the night, arrived with Andres Garcia and with the four other gentlemen that had been helping Andres Garcia at the creek. They were: Faustino, the drunkard, who had noticed Andres Garcia at the creek in the first place; Amandito, the fat one, who had already been there helping Andres Garcia placate the disturbed locusts; Bernabe, the crazy one, who was helping at the creek when the Priest had arrived; and Fecundo, the prolific, the man with many children, who had also joined the other three in helping Andres Garcia. Andres Garcia walked erectly in the center of the group as they neared the house. "This reminds me," he said making a circle with his arms to signify the group, "of the death of James Bowie after the battle of the Alamo. Just as you are surrounding me, so did General Santa Anna's men surround the hated Bowie. Do you know that Bowie had the nerve to spit on my father's boots, while my father was trying to convince Travis that Santa Anna did not want a battle at the Alamo? What ignorance! There you had Captain Agustin Garcia, right hand man to the great General Santa Anna, educated in Spain at the most prestigious academies. . . . And then the ignorant Bowie, whose claim to fame was that he made a knife."

"What happened to the man?" Faustino asked him, as they walked.

"What man?"

"Bowie."

"Bowie was found alive after the Alamo. So was Crockett. Crockett hated Sam Houston for what Houston had done to General Santa Anna at the Alamo. Hated him so much that he joined Santa Anna's troups at San Jacinto." Andres Garcia adjusted his collar with both hands and tried to walk even more erect. "By that time Crockett had changed his name officially to David Cruz."

"This man knows everything," Bernabe said in awe. "Didn't I tell you that he knows everything?" . . .

"What happened to Bowie?" Fecundo asked. . . .

Don Andres Garcia stopped abruptly to gather his thoughts. He had been thinking of what Father Procopio had said about purgatory. Everyone stopped with him. At the same time he thought that he could still smell the honeysuckle blossoms from the front of his house. "My father killed James Bowie with his trusty derringer," he said. "Shot him in the head after he tied him to a horse ring on the wall of the Alamo. General Santa Anna asked him to. My father had been very pleased that Bowie had begged for his life . . . that Bowie had lied and said that his mother was a Mexican and he should be allowed to live. Bowie's death was the highlight of my father's life up to that point. . . .

". . . I had other men in mind, the priest's cousin who came to visit from Spain. How educated he was. I could sit and talk to him for hours without being bored. He understood the history of Texas as I explained it to him. The treachery of Sam

Lionel G. Garcia, *A Shroud in the Family* (Houston: Arte Publico Press, 1987): 23–28, 47–48. Reprinted with permission from the publisher of *A Shroud in the Family.*

Houston. The integrity and honor that dominated General Santa Anna's life. I could explain to him the battles of the Alamo and Goliad and San Jacinto. Logically, as my father had lived them. He knew that the Texas Rangers were men that were not to be trusted. He knew how the Mexican people had been exploited by Anglo justice. I could make him understand the destruction of culture that took place when the ignorant Anglo came to Texas. How they made everyone into an animal of greed and avarice. This is mine, the Anglo would say to the Mexican. Give it to me or I'll kill you. How much is that? Sell it to me or I'll kill you or I'll steal it. Through hook or crook, I'll get it. With or without the law. And if the law is against me, why I'll change the law. That's what a gentleman of breeding understands. That no one of culture ever came to save Texas from Mexico. They were castoffs of other states, dumb enough to come here just to die." . . .

4. The League of Latin American Citizens (LULAC) States Its Objectives, Goals, and Code, 1932, 1933

Objectives and Goals of the League of United Latin American Citizens

The goals and objectives of this Organization will be:

1. –To develop among the members of our race the best, purest and most perfect type of true and loyal citizen of the United States of America.
2. –To yank from the roots of our political body any tendency to make distinctions among our fellow citizens based on race, religion or social position, as contrary to the true spirit of Democracy, our Constitution and our Laws.
3. –To use all the legal means at our disposal to ensure that all citizens of our nation enjoy equal rights, equal protection under this nation's laws, and equal opportunities and privileges.
4. –The acquisition of the English language, which is the official language of our nation and necessary for the full enjoyment of our rights and privileges, is declared for that reason to be the official language of this Organization. We affirm our intention to learn it, to speak it, and to teach it to our children.
5. –To define clearly and with absolute precision our indisputable loyalty toward the ideals, principles, and citizenship of the United States of America.
6. –To assume complete responsibility for the education of our children in the knowledge of their rights and responsibilities as well as knowledge of the language and customs of this nation in terms of their good features.
7. –We solemnly declare once and for all to pay respectful and sincere homage to our racial origins, of which we are proud.
8. –Secretly or openly, by all legal means at our disposal, we will help with the cultural level and guidance of Latin Americans. We will protect and defend their lives and interests whenever necessary.

From "Objectos y Fines de la Liga de Cuidadanos Unidos Latino-Americanos," *LULAC News* (September 1932) and "L.U.L.A.C. Code," *LULAC News* (January 1933). [E. E. Mireles and Jovita Gonzalez de Mireles Papers, Special Collections and Archives, Texas A&M University—Corpus Christi Library]. "Objectives and Goals" translated by Francine Cronshaw. Reprinted with permission from the League of Latin American Citizens (LULAC).

9. –We will block any momentum leading to the creation of racial prejudices against our people. We will fight any degrading stigma imposed on them. We claim on their behalf the respect and the prerogatives granted to all under the Constitution of our nation.

10. –Each one of us is considered to have equal responsibility in our Organization, to which we voluntarily pledge our subordination and obedience.

11. –We will create funds for our mutual protection, for the defense of any among us who might be unfairly indicted, and for the education and cultural development of our people.

12. –This Society is not a political club, but as citizens we will participate in the electoral contests at local, state and federal levels. However, in the process we will always keep in mind the general welfare of our people. We disavow and renounce once and for all any commitment of a personal nature not in harmony with the above principles.

13. –We will lend our votes and influence to building the political stature of individuals whose actions show respect and consideration for our people.

14. –We will elect as our leaders those among us who show by their integrity and cultural attainments that they are capable of guiding and leading us in an upright manner.

15. –We will maintain publicity efforts to communicate these principles, increase the number of branches of our Organization, and work for its consolidation.

16. –We will pay our share of the poll tax for ourselves and our families in order to fully enjoy our political rights.

17. –We will spread the word about our ideals through the press, conferences, and pamphlets.

18. –We are opposed to any kind of racial and violent demonstration that might tend to create conflicts and consequently infringe on the peace and tranquility of this nation.

19. –We will respect the religious ideas of each individual and moreover we refer to religious ideas in our institutions.

20. –We will stimulate the creation of educational institutions for Latin Americans and we will lend our support to those already in existence.

21. –We will work toward obtaining equal representation for our people on juries and in public administration in general.

22. –We will denounce all instances of peonage and mistreatment as well as child labor among our people.

23. –We will resist and forcefully combat all machinations tending to prevent our social and political unity.

24. –We will unite against any effort leading to the segregation of our children in the schools of our nation.*

25. –We will set up statistics to orient our people in regards to working and living conditions and agricultural and business activity in different parts of the country.

---

*The original Spanish uses the verb "combinaremos" (we will unite). The resulting translation says that LULAC will unite to support any effort to segregate their children. Obviously, either the negative was omitted (we will unite against), or the writers meant to use the verb "combatiremos" (we will fight).

L. U. L. A. C. CODE

Respect your citizenship and preserve it: honor your country, maintain its traditions in the spirit of its citizens, and embody yourself into its culture and civilization;

Love the men of your race, be proud of your origin and maintain it immaculate, respect your glorious past and help to defend the rights of your own people.

Learn how to fulfill your duties before you learn how to claim your rights; educate and make yourself worthy, and stand high in the light of your own deeds; you must always be loyal and courageous;

Filled with optimism make yourself sociable, upright, judicious, and above all things be sober and collected in your habits, cautious in your actions and sparing in your speech;

Study the past of your own, and of the country to which you owe your allegiance, learn how to master with purity the two most essential languages—English and Spanish.

Always be honorable and high-minded, learn how to be self-reliant upon your own qualifications and resources;

Believe in God, love Humanity and rely upon the framework of human progress, slow and sound, unequivocal and firm;

In war serve your country, in peace your convictions; discern, investigate, meditate and think, study, at all times be honest and generous.

Let your firmest purpose be that of helping to see that each new generation of your own shall be of a youth more efficient and capable, and in this, let your own children be included.

5. The Chapultepec Club, a Mexican American Women's Club in Houston, Lists Complaints Concerning Treatment of Minorities, 1937

June 11, 1937

Miss Leona B. Hendrix
2219 Tracy Street
Kansas City, Missouri

My dear Miss Hendrix:

The Chapultepec Club of the Houston Y.W.C.A. has the following to offer as findings from their study of minorities. Here in Texas they [the club members] happen to constitute a minority group themselves and are called Mexicans. Some of the group were born in Mexico and have not taken out citizenship papers. [The] reason [is as] follows: Many were born in Texas and are therefore American citizens but are

---

Thomas Krenick, "The Chapultepec Club: A Mexican American Women's Club in Houston" from *Houston Review* 3 (Summer 1981): 269–71. Copyright © 1981 University of Houston. Reprinted with permission.

still called Mexicans. The group is made up of an excellent cross section of the Mexican colony in Houston. There are several high school graduates in the group and of course every year more Mexicans are staying in school until graduation.

These are the problems which these young Mexican girls and women face in Texas and they wonder what the future will be for them and their children. From this study, they hope sincerely for recommendations from the National B. & P. Council on action they can take to better understanding, respect and opportunity. They recognize that minority groups elsewhere in the United States face some, though not all, of the same problems.

1. Texas is next door to Mexico and there are border town problems to be considered, historically as well as at present.

   Texas history is founded on troubles, oft created by Texans, to get land and cattle from the Mexican people. [N]ow the problem of stolen automobiles is causing the same problem and also the water power of the Rio Grande River is causing hard feelings.

2. Texas cannot, due to Chamber of Commerce and patriotic society activities, forget that Texas lost a tragic battle at the [A]lamo in San Antonio and won a battle at San Jacinto. This causes teachers to preach a patriotism not kind to Mexican children. Mexicans have been known to stay out of school [in Houston] when that part of history was being taught because of abuses inflicted by pupils and even teachers.

3. Mexicans in [a] desire to get ahead have at times denied their nationality calling themselves French, Italian, and Spanish. This induces the Mexican colony's disfavor. Nationalistic spirit [is] being cultured at present [and] this of course can be as dangerous an attitude as the denial [of] one.

   If they should move back to Mexico they are considered traitors for having lived in Texas.

4. They do not take out citizenship papers because those who have are still called Mexicans and treated as such.

5. The Mexican people find it impossible to rent or buy in any decent section of town and are forced to live in dirty crowded conditions in houses out of which Americans have moved.

6. Playgrounds and parks show distinct distaste to their presence on them and in some cases they are ordered off or forbidden on. This problem is caused by the youth and not the recreation leaders.

7. Falsely accused of many crimes in the city and because of some difficulty with the English language they are taken advantage of frequently.

8. Mexican people are paid less in wages on all jobs and a great many jobs and industries are closed to them.

9. Mexican lawyers receive no respect from other lawyers nor even from our judges. It is a well known fact that a case is practically lost if a Mexican lawyer handles it. Justice is very one-sided, and they have had some rather serious cases recently.

10. They are called "brown people," "greasers," et cetera and of course want to be called white.

This letter is also going to Beatrice Langley and at the same time the group is also sending a letter to the American Youth Congress protesting certain movies which have been shown in Texas portraying the Mexicans in a very bad light.

Very truly yours,
Stella Quintenella
Carmen Cortez
Olive Lewis

P.S. These statements were verified by outstanding men in the Mexican colony, such as the consul, doctors, and teachers.

6. Emma Tenayuca and Homer Brooks, Officers of the Texas Communist Party, Outline Their Vision for Mexican Unification, 1939

Upon what is this movement for Mexican unification based? What are its main objectives?

It is a people's movement, uniting the interests of large and important sections of the population, over two million strong, who, in alliance with the country's democratic forces, in the Southwest and nationally, can free themselves from the special oppression and discrimination in all its phases that have existed for almost a century.

The struggle is directed:

1. Against economic discrimination—extra low wages; expropriation of small land holders; discrimination in the right to work in all trades and crafts, particularly skilled trades; discrimination against professional and white collar workers; discrimination in relief and right to employment in W.P.A.

2. For educational and cultural equality—equal educational facilities for the Mexican population; no discrimination against children of Mexican parentage; a special system of schooling to meet the needs of the migratory families; the study of the Spanish language and *the use of Spanish as well as English in the public schools and universities* in communities where Mexicans are a majority; the granting of equal status to the Spanish language, as has been done in New Mexico and in those counties and states where the Mexican people form a large part of the total population.

3. Against social oppression—for laws making illegal the various forms of Jim-Crowism, segregation in living quarters, schools, parks, hotels, restaurants, etc. This struggle must be linked with that of the Negro people.

4. Against political repression. The struggle for the right to vote is divided into two phases:

    (a) The majority of the Mexicans are American-born. The problem is, therefore, one of enforcing their citizenship right. This means demanding that all

Emma Tenayuca and Homer Brooks, "What Path to Follow" in "The Mexican Questions in the Southwest," *The Communist* 18 (March 1939): 264–265.

legal and extra-legal restrictions to the free exercise of the ballot be re-moved. These include residence qualifications, difficult for semi-migratory workers to meet; and in Texas, the elimination of the poll tax.

(b) Those who are foreign born must join with all of the immigrant groups in the United States to secure the democratization of the federal regulations pertaining to *length of time, cost,* and *language conditions* required for citizenship; the aim being to simplify the process whereby all who intend to remain permanent residents of the United States—and this includes nearly all of the Mexicans—and who express a desire for naturalization, can become citizens.

In some states, as in Texas, it may become feasible to restore, at least until federal requirements for becoming citizens become less onerous, the provisions in the Texas state constitution which, until 1921, granted vot-ing rights to all Mexicans and other foreign born, citizens and non-citi-zens, providing they met residence requirements and declared their desire for American citizenship.

In this general movement the leading role will undoubtedly be played by the proletarian base of the Mexican population, its overwhelming majority. This is al-ready evident from the impetus given the movement for Mexican rights by the large strike struggles in Texas, California and Colorado. The surest guarantee for the full and successful development of the people's movement will be in further trade union organization among the Mexican workers.

7. Poet Américo Paredes Manzano Laments the Oppression of the Mexico-Texan, 1939

"The Mexico-Texan, he's one fonny man
Who lives in the region that's north of the Gran';
Of Mexican father, he born in thees part.
For the Mexico-Texan, he no gotta lan';
And sometimes he rues it, deep down in hees heart.
He stomped on da neck on both sides of the Gran';
The dam gringo lingo he no cannot spick,
It twista da tong and it maka heem sik;
A cit'zen of Texas they say that he ees!
But then,—why they call heem da Mexican Grease?
Soft talk and hard action, he can't understan',
The Mexico-Texan, he no gotta' lan'."

—Américo Paredes Manzano
"The Mexico-Texan," 1939

Américo Paredes Manzano, "The Mexico-Texan," 1939 in David Montejano, *Anglos and Mexicans in the Making of Texas, 1836–1986* (Austin: Arte Publico Press, University of Texas Press, 1991): 158. Reprinted with permission from the publisher.

8. The Constitution of the American G.I. Forum of Texas Seeks Equal Rights for Mexican Americans in the Post-World War II Era

Section 1: NAME

The official name of this organization shall be "The American GI Forum of Texas, Inc." and can be shortened for practical use to "GI Forum".

Section 2: PURPOSE

As veterans, this organization will strive for the procurement, of all veterans and their families, regardless of race, color or creed, the equal privileges to which they are entitled under the laws of our country. Also, this organization will strive for the preservation of the Democratic ideals for which this country has fought in all wars, and we propose to ever maintain as well as advance these ideals wherever possible; to foster the training and education of our citizens in order that a true and real democracy may exist in the lowest as well as the highest unit so that our loyalty to these principles may never be questioned.

As loyal citizens of the United States of America, we sincerely believe that one of the principles of Democracy is religious and political freedom for the individual and that all citizens are entitled to the right of equality in social and economic opportunities and that to produce a stronger American society we must advance understanding between the different nationalities.

★ E S S A Y S

By the 1920s, the growing Mexican American population began organizing to achieve economic, social, and political rights. In the first essay, Mario T. Garcia of the University of California at Santa Barbara, discusses the efforts of the rising middle class to create an organization that would enable them to win the respect of the Anglo majority and smooth their assimilation into American life. In spite of the underlying conservatism of LULAC, it did give voice to the Mexican American demand for civil rights and an end to discrimination. Mexican American workers also addressed the injustices they confronted in Texas. In the second essay, the late Irene Ledesma, who was a professor at the University of Texas Pan American, examines the efforts of Mexican American women to organize in defense of their rights in the workplace and to achieve economic and social justice. Ledesma argues that as they became labor activists, Mexican American women confronted a mixed response from the media. She analyzes the complex and often contradictory response to the workplace struggles for these women, not only in the mainstream press, but also among the labor press and the Mexican American newspapers.

From "Constitution of the American G.I. Forum of Texas," Article I, Section 2, "Purpose" 1949. [Dr. Hector P. Garcia Papers Special Collections and Archives, Texas A&M University—Corpus Christi Library].

LULAC, Mexican American Identity, and Civil Rights

MARIO T. GARCÍA

The search for America and their place in it shaped the consciousness and politics of the Mexican-American Generation. Mexican Americans, however, did not define "Americanization" in the patronizing and ethnocentric terms characteristic of many Anglo-American educators and welfare workers. They interpreted Americanization in light of the perceived need to forge a movement that would help break the economic, political, and cultural isolation of Mexican Americans in the United States during the early twentieth century. The Mexican-American Generation aspired to move into the mainstream of American life. They recognized that Mexican Americans could no longer adequately function in the marginal ethnic enclaves of the Southwest that had survived the nineteenth century or in the immigrant culture superimposed after 1900 as thousands of Mexicans crossed the border seeking work and political asylum. Instead, the Mexican-American Generation sought to advance from their past and to see themselves as permanent citizens of the United States with all the rights and privileges of American citizenship. . . . No Mexican-American organization better exemplified this search for America than the League of United Latin American Citizens, founded in 1929 and the oldest Mexican-American civil rights association in the United States.

Origins of a Political Generation

The Mexican-American Generation, as a political entity, began to come of age in the 1930s, but its embryo can be detected in the Roaring Twenties. In this decade, Mexican Americans already stressed the need for a new political direction for themselves based on two basic needs: the importance of instilling a new consciousness among Mexican Americans—to develop a "new Mexican" in the United States—and the need to organize new forms of political and civic organizations—a "new politics"—that would best serve their interests separate from those of Mexican immigrants. The confluence of these two needs can be seen in south Texas, the cradle of the Mexican-American Generation.

The importance of a new political movement for Mexican Americans in south Texas was emphasized by the economic and social transformations affecting the region. Increased agricultural production during World War I integrated south Texas into the market economy of the United States. Possessing a year-long warm climate, south Texas became the "winter garden" of the nation, producing a variety of commercial fruits and vegetables. Economic development along capitalist agricultural lines in turn changed the class structure of south Texas. Texas-born Mexican-American farmers and ranchers as well as sharecroppers found themselves unable to compete with agribusiness and some lost what small family lands they possessed. In their place, or alongside them, came thousands of Mexican immigrant

Mario T. García, "In Search of America: The League of United Latin American Citizens (LULAC)," in *Mexican Americans: Leadership, Ideology & Identity, 1930–1960*. (New Haven: Yale University Press, 1989): 25–61. Copyright © 1989 by Yale University Press. Reprinted with permission.

wageworkers to pick the crops produced by the new mode of production. The introduction of this large immigrant work force plus the need to segregate Mexican immigrants and dislocated Mexican-Americans as a cheap agricultural labor force responsible for producing surplus value intensified earlier patterns of discrimination and racial hostility toward people of Mexican descent.

Indeed, the "Mexican problem" emerged in the 1920s. Anglos adversely affected by the rise of agribusiness vented their resentments and frustrations toward Mexican immigrants, whom they characterized as an economic and social threat to Texas and the rest of the country. They charged mexicanos with introducing crime, illiteracy, and diseases and with mongrelizing the social-ethnic base of American society. . . .

Such antagonisms in conjunction with labor exploitation directed at people of Mexican descent during the 1920s, plus a previous history of racism in Texas and elsewhere, created objective conditions for efforts toward Mexican-American political unity. M. C. González . . . categorized five types of discrimination faced by all Mexicans in Texas during the 1920s. These included (1) public school segregation of Mexican-American children; (2) segregation and discrimination in public facilities such as restaurants, movie theaters, swimming pools, and barbershops; (3) the establishment of "white man's" primaries to prevent blacks and Mexican Americans from exercising their right of suffrage; (4) discrimination in housing by not allowing Mexicans to purchase real estate in certain sections of towns and cities such as San Antonio; and (5) discrimination in the administration of justice by preventing Mexican Americans from serving on juries. . . . Of course most Mexicans also faced job discrimination. Both rural and urban employers profited from Mexicans as cheap unskilled labor and refused to jeopardize such a lucrative labor pool by supporting educational and job opportunities.

Yet, despite heightened discrimination against Mexicans in south Texas, economic development plus the needs of an expanding Mexican population produced some advances and even relative prosperity for a few Mexican Americans in the growing towns and cities of the region. Those whose families had previously been merchants or who had recently migrated from the rural areas with sufficient capital to open small stores shared, although unequally, in the south Texas boom. Most catered to the Mexican communities—the "Mexiquitos"—and hence experienced mobility within a Mexican-American context. A few *comerciantes,* especially along the border, expanded enough to also serve Anglo customers. An even smaller number with better opportunities for education became lawyers, teachers, journalists, and politicians. In effect, a small Mexican-American middle class emerged or survived from an earlier period.

The Mexican-American middle class, however, confronted a contradiction. It participated in the new prosperity of south Texas but still faced racial, cultural, and social discrimination. The notice No Mexicans Allowed affected them just as it did immigrant workers. Hence, the Mexican-American middle class sowed the seeds of discontent over the magnitude and persistence of racial discrimination and called for its eradication. Yet the middle class recognized that the struggle against racism would have to take a different form and have a different emphasis than before. Mexicans through older forms of organization such as mutual aid societies and through Mexican consulates had historically protested against discrimination.

But antidiscrimination was never effectively linked with the issue of integration. This was mainly because previous generations of both native-born citizens, still living in a predominantly Mexican world, and recent immigrants from Mexico did not share an interest in Americanizing their experiences. . . .

Besides a change of consciousness, a "new politics" was in order. Unlike the older generation of Mexican-American politicos who subordinated themselves to Anglo political machines, purchased the Mexican-American vote, and literally herded Mexican Americans to the polls, those involved in the "new politics" hoped to cleanse Mexican-American politics by stressing nonpartisan civic action and avoidance of machine politics. . . . This new consciousness and new politics would give birth to a new citizen: the Mexican American.

The Formation of LULAC

The initial effort at a new political movement among Mexican Americans commenced in 1921 with the organization of the Sons of America in San Antonio. Comprised of mostly lower middle-class professionals, the Sons stressed socializing Mexican Americans to their rights as U.S. citizens and obtaining equal rights for them. Unfortunately, personal rivalries within the Sons soon splintered the organization. . . . To remedy the situation and redirect efforts toward political unity, Ben Garza of Council No. 4 of the Sons of America and González of the Knights took the lead in advocating a merger of the different organizations. . . . With Perales's* support as well as that of González,** . . . Garza . . . called for a unity convention to be held in Corpus Christi on February 17, 1929, for the purpose of founding a new Mexican-American association.

Twenty-five designated delegates attended the convention held in Obreros Hall. An additional 150 Mexican Americans participated as nonvoting members. They came from throughout south Texas. . . .

The convention unanimously agreed to fuse all three represented organizations and to form . . . the League of United Latin-American Citizens (LULAC). The convention also agreed to restrict its membership to U.S. citizens of Latin extraction. English would be the official language of LULAC. . . .

Mexican Americans were to be socialized to U.S. citizenship. The goal was "to develop within the members of our race the best, purest and most perfect type of a true and loyal citizen of the United States of America." However, Mexican Americans could not assume their rightful place alongside other Americans as long as they faced discrimination. LULAC committed itself to a campaign, if not crusade, against such un-American practices. Reforms would be achieved not by radical measures but within the confines of the law. Americanization for LULAC meant struggling within the system not outside it and certainly not against it. Of course, Americanizing the Mexican-American experience also involved a cultural question. LULAC emphasized a dual cultural approach. For one, LULAC emphatically reiterated its support of English as the organization's official language and noted that

---

*Alonso S. Perales
**M. C. González

only by learning English could Mexican Americans be integrated as full citizens. Yet, organizers of LULAC believed that they were of such an ethnic, class, and cultural background that they did not have to apologize for their Mexican roots and cultural traditions. Lulacers were not begging for integration. They were proud middle-class Mexican Americans who at the same time understood the need to adapt to American conditions. Consequently, Americanization was not perceived as a one-way street. Anglo Americans would also have to accommodate to the best of middle-class Mexican-American life. "We solemnly declare once and for all to maintain a sincere and respectful reverence for our racial origin of which we are proud." The LULAC constitution reaffirmed the need to maintain bilingualism and ethnic pride.

Despite the affirmation of their ethnicity, or what Conzen regards as the invention of ethnicity, Lulacers still recognized the controversial nature of their exclusion of Mexican nationals and their adoption of English as LULAC's official language. Indeed, the exclusion of Mexican nationals had not been a unanimous decision. M. C. González, for example, had argued that ethnic unity required inclusion of Mexican nationals and that LULAC could utilize the support of the Mexican consulates along with mexicano self-help organizations. . . . Alonso Perales stressed that exclusion of Mexican nationals was based solely on pragmatism. . . . State and local authorities, especially in Texas, did not respect or fear groupings of noncitizens. Perales argued that only an association of U.S. citizens, such as LULAC, could effectively pressure and lobby for concrete reforms. Practicality also involved a recognition that Mexican Americans and Mexican nationals possessed certain distinct political interests that separated them. Whereas Mexican nationals looked toward their eventual repatriation to Mexico, Mexican Americans hoped for integration within the United States. . . .

On the question of the use of English, Lulacers reemphasized that this did not imply an abandonment of Spanish. Instead, *La Verdad* of Corpus Christi, a LULAC supporter, advocated bilingualism and called on Mexican Americans as well as Mexican nationals to retain their knowledge of Spanish. English, however, could not be avoided. It was indispensable for adjusting to life north of the border and it behooved Mexicans—of whatever nationality—to learn it. Moreover, Mexican Americans would be aided in their efforts to secure their rights and privileges as U.S. citizens by learning English and the customs of the country. . . .

Finally, the Corpus Christi constitutional convention underscored the need for Mexican-American unity. Without it, LULAC efforts to remove the barriers excluding Mexican Americans from full participation in American life would come to naught. "We should resist and attack energetically," the constitution proclaimed, "all machinations tending to prevent our social and political unification." . . .

From a few initial chapters in south Texas, LULAC expanded throughout the 1930s. By the commencement of World War II, it included more than 80 councils in Texas, New Mexico, Arizona, California, and Kansas. "Tejanos" with their more numerous councils, however, continued to dominate the organization. Indeed, most of LULAC's principal issues and activities took place in Texas until the postwar period. . . .

As pioneers searching for a Mexican-American place in the American sun, LULAC leaders attempted to define what Americanization meant to them. This involved both the evolution of a set of principles, what one historian has termed the "Mexican-American mind," as well as a praxis through particular struggles. Mexican Americans in LULAC desired integration and acceptance as U.S. citizens but at the same time wanted to negotiate maintaining their Mexican heritage, or portions of it. Could such a pluralistic assimilation be accomplished? This was one of the questions faced by the initial LULAC generation. This and other issues were magnified by the pressures and transforming conditions of the Great Depression, World War II, and the cold war. LULAC's responses to these historical periods set the tone for much of the politics of the Mexican-American Generation. Although more radical Mexican Americans would challenge LULAC for political hegemony, they supplemented rather than replaced LULAC's basic reformism. Reform not revolution characterized Mexican-American politics. . . . Devoid of a radical political culture such as existed in California, which was characterized by the greater activism of white radicals as well as a more militant labor movement, Texas proved to be less than fertile ground for a more radical form of Mexican-American politics. . . . Fundamental to LULAC's reform initiatives was the stress on Americanization as LULAC's interpretation of Americanization, for the purpose of preparing Mexican Americans for their roles in American society and proving to other citizens the assimilable character of people of Mexican descent. Americanization for LULAC revolved around the following issues: (1) adjustment to American values and culture, (2) political socialization, (3) cultural pluralism, (4) desegregation, and (5) education. . . .

Fundamental to LULAC's effort to assimilate American democratic ideals was the need to reinforce the idea among Mexican Americans that they were as American as anyone else in the United States. . . . Mexican Americans had to see themselves as Americans not Mexicans. LULAC rejected any suggestion that "real Americans" belonged to a particular ethnic group. "When Columbus came here he brought with him our forefathers," one LULAC official wrote, "but he did not bring a blood. Later, when Americo Vespucius named the country America, he had no particular racial blood in mind. So therefore we are all Americans because we live in America, and don't let anyone kid you." No basic human differences existed between the average Mexican American and the average Anglo American.

LULAC accentuated the inherent Americanism of Mexican Americans but still had to confront ethnic labeling. This involved the term "Latin American." The *LULAC News* acknowledged that the term had been a compromise to accommodate the particular position of Mexican Americans in the Southwest. LULAC needed a term that would not offend Anglos but at the same time convince them that Mexican Americans were American citizens and not just "Mexican." . . .

Acculturation also meant rejecting competing ideologies. During the 1930s, LULAC condemned both fascism and communism. In an editorial entitled "Beware of Communism," M. C. González pledged that LULAC would not only be an agent of Americanization, but that it enlisted in the combat against "communistic propaganda that is so destructive of the basic principles of Democracy and of American ideals." At its 1938 convention in El Paso, LULAC furthered its antitotalitarian posture by adopting resolutions opposing "all seditious propaganda courting our subscription to the un-American doctrines of Communism, Nazism, fascism, and all other 'isms' detrimental to the present and future well-being of all Americans." . . .

As part of its effort to Americanize the Mexican-American image, LULAC upheld middle-class role models. "Most of us in LULAC enjoy a fairly good standard of living," the *LULAC News* reported in 1954, "bringing about our desire to 'keep up with the Jones.'" Both middle-class and working-class Mexican Americans joined LULAC, but the middle class dominated leadership positions at the local and national levels. Attorneys, for example, formed the overwhelming majority of national LULAC presidents. In addition, the *LULAC News* extolled the life histories and achievements of its middle-class leaders. A composite picture of such role models included the following characteristics: American born, rising from poor backgrounds to achieve education, veterans of World War I or World War II, high school or college graduates, and professionally either a lawyer, teacher, physician, or government employee. In all, LULAC equated Americanism with middle-class success and believed that true leadership could emanate only from the middle class.

Although an organization of Mexican Americans, LULAC also aimed to Americanize Mexican nationals. Mexicanos could not be official members of LULAC, but they could become honorary members and some apparently joined under this status. LULAC in Victoria, Texas, in 1944 sponsored a meeting chaired by the Mexican consul of Corpus Christi that discussed discrimination against Mexican nationals and organized a committee composed of Mexican nationals to investigate the situation. Moreover, LULAC through the Spanish-language sections of the *LULAC News* during the 1930s counseled Mexican nationals about adjustment to life in the United States. It organized English and citizenship classes for Mexican nationals. LULAC councils in south Texas in the post-World War II period, for example, expressed shock at the number of Mexican nationals who failed citizenship examinations due to lack of both English and a knowledge of American civics. Consequently, Laredo Council No. 12 commenced its own adult night school for Mexican nationals. In 1953 the school taught English and citizenship to more than two thousand persons. LULAC teachers provided citizenship classes in both English and Spanish. "I teach them in English hoping they will pick up the language," one teacher in El Paso told a reporter about his students, "and I teach Spanish to be sure they learn the essentials of the American form of government in which they will be tested when they apply for naturalization." . . .

Although LULAC's constitution prohibited councils from engaging in electoral politics, still, men and women members were encouraged to participate in politics. However, they had to do so in a nonpartisan fashion. LULAC believed that it would lose effectiveness if perceived as a partisan front for a political party. According to M. C. González, given the hostile climate against Mexican Americans in Texas, LULAC could organize politically only by stressing citizenship and Americanism and avoiding being labeled as "political agitators." Hence LULAC reacted strongly to implications that it was a political organization. When the *Harlingen Morning Star,* in noting the formation of a LULAC council in this south Texas city, referred to it as a "Vote League," the neighboring Brownsville LULAC council quickly refuted the statement. "This is absolutely wrong," officer Federico Recio wrote the Chamber of Commerce. "The League of United Latin American Citizens is not a political organization, it stands for something better and higher than that; it is a Civic and Patriotic Organization." Shunning the label of "political club,"

LULAC insisted that members as individuals actively work in local, state, and national politics. In doing so, they should be guided by LULAC principles. T. G. Giron of El Paso stressed that nonpartisan political activity conformed to the need for a new political direction and abandonment of machine politics that had characterized much of Mexican-American politics, especially in Texas. Under the "old politics," politicians saw Mexican Americans only as commodities to be bought or sold during election time. This was also the politics of "old Mexico" and it had to change and become Americanized by Mexican Americans acting independently in politics.

LULAC considered voting to be the most important political act. Voting was a right and a duty for citizens. For Mexican Americans, it was also an Americanizing exercise. Good citizenship was more than fighting to protect one's country in war or being patriotic in time of peace. Good citizenship also involved participating in the making of the country's laws. Citizens did this through voting and electing their representatives. . . .

In Texas, however, voting was no simple matter. Like other southern states. Texas required a poll tax until the 1960s. The tax in the South prevented blacks from voting, but in Texas it likewise discriminated against thousands of poor Mexican Americans. Some counties excluded Mexican Americans from voting in "white primaries" of the Democratic party until the 1930s. LULAC detested the poll tax but faced a dilemma. It could boycott the tax and attempt to eliminate it or it could encourage Mexican Americans to pay the tax and build up Mexican-American political strength. Recognizing that not to pay would be the greater evil, LULAC organized Poll Tax Committees and conducted voter registration drives. . . .

Voting also assumed importance in encouraging Mexican Americans to run for office. LULAC acknowledged that one of the main political problems faced by Mexican Americans was their lack of representation. However, Mexican-American candidates had to run free of entangling alliances with machine politics. M. C. González, who unsuccessfully campaigned in San Antonio for the Texas legislature in 1930, sought votes under the banner of the Citizens League, a reform political movement. "It is obvious from my name that I am of Mexican descent," González told a reporter during the campaign. "I was born and raised in Texas, however; I served my country during the war. I am an American and am proud of it." Other Mexican American candidates ran for office and failed, but in time some succeeded. LULAC celebrated the election in 1932 of Mexican-American Griff Jones as county commissioner of Maverick County in south Texas. "As he is Vice President of the Eagle Pass Council of LULAC," the *LULAC News* observed of Jones, "rumor has it that LULAC is responsible for his election, as all the Eagle Pass Lulacers supported him individualby [*sic*]." . . .

LULAC's efforts at political socialization finally consisted of getting Mexican Americans to become interested and involved in state and national politics. The economic crisis of the 1930s, of course, and the activist response by President Roosevelt's New Deal attracted Mexican-American adherents, as they did Afro-American and other previously unrecognized minorities, to FDR and the standard of the national Democratic party. LULAC furthered the nationalization of Mexican-American politics by passing resolutions at its national conventions endorsing federal legislation that would benefit Mexican Americans. In all, LULAC through its political socialization sanctioned the Mexican-American Generation's need to engage in a new type of politics in the Southwest aimed at its integration into American life. . . .

Desegregation Struggles

Desiring to be integrated as first-class citizens, Mexican Americans in LULAC, like their middle-class Afro-American counterparts in the NAACP, struggled against various forms of racial discrimination. . . . They did not want to be singled out for discrimination or for patronization. All they aspired to was equal access to the rights enjoyed by other Americans. Lulacers believed that Mexican Americans were entitled to first-class citizenship not only under the Constitution but also under guarantees of the Treaty of Guadalupe Hidalgo (1848), which ended the Mexican War. . . .

LULAC in particular protested against discrimination in public facilities, considered a major affront to Mexican Americans. Not shy about resorting to the courts, LULAC preferred diplomacy and pressure group politics to achieve desegregation. . . . Lockhart Council No. 38 in Texas, for example, after hearing in 1938 that a new movie theater was going to segregate Mexicans and blacks in the balcony, vehemently objected to the management and succeeded in desegregating the theater, at least for Mexican Americans. . . .

On certain occasions diplomacy and pressure group politics had to include the threat of an economic boycott to achieve desegregation of public facilities. In 1940 LULAC again protested in San Angelo over the efforts of a new movie theater to segregate Mexicans along with blacks in the balcony. President General A. M. Fernández at first counseled firm diplomacy. He advised LULAC's newly created Public Relations Board headed by E. D. Salinas to investigate the issue and "courteously" request that the theater drop its segregated policy toward Mexicans. Fernández also proposed publicizing this local affront to Mexican Americans by linking it with the harm such a case of prejudice did to President Roosevelt's efforts to advance the Good Neighbor Policy. If the management still demurred, Fernández proposed appealing to Washington, where Senator Dennis Chávez, the lone Mexican American in the Congress, and other supporters of the Good Neighbor Policy might be able to intervene. These political channels would first be exhausted before possibly pursuing adjudication. Yet diplomacy had to be reinforced by more direct action. Fernández called on Mexican Americans to boycott the theater until its segregated policies ended. LULAC's strategy succeeded. The management agreed to seat Mexicans throughout the theater and publicly apologized for the controversy. Besides theaters, LULAC protested, in many cases successfully, the segregation of Mexican Americans in swimming pools, restaurants, hospitals, and other forms of public accommodations.

In these antisegregation efforts, LULAC rejected any attempt to segregate Mexican Americans as a nonwhite population. Mexican Americans expressed ambivalences about race identity and possessed their own prejudices against blacks. However, they also recognized that irrespective of how they saw themselves, reclassification as colored, especially in Texas, would subject Mexicans not only to de facto segregation but to de jure as well. This was intolerable. Lulacers consistently argued that Mexicans were legally recognized members of the white race and that no legal or physical basis existed for racial discrimination. Lulacers specifically objected to Anglos excluding Mexican Americans from the political process because Mexicans were colored. In 1937 Council No. 69 in Wharton, Texas, successfully stopped the county tax collector from designating Mexican Americans holding receipts as "colored." . . .

Public discrimination against Mexican Americans likewise involved the exclusion of Mexican Americans from juries in Texas. Although this practice had a long history, Mexican Americans in LULAC vowed to eliminate this blatant type of discrimination. Despite earlier efforts to achieve proportional representation on grand juries in Texas counties with significant Mexican-American populations, by 1951 LULAC concluded that only through court action could jury discrimination be abolished. In September of that year, LULAC lawyer Gus García agreed to represent Pete Hernández, a laborer charged with murdering another Mexican American in Jackson County, Texas. García defended Hernández not only because he believed that authorities were determined to condemn the 26-year old to the electric chair, but because García concluded that he could use the case to combat the systematic exclusion of Mexican Americans from jury commissions, grand juries, and petit juries in Texas. Exclusion could be attacked as a violation of the Fourteenth Amendment, which insisted on equal protection of the law. With the assistance of Houston lawyer John J. Herrera, who also served as first national vice president of LULAC, García defended Hernández in his preliminary hearing and in the initial trial. . . . Despite García's and Herrera's labors, a Jackson County jury, containing no Mexican Americans, found Hernández guilty and sentenced him to life imprisonment.

Not discouraged, García and Herrera filed a motion for a new trial with the Texas Court of Criminal Appeals. In the appeal process, Carlos Cadena, a law professor at St. Mary's University in San Antonio, assisted García and Herrera. The court heard the Mexican-American arguments but still rejected Hernández's request for a new trial. It argued that the Fourteenth Amendment did not apply to the case. The amendment, so the court asserted, recognized only two classes under its equal protection of the law clause: whites and blacks. Mexican Americans were considered whites, hence they could not claim that they had been discriminated against in jury selection. As long as other whites served on these juries, Mexican Americans were represented. . . .

Despite some misgivings over the case, García and Cadena filed an application for a writ of certiorari (review) with the U.S. Supreme Court on January 19, 1953. . . . The U.S. Supreme Court on May 3, 1954, in a decision written by Chief Justice Earl Warren, overturned the Texas Court of Appeals and ruled that Hernández had not received a fair trial due to jury discrimination against Mexican Americans depriving him of the equal protection of the laws under the Fourteenth Amendment. Warren and the Court rejected the "two classes" theory and stated that the Fourteenth Amendment did not restrict itself to whites and blacks.

The Hernández decision represented a major legal victory for Mexican Americans. . . . The Supreme Court's rejection of the "two classes" theory under the Fourteenth Amendment meant that other ethnic groups besides blacks could appeal for protection under the amendment. . . .

Besides acting against discrimination in public facilities and on juries, LULAC struggled against varied forms of job discrimination. It investigated charges of discrimination in WPA jobs during the 1930s depression. LULAC also protested efforts to exclude Mexican Americans from skilled jobs. In 1941 El Paso Council No. 132 expressed anger over the Southern Pacific Railroad's refusal to provide skilled apprenticeships to Mexican Americans. . . .

Yet eliminating discrimination would not mean much unless accompanied by education. Consequently, education became basic to LULAC's ideology and the foundation of its Americanization program. As political liberals, Lulacers perceived education as the key solution to the social problems facing Mexican Americans. LULAC linked its commitment to education to the belief that Americans possessed a universal right to education with no limit to individual educational achievement. Mexican Americans would no longer accept, as they had experienced for many years, limited education in inferior Mexican schools throughout the Southwest. Such an education reproduced a low-skilled work force and kept Mexican Americans in a state of economic underdevelopment. . . .

LULAC also visualized education as a means of developing permanent leadership for the Mexican-American community. This leadership would, of course, be based on a professional middle class. The linkage of education with leadership, however, would require access to university education. Carlos Castañeda of the University of Texas expressed delight with the increased number of young Mexican Americans studying at Austin in the 1930s. He especially noted the importance of many of them studying law. "This is essential to the best interests of our Latin American citizens," he wrote to lawyer M. C. González. "What we need most of all in this state is a group of well trained and representative Latin-American lawyers to whom our people can go for legal advice and who can defend their rights when these are trampled upon."

Embracing education as perhaps the chief vehicle for the integration of Mexican Americans, LULAC at the same time understood that Mexican Americans would have to wage desegregation struggles to achieve quality education. . . .

LULAC pursued dual strategies in its attempt to achieve educational integration and quality education for Mexican-American children. It first sought through a combination of protests, negotiations, and community pressure to convince school authorities to institute changes voluntarily. LULAC councils, for example, investigated charges by Mexican parents concerning discriminatory acts by teachers against their children and when warranted brought such incidents to the attention of the proper authorities. Councils also publicized the unequal distribution of educational resources between schools predominantly attended by Mexican Americans and those attended by Anglos. Moreover, councils protested against de facto segregated schools for Mexican-American children. In particular cases, local community pressure by itself succeeded in desegregating the schools. In 1934, Goliad Council No. 21 assisted by Lulacers from San Antonio obtained the integration of Mexican-American students into the primarily Anglo Goliad High School. Five years later, Council No. 2 of San Antonio achieved the desegregation of the high school in Beeville, Texas. Still other actions involved meetings with state educational authorities concerning desegregation and increased resources for Mexican-American students as well as the hiring of attorneys to investigate segregated conditions. Some of these efforts resulted in reforms, while others encountered more obstacles.

Because of the difficulties in eradicating de facto school segregation in Texas and throughout the Southwest, LULAC also pursued a policy of instigating or assisting in legal actions. In 1930, one year after its formation, LULAC organized its first school desegregation case in Del Rio, Texas. Jesús Salvatierra and several parents, assisted by LULAC lawyers . . . requested and obtained a local injunction from a state court prohibiting the Del Rio School District from using recently approved bond monies to construct new facilities that Mexican Americans claimed would only further the existing segregation of Mexican-American children. . . .

After hearing the arguments, a local trial court ruled in favor of Salvatierra and the other Mexican-American appellants and issued an injunction restraining the school district from expanding the de facto segregated Mexican school. However, on appeal the court of appeals in San Antonio overturned the injunction. The court in the Salvatierra case dismissed the contention by the appellates that the Del Rio school district deliberately segregated Mexican-American children on the basis of race. . . . The Salvatierra case had displayed LULAC's ability to lead in this matter and to organize support. Numerous individuals as well as local LULAC councils throughout Texas contributed to the legal defense fund. The Salvatierra case became the first step in a legal campaign for school integration.

Sixteen years later, in 1946, LULAC helped achieve a major legal breakthrough in the Westminster case in California. . . . LULAC endorsed and supported a class suit by Gonzalo Méndez and other Mexican Americans against the school districts of Westminster, Garden Grove, El Modeno, and Santa Ana of Orange county. Mexican Americans alleged that these districts' policies of segregating Mexican-American students throughout most if not all the elementary grades was discriminatory and a violation of the Fourteenth Amendment. . . .

The Federal District Court agreed and ruled that such segregation not only violated California educational laws that prohibited segregation of Mexican-American children, but also violated the Fourteenth Amendment of the U.S. Constitution. . . .

On appeal the Ninth Circuit Court of Appeals one year later affirmed the decision in the Westminster case. Closely resembling the more famous Brown case in 1954, in which the U.S. Supreme Court declared separate schools for blacks unconstitutional, the Westminster case signaled a major victory for Mexican Americans and for LULAC, which had helped provide the funding support for the adjudication of the case. . . .

The Westminster case had a ripple effect and in 1948 LULAC sponsored and funded a similar legal challenge to school segregation in Texas. In *Delgado v. Bastrop Independent School District,* a federal district court again ruled, as in the Westminster case, that the segregation of Mexican-American pupils violated the Fourteenth Amendment. The Delgado case went one step further and specifically declared unconstitutional the segregation of Mexican Americans in separate classrooms within "integrated" schools. . . .

. . . LULAC's legal battles did not end educational underdevelopment for many Mexican Americans. They continued to face inequalities in comparison to Anglo students. Still, LULAC's path-breaking litigation forced the southwestern education system on the defensive and obtained the force of law behind Mexican-American efforts to achieve educational equality. It also furthered the "nationalization" of Mexican-American politics through LULAC's reliance on the powers of the federal courts to institute changes for Mexican Americans.

Conclusion

For over thirty years LULAC served as the principal and most visible Mexican-American organization in the United States. Although founded in Texas and initially concentrating on Mexican-American issues in that state, LULAC by 1960 had become a national organization with councils throughout the Southwest and Midwest, the regions containing the majority of Mexican Americans. In later decades it would spread even more and include other Latino peoples such as Puerto Ricans and to a lesser extent Cuban Americans. As one of the few organizations working on basic civil rights for Mexican Americans, LULAC, despite its idealistic faith in the ability of the American system to reform itself, provided a degree of ethnic protection for Mexican Americans and through its struggles achieved breakthroughs in advancing civil rights.

Race, Gender, Class, and Image in the Chicana Labor Struggle, 1918–1938

IRENE LEDESMA

During the 1935 organizing of Dorothy Frocks workers in San Antonio, Mexican women, members of the International Ladies Garment Workers Union (ILGWU) advertised for a fund-raising dance in the local labor-union paper. In the advertisement, union leaders described the women workers as "some of the most comely of the female sex to be found anywhere. They are good seamstresses besides." Although the editors of the paper recognized the women's struggle, they portrayed the dance merely as a social event. This incident was not unique. The press image of Mexican women workers frequently diverged from the women's pronouncements and actions. In this article, I would like to show that Texas-press images of Mexican-American strikers depended on Anglo, "American," and male criteria, and therefore touched only peripherally on the women's experiences. . . .

Texas newspapers reported numerous union disputes and constructed images of Chicana strikers. . . . In El Paso, in 1919, Mexican laundry women protested the firing of two workers for union activity. During the 1930s, Mexican women in San Antonio—cigarmakers, pecan shellers, and dressmakers—went on strike for higher wages and for improved working-conditions. . . .

The Mexican women strikers in El Paso contended with a particularly antagonistic, Anglo-dominated economy. World War I anti-foreign propaganda and Pancho Villa raids into New Mexico generated hostile anti-Mexican sentiments. Accordingly, in 1919, the Anglo-American population of El Paso generally viewed Mexican

Irene Ledesma, "Texas Newspapers and Chicana Workers' Activism, 1918–1974," *Western Historical Quarterly* 26 (Autumn 1995): 309–332. Copyright © 1995 by The Western Historical Quarterly. Reprinted with permission.

immigrants as an alien force. This hostility was compounded by the anti-labor sentiments of local officials, who expressed themselves by creating an ordinance against
picketing.

Organized labor also resented Mexican immigrants. Union officials blamed
them for low wages, claimed they took jobs from Americans, and declared that they
served as strikebreakers. El Paso's light industrial economy and the discriminatory
practices of American employers placed unskilled Mexican workers in low-paying,
segmented, and stratified jobs. Married Mexican immigrant women usually did not
work; young, single Mexican women were employed in domestic service and in
laundries.

When the Mexican women's laundry strike broke out, however, xenophobic
labor leaders momentarily stopped their racially-based campaigns against the employment of Mexicans. The story of the laundry workers is a good example of
how labor leaders seemingly change their attitudes toward Mexican workers. On
24 October 1919, Mexican women workers organized a local of the International
Laundry Workers Union. Soon after, the Acme Laundry of El Paso fired two veteran
workers—one sorter and one marker—because they were recruiting new members
to the union. According to sorter Francisca Saenz, the remaining Mexican women at
Acme then refused to cooperate with Acme's attempt to send their work to other
local laundries. Within a few days, almost five hundred laundry women walked
out of the six laundries in the city.

On the evening of the walkout at Acme, several hundred Mexican laundry
women voted to stay out until the company reinstated the two fired workers. Subsequently, William Moran, editor of the labor paper and head of the Central Labor
Union (CLU), the labor leadership in El Paso, assumed control of the strike. He
took responsibility for all public statements on the strike and created a fund-raising
committee from the CLU membership. A few Mexican women were assigned the
task of persuading strikebreakers to refrain from taking the places of union members; all other Mexican women union members were relegated to the union hall.
The CLU leadership takeover reflected a belief generally held among unionists
that working women could be dominated by male leaders. The takeover further
suggested that Anglo CLU leaders perceived Mexicans as docile people.

From previous experience, labor leaders understood the difficulty of presenting a favorable image of Mexican immigrants to the Anglos in El Paso. Like many
Progressive reformers of the era, the editors of the *El Paso City and County Labor
Advocate* called on employers to prevent vice among the unmarried Mexican
women workers. Labor leaders focused on the low wages of the laundry strikers,
asking, "What chance has a girl or woman to live a decent respectable life at the
wages of this kind?" In another article concerning wages, the union leadership
claimed that many of the laundry stockholders were two-faced in calling for "clean-
up campaigns" while "breeding prostitution and every thing that can possibly be
vicious" and by paying a four dollar a week wage. As the strike intensified, the paper
attempted to counter El Pasoans' notions that Mexicans were morally lax. To do
this, they imposed on the public images of the women's vulnerability.

In this attempt to help, the labor leadership itself ignored other roles of the Mexican women unionists. In November, a Texas Welfare Commission study of wages—
in a variety of industries—revealed that many of the laundry women supported their

families. One laundry worker told the committee, "I find it difficult to live on my wages, which I turn in to the family budget." Despite the report and personal testimony, union leaders continued to portray these workers as women in need of moral protection and guidance. . . .

In their attempt to create new images of the women, the labor press fought employer practices that were acceptable to business-dominated civic leaders. The labor paper raised the issue of the women's citizenship, hoping to turn the public against the practice of hiring Mexican aliens to replace strikers. Labor leaders intended to reach any reform-minded unionist through the use of Progressive rhetoric. These leaders emphasized that the striking women were asking for fundamental rights expressed in the Constitution. They admitted, too, that many Americans regarded all Mexican Americans as Mexicans. . . . Acknowledging members' prejudices, the labor paper sought its members' support by defining Mexicans in a manner consistent with Progressive ideals.

Labor leaders used the citizenship angle to reverse other working El Pasoans' chronic antagonism toward Mexican immigrants. Pressing the issue, the *Labor Advocate* insisted that "nothing will be left undone to see that they receive just treatment and a square deal . . . which the Constitution of the American government guarantees to its every citizen." Fortunately for El Paso labor leaders, Theodore Roosevelt's Progressive language and Americans' ideal vision of the Constitution proved perfect for turning Mexicans from aliens into American citizens.

The laborites did not limit to editorials their representation of the strikers. Having banished the Mexican women strikers to the union hall or to the picket line, the CLU leadership sent out agents to garner support from other locals, Mexican-American civic groups, and Anglo-American organizations. The American Federation of Labor (AFL) sent in C.N. Idar to help. Idar, in a speech before the El Paso Ministerial Alliance, took the opportunity to impress upon his listeners the image of the strikers as both morally vulnerable women and as citizens. He told the group that prevailing wages did not permit the Mexican laundry women to "live decent and respectable lives as American citizens." Both appeals succeeded: locals sent funds totaling more than $3,000. Local ministers promised to look into the situation.

But union leaders' appeals on the issue of morality posed a problem. When Mexican women strikers positioned themselves at the El Paso-Ciudad Juarez border bridge to prevent Mexican citizens from taking their places, they contradicted union images of vulnerability. Those that remained picketing at plant sites issued verbal threats. They told one worker they would "pull her hair out if she crossed the line." They also knitted and sold items for strike coffers, even as a male unionist took a leave of absence from his job to raise strike funds. Such actions clearly contradicted the prevailing image of these workers as defenseless women.

On the issue of anti-Mexican biases, the union faced overwhelming obstacles. In 1919, Anglo El Pasoans regarded Mexicans as foreigners, regardless of their citizenship status. Anglos saw non-English speaking Mexicans as unlikely Americans. They perceived a link between corrupt local government officials and Mexican votes. Protestant Anglos considered Catholics non-Christians, and Mexicans were mostly Catholic. These Protestants also held Mexicans responsible for bootlegging and for the excessive drinking in the area. And Anglos believed that Mexicans, as dark-skinned people, expressed a threatening sexual licentiousness through prostitution.

Clashes between Mexican revolutionaries and American citizens in Columbus, New Mexico, added to Anglo El Pasoans' convictions that Mexicans spelled trouble. Despite Anglo preconceptions, the Mexican strikers in El Paso saw themselves to be Americans, and they viewed those crossing over from Juarez to be the "aliens."

Laundry owners rallied, turning the tables on their opponents by seizing these negative preconceptions and applying them to union members. The daily press was quick to echo the owners' cause. Reiterating that the strike had no effect on his business, the owner of the Excelsior Laundry boasted in the *El Paso Herald,* "[S]ome of my Mexicans quit and I put Americans in their place. The American used just half as much materials as the Mexican. The work was cleaner and whiter and better in every way." In a news advertisement in the same paper, the owner of the Elite Laundry reinforced notions of Mexican workers as less capable of good work. He argued that the walkout had started when a girl was fired for not doing her work. The *El Paso Herald* added to the negative image by describing strikers as "Mexican girls" who "are enjoying their vacation." The paper declared, "At the central Labor Union hall the girls are singing and dancing." In these depictions, the Mexicans seemed childlike. As one school principal said of them, "The Mexicans are particulary gifted in art work and music."

Without evidence, the commercial press disparaged the Mexican strikers by linking them to radical groups. The *Herald* published the mayor's instructions to the police chief "to permit no disorders of rioting in this city no matter what the cause." The *El Paso Morning Times,* at least, noted that the women had acted peacefully during the strike. The press gave inordinate attention to materials written in Spanish that had been seized from the Industrial Workers of the World (IWW). The daily papers played up the actions of scab laundry drivers as a first blow against Bolshevism. Although the Mexican women strikers had not gone beyond verbal jousting against strikebreakers, the daily press insisted on associating them with so-called un-American activities.

The daily press fueled ethnic slurs by quoting employers. One such quote included the Acme Laundry owner's pernicious statements on wages to the Welfare Commission. In his testimony, he argued that Mexican women worked too slowly, lacked interest in their work, and completed less items than American employees. He referred to twenty striking women from his plant as, "the cheaper sort of work." He said he found it difficult to find workers for the better jobs because Mexican women could only do routine back labor. Although the two Mexican women he fired had worked (one as a sorter and one as a marker) for at least six years, he testified that American women served better at those positions. Such public observations fueled existing prejudices, intensifying the image of the Mexican women strikers as "un-American," subversive, or inept.

The sentiments of Anglo-American society complicated the strike situation for the women. These El Pasoans seemed to share with other Americans a fear that organized labor might lead the way to Bolshevism. The local American Legion members searched the city for "Reds" but found none. The press, meanwhile, exploited strike stories involving the IWW, and the hysteria reached such heights that the press interpreted unintelligible graffiti found in a men's room as the advance guard of the IWW. Stories such as these gained credibility in light of the other negative images of Mexicans.

The Spanish-language press, with its largely Mexican audience, was enthusiastic, but patronizing, in its portrayal of laundry strikers. The paper covered the visit of Mexican women strikers to local Mexican civic groups, proudly and frequently referring to the women's Mexican antecedents and emphasizing their goals as a struggle for respect for their rights. Stressing the women's peacefulness, the press claimed, "pero no han pasado de eso[1] [shouting at scabs]," the papers expressed outright admiration for them, saying "nuestras mujeres están dando un ejemplo de carácter, energía y solidaridad racial."[2] Interestingly, the Mexican umbrella union that supported the women declared itself the voice of the Mexican community, announcing that the latter was "muy dignamente representada en las sociedades."[3]

For all its posturing in support of the laundry strikers, *La Patria* was often condescending. An article calling the women "compatriots" expressed appreciation to all who had helped the women in their struggle and exhorted the latter to remain united in the view of the union's efforts on their behalf. Earlier in the article, *La Patria*, recounting how the mayor had ordered the police to enforce peace on both sides, considered the situation grave. The journalist stressed that the women "se han portado con toda corrección."[4] This writer added that the violence would be eschewed by the organizers and indicated that any violence would undercut the women's final goal. The ones who wrote these words offered solidarity only because the strikers behaved correctly, and such writers took upon themselves the task of showing to whom the women ought to be grateful as well as what the women's goals should be.

Editors of *La Patria,* and others, appeared intent on educating the women on the conduct of labor disputes. In a discussion of the problems facing the strikers, they predicted the negative outcome of the strike. With a hint of censure, they concluded that too many unemployed women resided in El Paso and Ciudad Juarez. Both strikers and the union realized the extent of the unemployment problem. The CLU sought a solution, asking city officials to demand that laundry owners not hire alien labor. The effort was rebuffed. Another Mexican-American organization added a *machismo* element. In calling for a conference on the strike, the umbrella civic group noted the high percentage of *women* [my emphasis] strikers and asked that "no por esa misma razón [deben] abandonarlas en este momento."[5] Thus, they implied the women needed their help. Mention of the strike by the press had diminished by early December, an indication that the prediction of the Spanish press that the strike would fail had been realized.

Those civic groups to whom *La Patria* appealed clearly reflected the class interests of the Spanish press and of their own membership. In particular, the Mexican Alliance's denial of rumors that it was contemplating supporting a general strike by Mexican workers showed the members' eagerness to appease the owners. When questioned on the issue, members responded that "they were in full sympathy with the striking girls [but] no proposition of a sympathetic strike by local Mexican workers was favored or had even been considered." Seeing themselves as

---

[1]But they have not gone beyond this.
[2]Our women are giving an example of character, enthusiasm, and racial solidarity.
[3]Very well represented in the groups.
[4]They have behaved quite correctly.
[5]For the same reason, we should not abandon them at this time.

representatives of El Paso's Mexican community, the Mexican Alliance quickly discounted any connection to extremist actions.

By 1920, many CLU members withdrew into an alliance with a Ku Klux Klan-dominated good-government movement. With this retreat, organized labor and Mexican immigrants lost the opportunity for an alliance. Nativism in the 1920s and bad economic conditions in the 1930s widened the rift. It would not be until the 1950s that organized labor in El Paso allied itself once again with those workers of Mexican heritage.

Labor union activity in the United States increased enormously in the 1930s because of economic conditions and encouragement from the national government in the form of the Wagner Act. The creation of the Congress of Industrial Organization (CIO) made trade unionism possible to the "unorganizable." In San Antonio, between 12,000 and 15,000 mainly unorganized pecan shellers worked in the pecan industry. Pecan shelling was normally a young, single woman's job, but Depression conditions had forced men into the industry, and home-shelling by entire families became common. When the CIO began unionizing efforts among the shellers, business and community leaders, who touted the city as a haven of cheap labor and who relied on bought Mexican votes, worried that the Chicano masses might become politically conscious.

Conditions and pay in pecan plants in San Antonio early in this century can best be described as poor, but the economic situation of the 1930s made it worse. Workers sat in filthy rooms on backless benches with boxes of pecans in front of them. They were surrounded by the dust from broken shells, and they cracked the nuts by hand. The average weekly wage was $2.25. In 1934, and again in 1935, the pecan shellers forced companies to rescind pay cuts. The owner of Southern Pecan Shelling Company solved this problem by funding the president of the largest local, making it, for all intents and purposes, a company union. In 1936, the president of Southern Pecan proclaimed that five cents a day was plenty for the shellers, who, he said, daily consumed nuts as they worked. That year the company made a profit of $500,000.

On 1 February 1938, thousands of pecan shellers walked out in protest of yet another wage reduction. The pecan shellers chose a non-sheller, twenty-three-year-old Emma Tenayuca, as strike committee chair. The shellers told the Spanish paper that, "la repetida líder no ha tomado participación en este movimiento de manera espontánea, sino obedeciendo la persistente solicitud de los obreros."[6] Tenayuca had earned the Mexican-American workers' respect through her activities as secretary of the local chapter of the Workers' Alliance. During the 1937 winter layoff of relief recipients on public works projects, Tenayuca and the Alliance staged a workers' protest in front of city hall. Additionally, in Tenayuca's words, "the Workers' Alliance continued, carrying grievances, meeting on Sunday." According to Tenayuca, the Alliance "had more than 10,000 members," and its attempts to inform Mexican-American workers of their rights and to alleviate their work-related problems angered city government officials. For years, they had counted on an acquiescent Mexican-American work force to prop their political machine.

---

[6]The above-mentioned leader did not take part in this movement spontaneously but to obey the persistent requests of the workers.

In support of city government's contention that no strike existed, police committed violence on the picket line almost daily. San Antonio did not have Mexican policemen in the 1930s, but strikers, and most of their leaders, came from the Mexican community. Both male and female strikers were arrested during the strike, although on occasion police released from jail women with children. The governor of Texas initiated an investigation on blatant police harassment after the Mexican consul and a U.S. congressman protested the worker's treatment.

Police used lawful and unlawful means to suppress the strike. Capturing national attention with their actions, they tear-gassed pickets indiscriminately, jailed pecan shellers for days without charging them, and took workers outside city limits, forcing them to walk miles back to town. At one point, the police chief doused male strikers with hoses for protesting jail conditions. A local study by a woman's group revealed that Mexican women strikers were crowded into cells with prostitutes. The treatment of the women reflected city officials' bias in categorizing women into what historians call the whore/Madonna complex. The police chief justified his handling of the strike situation by claiming, "It is my duty to interfere with revolution, and communism is revolution." The archbishop of San Antonio, Arthur Drossaerts, praised the chief's efforts.

Fearing the political consequences of a successful strike, the Democratic machine at city hall denounced the strikers and their leaders as outsiders and Communists. The local papers published the police chief's comment that no strike existed because Communist leaders—and he named Tenayuca and Minnie Rendon, the local's secretary—duped the Mexican-American workers. In addition, the mayor and the head of the city vigilance committee questioned the credentials of Cassie Jane Winifree, state chairperson of the Women's National League for Peace and Freedom, after she requested approval to seek funds for strikers' meals. The daily paper wrote approvingly of the mayor's visit to pecan sheds, where he told workers,

> I am convinced that you will not be able to receive calm and dispassionate hearing if you permit Communistic leaders to excite and agitate your people . . . I have reference to such well-known Communistic leaders as Mrs. Emma Tenayuca Brooks, Jim Sager and their co-workers and advisors in the Communist or Red movement.

The police chief told a state inquiry commission, "if the [Mexican] westside workers were organized by UCAPAWA [United Cannery, Agricultural, Pacing and Allied Workers of America], 25,000 persons would be lost to the 'Red Banner.'" The daily press accepted the mayor's and the chief's characterizations and disseminated them without further inquiry. Refusing to consider the frustrations of a destitute people, the mayor and chief gave voice to Anglo San Antonians' views of Mexican immigrants as ignorant, tractable people open to subversive influences.

Daily press accounts of the strike focused on similar allegations about Tenayuca. They centered on Tenayuca's connection to Communism. Even after UCAPAWA's national president, Donald Henderson, took over the strike, the papers continued to allude to Tenayuca's Communist affiliations. The journalists concentrated on her marriage to Homer Brooks, onetime candidate for governor on the Communist ticket. Tenayuca's marriage to an Anglo failed to endear her to other Anglos, not only because she was breaking a social taboo with the marriage but because the marriage reflected her ties to outsiders and Communists. The Mexican community preferred to see her in terms of her activism on their behalf. It typically referred to her as "la pasionaría" rather than by her married name.

In addition to frequent references of her marriage to a Communist, the press detailed Tenayuca's protest activities as chair of the state chapter of the Workers' Alliance. The *San Antonio Express,* reporting the findings of the state industrial commission on police harassment, noted that she had previously been "acquitted of a charge of unlawful assemblage and disturbing the peace." In this article on police wrong-doing, the journalist discredited Tenayuca by associating her with anarchy, lawlessness, and even subversion.

In contrast to the obviously hostile attitude of the Anglo press and aggressive actions of the police, the middle-class Spanish-language paper *La Prensa* expressed some support for the Mexican strikers. The paper approvingly described them as "los miembros de la Texas Pecan Shelling Workers Union han guardado completo orden durante su huelga, sin recurrir a actos de violencia."[7] The journalist at *La Prensa* attempted to dilute the negative images of the strikers by noting that "unos cuantos radicales, sin conección alguna con la industria de nuez, intentaron de tomar parte en la huelga y algunos fueron aprehendidos."[8] The paper, however, also noted that two Mexican-American civic groups—the League of Loyal Americans and the Mexican Chamber of Commerce—demanded that strike leaders sign a loyalty pledge. These groups proclaimed, "We are interested in Mexican workers getting a living wage because we want them to be loyal and progressive citizens of the United States." Two weeks later a worker's rally featured the archbishop, a University of Mexico student, and two representatives from Mexican civic groups. Speakers denounced Communist support and reinforced middle-class Mexican-Americans' stance.

At the same time, the paper offered stories on other aspects of the strike that showed the Mexican unionists' viewpoint. The paper published the workers' defense of Tenayuca and a statement of their intent to protest her arrest. *La Prensa* also published references to the strike that the daily press ignored, such as a charge by Henderson that city opposition was racially motivated. In addition, *La Prensa* proudly noted that the Mexican vice-consul defended the rights of arrested Mexican strikers by attending their court appearances. As had *La Patria* in El Paso in 1919, *La Prensa* offered support only when the women behaved according to middle-class standards. Additionally, by the 1930s, the owner of the paper, favoring American citizenship, lost interest in returning to Mexico. His editors reflected this shift in mindset by emphasizing that the Mexican strikers were peaceful, citizenship-worthy people.

The Anglo-labor leadership in San Antonio shared city government fears that the Mexican masses might revolt. This concern explained the labor paper's lack of coverage of the shellers' strike. In the four years prior to the 1938 strike, the labor press occasionally expressed its dismay over work conditions in the pecan industry,

---

[7]The members of the Texas Pecan Shelling Workers Union have maintained complete order during their strike, without resorting to violence.

[8]A few radicals without connection to the pecan industry have tried to take part in the strike and a few were apprehended.

and referred to the Mexican strikers as "that class of citizenship that are located on our West side." This was a weak gesture made to represent the strikers as Americans. Laborites knew that during a depression American workers' resentment of aliens increased. In the case of Mexicans, this animosity was so intense that repatriation efforts in some cities had succeeded.

When the unionist newspaper did take up the topic, labor leaders' resentment was clear. The paper had indicated its biases in the 1934 strike by declaring that a "more intelligent class of workers" would not have brooked the interference that the sheriff had inflicted on the Mexican strikers' rights. The attorney for the ILGWU may have expressed local labor leaders' attitude most cogently by saying that the pecan strike concerned "un grupo de radicales que se declararon en huelga bajo la guía de Emma Tenayuca de Brooks y Homer Brooks."[9] During the dispute some presidents of locals joined pecan-sheller representatives at behind-the-scenes meetings with town officials. But, in fact, by 1938, the AF of L leadership had done nothing to organize the largely female shellers, and it expressed surprise and perturbation in the *Weekly Dispatch* over CIO efforts to do so that year.

The Mexican pecan shellers won the dispute. Three Mexican women—Amelia De La Rosa, Natalia Camareno, and Velia Quinones—served on the committee arranging for an arbitration board settlement that restored wages to pre-strike levels. Other women did not fare as well. Tenayuca left San Antonio in 1939 when in August a mob stormed the city auditorium in a successful effort to prevent an Alliance rally. Tired of her protest activities, city leaders advised her to leave or face the consequences. Pecan-shelling companies reverted to machine labor in 1939 to avoid paying the wage rates of 25 cents an hour that had been set by Fair Labor Standards Act. This measure reduced the work force in the sheds by thousands. . . .

Guided by accepted ideas of gender, class, and ethnicity in American society, Texas newspapers expressed unwarranted assumptions in their representations of the Chicana strikers. The daily, local papers maintained a consistent profile of the strikers as outside mainstream America—as Bolsheviks, Communists, and as evil and filthy foreigners. When the local press was not focusing on the alleged anti-social and anti-American behavior of the women, it tended to ignore them and concentrate on the males instead. San Antonio and El Paso papers emphasized the Mexican heritage of the strikers in negative ways, usually through the comments of company owners or city officials. These papers pictured the Chicanas as lazy, impressionable, and stupid—or simply as "Mexicans." The daily paper's representations illustrated their bonds with Anglo government at the local level.

The daily press did not seem bothered by their contradictory depictions of the strikers. Their efforts *meant* to alienate the women from the rest of the community. At times, the papers portrayed the women as the antithesis of American good. In the next breath, the papers called them gullible and too indolent even to realize the American work ethic. Anglo readers could be comfortable with these representations because they fit into the accepted notion of Chicanas as an alien and unassimilable

---

[9]A group of radicals who went on strike under the guidance of Emma Tenayuca Brooks and Henry Brooks.

element. It was this shared understanding with other establishment institutions that the commercial press pushed incomplete images of the striker.

To gain support, the labor press would periodically change its image of the Chicana strikers. It would select what was socially palatable in an effort to make acceptable a group of strikers who stood on the margins of society. . . . [T]he labor papers overlooked the Mexican heritage of the strikers to stress their American citizenship and their roles as vulnerable women and mothers. . . .

Labor editors operated with many of the same prejudices as the rest of the community. In 1919, the labor paper pulled back from earlier anti-Mexican diatribes and supported the Mexican women strikers only to retreat into a KKK alliance by 1920. In the pecan strike of 1938, the labor paper, run by AFL leaders, gave coverage only in reaction to CIO interest or involvement in it. . . .

Spanish-language papers . . . caught between their Mexican origins and ties to Chicana strikers and their hopes of becoming Americans, tried to play it both ways be stressing the Mexican heritage of the women in a positive way and at the same time stressing their good behavior. By emphasizing proper behavior, the Spanish press, with its own middle-and-upper class management, clearly exhibited patronizing attitudes towards the strikers as women and as working-class people.

In reality, the seeming ambivalence of the Spanish press lay purely on the surface. Its concerns over its own status in the U.S. inhibited its sense of solidarity, as evidenced by the civic club's attitude in 1919 that the women's good behavior had earned them the former's support as representatives of the Mexican community. The striking women's often violent responses served to place them beyond the pale of traditional middle-class ideology, and the male hierarchy in the Spanish language press preferred instructing the women on strategy and conduct. Particularly after the 1920s, the middle- and upper-class Mexican immigrant embraced American ideals, and they pushed their ideals on their less well-placed ethnic sisters. . . .

The newspapers in El Paso and San Antonio proved unable to move beyond established notions of gender, class, and ethnicity in their coverage of the Chicana strikers . . . but in the process, the press provided information on the overwhelming forces the women faced during protest situations. The Chicanas fought not only great opposition from the companies, but a powerful daily press ready to condemn their actions in support of the established order. Even their supporters, the unions and Spanish-language papers, expected certain behavior from them based on each paper's particular agenda in a given period. Despite these complex odds arrayed against them, Chicanas in Texas demonstrated the power of persistence in the battle for labor justice.

FURTHER READING

Carl Allsup, *The American G.I. Forum: Origins and Evolution* (1982)

Francisco E. Balderrama and Raymond Rodríguez, *Decade of Betrayal: Mexican Repatriation in the 1930s* (1995)

Julia Blackwelder, *Women of the Depression: Caste and Culture in San Antonio, 1929–1939* (1984)

Armando C. Alonzo, *Tejano Legacy: Rancheros and Settlers in South Texas, 1734–1900* (1998)

Arnoldo De León, *Ethnicity in the Sunbelt: A History of Mexican Americans in Houston* (1989)

——*The Tejano Community, 1836–1900* (1982)

——*They Call Them Greasers: Anglo Attitudes toward Mexicans in Texas, 1821–1900* (1983)

Arnold De León and Kenneth L. Stewart, *Not Room Enough: Mexicans, Anglos, and Socioeconomic Change in Texas, 1850–1900* (1993)

——*Tejanos and the Numbers Game: A Socio-Historical Interpretation from the Federal Censuses, 1850–1900* (1989)

Neil Foley, *The White Scourge: Mexicans, Blacks, and Poor Whites in Texas Cotton Culture* (1997)

Mario T. García, *Desert Immigrants: The Mexicans of El Paso, 1880–1920* (1981)

——*Mexican Americans: Leadership, Ideology & Identity, 1930–1960* (1989)

Richard Griswald del Castillo and Arnoldo De León, *North to Aztlán: A History of Mexican Americans in the United States* (1996)

Thomas H. Kreneck, *Mexican American Odyssey: Felix Tijerina, Entrepreneur and Civic Leader, 1905–1965* (2001)

Benjamin Marques, *LULAC: The Evolution of a Mexican American Political Organization* (1993)

David Montejano, *Anglos and Mexicans in the Making of Texas, 1836–1986* (1987)

Guadalupe San Miguel, Jr.,*"Let All of them Take Heed": Mexican Americans and the Campaign for Educational Equality in Texas, 1910–1981* (1987)

Emilio Zamora, Cynthia Orozco, and Rodolfo Rocha, eds., *Mexican Americans in Texas History: Selected Essays* (2000)

The African American Struggle for Civil Rights in Texas, 1940–1960

The African American civil rights movement is generally viewed as a post-World War II phenomenon that followed the Supreme Court decision against school segregation in Brown v. Topeka Board of Education *and was dominated by the leadership of Martin Luther King. In Texas the struggle for racial equality was well underway in the 1930s, and achieved major victories in the 1940s and early 1950s under the leadership of local NAACP (National Association for the Advancement of Colored People) organizers like Lulu B. White of Houston and Juanita Craft of Dallas. Black Texans never accommodated themselves to discrimination and disfranchisement. Primarily through the NAACP, which established its first local chapter in the state in 1912 and had grown to 31 chapters and 7,000 members by 1919, blacks organized themselves on the local level to resist the attack on their civil and political rights.*

In the 1920s and 1930s the struggle for civil rights in Texas took several forms. First, beginning in 1924 in El Paso local blacks, with support from the national NAACP, launched a legal challenge to the white primary, the principal tool used to disfranchise African Americans. Blacks would win this battle in 1944. Meanwhile in a number of communities, blacks challenged segregation in public transportation; others campaigned to improve segregated facilities like schools and hospitals. In the 1940s conflict developed about the appropriate strategy to combat discrimination. Should African Americans accept equal funding or even high quality segregated facilities, or should they insist on desegregation, even if it meant that existing black institutions would suffer? This conflict divided the black community when the state legislature voted in 1947 to create the Texas State University for Negroes in an effort to block the lawsuit to desegregate the University of Texas Law School. Blacks also faced serious opposition from whites anytime they demanded equal rights. Although highly publicized confrontations between civil rights activists and political leaders were rare in Texas, resistance to racial equality was widespread, both among white supremacist fringe groups and public officials. Still, black Texans won their major civil rights battles and, for the most part, won them sooner with less violence than did blacks in the deep South.

How did the civil rights struggle in Texas differ from that of other former Confederate states? How significant were local leadership and local movements compared with the struggle at the national level? How was the struggle for civil rights in Texas affected by national political and civil rights movements?

🔖 D O C U M E N T S

The first three documents illustrate the campaign of African Americans to regain the right to vote. This struggle to regain the right to vote in Texas began in 1924 when an El Paso dentist, Lawrence A. Nixon, filed suit challenging the white primary. Document 1 is a memo from NAACP attorney Thurgood Marshall to the NAACP describing efforts to organize a new legal challenge to the white primary in 1940. Document 2 presents the 1944 Supreme Court decision in the case of *Smith v. Allwright* that declared the white primary unconstitutional. Document 3 illustrates the resurgence of African American political activity in the late 1940s following the decision.

The next three documents relate to the struggle for equal access to higher education in Texas. As in the struggle against the white primary, local NAACP chapters worked with the national office of the NAACP to organize a legal challenge to segregate colleges and universities. In 1947 Heman Sweatt filed suit when he was denied admission to the University of Texas Law School. As Document 4 demonstrates, in a ploy to maintain "separate but equal" facilities, the Texas legislature voted to create the Texas State University for Negroes (with a law school) in 1947. Three years later, in a decision that anticipated *Brown v. The Topeka Board of Education,* the Supreme Court ruled against the state of Texas (Document 5). As desegregation spread in the 1950s, reactionary groups organized to resist the assault on white supremacy. In Document 6, an unidentified El Paso investigator gathered intelligence on civil rights activities in that community, including the efforts to desegregate Texas Western College (now the University of Texas at El Paso).

Texas civil rights groups and their political allies attempted to resist efforts of segregationists and white supremacists to derail the civil rights movement. In Document 7, the Texas Citizen's Council of Greater Houston attempted to link civil rights to communism and arouse fears of miscegenation. When the Texas legislature introduced a series of anti-desegregation bills in 1957, liberal state senator Henry B. Gonzalez employed the favorite legislative weapon of southern segregationists, the filibuster, in an effort to defeat the proposals. In Document 8, *The Texas Observer* describes Gonzalez's filibuster. Document 9 describes the Dallas NAACP's fundraising efforts aimed at combating the state's segregationist legislation.

1. NAACP Attorney Thurgood Marshall Describes Efforts to Challenge the White Primary, 1941

November 17, 1941.

Memorandum: to office
From: Thurgood Marshall
Re: *"Saving the Race"*

Background

Left New York October 31 for two days in Washington with enough clothes for one day and a tooth brush—still on the road.

Old Texas Primary Case

Only way to get to Dallas in time for the meeting on Wednsday, [sic] November 5th was to fly by way of New Orleans to Houston and then to Dallas. On Tuesday night before I arrived in Dallas Charlie Brackins and some other members of the local committee made some rather bad statements about "messing up" the case etc. Had to take most of the time Wednesday pointing out to Brackins and others the true difficulties in the case and the benefits of filing another case. All agreed that if we did not get another case started all of us would have to leave the U.S. and go live with Hitler or some other peace loving individual who would be less difficult then the Negroes in Texas who had put up the money for the case.

New Case????

The gang in Dallas swore that they had a good plaintiff for a new case. We immediately started drafting a new complaint to fit this situation. By the time the man returned to town we discovered that he was not sure when he tried to vote. On checking the dailies we found that he had attempted to vote in the "run-off" primary in 1940 and we were right where we started—out in the street. Checked again and could find no cases in Dallas. Next stop Houston—still not anxious to go live with Hitler. This was on November 8th.

In Houston talked with Dr. L. E. Smith who is alleged to have attempted to vote at the right time. Checked his story as best I could. Started drafting complaint. Davis' stenographer can't type worth a dime. Tried for a day to get a stenographer who specialized in typing—no such animal available. Called Carter Wesley and drafted his secretary who really can type.

Had to go to Court House to find names of officials involved in case. Got the name of the County Clerk. Tried to get the names of the elections judges. Could only get the name of the election judge. Called this man and told him I was a reporter

"Saving the Race," Memo, Thurgood Marshall to [NAACP] Office, November 17, 1941, in NAACP Collection, Manuscript Division (8–16) Library of Congress. Available from lcweb.loc.gov/exhibits/odyssey/archive/08/0816001r.jpg.

for a local daily and wanted the name of his associated judge. Got the name and called this man who admitted he was the associate judge in the particular precinct. Drafted complaint Thursday.

2. *Smith v. Allwright* Declares the White Primary Unconstitutional, April 3, 1944

Mr. Justice Reed delivered the opinion of the Court.

This writ of certiorari brings here for review a claim for damages in the sum of $5,000 on the part of petitioner, a Negro citizen of the 48th precinct of Harris County, Texas, for the refusal . . . to give petitioner a ballot or to permit him to cast a ballot in the primary election of July 27, 1940. . . . The refusal is alleged to have been solely because of the race and color of the proposed voter. . . .

The State of Texas by its Constitution and statutes provides that every person, if certain other requirements are met which are not here in issue, qualified by residence in the district or county "shall be deemed a qualified elector." . . . Primary elections for United States Senators, Congressmen and state officers are provided for by Chapters Twelve and Thirteen of the statutes. Under these chapters, the Democratic Party was required to hold the primary which was the occasion of the alleged wrong to petitioner. . . .

The Democratic party, on May 24, 1932, in a state convention adopted the following resolution: . . .

> Be it resolved that all white citizens of the State of Texas who are qualified to vote under the Constitution and laws of the State shall be eligible to membership in the Democratic party and, as such, entitled to participate in its deliberations.

It was by virtue of this resolution that the respondents refused to permit the petitioner to vote.

Texas is free to conduct her elections and limit her electorate as she may deem wise, save only as her action may be affected by the prohibitions of the United States Constitution or in conflict with powers delegated to and exercised by the National Government. The Fourteenth Amendment forbids a state from making or enforcing any law which abridges the privileges or immunities of citizens of the United States and the Fifteenth Amendment specifically interdicts any denial or abridgement by a state of the right of citizens to vote on account of color. . . .

The statutes of Texas relating to primaries and the resolution of the Democratic party of Texas extending the privileges of membership to white citizens only are the same in substance and effect today as they were when *Grovey v. Townsend* was decided by a unanimous Court. The question as to whether the exclusionary action of the party was the action of the State persists as the determinative factor. . . .

We are thus brought to an examination of the qualifications for Democratic primary electors in Texas, to determine whether state action or private action has

Smith v. Allwright, 321 U.S. 649 (April 3, 1944).

excluded Negroes from participation. . . . Texas requires electors in a primary to pay a poll tax. Every person who does so pay and who has the qualifications of age and residence is an acceptable voter for the primary. . . . Texas requires by the law the election of the county officers of a party. . . . The county chairmen so selected are members of the district executive committee and choose the chairman for the district. Precinct primary election officers are named by the county executive committee. . . . Texas thus directs the selection of all party officers.

Primary elections are conducted by the party under state statutory authority. . . .

We think that this statutory system for the selection of party nominees for inclusion on the general election ballot makes the party which is required to follow these legislative directions an agency of the state in so far as it determines the participants in a primary election. . . .

The United States is a constitutional democracy. Its organic law grants to all citizens a right to participate in the choice of elected officials without restriction by any state because of race. This grant to the people of the opportunity for choice is not to be nullified by a state through casting its electoral process in a form which permits a private organization to practice racial discrimination in the election. Constitutional rights would be of little value if they could be thus indirectly denied. . . .

The privilege of membership in a party may be, as this Court said in *Grovey v. Townsend*, . . . no concern of a state. But when, as here, that privilege is also the essential qualification for voting in a primary to select nominees for a general election, that state makes the action of the party the action of the state. . . . Here, we are applying, contrary to the recent decision in *Grovey v. Townsend,* the well established principle of the Fifteenth Amendment, forbidding the abridgement by a state of a citizen's right to vote. *Grovey v. Townsend* is overruled.

Judgment reversed.

3. Broadside Documents Political Action of African Americans After Defeat of the White Primary, 1948

CITY-WIDE
Political Rallies

Hear ATTORNEY C. B. BUNKLEY, Jr., candidate for Precinct Committee-
man, Precinct 6, and MR. GEORGE ALLEN, candidate for Precinct Commit-
teeman, Precinct 45, along with other Candidates on the following dates
and places:

Tuesday, July 20th, 1948   8 P. M.
ST. PAUL A. M. E. CHURCH
Rev. F. W. Grant, Pastor

Friday, July 23rd, 1948   8 P. M.
ST. JOHN BAPTIST CHURCH

Allen Street   Rev. E C. Estelle, Pastor

Every citizen and voter is invited to hear the candidates discuss the issues
in this campaign.   After hearing the issues discussed then go to the polls
and vote your honest conviction for the best qualified candidate.

Attend these meetings and hear the facts concerning certain political leaders in
this campaign.

TEXAS CLUB OF DEMOCRATIC VOTERS
BY: CAMPAIGN COMMITTEE

D. B. Garner, President; Raymond Rogers, Lynn Townsend, Mrs. Mary Clark, Mrs. R. V.
Smith, Mrs. Edith Richardson, Rev. J. R. McGee, Rev. B. E. Joshua, Rev. C. D. Knight,
C. A. Ventress, Jimmie Walker, Mrs. J. E. Craft, W. J. Durham.

"City-Wide Political Rallies," Dallas, TX, July 20, 1948 and July 23, 1948, Juanita Jewel Shanks Craft Collection, The Center for American History, The University of Texas at Austin. (3N325). Reprinted with permission.

4. The Founding of Texas Southern University Affirms "Separate But Equal" Education, 1947

Art. 2643b. Texas Southern University; The Prairie View Agricultural and Mechanical College of Texas

Purpose of act

Sec. 1.   The Legislature of Texas deems it impracticable to establish and maintain a college or branch of the University of Texas for the instruction of the colored youths of this state without the levy of taxes and the use of the general revenue for the establishment, maintenance and erection of buildings as would be required by Section 14 of Article VII of the Constitution of Texas, if such institution were established as a college or branch of the University of Texas. Further, the Legislature of Texas deems that establishment of a negro university with such limitations as to funds and operation would be unfair and wholly inadequate for the purpose of providing an equivalent university of the first class for negroes of this state. Therefore, it is the purpose of this Act to establish an entirely separate and equivalent university of the first class for negroes with full rights to the use of tax money and the general revenue fund for establishment, maintenance, erection of buildings and operation of such institution as provided in Section 48, Article III of the Constitution of the State of Texas.

Establishment; courses; governing body of agricultural and mechanical college

Sec. 2.   To provide instruction, training, and higher education for colored people, there is hereby established a university of the first class in two divisions: the first, styled "The Texas State University for Negroes" to be located at Houston, Harris County, Texas, to be governed by a Board of Directors as provided in Section 3 hereof; the second, to be styled "The Prairie View Agricultural and Mechanical College of Texas" at Prairie View, Waller County, Texas, formerly known as Prairie View University, originally established in 1876, which shall remain under the control and supervision of the Board of Directors of The Agricultural and Mechanical College of Texas. At the Prairie View Agricultural and Mechanical College shall be offered courses in agriculture, the mechanic arts, engineering, and the natural sciences connected therewith, together with any other courses authorized at Prairie View at the time of the passage of this Act, all of which shall be equivalent to those offered at The Agricultural and Mechanical College of Texas. The Texas State University for Negroes shall offer all other courses of higher learning, including, but without limitation, (other than as to those professional courses designated for the Prairie View Agricultural and Mechanical College), arts and sciences, literature, law, medicine, pharmacy, dentistry, journalism, education, and other professional courses, all of which shall be equivalent to those offered at The University of Texas.

"Legislation Establishing Texas State University for Negroes," in *Coordinating Board, Texas College and University System. Compilation of Constitutional and Statutory Laws Affecting Public Colleges and Universities* (Austin: November 1967): 305.

Upon demand being made by any qualified applicant for any present or future course of instruction offered at The University of Texas, or its branches, such course shall be established or added to the curriculum of the appropriate division of the schools hereby established in order that the separate universities for Negroes shall at all times offer equal educational opportunities and training as that available to other persons of this state.

5. The Supreme Court Rules Separate Education Is Unequal in *Sweatt v. Painter,* April 4, 1950

Mr. Chief Justice Vinson delivered the opinion of the Court.

This case and *McLaurin v. Oklahoma State Regents, post,* p. *637,* present different aspects of this general question: to what extent does the Equal Protection Clause of the Fourteenth Amendment limit the power of a state to distinguish between students of different races in professional and graduate education in a state university? Broader issues have been urged for our consideration, but we adhere to the principle of deciding constitutional questions only in the context of the particular case before the Court. . . .

In the instant case, petitioner filed an application for admission to the University of Texas Law School for the February, 1946, term. His application was rejected solely because he is a Negro. . . . At that time, there was no law school in Texas which admitted Negroes.

The state trial court recognized that the action of the State in denying petitioner the opportunity to gain a legal education while granting it to others deprived him of the equal protection of the laws guaranteed by the Fourteenth Amendment. The court did not grant the relief requested, however, but continued the case for six months to allow the State to supply substantially equal facilities. At the expiration of the six months, in December, 1946, the court denied the writ on the showing that the authorized university officials had adopted an order calling for the opening of a law school for Negroes the following February. . . .

. . . We granted certiorari, because of the manifest importance of the constitutional issues involved.

The University of Texas Law School, from which petitioner was excluded, was staffed by a faculty of sixteen full-time and three part-time professors, some of whom are nationally recognized authorities in their field. Its student body numbered 850. The library contained over 65,000 volumes. Among the other facilities available to the students were a law review, moot court facilities, scholarship funds, and Order of the Coif affiliation. The school's alumni occupy the most distinguished positions in the private practice of the law and in the public life of the State. It may properly be considered one of the nation's ranking law schools.

The law school for Negroes which was to have opened in February, 1947, would have had no independent faculty or library. The teaching was to be carried on by four members of the University of Texas Law School faculty, who were to maintain their offices at the University of Texas while teaching at both institutions.

Sweatt v. Painter, 339 U.S. 629, (April 4, 1950).

Few of the 10,000 volumes ordered for the library had arrived, nor was there any full-time librarian. The school lacked accreditation.

Since the trial of this case, respondents report the opening of a law school at the Texas State University for Negroes. It is apparently on the road to full accreditation. It has a faculty of five full-time professors; a student body of 23; a library of some 16,500 volumes serviced by a full-time staff; a practice court and legal aid association, and one alumnus who has become a member of the Texas Bar.

Whether the University of Texas Law School is compared with the original or the new law school for Negroes, we cannot find substantial equality in the educational opportunities offered white and Negro law students by the State. In terms of number of the faculty, variety of courses and opportunity for specialization, size of the student body, scope of the library, availability of law review and similar activities, the University of Texas Law School is superior. What is more important, the University of Texas Law School possesses to a far greater degree those qualities which are incapable of objective measurement but which make for greatness in a law school. Such qualities, to name but a few, include reputation of the faculty, experience of the administration, position and influence of the alumni, standing in the community, traditions and prestige. It is difficult to believe that one who had a free choice between these law schools would consider the question close. . . .

In accordance with these cases, petitioner may claim his full constitutional right: legal education equivalent to that offered by the State to students of other races. Such education is not available to him in a separate law school as offered by the State. We cannot, therefore, agree with respondents that the doctrine of *Plessy v. Ferguson,* (1896), requires affirmance of the judgment below. Nor need we reach petitioner's contention that *Plessy v. Ferguson* should be reexamined in the light of contemporary knowledge respecting the purposes of the Fourteenth Amendment and the effects of racial segregation.

We hold that the Equal Protection Clause of the Fourteenth Amendment requires that petitioner be admitted to the University of Texas Law School. The judgment is reversed, and the cause is remanded for proceedings not inconsistent with this opinion.

Reversed.

6. An Unidentified Investigator Gathers Intelligence on Desegregation Activities in El Paso, 1955

April 9, 1955

Subject: Segregation.   *(Suit Thelma White)*

Pursuant to instructions the undersigned contacted a number of information sources regarding the back ground of the *Ray White Family.* I secured through several reliable sources the following information regarding activities of Ray White and his family back ground.

"Segregation Suit: Thelma White," April 9, 1955, Juanita Jewel Shanks Craft Collection, The Center for American History, The University of Texas at Austin. (3N164). Reprinted with permission.

Ray White (Negro male) was born in Marlin, Texas about 1908, and was one of a family of five children. His parents were common working people and worked for wages on various farms and worked a small farm on shares with the [l]and for the land-lord. White obtained a 5th grade education in the colored school of Marlin, Texas, and worked on the farm with his parents, and worked some odd jobs receiving a laborers wage. White, moved away from his parents at the age of 19 years old and worked on farms, and at other jobs and in the early part of 1931 married a Marlin colored girl. Two children were born to this family—namely *Ray White Junior,* who is serving in the United States Navy at this time, and *Thelma White*—party involved in the suit against Texas Western College. White's wife died when the two children were very young. . . .

From a reliable source the under signed learned that Ray White had financial difficulties and secured a number of loans as indicated below . . .

Investigation revealed that *Thelma White* was an honor student of the Douglas High School and was give two Scholorships of $100.00 each from the Las Amigas Club for application to any school she chose and a $75.00 scholarship to Prairie View A & M College. At registeration time in the fall of 1954 she (Thelma White) accompanied by Mrs E. M. Williams (Widow of the late Dr. E. M. Williams), Council for National Association for Advancement for colored people for the El Paso area, went to the Registar, Texas Wester[n] College, El Paso, Texas and attempted to enroll where she was refused admittance due to her *color.* . . .

Investigation reveals that Thelma White, began to associate with Mrs. E. M. Williams by meeting her at the Church, and Mrs E. M. Williams taking a liking to Thelma White and began to push her for advancement and encouraged her to seek admittance to a *White State College or University.*

Thelma White, was also promised the support and backing of the Local Chapter of National Association for Advancement of Colored People, and on a state level also. This writer learned from a reliable source that Doctor Vernon Collins, Acting President, of the National Association of advancement of Colored People (NAACP) through Mrs. E. M. Williams got interested in Thelma White and began to seek support of the local groups, regional, State and National level of the National Association for Advancement of Colored People to get her enrolled in one of the *State Colleges, or Universities.* . . . The undersigned recieved information from a reliable informant that after Thelma White attempted to secure admission to Texas Western College and finally entered New Mexico A & M that Dr. Vernon Collins, U. Simpson Tate and other leaders of the NAACP, State level organization met and discussed the case of Thelma White, this leading up to the suit being filed in the U.S. District Court, El Paso, Texas. . . .

At the time that the petition was filed in the United States District Court (Texas Western District), El Paso, Texas, wide publicity was given by the El Paso Times, El Paso Herald Post, and some Radio Station on their news cast. This writer received information from a relieable source that Airforce Personnel (NEGRO) station at Biggs Field, contacted Social Workers at agencies located on the base and complained of discrimination against the negro personnel in El Paso, naming places of businesses as *Bar-rooms, eating establishments, theaters and hotels and other places,* and some places of *recreation.* Negro airmen accompanied by one or two white airmen entered some of the first class eating establishments and demanded service and due to existing laws the management refused service due to subjects being incompany with negro personnel. After a lengthy argument between the management and the negro subjects the white personnel would take up the argument and ask the management if they did not respect the United States Air Force Uniform and not the color or race of the man that was wearing it. And upon leaving the establishment would threaten the management with having them put off limits for not serving the colored personnel. This same type disturbance occurred at a local first class theater.

This writer received information that during the second week of March 1954, the speech class at TWC were assigned the topic of "BROTHERHOOD." With the assistance of the instructor, Mrs. Ball, many of the students chose to discuss the problem of *segregation*. The idea of the talks, according to Mrs. Ball, was to encourage *kindness* and *understanding* for the fellow-man. Since the issue of admitting colored students to TWC has been much publicized, several students used this as the subject for their talks. None of the students who spoke on this issue were against it. . . .

This writer contacted a informant (Reliable). . . . This informant is a colored man and is a business man in El Paso and owns a large amount of property. He stated to this writer that as far as he was concerned that he was happy as he was and had no desire to be come involved in a segregation questions and also had no desire to mix and mingle with the white race and they have always been good to him and that he knew he was a negro and was going to stay in his place. . . . This informant stated that as far as Doctor Vernon Collin's was concerned that the only reason that he wanted to be on the equal with the white man was that he wanted to move upon the hill along with the white doctors and have the opportunity to examine and *play*, and when he stated play, he stated you know what I mean, as he thinks that he is a lady's man either white or black. . . . This informant stated that a large number of the local members of the NAACP are the young buck negros that have the same desire as Dr. Collins, and are former Army, Navy, or Marine personnel and want to get an education and live off of the Government taxes that you and I are paying.

7. White Backlash: The Texas Citizens' Council of Houston Describes Links Between Civil Rights Activities and Communists, 1956

Our guest speaker for last Thursday night, Feb. 23, 1956, was Mr Curt Copeland. Mr Copeland is editor and publisher of "Arkansas Faith", 111 Caddo St., Crossett, Ark. Subscription to this publication—$3.00 per year. We urge our members and their friends to subscribe to this and other publications that will furnish you with the only source of truth and imformation about what is taking place on our side of this fight to preserve the racial integrity of the White people of this country. Send Mr Copeland a postcard thanking him for his speech—it will cost you only two

"Newsletter," Texas Citizens' Council of Greater Houston, February 27, 1956, Juanita Jewel Shanks Craft Collection, The Center for American History, The University of Texas at Austin. (3N164). Reprinted with permission.

cents, but will be worth many many times that amount to him. We must encourage all of our people who have the courage and intestinal fortitude to lead this fight. . . .

JOIN US NOW * BECOME ACTIVE!
IF YOU ARE TOO TIMID TO GET INTO THIS FIGHT THEN
LEND US YOUR FINANCIAL, MORAL AND SPIRITUAL HELP.

If the communists are allowed to lead the negro into such unwise participation as their transportation boycott in Alabama, to force their unwelcome association upon the majority of American White people, to corrupt our Churches and our schools, and to eventually lead our children into the BLACK HELL of miscegenation—without our willingness to resist this communist inspired and directed plot—THEN WE SHALL DESERVE THE HOUSE FULL OF MULATTO GRANDCHILDREN WE SHALL HAVE. . . .

. . .—*YOU BE THE JUDGE.* Senator James O. Eastland of Mississippi, said in a speech on the floor of the U.S. Senate, Thursday May 26, 1955, quote;

"Mr President, somewhat more than 1 year ago I pointed out in an adress on this floor that the Supreme Court had been indoctrinated and brainwashed by left-wing pressure groups; that individual members of the Court *were influenced by and were guilty of* grossly improper conduct in accepting *awards and emoluments* from groups and organizations interested in political litigation before the Court and bent on changing and destroying our American way of life; that such reprehensible conduct placed a question mark by the validity and integrity of their decisions in cases which these groups were interested, of which the school segregation case is one.

Today, I am calling upon the members of the Senate to consider an even more serious problem. *The Court has not only arrogated to itself powers which were not delegated to it under the Constitution of the United States* and has entered fields of the legislative and executive branches of the Government, but they are attempting to graft into the organic law of the land the teachings, preachments, and social doctrines arising from a political philosophy which is the antithesis of the principles upon which this Government was founded. The origin of the doctrines can be traced to Karl Marx, and their propagation is part and parcel of the conspiracy to divide and destroy this Government through internal controversy. The Court adopts this propaganda as "modern scientific authority". Emphasis added.

Texas Citizens' Council of Greater Houston
P.O. Box 2316
Houston 1, Texas

8. Liberal State Senator Henry B. Gonzalez Uses the Filibuster to Oppose Anti-Desegregation Bills, 1957

No one in the capitol this week will deny that Henry Gonzalez registered it—that through him and Sen. Abraham (Chick) Kazen of Laredo and four other senators who spelled the two talkers-in-chief during their 36-hour marathon on the Senate floor, the minorities were heard with eloquence and impact as never before in Texas.

Ronnie Dugger, "The Segregation Filibuster of 1957," reprinted in *The Texas Observer* 66 (December 27, 1974): 46–47. Copyright © 1974 by The Texas Observer. Reprinted with permission.

In the larger way the filibuster was the splitting up of the Texas culture into some of its varied ways of life. On one side of the Senate chamber stood South and far West Texans with more than a million Latin-Americans behind them—Latin-Americans they think are threatened by general segregation bills which do not say they aim at Negroes. On the other side of the chamber were white East Texans with a million Negroes behind them, some of them restive for what the Supreme Court says are their rights. In the middle stood senators of moderate persuasion, some of whom voted with the minorities, some of whom voted with the East Texans—then switched at the last minute to vote their personal convictions. . . .

The talkers won their point for the week: Sen. Wardlow Lane, Center, who originally wanted to pass out all five bills before the Senate, except the one barring NAACP members from public employment, gave in when Gonzalez refused all blandishments and importunations and talked on into early Friday morning. Only HB 231 was passed. . . . It was due Wednesday.

Monday, Senate State Affairs passed out two more bills but (by a 9-7 vote) referred to Atty. Gen. Will Wilson one requiring some advocates of integration and segregation to register with the secretary of state.

"I intend to fight every one of 'em to the last ditch—every one of 'em. It's the least I can do," said Gonzalez after 22 hours and 2 minutes of continuous argument. . . .

Sen. Wardlow Lane of Center, the Senate leader of the East Texans, explained very briefly that H.B. 231 permits school boards to use 17 factors (not including race) in assigning students to schools. It ought to be passed. . . .

As passed by the House, HB 231 also permits parents who object to integration to withdraw their children from the public schools, all other laws to the contrary notwithstanding, and says they will then get education grants as provided by law. . . .

The argument was advanced, Gonzalez said, that the bills had to be passed of necessity. "Necessity is the creed of slaves and the argument of tyrants. They have sown to the wind and reaped a whirlwind!" he shouted. . . .

Gonzalez told of times he had been discriminated against because of his ancestry. "The Irish have a saying, 'It's easy to sleep on another man's wounds,'" he said. "Well, what's the difference? Mexican, Negro, what have you. The assault on the inward dignity of man, which our society protects, has been made . . . We all know in our hearts and our minds that it is wrong." . . .

About 3:30 negotiations started for a compromise. At 5:07 Lane asked him if he had yielded the floor because he was sitting against his desk. At 5:13 his friends came to him and asked him to quit. . . .

"Henry," said Reagan to Gonzalez, "I think we ought to go." Willis told him they were going to move the previous question. Reagan said something to him about getting "urban renewal up." Hudson said, "We've done all we can, Henry." Owen said to him, "It's how far we're gonna push the chair."

Gonzalez replied to them: "I think compromise on one, you're sunk on all. They're fanatical!" . . .

About 1:45 Lane came in unhappily. They would pass only HB 231. The call for a quorum went out, and the senators started dragging in sleepily. The voting was finished, the Senate adjourned. . . .

He held the floor 22 hours and two minutes. He and Mrs. Gonzalez, and Senator and Mrs. Kazen, went on home to bed.

Later in the year, Gonzalez was filibustering again—this time alone—in opposition to a bill allowing local boards to close schools if they thought violence or the threat thereof could not be controlled without military troops. Gonzales talked all night long, and when he sat down at 7 a.m., the Senate passed the bill. A total of nine segregation bills were passed in 1957.

9. The Dallas NAACP Organizes Against the Segregationists, 1957

1. The recent session of the Texas Legislature passed certain laws which the Legislators, in debate, admitted were directed at the NAACP and Negro citizens for the purpose of preventing Negroes from lawfully pursuing a course for the protection of their constitutional rights.

2. The State of Texas has already appropriated an initial sum of $50,000.00 to be used and spent by the Attorney General to prevent Negroes from enjoying rights and privileges which the United States Constitution guarantees and the Supreme Court of the United States has already declared that Negroes are entitled to.

3. The Registration Law was passed for the sole purpose of destroying the NAACP and its work; the most powerful organization in the world today fighting to protect the rights of Negro citizens.

4. The Registration Law does not only affect the NAACP and its members, but the same can and will be used by unscrupulous politicians and hate masters against any other organization that works for and advocates equal rights for Negroes.

5. The Registration Law can be used against a church when the minister and the members advocate justice for Negroes if the manipulators of this law so choose.

6. The Registration Law can be used to intimidate members of social clubs, fraternities, sororities, labor unions, charitable, educational, literary and any other type of organization that the officials of the State consider to be against their interest, or is advocating justice for Negroes.

7. The most vicious effect of the Registration Law is that unscrupulous politicians confederating with the members of the White Citizens Council will have their power to examine the lists of members of any organization since the list of membership of any organization, under the Registration statute, is to be made public, thus, when any Negro is compelled to take an examination by any board set up by the State or City, to wit, Plumbers, Barbers, Beauticians, Morticians, Electricians, Doctors, Lawyers, Teachers, Pharmacists, et cetera, will be subject to the whims of the members of the examining boards. No Negro applicant would be able to pass any examination given by unscrupulous members of the board where it was shown that he was affiliated with or a member of a church or other organization fighting for the protection of the rights of Negroes.

"Information: For Use by the Members of the Finance Department and Workers in Raising the Special Defense Fund," [Dallas NAACP Chapter] c. 1957, Juanita Jewel Shanks Craft Collection, The Center for American History, The University of Texas at Austin. (3N321). Reprinted with permssion.

8. Negroes in the State of Mississippi, for many years, it has been disclosed, are allowed to pass the examinations given provided they will settle only in areas where white applicants do not desire to locate.

9. To further emphasize that such laws can and will be used against other organizations, is the incident which occurred at Jackson, Mississippi, when the charter of an all-Negro American Legion post was cancelled because of alleged "radical agitators" in the membership and because the post's commander was "very much active in the NAACP." This is a patriotic organization.

10. It is reliably reported that the leaders of the White Citizens Council have reached the conclusion that the bulk of the money furnished for the fight for Negroes' rights comes from Negro citizens who are required to pass examinations such as Plumbers, Barbers, Beauticians, Morticians, Electricians, Doctors, Lawyers, Teachers, Pharmacists, and the like, and that the effective way to destroy the NAACP and other organizations is to make it impossible for Negroes to pass these examinations and enter into and engage in the above professions and callings.

11. It is the plan of the reactionaries to whip the Negro into submission economically, and a part of their strategy is above indicated. These laws must be attacked in the courts on the grounds that they are unconstitutional. *It will require money to do this!*

 E S S A Y S

The two essays in this chapter examine the leadership of the civil rights movement in Texas' two largest cities, Houston and Dallas. Merline Pitre, of Texas Southern University, emphasizes the local nature of the civil rights struggle. She describes how Lulu White of Houston confronted opposition both from within the leadership of the African American community and from white segregationists. Pitre also describes how national events and issues affected local movements. Yvonne Davis Freer, a doctoral candidate at Texas A & M University, argues that while there was a successful grassroots civil rights movement in North Texas under the direction of Juanita Craft, this movement was essentially a local manifestation of the national civil rights struggle and drew its strength from national events, especially the Supreme Court decision in *Brown v. The Topeka Board of Education*.

Lulu B. White, the NAACP, and Launching the Fight Against Segregation in Houston

MERLINE PITRE

Lulu White, female and civil rights activist, was a significant force in the struggle against Jim Crow in Texas during the 1940s and 1950s. A mobilizer, organizer, and foot soldier, White dedicated her entire life to fighting to dismantle the apartheid system in this country and used almost every means necessary to accomplish this

Merline Pitre, original essay drawn from Merline Pitre, *In Struggle Against Jim Crow: Lulu B. White and the NAACP, 1900–1957* (College Station: Texas A&M University Press, 1999). Reprinted by permission of the Texas A&M University Press.

goal. She led mass movements, delighted in controversies, and encouraged coalitions. Her name was far more likely to appear in a headline than a byline. Yet her role as a radical, black leader, as one of those giants on whose shoulders Barbara Jordan and other civil rights leaders have stood, has been obscured and ignored by historians. White's activities and positions with the NAACP, as well as her philosophy of integrating African Americans into the mainstream of American life is no less substantial for its lack of publicity. It is the purpose of this essay to provide a glimpse of the activities and ideologies that made White vulnerable to charges that she was a participant in the Communist conspiracy.

Born in 1900 in Elmo, Texas to Henry Madison, a farmer, and Easter Madison, a domestic worker, Lulu Belle Madison White, received her early education in the public schools of Elmo and Terrell, Texas. Following her high school graduation, she attended Butler College for one year before transferring to Prairie View College where she received a bachelor's degree in English in 1928. After her marriage to Julius White and teaching school for nine years, White resigned her post to devote full time service to the NAACP. In 1937 she became Director of Youth Council and field worker and in 1939, acting president of the Houston branch of the NAACP. In 1943, she was elevated to full-time executive secretary of the Houston branch, making her the first women in the South to hold such a post. Finally, in 1946, she was named director of state branches for the state of Texas.

In size and appearance, Lulu White presented a formidable image to confront the state of Texas. Standing five feet, six inches tall and weighing more than two hundred and fifty pounds, she was bold, brave, and loud, but also amiable, dignified, and respected by friends and foes alike. An acid tongued individual who was not afraid to speak her mind to powerful whites and to differing black factions, White combined political radicalism with the administrative skills needed to effect change. When milder techniques did not work, she became openly defiant. To many, she seemed exactly what the doctor ordered for the civil rights movement in Houston and in Texas during the 1940s and 1950s.

Lulu White's political sensibility was informed by a belief in racial equality and in federally protected citizenship rights. Guided by this philosophy, she was not hesitant about raising her voice on any issue pertaining to the civil rights of blacks. She publicly advocated the right of blacks to vote and to participate at all levels of government. She pushed for equal access to jobs and education. She defended the political and civil rights of blacks and complained loudly whenever anyone trampled upon them. In her various capacities with the NAACP, White increasingly adopted an outspoken, almost deliberately provocative style. Both her natural speaking talent and her defense of free expression reinforced her candor. The NAACP's legal success in breaking down racial barriers in the 1940s, the growth of its branches, an increase in the number of black organizations and liberal labor unions—all of these broadened the parameters of Lulu White's activism. Needless to say, White thrived on the activities of her office, as the city of Houston and the state of Texas offered new opportunities and challenges to those working to move the South beyond the politics of racial differences.

Upon assuming her post as head of the NAACP, Lulu White acquired firsthand knowledge of how deeply race prejudice was embedded in the American economic and political system. Moreover, she was cognizant of the fact that the NAACP had waged a two-decade struggle to garner support for an anti-lynching bill, all to no avail. She knew that although the white Democratic primary had been overturned via *Smith v. Allwright* (1944), there were still impediments to the black franchise, such as poll taxes. With these facts in mind, Lulu White reasoned that if blacks were to overcome such obstacles, assistance from other sources was imperative. They would need to unite or join forces with other groups with shared political and economic interests.

As Lulu White traversed Texas' racialized terrain and experimented with different groups, strategies, and tactics, she embraced organized labor, the leftist proclivities of the Congress of Industrial Opportunities (CIO) notwithstanding. For as she put it: "You take your friends where you find them." White's idea to coalesce with labor was neither novel nor original. Blacks and labor faced many common problems in the South during the first half of the twentieth century. The South was a stronghold of antiunion, antiblack and antifemale sentiments. Its powerful elected officials, from the local to the national level, defied the political winds of change that threatened to undermine the established order and way of life. Facing this reality, the national office of the NAACP and labor entered an alliance in 1941. This alliance was a marriage of convenience because blacks and labor were facing some of the same enemies—city halls, state legislatures, Congress, southern Democrats, conservative Northerners, western Republicans, and other individuals who saw the two as a threat to their jobs and the status quo.

With few exceptions, efforts to organize workers, white or black, remained extremely weak in Texas, including in Houston until 1930, at which time both the American Federation of Labor (AFL), a craft-oriented union, and the Congress of Industrial Opportunities (CIO) a semiskilled union, initiated a general campaign in Dixie. Prior to 1935, the International Longshoreman's Association, a separate affiliate of the AFL, conducted most union activities in the city involving blacks. After 1935, the CIO would be most visible in union activities among blacks. Between 1935 and 1945, the CIO was responsible for organizing blacks in several industries including workers in oil and sugar refineries, and in fruits and tobacco industries. CIO field workers proved especially effective in organizing black steelworkers at Hughes Tool Company, Sheffield Steel Company, and the Dedman Foundry. Through these industries, almost two thousand blacks had joined the United Steel Workers of America Local Union by 1945.

While these efforts of the CIO's campaign to attract formerly unorganized black workers would prove beneficial in the early 1940s, labor unions still posed a problem for blacks, whites, and the NAACP. Sometimes, black workers joined enthusiastically; but in other cases, they were skeptical and distrustful, as wisdom born from the bitter experience of discrimination had taught them. The CIO's interest in and activities with black workers impressed the NAACP, but the Association was hesitant to commit to a total alliance with the union because of the latter's alleged communist ties. Likewise, many whites opposed unions in general and the CIO in particular for its interracial character and Communist affiliation. To many white southern conservatives, the push for civil rights by the CIO and the NAACP was nothing more than a communist conspiracy. In their mind, both the NAACP and the CIO were communist—led, inspired, and dominated.

Because of this recurring Communist label, by 1945 the NAACP leadership began to wean itself from the CIO. This was not so, however, for Lulu White, who retained her relationship with labor and used the Communist threat to her advantage.

While White was willing and eager to say that she did not embrace Communism, she used the threat posed by Communism to press the NAACP agenda against racism and discrimination in the workplace. In a word, she became more visible and more vocal in her support of labor.

Through an association with a number of friends who were members, supporters, and organizers of union activities, Lulu White had acquired some knowledge of the labor movement in Houston and in Texas. Yet it was not until she became executive secretary that she acquired firsthand knowledge of the activities of the major unions, especially those of the CIO. White was impressed with the educational program of the CIO, a program that increased blacks' militancy by making them more desirous of waging the struggle for racial equality and less willing to tolerate gradualism. Administering this program was a CIO Political Action Committee (PAC), formed in the summer of 1943. The purpose of the PAC was to build a political machine rooted in the national network of local unions, and city and state industrial councils that embraced liberal, progressive, and civil rights activities. This PAC divided the nation into fourteen regional centers and organized branches in states, cities, and wards. Operating under the premise that organized, informed, and active voters were essential for meeting antiunion conservatives at the polls, the PAC had voter education and registration as the core of its activities.

These PAC activities went hand in hand with the civil rights movement in Texas and were very encouraging to Lulu White. The CIO union's campaign for voting rights was creative and wide-ranging, combining such activities as education, organizing, and publicity strategies. Partially due to PAC's campaign efforts in 1943, three powerful southern congressmen lost their house seats. Two lost their bid for reelection and Texas Congressman Martin Dies, Chairman of the House Un-American Activities Committee, withdrew from the race once he learned that the CIO PAC was campaigning against him. Recognizing their effectiveness, White utilized PAC members as teachers for the many citizenship classes that the local chapter NAACP sponsored before and after *Smith v. Allwright* (1944). Also, PAC aided union members in paying poll taxes and in sponsoring rallies to get out the vote in elections held after 1944.

Because Lulu White established a special bond with labor early in her career, it did not take much prodding for her to support the CIO-led United Steel Workers Strike of 1946 and the 1946 Houston Municipal strike engineered by the AFL. For Lulu White, to the extent that these and other labor unions protected all workers from discrimination by employers and raised the wages of lower paid workers, they advanced the interests of their black workers and furthered the cause of the NAACP in eradicating economic injustice.

By 1946, White had come to view the labor movement as a liberalizing force in the civil rights struggle, a force that could help bring the country nearer to the reality of democracy. Because she viewed the movement as a voice of domestic liberalism, White helped to organize a Houston Area Labor Conference on September 28, 1946. She was the only female on the program when the conference adopted resolutions that called for unity of labor; an end to Jim Crow schools, poll taxes, lynching; and the abolition of the House Un-American Activities Committee. The conference also adopted a controversial resolution calling for "World Peace and the Freedom of Oppressed People." This resolution literally raised the eyebrows of Gloster Current, national director of branches of the NAACP, who sent a memorandum to Walter White noting that the "Houston NAACP Labor Committee saw fit to take a position on foreign policy which paralleled that of Moscow. This is friendship and collaboration of USSR." Current commented further that the political orientation of several of these unions was obvious.

While the above resolutions expressed the philosophy of Lulu White, they do not shed much light on her active role in the labor movement. When viewed from the perspective that the labor movement among blacks in Houston was a combination of public spokesperson and network activators, rather than simply people following an articulate leader, one gets a better sense of Lulu White's activities in the movement. To be sure, White's effectiveness was closely connected to the work of advance men in the labor movement such as Richard Grovey, Sid Hilliard, Sidney Hasgett, Heman Sweatt, and Moses Leroy. These men worked publicly in organizing black workers and privately in negotiating with white employers for better wages and working conditions. They risked their reputations and livelihoods by accepting leadership roles in the fledgling labor movement, by informing Lulu White of the discrimination heaped on black workers, and by developing strategies with her that were designed to reach economic parity. Lulu White's sharp tongue and bold speeches made her widely popular with the labor movement. Yet she was essentially a network activator and gadfly for the movement. For example, in the elections of 1946, she posed the following question to many candidates: "Are you in favor of equal opportunity? Do you support organized labor? Will you support or oppose legislation planned to curb organized labor in our state?" Depending on the response given, White elicited support for or against the candidate.

Lulu White's pro-labor stance was probably magnified most during the summer of 1946 when the death of a black man gave rise to the largest mass protest demonstration that the city of Houston had ever witnessed. White and the NAACP converted the funeral for Berry Branch, killed by a white bus driver, into a rally, but used this occasion to denounce discrimination and to call for the need to build a coalition with labor. Blacks of all classes, as well as socialists, labor leaders and white radicals were there. Not only were all labor unions in the city present at the funeral, but representatives from the CIO and AFL participated on the program and served as pallbearers. What was interesting about this funeral was not that both of Houston's white newspapers carried stories about it, but that both branded Lulu White as an agent of the "red" movement.

At this point, the communist label seemed not to have bothered Lulu White, for she continued to stand up for labor. In response to strikes throughout the city and state, in 1947 the Texas legislature passed a Right to Work Act designed to curtail and restrict labor unions' activities. More specifically, this law denied public employees the right to bargain collectively. To add insult to injury, the state of Texas embraced the Taft-Hartley Bill that outlawed the closed shop but allowed a measure of union security. This bill called for a contract that required workers to join the union after signing a contract, as opposed to joining before employment. It also legalized the right to work by which states could forbid the requirement of union membership as a condition of employment. Additionally, the bill provided for a "cooling off" period for both sides before they resorted to strike. Labor leaders throughout the country denounced the law. Lulu White joined the chorus and made several speeches across the state, trying to garner support for its repeal. When she appeared in Galveston, to speak on this subject, Carter Wesley, who White had chided for supporting Taft-Hartley, reported in the *Informer* that "the Galveston Branch had been taken over by Communists like the Houston Branch." White shrugged off this allegation by saying these newspaper writers (including Wesley) and the FBI were present at the meeting at the urging of a "stool pigeon black woman who wanted to discredit [her]." In part because of such black critics as Carter Wesley, most whites interpreted Lulu White's support for labor as the work of outside agitators who were using White to surreptitiously change the economic order of this country. Hence, the Communist label would come to haunt White like a fire bell in the night.

To make matters worse, in June 1947, Arthur J. Mandell and Herman Wright, labor lawyers, added the civil rights struggle to their list of reforms in America and joined the local chapter of the [NAACP]. Needless to say, the membership of these radical, socialist labor lawyers was not greeted by instant jubilation in the black community. In fact, their membership attracted the attention of many members of the NAACP, especially those caught up in the anticommunist hysteria. But White responded to this criticism by noting again that in the struggle against Jim Crow, "you take your friends where you find them." Furthermore, at the time that Mandell and Wright joined the NAACP, Lulu White and Carter Wesley were in a bitter dispute over the integration of the University of Texas versus the establishment of a separate black University in Houston. White was opposed to creating another black university because in her opinion, "there could be no equality in separation." Wesley held just the opposite view—blacks could force the state to make separate equal and thus African Americans could have an institution of their own and still attend the University of Texas. Because White did not agree with Wesley on this issue, he began an unrelenting attack against her for what he called "Communist influence in the NAACP." In July 1947, he wrote in his *Informer* that "our NAACP [is] taken over by the infiltration of the Communists through the stupidity and nearsightedness of our leaders." In Wesley's opinion, these Communists were not merely allies of Lulu White, but they were dominating her thinking and aiding the formulation of policies. "They [helped] mimeograph sharp attacks against race prejudice and organized committees to go before City Council and protest discrimination. Our leaders think they are God," wrote Wesley.

Wesley would later admit that he did not know if White was a Communist, but that he knew the company she kept: "When a Communist is willing to go to Negro houses and drink liquor with them and call them by their first name, they know that as far as these white people are concerned, the race question is solved," wrote Wesley. Everyone in town knew that Lulu White and Herman Wright had established a close friendship, and that Wright was one among many whites who frequented her house and attended her twentieth wedding anniversary. Lulu White's history and demeanor indicate she that could hardly be accused of allowing anyone to do her thinking. Whatever White did, she did because it was what she wanted or because of her belief in integration, criticism notwithstanding.

While Wesley was making his allegations, the Federal Bureau of Investigation (FBI) was launching a concerted effort to monitor all black organizations and individuals whom it deemed as subversive. The surveillance of black Americans was established as part of the FBI's responsibilities during Franklin D. Roosevelt's administration, but it would intensify during the cold war era. Thus, in 1938, in the area of domestic intelligence, Roosevelt both expanded and encouraged the FBI to gather information on the activities of individuals labeled as subversive. In that same year, the FBI included a special Negro Question Category as part of its regular Communist infiltration investigations. One year later, President Roosevelt expanded the FBI's civil and criminal jurisdiction to include at least a cursory examination, if not a complete investigation of almost every type of civil rights case from voter registration to police brutality and lynching. For more than twenty years, the FBI and its director, J. Edgar Hoover, pursued these dual mandates at their own discretion, investigating the political affairs of black activists and organizations thoroughly, while treating civil rights investigations nonchalantly (if at all). Such was the fate of Lulu White and the NAACP.

In September 1947, the FBI sent out a circular letter to all its directors and field workers "to submit to the Bureau any information obtained from reliable and established sources indicating Communist infiltration, influence or connection of the local NAACP chapters." While admitting that the national office of the NAACP was not associated with Communist activities, the FBI was adamant that some local chapters were "under the direct influence of the Communist elements." Because of this belief, whether real or imagined, the FBI began a "dead file" designed for local chapters but entitled "Communist Infiltration of the National Office." Information contained in this file was sent to the attorney general's Loyal Review Board, which had been established to analyze the information and to make a determination if any of it was subversive to the government. Once such analysis was completed, the attorney general published a list of individuals and organizations that were deemed antigovernment. The list, published in December of 1947, named the Civil Rights Congress and all of its affiliates as antigovernment forces. One of the affiliates mentioned was located in Houston and had the same office and address as the Houston chapter of the NAACP.

The Civil Rights Congress was formed in April 1946 as a merger between two organizations, the International Labor Defense and the National Federation of Constitutional Liberties. According to FBI records, this organization was not "dedicated to the broader issue of civil liberties, but to the defense of individual Communists and the Communist Party, and controlled by individuals who were either members of the Communist Party or openly loyal to it." In December of 1947, the Civil Rights Congress put out a call for a legislative conference scheduled in Washington, D.C. on January 17–18, 1948. Members of the Civil Rights Congress asked Lulu White to sign the call for this conference, but she failed to respond. Nevertheless, when the flyer was sent out announcing the conference, White's name was listed as one of its sponsors. No doubt, this was one of the reasons why the local branch was viewed as an affiliate of the Civil Rights Congress.

Upon hearing and reading that the Civil Rights Congress was being linked to the Houston branch, Thurgood Marshall moved quickly to squash any speculations of the FBI. First, he contacted Lulu White, then relayed her reply to J. Edgar Hoover in order "to keep the record straight." "I have received the following report form our Houston Branch," wrote Marshall. "Neither at this time nor any other time has this office been affiliated with the Office of the Civil Rights Congress. It is true that they did hold about three meetings here about a year ago [but they are not part of the organization]." When Hoover replied and denied that the list had been sent from his office to the Dallas newspaper or that his office had anything to do with the compilation of the list, Marshall then responded in kind, either facetiously or naively saying, "I am happy to know that the listing does not appear in your file."

Evidence reveals that when Marshall requested that Hoover clear up this matter, he probably was unaware that Hoover had instructed a field agent to make a "very discreet check on the Pilgrim Building #228" the day after the Dallas newspaper published the subversive list, and instructed the agent "to furnish the results [to Hoover] telephonically." The agent reported his finding the same day he received the communiqué. There was nothing in the office to the effect that the Civil Rights Congress maintained an office in Houston. But "a check at the post office reflect[ed] that P.O. Box 1988 was rented on July 1, 1946. The application was signed by [an unidentified woman] who gave as her business address: Civil Rights Congress, 228 Pilgrim Building, Houston Texas . . . On the letterhead she is listed as the Temporary Executive Secretary." A further check showed that White had received two copies of the pamphlet, *The Southern People's Congress Program.* Throughout this investigation, Lulu White maintained that neither she nor the Civil Rights Congress was Communist, and that her association with any labor organization reflected her concern for civil liberties. So strong were the communist attacks from both whites and blacks that Lulu White could no longer ignore them. Responding to Carter Wesley's charge of her affiliation with Communists (Mandell and Wright), Lulu White wrote Gloster Current: "I have talked to Maceo about this Communist business. He told me that the NAACP did not ask persons to declare their party affiliation before they join the organization." In this civil rights movement, White was of the opinion that "Negroes are supposed to take friends where they find them."

To many, Lulu White moved even further to the "left" when she openly supported Henry A. Wallace's candidacy for president of the United States in 1948. Wallace, the Progressive Party presidential nominee, was a former Secretary of Agriculture in the 1930s and a former Vice President during Franklin Roosevelt's third term. The four individuals who ran for the presidency in 1948 were Republican governor Thomas E. Dewey, Democratic incumbent Harry S Truman, Progressive Party candidate Henry A. Wallace, and the anti–civil rights Dixiecrat candidate, Strom Thurmond. Neither Dewey's personality nor his campaign aroused enthusiasm among his supporters. As far as Truman was concerned, there were signs as early as 1946 that he and lost control of the economic and political situation in this country. Labor resented his reaction to the railroad strikes. Farmers attempted to roll back Truman's meat prices. Conservatives denounced his civil rights proposals, and his "Doctrine of Containment" outraged communist sympathizers in the North. Because of these views, the Progressives thought that their candidate, Henry Wallace, had a good chance of winning.

Between 1941 and 1945, there were few politicians more highly praised by the NAACP than Wallace. He was lauded for his stance on racism, poll taxes, and Jim Crow. Even when President Harry S Truman dropped him from the ticket, the NAACP still supported him. This situation changed, however, when it became apparent to the NAACP in 1948 that Wallace's candidacy would take black voters away from the Democratic party. Yet, a number of blacks continued to support Henry Wallace. Included were such notables as Lulu White, W.E.B. Du Bois, Lena

Horne, Roscoe Dunjee, Margaret Bush Wilson, Paul Robeson, and Gordon Hancock. For these individuals, Wallace's campaign represented a radical, forward-looking approach to solving the race problems and to bringing about economic parity in this country. Moreover, Wallace's platform included demands for a one-dollar per hour minimum wage, abolition of the poll tax, desegregation, repeal of the Taft-Hartley labor law, day care centers for working mothers, and opposition to the military draft.

The day after Wallace announced his candidacy, the pro-Wallace forces began working to establish a Texas Wallace campaign headquarters. This project came to fruition on March 21, 1948, when the Wallace for President Committee held its first state meeting in Austin. The organizers included Elvierto Bela of Laredo, Harriet Leary of San Antonio, H. K. Deuchare of Galveston, Pat Lunford of Baytown, and Herman Wright of Houston. There were reports that Lulu White was a party to this group, rumors which she denied. When the news media heard of Lulu White's alleged involvement with this group, all pandemonium broke loose. Many newspapers carried headlines such as "An NAACP Official Endorses Wallace." *The Austin American Statesman* reported that the "Director of the NAACP was elected Vice Chair of a Statewide Movement for Wallace." The hierarchy of the NAACP became very disturbed over this matter and called Lulu White's actions into question. White denied such involvements and asked these newspapers for a retraction. Never cast as a moderate, in writing to the editors of these newspapers, Lulu White made it clear that she did not endorse Wallace in her official capacity, but that she "reserve[d] the right to support the candidate of her choice in any election."

With her position made clear to the public and to the NAACP, Lulu White was active and visible in Wallace's two-day whistle stop tour of Houston on September 28 and 29, 1948. The first of these hectic days included a Wallace press conference, speeches by the candidate at radio station KPRC, at the Black Businessmen Club's luncheon, and at a tea in the home of Lulu White. Present at White's reception was Paul Robeson, black actor, singer, and a professed socialist, whose passport had been revoked. Already a thorn in the side of many white conservatives, White now became a menace to be reckoned with as a result of publicly supporting Wallace, embracing Paul Robeson, and holding a mixed audience reception at her home. White's position was undergirded by Wallace on the next day of his tour when he spoke to approximately four hundred persons—blacks and whites—at the Music Hall.

While in Houston, Wallace encountered many hecklers who threw omelets and eggs at him and almost forced him out of town. The newspaper account of his two-day visit could give one the impression that Wallace was a viable candidate, although he was only a Third Party candidate who stood no chance of winning. Although Lulu White supported Wallace, along with a small number of blacks throughout the country, there is no evidence that she persuaded other blacks to do likewise. She took a fearless stand on Wallace's candidacy because she believed that Wallace shared some of her views on bettering the conditions of "the common man and woman." In part, because of Wallace's campaign, Wesley's labeling of White as a communist, and her affiliation with several socialists, Lulu White's name appeared on the list of the House Un-American Activities Committee in 1948.

The indomitable Lulu White was not one to walk away from a struggle, and silently endured the pains of discrimination. She resolved to fight back, the Communist label notwithstanding. But her fortitude and courage were equally matched by the doggedness and cynicism of many of her critics, not the least of whom was

Carter Wesley. Wesley's constant bashing in his newspaper was enough to convince many blacks that in the struggle for civil rights, Lulu White's behavior had moved from disorderly conduct to radicalism. In his June 11, 1949 editorial citing yet another case of her flirtation with socialists, Wesley pointed out that Lulu White had joined forces with the CIO, the Civil Rights Congress, and the Texas Progressive Party in signing a petition to protest Judge Harold Medina's jailing of *The Daily Worker's* editor along with three socialists for contempt of court in a New York conspiracy trial. In Wesley's opinion, the actions of the petitioners did not result from spontaneous protest of aggrieved citizens, but were carefully orchestrated. Wesley was partially right in his assessment. Lulu White was an adept practitioner of coalition-building politics and would ally herself with almost any group if it would bring about political and economic parity for blacks. Her action in the above case, however, only fueled further speculation that she was doing the bidding of the Communists. Because of this incident, Carter Wesley again called for White's resignation as executive secretary of the Houston Branch. This time she acquiesced. She stepped down almost immediately after the publication of his editorial.

Even after Lulu White left the helm of the local branch of the NAACP in 1949, the FBI still followed her. In 1951 an informant reported that although she was no longer working in the office of the local chapter, Communist literature was still being sent to her at that address. In 1953 the same informant reported that Lulu White was not as active in the Communist Party as she had been in the past; and that she did not influence her successor, Christia Adair, who was described as anticommunist. In 1956, when students at Texas Southern University (TSU) staged a protest against Governor Alan Shivers, who was the guest speaker for the inauguration of Samuel M. Nabrit, the University's second president, Lulu White was listed by the FBI as the instigator of that activity. The field agent confirmed and enhanced this speculation by sending a newspaper clipping to the FBI director that carried the following headline: "New President Inaugurated: Shivers Ignores Pickets to Give T.S.U. Speech."

The TSU demonstration was a reaction to a speech made by Shivers against the Supreme Court's decision in *Brown v. Board of Education* (1954) and against his stance on the integration of schools in particular. A poll taken by the informant revealed that most of the student body at Texas Southern University favored the protest because of the governor's pro-segregationist stand. When Shivers arrived on campus on March 14, 1956, he met the protestors carrying placards that read "We want integration, not Shivers"; "Not anti-T.S.U., just anti-Shivers"; "Alan Shivers, you sent your boy to an integrated school, but why object to others." The local chapter of the NAACP, along with TSU students, supposedly staged this demonstration. But as Carter Wesley would later write: "Those on the inside knew that Lulu was the reason why the picketing came off. The people of the local chapter gave every indication of not wanting the picket to go forward . . . but Lulu consulted her lawyers and when told it would not be illegal to picket, she gathered her forces and went out to Texas Southern University." The demonstration went on without incident, but the FBI hounded Lulu White until her death.

There is no hard data to support the claim that White was a Communist. But as was true for many whites, the combined forces of the Great Depression, the New Deal, and World War II pushed black political activists and thought in a leftward direction. Like their white counterparts, a number of African American reformers were affected by Marxist and non-Marxist class theories. Neither the NAACP nor the Urban League was immune to the economic and political impulses of the thirties and forties. Within the ranks of both organizations were individuals who advocated a more militant course of economic action. Young intellectuals such as E. Franklin Frazier and Ralph Bunch held that an expanded federal authority in the economy required new strategies and a more radical response by blacks for a more comprehensive economic program. Made somewhat impatient by what she felt was the unwillingness of the federal government to provide blacks with equal economic opportunities, Lulu White turned to building coalitions with other groups of similar fate. What complicated her willingness to embrace an alternative economic perspective was her inclination to entertain an organized political struggle outside the traditional, legal, educational and personal lobbying tactics associated with the NAACP. But if the means she employed were different, her objective was the same as that of the NAACP: to force the government into extending and expanding the scope of its efforts to become more inclusive of African Americans. Lulu White's flirtation with alleged Communists in relation to her role in the NAACP was one of loyal opposition. There is no record to indicate that she tried to convince anyone to join the leftist cause. In fact, her husband's business venture would have militated against that course. Her association with individuals with socialist proclivities was sometimes used for coalition building. At other times, it amounted to little more than White's own personal protest when government policies appeared antithetical to black needs.

Juanita Craft and the Struggle to End Segregation in Dallas, 1945–1955

YVONNE DAVIS FREER

Until the middle of the twentieth century, Jim Crow laws defined race relations in the South and many of the border states. These laws and de facto practices of segregation in housing, public accommodations, transportation, politics, and education, denied most blacks the right to vote and restricted blacks to segregated, low-paying, unskilled jobs. In 1954, the United States Supreme Court handed down the landmark decision, *Brown v. Board of Education of Topeka,* 347 U.S.483 (1954), which brought an end to Jim Crow, at least in *de jure* form. *Brown v. Board of Education of Topeka* reversed the racist "separate but equal doctrine" handed down fifty-eight years prior in the *Plessy v. Ferguson* case. In 1896, the jurists in *Plessy v. Ferguson,* 163 U.S.537 (1896), held that racial segregation of public train passengers in separate but equal facilities complied with the equal protection clause under the Fourteenth Amendment. This decision served as legal justification of segregation in public facilities and accommodations until the Supreme Court ruled in the *Brown* case that mandatory racial separation contradicted the guarantee of equal protection

Yvonne Davis Freer, original essay based on " 'The Fight Is On!': One Woman's Battle to End Segregation in Dallas, Texas, 1945–1965," a paper presented at the annual meeting of the Texas State Historical Association, Dallas, March 4, 1999. Reprinted with permission.

laws outlined in the Fourteenth Amendment. In short, the ruling held that the discriminatory laws that enforced the segregation of the races were unconstitutional, thus providing the legal basis of dismantling the system of Jim Crow laws.

The Supreme Court's decision in *Brown* energized the existing struggle against racial segregation in the United States. Blacks had struggled both in the political and legal arenas against segregation ever since the *Plessy* decision, but had not established a successful strategy to challenge racial segregation. African American leadership in the United States saw the *Brown* decision as the catalyst to end segregation in the public schools, one of the areas where segregation was most visible and most resented. Unfortunately, the end of segregated schools occurred all too slowly after the ruling.

Despite the 1954 court ruling in *Brown v. Board of Education,* segregation survived in Texas for a number of years. While the state's civil rights movement certainly was stimulated by the *Brown* decision, its origins predated that decision by several decades. For many years prior to *Brown,* the state's African American leaders concentrated their physical, emotional, and financial resources on efforts to gain racial equality through a statewide movement. Black leaders in most cities and counties in Texas challenged the degrading practices of segregation that undermined their basic constitutional and human rights. In 1954, the struggle escalated as the national civil rights movement gained momentum in the post-*Brown* years. African Americans seized the opportunity not merely to scale the walls of segregation, but to tear the walls down. With a national mandate and statewide momentum, significant political and social transformation in Texas was inevitable.

Texas African American leaders recognized the significance of the Supreme Court's decision and the opportunity it provided in their struggle for the total integration of the state's educational system. In the same year as the *Brown* decision, these civil rights leaders attending the General Convention of the National Association for the Advancement of Colored People (NAACP) outlined their long range plans for the fight for first-class citizenship at all levels. This struggle brought to the forefront already established civil rights leaders such as Lulu White of Houston, and Antonio Maceo Smith and Juanita Craft of Dallas. White, Smith, and Craft understood that segregation implied the inferiority of African Americans and that it restricted the educational, mental, and social development of the race. In the aftermath of *Brown,* the elimination of de jure segregation in Texas schools was no longer an unattainable dream, but a constitutional reality.

One woman who was particularly influential in the battle to end segregation in Texas was Juanita Jewel Shanks Craft. Craft had lived in Dallas for more than twenty-five years prior to the *Brown* decision, so she experienced firsthand segregation in all of its forms. She had attended a segregated high school in Austin, a segregated college in Prairie View, and experienced discrimination at her job at the Adolphus Hotel in Dallas. These experiences, as well as the Court's ruling and the burgeoning civil rights movement fueled the fervor that Craft brought to the struggle to end segregation in Dallas and to establish a more egalitarian social order. Her dream was a social order that would extinguish the racial caste system that had penetrated a significant portion of Craft's life and prevented African Americans from interacting with whites. Her struggle to achieve this dream began years before the *Brown* decision and continued throughout her life.

During the postwar years, Dallas rose to prominence as one of the nation's leading textile, technological, and financial centers, and the state's second largest city. Spread over 893 square miles with an estimated metropolitan area population of greater than 600,000, Dallas offered its population real opportunities in the economic, political, and educational arenas, but only if they were white. However for thirteen percent of the city—the African American population—opportunities in these areas were quite limited, not because of competition, but because of entrenched racial segregation and discrimination. Segregation was as fundamental to Texas's identity as the bluebonnet, the state flower. African Americans in Dallas suffered from segregation in the workplace, public accommodations, housing, and education. Although individuals of both races protested segregationist policies in Texas, the majority supported the system, arguing that it was easier and safer to establish and implement "separate" policies and facilities for the races than to integrate them. Despite this belief, key leaders in Dallas's African American community made significant strides to remove these antiquated barriers and move toward racial equality.

African Americans in Dallas concluded that the process of desegregation could only begin if they presented an organized and unified front and demanded that supporters of segregation recognize the legal and constitutional rights of African Americans. Juanita Craft, as the NAACP field organizer in Dallas, organized and led the struggle against segregation in Dallas. Craft joined the Dallas chapter of the NAACP in 1935, and by 1942 she had become instrumental in increasing the city's recorded membership to 1,200. Under her guidance, it grew to an amazing 7,000 members by 1946. This increase in NAACP membership reflected the unity among African Americans in Dallas as well as their commitment to confront inequality and racial injustice in Dallas through systematic organization. Craft's strident oratorical style at membership rallies infused the public with a desire for justice. Donald Jones, a local leader in Dallas, recalled that Craft's membership campaigns were "like a blood transfusion," that she invigorated individuals to join the NAACP in its campaign against segregation and for civil rights.

Craft's success in increasing the NAACP membership in Dallas provided her with a formidable army for the battle against segregation. Craft had lived under varying forms of segregation for most of her life and personally abhorred the institutional barriers that limited her access to the political, social, and economic benefits that Texas and Dallas had to offer. Reacting against her early years as a marginalized citizen, Craft emphasized action through activism. However, she recognized that the implementation of any action would take more than the efforts of one woman. Craft, along with Lulu White, executive secretary of the Houston branch of the NAACP, merged their energies and traveled thousands of miles throughout Texas on massive NAACP membership campaigns. Craft and White organized membership meetings, collected membership fees, and established local chapters. They employed the oratorical style of the pulpit and infused the masses they met, primarily at church meetings and voter registration drives, with the passion and courage to rebel against the stagnated structure of segregation and join in the fight for full civil rights. Their successful grassroots approach increased NAACP membership across the state and informed the new members about NAACP programs for equality in politics and educational opportunity. By garnering interest in the NAACP and increasing the membership rolls, Craft and White gathered the resources they needed to launch a well-organized and coordinated attack on the "old" segregationist leadership of the state and their bastions of racial injustice and discrimination.

To launch her civil rights campaign in Dallas, Juanita Craft joined forces with Antonio Maceo Smith, executive secretary of the Texas State Conference of Branches, NAACP. Craft and Smith understood that revitalization of the Dallas Chapter of the NAACP was essential to the successful promotion of its statewide efforts. Smith was instrumental in reviving the foundering state branches and worked tirelessly to encourage participation among African Americans in the state's political, economic, and civil rights affairs. Craft and Smith focused their initial efforts on securing public sector jobs for African Americans in Dallas. They reasoned that if members and potential members saw the NAACP achieve success in integrating public sector jobs, then they would commit their energy and resources to the civil rights struggle.

During the mid-1940s to early 1950s, Craft joined the NAACP in challenging racial discrimination in employment and education. The Texas State Conference of Branches of the NAACP targeted the inequity in teachers' salaries as their first point of attack. This was a moderate approach, which did not directly confront segregation, but which demanded equality in pay for black and white teachers and principals. In 1942, Craft allied with the Texas State Conference of Branches and the Dallas Council of Negro Organizations (DCNO), which consisted of about twenty other African American organizations in Dallas, to support a lawsuit against the Dallas school board for its racially biased salary structure. Prominent black civil rights activist and attorney William J. Durham, with the cooperation of the Texas State Conference of Branches and the DCNO, filed the civil action on the behalf of plaintiff, Thelma Page and the Negro Teachers Alliance of Dallas.

In the late 1930s, the African American teachers and principals in Dallas had organized to challenge salary discrimination in the Dallas public school system by forming the Dallas Teachers Alliance. By the early 1940s, the Alliance had raised a legal defense fund and after several special meetings agreed that it was time to enter into legal proceedings against the Board of Education, City of Dallas. William Durham and Thurgood Marshall, representing the NAACP legal team, argued for a summary judgment against the Board of Education for its system of salary discrimination. In a judgment rendered by the court in February 1943, African American teachers were granted salary increases designed to equalize pay over a two-year period.

The early judgment by the United States District Court for the Northern District of Dallas in 1943 forced an out of court settlement with a three-step plan. The key element of the plan that signaled victory for the NAACP and the DCNO was that one third of the amount needed for salary equalization would immediately be added to African American teacher salary contracts. The settlement forced the Dallas school board to pay African American teachers on the same scale as its white teachers. This victory set the precedence for other school districts in Texas to adjust their pay scales and pay African American teachers an equitable salary.

The success in getting the Dallas school board to equalize pay for black and white teachers encouraged Craft to seek additional changes, especially in education. Craft was appointed the advisor of the Dallas NAACP Youth Council in 1946. Although the primary purpose of NAACP youth councils was to act as social organizations, Craft organized the Dallas chapter to be active in the civil rights movement. She instructed the members about the importance of education and its connection to ending discrimination. In that same year, Craft organized the youth to raise money and picket in support of ending segregation in higher education. Heman Marion Sweatt, a Houston letter carrier, had applied for admission to the all-white University of Texas law school in 1946 and was denied admission based on his race. The University of Texas offered the best legal education in the southern region of the United States, but routinely denied admission to African American applicants. Initially, the state legislature tried to appease Heman Sweatt and provide legal education for blacks by establishing a law school at the colored Prairie View University. Then they created a makeshift school in a basement office building that was located blocks from University of Texas in Austin, and finally, in 1947 created the Texas State University for Negroes in Houston with a law school. Sweatt and the NAACP refused to accept a segregated law school and continued their suit against Jim Crow education. Again, William Durham and Thurgood Marshall directed the lawsuit.

Craft's grassroots involvement in the Sweatt case was effective. Youth Council members demonstrated and helped raise money for the NAACP's legal fees, and Craft used the struggle to educate them about the importance of confronting racial segregation in public higher education. Craft supported the tempestuous four-year battle to gain Sweatt's admission into the Texas law school because she believed that a truly first-class education was impossible in segregated facilities. Sweatt and the NAACP won their case June 6, 1950. The Supreme Court ruled that a black law student must be admitted to the all-white University of Texas because separate facilities for Negroes were inherently not equal. The Court's ruling paved the way for a series of education desegregation cases that would lead to the landmark *Brown* ruling and defiance of segregation.

The *Sweatt* decision may have ignited the embers in the battle against segregation, but it was the *Brown* decision that fueled the fire of interest and support for the civil rights movement. Craft's participation in the battle to end segregation increased as the problems of African Americans in Dallas escalated. The national push toward civil rights for African Americans confirmed to Craft that "there was a lot to be done." Craft disliked being discriminated against because of her color or her condition. She fervently believed that she and others of the African American race deserved an opportunity to participate fully and equally in all the rights and privileges outlined in the United States Constitution and that drawing arbitrary lines based on prejudicial traditions or opinions served only to strengthen injustice and discrimination. Unfortunately, proponents of segregation in Dallas did not share Craft's beliefs and they worked vigorously to maintain a segregated city.

The legal assaults for racial equality orchestrated by the NAACP were virtually ineffective as racial discrimination in Dallas continued unabated. The Dallas Board of Education refused to comply with the 1954 Supreme Court school desegregation order. The local chapter of the NAACP responded with a petition demanding that the school board immediately comply with the Supreme Court ruling. However, Dallas School Superintendent W. T. White refused to provide equal education for African American children and white children because, he argued, the Dallas schools operated solely under state legislation, not federal law. The obstinacy exhibited by the Dallas school system in refusing to end segregation filtered into other public arenas in the city. Retail stores in downtown Dallas refused to allow African American customers to try on clothing. The NAACP responded by peaceful protests and sit-ins, but was relatively unsuccessful in attaining speedy desegregation of the stores. Not until the early 1960s did most downtown department stores desegregate in Dallas, and then only to "promote a good national image of the city." Housing codes and localized acts of violence deterred African Americans from moving into in nonsegregated residential neighborhoods in Dallas. Housing for African Americans in Dallas was never a great priority of the city's leaders, but a restrictive process. Segregated housing patterns forced at least ninety percent of the African American population in Dallas to reside in South Dallas. Despite the legal maneuvers of the NAACP and federal legislation, most African Americans who could afford housing remained in the southern sector of the city for fear of being bombed, like several other African Americans who attempted to move into North or East Dallas. The only visible gesture to provide better housing for blacks was the development of Hamilton Park in 1954, a model, segregated residential housing community for those middle-class African Americans who could afford to purchase a home. Even though the outlook on ending segregation in Dallas looked bleak based on these setbacks experienced by the NAACP and other key African American organizations, Craft continued to commit herself to the struggle for equality.

As the struggle for civil rights continued, Craft continued to use her position as advisor of the Youth Council to involve African American students in the process of school desegregation. She continuously lectured the youth about their rights as Americans and the importance of ending segregation in Dallas and opening the doors of equal opportunity in politics, employment, and education. In 1955 she directed her attention to the desegregation of North Texas State College (now the University of North Texas). Joe L. Atkins, a member of the Youth Council and high school honor student, applied for admission to North Texas State College in Denton, Texas, approximately forty miles north of Dallas. Atkins, his mother, Mable Atkins, and Craft traveled to Denton to meet the school's president, James Carl Matthews and Vice President Arthur Sampley about Atkins' admission. According to Craft, a week later Atkins received a letter from the president of North Texas State University refusing to admit him because of his race. This correspondence from President Matthews blatantly violated the Supreme Court mandate in the *Brown* decision. However, President Matthews intended to avoid desegregation of his campus as long as possible, despite the Court's ruling. Joe Atkins responded to the letter by filing a lawsuit against North Texas State College for failing to admit him based on his race.

The Dallas NAACP legal team headed by U. Simpson Tate, a Howard University graduate and confidant of Thurgood Marshall, represented Atkins in his case. Tate filed an immediate motion to force North Texas to allow Atkins to be admitted for the fall semester. He also argued that the school violated the Fourteenth Amendment by admitting African American students only to the college's doctoral program, not its undergraduate and masters level programs. Counsel for the university replied to the injunction by stating that the campus was not prepared administratively or financially to address the needs of approximately two hundred or more African American students, especially since Texas Southern University and Prairie

View A&M University were available to this group. The order overruling Tate's request for an injunction forced Atkins to enroll at the integrated Texas Western College in El Paso so he would not lose a semester of study during the trial.

By late fall semester 1955, federal magistrate Judge Joe Sheehy in the Eastern District court ruled that North Texas had to admit Atkins without delay. Judge Sheehy ruled that North Texas had admitted many other white students to its campus without any administrative or financial difficulties since Atkins made application to the campus and that any further delay of admissions to African Americans directly violated the Fourteenth Amendment, the Supreme Court ruling in *Brown*, and subsequent desegregation cases. The permanent injunction rendered by Judge Sheehy ended the exclusion of admission to the university based solely on race. For Atkins, the judge's ruling was bittersweet, as he already was attending the integrated Texas Western College and did not wish to transfer. However, for Craft, the victory was sweet justice, because she had played an instrumental role in ending segregation in education and opening North Texas State College's doors to African American students.

Juanita Craft focused the public's attention on the inequitable treatment of African Americans because of segregationist policies and practices. Because of her own experiences with segregation and racial discrimination, Craft worked unselfishly to end segregation and to increase equal opportunities regardless of race. Her contributions stimulated by her participation in the NAACP, the *Brown* decision, and the burgeoning civil rights movement catapulted her into the mainstream battle for racial equality. In a ten-year span, her battles against segregation in Dallas pecked away at the bastions of exclusion and segregation. Despite deeply-rooted resistance to desegregation, Craft, along with others, continued to press for full integration in education, politics, housing, and public accommodations. *"The Fight is On!"* served no longer as a catchy membership slogan, but as an electrically charged statement of action. This statement of action would dominate the civil rights movement in Dallas well beyond the 1950s.

EPILOGUE

Juanita Craft's vision and dedication to ending segregation in Dallas did not go unnoticed. On the national level she received personal invitations from Presidents Kennedy, Johnson, Nixon, and Carter to attend conferences focusing on the escalating problems among the nation's youth. The national office of the NAACP presented her with two major awards for her guidance in the Dallas Youth Council's fight against segregation. And locally in Dallas, Mayor Erik Jonsson invited Craft to attend several of the conferences, "Goals for Dallas."

Craft's continued interest in and love for her city pushed her into the political arena at the age of seventy-three. She ran for city council in 1975, winning over six opponents. Although critics chided her for her age, she resisted their verbal attacks and became the second African American female elected to the Dallas City Council. During her two council terms, she carried out her election platform of cleaning up the deteriorating inner-city areas of Dallas and revitalizing downtown Dallas.

Juanita Craft held what scholars identify as a utopian vision. She pushed for African American civil rights because she knew something was wrong and she "had to help change the system." The events that occurred during the civil rights movement were inevitable actions that Craft was able to use in her arsenal for the assault on segregation. Her involvement in the battles became infectious actions that encouraged youth and adults to envision a life that went beyond merely hoping for a desegregated society, to actively seize the opportunity promised by the Constitution. Craft believed in and insisted race relations improve in her city, so that racial tolerance and harmony was not an elusive goal, but a potential reality.

⭐ F U R T H E R   R E A D I N G

Alwyn Barr, *Black Texans: A History of African Americans in Texas, 1528–1995,* 2d ed. (1996)

Howard Beeth and Cary D. Wintz, eds., *Black Dixie: Afro-Texan History and Culture in Houston* (1992)

Thomas R. Cole, *No Color Is My Kind: The Life of Eldrewey Stearns and the Integration of Houston* (1997)

Vicki Crawford, Jacqueline Anne Rouse, and Barbara Woods, eds., *Women in the Civil Rights Movement: Trailblazers and Torchbearers, 1941–1965* (1990)

W. Marvin Dulaney, "Whatever Happened to the Civil Rights Movement in Dallas, Texas?" in *Essays on the American Civil Rights Movement,* eds. John Dittmer, W. Marvin Dulaney, Kathleen Underwood, and George C. Wright (1993)

Michael L Gillette, "The Rise of the NAACP in Texas," *Southwestern Historical Quarterly* 81 (1978): 393–416

William Henry Kellar, *Make Haste Slowly: Moderates, Conservatives, and School Desegregation in Houston* (1999)

Robyn Duff Ladino, *Desegregating Texas Schools: Eisenhower, Shivers, and the Crisis at Mansfield High* (1996)

Ronald E. Marcello, "Reluctance versus Reality: The Desegregation of North Texas State College, 1954–1956," *Southwestern Historical Quarterly* 99 (1996): 153–185

Ernest Obadele-Starks, *Black Unionism in the Industrial South* (2000)

Merline Pitre, "Black Houstonians and the 'Separate But Equal' Doctrine: Carter W. Wesley versus Lulu White" *The Houston Review* 12 (1990): 23–36

———, *In Struggle against Jim Crow: Lulu B. White and the NAACP, 1900–1957* (1999)

William H. Wilson, *Hamilton Park: A Planned Black Community in Dallas* (1998)

Ruthe Winegarten, *Black Texas Women: 150 Years of Trial and Triumph* (1995)